MODERN IRISH
DRAMA

Cathleen Ni Houlihan • On Baile's Strand • Purgatory
Spreading the News • The Rising of the Moon
Riders to the Sea • The Playboy of the Western World
John Bull's Other Island • Juno and the Paycock
The Quare Fellow • Krapp's Last Tape
Translations

BACKGROUNDS AND CRITICISM

A NORTON CRITICAL EDITION

MODERN IRISH DRAMA

Cathleen Ni Houlihan • On Baile's Strand • Purgatory
Spreading the News • The Rising of the Moon
Riders to the Sea • The Playboy of the Western World
John Bull's Other Island • Juno and the Paycock
The Quare Fellow • Krapp's Last Tape
Translations

BACKGROUNDS AND CRITICISM

Edited by
JOHN P. HARRINGTON

THE COOPER UNION

W·W·NORTON   &   COMPANY • *New   York • London*

Printed in the United States of America.

The text of this book is composed in Electra,
with the display set in Bernhard Modern.
Composition by Vail-Ballou.
Manufacturing by the Maple-Vail Book Group.
Book design by Antonina Krass.

First Edition

Library of Congress Cataloging-in-Publication Data
Modern Irish drama / edited by John P. Harrington.
p.   cm.—(A Norton critical edition)
Includes bibliographical references (p.   ).
1. English drama—Irish authors.   2. English drama—Irish authors—
History and criticism.   3. English drama—20th century—History and
criticism.   4. English drama—20th century.   5. Ireland in
literature.   6. Ireland—Drama.   I. Harrington, John P.
PR8869.M63   1991
822'.910809415—dc20   90-38999

ISBN 0-393-96063-3
W.W. Norton & Company, Inc., 500 Fifth Avenue, New York, N.Y. 10110
W.W. Norton & Company, Ltd., 10 Coptic Street, London WC1A 1PU

1 2 3 4 5 6 7 8 9 0

Contents

Preface

The seminal document of modern Irish drama is the declaration of intentions agreed upon in 1897 by William Butler Yeats, Lady Augusta Gregory, and Edward Martyn. The crucial text, composed at Lady Gregory's western Ireland estate, Coole Park, which was near Edward Martyn's estate, Tillyra Castle, and Yeats's future summer home, Thoor Ballylee, is that reproduced in Lady Gregory's memoir *Our Irish Theatre*:

> We propose to have performed in Dublin, in the spring of every year certain Celtic and Irish plays, which whatever be their degree of excellence will be written with a high ambition, and so to build up a Celtic and Irish school of dramatic literature. We hope to find in Ireland an uncorrupted and imaginative audience trained to listen by its passion for oratory, and believe that our desire to bring upon the stage the deeper thoughts and emotions of Ireland will ensure for us a tolerant welcome, and that freedom to experiment which is not found in theatres of England, and without which no new movement in art or literature can succeed. We will show that Ireland is not the home of buffoonery and of easy sentiment, as it has been represented, but the home of an ancient idealism.

Some local context for this statement is provided in the selection from Lady Gregory's book reprinted in this volume on pp. 377–86. The more general context can be sketched here as introduction to this collection of plays, all of which follow, in assent or in dissent, willingly or unwillingly, from the thesis of this prospectus.

The idea of a national drama, which is not at all specific to Ireland, is to represent the theater's audience on its stage ("to bring upon the stage the deeper thoughts and emotions of Ireland") and at the same time to elevate that audience (to perform plays written "with a high ambition"). Thus national drama has a contradictory relation to its audience: to reflect the audience as it is, and to improve it. Both roles are presumptuous. The first presumes the authority to identify the nation, an exercise of radical reduction even in so small a country as Ireland. The exercise entails evaluating segments of a national society and determining which will occupy center stage as "the real Ireland," or the "Irish

Ireland." Early in the century, especially in the works of John Millington Synge, the rural peasantry prevailed as "the real Ireland," and by
mid-century, in the face of modernization, this identification of "the
real Ireland" ossified into a convention whereby, many complained, Irish
plays were ranked by measure of "PQ," or peasant quality. Also, in identification of a "real Ireland" empiricism was of little use. Roger McHugh,
a contributor to the Abbey Theatre in a variety of roles, recalled how he
defended Sean O'Casey's *The Plough and the Stars* before an audience
outraged by one character because, they argued, there were no prostitutes in Dublin, and how he, McHugh, was that evening solicited by
prostitutes on his way home. The real Ireland, then, could be fictional-
ized by dramatists or by audiences alike.

The second role in national drama, improving the audience, presumes to identify the people's proper aspirations and to require their
enrollment, by attendance, in an improving program. The historical
record indicates that the Irish audience was generally quite happy with
its current aspirations and so preferred self-congratulatory drama over
any "new movement in art or literature." Further, its "passion for oratory" evidently trained the "uncorrupted and imaginative audience" in
speaking as well as in listening, for modern Irish drama is notable for
obstreperous objections to the images of the Irish people presented to the
Irish people by Irish playwrights. "What is the meaning of this rubbish?"
asked one notable, enraged objector, Frank Hugh O'Donnell, of the first
Yeats contribution in 1899 to the Celtic and Irish school of dramatic
literature promised by the Coole Park manifesto. "How will it help the
national cause? How is it to help any cause at all?" The same questions
were asked at mid-century. At that time plays, now much-maligned,
prevailed that were, if not wholly self-congratulatory, certainly of manageable demands. In 1958 O'Casey had a follow-up bout when the
Catholic church, acting for its parishioners, objected to immorality in
The Drums of Father Ned: O'Casey simply withdrew his play, and in
this action he was followed by producers of a dramatization of James
Joyce's *Ulysses* and by Samuel Beckett. In sufficient ire, then, the audience can walk away and the playwrights can close their own plays. Small
surprise that the word "theater" is also used in reference to military
maneuvers.

In Ireland in 1899 the cause in question was national independence.
To this national drama was a contribution, though a problematic contribution. It could please, as with *Cathleen Ni Houlihan*, and it could
infuriate, as with *The Playboy of the Western World*. Nationalism, one
of the principal factors in modern history, is organization and agitation
to establish or to preserve a government that reflects its constituency.

Nationalism takes shape in the wake of colonialism, a prior factor in history, in which single imperialist states amassed global territories and administered them with policies that reflected home base more than local population. Ireland was claimed by England as long ago as 1141, and it was with considerable difficulty maintained as a tenuously manageable colony by Elizabeth I in 1601 and by successive monarchs. The persistent, contrary Irish movement for self-rule entered a modern phase in the mid-nineteenth century, when the Young Ireland movement addressed its people in the literary medium of patriotic poems and ballads, a medium that, like theater, demands group performance. Some argue that the Irish independence movement concluded in 1922, with the establishment of the Irish Free State; others argue that it continues today, when the island is partitioned into an autonomous Irish Republic and a smaller Northern Ireland territory that continues to be administered from London. As the Yeats / Gregory / Martyn prospectus for an Irish national drama dates from 1897, and as Irish playwrights continue to address the issue of self-determination and continuing civil strife today, nationalism is the informing focus of modern Irish drama in this century. Nationalism is a focus, but not a position; drama helps articulate both arguments and counterarguments. Bernard Shaw noted this in a 1913 essay on nationalism written about ten years after *John Bull's Other Island* and its preface: "The modern Irish theatre began with the *Cathleen Ni Houlihan* of Mr. Yeats and Lady Gregory's *Rising of the Moon*, in which the old patriotism stirred and wrung its victims; but when the theatre thus established called on Young Ireland to write plays and found a national school of drama, the immediate result was a string of plays of Irish life—and very true to life they were—in which heroines proclaimed that they were sick of Ireland and [be]rated their Nationalist husbands for sacrificing all the realities of life to senseless Fenian maunderings." Such was the outcome of the Yeats / Martyn / Gregory call for a "Celtic and Irish school of dramatic literature": not a common set of unimpeachable axioms but an extended and ongoing critique.

Political nationalism is a pragmatic program in which a native population or spokespeople for a native population organize formidable resistance to outside, colonial government. Though he was not one, a political pragmatist must ask Frank Hugh O'Donnell's question: How will it help the cause? In *Juno and the Paycock* Sean O'Casey gives a particularly chilling portrait of political nationalists, members of the Irish Republican Army, assassinating one of their own, Johnny Boyle, as a matter of praxis: elimination of a suspected informer. Cultural nationalism, generally a corollary movement, is an aesthetic program to organize for a native population a sustaining image of itself, its uniqueness, and its dignity, all contrary to the subordinate and submissive identity nurtured by outside administration. Much of the thrust of cultural nationalism is rescue of a dignified indigenous culture previously submerged by powerful colonial culture. Thus a national drama often focuses on local culture as yet unspoiled by the influence of foreign colonialism, as in Synge's *Riders to the Sea*, or, better yet, in plays written and performed in Irish Gaelic, like Douglas Hyde's *Casadh an tSugain (The Twisting of the Rope)*. Thus a national literary movement, like Ireland's at the turn of the century, is termed a "revival": restoration of a culture temporarily marginalized by outsiders to its proper, central place. A key component of this effort is reinterpretation of local history from a native perspective. The first and last plays in this collection, *Cathleen Ni Houlihan* and *Translations*, are historical dramas that restore Irish dignity to historical episodes previously regarded from a British perspective as evidence of Irish inferiority.

Cultural nationalism, however, is not as pragmatic or didactic as political nationalism, and that accounts for drama's lack of unanimity. Lady Gregory, despite the prospectus of an Irish National Theatre, admits buffoonery in depiction of folk culture in *Spreading the News*. Shaw depicts Irish nationalism as a clever scam in *John Bull's Other Island*. One might well ask how these works were to help the national cause. Further, political nationalists, seeking unanimity, could and did argue that the dramatists establishing images of folk culture were not of it. Yeats, Gregory, and Martyn, who presumed to tell the people who they were and who they should be, were landed gentry or, in Yeats's case, at least of such pretension. Synge, authorized dramatist of peasant culture, could be termed an urban, professorial linguist with equal enthusiasms for Gaelic folk culture and the very latest in Parisian intellectual fashion. Thus the landmark early plays of Irish national drama could plausibly be viewed, as they have been by some, as an invented folk culture that served the needs of artists and intellectuals. The notable theater riots in Dublin over Synge and O'Casey plays were audience counterarguments that the plays in question were neither useful nor accurate. Playwrights often responded without challenging that point. In his autobiography, Yeats wrote that the national drama, and in particular the Abbey Theatre that epitomizes it, "will fail to do its full work because there is no accepted authority to explain why the more difficult pleasure is the nobler pleasure. The fascination of the National Movement for me in my youth was, I think, that it seemed to promise such authority." Synge was blunter. "I have the wildest admiration for the Irish Peasants and for Irishmen of known or unknown genius," he wrote to fellow literary nationalist Stephen McKenna, "but between the two there's an ungodly ruck of fatfaced sweaty-headed swine." Thus the playwright position might be that the questions of usefulness and accuracy were simply irrelevant.

The theatergoer in Dublin at the turn of the century might also wonder if the playwrights considered entertainment a further irrelevance. Though the comic mode was an element of modern Irish drama from its beginning, the national drama scarcely matched the popular draw of other theater fare already well-established in Dublin. Dublin was in fact the site of the first licensed English theater outside London: it was established by a new lord deputy of Ireland, Thomas Wentworth, and opened in 1637 on Werburgh Street near the center of colonial administration at Dublin Castle. There the estimable dramatist and resident playwright James Shirley wrote *St. Patrick for Ireland* (1639), generally considered the first play with Irish subject matter. After the restoration of Stuart monarchy reopened theaters briefly closed by Puritan government, Dublin was notable for the Smock Alley Theatre and for a series of playwrights, Irish by birth or association, critical to English drama; William Congreve, George Farquhar, Richard Steele, Oliver Goldsmith, Richard Brinsley Sheridan, and others. These, like Oscar Wilde and Bernard Shaw in a later period, gravitated to London, to its dramatic traditions and innovations, and to its English audiences. Dublin theater functioned as a provincial theater, or a straw-hat circuit theater, trying out productions that hoped to reach London or wringing last earnings from productions already closed in London. By the late nineteenth century Dublin houses offered light operas, melodramas, the "well-made" plays of curtain solutions, and musical variety shows. This was entertainment indeed. Robert Hogan and James Kilroy's *The Irish Literary Theatre* lists offerings in the late 1890s that included the musical comedies *The Skirt Dancer* and *A Greek Slave*, respectable British dramas such as Arthur Wing Pinero's *The Second Mrs. Tanqueray*, and a musical card with Virto, the Man of Many Instruments; Werner and Rieder, Duettists and Swiss Warblers; *and* the Eight Eldorados. Some of this could be done with an Irish angle: there was the light opera *Lily of Killarney* or the drama *An Irish Gentleman*. There were as well the Irish melodramas of Dion Boucicault, such as *Arrah-na-Pogue* and *The Coleen Bawn*: these were and are thought to have more than purely melodramatic potential. But all this Irish material was done with an eye to export, usually to London, though Boucicault went to New York. Hence the "Irish" quality—conspicuous drunkenness, clownishness, and sentimentality—was exaggerated for recognition by a foreign audience, and the result was a caricature known as "the stage Irishman."

This was the condition the Irish Literary Theatre hoped to offset, to "show that Ireland is not the home of buffoonery and of easy sentiment."

The prospectus written by W. B. Yeats, Edward Martyn, and Lady Gregory resulted most immediately in productions in 1899 intended to add to this functioning Dublin theatrical scene artistic idealism and native culture. The project operated in conjunction with an Irish literary revival in all genres: poetry, fiction, criticism, new histories, and translation from and into Irish Gaelic. Because drama is fundamentally a group event, involving authors, production personnel, and a group audience, Irish drama took a critical public role in this revival. The dramatic movement, in particular, took on the role of the Young Ireland movement of the mid-nineteenth century. The Young Ireland movement had hoped to catalyze nationalistic unity with ballads. It lost influence when political nationalism, particularly agitation over ownership known as the land wars, was more influential than cultural nationalism. In 1890 the political movement for Home Rule, or parliamentary autonomy, collapsed with the fortunes of its charismatic leader, Charles Stewart Parnell. With political nationalism in eclipse, cultural nationalism could and did regain its influence. Yeats organized a London Irish Literary Society in 1891 and a National Literary Society in Dublin in 1892. The conception of a national drama in Dubin benefited from the local literary revival, and participants in the Irish Literary Theatre usually had sidelines in other genres. However, the dramatic movement also benefited immensely from external models, a foreign influence that, though distinctly not English, was to engender its own complications. In 1850 Ole Bull had established a national theater in Norway, to which Henrik Ibsen, especially when young, contributed plays based on Norwegian life, history, and cultural traditions. The later, better-known Ibsen plays had direct impact on the Irish Literary Theatre, especially through Martyn, for whom Ibsen was a model, and Yeats, for whom Ibsen's social drama was a perfect example of how not to proceed. Other Continental models, to be taken for positive and negative instruction, included André Antoine, who founded Théâtre Libre in Paris in 1887, and Otto Brahm, who founded the Freie Bühne in Berlin in 1889. In addition, Richard Wagner's Bayreuth theater festival was a great personal influence on the founding participants of the Irish Literary Theatre.

All these factors, local and Continental, nationalistic and aesthetic, came to bear on the first, formative production of the Irish Literary Theatre in May 1899: Yeats's *The Countess Cathleen* and Martyn's *The Heather Field*. The first represented the theater of art, of aesthetics, initially bound up in Yeats's own emerging philosophy of drama. The second represented the theater of praxis, of social drama, immediately descended from Ibsen. The organizing force joining them was Lady Gregory, assuming a managerial role that would continue. The result was general clamor. The Yeats play, for its personification of a feminine Ireland bartering immortality for food, was denounced as heresy by the keepers of a distinctly Catholic public morality of "Irish Ireland." Police protection was required for performance, and newspapers were filled with letters from those outraged by the play's representation of Ireland. The Martyn play, for its extended consideration of agricultural ethics, was denounced as pedestrian by keepers of literary standards, and reviews decried its mechanical exhaustion of a predictable liberal thesis. At issue was both the accuracy of the representation of Ireland on the stage and the formulation of Ireland's proper ambition: the central conflict in nationalism between the pragmatic and the aesthetic. Martyn saw no benefit in alienating the audience or, most important, the Catholic church; he saw the benefit of addressing the audience on its own terms, with its own problems, and with realistic resolutions. Yeats instead took the course of a drama that would be "remote, spiritual, and ideal." These remain options today: for playwrights, for production directors, and for audiences.

All participants in that general clamor of 1899, however critical, were active participants in a debate about a drama with national pretensions and so about the nation itself. This same debate, sustained by Lady Gregory and successors under auspices of the national theater, the Abbey, and the dissenting competitors it inspired, has continued throughout the history of modern Irish drama represented in this volume in the dramatic texts themselves and in the critical texts they have provoked. The most noteworthy public clamors followed the plays of Synge and O'Casey, but the work of Shaw, Behan, and Beckett also demanded, on public performance, a public response to dramatic provocation. Brian Friel's *Translations*, and indeed the whole Field Day program of which it was the first production, is the most recent installment in this continuing debate. What joins all these plays is not the birthplace of the authors but their collective contemplation of Ireland's identity. These plays dwell on shared national symbols, such as Cathleen Ni Houlihan or the Shan Van Vocht; events, such as the 1798 rising; political movements, such as Home Rule; and emblematic places, such as the political landmark Kilmainham Jail or the open wilds of Connaught. In response to this common framework these plays offer plural commentaries. Irish drama is notable for shifting allegiances to self or to place, to the individual or to the collective obligation, to liberatory aesthetics or to unifying traditions. At issue throughout is the relation between individual writer and national state, a relation that binds even in dissent. "The first duty of a writer," Brendan Behan wrote, "is to let his Fatherland down, otherwise he is no writer."

THE TEXTS OF THE PLAYS

W. B. YEATS

Cathleen Ni Houlihan†

Persons in the Play

PETER GILLANE
MICHAEL GILLANE, *his son, going to be married*
PATRICK GILLANE, *a lad of twelve, Michael's brother*
BRIDGET GILLANE, *Peter's wife*
DELIA CAHEL, *engaged to Michael*
THE POOR OLD WOMAN
NEIGHBOURS

Interior of a cottage close to Killala, in 1798.[1] BRIDGET *is standing at a table undoing a parcel.* PETER *is sitting at one side of the fire,* PATRICK *at the other.*

PETER.   What is the sound I hear?
PATRICK.   I don't hear anything. [*He listens.*] I hear it now. It's like cheering. [*He goes to the window and looks out.*] I wonder what they are cheering about. I don't see anybody.
PETER.   It might be a hurling.[2]
PATRICK.   There's no hurling to-day. It must be down in the town the cheering is.
BRIDGET.   I suppose the boys must be having some sport of their own. Come over here, Peter, and look at Michael's wedding clothes.
PETER [*shifts his chair to table*].   Those are grand clothes, indeed.
BRIDGET.   You hadn't clothes like that when you married me, and no coat to put on of a Sunday more than any other day.
PETER.   That is true, indeed. We never thought a son of our own would be wearing a suit of that sort for his wedding, or have so good a place to bring a wife to.

† From *The Collected Plays of W. B. Yeats*, rev. ed. (New York: Macmillan, 1953).
1. Site, in western Ireland, and date, on August 22, of the landing of a French force supporting Irish rebellion against British control; the French and the Irish alike surrendered to the British on September 8.
2. Game, somewhat like field hockey, with origins in Celtic Ireland.

PATRICK [*who is still at the window*].   There's an old woman coming down the road. I don't know is it here she is coming.

BRIDGET.   It will be a neighbour coming to hear about Michael's wedding. Can you see who it is?

PATRICK.   I think it is a stranger, but she's not coming to the house. She's turned into the gap that goes down where Maurteen and his sons are shearing sheep. [*He turns towards* BRIDGET.] Do you remember what Winny of the Cross-Roads was saying the other night about the strange woman that goes through the country whatever time there's war or trouble coming?

BRIDGET.   Don't be bothering us about Winny's talk, but go and open the door for your brother. I hear him coming up the path.

PETER.   I hope he has brought Delia's fortune with him safe, for fear the people might go back on the bargain and I after making it. Trouble enough I had making it.

[PATRICK *opens the door and* MICHAEL *comes in.*]

BRIDGET.   What kept you, Michael? We were looking out for you this long time.

MICHAEL.   I went round by the priest's house to bid him be ready to marry us to-morrow.

BRIDGET.   Did he say anything?

MICHAEL.   He said it was a very nice match, and that he was never better pleased to marry any two in his parish than myself and Delia Cahel.

PETER. Have you got the fortune, Michael?

MICHAEL.   Here it is.

[MICHAEL *puts bag on table and goes over and leans against chimney-jamb.* BRIDGET, *who has been all this time examining the clothes, pulling the seams and trying the lining of the pockets, etc., puts the clothes on the dresser.*]

PETER [*getting up and taking the bag in his hand and turning out the money*].   Yes, I made the bargain well for you, Michael. Old John Cahel would sooner have kept a share of this a while longer. 'Let me keep the half of it until the first boy is born,' says he. 'You will not,' says I. 'Whether there is or is not a boy, the whole hundred pounds must be in Michael's hands before he brings your daughter to the house.' The wife spoke to him then, and he gave in at the end.

BRIDGET.   You seem well pleased to be handling the money, Peter.

PETER.   Indeed, I wish I had had the luck to get a hundred pounds, or twenty pounds itself, with the wife I married.

BRIDGET.   Well, if I didn't bring much I didn't get much. What had you the day I married you but a flock of hens and you feeding them, and a few lambs and you driving them to the market at Ballina? [*She is vexed and bangs a jug on the dresser.*] If I brought no fortune I worked it out in my bones, laying down the baby, Michael that is standing there now, on a stook of straw, while I dug the potatoes, and never asking big dresses or anything but to be working.

PETER. That is true, indeed. [*He pats her arm.*]

BRIDGET. Leave me alone now till I ready the house for the woman that is to come into it.

PETER. You are the best woman in Ireland, but money is good, too [*He begins handling the money again and sits down.*] I never thought to see so much money within my four walls. We can do great things now we have it. We can take the ten acres of land we have the chance of since Jamsie Dempsey died, and stock it. We will go to the fair at Ballina to buy the stock. Did Delia ask any of the money for her own use, Michael?

MICHAEL. She did not, indeed. She did not seem to take much notice of it, or to look at it at all.

BRIDGET. That's no wonder. Why would she look at it when she had yourself to look at, a fine, strong young man? It is proud she must be to get you; a good steady boy that will make use of the money, and not be running through it or spending it on drink like another.

PETER. It's likely Michael himself was not thinking much of the fortune either, but of what sort the girl was to look at.

MICHAEL [*coming over towards the table*]. Well, you would like a nice comely girl to be beside you, and to go walking with you. The fortune only lasts for a while, but the woman will be there always.

PATRICK [*turning round from the window*]. They are cheering again down in the town. Maybe they are landing horses from Enniscrone. They do be cheering when the horses take the water well.

MICHAEL. There are no horses in it. Where would they be going and no fair at hand? Go down to the town, Patrick, and see what is going on.

PATRICK [*opens the door to go out, but stops for a moment on the threshold*]. Will Delia remember, do you think, to bring the greyhound pup she promised me when she would be coming to the house?

MICHAEL. She will surely.

[PATRICK *goes out, leaving the door open.*]

PETER. It will be Patrick's turn next to be looking for a fortune, but he won't find it so easy to get it and he with no place of his own.

BRIDGET. I do be thinking sometimes, now things are going so well with us, and the Cahels such a good back to us in the district, and Delia's own uncle a priest, we might be put in the way of making Patrick a priest some day, and he so good at his books.

PETER. Time enough, time enough. You have always your head full of plans, Bridget.

BRIDGET.   We will be well able to give him learning, and not to send him tramping the country like a poor scholar that lives on charity.

MICHAEL.   They're not done cheering yet. [*He goes over to the door and stands there for a moment, putting up his hand to shade his eyes.*]

BRIDGET.   Do you see anything?

MICHAEL.   I see an old woman coming up the path.

BRIDGET.   Who is it, I wonder? It must be the strange woman Patrick saw a while ago.

MICHAEL.   I don't think it's one of the neighbours anyway, but she has her cloak over her face.

BRIDGET.   It might be some poor woman heard we were making ready for the wedding and came to look for her share.

PETER.   I may as well put the money out of sight. There is no use leaving it out for every stranger to look at.

[*He goes over to a large box in the corner, opens it and puts the bag in and fumbles at the lock.*]

MICHAEL.   There she is father!

[*An* OLD WOMAN *passes the window slowly. She looks at* MICHAEL *as she passes.*]

I'd sooner a stranger not to come to the house the night before my wedding.

BRIDGET.   Open the door, Michael; don't keep the poor woman waiting.

[*The* OLD WOMAN *comes in.* MICHAEL *stands aside to make way for her.*]

OLD WOMAN.   God save all here!

PETER.   God save you kindly!

OLD WOMAN.   You have good shelter here.

PETER.   You are welcome to whatever shelter we have.

BRIDGET.   Sit down there by the fire and welcome.

OLD WOMAN [*warming her hands*].   There is a hard wind outside.

[MICHAEL *watches her curiously from the door.* PETER *comes over to the table.*]

PETER.   Have you travelled far to-day?

OLD WOMAN.   I have travelled far, very far; there are few have travelled so far as myself, and there's many a one that doesn't make me welcome. There was one that had strong sons I thought were friends of mine, but they were shearing their sheep, and they wouldn't listen to me.

PETER.   It's a pity indeed for any person to have no place of their own.

OLD WOMAN.   That's true for you indeed, and it's long I'm on the roads
since I first went wandering.

BRIDGET.   It is a wonder you are not worn out with so much wandering.

OLD WOMAN.   Sometimes my feet are tired and my hands are quiet, but
there is no quiet in my heart. When the people see me quiet, they
think old age has come on me and that all the stir has gone out of
me. But when the trouble is on me I must be talking to my friends.

BRIDGET.   What was it put you wandering?

OLD WOMAN.   Too many strangers in the house.

BRIDGET.   Indeed you look as if you'd had your share of trouble.

OLD WOMAN.   I have had trouble indeed.

BRIDGET.   What was it put the trouble on you?

OLD WOMAN.   My land that was taken from me.

PETER.   Was it much land they took from you?

OLD WOMAN.   My four beautiful green fields. [3]

PETER [*aside to* BRIDGET].   Do you think could she be the widow Casey
that was put out of her holding at Kilglass a while ago?

BRIDGET.   She is not. I saw the widow Casey one time at the market in
Ballina, a stout fresh woman.

PETER [*to* OLD WOMAN].   Did you hear a noise of cheering, and you
coming up the hill?

OLD WOMAN.   I thought I heard the noise I used to hear when my friends
came to visit me. [*She begins singing half to herself.*]

> I will go cry with the woman,
> For yellow-haired Donough is dead,
> With a hempen rope for a neckcloth,
> And a white cloth on his head,— [4]

MICHAEL [*coming from the door*].   What is it that you are singing, ma'am?

OLD WOMAN.   Singing I am about a man I knew one time, yellow-
haired Donough that was hanged in Galway. [*She goes on singing,
much louder.*]

> I am come to cry with you, woman,
> My hair is unwound and unbound;
> I remember him ploughing his field,
> Turning up the red side of the ground,
> And building his barn on the hill
> With the good mortared stone;
> O! we'd have pulled down the gallows
> Had it happened in Enniscrone!

3. The island of Ireland's traditional division is into
four provinces: Ulster, Munster, Leinster, and
Connacht.

4. In a 1904 note Yeats identified music of this

original lyric as "an old Irish air" and the music
for the two original lyrics below as airs heard in a
dream by a member of the original cast.

MICHAEL. What was it brought him to his death?

OLD WOMAN. He died for love of me: many a man has died for love of me.

Peter [*aside to* BRIDGET]. Her trouble has put her wits astray.

MICHAEL. Is it long since that song was made? Is it long since he got his death?

OLD WOMAN. Not long, not long. But there were others that died for love of me a long time ago.

MICHAEL. Were they neighbours of your own, ma'am?

OLD WOMAN. Come here beside me and I'll tell you about them.

[MICHAEL *sits down beside her on the hearth.*]

There was a red man of the O'Donnells from the north, and a man of the O'Sullivans from the south, and there was one Brian that lost his life at Clontarf by the sea,[5] and there were a great many in the west, some that died hundreds of years ago, and there are some that will die to-morrow.

MICHAEL. Is it in the west that men will die to-morrow?

OLD WOMAN. Come nearer, nearer to me.

BRIDGET. Is she right, do you think? Or is she a woman from beyond the world?

PETER. She doesn't know well what she's talking about, with the want and the trouble she has gone through.

BRIDGET. The poor thing, we should treat her well.

PETER. Give her a drink of milk and a bit of the oaten cake.

BRIDGET. Maybe we should give her something along with that, to bring her on her way. A few pence or a shilling itself, and we with so much money in the house.

PETER. Indeed I'd not begrudge it to her if we had it to spare, but if we go running through what we have, we'll soon have to break the hundred pounds, and that would be a pity.

BRIDGET. Shame on you, Peter. Give her the shilling and your blessing with it, or our own luck will go from us.

[PETER *goes to the box and takes out a shilling.*]

BRIDGET [*to the* OLD WOMAN]. Will you have a drink of milk, ma'am?

OLD WOMAN. It is not food or drink that I want.

PETER [*offering the shilling*]. Here is something for you.

OLD WOMAN. This is not what I want. It is not silver I want.

PETER. What is it you would be asking for?

OLD WOMAN. If anyone would give me help he must give me himself, he must give me all.

5. Red Hugh O'Donnell (1571–1602), Donal O'Sullivan Beare (c. 1560–1618), and Brian Boru (926–1014).

[PETER *goes over to the table staring at the shilling in his hand in a bewildered way, and stands whispering to* BRIDGET.]

MICHAEL. Have you no one to care you in your age, ma'am?

OLD WOMAN. I have not. With all the lovers that brought me their love I never set out the bed for any.

MICHAEL. Are you lonely going the roads, ma'am?

OLD WOMAN. I have my thoughts and I have my hopes.

MICHAEL. What hopes have you to hold to?

OLD WOMAN. The hope of getting my beautiful fields back again; the hope of putting the strangers out of my house.

MICHAEL. What way will you do that, ma'am?

OLD WOMAN. I have good friends that will help me. They are gathering to help me now. I am not afraid. If they are put down to-day they will get the upper hand to-morrow. [*She gets up.*] I must be going to meet my friends. They are coming to help me and I must be there to welcome them. I must call the neighbours together to welcome them.

MICHAEL. I will go with you.

BRIDGET. It is not her friends you have to go and welcome, Michael; it is the girl coming into the house you have to welcome. You have plenty to do; it is food and drink you have to bring to the house. The woman that is coming home is not coming with empty hands; you would not have an empty house before her. [*To the* OLD WOMAN.] Maybe you don't know, ma'am, that my son is going to be married to-morrow.

OLD WOMAN. It is not a man going to his marriage that I look to for help.

PETER [*to* BRIDGET]. Who is she, do you think, at all?

BRIDGET. You did not tell us your name yet, ma'am.

OLD WOMAN. Some call me the Poor Old Woman, and there are some that call me Cathleen, the daughter of Houlihan.

PETER. I think I knew some one of that name, once. Who was it, I wonder? It must have been some one I knew when I was a boy. No, no; I remember, I heard it in a song.

OLD WOMAN [*who is standing in the doorway*]. They are wondering that there were songs made for me; there have been many songs made for me. I heard one on the wind this morning. [*Sings.*]

> Do not make a great keening
> When the graves have been dug to-morrow.
> Do not call the white-scarfed riders
> To the burying that shall be to-morrow.
> Do not spread food to call strangers
> To the wakes that shall be to-morrow;
> Do not give money for prayers
> For the dead that shall die to-morrow. . . .

They will have no need of prayers, they will have no need of prayers.

MICHAEL.   I do not know what that song means, but tell me something I can do for you.

PETER.   Come over to me, Michael.

MICHAEL.   Hush, father, listen to her.

OLD WOMAN.   It is a hard service they take that help me. Many that are red-cheeked now will be pale-cheeked; many that have been free to walk the hills and the bogs and the rushes will be sent to walk hard streets in far countries; many a good plan will be broken; many that have gathered money will not stay to spend it; many a child will be born and there will be no father at its christening to give it a name. They that have red cheeks will have pale cheeks for my sake, and for all that, they will think they are well paid. [*She goes out; her voice is heard outside singing.*]

> They shall be remembered for ever,
> They shall be alive for ever,
> They shall be speaking for ever,
> The people shall hear them for ever.

BRIDGET [*to* PETER].   Look at him, Peter; he has the look of a man that has got the touch. [*Raising her voice*] Look here, Michael, at the wedding clothes. Such grand clothes as these are! You have a right to fit them on now; it would be a pity to-morrow if they did not fit. The boys would be laughing at you. Take them, Michael, and go into the room and fit them on [*She puts them on his arm.*]

MICHAEL.   What wedding are you talking of? What clothes will I be wearing to-morrow?

BRIDGET.   These are the clothes you are going to wear when you marry Delia Cahel to-morrow.

MICHAEL.   I had forgotten that. [*He looks at the clothes and turns towards the inner room, but stops at the sound of cheering outside.*]

PETER.   There is the shouting come to our own door. What is it has happened?

[*Neighbours come crowding in,* PATRICK *and* DELIA *with them.*]

PATRICK.   There are ships in the Bay; the French are landing at Killala!

[PETER *takes his pipe from his mouth and his hat off, and stands up. The clothes slip from* MICHAEL'S *arm.*]

DELIA.   Michael!

[*He takes no notice.*]

Michael!

[*He turns towards her.*]

Why do you look at me like a stranger?

[*She drops his arm.* BRIDGET *goes over towards her.*]

PATRICK. The boys are all hurrying down the hillside to join the French.

DELIA. Michael won't be going to join the French.

BRIDGET [*to* PETER]. Tell him not to go, Peter.

PETER. It's no use. He doesn't hear a word we're saying.

BRIDGET. Try and coax him over to the fire.

DELIA. Michael, Michael! You won't leave me! You won't join the French, and we going to be married!

[*She puts her arms about him, he turns towards her as if about to yield.*]

OLD WOMAN'S *voice outside.*

They shall be speaking for ever,
The people shall hear them for ever.

[MICHAEL *breaks away from* DELIA, *stands for a second at the door, then rushes out, following the* OLD WOMAN'S *voice.* BRIDGET *takes* DELIA, *who is crying silently, into her arms.*]

PETER [*to* PATRICK, *laying a hand on his arm*]. Did you see an old woman going down the path?

PATRICK. I did not, but I saw a young girl, and she had the walk of a queen.

W. B. YEATS

On Baile's Strand †

Persons in the Play

A FOOL
A BLIND MAN
CUCHULAIN, *King of Muirthemne* [1]
CONCHUBAR, *High King of Uladh*
A YOUNG MAN, *son of Cuchulain*
KINGS AND SINGING WOMEN

A great hall at Dundealgan, not 'CUCHULAIN's *great ancient house' but
an assembly-house nearer to the sea. A big door at the back, and through
the door the misty light as of sea-mist. There are many chairs and one
long bench. One of these chairs, which is towards the front of the stage,
is bigger than the others. Somewhere at the back there is a table with
flagons of ale upon it and drinking-horns. There is a small door at one
side of the hall. A* FOOL *and* BLIND MAN, *both ragged, and their features
made grotesque and extravagant by masks, come in through the door at
the back. The* BLIND MAN *leans upon a staff.*

FOOL.   What a clever man you are though you are blind! There's nobody
with two eyes in his head that is a clever as you are. Who but you
could have thought that the henwife sleeps every day a little at noon?
I would never be able to steal anything if you didn't tell me where to
look for it. And what a good cook you are! You take the fowl out of
my hands after I have stolen it and plucked it, and you put it into the
big pot at the fire there, and I can go out and run races with the
witches at the edge of the waves and get an appetite, and when I've
got it, there's the hen waiting inside for me, done to the turn.
BLIND MAN [*who is feeling about with his stick*].   Done to the turn.
FOOL [*putting his arm round* BLIND MAN's *neck*].   Come now, I'll have

† From *The Collected Plays of W. B. Yeats*, rev.
ed. (New York: Macmillan, 1953).
1. Proper names and place names throughout the
play are taken from the Red Branch cycle of pre-
Christian, Celtic mythology and epic poetry.

a leg and you'll have a leg, and we'll draw lots for the wish-bone. I'll
be praising you, I'll be praising you while we're eating it, for your
good plans and for your good cooking. There's nobody in the world
like you, Blind Man. Come, come. Wait a minute. I shouldn't have
closed the door. There are some that look for me, and I wouldn't like
them not to find me. Don't tell it to anybody, Blind Man. There are
some that follow me. Boann herself out of the river and Fand out of
the deep sea. Witches they are, and they come by in the wind, and
they cry, 'Give a kiss, Fool, give a kiss', that's what they cry. That's
wide enough. All the witches can come in now. I wouldn't have them
beat at the door and say, 'Where is the Fool? Why has he put a lock
on the door?' Maybe they'll hear the bubbling of the pot and come in
and sit on the ground. But we won't give them any of the fowl. Let
them go back to the sea, let them go back to the sea.

BLIND MAN [*feeling legs of big chair with his hands*].   Ah! [*Then, in a
louder voice as he feels the back of it*] Ah—ah—

FOOL.   Why do you say 'Ah-ah'?

BLIND MAN.   I know the big chair. It is to-day the High King Conchubar
is coming. They have brought out his chair. He is going to be Cuchulain's master in earnest from this day out. It is that he's coming for.

FOOL.   He must be a great man to be Cuchulain's master.

BLIND MAN.   So he is. He is a great man. He is over all the rest of the
kings of Ireland.

FOOL.   Cuchulain's master! I thought Cuchulain could do anything he
liked.

BLIND MAN.   So he did, so he did. But he ran too wild, and Conchubar
is coming to-day to put an oath upon him that will stop his rambling
and make him as biddable[2] as a house-dog and keep him always at
his hand. He will sit in this chair and put the oath upon him.

FOOL.   How will he do that?

BLIND MAN.   You have no wits to understand such things. [*The* BLIND
MAN *has got into the chair.*] He will sit up in this chair and he'll say:
'Take the oath, Cuchulain. I bid you take the oath. Do as I tell you.
What are your wits compared with mine, and what are your riches
compared with mine? And what sons have you to pay your debts and
to put a stone over you when you die? Take the oath, I tell you. Take
a strong oath.'

FOOL [*crumpling himself up and whining*].   I will not. I'll take no oath.
I want my dinner.

BLIND MAN.   Hush, hush! It is not done yet.

FOOL.   You said it was done to a turn.

BLIND MAN.   Did I, now? Well, it might be done, and not done. The
wings might be white, but the legs might be red. The flesh might stick

2. Obedient.

hard to the bones and not come away in the teeth. But, believe me, Fool, it will be well done before you put your teeth in it.

FOOL.   My teeth are growing long with the hunger.

BLIND MAN.   I'll tell you a story—the kings have story-tellers while they are waiting for their dinner—I will tell you a story with a fight in it, a story with a champion in it, and a ship and a queen's son that has his mind set on killing somebody that you and I know.

FOOL.   Who is that? Who is he coming to kill?

BLIND MAN.   Wait, now, till you hear. When you were stealing the fowl, I was lying in a hole in the sand, and I heard three men coming with a shuffling sort of noise. They were wounded and groaning.

FOOL.   Go on. Tell me about the fight.

BLIND MAN.   There had been a fight, a great fight, a tremendous great fight. A young man had landed on the shore, the guardians of the shore had asked his name, and he had refused to tell it, and he had killed one, and others had run away.

FOOL.   That's enough. Come on now to the fowl. I wish it was bigger. I wish it was as big as a goose.

BLIND MAN.   Hush! I haven't told you all. I know who that young man is. I heard the men who were running away say he had red hair, that he had come from Aoife's country, that he was coming to kill Cuchulain.

FOOL.   Nobody can do that. [*To a tune.*]

> Cuchulain has killed kings,
> Kings and sons of kings,
> Dragons out of the water,
> And witches out of the air,

Banachas and Bonachas and people of the woods.

BLIND MAN.   Hush! hush!

FOOL [*still singing*].

> Witches that steal the milk,
> Fomor[3] that steal the children,
> Hags that have heads like hares,
> Hares that have claws like witches,
> All riding a-cock-horse[4]

[*Spoken.*] Out of the very bottom of the bitter black North.

BLIND MAN.   Hush, I say!

FOOL.   Does Cuchulain know that he is coming to kill him?

BLIND MAN.   How would he know that with his head in the clouds? He doesn't care for common fighting. Why would he put himself out,

---

3. Fomorians, creatures of the night.   4. On horseback.

and nobody in it but that young man? Now if it were a white fawn
that might turn into a queen before morning—

FOOL.   Come to the fowl. I wish it was as big as a pig; a fowl with goose
grease and pig's crackling.

BLIND MAN.   No hurry, no hurry. I know whose son it is. I wouldn't tell
anybody else, but I will tell you,—a secret is better to you than your
dinner. You like being told secrets.

FOOL.   Tell me the secret.

BLIND MAN.   That young man is Aoife's son. I am sure it is Aoife's son,
it flows in upon me that it is Aoife's son. You have often heard me
talking of Aoife, the great woman-fighter Cuchulain got the mastery
over in the North?

FOOL.   I know, I know. She is one of those cross queens that live in
hungry Scotland.

BLIND MAN.   I am sure it is her son. I was in Aoife's country for a long
time.

FOOL.   That was before you were blinded for putting a curse upon the
wind.

BLIND MAN.   There was a boy in her house that had her own red colour
on him, and everybody said he was to be brought up to kill Cuchulain, that she hated Cuchulain. She used to put a helmet on a pillar-
stone and call it Cuchulain and set him casting at it. There is a step
outside—Cuchulain's step.

[CUCHULAIN *passes by in the mist outside the big door.*]

FOOL.   Where is Cuchulain going?

BLIND MAN.   He is going to meet Conchubar that has bidden him to
take the oath.

FOOL.   Ah, an oath, Blind Man. How can I remember so many things
at once? Who is going to take an oath?

BLIND MAN.   Cuchulain is going to take an oath to Conchubar who is
High King.

FOOL.   What a mix-up you make of everything, Blind Man! You were
telling me one story, and now you are telling me another story. . . .
How can I get the hang of it at the end if you mix everything at the
beginning? Wait till I settle it out. There now, there's Cuchulain [*he
points to one foot*], and there is the young man [*he points to the other
foot*] that is coming to kill him, and Cuchulain doesn't know. But
where's Conchubar? [*Takes bag from side.*] That's Conchubar with all
his riches—Cuchulain, young man, Conchubar.—And where's Aoife?
[*Throws up cap.*] There is Aoife, high up on the mountains in high
hungry Scotland. Maybe it is not true after all. Maybe it was your
own making up. It's many a time you cheated me before with your
lies. Come to the cooking-pot, my stomach is pinched and rusty.
Would you have it to be creaking like a gate?

BLIND MAN. I tell you it's true. And more than that is true. If you listen to what I say, you'll forget your stomach.

FOOL. I won't.

BLIND MAN. Listen. I know who the young man's father is, but I won't say. I would be afraid to say. Ah, Fool, you would forget everything if you could know who the young man's father is.

FOOL. Who is it? Tell me now quick, or I'll shake you. Come, out with it, or I'll shake you.

[A *murmur of voices in the distance.*]

BLIND MAN. Wait, wait. There's something coming . . . It is Cuchulain is coming. He's coming back with the High King. Go and ask Cuchulain. He'll tell you. It's little you'll care about the cooking-pot when you have asked Cuchulain that . . . [BLIND MAN *goes out by side door.*]

FOOL. I'll ask him. Cuchulain will know. He was in Aoife's country. [*Goes up stage.*] I'll ask him. [*Turns and goes down stage.*] But, no, I won't ask him, I would be afraid. [*Going up again.*] Yes, I will ask him. What harm in asking? The Blind Man said I was to ask him. [*Going down.*] No, no. I'll not ask him. He might kill me. I have but killed hens and geese and pigs. He has killed kings. [*Goes up again almost to big door.*] Who says I'm afraid? I'm not afraid. I'm no coward. I'll ask him. No, no, Cuchulain, I'm not going to ask you.

> He has killed kings,
> Kings and the sons of kings,
> Dragons out of the water,
> And witches out of the air,
> Banachas and Bonachas and people of the woods.

[FOOL *goes out by side door, the last words being heard outside.* CUCHULAIN *and* CONCHUBAR *enter through the big door at the back. While they are still outside,* CUCHULAIN's *voice is heard raised in anger. He is a dark man, something over forty years of age.* CONCHUBAR *is much older and carries a long staff, elaborately carved or with an elaborate gold handle.*]

CUCHULAIN. Because I have killed men without your bidding
And have rewarded others at my own pleasure,
Because of half a score of trifling things,
You'd lay this oath upon me, and now—and now
You add another pebble to the heap,
And I must be your man, well-nigh your bondsman,
Because a youngster out of Aoife's country
Has found the shore ill-guarded.

CONCHUBAR. He came to land

While you were somewhere out of sight and hearing,
Hunting or dancing with your wild companions.
CUCHULAIN. He can be driven out. I'll not be bound.
I'll dance or hunt, or quarrel or make love,
Wherever and whenever I've a mind to.
If time had not put water in your blood,
You never would have thought it.
CONCHUBAR. I would leave
A strong and settled country to my children.
CUCHULAIN. And I must be obedient in all things;
Give up my will to yours; go where you please;
Come when you call; sit at the council-board
Among the unshapely bodies of old men;
I whose mere name has kept this country safe,
I that in early days have driven out
Maeve of Cruachan and the northern pirates,
The hundred kings of Sorcha, and the kings
Out of the Garden in the East of the World.
Must I, that held you on the throne when all
Had pulled you from it, swear obedience
As if I were some cattle-raising king?
Are my shins speckled with the heat of the fire,
Or have my hands no skill but to make figures
Upon the ashes with a stick? Am I
So slack and idle that I need a whip
Before I serve you?
CONCHUBAR. No, no whip, Cuchulain,
But every day my children come and say:
'This man is growing harder to endure.
How can we be at safety with this man
That nobody can buy or bid or bind?
We shall be at his mercy when you are gone;
He burns the earth as if he were a fire,
And time can never touch him'
CUCHULAIN. And so the tale
Grows finer yet; and I am to obey
Whatever child you set upon the throne,
As if it were yourself!
CONCHUBAR Most certainly
I am High King, my son shall be High King;
And you for all the wildness of your blood,
And though your father came out of the sun,
Are but a little king and weigh but light
In anything that touches government,
If put into the balance with my children.

CUCHULAIN.   It's well that we should speak our minds out plainly,
    For when we die we shall be spoken of
    In many countries. We in our young days
    Have seen the heavens like a burning cloud
    Brooding upon the world, and being more
    Than men can be now that cloud's lifted up,
    We should be the more truthful. Conchubar,
    I do not like your children—they have no pith,
    No marrow in their bones, and will lie soft
    Where you and I lie hard.
CONCHUBAR.   You rail at them
    Because you have no children of your own.
CUCHULAIN.   I think myself most lucky that I leave
    No pallid ghost or mockery of a man
    To drift and mutter in the corridors
    Where I have laughed and sung.
CONCHUBAR.   That is not true,
    For all your boasting of the truth between us;
    For there is no man having house and lands,
    That have been in the one family, called
    By that one family's name for centuries,
    But is made miserable if he know
    They are to pass into a stranger's keeping,
    As yours will pass.
CUCHULAIN.   The most of men feel that,
    But you and I leave names upon the harp.
CONCHUBAR.   You play with arguments as lawyers do,
    And put no heart in them. I know your thoughts,
    For we have slept under the one cloak and drunk
    From the one wine-cup. I know you to the bone,
    I have heard you cry, aye, in your very sleep,
    'I have no son', and with such bitterness
    That I have gone upon my knees and prayed
    That it might be amended.
CUCHULAIN.   For you thought
    That I should be as biddable as others
    Had I their reason for it; but that's not true;
    For I would need a weightier argument
    Than one that marred me in the copying,
    As I have that clean hawk out of the air
    That, as men say, begot this body of mine
    Upon a mortal woman.
CONCHUBAR.   Now as ever
    You mock at every reasonable hope,
    And would have nothing, or impossible things.

What eye has ever looked upon the child
Would satisfy a mind like that?
CUCHULAIN.   I would leave
My house and name to none that would not face
Even myself in battle.
CONCHUBAR.   Being swift of foot,
  And making light of every common chance,
  You should have overtaken on the hills
  Some daughter of the air, or on the shore
  A daughter of the Country-under-Wave.
CUCHULAIN.   I am not blasphemous.
CONCHUBAR.   Yet you despise
Our queens, and would not call a child your own,
  If one of them had borne him.
CUCHULAIN.   I have not said it.
CONCHUBAR.   Ah! I remember I have heard you boast,
  When the ale was in your blood, that there was one
  In Scotland, where you had learnt the trade of war,
  That had a stone-pale cheek and red-brown hair;
  And that although you have loved other women,
  You'd sooner that fierce woman of the camp
  Bore you a son than any queen among them.
CUCHULAIN.   You call her a 'fierce woman of the camp',
  For, having lived among the spinning-wheels,
  You'd have no woman near that would not say,
  'Ah! how wise!' 'What will you have for supper?'
  'What shall I wear that I may please you, sir?'
  And keep that humming through the day and night
  For ever. A fierce woman of the camp!
  But I am getting angry about nothing.
  You have never seen her. Ah! Conchubar, had you seen her
  With that high, laughing, turbulent head of hers
  Thrown backward, and the bowstring at her ear,
  Or sitting at the fire with those grave eyes
  Full of good counsel as it were with wine,
  Or when love ran through all the lineaments
  Of her wild body—although she had no child,
  None other had all beauty, queen or lover,
  Or was so fitted to give birth to kings.
CONCHUBAR.   There's nothing I can say that drifts you farther
  From the one weighty matter. That very woman—
  For I know well that you are praising Aoife—
  Now hates you and will leave no subtlety
  Unknotted that might run into a noose
  About your throat, no army in idleness

That might bring ruin on this land you serve.
CUCHULAIN.   No wonder in that, no wonder at all in that.
I never have known love but as a kiss
In the mid-battle, and a difficult truce
Of oil and water, candles and dark night,
Hillside and hollow, the hot-footed sun
And the cold, sliding, slippery-footed moon—
A brief forgiveness between opposites
That have been hatreds for three times the age
Of this long-'stablished ground.
CONCHUBAR.   Listen to me.
Aoife makes war on us, and every day
Our enemies grow greater and beat the walls
More bitterly, and you within the walls
Are every day more turbulent; and yet,
When I would speak about these things, your fancy
Runs as it were a swallow on the wind.

> [*Outside the door in the blue light of the sea-mist are many old
> and young* KINGS; *amongst them are three* WOMEN, *two of whom
> carry a bowl of fire. The third, in what follows, puts from time
> to time fragrant herbs into the fire so that it flickers up into
> brighter flame.*]

Look at the door and what men gather there—
Old counsellors that steer the land with me,
And younger kings, the dancers and harp-players
That follow in your tumults, and all these
Are held there by the one anxiety.
Will you be bound into obedience
And so make this land safe for them and theirs?
You are but half a king and I but half;
I need your might of hand and burning heart,
And you my wisdom.
CUCHULAIN [*going near to door*].   Nestlings of a high nest,
Hawks that have followed me into the air
And looked upon the sun, we'll out of this
And sail upon the wind once more. This king
Would have me take an oath to do his will,
And having listened to his tune from morning,
I will no more of it. Run to the stable
And set the horses to the chariot-pole,
And send a messenger to the harp-players.
We'll find a level place among the woods,
And dance awhile.
A YOUNG KING.   Cuchulain, take the oath.

There is none here that would not have you take it.
CUCHULAIN.   You'd have me take it? Are you of one mind?
THE KINGS.   All, all, all, all!
A YOUNG KING.   Do what the High King bids you.
CONCHUBAR.   There is not one but dreads this turbulence
  Now that they're settled men.
CUCHULAIN.   Are you so changed,
  Or have I grown more dangerous of late?
  But that's not it. I understand it all.
  It's you that have changed. You've wives and children now,
  And for that reason cannot follow one
  That lives like a bird's flight from tree to tree.—
  It's time the years put water in my blood
  And drowned the wildness of it, for all's changed,
  But that unchanged.—I'll take what oath you will:
  The moon, the sun, the water, light, or air,
  I do not care how binding.
CONCHUBAR.   On this fire
  That has been lighted from your hearth and mine;
  The older men shall be my witnesses,
  The younger, yours. The holders of the fire
  Shall purify the thresholds of the house
  With waving fire, and shut the outer door,
  According to the custom; and sing rhyme
  That has come down from the old law-makers
  To blow the witches out. Considering
  That the wild will of man could be oath-bound,
  But that a woman's could not, they bid us sing
  Against the will of woman at its wildest
  In Shape-Changers that run upon the wind.

  [CONCHUBAR *has gone on to his throne.*]

THE WOMEN.   [*They sing in a very low voice after the first few words so
  that the others will all but drown their words.*]

            May this fire have driven out
            The Shape-Changers that can put
            Ruin on a great king's house
            Until all be ruinous.
            Names whereby a man has known
            The threshold and the hearthstone,
            Gather on the wind and drive
            The women none can kiss and thrive,
            For they are but whirling wind,
            Out of memory and mind.

They would make a prince decay
With light images of clay
Planted in the running wave;
Or, for many shapes they have,
They would change them into hounds
Until he had died of his wounds,
Though the change were but a whim;
Or they'd hurl a spell at him,
That he follow with desire
Bodies that can never tire
Or grow kind, for they anoint
All their bodies, joint by joint,
With a miracle-working juice
That is made out of the grease
Of the ungoverned unicorn.
But the man is thrice forlorn,
Emptied, ruined, wracked, and lost,
That they follow, for at most
They will give him kiss for kiss
While they murmur, 'After this
Hatred may be sweet to the taste'.
Those wild hands that have embraced
All his body can but shove
At the burning wheel of love
Till the side of hate comes up.
Therefore in this ancient cup
May the sword-blades drink their fill
Of the home-brew there, until
They will have for masters none
But the threshold and hearthstone.

CUCHULAIN [*speaking, while they are singing*]. I'll take and keep this
oath, and from this day
I shall be what you please, my chicks, my nestlings.
Yet I had thought you were of those that praised
Whatever life could make the pulse run quickly,
Even though it were brief, and that you held
That a free gift was better than a forced.—
But that's all over.—I will keep it, too;
I never gave a gift and took it again.
If the wild horse should break the chariot-pole,
It would be punished. Should that be in the oath?

[*Two of the* WOMEN, *still singing, crouch in front of him holding
the bowl over their heads. He spreads his hands over the flame.*]

I swear to be obedient in all things
To Conchubar, and to uphold his children.
CONCHUBAR.   We are one being, as these flames are one:
I give my wisdom, and I take your strength.
Now thrust the swords into the flame, and pray
That they may serve the threshold and the hearthstone
With faithful service.

> [*The* KINGS *kneel in a semicircle before the two* WOMEN *and* CUCHULAIN, *who thrusts his sword into the flame. They all put the points of their swords into the flame. The third* WOMAN *is at the back near the big door.*]

CUCHULAIN.   O pure, glittering ones
That should be more than wife or friend or mistress,
Give us the enduring will, the unquenchable hope,
The friendliness of the sword!—

> [*The song grows louder, and the last words ring out clearly. There is a loud knocking at the door, and a cry of* 'Open! open!']

CONCHUBAR.   Some king that has been loitering on the way.
Open the door, for I would have all know
That the oath's finished and Cuchulain bound,
And that the swords are drinking up the flame.

> [*The door is opened by the third* WOMAN, *and a* YOUNG MAN *with a drawn sword enters.*]

YOUNG MAN.   I am of Aoife's country.

> [*The* KINGS *rush towards him.* CUCHULAIN *throws himself between.*]

CUCHULAIN.
He is but one. Aoife is far away.
YOUNG MAN.   I have come alone into the midst of you
To weigh this sword against Cuchulain's sword.
CONCHUBAR.   And are you noble? for if of common seed,
You cannot weigh your sword against his sword
But in mixed battle.
YOUNG MAN.   I am under bonds
To tell my name to no man; but it's noble.
CONCHUBAR.   But I would know your name and not your bonds.
You cannot speak in the Assembly House,
If you are not noble.
FIRST OLD KING.   Answer the High King!
YOUNG MAN.   I will give no other proof than the hawk gives
That it's no sparrow! [*He is silent for a moment, then speaks to all.*]
                    Yet look upon me, Kings.

I, too, am of that ancient seed, and carry
The signs about this body and in these bones.
CUCHULAIN.   To have shown the hawk's grey feather is enough,
And you speak highly, too. Give me that helmet.
I'd thought they had grown weary sending champions.
That sword and belt will do. This fighting's welcome.
The High King there has promised me his wisdom;
But the hawk's sleepy till its well-beloved
Cries out amid the acorns, or it has seen
Its enemy like a speck upon the sun.
What's wisdom to the hawk, when that clear eye
Is burning nearer up in the high air?

> [*Looks hard at* YOUNG MAN; *then comes down steps and grasps*
> YOUNG MAN *by shoulder.*]

Hither into the light.
[*To* CONCHUBAR.]   The very tint
Of her that I was speaking of but now.
Not a pin's difference.
[*To* YOUNG MAN.]   You are from the North,
Where there are many that have that tint of hair—
Red-brown, the light red-brown. Come nearer, boy,
For I would have another look at you.
There's more likeness—a pale, a stone-pale cheek.
What brought you, boy? Have you no fear of death?
YOUNG MAN.   Whether I live or die is in the gods' hands.
CUCHULAIN.   That is all words, all words; a young man's talk.
I am their plough, their harrow, their very strength;
For he that's in the sun begot this body
Upon a mortal woman, and I have heard tell
It seemed as if he had outrun the moon
That he must follow always through waste heaven,
He loved so happily. He'll be but slow
To break a tree that was so sweetly planted.
Let's see that arm. I'll see it if I choose.
That arm had a good father and a good mother,
But it is not like this.
YOUNG MAN.   You are mocking me;
You think I am not worthy to be fought.
But I'll not wrangle but with this talkative knife.
CUCHULAIN.   Put up your sword; I am not mocking you.
I'd have you for my friend, but if it's not
Because you have a hot heart and a cold eye,
I cannot tell the reason.
[*To* CONCHUBAR.]   He has got her fierceness,

And nobody is as fierce as those pale women.
But I will keep him with me, Conchubar,
That he may set my memory upon her
When the day's fading.—You will stop with us,
And we will hunt the deer and the wild bulls;
And, when we have grown weary, light our fires
Between the wood and water, or on some mountain
Where the Shape-Changers of the morning come.
The High King there would make a mock of me
Because I did not take a wife among them.
Why do you hang your head? It's a good life:
The head grows prouder in the light of the dawn,
And friendship thickens in the murmuring dark
Where the spare hazels meet the wool-white foam.
But I can see there's no more need for words
And that you'll be my friend from this day out.

CONCHUBAR.   He has come hither not in his own name
But in Queen Aoife's, and has challenged us
In challenging the foremost man of us all.

CUCHULAIN.   Well, well, what matter?

CONCHUBAR.   You think it does not matter,
And that a fancy lighter than the air,
A whim of the moment, has more matter in it.
For, having none that shall reign after you,
You cannot think as I do, who would leave
A throne too high for insult.

CUCHULAIN.   Let your children
Re-mortar their inheritance, as we have,
And put more muscle on.—I'll give you gifts,
But I'd have something too—that arm-ring, boy.
We'll have this quarrel out when you are older.

YOUNG MAN.   There is no man I'd sooner have my friend
Than you, whose name has gone about the world
As if it had been the wind; but Aoife'd say
I had turned coward.

CUCHULAIN.   I will give you gifts
That Aoife'll know, and all her people know,
To have come from me.

    [*Showing cloak.*]

My father gave me this.
He came to try me, rising up at dawn
Out of the cold dark of the rich sea.
He challenged me to battle, but before
My sword had touched his sword, told me his name,

Gave me this cloak, and vanished. It was woven
By women of the Country-under-Wave
Out of the fleeces of the sea. O! tell her
I was afraid, or tell her what you will.
No; tell her that I heard a raven croak
On the north side of the house, and was afraid.
CONCHUBAR.   Some witch of the air has troubled Cuchulain's mind.
CUCHULAIN.   No witchcraft. His head is like a woman's head
  I had a fancy for.
CONCHUBAR.   A witch of the air
  Can make a leaf confound us with memories.
  They run upon the wind and hurl the spells
  That make us nothing, out of the invisible wind.
  They have gone to school to learn the trick of it.
CUCHULAIN.   No, no—there's nothing out of common here;
  The winds are innocent.—That arm-ring, boy.
A KING.   If I've your leave I'll take this challenge up.
ANOTHER KING.   No, give it me, High King, for this wild Aoife
  Has carried off my slaves   .
ANOTHER KING.   No, give it me,
  For she has harried me in house and herd.
ANOTHER KING.   I claim this fight.
OTHER KINGS [together].   And I! And I! And I!
CUCHULAIN.   Back! back! Put up your swords! Put up your swords!
  There's none alive that shall accept a challenge
  I have refused. Laegaire, put up your sword!
YOUNG MAN.   No, let them come. If they've a mind for it,
  I'll try it out with any two together.
CUCHULAIN.   That's spoken as I'd have spoken it at your age.
  But you are in my house. Whatever man
  Would fight with you shall fight it out with me.
  They're dumb, they're dumb. How many of you would meet

      [Draws sword.]

This mutterer, this old whistler, this sand-piper,
This edge that's greyer than the tide, this mouse
That's gnawing at the timbers of the world,
This, this—Boy, I would meet them all in arms
If I'd a son like you. He would avenge me
When I have withstood for the last time the men
Whose fathers, brothers, sons, and friends I have killed
Upholding Conchubar, when the four provinces [5]

---

5. The traditional provinces of Ireland (Ulster, Munster, Leinster, and Connacht), as in *Cathleen Ni Houlihan*.

Have gathered with the ravens over them.
But I'd need no avenger. You and I
Would scatter them like water from a dish.
YOUNG MAN.   We'll stand by one another from this out.
Here is the ring.
CUCHULAIN.   No, turn and turn about.
But my turn's first because I am the older. [*Spreading out cloak.*]
Nine queens out of the Country-under-Wave
Have woven it with the fleeces of the sea
And they were long embroidering at it.—Boy
If I had fought my father, he'd have killed me,
As certainly as if I had a son
And fought with him, I should be deadly to him;
For the old fiery fountains are far off
And every day there is less heat o' the blood.
CONCHUBAR [*in a loud voice*].   No more of this. I will not have
     this friendship.
Cuchulain is my man, and I forbid it.
He shall not go unfought, for I myself—
CUCHULAIN.   I will not have it.
CONCHUBAR.   You lay commands on me?
CUCHULAIN [*seizing* CONCHUBAR].   You shall not stir, High King. I'll
     hold you there.
CONCHUBAR.   Witchcraft has maddened you.
THE KINGS [*shouting*].   Yes, witchcraft! witchcraft!
FIRST OLD KING.   Some witch has worked upon your mind, Cuchulain.
The head of that young man seemed like a woman's
You'd had a fancy for. Then of a sudden
You laid your hands on the High King himself!
CUCHULAIN.   And laid my hands on the High King himself?
CONCHUBAR.   Some witch is floating in the air above us.
CUCHULAIN.   Yes, witchcraft! witchcraft! Witches of the air!
   [*To* YOUNG MAN.] Why did you? Who was it set you to this work?
Out, out! I say, for now it's sword on sword!
YOUNG MAN.   But . . . but I did not.
CUCHULAIN.   Out, I say, out, out!

   [YOUNG MAN *goes out followed by* CUCHULAIN. *The* KINGS *follow
   them out with confused cries, and words one can hardly hear
   because of the noise. Some cry,* 'Quicker, quicker!' 'Why are you
   so long at the door?' 'We'll be too late!' 'Have they begun to
   fight?' 'Can you see if they are fighting?' *and so on. Their voices
   drown each other. The three* WOMEN *are left alone.*]

FIRST WOMAN.   I have seen, I have seen!
SECOND WOMAN.   What do you cry aloud?
FIRST WOMAN.   The Ever-living have shown me what's to come.

THIRD WOMAN. How? Where?
FIRST WOMAN.   In the ashes of the bowl.
SECOND WOMAN. While you were holding it between your hands?
THIRD WOMAN. Speak quickly!
FIRST WOMAN.   I have seen Cuchulain's roof-tree
  Leap into fire, and the walls split and blacken.
SECOND WOMAN. Cuchulain has gone out to die.
THIRD WOMAN.   O! O!
SECOND WOMAN. Who could have thought that one so great as he
  Should meet his end at this unnoted sword!
FIRST WOMAN. Life drifts between a fool and a blind man
  To the end, and nobody can know his end.
SECOND WOMAN. Come, look upon the quenching of this greatness.

> [*The other two go to the door, but they stop for a moment upon the threshold and wail.*]

FIRST WOMAN. No crying out, for there'll be need of cries
  And rending of the hair when it's all finished.

> [*The* WOMEN *go out. There is the sound of clashing swords from time to time during what follows. Enter the Fool, dragging the Blind Man.*]

FOOL. You have eaten it, you have eaten it! You have left me nothing but the bones. [*He throws* BLIND MAN *down by big chair.*]
BLIND MAN. O, that I should have to endure such a plague! O, I ache all over! O, I am pulled to pieces! This is the way you pay me all the good I have done you.
FOOL. You have eaten it! You have told me lies. I might have known you had eaten it when I saw your slow, sleepy walk. Lie there till the kings come. O, I will tell Conchubar and Cuchulain and all the kings about you!
BLIND MAN. What would have happened to you but for me, and you without your wits? If I did not take care of you, what would you do for food and warmth?
FOOL. You take care of me? You stay safe, and send me into every kind of danger. You sent me down the cliff for gulls' eggs while you warmed your blind eyes in the sun; and then you ate all that were good for food. You left me the eggs that were neither egg nor bird.

> [BLIND MAN *tries to rise;* FOOL *makes him lie down again.*]

Keep quiet now, till I shut the door. There is some noise outside—a high vexing noise, so that I can't be listening to myself. [*Shuts the big door.*] Why can't they be quiet? Why can't they be quiet?

> [BLIND MAN *tries to get away.*]

Oh! you would get away, would you?

[*Follows* BLIND MAN *and brings him back.*]

Lie there! lie there! No, you won't get away! Lie there till the kings come. I'll tell them all about you. I will tell it all. How you sit warming yourself, when you have made me light a fire of sticks, while I sit blowing it with my mouth. Do you not always make me take the windy side of the bush when it blows, and the rainy side when it rains?

BLIND MAN.   O, good Fool! listen to me. Think of the care I have taken of you. I have brought you to many a warm hearth, where there was a good welcome for you, but you would not stay there; you were always wandering about.

FOOL.   The last time you brought me in, it was not I who wandered away, but you that got put out because you took the crubeen [6] out of the pot when nobody was looking. Keep quiet, now!

CUCHULAIN [*rushing in*].   Witchcraft! There is no witchcraft on the earth, or among the witches of the air, that these hands cannot break.

FOOL.   Listen to me, Cuchulain. I left him turning the fowl at the fire. He ate it all, though I had stolen it. He left me nothing but the feathers.

CUCHULAIN.   Fill me a horn of ale!

BLIND MAN.   I gave him what he likes best. You do not know how vain this Fool is. He likes nothing so well as a feather.

FOOL.   He left me nothing but the bones and feathers. Nothing but the feathers, though I had stolen it.

CUCHULAIN.   Give me that horn. Quarrels here, too! [*Drinks.*] What is there between you two that is worth a quarrel? Out with it!

BLIND MAN.   Where would he be but for me? I must be always thinking—thinking to get food for the two of us, and when we've got it, if the moon is at the full or the tide on the turn, he'll leave the rabbit in the snare till it is full of maggots, or let the trout slip back through his hands into the stream.

[*The* FOOL *has begun singing while the* BLIND MAN *is speaking.*]

FOOL [*singing*].

> When you were an acorn on the tree-top,
>   Then was I an eagle-cock;
> Now that you are a withered old block,
>   Still am I an eagle-cock.

BLIND MAN.   Listen to him, now. That's the sort of talk I have to put up with day out, day in

[*The* FOOL *is putting the feathers into his hair.* CUCHULAIN *takes a handful of feathers out of a heap the* FOOL *has on the bench*

6. Pig's foot.

beside him, and out of the FOOL's *hair, and begins to wipe the blood from his sword with them.*]

FOOL. He has taken my feathers to wipe his sword. It is blood that he is wiping from his sword.

CUCHULAIN [*goes up to door at back and throws away feathers*]. They are standing about his body. They will not awaken him, for all his witchcraft.

BLIND MAN. It is that young champion that he has killed. He that came out of Aoife's country.

CUCHULAIN. He thought to have saved himself with witchcraft.

FOOL. That Blind Man there said he would kill you. He came from Aoife's country to kill you. That Blind Man said they had taught him every kind of weapon that he might do it. But I always knew that you would kill him.

CUCHULAIN [*to the* BLIND MAN]. You knew him, then?

BLIND MAN. I saw him, when I had my eyes, in Aoife's country.

CUCHULAIN. You were in Aoife's country?

BLIND MAN. I knew him and his mother there.

CUCHULAIN. He was about to speak of her when he died.

BLIND MAN. He was a queen's son.

CUCHULAIN. What queen? what queen? [*Seizes* BLIND MAN, *who is now sitting upon the bench.*] Was it Scathach? There were many queens. All the rulers there were queens.

BLIND MAN. No, not Scathach.

CUCHULAIN. It was Uathach, then? Speak! speak!

BLIND MAN. I cannot speak; you are clutching me too tightly.

[CUCHULAIN *lets him go.*]

I cannot remember who it was. I am not certain. It was some queen.

FOOL. He said a while ago that the young man was Aoife's son.

CUCHULAIN. She? No, no! She had no son when I was there.

FOOL. That Blind Man there said that she owned him for her son.

CUCHULAIN. I had rather he had been some other woman's son. What father had he? A soldier out of Alba? She was an amorous woman— a proud, pale, amorous woman.

BLIND MAN. None knew whose son he was.

CUCHULAIN. None knew! Did you know, old listener at doors?

BLIND MAN. No, no; I knew nothing.

FOOL. He said a while ago that he heard Aoife boast that she'd never but the one lover, and he the only man that had overcome her in battle. [*Pause.*]

BLIND MAN. Somebody is trembling, Fool! The bench is shaking. Why are you trembling? Is Cuchulain going to hurt us? It was not I who told you, Cuchulain.

FOOL. It is Cuchulain who is trembling. It is Cuchulain who is shaking the bench.

BLIND MAN. It is his own son he has slain.

CUCHULAIN. 'Twas they that did it, the pale windy people.
Where? where? where? My sword against the thunder!
But no, for they have always been my friends;
And though they love to blow a smoking coal
Till it's all flame, the wars they blow aflame
Are full of glory, and heart-uplifting pride,
And not like this. The wars they love awaken
Old fingers and the sleepy strings of harps.
Who did it then? Are you afraid? Speak out!
For I have put you under my protection,
And will reward you well. Dubthach the Chafer?
He'd an old grudge. No, for he is with Maeve.
Laegaire did it! Why do you not speak?
What is this house? [*Pause.*] Now I remember all.

[*Comes before* CONCHUBAR's *chair, and strikes out with his sword, as if* CONCHUBAR *was sitting upon it.*]

'Twas you who did it—you who sat up there
With your old rod of kingship, like a magpie
Nursing a stolen spoon. No, not a magpie,
A maggot that is eating up the earth!
Yes, but a magpie, for he's flown away.
Where did he fly to?

BLIND MAN.   He is outside the door.

CUCHULAIN.   Outside the door?

BLIND MAN.   Between the door and the sea.

CUCHULAIN.   Conchubar, Conchubar! the sword into your heart!

[*He rushes out. Pause.* FOOL *creeps up to the big door and looks after him.*]

FOOL. He is going up to King Conchubar. They are all about the young man. No, no, he is standing still. There is a great wave going to break, and he is looking at it. Ah! now he is running down to the sea, but he is holding up his sword as if he were going into a fight. [*Pause.*] Well struck! well struck!

BLIND MAN. What is he doing now?

FOOL. O! he is fighting the waves!

BLIND MAN. He sees King Conchubar's crown on every one of them.

FOOL. There, he has struck at a big one! He has struck the crown off it; he has made the foam fly. There again, another big one!

BLIND MAN. Where are the kings? What are the kings doing?

FOOL. They are shouting and running down to the shore, and the people are running out of the houses. They are all running.

BLIND MAN.   You say they are running out of the houses? There will be nobody left in the houses. Listen, Fool!

FOOL.   There, he is down! He is up again. He is going out in the deep water. There is a big wave. It has gone over him. I cannot see him now. He has killed kings and giants, but the waves have mastered him, the waves have mastered him!

BLIND MAN.   Come here, Fool!

FOOL.   The waves have mastered him.

BLIND MAN.   Come here!

FOOL.   The waves have mastered him.

BLIND MAN.   Come here, I say.

FOOL.   [coming towards him, but looking backwards towards the door].   What is it?

BLIND MAN.   There will be nobody in the houses. Come this way; come quickly! The ovens will be full. We will put our hands into the ovens.

[They go out.]

W. B. YEATS

Purgatory †

Persons in the Play

A BOY
AN OLD MAN

SCENE.—*A ruined house and a bare tree in the background.*

BOY.   Half-door, hall door,
   Hither and thither day and night,
   Hill or hollow, shouldering this pack,
   Hearing you talk.
OLD MAN.   Study that house.
   I think about its jokes and stories;
   I try to remember what the butler
   Said to a drunken gamekeeper
   In mid-October, but I cannot.
   If I cannot, none living can.
   Where are the jokes and stories of a house,
   Its threshold gone to patch a pig-sty?
BOY.   So you have come this path before?
OLD MAN.   The moonlight falls upon the path,
   The shadow of a cloud upon the house,
   And that's symbolical; study that tree,
   What is it like?
BOY.   A silly old man.
OLD MAN. It's like—no matter what it's like.
   I saw it a year ago stripped bare as now,
   So I chose a better trade.
   I saw it fifty years ago
   Before the thunderbolt had riven it,

† Reprinted with permission of Macmillan Publishing Company from *The Collected Plays of W.
B. Yeats*, rev. ed. (New York: Macmillan, 1953).

Copyright 1952 by Macmillan Publishing Company, renewed 1980 by Anne Yeats.

Green leaves, ripe leaves, leaves thick as butter,
Fat, greasy life. Stand there and look,
Because there is somebody in that house.

[*The* BOY *puts down pack and stands in the doorway.*]

BOY.   There's nobody here.
OLD MAN.   There's somebody there.
BOY.   The floor is gone, the windows gone,
    And where there should be roof there's sky,
    And here's a bit of an egg-shell thrown
    Out of a jackdaw's nest.
OLD MAN.   But there are some
    That do not care what's gone, what's left:
    The souls in Purgatory that come back
    To habitations and familiar spots.
BOY.   Your wits are out again.
OLD MAN.   Re-live
    Their transgressions, and that not once
    But many times; they know at last
    The consequence of those transgressions
    Whether upon others or upon themselves;
    Upon others, others may bring help,
    For when the consequence is at an end
    The dream must end; if upon themselves,
    There is no help but in themselves
    And in the mercy of God.
BOY.   I have had enough!
    Talk to the jackdaws, if talk you must.
OLD MAN.   Stop! Sit there upon that stone.
    That is the house where I was born.
BOY.   The big old house that was burnt down?
OLD MAN.   My mother that was your grand-dam owned it,
    This scenery and this countryside,
    Kennel and stable, horse and hound—
    She had a horse at the Curragh,[1] and there met
    My father, a groom in a training stable,
    Looked at him and married him.
    Her mother never spoke to her again,
    And she did right.
BOY.   What's right and wrong?
    My grand-dad got the girl and the money.
OLD MAN.   Looked at him and married him,
    And he squandered everything she had.

---

1. Center for Irish horse racing in county Kildare.

She never knew the worst, because
She died in giving birth to me,
But now she knows it all, being dead.
Great people lived and died in this house;
Magistrates, colonels, members of Parliament,
Captains and Governors, and long ago
Men that had fought at Aughrim and the Boyne.[2]
Some that had gone on Government work
To London or to India came home to die,
Or came from London every spring
To look at the may-blossom in the park.
They had loved the trees that he cut down
To pay what he had lost at cards
Or spent on horses, drink and women;
Had loved the house, had loved all
The intricate passages of the house,
But he killed the house; to kill a house
Where great men grew up, married, died,
I here declare a capital offence.

BOY.   My God, but you had luck! Grand clothes,
And maybe a grand horse to ride.

OLD MAN.   That he might keep me upon his level
He never sent me to school, but some
Half-loved me for my half of her:
A gamekeeper's wife taught me to read,
A Catholic curate taught me Latin.
There were old books and books made fine
By eighteenth-century French binding, books
Modern and ancient, books by the ton.

BOY.   What education have you given me?

OLD MAN.   I gave the education that befits
A bastard that a pedlar got
Upon a tinker's[3] daughter in a ditch.
When I had come to sixteen years old
My father burned down the house when drunk.

BOY.   But that is my age, sixteen years old,
At the Puck Fair.[4]

OLD MAN.   And everything was burnt;
Books, library, all were burnt.

BOY.   Is what I have heard upon the road the truth,
That you killed him in the burning house?

2. The conquest of Ireland by William of Orange
included crucial victories over the Irish at the Boyne
River on July 1, 1690, and at Aughrim on July 12,
1691.

3. An itinerant peddler's.
4. August festival in county Kerry notable for folk
traditions, including the crowning as king of a goat,
and for attendance by tinkers.

OLD MAN.   There's nobody here but our two selves?
BOY.   Nobody, Father.
OLD MAN.   I stuck him with a knife,
   That knife that cuts my dinner now,
   And after that I left him in the fire.
   They dragged him out, somebody saw
   The knife-wound but could not be certain
   Because the body was all black and charred.
   Then some that were his drunken friends
   Swore they would put me upon trial,
   Spoke of quarrels, a threat I had made.
   The gamekeeper gave me some old clothes,
   I ran away, worked here and there
   Till I became a pedlar on the roads,
   No good trade, but good enough
   Because I am my father's son,
   Because of what I did or may do.
   Listen to the hoof-beats! Listen, listen!
BOY.   I cannot hear a sound
OLD MAN.   Beat! Beat!
   This night is the anniversary
   Of my mother's wedding night,
   Or of the night wherein I was begotten.
   My father is riding from the public-house, [5]
   A whiskey-bottle under his arm.

   [A *window is lit showing a young girl.*]

   Look at the window; she stands there
   Listening, the servants are all in bed,
   She is alone, he has stayed late
   Bragging and drinking in the public-house.
BOY.   There's nothing but an empty gap in the wall.
   You have made it up. No, you are mad!
   You are getting madder every day.
OLD MAN.   It's louder now because he rides
   Upon a gravelled avenue
   All grass to-day. The hoof-beat stops,
   He has gone to the other side of the house,
   Gone to the stable, put the horse up.
   She has gone down to open the door.
   This night she is no better than her man
   And does not mind that he is half drunk,
   She is mad about him. They mount the stairs,

---

5. Tavern, or, in short form, pub.

She brings him into her own chamber.
And that is the marriage-chamber now.
The window is dimly lit again.

Do not let him touch you! It is not true
That drunken men cannot beget,
And if he touch he must beget
And you must bear his murderer.
Deaf! Both deaf! If I should throw
A stick or a stone they would not hear;
And that's a proof my wits area out.
But there's a problem: she must live
Through everything in exact detail,
Driven to it by remorse, and yet
Can she renew the sexual act
And find no pleasure in it, and if not,
If pleasure and remorse must both be there,
Which is the greater?
                    I lack schooling.
Go fetch Tertullian;[6] he and I
Will ravel all that problem out
Whilst those two lie upon the mattress
Begetting me.
              Come back! Come back!
And so you thought to slip away,
My bag of money between your fingers,
And that I could not talk and see!
You have been rummaging in the pack.

    [*The light in the window has faded out.*]

BOY.   You never gave me my right share.
OLD MAN.   And had I given it, young as you are,
   You would have spent it upon drink.
BOY.   What if I did? I had a right
   To get it and spend it as I chose.
OLD MAN.   Give me that bag and no more words.
BOY.   I will not.
OLD MAN.   I will break your fingers.

    [*They struggle for the bag. In the struggle it drops, scattering the
    money. The* OLD MAN *staggers but does not fall. They stand look-
    ing at each other. The window is lit up. A man is seen pouring
    whiskey into a glass.*]

6. Latin rhetorician and early Christian theologian (c. 160–240).

BOY.   What if I killed you? You killed my grand-dad,
Because you were young and he was old.
Now I am young and you are old.
OLD MAN.   [*staring at window*]. Better-looking, those sixteen years—
BOY.   What are you muttering?
OLD MAN.   Younger—and yet
She should have known he was not her kind.
BOY.   What are you saying? Out with it! [OLD MAN *points to window.*]
My God! The window is lit up
And somebody stands there, although
The floorboards are all burnt away.
OLD MAN.   The window is lit up because my father
Has come to find a glass for his whiskey.
He leans there like some tired beast.
BOY.   A dead, living, murdered man!
OLD MAN.   'Then the bride-sleep fell upon Adam':
Where did I read those words? [7]
                                        And yet
There's nothing leaning in the window
But the impression upon my mother's mind;
Being dead she is alone in her remorse.
BOY.   A body that was a bundle of old bones
Before I was born. Horrible! Horrible!

        [*He covers his eyes.*]

OLD MAN.   That beast there would know nothing, being nothing,
If I should kill a man under the window
He would not even turn his head.

        [*He stabs the* BOY.]

My father and my son on the same jack-knife!
That finishes—there—there—there—

        [*He stabs again and again. The window grows dark.*]

'Hush-a-bye baby, thy father's a knight,
Thy mother a lady, lovely and bright.'[8]
No, that is something that I read in a book,
And if I sing it must be to my mother,
And I lack rhyme.

        [*The stage has grown dark except where the tree stands in white
        light.*]

---

7. In "Eden Bower," by Dante Gabriel Rossetti   8. "Lullaby of an Infant Chief," by Sir Walter Scott
(1828–82), English poet.   (1771–1832).

Study that tree.
It stands there like a purified soul,
All cold, sweet, glistening light.
Dear mother, the window is dark again,
But you are in the light because
I finished all that consequence.
I killed that lad because had he grown up
He would have struck a woman's fancy,
Begot, and passed pollution on.
I am a wretched foul old man
And therefore harmless. When I have stuck
This old jack-knife into a sod
And pulled it out all bright again,
And picked up all the money that he dropped,
I'll to a distant place, and there
Tell my old jokes among new men.

[*He cleans the knife and begins to pick up money.*]

Hoof-beats! Dear God,
How quickly it returns—beat—beat—!

Her mind cannot hold up that dream.
Twice a murderer and all for nothing,
And she must animate that dead night
Not once but many times!
              O God,
Release my mother's soul from its dream!
Mankind can do no more. Appease
The misery of the living and the remorse of the dead.

LADY GREGORY

Spreading the News †

Persons

BARTLEY FALLON
MRS. FALLON
JACK SMITH
SHAWN EARLY
TIM CASEY
JAMES RYAN
MRS. TARPEY
MRS. TULLY
A POLICEMAN (JO MULDOON)
A REMOVABLE MAGISTRATE [1]

SCENE. *The outskirts of a Fair. An Apple Stall.* MRS. TARPEY *sitting at it.* MAGISTRATE *and* POLICEMAN *enter.*

MAGISTRATE. So that is the Fair Green. Cattle and sheep and mud. No system. What a repulsive sight!
POLICEMAN. That is so, indeed.
MAGISTRATE. I suppose there is as good deal of disorder in this place?
POLICEMAN. There is.
MAGISTRATE. Common assault?
POLICEMAN. It's common enough.
MAGISTRATE. Agrarian crime, no doubt?
POLICEMAN. That is so.
MAGISTRATE. Boycotting? Maiming of cattle? Firing into houses?
POLICEMAN. There was one time, and there might be again.
MAGISTRATE. That is bad. Does it go any farther than that?
POLICEMAN. Far enough, indeed.
MAGISTRATE. Homicide, then! This district has been shamefully

---

† From *The Collected Plays of Lady Gregory*, Coole Edition, published by Oxford University Press and Colin Smythe Limited.

1. An appointed, rather than elected, magistrate subject to removal from office; in Ireland, where most common, often called a "Removable."

neglected! I will change all that. When I was in the Andaman Islands,[2] my system never failed. Yes, yes, I will change all that. What has that woman on her stall?

POLICEMAN.   Apples mostly—and sweets.

MAGISTRATE.   Just see if there are any unlicensed goods underneath— spirits or the like. We had evasions of the salt tax in the Andaman Islands.

POLICEMAN [*sniffing cautiously and upsetting a heap of apples*].   I see no spirits here—or salt.

MAGISTRATE [*to* MRS. TARPEY].   Do you know this town well, my good woman?

MRS. TARPEY [*holding out some apples*].   A penny the half-dozen, your honor.

POLICEMAN [*shouting*].   The gentleman is asking do you know the town! He's the new magistrate!

MRS. TARPEY [*rising and ducking.*].   Do I know the town? I do, to be sure.

MAGISTRATE [*shouting*].   What is its chief business?

MRS. TARPEY.   Business, is it? What business would the people here have but to be minding one another's business?

MAGISTRATE.   I mean what trade have they?

MRS. TARPEY.   Not a trade. No trade at all but to be talking.

MAGISTRATE.   I shall learn nothing here.

[JAMES RYAN *comes in, pipe in mouth. Seeing* MAGISTRATE *he retreats quickly, taking pipe from mouth.*]

MAGISTRATE.   The smoke from that man's pipe had a greenish look; he may be growing unlicensed tobacco at home. I wish I had brought my telescope to this district. Come to the post-office, I will telegraph for it. I found it very useful in the Andaman Islands.

[MAGISTRATE *and* POLICEMAN *go out left.*]

MRS. TARPEY.   Bad luck to JO MULDOON, knocking my apples this way and that way. [*Begins arranging them.*] Showing off he was to the new magistrate.

[*Enter* BARTLEY FALLON *and* MRS. FALLON.]

BARTLEY.   Indeed it's a poor country and a scarce country to be living in. But I'm thinking if I went to America it's long ago the day I'd be dead!

MRS. FALLON.   So you might, indeed. [*She puts her basket on a barrel and begins putting parcels in it, taking them from under her cloak.*]

---

2. An archipelago of more than two hundred islands in the Bay of Bengal that served as a British penal colony from 1858 to 1942.

BARTLEY.   And it's a great expense for a poor man to be buried in America.

MRS. FALLON.   Never fear, Bartley Fallon, but I'll give you a good burying the day you'll die.

BARTLEY.   Maybe it's yourself will be buried in the graveyard of Cloonmara before me, Mary Fallon, and I myself that will be dying unbeknownst some night, and no one a-near me. And the cat itself may be gone straying through the country, and the mice squealing over the quilt.

MRS. FALLON.   Leave off talking of dying. It might be twenty years you'll be living yet.

BARTLEY [*with a deep sigh*].   I'm thinking if I'll be living at the end of twenty years, it's a very old man I'll be then!

MRS. TARPEY [*turns and sees them*].   Good morrow, Bartley Fallon; good morrow, Mrs. Fallon. Well, Bartley, you'll find no cause for complaining to-day; they are all saying it was a good fair.

BARTLEY [*raising his voice*].   It was not a good fair, Mrs. Tarpey. It was a scattered sort of a fair. If we didn't expect more, we got less. That's the way with me always; whatever I have to sell goes down and whatever I have to buy goes up. If there's ever any misfortune coming to this world, it's on myself in pitches, like a flock of crows on seed potatoes.

MRS. FALLON.   Leave off talking of misfortunes, and listen to Jack Smith that is coming the way, and he singing.

[*Voice of* JACK SMITH *heard singing.*]

I thought, my first love,
    There'd be but one house between you and me,
And I thought I would find
    Yourself coaxing my child on your knee.
Over the tide
    I would leap with the leap of a swan,
Till I came to the side
    Of the wife of the Red-haired man!

[JACK SMITH *comes in; he is a red-haired man, and is carrying a hayfork.*]

MRS. TARPEY.   That should be a good song if I had my hearing.

MRS. FALLON [*shouting.*].   It's "The Red-haired Man's Wife."

MRS. TARPEY.   I know it well. That's the song that has a skin on it! [*She turns her back to them and goes on arranging her apples.*]

MRS. FALLON.   Where's herself, Jack Smith?

JACK SMITH.   She was delayed with her washing; bleaching the clothes on the hedge she is, and she daren't leave them, with all the tinkers

that do be passing to the fair. It isn't to the fair I came myself, but up
to the Five Acre Meadow I'm going, where I have a contract for the
hay. We'll get a share of it into tramps to-day. [*He lays down hayfork
and lights his pipe.*]

BARTLEY.   You will not get it into tramps to-day. The rain will be down
on it by evening, and on myself too. It's seldom I ever started on a
journey but the rain would come down on me before I'd find any
place of shelter.

JACK SMITH.   If it didn't itself, Bartley, it is my belief you would carry a
leaky pail on your head in place of a hat, the way you'd not be without
some cause of complaining.

[*A voice heard,* "God on, now, go on that o' that. Go on I say."]

JACK SMITH.   Look at that young mare of Pat Ryan's that is backing into
Shaughnessy's bullocks with the dint of the crowd! Don't be daunted,
Pat, I'll give you a hand with her. [*He goes out, leaving his hayfork.*]

MRS. FALLON.   It's time for ourselves to be going home. I have all I
bought put in the basket. Look at there, Jack Smith's hayfork he left
after him! He'll be wanting it. [*Calls.*] Jack Smith! Jack Smith!—He's
gone through the crowd—hurry after him, Bartley, he'll be wanting
it.

BARTLEY.   I'll do that. This is no safe place to be leaving it. [*He takes
up fork awkwardly and upsets the basket.*] Look at that now! If there
is any basket in the fair upset, it must be our own basket! [*He goes out
to right.*]

MRS. FALLON.   Get out of that! It is your own fault, it is. Talk of misfortunes and misfortunes will come. Glory be! Look at my new eggcups rolling in every part—and my two pound of sugar with the paper
broke—

MRS. TARPEY [*turning from stall*].   God help us, Mrs. Fallon, what happened your basket?

MRS. FALLON.   It's himself that knocked it down, bad manners to him.
[*Putting things up.*] My grand sugar that's destroyed, and he'll not
drink his tea without it. I had best go back to the shop for more, much
good may it do him!

[*Enter* TIM CASEY.]

TIM CASEY.   Where is Bartley Fallon, Mrs. Fallon? I want a word with
him before he'll leave the fair. I was afraid he might have gone home
by this, for he's a temperate man.

MRS. FALLON.   I wish he did go home! It'd be best for me if he went
home straight from the fair green, or if he never came with me at all?
Where is he, is it? He's gone up the road [*jerks elbow*] following Jack
Smith with a hayfork. [*She goes out to left.*]

TIM CASEY.   Following Jack Smith with a hayfork! Did ever any one hear the like of that. [*Shouts*]. Did you hear that news, Mrs. Tarpey?

MRS. TARPEY.   I heard no news at all.

TIM CASEY.   Some dispute I suppose it was that rose between Jack Smith and Bartley Fallon, and it seems Jack made off, and Bartley is following him with a hayfork!

MRS. TARPEY.   Is he now? Well, that was quick work! It's not ten minutes since the two of them were here, Bartley going home and Jack going to the Five Acre Meadow; and I had my apples to settle up, that Jo Muldoon of the police had scattered, and when I looked round again Jack Smith was gone, and Bartley Fallon was gone, and Mrs. Fallon's basket upset, and all in it strewed upon the ground—the tea here—the two pound of sugar there—the eggcups there—Look, now, what a great hardship the deafness puts upon me, that I didn't hear the commincement of the fight! Wait till I tell James Ryan that I see below; he is a neighbour of Bartley's, it would be a pity if he wouldn't hear the news!

[*She goes out. Enter* SHAWN EARLY *and* MRS. TULLEY.]

TIM CASEY.   Listen, Shawn Early! Listen, Mrs. Tully, to the news! Jack Smith and Bartley Fallon had a falling out, and Jack knocked Mrs. Fallon's basket into the road, and Bartley made an attack on him with a hayfork, and away with Jack, and Bartley after him. Look at the sugar here yet on the road!

SHAWN EARLY.   Do you tell me so? Well, that's a queer thing, and Bartley Fallon so quiet a man!

MRS. TULLY.   I wouldn't wonder at all. I would never think well of a man that would have that sort of a mouldering look. It's likely he has overtaken Jack by this.

[*Enter* JAMES RYAN *and* MRS. TARPEY.]

JAMES RYAN.   That is great news Mrs. Tarpey was telling me! I suppose that's what brought the police and the magistrate up this way. I was wondering to see them in it a while ago.

SHAWN EARLY.   The police after them? Bartley Fallon must have injured Jack so. They wouldn't meddle in a fight that was only for show!

MRS. TULLY.   Why wouldn't he injure him? There was many a man killed with no more of a weapon than a hayfork.

JAMES RYAN.   Wait till I run north as far as Kelly's bar to spread the news! [*He goes out.*]

TIM CASEY.   I'll go tell Jack Smith's first cousin that is standing there south of the church after selling his lambs. [*Goes out.*]

MRS. TULLY.   I'll go telling a few of the neighbours I see beyond to the west. [*Goes out.*]

SHAWN EARLY.   I'll give word of it beyond at the east of the green.

[*Is going out when* MRS. TARPEY *seizes hold of him.*]

MRS. TARPEY. Stop a minute, Shawn Early, and tell me did you see red Jack Smith's wife, Kitty Keary, in any place?

SHAWN EARLY. I did. At her own house she was, drying clothes on the hedge as I passed.

MRS. TARPEY. What did you say she was doing?

SHAWN EARLY [*breaking away*]. Laying out a sheet on the hedge. [*He goes.*]

MRS. TARPEY. Laying out a sheet for the dead! The Lord have mercy on us! Jack Smith dead, and his wife laying out a sheet for his burying! [*Calls out.*] Why didn't you tell me that before, Shawn Early? Isn't the deafness the great hardship? Half the world might be dead without me knowing of it or getting word of it all! [*She sits down and rocks herself.*] O my poor Jack Smith! To be going to his work so nice and so hearty, and to be left stretched on the ground in the light of the day!

[*Enter* TIM CASEY.]

TIM CASEY. What is it, Mrs. Tarpey? What happened since?

MRS. TARPEY. O my poor Jack Smith!

TIM CASEY. Did Bartley overtake him?

MRS. TARPEY. O the poor man!

TIM CASEY. Is it killed he is?

MRS. TARPEY. Stretched on the Five Acre Meadow!

TIM CASEY. The Lord have mercy on us! Is that a fact?

MRS. TARPEY. Without the rites of the Church or a ha'porth!

TIM CASEY. Who was telling you?

MRS. TARPEY. And the wife laying out a sheet for his corpse. [*Sits up and wipes her eyes.*] I suppose they'll wake him the same as another?

[*Enter* MRS. TULLY, SHAWN EARLY, AND JAMES RYAN.]

MRS. TULLY. There is great talk about this work in every quarter of the fair.

MRS. TARPEY. Ochone![3] cold and dead. And myself maybe the last he was speaking to!

JAMES RYAN. The Lord save us! Is it dead he is?

TIM CASEY. Dead surely, and the wife getting provision for the wake.

SHAWN EARLY. Well, now, hadn't Bartley Fallon great venom in him?

MRS. TULLY. You may be sure he had some cause. Why would he have made an end of him if he had not? [*To* MRS. TARPEY, *raising her voice.*] What was it rose the dispute at all, Mrs. Tarpey?

MRS. TARPEY. Not a one of me knows. The last I saw of them, Jack

---

3. An expression of lamentation.

Smith was standing there, and Bartley Fallon was standing there, quiet and easy, and he listening to "The Red-haired Man's Wife."

MRS. TULLY.   Do you hear that, Tim Casey? Do you head that, Shawn Early and James Ryan? Bartley Fallon was there this morning listening to red Jack Smith's wife, Kitty Keary that was! Listening to her and whispering with her! It was she started the fight so!

SHAWN EARLY.   She must have followed him from her own house. It is likely some person roused him.

TIM CASEY.   I never knew, before, Bartley Fallon was great with Jack Smith's wife.

MRS. TULLY.   How would you know it? Sure it's not in the streets they would be calling it. If Mrs. Fallon didn't know of it, and if I that have the next house to them didn't know of it, and if Jack Smith himself didn't know of it, it is not likely you would know of it, Tim Casey.

SHAWN EARLY.   Let Bartley Fallon take charge of her from this out so, and let him provide for her. It is little pity she will get from any person in this parish.

TIM CASEY.   How can he take charge of her? Sure he has a wife of his own. Sure you don't think he'd turn souper and marry her in a Protestant church?

JAMES RYAN.   It would be easy for him to marry her if he brought her to America.

SHAWN EARLY.   With or without Kitty Keary, believe me it is for America he's making at this minute. I saw the new magistrate and Jo Muldoon of the police going into the post-office as I came up—there was hurry on them—you may be sure it was to telegraph they went, the way he'll be stopped in the docks at Queenstown!

MRS. TULLY.   It's like Kitty Keary is gone with him, and not minding a sheet or a wake at all. The poor man, to be deserted by his own wife, and the breath hardly gone out yet from his body that is lying bloody in the field!

[*Enter* MRS. FALLON.]

MRS. FALLON.   What is it the whole of the town is talking about? And what is it you yourselves are talking about? Is it about my man Bartley Fallon you are talking? Is it lies about him you are telling, saying that he went killing Jack Smith? My grief that ever he came into this place at all!

JAMES RYAN.   Be easy now, Mrs. Fallon. Sure there is no one at all in the whole fair but is sorry for you!

MRS. FALLON.   Sorry for me, is it? Why would any one be sorry for me? Let you be sorry for yourselves, and that there may be shame on you for ever and at the day of judgment, for the words you are saying and the lies you are telling to take away the character of my poor man, and to take the good name off of him, and to drive him to destruction! That is what you are doing!

SHAWN EARLY.   Take comfort now, Mrs. Fallon. The police are not so smart as they think. Sure he might give them the slip yet, the same as Lynchehaun.

MRS. TULLY.   If they do get him, and if they do put a rope around his neck, there is no one can say he does not deserve it!

MRS. FALLON.   Is that what you are saying, Bridget Tully, and is that what you think? I tell you it's too much talk you have, making yourself out to be such a great one, and to be running down every respectable person! A rope, is it? It isn't much of a rope was needed to tie up your own furniture the day you came into Martin Tully's house, and you never bringing as much as a blanket, or a penny, or a suit of clothes with you and I myself bringing seventy pounds and two feather beds. And now you are stiffer than a woman would have a hundred pounds! It is too much talk the whole of you have. A rope is it? I tell you the whole of this town is full of liars and schemers that would hang you up for half a glass of whiskey. [*Turning to go.*] People they are you wouldn't believe as much as daylight from without you'd get up to have a look at it yourself. Killing Jack Smith indeed! Where are you at all, Bartley, till I bring you out of this? My nice quiet little man! My decent comrade! He that is as kind and as harmless as an innocent beast of the field! He'll be doing no harm at all if he'll shed the blood of some of you after this day's work! That much would be no harm at all. [*Calls out.*] Bartley! Bartley Fallon! Where are you? [*Going out.*] Did any one see Bartley Fallon?

[*All turn to look after her.*]

JAMES RYAN.   It is hard for her to believe any such a thing, God help her!

[*Enter* BARTLEY FALLON *from right, carrying hayfork.*]

BARTLEY.   It is what I often said to myself, if there is ever any misfortune coming to this world it is on myself it is sure to come!

[*All turn round and face him.*]

BARTLEY.   To be going about with this fork and to find no one to take it, and no place to leave it down, and I wanting to be gone out of this—Is that you, Shawn Early? [*Holds out fork.*] It's well I met you. You have no call to be leaving the fair for a while the way I have, and how can I go till I'm rid of this fork? Will you take it and keep it until such time as Jack Smith—

SHAWN EARLY [*backing*].   I will not take it, Bartley Fallon, I'm very thankful to you!

BARTLEY [*turning to apple stall*].   Look at it now, Mrs. Tarpey, it was here I got it; let me thrust it in under the stall. It will lie there safe enough, and no one will take notice of it until such time as Jack Smith—

MRS. TARPEY. Take your fork out of that! Is it to put trouble on me and to destroy me you want? putting it there for the police to be rooting it out maybe. [*Thrusts him back.*]

BARTLEY. That is a very unneighbourly thing for you to do, Mrs. Tarpey. Hadn't I enough care on me with that fork before this, running up and down with it like the swinging of a clock, and afeard to lay it down in any place! I wish I never touched it or meddled with it at all!

JAMES RYAN. It is a pity, indeed, you ever did.

BARTLEY. Will you yourself take it, James Ryan? You were always a neighbourly man.

JAMES RYAN [*backing*]. There is many a thing I would do for you, Bartley Fallon, but I won't do that!

SHAWN EARLY. I tell you there is no man will give you any help or any encouragement for this day's work. If it was something agrarian now—

BARTLEY. If no one at all will take it, maybe it's best to give it up to the police.

TIM CASEY. There'd be a welcome for it with them surely! [*Laughter.*]

MRS. TULLY. And it is to the police Kitty Keary herself will be brought.

MRS. TARPEY [*rocking to and fro*]. I wonder now who will take the expense of the wake for poor Jack Smith?

BARTLEY. The wake for Jack Smith!

TIM CASEY. Why wouldn't he get a wake as well as another? Would you begrudge him that much?

BARTLEY. Red Jack Smith dead! Who was telling you?

SHAWN EARLY. The whole town knows of it by this.

BARTLEY. Do they say what way did he die?

JAMES RYAN. You don't know that yourself, I suppose, Bartley Fallon? You don't know he was followed and that he was laid dead with a stab of a hayfork?

BARTLEY. The stab of a hayfork!

SHAWN EARLY. You don't know, I suppose, that the body was found in the Five Acre Meadow?

BARTLEY. The Five Acre Meadow!

TIM CASEY. It is likely you don't know that the police are after the man that did it?

BARTLEY. The man that did it!

MRS. TULLY. You don't know, maybe, that he was made away with for the sake of Kitty Keary, his wife?

BARTLEY. Kitty Keary, his wife! [*Sits down bewildered.*]

MRS. TULLY. And what have you to say now, Bartley Fallon?

BARTLEY [*crossing himself*]. I to bring that fork here, and to find that news before me! It is much if I can ever stir from this place at all, or reach as far as the road!

TIM CASEY. Look, boys, at the new magistrate, and Jo Muldoon along with him! It's best for us to quit this.

SHAWN EARLY. That is so. It is best not to be mixed in this business at all.

JAMES RYAN. Bad as he is, I wouldn't like to be an informer against any man.

[*All hurry away except* MRS. TARPEY, *who remains behind her stall. Enter* MAGISTRATE *and* POLICEMAN.]

MAGISTRATE. I knew the district was in a bad state, but I did not expect to be confronted with a murder at the first fair I came to.

POLICEMAN. I am sure you did not, indeed.

MAGISTRATE. It was well I had not gone home. I caught a few words here and there that roused my suspicions.

POLICEMAN. So they would, too.

MAGISTRATE. You heard the same story from everyone you asked?

POLICEMAN. The same story—or if it was not altogether the same, anyway it was no less than the first story.

MAGISTRATE. What is that man doing? He is sitting alone with a hayfork. He has a guilty look. The murder was done with a hayfork!

POLICEMAN [*in a whisper*]. That's the very man they say did the act; Bartley Fallon himself!

MAGISTRATE. He must have found escape difficult—he is trying to brazen it out. A convict in the Andaman Islands tried the same game, but he could not escape my system! Stand aside—Don't go far—have the handcuffs ready. [*He walks up to Bartley, folds his arms, and stands before him.*] Here, my man, do you know anything of John Smith?

BARTLEY. Of John Smith! Who is he, now?

POLICEMAN. Jack Smith, sir—Red Jack Smith!

MAGISTRATE. [*coming a step nearer and tapping him on the shoulder*]. Where is Jack Smith?

BARTLEY [*with a deep sigh, and shaking his head slowly*]. Where is he, indeed?

MAGISTRATE. What have you to tell?

BARTLEY. It is where he was this morning, standing in this spot, singing his share of songs—no, but lighting his pipe—scraping a match on the sole of his shoes—

MAGISTRATE. I ask you, for the third time, where is he?

BARTLEY. I wouldn't like to say that. It is a great mystery, and it is hard to say of any man, did he earn hatred or love.

MAGISTRATE. Tell me all you know.

BARTLEY. All that I know—Well, there are the three estates; there is Limbo, and there is Purgatory, and there is—

MAGISTRATE. Nonsense! This is trifling! Get to the point.

BARTLEY. Maybe you don't hold with the clergy so? That is the teaching of the clergy. Maybe you hold with the old people. It is what they do be saying, that the shadow goes wandering, and the soul is tired, and the body is taking a rest—The shadow! [*Starts up.*] I was nearly sure I saw Jack Smith not ten minutes ago at the corner of the forge, and I lost him again—Was it his ghost I saw, do you think?

MAGISTRATE [*to policeman*].   Conscience-struck! He will confess all now!

BARTLEY.   His ghost to come before me! It is likely it was on account of the fork! I to have it and he to have no way to defend himself the time he met with his death!

MAGISTRATE [*to policeman*].   I must note down his words. [*Takes out notebook. To* BARTLEY.] I warn you that your words are being noted.

BARTLEY.   If I had ha' run faster in the beginning, this terror would not be on me at the latter end! Maybe he will cast it up against me at the day of judgment—I wouldn't wonder at all at that.

MAGISTRATE [*writing.*].   At the day of judgment—

BARTLEY.   It was soon for his ghost to appear to me—is it coming after me always by day it will be, and stripping the clothes off in the night time?—I wouldn't wonder at all at that, being as I am an unfortunate man!

MAGISTRATE [*sternly*].   Tell me this truly. What was the motive of this crime?

BARTLEY.   The motive, is it?

MAGISTRATE.   Yes; the motive; the cause.

BARTLEY.   I'd sooner not say that.

MAGISTRATE.   You had better tell me truly. Was it money?

BARTLEY.   Not at all! What did poor Jack Smith ever have in his pockets unless it might be his hands that would be in them?

MAGISTRATE.   Any dispute about land?

BARTLEY [*indignantly*].   Not at all! He never was a grabber or grabbed from any one!

MAGISTRATE.   You will find it better for you if you tell me at once.

BARTLEY.   I tell you I wouldn't for the whole world wish to say what it was—it is a thing I would not like to be talking about.

MAGISTRATE.   There is no use in hiding it. It will be discovered in the end.

BARTLEY.   Well, I suppose it will, seeing that mostly everybody knows it before. Whisper here now. I will tell no lie; where would be the use?

[*Puts his hand to his mouth, and* MAGISTRATE *stoops.*]

Don't be putting the blame on the parish, for such as thing was never done in the parish before—it was done for the sake of Kitty Keary, Jack Smith's wife.

MAGISTRATE [*to policeman*].   Put on the handcuffs. we have been saved some trouble. I knew he would confess if taken in the right way.

[*Policeman puts on handcuffs.*]

BARTLEY.   Handcuffs now! Glory be! I always said, if there was ever any misfortune coming to this place it was on myself it would fall. I to be in handcuffs! There's no wonder at all in that.

[*Enter* MRS. FALLON, *followed by the rest. She is looking back at them as she speaks.*]

MRS. FALLON.   Telling lies the whole of the people of his town are; telling lies, telling lies as fast as a dog will trot! Speaking against my poor respectable man! Saying he made an end of Jack Smith! My decent comrade! There is no better man and no kinder man in the whole of the five parishes! It's little annoyance he ever gave to any one! [*Turns and sees him.*] What in the earthly world do I see before me? Bartley Fallon in charge of the police! Handcuffs on him! O Bartley, what did you do at all at all?

BARTLEY.   O Mary, there has a great misfortune come upon me! It is what I always said, that if there is ever any misfortune—

MRS. FALLON.   What did he do at all, or is it bewitched I am?

MAGISTRATE.   This man has been arrested on a charge of murder.

MRS. FALLON.   Whose charge is that? Don't believe them! They are all liars in this place! Give me back my man!

MAGISTRATE.   It is natural you should take his part, but you have no cause of complaint against your neighbors. He has been arrested for the murder of John Smith, on his own confession.

MRS. FALLON.   The saints of heaven protect us! And what did he want killing Jack Smith?

MAGISTRATE.   It is best you should know all. He did it on account of a love affair with the murdered man's wife.

MRS. FALLON [*sitting down*].   With Jack Smith's wife! With Kitty Keary!— Ochone, the traitor!

THE CROWD.   A great shame, indeed. He is a traitor indeed.

MRS. TULLY.   To America he was bringing her, Mrs. Fallon.

BARTLEY.   What are you saying, Mary? I tell you—

MRS. FALLON.   Don't say a word! I won't listen to any word you'll say! [*Stop her ears.*] O, isn't he the treacherous villain? Ochone go deo!

BARTLEY.   Be quiet till I speak! Listen to what I say!

MRS. FALLON.   Sitting beside me on the ass car coming to the town, so quiet and so respectable, and treachery like that in his heart!

BARTLEY.   Is it your wits you have lost or is it I myself that have lost my wits?

MRS. FALLON.   And it's hard I earned you, slaving—and you grumbling, and sighing, and coughing, and discontented, and the priest wore out anointing you, with all the times you threatened to die!

BARTLEY.   Let you be quiet till I tell you!

MRS. FALLON. You to bring such a disgrace into the parish. A thing that was never heard of before!

BARTLEY. Will you shut your mouth and hear me speaking?

MRS. FALLON. And if it was for any sort of a fine handsome woman, but for a little fistful of a woman like Kitty Keary, that's not four feet high hardly, and not three teeth in her head unless she got new ones! May God reward you, Bartley Fallon, for the black treachery in your heart and the wickedness in your mind, and the red blood of poor Jack Smith that is wet upon your hand!

[*Voice of Jack Smith heard singing.*]

> The sea shall be dry,
> The earth under mourning and ban!
> Then loud shall he cry
> For the wife of the red-haired man!

BARTLEY. It's Jack Smith's voice—I never knew a ghost to sing before—

It is after myself and the fork he is coming! [*Goes back.*]

[*Enter* JACK SMITH.]

Let one of you give him the fork and I will be clear of him now and for eternity!

MRS. TARPEY. The Lord have mercy on us! Red Jack Smith! The man that was going to be waked!

JAMES RYAN. Is it back from the grave you are come?

SHAWN EARLY. Is it alive you are, or is it dead you are?

TIM CASEY. Is it yourself at all that's in it?

MRS. TULLY. Is it letting on you were to be dead?

MRS. FALLON. Dead or alive, let you stop Kitty Keary, your wife, from bringing my man away with her to America!

JACK SMITH. It is what I think, the wits are gone astray on the whole of you. What would my wife want bringing Bartley Fallon to America?

MRS. FALLON. To leave yourself, and to get quit of you she wants, Jack Smith, and to bring him away from myself. That's what the two of them had settled together.

JACK SMITH. I'll break the head of any man that says that! Who is it says it? [*To* TIM CASEY.] Was it you said it? [*To* SHAWN EARLY.] Was it you?

ALL TOGETHER [*backing and shaking their heads.*] It wasn't I said it!

JACK SMITH. Tell me the name of any man that said it!

ALL TOGETHER [*pointing to Bartley.*] It was *him* that said it!

JACK SMITH. Let me at him till I break his head!

[BARTLEY *backs in terror. Neighbours hold* JACK SMITH *back.*]

JACK SMITH [*trying to free himself*].   Let me at him! Isn't he the pleasant sort of a scarecrow for any woman to be crossing the ocean with! It's back from the docks of New York he'd be turned [*trying to rush at him again*], with a lie in his mouth and treachery in his heart, and another man's wife by his side, and he passing her off as his own! Let me at him can't you.

[*Makes another rush, but is held back.*]

MAGISTRATE [*pointing to* JACK SMITH.]   Policeman, put the handcuffs on this man. I see it all now. A case of false impersonation, a conspiracy to defeat the ends of justice. There was a case in the Andaman Islands, a murderer of the Mopsa tribe, a religious enthusiast—

POLICEMAN.   So he might be, too.

MAGISTRATE.   We must take both these men to the scene of the murder. We must confront them with the body of the real Jack Smith.

JACK SMITH.   I'll break the head of any man that will find my dead body!

MAGISTRATE.   I'll call more help from the barracks. [*Blows* POLICEMAN'S *whistle.*]

BARTLEY.   It is what I am thinking, if myself and Jack Smith are put together in the one cell for the night, the handcuffs will be taken off him, and his hands will be free, and murder will be done that time surely!

MAGISTRATE.   Come on!

[*They turn to the right.*] [4]

---

4. *The earliest printings of this play left the last word to Mrs. Tarpey.* The two of them in charge now, and a great hoop of people going by from the fair. Come up here the whole of you! It would be a pity you to be passing, and I not spreading the news! [*Oxford UP note*].

LADY GREGORY

The Rising of the Moon †

Persons

SERGEANT
POLICEMAN X
POLICEMAN B
A RAGGED MAN

SCENE. *Side of a quay in a seaport town. Some posts and chains. A large barrel. Enter three policemen. Moonlight.*

> [SERGEANT, *who is older than the others, crosses the stage to right and looks down steps. The others put down a pastepot and unroll a bundle of placards.*]

POLICEMAN B.   I think this would be a good place to put up a notice. [*He points to barrel.*]

POLICEMAN X.   Better ask him. [*Calls to* SERGEANT.] Will this be a good place for a placard?

> [*No answer.*]

POLICEMAN B.   Will we put up a notice here on the barrel?

> [*No answer.*]

SERGEANT.   There's a flight of steps here that leads to the water. This is a place that should be minded well. If he got down here, his friends might have a boat to meet him; they might send it in here from outside.

POLICEMAN B.   Would the barrel be a good place to put a notice up?

SERGEANT.   It might; you can put it there.

> [*They paste the notice up.*]

---

† From *The Collected Plays of Lady Gregory*, Coole Edition, published by Oxford University Press and Colin Smythe Limited.

SERGEANT [*reading it*].   Dark hair—dark eyes, smooth face, height five feet five—there's not much to take hold of in that—It's a pity I had no chance of seeing him before he broke out of gaol. They say he's a wonder, that it's he makes all the plans for the whole organization. There isn't another man in Ireland would have broken gaol the way he did. He must have some friends among the gaolers.

POLICEMAN B.   A hundred pounds is little enough for the Government to offer for him. You may be sure any man in the force that takes him will get promotion.

SERGEANT.   I'll mind this place myself. I wouldn't wonder at all if he came this way. He might come slipping along there [*points to side of quay*], and his friends might be waiting for him there [*points down steps*], and once he got away it's little chance we'd have of finding him; it's maybe under a load of kelp he'd be in a fishing boat, and not one to help a married man that wants it to the reward.

POLICEMAN X.   And if we get him itself, nothing but abuse on our heads for it from the people, land maybe from our own relations.

SERGEANT.   Well, we have to do our duty in the force. Haven't we the whole country depending on us to keep law and order? It's those that are down would be up and those that are up would be down, if it wasn't for us. Well, hurry on, you have plenty of other places to placard yet, and come back here then to me. You can take the lantern. Don't be too long now. It's very lonesome here with nothing but the moon.

POLICEMAN B.   It's a pity we can't stop with you. The Government should have brought more police into the town, with *him* in gaol, and at assize [1] time too. Well, good luck to your watch.

[*They go out.*]

SERGEANT [*walks up and down once or twice and looks at placard*].   A hundred pounds and promotion sure. There must be a great deal of spending in a hundred pounds. It's a pity some honest man not to be better of that.

[A RAGGED MAN *appears at left and tries to slip past.* SERGEANT *suddenly turns.*]

SERGEANT.   Where are you going?

MAN.   I'm a poor ballad-singer, your honor. I thought to sell some of these [*holds out bundle of ballads*] to the sailors. [*He goes on.*]

SERGEANT.   Stop! Didn't I tell you to stop? You can't go on there.

MAN.   Oh, very well. It's a hard thing to be poor. All the world's against the poor!

SERGEANT.   Who are you?

---

1. Periodical legal proceedings.

MAN. You'd be as wise as myself if I told you, but I don't mind. I'm one Jimmy Walsh, a ballad-singer.

SERGEANT. Jimmy Walsh? I don't know that name.

MAN. Ah, sure, they know it well enough in Ennis. Were you ever in Ennis, sergeant?

SERGEANT. What brought you here?

MAN. Sure, it's to the assizes I came, thinking I might make a few shillings here or there. It's in the one train with the judges I came.

SERGEANT. Well, if you came so far, you may as well go farther, for you'll walk out of this.

MAN. I will, I will; I'll just go on where I was going. [Goes toward steps.]

SERGEANT. Come back from those steps; no one has leave to pass down them to-night.

MAN. I'll just sit on the top of the steps till I see will some sailor buy a ballad off me that would give me my supper. They do be late going back to the ship. It's often I saw them in Cork carried down the quay in a hand-cart.

SERGEANT. Move on, I tell you. I won't have any one lingering about the quay to-night.

MAN. Well, I'll go. It's the poor have the hard life! Maybe yourself might like one, sergeant. Here's a good sheet now. [Turns one over.] "Content and a pipe"—that's not much. "The Peeler and the goat"— you wouldn't like that. "Johnny Hart"—that's a lovely song.

SERGEANT. Move on.

MAN. Ah, wait till you hear it. [Sings.]

There was a rich farmer's daughter lived near the town of Ross;
She courted a Highland soldier, his name was Johnny Hart;
Says the mother to her daughter, "I'll go distracted mad
If you marry that Highland soldier dressed up in Highland plaid."

SERGEANT. Stop that noise.

[MAN wraps up his ballads and shuffles towards the steps.]

SERGEANT. Where are you going?

MAN. Sure you told me to be going, and I am going.

SERGEANT. Don't be a fool. I didn't tell you to go that way; I told you to go back to the town.

MAN. Back to the town, is it?

SERGEANT [taking him by the shoulder and shoving him before him]. Here, I'll show you the way. Be off with you. What are you stopping for?

MAN [who has been keeping his eye on the notice, points to it]. I think I know what you're waiting for, sergeant.

SERGEANT. What's that to you?

MAN.   And I know well the man you're waiting for—I know him well—
I'll be going. [*He shuffles on.*]

SERGEANT.   You know him? Come back here. What sort is he?

MAN.   Come back is it, sergeant? Do you want to have me killed?

SERGEANT.   Why do you say that?

MAN.   Never mind. I'm going. I wouldn't be in your shoes if the reward
was ten times as much. [*Goes on off stage to left.*] Not if it was ten
times as much.

SERGEANT [*rushing after him*].   Come back here, come back. [*Drags
him back.*] What sort is he? Where did you see him?

MAN.   I saw him in my own place, in the County Clare. I tell you you
wouldn't like to be looking at him. You'd be afraid to be in the one
place with him. There isn't a weapon he doesn't know the use of, and
as to strength, his muscles are as hard as that board. [*Slaps barrel.*]

SERGEANT.   Is he as bad as that?

MAN.   He is then.

SERGEANT.   Do you tell me so?

MAN.   There was a poor man in our place, a sergeant from Bally-
vaughan.—It was with a lump of stone he did it.

SERGEANT.   I never heard of that.

MAN.   And you wouldn't, sergeant. It's not everything that happens gets
into the papers. And there was a policeman in plain clothes, too . . .
It is in Limerick he was. . . . It was after the time of the attack on the
police barrack in Kilmallock. . . . Moonlight . . . just like this . . .
waterside. . . . Nothing was known for certain.

SERGEANT.   Do you say so? It's a terrible county to belong to.

MAN.   That's so, indeed! You might be standing there, looking out that
way, thinking you saw him coming up this side of the quay [*points*],
and he might be coming up this other side [*points*], and he'd be on
you before you knew where you were.

SERGEANT.   It's a whole troop of police they ought to put here to stop a
man like that.

MAN.   But if you'd like me to stop with you, I could be looking down
this side. I could be sitting up here on this barrel.

SERGEANT.   And you know him well, too?

MAN.   I'd know him a mile off, sergeant.

SERGEANT.   But you wouldn't want to share the reward?

MAN.   Is it a poor man like me, that has to be going the roads and
singing in fairs, to have the name on him that he took a reward? but
you don't want me. I'll be safer in the town.

SERGEANT.   Well, you can stop.

MAN [*getting up on barrel*].   All right, sergeant, I wonder, now, you're
tired out, sergeant, walking up and down the way you are.

SERGEANT.   If I'm tired I'm used to it.

MAN.   You might have hard work before you to-night yet. Take it easy while you can. There's plenty of room up here on the barrel, and you see farther when you're higher up.

SERGEANT. Maybe so. [*Gets up beside him on barrel, facing right.*]

[*They sit back to back, looking different ways.*]

You made me feel a bit queer with the way you talked.

MAN. Give me a match, sergeant [*he gives it and* MAN *lights pipe*]; take a draw yourself? It'll quiet you. Wait now till I give you a light, but you needn't turn round. Don't take your eye off the quay for the life of you.

SERGEANT. Never fear, I won't. [*Lights pipe.*]

[*They both smoke.*]

Indeed it's a hard thing to be in the force, out at night and no thanks for it, for all the danger we're in. And it's little we get but abuse from the people, and no choice but to obey our orders, and never asked when a man is sent into danger, if you are a married man with a family.

MAN [*sings*].

As through the hills I walked to view the hills and shamrock plain,
I stood awhile where nature smiles to view the rocks and streams,
On a matron fair I fixed my eyes beneath a fertile vale,
And she sang her song it was on the wrong of poor old Granuaile.

SERGEANT. Stop that; that's no song to be singing in these times.

MAN. Ah, sergeant, I was only singing to keep my heart up. It sinks when I think of him. To think of us two sitting here, and he creeping up the quay, maybe, to get to us.

SERGEANT. Are you keeping a good lookout?

MAN. I am; and for no reward too. Amn't I the fool man? But when I saw a man in trouble, I never could help trying to get him out of it. What's that? Did something hit me? [*Rubs his heart.*]

SERGEANT [*patting him on the shoulder*]. You will get your reward in heaven.

MAN. I know that, I know that, sergeant, but life is precious.

SERGEANT. Well, you can sing if it gives you more courage.

MAN [*sings*].

Her head was bare, her hands and feet with iron bands were bound,
Her pensive strain and plaintive wail mingles with the evening gale,
And the song she sang with mournful air, I am old Granuaile.
Her lips so sweet that monarchs kissed . . .

SERGEANT. That's not it. . . . "Her gown she wore was stained with gore." . . . That's it—you missed that.

MAN.   You're right, sergeant, so it is; I missed it. [*Repeats line.*] But to think of a man like you knowing a song like that.

SERGEANT.   There's many a thing a man might know and might not have any wish for.

MANA.   Now, I daresay, sergeant, in your youth, you used to be sitting up on a wall, the way you are sitting up on this barrel now, and the other lads beside you, and you singing "Granuaile"? . . .

SERGEANT.   I did then.

MAN.   And the "Shan Van Vocht"?[2] . . .

SERGEANT,   I did then.

MAN.   And the "Green on the Cape?"

SERGEANT,   That was one of them.

MAN.   And maybe the man you are watching for to-night used to be sitting on the wall, when he was young, and singing those same songs. . . . It's a queer world. . . .

SERGEANT.   Whisht! . . . I think I see something coming. . . . It's only a dog.

MAN.   And isn't it a queer world? . . . Maybe it's one of the boys you used to be singing with that time you will be arresting to-day or to-morrow, and sending into the dock. . . .

SERGEANT.   That's true indeed.

MAN.   And maybe one night, after you had been singing, if the other boys had told you some plan they had, some plan to free the country, you might have joined with them . . . and maybe it is you might be in trouble now.

SERGEANT.   Well, who knows but I might? I had a great spirit in those days.

MAN.   It's a queer world, sergeant, and it's little any mother knows when she sees her child creeping on the floor what might happen to it before it has gone through its life, or who will be who in the end.

SERGEANT.   That's a queer thought now, and a true thought. Wait now till I think it out. . . . If it wasn't for the sense I have, and for my wife and family, and for me joining the force the time I did, it might be myself now would be after breaking gaol and hiding in the dark, and it might be him that's hiding in the dark and that got out of gaol would be sitting up here where I am on this barrel. . . . And it might be myself would be creeping up trying to make my escape from himself, and it might be himself would be keeping the law, and myself would be breaking it, and myself would be trying to put a bullet in his head, or to take up a lump of stone the way you said he did . . . no, that myself did. . . . Oh! [*Gasps. After a pause*] What's that? [*Grasps man's arm.*]

2. Song of a poor old woman, personification of Ireland, foretelling the coming of the French to aid Irish rebellion; the Shan Van Vocht personifi-cation of Ireland also informs Yeats's *Cathleen Ni Houlihan*, pp. 3–11, above.

MAN [*jumps off barrel and listens, looking out over water*]. It's nothing, sergeant.

SERGEANT. I thought it might be a boat. I had a notion there might be friends of his coming about the quays with a boat.

MAN. Sergeant, I am thinking it was with the people you were, and not with the law you were, when you were a young man.

SERGEANT. Well, if I was foolish then, that time's gone.

MAN. Maybe, sergeant, it comes into your head sometimes, in spite of your belt and your tunic, that it might have been as well for you to have followed Granuaile.

SERGEANT. It's no business of yours what I think.

MAN. Maybe, sergeant, you'll be on the side of the country yet.

SERGEANT [*gets off barrel*]. Don't talk to me like that. I have my duties and I know them. [*Looks round.*] That was a boat; I hear the oars. [*Goes to the steps and looks down.*]

MAN [*sings*]

> O, then, tell me, Shawn O'Farrell,
> Where the gathering is to be.
> In the old spot by the river
> Right well known to you and me!

SERGEANT. Stop that! Stop that, I tell you!

MAN [*sings louder*].

> One word more, for signal token,
> Whistle up the marching tune,
> With your pike upon your shoulder,
> At the Rising of the Moon.

SERGEANT. If you don't stop that, I'll arrest you.

> [*A whistle from below answers, repeating the air.*]

SERGEANT. That's a signal. [*Stands between him and steps.*] You must not pass this way. . . . Step farther back. . . . Who are you? You are no ballad-singer.

MAN. You needn't ask who I am; that placard will tell you. [*Points to placard.*]

SERGEANT. You are the man I am looking for.

MAN [*takes off hat and wig*].

> [SERGEANT *seizes them.*]

I am. There's a hundred pounds on my head. There is a friend of mine below in a boat. He knows a safe place to bring me to.

SERGEANT [*looking still at hat and wig*]. It's a pity! It's a pity. You deceived me. You deceived me well.

MAN. I am a friend of Granuaile. There is a hundred pounds on my head.

SERGEANT. It's a pity, it's a pity!

MAN. Will you let me pass, or must I make you let me?

SERGEANT. I am in the force. I will not let you pass.

MAN. I thought to do it with my tongue. [*Puts hand in breast.*] What is that?

Voice of POLICEMAN X *outside*. Here, this is where we left him.

SERGEANT. It's my comrades coming.

MAN. You won't betray me . . . the friend of Granuaile. [*Slips behind barrel.*]

Voice of POLICEMAN B. That was the last of the placards.

POLICEMAN X [*as they come in*]. If he makes his escape it won't be unknown he'll make it.

[SERGEANT *puts hat and wig behind his back.*]

POLICEMAN B. Did any one come this way?

SERGEANT [*after a pause*]. No one.

POLICEMAN B. No one at all?

SERGEANT. No one at all.

POLICEMAN B. We had no orders to go back to the station; we can stop along with you.

SERGEANT. I don't want you. There is nothing for you to do here.

POLICEMAN B. You bade us to come back here and keep watch with you.

SERGEANT. I'd sooner be alone. Would any man come this way and you making all that talk? It is better the place to be quiet.

POLICEMAN B. Well, we'll leave you the lantern anyhow.

[*Hands it to him.*]

SERGEANT. I don't want it. Bring it with you.

POLICEMAN B. You might want it. There are clouds coming up and you have the darkness of the night before you yet. I'll leave it over here on the barrel. [*Goes to barrel.*]

SERGEANT. Bring it with you I tell you. No more talk.

POLICEMAN B. Well, I thought it might be a comfort to you. I often think when I have it in my hand and can be flashing it about into every dark corner [*doing so*] that it's the same as being beside the fire at home, and the bits of bogwood blazing up now and again. [*Flashes it about, now on the barrel, now on* SERGEANT.]

SERGEANT [*furious*]. Be off the two of you, yourselves and your lantern!

[*They go out.* MAN *comes from behind barrel. He and* SERGEANT *stand looking at one another.*]

SERGEANT. What are you waiting for?

MAN. For my hat, of course, and my wig. You wouldn't wish me to get my death of cold?

[SERGEANT *gives them.*]

MAN [*going towards steps*]. Well, good-night, comrade, and thank you. You did me a good turn to-night, and I'm obliged to you. Maybe I'll be able to do as much for you when the small rise up and the big fall down . . . when we all change places at the rising [*waves his hand and disappears*] of the Moon.

SERGEANT [*turning his back to audience and reading placard*]. A hundred pounds reward! A hundred pounds! [*turns towards audience.*] I wonder, now, am I as great a fool as I think I am?

J. M. SYNGE

Riders to the Sea†

Persons in the Play

MAURYA, *an old woman*
BARTLEY, *her son*
CATHLEEN, *her daughter*
NORA, *a younger daughter*
MEN AND WOMEN

SCENE. *An Island off the West of Ireland.*

> [*Cottage kitchen, with nets, oil-skins, spinning wheel, some new boards standing by the wall, etc.* CATHLEEN, *a girl of about twenty, finishes kneading cake, and puts it down in the pot-oven by the fire; then wipes her hands, and begins to spin at the wheel.* NORA, *a young girl, puts her head in at the door.*]

NORA [*in a low voice*]. Where is she?
CATHLEEN. She's lying down, God help her, and may be sleeping, if she's able.

> [NORA *comes in softly, and takes a bundle from under her shawl.*]

CATHLEEN [*spinning the wheel rapidly*]. What is it you have?
NORA. The young priest is after bringing them. It's a shirt and a plain stocking were got off a drowned man in Donegal.

> [CATHLEEN *stops her wheel with a sudden movement, and leans out to listen.*]

NORA. We're to find out if it's Michael's they are, some time herself will be down looking at the sea.
CATHLEEN. How would they be Michael's, Nora. How would he go the length of that way to the far north?
NORA. The young priest says he's known the like of it. "If it's Michael's

† From *The Complete Plays of John M. Synge* (New York: Random House, 1935), Vintage Books edition.

they are," says he, "you can tell herself he's got a clean burial by the grace of God, and if they're not his, let no one say a word about them, for she'll be getting her death," says he, "with crying and lamenting."

[*The door which* NORA *half closed is blown open by a gust of wind.*]

CATHLEEN [*looking out anxiously*].   Did you ask him would he stop Bartley going this day with the horses to the Galway fair? [1]

NORA.   "I won't stop him," says he, "but let you not be afraid. Herself does be saying prayers half through the night, and the Almighty God won't leave her destitute," says he, "with no son living."

CATHLEEN.   Is the sea bad by the white rocks, Nora?

NORA.   Middling bad, God help us. There's a great roaring in the west, and it's worse it'll be getting when the tide's turned to the wind. [*She goes over to the table with the bundle.*] Shall I open it now?

CATHLEEN.   Maybe she'd wake up on us, and come in before we'd done. [*Coming to the table.*] It's a long time we'll be, and the two of us crying.

NORA [*goes to the inner door and listens*].   She's moving about on the bed. She'll be coming in a minute.

CATHLEEN.   Give me the ladder, and I'll put them up in the turf-loft, the way she won't know of them at all, and maybe when the tide turns she'll be going down to see would he be floating from the east.

[*They put the ladder against the gable of the chimney;* CATHLEEN *goes up a few steps and hides the bundle in the turf-loft.* MAURYA *comes from the inner room.*]

MAURYA [*looking up at Cathleen and speaking querulously*].   Isn't it turf enough you have for this day and evening?

CATHLEEN.   There's a cake baking at the fire for a short space [*throwing down the turf*] and Bartley will want it when the tide turns if he goes to Connemara. [2]

[NORA *picks up the turf and puts it round the pot-oven.*]

MAURYA [*sitting down on a stool at the fire*].   He won't go this day with the wind rising from the south and west. He won't go this day, for the young priest will stop him surely.

NORA.   He'll not stop him, mother, and I heard Eamon Simon and Stephen Pheety and Colum Shawn saying he would go.

MAURYA.   Where is he itself?

NORA.   He went down to see would there be another boat sailing in the week, and I'm thinking it won't be long till he's here now, for the

---

1. Going to the mainland.   2. Nearest mainland point on the route to Galway.

tide's turning at the green head, and the hooker's tacking from the east.

CATHLEEN. I hear some one passing the big stones.

NORA [looking out]. He's coming now, and he in a hurry.

BARTLEY [comes in and looks round the room. Speaking sadly and quietly]. Where is the bit of new rope, Cathleen, was bought in Connemara?

CATHLEEN [coming down]. Give it to him, Nora; it's on a nail by the white boards. I hung it up this morning, for the pig with the black feet was eating it.

NORA [giving him a rope]. Is that it, Bartley?

MAURYA. You'd do right to leave that rope, Bartley, hanging by the boards.

[BARTLEY takes the rope.]

It will be wanting in this place, I'm telling you, if Michael is washed up to-morrow morning, or the next morning, or any morning in the week, for it's a deep grave we'll make him by the grace of God.

BARTLEY [beginning to work with the rope]. I've no halter the way I can ride down on the mare, and I must go now quickly. This is the one boat going for two weeks or beyond it, and the fair will be a good fair for horses I heard them saying below.

MAURYA. It's a hard thing they'll be saying below if the body is washed up and there's no man in it to make the coffin, and I after giving a big price for the finest white boards you'd find in Connemara. [She looks round at the boards.]

BARTLEY. How would it be washed up, and we after looking each day for nine days, and a strong wind blowing a while back from the west and south?

MAURYA. If it wasn't found itself, that wind is raising the sea, and there was a star up against the moon, and it rising in the night. If it was a hundred horses, or a thousand horses you had itself, what is the price of a thousand horses against a son where there is one son only?

BARTLEY [working at the halter, to CATHLEEN]. Let you go down each day, and see the sheep aren't jumping in on the rye, and if the jobber comes you can sell the pig with the black feet if there is a good price going.

MAURYA. How would the like of her get a good price for a pig?

BARTLEY [to CATHLEEN]. If the west wind holds with the last bit of the moon let you and Nora get up weed enough for another cock for the kelp. It's hard set we'll be from this day with no one in it but one man to work.

MAURYA. It's hard set we'll be surely the day you're drown'd with the rest. What way will I live and the girls with me, and I an old woman looking for the grave?

[BARTLEY *lays down the halter, takes off his old coat, and puts on a newer one of the same flannel.*]

BARTLEY [*to Nora*]. Is she coming to the pier?

NORA [*looking out*]. She's passing the green head and letting fall her sails.

BARTLEY [*getting his purse and tobacco*]. I'll have half an hour to go down, and you'll see me coming again in two days, or in three days, or maybe in four days if the wind is bad.

MAURYA [*turning round to the fire, and putting her shawl over her head*]. Isn't it a hard and cruel man won't hear a word from an old woman, and she holding him from the sea?

CATHLEEN. It's the life of a young man to be going on the sea, and who would listen to an old woman with one thing and she saying it over?

BARTLEY [*taking the halter*]. I must go now quickly. I'll ride down on the red mare, and the gray pony 'll run behind me. . . . The blessing of God on you. [*He goes out.*]

MAURYA [*crying out as he is in the door*]. He's gone now, God spare us, and we'll not see him again. He's gone now, and when the black night is falling I'll have no son left me in the world.

CATHLEEN. Why wouldn't you give him your blessing and he looking round in the door? Isn't it sorrow enough is on every one in this house without your sending him out with an unlucky word behind him, and a hard word in his ear?

[MAURYA *takes up the tongs and begins raking the fire aimlessly without looking round.*]

NORA [*turning towards her*]. You're taking away the turf from the cake.

CATHLEEN [*crying out*]. The Son of God forgive us, Nora, we're after forgetting his bit of bread. [*She comes over to the fire.*]

NORA. And it's destroyed he'll be going till dark night, and he after eating nothing since the sun went up.

CATHLEEN [*turning the cake out of the oven*]. It's destroyed he'll be, surely. There's no sense left on any person in a house where an old woman will be talking for ever.

[MAURYA *sways herself on her stool.*]

CATHLEEN [*cutting off some of the bread and rolling it in a cloth; to Maurya*]. Let you go down now to the spring well and give him this and he passing. You'll see him when the dark word will be broken, and you can say "God speed you," the way he'll be easy in his mind.

MAURYA [*taking the bread*]. Will I be in it as soon as himself?

CATHLEEN. If you go now quickly.

MAURYA [*standing up unsteadily*]. It's hard set I am to walk.

CATHLEEN [*looking at her anxiously*]. Give her the stick, Nora, or maybe she'll slip on the big stones.

NORA. What stick?

CATHLEEN. The stick Michael brought from Connemara.

MAURYA [*taking a stick* NORA *gives her*]. In the big world the old people do be leaving things after them for their sons and children, but in this place it is the young men do be leaving things behind for them that do be old. [*She goes out slowly.*]

[NORA *goes over to the ladder.*]

CATHLEEN. Wait, Nora, maybe she'd turn back quickly. She's that sorry, God help her, you wouldn't know the thing she'd do.

NORA. Is she gone round by the bush?

CATHLEEN [*looking out*]. She gone now. Throw it down quickly, for the Lord knows when she'll be out of it again.

NORA [*getting the bundle from the loft*]. The young priest said he'd be passing to-morrow, and we might go down and speak to him below if it's Michael's they are surely.

CATHLEEN [*taking the bundle*]. Did he say what way they were found?

NORA [*coming down*]. "There were two men," says he, "and they rowing round with poteen [3] before the cocks crowed, and the oar of one of them caught the body, and they passing the black cliffs of the north."

CATHLEEN [*trying to open the bundle*]. Give me a knife, Nora, the string's perished with the salt water, and there's a black knot on it you wouldn't loosen in a week.

NORA [*giving her a knife*]. I've heard tell it was a long way to Donegal.

CATHLEEN [*cutting the string*]. It is surely. There was a man in here a while ago—the man sold us that knife—and he said if you set off walking from the rocks beyond, it would be seven days you'd be in Donegal.

NORA. And what time would a man take, and he floating?

[CATHLEEN *opens the bundle and takes out a bit of a stocking. They look at them eagerly.*]

CATHLEEN [*in a low voice*]. The Lord spare us, Nora! Isn't it a queer hard thing to say if it's his they are surely?

NORA. I'll get his shirt off the hook the way we can put the one flannel on the other. [*She looks through some clothes hanging in the corner.*] It's not with them, Cathleen, and where will it be?

CATHLEEN. I'm thinking Bartley put it on him in the morning, for his own shirt was heavy with the salt in it [*pointing to the corner*]. There's a bit of a sleeve was of the same stuff. Give me that and it will do.

[NORA *brings it to her and they compare the flannel.*]

3. Illegal, home-distilled spirits.

CATHLEEN.   It's the same stuff, Nora; but if it is itself aren't there great
   rolls of it in the shops of Galway, and isn't it many another man may
   have a shirt of it as well as Michael himself?
NORA [*who has taken up the stocking and counted the stitches, crying
   out*].   It's Michael, Cathleen, it's Michael; God spare his soul, and
   what will herself say when she hears this story, and Bartley on the sea?
CATHLEEN [*taking the stocking*].   It's a plain stocking.
NORA.   It's the second one of the third pair I knitted, and I put up three
   score stitches, and I dropped four of them.
CATHLEEN [*counts the stitches*].   It's that number is in it [*crying out*].
   Ah, Nora, isn't it a bitter thing to think of him floating that way to
   the far north, and no one to keen him [4] but the black hags that do be
   flying on the sea?
NORA [*swinging herself round, and throwing out her arms on the
   clothes*].   And isn't it a pitiful thing when there is nothing left of a
   man who was a great rower and fisher, but a bit of an old shirt and a
   plain stocking?
CATHLEEN [*after an instant*].   Tell me is herself coming, Nora? I hear
   a little sound on the path.
NORA [*looking out*].   She is, Cathleen. She's coming up to the door.
CATHLEEN.   Put these things away before she'll come in. Maybe it's
   easier she'll be after giving her blessing to Bartley, and we won't let
   on we've heard anything the time he's on the sea.
NORA [*helping* CATHLEEN *to close the bundle*].   We'll put them here in
   the corner.

>   [*They put them into a hole in the chimney corner.* CATHLEEN
>   *goes back to the spinning-wheel.*]

NORA.   Will she see it was crying I was?
CATHLEEN.   Keep your back to the door the way the light'll not be on
   you.

>   [NORA *sits down at the chimney corner, with her back to the door.*
>   MAURYA *comes in very slowly, without looking at the girls, and
>   goes over to her stool at the other side of the fire. The cloth with
>   the bread is still in her hand. The girls look at each other, and
>   NORA points to the bundle of bread.*]

CATHLEEN [*after spinning for a moment*].   You didn't give him his bit
   of bread?

>   [MAURYA *begins to keen softly, without turning round.*]

CATHLEEN.   Did you see him riding down?

>   [MAURYA *goes on keening.*]

4. To mourn by keening, or moaning and wailing, as at the end of the play.

CATHLEEN [*a little impatiently*].   God forgive you; isn't it a better thing to raise your voice and tell what you seen, than to be making lamentation for a thing that's done? Did you see Bartley, I'm saying to you.

MAURYA [*with a weak voice*].   My heart's broken from this day.

CATHLEEN [*as before*].   Did you see Bartley?

MAURYA.   I seen the fearfulest thing.

CATHLEEN [*leaves her wheel and looks out*].   God forgive you; he's riding the mare now over the green head, and the gray pony behind him.

MAURYA [*starts, so that her shawl falls back from her head and shows her white tossed hair. With a frightened voice*].   The gray pony behind him.

CATHLEEN [*coming to the fire*].   What is it ails you, at all?

MAURYA [*speaking very slowly*].   I've seen the fearfulest thing any person has seen, since the day Bride Dara seen the dead man with the child in his arms.

CATHLEEN AND NORA.   Uah.

[*They crouch down in front of the old woman at the fire.*]

NORA.   Tell us what it is you seen.

MAURYA.   I went down to the spring well, and I stood there saying a prayer to myself. Then Bartley came along, and he riding on the red mare with the gray pony behind him. [*She puts up her hands, as if to hide something from her eyes.*]   The Son of God spare us, Nora!

CATHLEEN.   What is it you seen.

MAURYA.   I seen Michael himself.

CATHLEEN [*speaking softly*].   You did not, mother; It wasn't Michael you seen, for his body is after being found in the far north, and he's got a clean burial by the grace of God.

MAURYA [*a little defiantly*].   I'm after seeing him this day, and he riding and galloping. Bartley came first on the red mare; and I tried to say "God speed you," but something choked the words in my throat. He went by quickly; and "the blessing of God on you," says he, and I could say nothing. I looked up then, and I crying, at the gray pony, and there was Michael upon it—with fine clothes on him, and new shoes on his feet.

CATHLEEN [*begins to keen*].   It's destroyed we are from this day. It's destroyed, surely.

NORA.   Didn't the young priest say the Almighty God wouldn't leave her destitute with no son living?

MAURYA [*in a low voice, but clearly*].   It's little the like of him knows of the sea. . . . Bartley will be lost now, and let you call in Eamon and make me a good coffin out of the white boards, for I won't live after them. I've had a husband, and a husband's father, and six sons in this house—six fine men, though it was a hard birth I had with every one of them and they coming to the world—and some of them were found and some of them were not found, but they're gone now the lot of them. . . . There were Stephen, and Shawn, were lost in the great wind, and found after in the Bay of Gregory of the Golden Mouth, and carried up the two of them on the one plank, and in by that door.

[*She pauses for a moment, the girls start as if they heard something through the door that is half open behind them.*]

NORA [*in a whisper*].   Did you hear that, Cathleen? Did you hear a noise in the north-east?

CATHLEEN [*in a whisper*].   There's some one after crying out by the seashore.

MAURYA [*continues without hearing anything*].   There was Sheamus and his father, and his own father again were lost in a dark night, and not a stick or sign was seen of them when the sun went up. There was Patch after was drowned out of a curagh[5] that turned over. I was sitting here with Bartley, and he a baby, lying on my two knees, and I seen two women, and three women and four women coming in, and they crossing themselves, and not saying a word. I looked out then, and there were men coming after them, and they holding a thing in the half of a red sail, and water dripping out of it—it was a dry day, Nora—and leaving a track to the door.

[*She pauses again with her hand stretched out towards the door. It opens softly and old* WOMEN *begin to come in, crossing themselves on the threshold, and kneeling down in front of the stage with red petticoats over their heads.*]

MAURYA [*half in a dream, to* CATHLEEN].   Is it Patch or Michael, or what is it at all?

CATHLEEN.   Michael is after being found in the far north, and when he is found there how could he be here in this place?

MAURYA.   There does be a power of young men floating round in the sea, and what way would they know if it was Michael they had, or another man like him, for when a man is nine days in the sea, and the wind blowing, it's hard set his own mother would be to say what man was it.

CATHLEEN.   It's Michael, God spare him, for they're after sending us a bit of his clothes from the far north.

[*She reaches out and hands* MAURYA *the clothes that belonged to* MICHAEL. MAURYA *stands up slowly and takes them in her hands.* NORA *looks out.*]

NORA.   They're carrying a thing among them and there's water dripping out of it and leaving a track by the big stones.

---

5. A frail boat of traditional construction, wood-frame and canvas shell, rowed in the open sea.

CATHLEEN [*in a whisper to the* WOMEN *who have come in*].   Is it Bartley
it is?
ONE OF THE WOMEN.   It is surely, God rest his soul.

[*Two younger* WOMEN *come in and pull out the table. Then* MEN
carry in the body of BARTLEY, *laid on a plank, with a bit of a
sail over it, and lay it on the table.*]

CATHLEEN [*to the women, as they are doing so*].   What way was he
drowned?
ONE OF THE WOMEN.   The gray pony knocked him into the sea, and he
was washed out where there is a great surf on the white rocks.

[MAURYA *has gone over and knelt down at the head of the table.
The* WOMEN *are keening softly and swaying themselves with a
slow movement.* CATHLEEN *and* NORA *kneel at the other end of
the table. The* MEN *kneel near the door.*]

MAURYA [*raising her head and speaking as if she did not see the people
around her*].   They're all gone now, and there isn't anything more
the sea can do to me. . . . I'll have no call now to be up crying and
praying when the wind breaks from the south, and you can hear the
surf is in the east, and the surf is in the west, making a great stir with
the two noises, and they hitting one on the other. I'll have no call
now to be going down and getting Holy Water in the dark nights after
Samhain,[6] and I won't care what way the sea is when the other women
will be keening. [*To* NORA.] Give me the Holy Water, Nora, there's a
small sup still on the dresser.

[NORA *gives it to her.*]

MAURYA [*drops* MICHAEL'S *clothes across* BARTLEY'S *feet, and sprinkles the
Holy Water over him*].   It isn't that I haven't prayed for you, Bartley,
to the Almighty God. It isn't that I haven't said prayers in the dark
night till you wouldn't know what I'd be saying; but it's a great rest I'll
have now, and it's time surely. It's a great rest I'll have now, and great
sleeping in the long nights after Samhain, if it's only a bit of wet flour
we do have to eat, and maybe a fish that would be stinking.

[*She kneels down again, crossing herself, and saying prayers under
her breath.*]

CATHLEEN [*to an old* MAN].   Maybe yourself and Eamon would make a
coffin when the sun rises. We have fine white boards herself bought,
God help her, thinking Michael would be found, and I have a new
cake you can eat while you'll be working.
THE OLD MAN [*looking at the boards*].   Are there nails with them?

6. All Saints' Day, November 1.

CATHLEEN. There are not, Colum; we didn't think of the nails.

ANOTHER MAN. It's a great wonder she wouldn't think of the nails, and all the coffins she's seen made already.

CATHLEEN. It's getting old she is, and broken.

[MAURYA *stands up again very slowly and spreads out the pieces of Michael's clothes beside the body, sprinkling them with the last of the Holy Water.*]

NORA [*in a whisper to* CATHLEEN]. She's quiet now and easy; but the day Michael was drowned you could hear her crying out from this to the spring well. It's fonder she was of Michael, and would any one have thought that?

CATHLEEN [*slowly and clearly*]. An old woman will be soon tired with anything she will do, and isn't it nine days herself is after crying and keening, and making great sorrow in the house?

MAURYA [*puts the empty cup mouth downwards on the table, and lays her hands together on* BARTLEY'S *feet*]. They're all together this time, and the end is come. May the Almighty God have mercy on Bartley's soul, and on Michael's soul, and on the souls of Sheamus and Patch, and Stephen and Shawn [*bending her head*]; and may He have mercy on my soul, Nora, and on the soul of every one is left living in the world.

[*She pauses, and the keen rises a little more loudly from the women, then sinks away.*]

MAURYA [*continuing*]. Michael has a clean burial in the far north, by the grace of the Almighty God. Bartley will have a fine coffin out of the white boards, and a deep grave surely. What more can we want than that? No man at all can be living for ever, and we must be satisfied.

[*She kneels down again and the curtain falls slowly.*]

J. M. SYNGE

The Playboy of the Western World†

Persons in the Play

CHRISTOPHER MAHON
OLD MAHON, *his father, a squatter*[1]
MICHAEL JAMES FLAHERTY, called MICHAEL JAMES, *a publican*
MARGARET FLAHERTY, called PEGEEN MIKE, *his daughter*
WIDOW QUIN, *a woman of about thirty*
SHAWN KEOGH, *her cousin, a young farmer*
PHILLY CULLEN AND JIMMY FARRELL, *small farmers*
SARA TANSEY, SUSAN BRADY, AND HONOR BLAKE, *village girls*
A BELLMAN
SOME PEASANTS

The action takes place near a village, on a wild coast of Mayo. The first Act passes on an evening of autumn, the other two Acts on the following day.

Act One

SCENE. *Country public-house or shebeen, very rough and untidy. There is a sort of counter on the right with shelves, holding many bottles and jugs, just seen above it. Empty barrels stand near the counter. At back, a little to left of counter, there is a door into the open air, then, more to the left, there is a settle with shelves above it, with more jugs, and a table beneath a window. At the left there is a large open fire-place, with turf fire, and a small door into inner room. Pegeen, a wild-looking but fine*

---

† From *The Complete Plays of John M. Synge* (New York: Random House, 1935), Vintage Books edition.

1. A settler without legal title, which was often unavailable in unsurveyed rural districts.

girl, of about twenty, is writing at table. She is dressed in the usual peasant dress.

PEGEEN [*slowly as she writes*].   Six yards of stuff for to make a yellow gown. A pair of lace boots with lengthy heels on them and brassy eyes. A hat is suited for a wedding-day. A fine tooth comb. To be sent with three barrels of porter in Jimmy Farrell's creel cart on the evening of the coming Fair to Mister Michael James Flaherty. With the best compliments of this season. Margaret Flaherty.

SHAWN KEOGH [*a fat and fair young man comes in as she signs, looks round awkwardly, when he sees she is alone*].   Where's himself?

PEGEEN [*without looking at him*].   He's coming. [*She directs the letter.*] To Mister Sheamus Mulroy, Wine and Spirit Dealer, Castlebar.

SHAWN [*uneasily*].   I didn't see him on the road.

PEGEEN.   How would you see him [*licks stamp and puts it on letter*] and it dark night this half hour gone by?

SHAWN [*turning towards the door again*].   I stood a while outside wondering would I have a right to pass on or to walk in and see you, Pegeen Mike [*comes to fire*], and I could hear the cows breathing, and sighing in the stillness of the air, and not a step moving any place from this gate to the bridge.

PEGEEN [*putting letter in envelope*].   It's above at the cross-roads he is, meeting Philly Cullen; and a couple more are going along with him to Kate Cassidy's wake.

SHAWN [*looking at her blankly*].   And he's going that length in the dark night?

PEGEEN [*impatiently*].   He is surely, and leaving me lonesome on the scruff of the hill. [*She gets up and puts envelope on dresser, then winds clock.*] Isn't it long the nights are now, Shawn Keogh, to be leaving a poor girl with her own self counting the hours to the dawn of day?

SHAWN [*with awkward humour*].   If it is, when we're wedded in a short while you'll have no call to complain, for I've little will to be walking off to wakes or weddings in the darkness of the night.

PEGEEN [*with rather scornful good humour*].   You're making might certain, Shaneen,[2] that I'll wed you now.

SHAWN.   Aren't we after making a good bargain, the way we're only waiting these days on Father Reilly's dispensation from the bishops, or the Court of Rome.

PEGEEN [*looking at him teasingly, washing up at dresser*].   It's a wonder, Shaneen, the Holy Father'd be taking notice of the likes of you; for if I was him I wouldn't bother with this place where you'll meet none but Red Linahan, has a squint in his eye, and Patcheen is lame in his

2. The *-een* suffix is an Irish diminutive, as in "Pegeen" or, later, "priesteen"; it may be used endearingly or contemptuously.

heel, or the mad Mulrannies were driven from California and they lost in their wits. We're a queer lot these times to go troubling the Holy Father on his sacred seat.

SHAWN [*scandalized*].   If we are, we're as good this place as another, maybe, and as good these times as we were for ever.

PEGEEN [*with scorn*].   As good, is it? Where now will you meet the like of Daneen Sullivan knocked the eye from a peeler,[3] or Marcus Quin, God rest him, got six months for maiming ewes, and he a great warrant to tell stories of hold Ireland till he'd have the old women shedding down tears about their feet. Where will you find the like of them, I'm saying?

SHAWN [*timidly*].   If you don't, it's a good job, maybe; for [*with peculiar emphasis on the words*] Father Reilly has small conceit to have that kind walking around and talking to the girls.

PEGEEN [*impatiently, throwing water from basin out of the door*].   Stop tormenting me with Father Reilly [*imitating his voice*] when I'm asking only what way I'll pass these twelve hours of dark, and not take my death with the fear. [*Looking out of door.*]

SHAWN [*timidly*].   Would I fetch you the Widow Quin, maybe?

PEGEEN.   Is it the like of that murderer? You'll not, surely.

SHAWN [*going to her, soothingly*].   Then I'm thinking himself will stop along with you when he sees you taking on, for it'll be a long nighttime with great darkness, and I'm after feeling a kind of fellow above in the furzy ditch, groaning wicked like a maddening dog, the way it's good cause you have, maybe, to be fearing now.

PEGEEN [*turning on him sharply*].   What's that? Is it a man you seen?

SHAWN [*retreating*].   I couldn't see him at all; but I heard him groaning out, and breaking his heart. It should have been a young man from his words speaking.

PEGEEN [*going after him*].   And you never went near to see was he hurted or what ailed him at all?

SHAWN.   I did not, Pegeen Mike. It was a dark, lonesome place to be hearing the like of him.

PEGEEN.   Well, you're a daring fellow, and if they find his corpse stretched above in the dews of dawn, what'll you say then to the peelers, or the Justice of the Peace?

SHAWN [*thunderstruck*].   I wasn't thinking of that. For the love of God, Pegeen Mike, don't let on I was speaking of him. don't tell your father and the men is coming above; for if they heard that story, they'd have great blabbing this night at the wake.

PEGEEN.   I'll maybe tell them, and I'll maybe not.

---

3. Policeman, a term originally applied to a member of the Royal Irish Constabulary force established by Robert Peel (1788–1850), chief secretary for Ireland (1812–18) and later prime minister.

SHAWN. They are coming at the door. Will you whisht, I'm saying?

PEGEEN. Whisht yourself.

[*She goes behind counter.* MICHAEL JAMES, *fat jovial publican, comes in followed by* PHILLY CULLEN, *who is thin and mistrusting, and* JIMMY FARRELL, *who is fat and amorous, about forty-five.*]

MEN [*together*]. God bless you. The blessing of God on this place.

PEGEEN. God bless you kindly.

MICHAEL [*to men who go to the counter*]. Sit down now, and take your rest. [*Crosses to* SHAWN *at the fire.*] And how is it you are, Shawn Keogh? Are you coming over the sands to Kate Cassidy's wake?

SHAWN. I am not, Michael James. I'm going home the short cut to my bed.

PEGEEN [*speaking across the counter*]. He's right too, and have you no shame, Michael James, to be quitting off for the whole night, and leaving myself lonesome in the shop?

MICHAEL [*good-humouredly*]. Isn't it the same whether I go for the whole night or a part only? and I'm thinking it's a queer daughter you are if you'd have me crossing backward through the Stooks of the Dead[4] Women, with a drop taken.

PEGEEN. If I am a queer daughter, it's a queer father'd be leaving me lonesome these twelve hours of dark, and I piling the turf with the dogs barking, and the calves mooing, and my own teeth rattling with the fear.

JIMMY [*flatteringly*]. What is there to hurt you, and you a fine, hardy girl would knock the head of any two men in the place?

PEGEEN [*working herself up*]. Isn't there the harvest boys with their tongues red for drink, and the ten tinkers is camped in the east glen, and the thousand militia—bad cess[5] to them!—walking idle through the land. There's lots surely to hurt me, and I won't stop alone in it, let himself do what he will.

MICHAEL. If you're afeard, let Shawn Keogh stop along with you. It's the will of God, I'm thinking, himself should be seeing to you now.

[*They all turn on* SHAWN.]

SHAWN [*in horrified confusion*]. I would and welcome, Michael James, but I'm afeard of Father Reilly; and what at all would the Holy Father and the Cardinals of Rome be saying if they heard I did the like of that?

MICHAEL [*with contempt*]. God help you! Can't you sit in by the hearth with the light lit and herself beyond in the room? You'll do that surely,

---

4. Shoreline rock formation named for a ship disaster and described in Synge's *Wicklow, West Kerry, and Connemara.*

5. Expression meaning "bad luck" derived from the practice of assessment of the Irish for provision of British military forces.

for I've heard tell there's a queer fellow above, going mad or getting his death, maybe, in the gripe of the ditch,[6] so she'd be safer this night with a person here.

SHAWN [*with plaintive despair*].   I'm afeard of Father Reilly, I'm saying. Let you not be tempting me, and we near married itself.

PHILLY [*with cold contempt*].   Lock him in the west room. He'll stay then and have no sin to be telling to the priest.

MICHAEL [*to* SHAWN, *getting between him and the door*].   Go up now.

SHAWN [*at the top of his voice*].   Don't stop me, Michael James. Let me out of the door, I'm saying, for the love of the Almighty God. Let me out [*trying to dodge past him*]. Let me out of it, and may God grant you His indulgence in the hour of need.

MICHAEL [*loudly*].   Stop your noising, and sit down by the hearth. [*Gives him a push and goes to counter laughing.*]

SHAWN [*turning back, wringing his hands*].   Oh, Father Reilly and the saints of God, where will I hide myself to-day? Oh, St. Joseph and St. Patrick and St. Brigid, and St. James, have mercy on me now! [SHAWN *turns round, sees door clear, and makes a rush for it.*]

MICHAEL [*catching him by the coat-tail.*].   You'd be going, is it?

SHAWN [*screaming*].   Leave me go, Michael James, leave me go, you old Pagan, leave me go, or I'll get the curse of the priests on you, and of the scarlet-coated bishops of the courts of Rome.

[*With a sudden movement he pulls himself out of his coat, and disappears out of the door, leaving his coat in* MICHAEL'S *hands.*]

MICHAEL [*turning round, and holding up coat*].   Well, there's the coat of a Christian man. Oh, there's sainted glory this day in the lonesome west; and by the will of God I've got you a decent man, Pegeen, you'll have no call to be spying after if you've a score of young girls, maybe, weeding in your fields.

PEGEEN [*taking up the defence of her property*].   What right have you to be making game of a poor fellow for minding the priest, when it's your own the fault is, not paying a penny pot-boy to stand along with me and give me courage in the doing of my work? [*She snaps the coat away from him, and goes behind counter with it.*]

MICHAEL [*taken aback*].   Where would I get a pot-boy? Would you have me send the bellman screaming in the streets of Castlebar?

SHAWN [*opening the door a chink and putting in his head, in a small voice*].   Michael James!

MICHAEL [*imitating him*].   What ails you?

SHAWN.   The queer dying fellow's beyond looking over the ditch. He's come up, I'm thinking, stealing your hens. [*Looks over his shoulder.*] God help me, he's following me now [*he runs into room*], and if he's

6. Trench at the edge of a hedge.

heard what I said, he'll be having my life, and I going home lonesome in the darkness of the night.

[*For a perceptible moment they watch the door with curiosity. Some one coughs outside. Then* CHRISTY MAHON, *a slight young man, comes in very tired and frightened and dirty.*]

CHRISTY [*in a small voice*]. God save all here!

MEN. God save you kindly.

CHRISTY [*going to the counter*]. I'd trouble you for a glass of porter, woman of the house. [*He puts down coin.*]

PEGEEN [*serving him*]. You're one of the tinkers,[7] young fellow, is beyond camped in the glen?

CHRISTY. I am not; but I'm destroyed walking.

MICHAEL [*patronizingly*]. Let you come up then to the fire. You're looking famished with the cold.

CHRISTY. God reward you. [*He takes up his glass and goes a little way across to the left, then stops and looks about him.*] Is it often the police do be coming into this place, master of the house?

MICHAEL. If you'd come in better hours, you'd have seen "Licensed for the sale of Beer and Spirits, to be consumed on the premises," written in white letters above the door, and what would the polis want spying on me, and not a decent house within four miles, the way every living Christian is a bona fide,[8] saving one widow alone?

CHRISTY [*with relief*]. It's a safe house, so. [*He goes over to the fire, sighing and moaning. Then he sits down, putting his glass beside him and begins gnawing a turnip, too miserable to feel the others staring at him with curiosity.*]

MICHAEL [*going after him*]. Is it yourself is fearing the polis? You're wanting, maybe?

CHRISTY. There's many wanting.

MICHAEL. Many surely, with the broken harvest and the ended wars.[9] [*He picks up some stockings, etc., that are near the fire, and carries them away furtively.*] It should be larceny, I'm thinking?

CHRISTY [*dolefully*]. I had it in my mind it was a different word and a bigger.

PEGEEN. There's a queer lad. Were you never slapped in school, young fellow, that you don't know the name of your deed?

CHRISTY [*bashfully*]. I'm slow at learning, a middling scholar only.

MICHAEL. If you're a dunce itself, you'd have a right to know that larceny's robbing and stealing. Is it for the like of that you're wanting?

CHRISTY [*with a flash of family pride*]. And I the son of a strong farmer

7. Itinerant peddlers.
8. A real traveler and so permitted to purchase spirits after closing time of licensed pubs.

9. The Land Wars, at peak in the 1880s, to nationalize ownership of land and so protect tenant farmers from eviction.

[*with a sudden qualm*], God rest his soul, could have bought up the whole of your old house a while since, from the butt of his tailpocket, and not have missed the weight of it gone.

MICHAEL [*impressed*].   If it's not stealing, it's maybe something big.

CHRISTY [*flattered*].   Aye; it's maybe something big.

JIMMY.   He's a wicked-looking young fellow. Maybe he followed after a young woman on a lonesome night.

CHRISTY [*shocked*].   Oh, the saints forbid, mister; I was all times a decent lad.

PHILLY [*turning on* JIMMY].   You're a silly man, Jimmy Farrell. He said his father was a farmer a while since, and there's himself now in a poor state. Maybe the land was grabbed from him, and he did what any decent man would do.

MICHAEL [*to* CHRISTY, *mysteriously*].   Was it baliffs?

CHRISTY.   The divil a one.

MICHAEL.   Agents?

CHRISTY.   The divil a one.

MICHAEL.   Landlords?

CHRISTY [*peevishly*].   Ah, not at all, I'm saying. You'd see the like of them stories on any little paper of a Munster town. But I'm not calling to mind any person, gentle, simple, judge or jury, did the like of me.

[*They all drew nearer with delighted curiosity.*]

PHILLY.   Well, that lad's a puzzle-the-world.

JIMMY.   He'd beat Dan Davies' circus, or the holy missioners making sermons on the villainy of man. Try him again, Philly.

PHILLY.   Did you strike golden guineas out of solder, young fellow, or shilling coins itself?

CHRISTY.   I did not, mister, not sixpence nor a farthing coin.

JIMMY.   Did you marry three wives maybe? I'm told there's a sprinkling have done that among the holy Luthers of the preaching north.

CHRISTY [*shyly*].   I never married with one, let alone with a couple or three.

PHILLY.   Maybe he went fighting for the Boers, the like of the man beyond, was judged to be hanged, quartered and drawn. Were you off east, young fellow, fighting bloody wars for Kruger and the freedom of the Boers?[1]

CHRISTY.   I never left my own parish till Tuesday was a week.

PEGEEN [*coming from counter*].   He's done nothing, so. [*To* CHRISTY.] If you didn't commit murder or a bad, nasty thing, or false coining, or robbery, or butchery, or the like of them, there isn't anything that

---

1. Paul Kruger, president of the South African Republic established by Boers, Dutch settlers, and suppressed by the British in the Boer War (1899–1902).

would be worth your troubling for to run from now. You did nothing at all.

CHRISTY [*his feelings hurt*].   That's an unkindly thing to be saying to a poor orphaned traveller, has a prison behind him, and hanging before, and hell's gap gaping below.

PEGEEN [*with a sign to the men to be quiet*].   You're only saying it. You did nothing at all. A soft lad the like of you wouldn't slit the windpipe of a screeching sow.

CHRISTY [*offended*].   You're not speaking the truth.

PEGEEN [*in mock rage*].   Not speaking the truth, is it? Would you have me knock the head of you with the butt of the broom?

CHRISTY [*twisting round on her with a sharp cry of horror*].   Don't strike me. I killed my poor father, Tuesday was a week, for doing the like of that.

PEGEEN [*with blank amazement*].   Is it killed your father?

CHRISTY [*subsiding*].   With the help of God I did surely, and that the Holy Immaculate Mother may intercede for his soul.

PHILLY [*retreating with* JIMMY].   There's a daring fellow.

JIMMY.   Oh, glory be to God!

MICHAEL [*with great respect*].   That was a hanging crime, mister honey. You should have had good reason for doing the like of that.

CHRISTY [*in a very reasonable tone*].   He was a dirty man, God forgive him, and he getting old and crusty, the way I couldn't put up with him at all.

PEGEEN.   And you shot him dead?

CHRISTY [*shaking his head*].   I never used weapons. I've no license, and I'm a law-fearing man.

MICHAEL.   It was with a hilted knife maybe? I'm told, in the big world it's bloody knives they use.

CHRISTY [*loudly, scandalized*].   Do you take me for a slaughter-boy?

PEGEEN.   You never hanged him, the way Jimmy Farrell hanged his dog from the license, and had it screeching and wriggling three hours at the butt of a string, and himself swearing it was a dead dog, and the peelers swearing it had life?

CHRISTY.   I did not then. I just riz the loy[2] and left fall the edge of it on the ridge of his skull, and he went down at my feet like an empty sack, and never let a grunt or groan from him at all.

MICHAEL [*making a sign to* PEGEEN *to fill* CHRISTY'S *glass*].   And what way weren't you hanged, mister? Did you bury him then?

CHRISTY [*considering*].   Aye. I buried him then. Wasn't I digging spuds in the field?

MICHAEL.   And the peelers never followed after you the eleven days that you're out?

---

2. Small spade, usually used for digging potatoes.

CHRISTY [*shaking his head*].   Never a none of them, and I walking forward facing hog, dog, or divil on the highway of the road.

PHILLY [*nodding wisely*].   It's only with a common week-day kind of a murderer them lads would be trusting their carcase, and that man should be a great terror when his temper's roused.

MICHAEL.   He should then. [*To* CHRISTY.] And where was it, mister honey, that you did the deed?

CHRISTY [*looking at him with suspicion*].   Oh, a distant place, master of the house, a windy corner of high, distant hills.

PHILLY [*nodding with approval*].   He's a close man, and he's right, surely.

PEGEEN.   That'd be a lad with the sense of Solomon to have for a pot-boy, Michael James, if it's the truth you're seeking one at all.

PHILLY.   The peelers is fearing him, and if you'd that lad in the house there isn't one of them would come smelling around if the dogs itself were lapping poteen[3] from the dung-pit of the yard.

JIMMY.   Bravery's a treasure in a lonesome place, and a lad would kill his father, I'm thinking, would face a foxy divil with a pitchpike on the flags of hell.

PEGEEN.   It's the truth they're saying, and if I'd that lad in the house, I wouldn't be fearing the loosed kharki[4] cut-throats, or the walking dead.

CHRISTY [*swelling with surprise and triumph*].   Well, glory be to God!

MICHAEL [*with deference*].   Would you think well to stop here and be pot-boy, mister honey, if we gave you good wages, and didn't destroy you with the weight of work?

SHAWN [*coming forward uneasily*].   That'd be a queer kind to bring into a decent quiet household with the like of Pegeen Mike.

PEGEEN [*very sharply*].   Will you whisht? Who's speaking to you?

SHAWN [*retreating*].   A bloody-handed murderer the like of . . .

PEGEEN [*snapping at him*].   Whisht I am saying; we'll take no fooling from your like at all. [*To* CHRISTY *with a honeyed voice.*] And you, young fellow, you'd have a right to stop, I'm thinking, for we'd do our all and utmost to content your needs.

CHRISTY [*overcome with wonder*].   And I'd be safe in this place from the searching law?

MICHAEL.   You would, surely. If they're not fearing you, itself, the peelers in this place is decent droughty[5] poor fellows, wouldn't touch a cur dog and not give warning in the dead of night.

PEGEEN [*very kindly and persuasively*].   Let you stop a short while anyhow. Aren't you destroyed walking with your feet in bleeding blisters, and your whole skin needing washing like a Wicklow sheep.

CHRISTY [*looking round with satisfaction*].   It's a nice room, and if it's not humbugging me you are, I'm thinking that I'll surely stay.

---

3. Illegal, home-distilled spirits.
4. Khaki, tan cotton associated with the British field

uniform.
5. Thirsty.

JIMMY [*jumps up*].   Now, by the grace of God, herself will be safe this
night, with a man killed his father holding danger from the door, and
let you come on, Michael James, or they'll have the best stuff drunk
at the wake.

MICHAEL [*going to the door with* MEN].   And begging your pardon, mister, what name will we call you, for we'd like to know?

CHRISTY.   Christopher Mahon.

MICHAEL.   Well, God bless you, Christy, and a good rest till we meet
again when the sun'll be rising to the noon of day.

CHRISTY.   God bless you all.

MEN.   God bless you.

[*They go out except* SHAWN, *who lingers at door.*]

SHAWN [*to* PEGEEN].   Are you wanting me to stop along with you and
keep you from harm?

PEGEEN [*gruffly*].   Didn't you say you were fearing Father Reilly?

SHAWN.   There'd be no harm staying now, I'm thinking, and himself
in it too.

PEGEEN.   You wouldn't stay when there was need for you, and let you
step off nimble this time when there's none.

SHAWN.   Didn't I say it was Father Reilly . . .

PEGEEN.   Go on, then, to Father Reilly [*in a jeering tone*], and let him
put you in the holy brotherhoods, and leave that lad to me.

SHAWN.   If I meet the Widow Quin . . .

PEGEEN.   Go on, I'm saying, and don't be waking this place with your
noise. [*She hustles him out and bolts the door.*] That lad would wear
the spirits from the saints of peace.

[*Bustles about, then takes off her apron and pins it up in the
window as a blind.* CHRISTY *watching her timidly. Then she comes
to him and speaks with bland good-humour.*]

Let you stretch out now by the fire, young fellow. You should be
destroyed travelling.

CHRISTY [*shyly again, drawing off his boots*].   I'm tired, surely, walking
wild eleven days, and waking fearful in the night. [*He holds up one of
his feet, feeling his blisters, and looking at them with compassion.*]

PEGEEN [*standing beside him, watching him with delight*].   You should
have had great people in your family, I'm thinking, with the little,
small feet you have, and you with a kind of a quality name, the like
of what you'd find on the great powers and potentates of France and
Spain.

CHRISTY [*with pride*].   We were great surely, with wide and windy acres
of rich Munster land.

PEGEEN.   Wasn't I telling you, and you a fine, handsome young fellow
with a noble brow?

CHRISTY [*with a flash of delighted surprise*].   Is it me?

PEGEEN.   Aye, Did you never hear that from the young girls where you come from in the west or south?

CHRISTY [*with venom*].   I did not then. Oh, they're bloody liars in the naked parish where I grew a man.

PEGEEN.   If they are itself, you've heard it these days, I'm thinking, and you walking the world telling out your story to young girls or old.

CHRISTY.   I've told my story no place till this night, Pegeen Mike, and it's foolish I was here, maybe, to be talking free, but you're decent people, I'm thinking, and yourself a kindly woman, the way I wasn't fearing you at all.

PEGEEN [*filling a sack with straw*].   You've said the like of that, maybe, in every cot and cabin where you've met a young girl on your way.

CHRISTY [*going over to her, gradually raising his voice*].   I've said it nowhere till this night, I'm telling you, for I've seen none the like of you the eleven long days I am walking the world, looking over a low ditch or a high ditch on my north or my south, into stony scattered fields, or scribes of bog, where you'd see young, limber girls, and fine prancing women making laughter with the men.

PEGEEN.   If you weren't destroyed travelling, you'd have as much talk and streeleen,[6] I'm thinking, as Owen Roe O'Sullivan or the poets of the Dingle Bay, and I've heard all times it's the poets are your like, fine fiery fellows with great rages when their temper's roused.

CHRISTY [*drawing a little nearer to her*].   You've a power of rings, God bless you, and would there be any offence if I was asking are you single now?

PEGEEN.   What would I want wedding so young?

CHRISTY [*with relief*].   We're alike, so.

PEGEEN [*she puts sack on settle and beats it up*].   I never killed my father. I'd be afeard to do that, except I was the like of yourself with blind rages tearing me within, for I'm thinking you should have had great tussling when the end was come.

CHRISTY [*expanding with delight at the first confidential talk he has ever had with a woman*].   We had not then. It was a hard woman was come over the hill, and if he was always a crusty kind when he'd a hard woman setting him on, not the divil himself or his four fathers could put up with him at all.

PEGEEN [*with curiosity*].   And isn't it a great wonder that one wasn't fearing you?

CHRISTY [*very confidentially*].   Up to the day I killed my father, there wasn't a person in Ireland knew the kind I was, and I there drinking, waking, eating, sleeping, a quiet, simple poor fellow with no man giving me heed.

PEGEEN [*getting a quilt out of the cupboard and putting it on the sack*].   It

6. Wandering, like Owen Roe O'Sullivan (1748–84), poet and scholar of county Kerry and its Dingle peninsula.

was the girls were giving you heed maybe, and I'm thinking it's most conceit you'd have to be gaming with their like.

CHRISTY [*shaking his head, with simplicity*]. Not the girls itself, and I won't tell you a lie. There wasn't anyone heeding me in that place saving only the dumb beasts of the field. [*He sits down at fire.*]

PEGEEN [*with disappointment*]. And I thinking you should have been living the like of a king of Norway or the Eastern world. [*She comes and sits beside him after placing bread and mug of milk on the table.*]

CHRISTY [*laughing piteously*]. The like of a king, is it? And I after toiling, moiling, digging, dodging from the dawn till dusk with never a sight of joy or sport saving only when I'd be abroad in the dark night poaching rabbits on hills, for I was a devil to poach, God forgive me, [*very naïvely*] and I near got six months for going with a dung fork and stabbing a fish.

PEGEEN. And it's that you'd call sport, is it, to be abroad in the darkness with yourself alone?

CHRISTY. I did, God help me, and there I'd be as happy as the sunshine of St. Martin's Day,[7] watching the light passing the north or the patches of fog, till I'd hear a rabbit starting to screech and I'd go running in the furze. Then when I'd my full share I'd come walking down where you'd see the ducks and geese stretched sleeping on the highway of the road, and before I'd pass the dunghill, I'd hear himself snoring out, a loud lonesome snore he'd be making all times, the while he was sleeping, and he a man 'd be raging all times, the while he was waking, like a gaudy officer you'd hear cursing and damning and swearing oaths.

PEGEEN. Providence and Mercy, spare us all!

CHRISTY. It's that you'd say surely if you seen him and he after drinking for weeks, rising up in the red dawn, or before it maybe, and going out into the yard as naked as an ash tree in the moon of May, and shying clods against the viságe of the stars till he'd put the fear of death into the banbhs[8] and the screeching sows.

PEGEEN. I'd be well-nigh afeard of that lad myself, I'm thinking. And there was no one in it but the two of you alone?

CHRISTY. The divil a one, though he'd sons and daughters walking all great states and territories of the world, and not a one of them, to this day, but would say their seven curses on him, and the rousing up to let a cough or sneeze, maybe, in the deadness of the night.

PEGEEN [*nodding her head*]. Well, you should have been a queer lot. I never cursed my father the like of that, though I'm twenty and more years of age.

CHRISTY. Then you'd have cursed mine, I'm telling you, and he a man

7. November 11, a festival day, Martinmas, before St. Martin's Lent, a period of penitence extending through Christmas.
8. Piglets.

never gave peace to any, saving when he'd get two months or three, or be locked in the asylums for battering peelers or assaulting men [*with depression*] the way it was a bitter life he led me till I did up a Tuesday and halve his skull.

PEGEEN [*putting her hand on his shoulder*].   Well, you'll have peace in this place, Christy Mahon, and none to trouble you, and it's near time a fine lad like you should have your good share of the earth.

CHRISTY.   It's the time surely, and I a seemly fellow with great strength in me and bravery of . . .

[*Someone knocks.*]

CHRISTY [*clinging to* PEGEEN].   Oh, glory! it's late for knocking, and this last while I'm in terror of the peelers, and the walking dead.

[*Knocking again.*]

PEGEEN.   Who's there?
VOICE [*outside*].   Me.
PEGEEN.   Who's me?
VOICE.   The Widow Quin.
PEGEEN [*jumping up and giving him the bread and milk*].   Go on now with your supper, and let on to be sleepy, for if she found you were such a warrant to talk, she'd be stringing gabble till the dawn of day.

[*He takes bread and sits shyly with his back to the door.*]

PEGEEN [*opening door, with temper*].   What ails you, or what is it you're wanting at this hour of the night?

WIDOW QUIN [*coming in a step and peering at* CHRISTY].   I'm after meeting Shawn Keogh and Father Reilly below, who told me of your curiosity man, and they fearing by this time he was maybe roaring, romping on your hands with drink.

PEGEEN [*pointing to* CHRISTY].   Look now is he roaring, and he stretched away drowsy with his supper and his mug of milk. Walk down and tell that to Father Reilly and to Shaneen Keogh.

WIDOW QUIN [*coming forward*].   I'll not see them again, for I've their word to lead that lad forward for to lodge with me.

PEGEEN [*in blank amazement*].   This night, is it?

WIDOW QUIN [*going over*].   This night. "It isn't fitting," says the priesteen, "to have his likeness lodging with an orphaned girl." [*To* CHRISTY.] God save you, mister!

CHRISTY [*shyly*].   God save you kindly.

WIDOW QUIN [*looking at him with half-amazed curiosity*].   Well, aren't you a little smiling fellow? It should have been great and bitter torments did rouse your spirits to a deed of blood.

CHRISTY [*doubtfully*].   It should, maybe.

WIDOW QUIN.   It's more than "maybe" I'm saying, and it'd soften my heart to see you sitting so simple with your cup and cake, and you fitter to be saying your catechism than slaying your da.

PEGEEN [*at counter, washing glasses*]. There's talking when any'd see he's fit to be holding his head high with the wonders of the world. Walk on from this, for I'll not have him tormented and he destroyed travelling since Tuesday was a week.

WIDOW QUIN [*peaceably*]. We'll be walking surely when his supper's done, and you'll find we're great company, young fellow, when it's of the like of you and me you'd hear the penny poets singing in an August Fair.

CHRISTY [*innocently*]. Did you kill your father?

PEGEEN [*contemptuously*]. She did not. She hit himself with a worn pick, and the rusted poison did corrode his blood the way he never overed it, and died after. That was a sneaky kind of murder did win small glory with the boys itself. [*She crosses to* CHRISTY's *left.*]

WIDOW QUIN [with good-humour]. If it didn't, maybe all knows a widow woman has buried her children and destroyed her man is a wiser comrade for a young lad than a girl, the like of you, who'd go helter-skeltering after any man would let you a wink upon the road.

PEGEEN [*breaking out into wild rage*]. And you'll say that, Widow Quin, and you gasping with the rage you had racing the hill beyond to look on his face.

WIDOW QUIN [*laughing derisively*]. Me, is it? Well, Father Reilly has cuteness to divide you now. [*She pulls* CHRISTY *up.*] There's great temptation in a man did slay his da, and we'd best be going, young fellow; so rise up and come with me.

PEGEEN [*seizing his arm*]. He'll not stir. He's pot-boy in this place, and I'll not have him stolen off and kidnabbed while himself's abroad.

WIDOW QUIN. It'd be a crazy pot-boy'd lodge him in the shebeen where he works by day, so you'd have a right to come on, young fellow, till you see my little houseen, a perch off on the rising hill.

PEGEEN. Wait till morning, Christy Mahon. Wait till you lay eyes on her leaky thatch is growing more pasture for her buck goat than her square of fields, and she without a tramp itself to keep in order her place at all.

WIDOW QUIN. When you see me contriving in my little gardens, Christy Mahon, you'll swear the Lord God formed me to be living lone, and that there isn't my match in Mayo for thatching, or mowing, or shearing a sheep.

PEGEEN [*with noisy scorn*]. It's true the Lord God formed you to contrive indeed. Doesn't the world know you reared a black lamb at your own breast, so that the Lord Bishop of Connaught felt the elements of a Christian, and he eating it after in a kidney stew? Doesn't the world know you've been seen shaving the foxy skipper from France for a threepenny bit and a sop of grass tobacco would wring the liver from a mountain goat you'd meet leaping the hills?

WIDOW QUIN [*with amusement*].   Do you hear her now, young fellow? Do you hear the way she'll be rating at your own self when a week is by?

PEGEEN [*to* CHRISTY].   Don't heed her. Tell her to go into her pigsty and not plague us here.

WIDOW QUIN.   I'm going; but he'll come with me.

PEGEEN [*shaking him*].   Are you dumb, young fellow?

CHRISTY [*timidly, to* WIDOW QUIN].   God increase you; but I'm pot-boy in his place, and it's here I'd liefer[9] stay.

PEGEEN [*triumphantly*].   Now you have heard him, and go on from this.

WIDOW QUIN [*looking round the room*].   It's lonesome this hour crossing the hill, and if he won't come along with me, I'd have a right maybe to stop this night with yourselves. Let me stretch out on the settle, Pegeen Mike; and himself can lie by the hearth.

PEGEEN [*short and fiercely*].   Faith, I won't. Quit off or I will send you now.

WIDOW QUIN [*gathering her shawl up*].   Well, it's a terror to be aged a score. [*To* CHRISTY.] God bless you now, young fellow, and let you be wary, or there's right torment will await you here if you go romancing with her like, and she waiting only, as they bade me say, on a sheep-skin parchment to be wed with Shawn Keogh of Killakeen.

CHRISTY [*going to* PEGEEN *as she bolts the door*].   What's that she's after saying?

PEGEEN.   Lies and blather, you've no call to mind. Well, isn't Shawn Keogh an impudent fellow to send up spying on me? Wait till I lay hands on him. Let him wait, I'm saying.

CHRISTY.   And you're not wedding him at all?

PEGEEN.   I wouldn't wed him if a bishop came walking for to join us here.

CHRISTY.   That God in glory may be thanked for that.

PEGEEN.   There's your bed now. I've put a quilt upon you I'm after quilting a while since with my own two hands, and you'd best stretch out now for your sleep, and may God give you a good rest till I call you in the morning when the cocks will crow.

CHRISTY [*as she goes to inner room*].   May God and Mary and St. Patrick bless you and reward you, for your kindly talk.

[*She shuts the door behind her. He settles his bed slowly, feeling the quilt with immense satisfaction.*]

Well, it's a clean bed and soft with it, and it's great luck and company I've won me in the end of time—two fine women fighting for the likes

_____
9. Willingly, gladly.

of me—till I'm thinking this night wasn't I a foolish fellow not to kill
my father in the years gone by.

Act Two

SCENE, *as before. Brilliant morning light.* CHRISTY, *looking bright and
cheerful, is cleaning a girl's boots.*

CHRISTY [*to himself, counting jugs on dresser*].   Half a hundred beyond.
Ten there. A score that's above. Eighty jugs. Six cups and a broken
one. Two plates. A power of glasses. Bottles, a school-master'd be
hard set to count, and enough in them, I'm thinking, to drunken all
the wealth and wisdom of the County Clare. [*He puts down the boot
carefully.*] There's her boots now, nice and decent for her evening
use, and isn't it grand brushes she has? [*He puts them down and goes
by degrees to the looking-glass.*] Well, this'd be a fine place to be my
whole life talking out with swearing Christians, in place of my old
dogs and cat, and I stalking around, smoking my pipe and drinking
my fill, and never a day's work but drawing a cork an odd time, or
wiping a glass, or rinsing out a shiny tumbler for a decent man. [*He
takes the looking-glass from the wall and puts it on the back of a chair;
then sits down in front of it and begins washing his face.*] Didn't I
know rightly I was handsome, though it was the divil's own mirror we
had beyond, would twist a squint across an angel's brow; and I'll be
growing fine from this day, the way I'll have a soft lovely skin on me
and won't be the like of the clumsy young fellows do be ploughing all
times in the earth and dung. [*He starts.*] Is she coming again? [*He
looks out.*] Stranger girls. God help me, where'll I hide myself away
and my long neck naked to the world? [*He looks out.*] I'd best go to
the room maybe till I'm dressed again.

> [*He gathers up his coat and the looking-glass, and runs into the
> inner room. The door is pushed open, and* SUSAN BRADY *looks in,
> and knocks on door.*]

SUSAN.   There's nobody in it. [*Knocks again.*]
NELLY [*pushing her in and following her, with* HONOR BLAKE *and* SARA
TANSEY].   It'd be early for them both to be out walking the hill.
SUSAN.   I'm thinking Shawn Keogh was making game of us and there's
no such man in it at all.
HONOR [*pointing to straw and quilt*].   Look at that. He's been sleeping
there in the night. Well, it'll be a hard case if he's gone off now, the
way we'll never set our eyes on a man killed his father, and we after
rising early and destroying ourselves running fast on the hill.
NELLY.   Are you thinking them's his boots?

SARA [*taking them up*].   If they are, there should be his father's track on them. Did you never read in the papers the way murdered men do bleed and drip?

SUSAN.   Is that blood there, Sara Tansey?

SARA [smelling it].   That's bog water, I'm thinking, but it's his own they are surely, for I never seen the like of them for whity mud, and red mud, and turf on them, and the fine sands of the sea. That man's been walking, I'm telling you. [*She goes down right, putting on one of his boots.*]

SUSAN [*going to window*].   Maybe he's stolen off to Belmullet with the boots of Michael James, and you'd have a right so to follow after him, Sara Tansey, and you the one yoked the ass cart and drove ten miles to set your eyes on the man bit the yellow lady's nostril on the northern shore. [*She looks out.*]

SARA [*running to window with one boot on*].   Don't be talking, and we fooled to-day. [*Putting on other boot.*] There's a pair do fit me well, and I'll be keeping them for walking to the priest, when you'd be ashamed this place, going up winter and summer with nothing worth while to confess at all.

HONOR [*who has been listening at the door*].   Whisht! there's someone inside the room. [*She pushes door a chink open.*] It's a man.

   [SARA *kicks off boots and puts them where they were. They all stand in a line looking through chink.*]

SARA.   I'll call him. Mister! Mister!

   [*He puts in his head.*]

Is Pegeen within?

CHRISTY [*coming in as meek as a mouse, with the looking-glass held behind his back*].   She's above on the cnuceen,[1] seeking the nanny goats, the way she'd have a sup of goat's milk for to colour my tea.

SARA.   And asking your pardon, is it you's the man killed his father?

CHRISTY [*sidling toward the nail where the glass was hanging*].   I am, God help me!

SARA [*taking eggs she has brought*].   Then my thousand welcomes to you, and I've run up with a brace of duck's eggs for your food to-day. Pegeen's ducks is no use, but these are the real rich sort. Hold out your hand and you'll see it's no lie I'm telling you.

CHRISTY [*coming forward shyly, and holding out his left hand*].   They're a great and weighty size.

SUSAN.   And I run up with a pat of butter, for it'd be a poor thing to have you eating your spuds dry, and you after running a great way since you did destroy your da.

1. Small hill.

CHRISTY.   Thank you kindly.

HONOR.   And I brought you a little cut of cake, for you should have a thin stomach on you, and you that length walking the world.

NELLY.   And I brought you a little laying pullet—boiled and all she is— was crushed at the fall of night by the curate's car. Feel the fat of that breast, mister.

CHRISTY.   It's bursting, surely. [*He feels it with the back of his hand, in which he holds the presents.*]

SARA.   Will you pinch it? Is your right hand too sacred for to use at all? [*She slips round behind him.*] It's a glass he has. Well, I never seen to this day a man with a looking-glass held to his back. Them that kills their fathers is a vain lot surely.

[*Girls giggle.*]

CHRISTY [*smiling innocently and piling presents on glass*].   I'm very thankful to you all to-day . . .

WIDOW QUIN [*coming in quickly, at door*].   Sara Tansey, Susan Brady, Honor Blake! What in glory has you here at this hour of day?

GIRLS [*giggling*].   That's the man killed his father.

WIDOW QUIN [*coming to them*].   I know well it's the man; and I'm after putting him down in the sports below for racing, leaping, pitching, and the Lord knows what.

SARA [*exuberantly*].   That's right, Widow Quin. I'll bet my dowry that he'll lick the world.

WIDOW QUIN.   If you will, you'd have a right to have him fresh and nourished in place of nursing a feast. [*Taking presents.*] Are you fasting or fed, young fellow?

CHRISTY.   Fasting, if you please.

WIDOW QUIN [*loudly*].   Well, you're the lot. Stir up now and give him his breakfast. [*To* CHRISTY.] Come here to me

[*she puts him on bench beside her while the girls make tea and get his breakfast*]

and let you tell us your story before Pegeen will come, in place of grinning your ears off like the moon of May.

CHRISTY [*beginning to be pleased*].   It's a long story; you'd be destroyed listening.

WIDOW QUIN.   Don't be letting on to be shy, a fine, gamey, treacherous lad the like of you. Was it in your house beyond you cracked his skull?

CHRISTY [*shy but flattered*].   It was not. We were digging spuds in his cold, sloping, stony, divil's patch of a field.

WIDOW QUIN.   And you went asking money of him, or making talk of getting a wife would drive him from his farm?

CHRISTY.   I did not, then; but there I was, digging and digging, and "You squinting idiot," says he, "let you walk down now and tell the priest you'll wed the Widow Casey in a score of days."

WIDOW QUIN.   And what kind was she?

CHRISTY [*with horror*].   A walking terror from beyond the hills, and she
two score and five years, and two hundredweights and five pounds in
the weighing scales, with a limping leg on her, and a blinded eye,
and she a woman of noted misbehaviour with the old and young.

GIRLS [*clustering round him, serving him*].   Glory be.

WIDOW QUIN.   And what did he want driving you to wed with her? [*She
takes a bit of the chicken.*]

CHRISTY [*eating with growing satisfaction*].   He was letting on I was
wanting a protector from the harshness of the world, and he without
a thought the whole while but how he'd have her hut to live in and
her gold to drink.

WIDOW QUIN.   There's maybe worse than a dry hearth and a widow
woman and your glass at night. So you hit him then?

CHRISTY [*getting almost excited*].   I did not. "I won't wed her," says I,
"when all know she did suckle me for six weeks when I came into the
world, and she a hag this day with a tongue on her has the crows and
seabirds scattered, the way they wouldn't cast a shadow on her garden
with the dread of her curse."

WIDOW QUIN [*teasingly*].   That one should be right company.

SARA [*eagerly*].   Don't mind her. Did you kill him then?

CHRISTY.   "She's too good for the like of you," says he, "and go on now
or I'll flatten you out like a crawling beast has passed under a dray."
"You will not if I can help it," says I. "Go on," says he, "or I'll have
the divil making garters of your limbs to-night." "You will not if I can
help it," says I. [*He sits up, brandishing his mug.*]

SARA.   You were right surely.

CHRISTY [*impressively*].   With that the sun came out between the cloud
and the hill, and it shining green in my face. "God have mercy on
your soul," says he, lifting a scythe; "or on your own," says I, raising
the loy.

SUSAN.   That's a grand story.

HONOR.   He tells it lovely.

CHRISTY [*flattered and confident, waving bone*].   He gave a drive with
the scythe, and I gave a lep to the east. Then I turned around with
my back to the north, and I hit a blow on the ridge of his skull, laid
him stretched out, and he split to the knob of his gullet. [*He raises the
chicken bone to his Adam's apple.*]

GIRLS [*together*].   Well, you're a marvel! Oh, God bless you! You're the
lad surely!

SUSAN.   I'm thinking the Lord God sent him this road to make a second
husband to the Widow Quin, and she with a great yearning to be
wedded, though all dread her here. Lift him on her knee, Sara Tansey.

WIDOW QUIN.   Don't tease him.

SARA [*going over to dresser and counter very quickly, and getting two glasses and porter*].   You're heroes surely, and let you drink a supeen with your arms linked like the outlandish lovers in the sailor's song.

[*She links their arms and gives them the glasses.*]

There now. Drink a health to the wonders of the western world, the pirates, preachers, poteen-makers, with the jobbing jockies; parching peelers, and the juries fill their stomachs selling judgments of the English law. [*Brandishing the bottle.*]

WIDOW QUIN.   That's a right toast, Sara Tansey. Now Christy.

[*They drink with their arms linked, he drinking with his left hand, she with her right. As they are drinking,* PEGEEN MIKE *comes in with a milk can and stands aghast. They all spring away from* CHRISTY. *He goes down left.* WIDOW QUIN *remains seated.*]

PEGEEN [*angrily, to* SARA].   What is it you're wanting?

SARA [*twisting her apron*].   An ounce of tobacco.

PEGEEN.   Have you tuppence?

SARA.   I've forgotten my purse.

PEGEEN.   Then you'd best be getting it and not fooling us here. [*To the* WIDOW QUIN, *with more elaborate scorn.*] And what is it you're wanting, Widow Quin?

WIDOW QUIN [*insolently*].   A penn'orth of starch.

PEGEEN [*breaking out*].   And you without a white shift or a shirt in your whole family since the drying of the flood. I've no starch for the like of you, and let you walk on now to Killamuck.

WIDOW QUIN [*turning to* CHRISTY, *as she goes out with the girls*].   Well, you're mighty huffy this day, Pegeen Mike, and, you young fellow, let you not forget the sports and racing when the noon is by.

[*They go out.*]

PEGEEN [*imperiously*].   Fling out that rubbish and put them cups away.

[CHRISTY *tidies away in great haste.*]

Shove in the bench by the wall.

[*He does so.*]

And hang that glass on the nail. What disturbed it at all?

CHRISTY [*very meekly*].   I was making myself decent only, and this a fine country for young lovely girls.

PEGEEN [*sharply*].   Whisht your talking of girls. [*Goes to counter—right.*]

CHRISTY.   Wouldn't any wish to be decent in a place . . .

PEGEEN.   Whisht I'm saying.

CHRISTY [*looks at her face for a moment with great misgivings, then as a last effort, takes up a loy, and goes towards her, with feigned assurance*].   It was with a loy the like of that I killed my father.

PEGEEN [*still sharply*].   You've told me that story six times since the dawn of day.

CHRISTY [*reproachfully*].   It's a queer thing you wouldn't care to be hearing it and them girls after walking four miles to be listening to me now.

PEGEEN [*turning round astonished*].   Four miles.

CHRISTY [*apologetically*].   Didn't himself say there were only four bona fides living in the place?

PEGEEN.   It's bona fides by the road they are, but that lot came over the river lepping the stones. It's not three perches when you go like that, and I was down this morning looking on the papers the post-boy does have in his bag. [*With meaning and emphasis.*] For there was great news this day, Christopher Mahon. [*She goes into room left.*]

CHRISTY [*suspiciously*].   Is it news of my murder?

PEGEEN [*inside*].   Murder, indeed.

CHRISTY [*loudly*].   A murdered da?

PEGEEN [*coming in again and crossing right*].   There was not, but a story filled half a page of the hanging of a man. Ah, that should be a fearful end, young fellow, and it worst of all for a man who destroyed his da, for the like of him would get small mercies, and when it's dead he is, they'd put him in a narrow grave, with cheap sacking wrapping him round, and pour down quicklime on his head, the way you'd see a woman pouring any frish-frash from a cup.

CHRISTY [*very miserably*].   Oh, God help me. Are you thinking I'm safe? You were saying at the fall of night, I was shut of jeopardy and I here with yourselves.

PEGEEN [*severely*].   You'll be shut of jeopardy no place if you go talking with a pack of wild girls the like of them do be walking abroad with the peelers, talking whispers at the fall of night.

CHRISTY [*with terror*].   And you're thinking they'd tell?

PEGEEN [*with mock sympathy*].   Who knows, God help you.

CHRISTY [*loudly*].   What joy would they have to bring hanging to the likes of me?

PEGEEN.   It's queer joys they have, and who knows the thing they'd do, if it'd make the green stones cry itself to think of you swaying and swiggling at the butt of a rope, and you with a fine, stout neck, God bless you! the way you'd be a half an hour, in great anguish, getting your death.

CHRISTY [*getting his boots and putting them on*].   If there's that terror of them, it'd be best, maybe, I went on wandering like Esau or Cain and Abel on the sides of Neifin or the Erris plain.[2]

2. Christy conflates biblical figures with Irish place names.

PEGEEN [*beginning to play with him*]. It would, maybe, for I've heard the Circuit Judges this place is a heartless crew.

CHRISTY [*bitterly*]. It's more than Judges this place is a heartless crew. [*Looking up at her.*] And isn't it a poor thing to be starting again and I a lonesome fellow will be looking out on women and girls the way the needy fallen spirits do be looking on the Lord?

PEGEEN. What call have you to be that lonesome when there's poor girls walking Mayo in their thousands now?

CHRISTY [*grimly*]. It's well you know what call I have. It's well you know it's a lonesome thing to be passing small towns with the lights shining sideways when the night is down, or going in strange places with a dog noising before you and a dog noising behind, or drawn to the cities where you'd hear a voice kissing and talking deep love in every shadow of the ditch, and you passing on with an empty, hungry stomach failing from your heart.

PEGEEN. I'm thinking you're an odd man, Christy Mahon. The oddest walking fellow I ever set my eyes on to this hour to-day.

CHRISTY. What would any be but odd men and they living lonesome in the world?

PEGEEN. I'm not odd, and I'm my whole life with my father only.

CHRISTY [*with infinite admiration*]. How would a lovely handsome woman the like of you be lonesome when all men should be thronging around to hear the sweetness of your voice, and the little infant children should be pestering your steps I'm thinking, and you walking the roads.

PEGEEN. I'm hard set to know what way a coaxing fellow the like of yourself should be lonesome either.

CHRISTY. Coaxing?

PEGEEN. Would you have me think a man never talked with the girls would have the words you've spoken today? It's only letting on you are to be lonesome, the way you'd get around me now.

CHRISTY. I wish to God I was letting on; but I was lonesome all times, and born lonesome, I'm thinking, as the moon of dawn. [*Going to door.*]

PEGEEN [*puzzled by his talk*]. Well, it's a story I'm not understanding at all why you'd be worse than another, Christy Mahon, and you a fine lad with the great savagery to destroy your da.

CHRISTY. It's little I'm understanding myself, saving only that my heart's scalded this day, and I going off stretching out the earth between us, the way I'll not be waking near you another dawn of the year till the two of us do arise to hope or judgment with the saints of God, and now I'd best be going with my wattle in my hand, for hanging is a poor thing [*turning to go.*], and it's little welcome only is left me in this house to-day.

PEGEEN [*sharply*]. Christy!

[*He turns round.*]

Come here to me.

[*He goes towards her.*]

Lay down that switch and throw some sods on the fire. You're pot-boy in this place, and I'll not have you mitch off from us now.

CHRISTY.   You were saying I'd be hanged if I stay.

PEGEEN [*quite kindly at last*].   I'm after going down and reading the fearful crimes of Ireland for two weeks or three, and there wasn't a word of your murder. [*Getting up and going over to the counter.*] They've likely not found the body. You're safe so with ourselves.

CHRISTY [*astonished, slowly*].   It's making game of me you were [*following her with fearful joy*], and I can stay so, working at your side, and I not lonesome from this mortal day.

PEGEEN.   What's to hinder you from staying, except the widow woman or the young girls would inveigle you off?

CHRISTY [*with rapture*].   And I'll have your words from this day filling my ears, and that look is come upon you meeting my two eyes, and I watching you loafing around in the warm sun, or rinsing your ankles when the night is come.

PEGEEN [*kindly, but a little embarrassed*].   I'm thinking you'll be a loyal young lad to have working around, and if you vexed me a while since with your leaguing with the girls, I wouldn't give a thraneen[3] for a lad hadn't a mighty spirit in him and a gamey heart.

[SHAWN KEOGH *runs in carrying a cleeve*[4] *on his back, followed by the* WIDOW QUIN.]

SHAWN [*to* PEGEEN].   I was passing below, and I seen your mountainy sheep eating cabbages in Jimmy's field. Run up or they'll be bursting surely.

PEGEEN.   Oh, God mend them! [*She puts a shawl over her head and runs out.*]

CHRISTY [*looking from one to the other. Still in high spirits*].   I'd best go to her aid maybe. I'm handy with ewes.

WIDOW QUIN [*closing the door*].   She can do that much, and there is Shaneen has long speeches for to tell you now. [*She sits down with an amused smile.*]

SHAWN [*taking something from his pocket and offering it to* CHRISTY].   Do you see that, mister?

CHRISTY [*looking at it*].   The half of a ticket to the Western States!

SHAWN [*trembling with anxiety*].   I'll give it to you and my new hat [*pulling it out of hamper*]; and my breeches with the double seat [*pull-*

3. Thread, song, scrap.   4. Basket.

ing it off]; and my new coat is woven from the blackest shearings for three miles around [*giving him the coat*]; I'll give you the whole of them, and my blessing, and the blessing of Father Reilly itself, maybe, if you'll quit from this and leave us in the peace we had till last night at the fall of dark.

CHRISTY [*with a new arrogance*].   And for what is it you're wanting to get shut of me?

SHAWN [*looking to the* WIDOW *for help*].   I'm a poor scholar with middling faculties to coin a lie, so I'll tell you the truth, Christy Mahon. I'm wedding with Pegeen beyond, and I don't think well of having a clever fearless man the like of you dwelling in her house.

CHRISTY [*almost pugnaciously*].   And you'd be using bribery for to banish me?

SHAWN [*in an imploring voice*].   Let you not take it badly, mister honey, isn't beyond the best place for you where you'll have golden chains and shiny coats and you riding upon hunters with the ladies of the land. [*He makes an eager sign to the* WIDOW QUIN *to come to help him.*]

WIDOW QUIN [*coming over*].   It's true for him, and you'd best quit off and not have that poor girl setting her mind on you, for there's Shaneen thinks she wouldn't suit you though all is saying that she'll wed you now.

[CHRISTY *beams with delight.*]

SHAWN [*in terrified earnest*].   She wouldn't suit you, and she with the divil's own temper the way you'd be strangling one another in a score of days. [*He makes the movement of strangling with his hands.*] It's the like of me only that she's fit for, a quiet simple fellow wouldn't raise a hand upon her if she scratched itself.

WIDOW QUIN [*putting* SHAWN's *hat on* CHRISTY].   Fit them clothes on you anyhow, young fellow, and he'd maybe loan them to you for the sports. [*Pushing him towards inner door.*] Fit them on and you can give your answer when you have them tried.

CHRISTY [*beaming, delighted with the clothes*].   I will then. I'd like herself to see me in them tweeds and hat. [*He goes into room and shuts the door.*]

SHAWN [*in great anxiety*].   He'd like herself to see them. He'll not leave us, Widow Quin. He's a score of divils in him the way it's well nigh certain he will wed Pegeen.

WIDOW QUIN [*jeering*].   It's true all girls are fond of courage and do hate the like of you.

SHAWN [*walking about in desperation*].   Oh, Widow Quin, what'll I be doing now? I'd inform again him, but he'd burst from Kilmainham[5]

5. Jail in Dublin.

and he'd be sure and certain to destroy me. If I wasn't so God-fearing, I'd near have courage to come behind him and run a pike into his side. Oh, it's a hard case to be an orphan and not to have your father that you're used to, and you'd easy kill and make yourself a hero in the sight of all. [*Coming up to her.*] Oh, Widow Quin, will you find me some contrivance when I've promised you a ewe?

WIDOW QUIN.   A ewe's a small thing, but what would you give me if I did wed him and did save you so?

SHAWN [*with astonishment*].   You?

WIDOW QUIN.   Aye. Would you give me the red cow you have and the mountainy ram, and the right of way across your rye path, and a load of dung at Michaelmas,[6] and turbary[7] upon the western hill?

SHAWN [*radiant with hope*].   I would surely, and I'd give you the wedding-ring I have, and the loan of a new suit, the way you'd have him decent on the wedding-day. I'd give you two kids for your dinner, and a gallon of poteen, and I'd call the piper on the long car to your wedding from Crossmolina or from Ballina. I'd give you . . .

WIDOW QUIN.   That'll do so, and let you whisht, for he's coming now again.

[CHRISTY *comes in very natty in the new clothes.* WIDOW QUIN *goes to him admiringly.*]

WIDOW QUIN.   If you seen yourself now, I'm thinking you'd be too proud to speak to us at all, and it'd be a pity surely to have your like sailing from Mayo to the Western World.

CHRISTY [*as proud as a peacock*].   I'm not going. If this is a poor place itself, I'll make myself contented to be lodging here.

[WIDOW QUIN *makes a sign to* SHAWN *to leave them.*]

SHAWN.   Well, I'm going measuring the race-course while the tide is low, so I'll leave you the garments and my blessing for the sports to-day. God bless you! [*He wriggles out.*]

WIDOW QUIN [*admiring* CHRISTY].   Well, you're mighty spruce, young fellow. Sit down now while you're quiet till you talk with me.

CHRISTY [*swaggering*].   I'm going abroad on the hillside for to seek Pegeen.

WIDOW QUIN.   You'll have time and plenty for to seek Pegeen, and you heard me saying at the fall of night the two of us should be great company.

CHRISTY.   From this out I'll have no want of company when all sorts is bringing me their food and clothing [*he swaggers to the door, tightening his belt*], the way they'd set their eyes upon a gallant orphan cleft his father with one blow to the breeches belt. [*He opens door, then*

6. Feast of St. Michael, September 29.   7. Right to cut turf, for fuel, on another's property.

staggers back.] Saints of glory! Holy angels from the throne of light!
WIDOW QUIN [*going over*]. What ails you?
CHRISTY.   It's the walking spirit of my murdered da?
WIDOW QUIN [*looking out*]. Is it that tramper?
CHRISTY [*wildly*].   Where'll I hide my poor body from that ghost of hell?

[*The door is pushed open, and old* MAHON *appears on threshold.*
CHRISTY *darts in behind door.*]

WIDOW QUIN [*in great amusement*].   God save you, my poor man.
MAHON [*gruffly*].   Did you see a young lad passing this way in the early
morning or the fall of night?
WIDOW QUIN.   You're a queer kind to walk in not saluting at all.
MAHON.   Did you see the young lad?
WIDOW QUIN [*stiffly*].   What kind was he?
MAHON.   An ugly young streeler with a murderous gob[8] on him, and a
little switch in his hand. I met a tramper seen him coming this way
at the fall of night.
WIDOW QUIN.   There's harvest hundreds do be passing these days for the
Sligo boat. For what is it you're wanting him, my poor man?
MAHON.   I want to destroy him for breaking the head on me with the
clout of a loy. [*He takes off a big hat, and shows his head in a mass of
bandages and plaster, with some pride.*] It was he did that, and amn't
I a great wonder to think I've traced him ten days with that rent in my
crown?
WIDOW QUIN [*taking his head in both hands and examining it with extreme
delight*].   That was a great blow. And who hit you? A robber maybe?
MAHON.   It was my own son hit me, and he the divil a robber, or anything else, but a dirty, stuttering lout.
WIDOW QUIN [*letting go his skull and wiping her hands in her
apron*].   You'd best be wary of a mortified scalp, I think they call it,
lepping around with that wound in the splendour of the sun. It was a
bad blow surely, and you should have vexed him fearful to make him
strike that gash in his da.
MAHON.   Is it me?
WIDOW QUIN [*amusing herself*].   Aye. And isn't it a great shame when
the old and hardened do torment the young?
MAHON [*raging*].   Torment him is it? And I after holding out with the
patience of a martyred saint till there's nothing but destruction on,
and I'm driven out in my old age with none to aid me.
WIDOW QUIN [*greatly amused*].   It's a sacred wonder the way that
wickedness will spoil a man.
MAHON.   My wickedness, is it? Amn't I after saying it is himself has me
destroyed, and he a liar on walls, a talker of folly, a man you'd see

8. That is, a worthless youth with a foul mouth.

stretched the half of the day in the brown ferns with his belly to the sun.

WIDOW QUIN.   Not working at all?

MAHON.   The divil a work, or if he did itself, you'd see him raising up a haystack like the stalk of a rush, or driving our last cow till he broke her leg at the hip, and when he wasn't at that he'd be fooling over little birds he had—finches and felts[9]—or making mugs at his own self in the bit of a glass we had hung on the wall.

WIDOW QUIN [*looking at* CHRISTY].   What way was he so foolish? It was running wild after the girls may be?

MAHON [*with a shout of derision*].   Running wild, is it? If he seen a red petticoat coming swinging over the hill, he'd be off to hide in the sticks, and you'd see him shooting out his sheep's eyes between the little twigs and the leaves, and his two ears rising like a hare looking out through a gap. Girls, indeed!

WIDOW QUIN.   It was drink maybe?

MAHON.   And he a poor fellow would get drunk on the smell of a pint. He'd a queer rotten stomach, I'm telling you, and when I gave him three pulls from my pipe a while since, he was taken with contortions till I had to send him in the ass cart to the females' nurse.

WIDOW QUIN [*clasping her hands*].   Well, I never till this day heard tell of a man the like of that!

MAHON.   I'd take a mighty oath you didn't surely, and wasn't he the laughing joke of every female woman where four baronies meet, the way the girls would stop their weeding if they seen him coming the road to let a roar at him, and call him the looney of Mahon's.

WIDOW QUIN.   I'd give the world and all to see the like of him. What kind was he?

MAHON.   A small low fellow.

WIDOW QUIN.   And dark?

MAHON.   Dark and dirty.

WIDOW QUIN [*considering*].   I'm thinking I seen him.

MAHON [*eagerly*].   An ugly young blackguard.

WIDOW QUIN.   A hideous, fearful villain, and the spit of you.

MAHON.   What way is he fled?

WIDOW QUIN.   Gone over the hills to catch a coasting steamer to the north or south.

MAHON.   Could I pull up on him now?

WIDOW QUIN.   If you'll cross the sands below where the tide is out, you'll be in it as soon as himself, for he had to go round ten miles by the top of the bay. [*She points to the door.*]   Strike down by the head beyond and then follow on the roadway to the north and east.

[MAHON *goes abruptly.*]

9. Thrushes.

WIDOW QUIN [*shouting after him*].   Let you give him a good vengeance when you come up with him, but don't put yourself in the power of the law, for it'd be a poor thing to see a judge in his black cap reading out his sentence on a civil warrior the like of you. [*She swings the door to and looks at* CHRISTY, *who is cowering in terror, for a moment, then she bursts into a laugh.*]

WIDOW QUIN.   Well, you're the walking Playboy of the Western World, and that's the poor man you had divided to his breeches belt.

CHRISTY [*looking out: then, to her*].   What'll Pegeen say when she hears that story? What'll she be saying to me now?

WIDOW QUIN.   She'll knock the head of you. I'm thinking, and drive you from the door. God help her to be taking you for a wonder, and you a little schemer making up the story you destroyed your da.

CHRISTY [*turning to the door, nearly speechless with rage, half to himself*].   To be letting on he was dead, and coming back to his life, and following after me like an old weazel tracing a rat, and coming in here laying desolation between my own self and the fine women of Ireland, and he a kind of carcase that you'd fling upon the sea . . .

WIDOW QUIN [*more soberly*].   There's talking for a man's one only son.

CHRISTY [*breaking out*].   His one son, is it? May I meet him with one tooth and it aching, and one eye to be seeing seven and seventy divils in the twists of the road, and one old timber leg on him to limp into the scalding grave. [*Looking out.*]   There he is now crossing the strands, and that the Lord God would send a high wave to wash him from the world.

WIDOW QUIN [*scandalized*].   Have you no shame? [*Putting her hand on his shoulder and turning him round.*]   What ails you? Near crying, is it?

CHRISTY [*in despair and grief*].   Amn't I after seeing the love-light of the star of knowledge shining from her brow, and hearing words would put you thinking on the holy Brigid speaking to the infant saints, and now she'll be turning again, and speaking hard words to me, like an old woman with a spavindy ass she'd have, urging on a hill.

WIDOW QUIN.   There's poetry talk for a girl you'd see itching and scratching, and she with a stale stink of poteen on her from selling in the shop.

CHRISTY [*impatiently*].   It's her like is fitted to be handling merchandise in the heavens above, and what'll I be doing now, I ask you, and I a kind of wonder was jilted by the heavens when a day was by.

> [*There is a distant noise of girls' voices.* WIDOW QUIN *looks from window and comes to him, hurriedly.*]

WIDOW QUIN.   You'll be doing like myself, I'm thinking, when I did destroy my man, for I'm above many's the day, odd times in great spirits, abroad in the sunshine, darning a stocking or stitching a shift;

and odd times again looking out on the schooners, hookers, trawlers is sailing the sea, and I thinking on the gallant hairy fellows are drifting beyond, and myself long years living alone.

CHRISTY [*interested*].   You're like me, so.

WIDOW QUIN.   I am your like, and it's for that I'm taking a fancy to you, and I with my little houseen above where there'd be myself to tend you, and none to ask were you a murderer or what at all.

CHRISTY.   And what would I be doing if I left Pegeen?

WIDOW QUIN.   I've nice jobs you could be doing, gathering shells to make a whitewash for our hut within, building up a little goose-house, or stretching a new skin on an old curragh I have, and if my hut is far from all sides, it's there you'll meet the wisest old men, I tell you, at the corner of my wheel, and it's there yourself and me will have great times whispering and hugging. . . .

VOICES [*outside, calling far away*].   Christy! Christy Mahon! Christy!

CHRISTY.   Is it Pegeen Mike?

WIDOW QUIN.   It's the young girls, I'm thinking, coming to bring you to the sports below, and what is it you'll have me to tell them now?

CHRISTY.   Aid me for to win Pegeen. It's herself only that I'm seeking now.

[WIDOW QUIN *gets up and goes to window.*]

Aid me for to win her, and I'll be asking God to stretch a hand to you in the hour of death, and lead you short cuts through the Meadows of Ease, and up the floor of Heaven to the Footstool of the Virgin's Son.

WIDOW QUIN.   There's praying.

VOICES [*nearer*].   Christy! Christy Mahon!

CHRISTY [*with agitation*].   They're coming. Will you swear to aid and save me for the love of Christ?

WIDOW QUIN [*looks at him for a moment*].   If I aid you, will you swear to give me a right of way I want, and a mountainy ram, and a load of dung at Michaelmas, the time that you'll be master here?

CHRISTY.   I will, by the elements and stars of night.

WIDOW QUIN.   Then we'll not say a word of the old fellow, the way Pegeen won't know your story till the end of time.

CHRISTY.   And if he chances to return again?

WIDOW QUIN.   We'll swear he's a maniac and not your da. I could take an oath I seen him raving on the sands to-day.

[*Girls run in.*]

SUSAN.   Come on to the sports below. Pegeen says you're to come.

SARA TANSEY.   The lepping's beginning, and we've a jockey's suit to fit upon you for the mule race on the sands below.

HONOR.   Come on, will you?

CHRISTY.   I will then if Pegeen's beyond.
SARA TANSEY.   She's in the boreen¹ making game of Shaneen Keogh.
CHRISTY.   Then I'll be going to her now.

[*He runs out followed by the girls.*]

WIDOW QUIN.   Well, if the worst comes in the end of all, it'll be great
   game to see there's none to pity him but a widow woman, the like of
   me, has buried her children and destroyed her man. [*She goes out.*]

Act Three

SCENE, *as before. Later in the day.* JIMMY *comes in, slightly drunk.*

JIMMY [*calls*].   Pegeen! [*Crosses to inner door.*] Pegeen Mike! [*Comes
   back again into the room.*] Pegeen!

   [PHILLY *comes in in the same state.*] [*To* PHILLY.]

Did you see herself?
PHILLY.   I did not; but I sent Shawn Keogh with the ass cart for to bear
   him home. [*Trying cupboards which are locked.*] Well, isn't he a nasty
   man to get into such staggers at a morning wake? and isn't herself the
   divil's daughter for locking, and she so fussy after that young gaffer,
   you might take your death with drought and none to heed you?
JIMMY.   It's little wonder she'd be fussy, and he after bringing bankrupt
   ruin on the roulette man, and the trick-o'-the-loop man, and breaking
   the nose of the cockshot-man, and winning all in the sports below,
   racing, lepping, dancing, and the Lord knows what! He's right luck,
   I'm telling you.
PHILLY.   If he has, he'll be rightly hobbled yet, and he not able to say
   ten words without making a brag of the way he killed his father, and
   the great blow he hit with the loy.
JIMMY.   A man can't hang by his own informing, and his father should
   be rotten by now.

   [OLD MAHON *passes window slowly.*]

PHILLY.   Supposing a man's digging spuds in that field with a long spade,
   and supposing he flings up the two halves of that skull, what'll be said
   then in the papers and the courts of law?
JIMMY.   They'd say it was an old Dane, maybe, was drowned in the
   flood.

   [OLD MAHON *comes in and sits down near door listening.*]

---

1. Small path.

Did you never hear tell of the skulls they have in the city of Dublin, ranged out like blue jugs in a cabin of Connaught?[1]

PHILLY.   And you believe that?

JIMMY [*pugnaciously*].   Didn't a lad see them and he after coming from harvesting in the Liverpool boat? "They have them there," says he, "making a show of the great people there was one time walking the world. White skulls and black skulls and yellow skulls, and some with full teeth, and some haven't only but one."

PHILLY.   It was no lie, maybe, for when I was a young lad there was a graveyard beyond the house with the remnants of a man who had thighs as long as your arm. He was a horrid man, I'm telling you, and there was many a fine Sunday I'd put him together for fun, and he with shiny bones, you wouldn't meet the like of these days in the cities of the world.

MAHON [*getting up*].   You wouldn't, is it? Lay your eyes on that skull, and tell me where and when there was another the like of it, is splintered only from the blow of a loy.

PHILLY.   Glory be to God! And who hit you at all?

MAHON [*triumphantly*].   It was my own son hit me. Would you believe that?

JIMMY.   Well, there's wonders hidden in the heart of man!

PHILLY [*suspiciously*].   And what way was it done?

MAHON [*wandering about the room*].   I'm after walking hundreds and long scores of miles, winning clean beds and the fill of my belly four times in the day, and I doing nothing but telling stories of that naked truth. [*He comes to them a little aggressively.*] Give me a supeen[2] and I'll tell you now.

[WIDOW QUIN *comes in and stands aghast behind him. He is facing* JIMMY *and* PHILLY, *who are on the left.*]

JIMMY.   Ask herself beyond. She's the stuff hidden in her shawl.

WIDOW QUIN [*coming to* MAHON *quickly*].   You here, is it? You didn't go far at all?

MAHON.   I seen the coasting steamer passing, and I got a drought upon me and a cramping leg, so I said, "The divil go along with him," and turned again. [*Looking under her shawl.*] And let you give me a supeen, for I'm destroyed travelling since Tuesday was a week.

WIDOW QUIN [*getting a glass, in a cajoling tone*].   Sit down then by the fire and take your ease for a space. You've a right to be destroyed indeed, with your walking, and fighting, and facing the sun [*giving him poteen from a stone jar she has brought in*]. There now is a drink for you, and may it be to your happiness and length of life.

---

1. Danish Vikings settled Dublic c. 850, but never penetrated Connacht in the west of Ireland.   2. Small drink.

MAHON [*taking glass greedily and sitting down by fire*].   God increase
you!

WIDOW QUIN [*taking men to the right stealthily*].   Do you know what?
That man's raving from his wound to-day, for I met him a while since
telling a rambling tale of a tinker had him destroyed. Then he heard
of Christy's deed, and he up and says it was his son had cracked his
skull. O isn't madness a fright, for he'll go killing someone yet, and
he thinking it's the man has struck him so?

JIMMY [*entirely convinced*].   It's a fright, surely. I knew a party was kicked
in the head by a red mare, and he went killing horses a great while,
till he eat the insides of a clock and died after.

PHILLY [*with suspicion*].   Did he see Christy?

WIDOW QUIN.   He didn't. [*With a warning gesture.*] *Let you not be putting him in mind of him, or you'll be likely summoned if there's murder
done.* [*Looking round at* MAHON.] Whisht! He's listening. Wait now
till you hear me taking him easy and unravelling all. [*She goes to*
MAHON.] And what way are you feeling, mister? Are you in content-
ment now?

MAHON [*slightly emotional from his drink*].   I'm poorly only, for it's a
hard story the way I'm left to-day, when it was I did tend him from
his hour of birth, and he a dunce never reached his second book, the
way he'd come from school, many's the day, with his legs lamed under
him, and he blackened with his beatings like a tinker's ass. It's a hard
story, I'm saying, the way some do have their next and nighest raising
up a hand of murder on them, and some is lonesome getting their
death with lamentation in the dead of night.

WIDOW QUIN [*not knowing what to say*].   To hear you talking so quiet,
who'd know you were the same fellow we seen pass to-day?

MAHON.   I'm the same surely. The wrack and ruin of three score years;
and it's a terror to live that length, I tell you, and to have your sons
going to the dogs against you, and you wore out scolding them, and
skelping them, and God knows what.

PHILLY [*to* JIMMY].   He's not raving. [*To* WIDOW QUIN.] Will you ask him
what kind was his son?

WIDOW QUIN [*to* MAHON, *with a peculiar look*].   Was your son that hit
you a lad of one year and a score maybe, a great hand at racing and
lepping and licking the world?

MAHON [*turning on her with a roar of rage*].   Didn't you hear me say he
was the fool of men, the way from this out he'll know the orphan's lot
with old and young making game of him and they swearing, raging,
kicking at him like a mangy cur.

[*A great burst of cheering outside, some way off.*]

MAHON [*putting his hands to his ears*].   What in the name of God do
they want roaring below?

WIDOW QUIN [*with the shade of a smile*].   They're cheering a young lad,
the champion Playboy of the Western World.

[*More cheering.*]

MAHON [*going to window*].   It'd split my heart to hear them, and I with
pulses in my brain-pan for a week gone by. Is it racing they are?

JIMMY [*looking from door*].   It is then. They are mounting him for the
mule race will be run upon the sands. That's the playboy on the
winkered[3] mule.

MAHON [*puzzled*].   That lad, is it? If you said it was a fool he was, I'd
have laid a mighty oath he was the likeness of my wandering son
[*uneasily, putting his hand to his head*]. Faith, I'm thinking I'll go
walking for to view the race.

WIDOW QUIN [*stopping him, sharply*].   You will not. You'd best take
the road to Belmullet, and not be dilly-dallying in this place where
there isn't a spot you could sleep.

PHILLY [*coming forward*].   Don't mind her. Mount there on the bench
and you'll have a view of the whole. They're hurrying before the tide
will rise, and it'd be near over if you went down the pathway through
the crags below.

MAHON [*mounts on bench*, WIDOW QUIN *beside him*].   That's a right view
again the edge of the sea. They're coming now from the point. He's
leading. Who is he at all?

WIDOW QUIN.   He's the champion of the world, I tell you, and there
isn't a hop'orth isn't falling lucky to his hands to-day.

PHILLY [*looking out, interested in the race*].   Look at that. They're pressing him now.

JIMMY.   He'll win it yet.

PHILLY.   Take your time, Jimmy Farrell. It's too soon to say.

WIDOW QUIN [*shouting*].   Watch him taking the gate. There's riding.

JIMMY [*cheering*].   More power to the young lad!

MAHON.   He's passing the third.

JIMMY.   He'll lick them yet!

WIDOW QUIN.   He'd lick them if he was running races with a score itself.

MAHON.   Look at the mule he has, kicking the stars.

WIDOW QUIN.   There was a lep! [*Catching hold of* MAHON *in her excitement.*] He's fallen! He's mounted again! Faith, he's passing them all!

JIMMY.   Look at him skelping her!

PHILLY.   And the mountain girls hooshing him on!

JIMMY.   It's the last turn! The post's cleared for them now!

MAHON.   Look at the narrow place. He'll be into the bogs! [*With a yell.*]
Good rider! He's through it again!

---

3. Wearing a harness with blinders.

JIMMY.   He neck and neck!
MAHON.   Good boy to him! Flames, but he's in!

[*Great cheering, in which all join.*]

MAHON [*with hesitation*].   What's that? They're raising him up. They're
coming this way. [*With a roar of rage and astonishment.*] It's Christy!
by the stars of God! I'd know his way of spitting and he astride the
moon.

[*He jumps down and makes for the door, but* WIDOW QUIN *catches
him and pulls him back.*]

WIDOW QUIN.   Stay quiet, will you. That's not your son. [*To* JIMMY.]
Stop him, or you'll get a month for the abetting of manslaughter and
be fined as well.
JIMMY.   I'll hold him.
MAHON [*struggling*].   Let me out! Let me out, the lot of you! till I have
my vengeance on his head to-day.
WIDOW QUIN [*shaking him, vehemently*].   That's not your son. That's a
man is going to make a marriage with the daughter of this house, a
place with fine trade, with a license, and with poteen too.
MAHON [*amazed*].   That man marrying a decent and a moneyed girl! Is
it mad yous are? Is it in a crazy-house for females that I'm landed
now?
WIDOW QUIN.   It's mad yourself is with the blow upon your head. That
lad is the wonder of the Western World.
MAHON.   I seen it's my son.
WIDOW QUIN.   You seen that you're mad.

[*Cheering outside.*]

Do you hear them cheering him in the zig-zags of the road? Aren't
you after saying that your son's a fool, and how would they be cheering a true idiot born?
MAHON [*getting distressed*].   It's maybe out of reason that that man's
himself.

[*Cheering again.*]

There's none surely will go cheering him. Oh, I'm raving with a madness that would fright the world! [*He sits down with his hand to his
head.*] There was one time I seen ten scarlet divils letting on they'd
cork my spirit in a gallon can; and one time I seen rats as big as
badgers sucking the life blood from the butt of my lug;[4] but I never
till this day confused that dribbling idiot with a likely man. I'm destroyed
surely.

4. My earlobe.

WIDOW QUIN.   And who'd wonder when it's your brain-pan that is gaping now?

MAHON.   Then the blight of the sacred drought upon myself and him, for I never went mad to this day, and I not three weeks with the Limerick girls drinking myself silly, and parlatic from the dusk to dawn. [*To* WIDOW QUIN, *suddenly.*] Is my visage astray?

WIDOW QUIN.   It is then. You're a sniggering maniac, a child could see.

MAHON [*getting up more cheerfully*].   Then I'd best be going to the union [5] beyond, and there'll be a welcome before me, I tell you [*with great pride*], and I a terrible and fearful case, the way that there I was one time, screeching in a straitened waistcoat, with seven doctors writing out my sayings in a printed book. Would you believe that?

WIDOW QUIN.   If you're a wonder itself, you'd best be hasty, for them lads caught a maniac one time and pelted the poor creature till he ran out, raving and foaming, and was drowned in the sea.

MAHON [*with philosophy*].   It's true mankind is the divil when your head's astray. Let me out now and I'll slip down the boreen, and not see them so.

WIDOW QUIN [*showing him out*].   That's it. Run to the right, and not a one will see.

[*He runs off.*]

PHILLY [*wisely*].   You're at some gaming, Widow Quin; but I'll walk after him and give him his dinner and a time to rest, and I'll see then if he's raving or as sane as you.

WIDOW QUIN [*annoyed*].   If you go near that lad, let you be wary of your head, I'm saying. Didn't you hear him telling he was crazed at times?

PHILLY.   I heard him telling a power; and I'm thinking we'll have right sport, before night will fall. [*He goes out.*]

JIMMY.   Well, Philly's a conceited and foolish man. How could that madman have his senses and his brain-pan slit? I'll go after them and see him turn on Philly now.

[*He goes;* WIDOW QUIN *hides poteen behind counter. Then hubbub outside.*]

VOICES.   There you are! Good jumper! Grand lepper! Darlint boy! He's the racer! Bear him on, will you!

[CHRISTY *comes in, in Jockey's dress, with* PEGEEN MIKE, SARA, *and other* GIRLS, *and* MEN.]

PEGEEN [*to crowd*].   Go on now and don't destroy him and he drenching with sweat. Go along, I'm saying, and have your tug-of-warring till he's dried his skin.

5. Public-assistance workhouse.

CROWD.   Here's his prizes! A bagpipes! A fiddle was played by a poet in
the years gone by! A flat and three-thorned blackthorn would lick the
scholars out of Dublin town!

CHRISTY [taking prizes from the MEN].   Thank you kindly, the lot of
you. But you'd say it was little only I did this day if you'd seen me a
while since striking my one single blow.

TOWN CRIER [outside, ringing a bell].   Take notice, last event of this
day! Tug-of-warring on the green below! Come on, the lot of you!
Great achievements for all Mayo men!

PEGEEN.   Go on, and leave him for to rest and dry. Go on, I tell you,
for he'll do no more.

[She hustles crowd out; WIDOW QUIN following them.]

MEN [going].   Come on then. Good luck for the while!

PEGEEN [radiantly, wiping his face with her shawl].   Well, you're the
lad, and you'll have great times from this out when you could win
that wealth of prizes, and you sweating in the heat of noon!

CHRISTY [looking at her with delight].   I'll have great times if I win the
crowning prize I'm seeking now, and that's your promise that you'll
wed me in a fortnight, when our banns is called.

PEGEEN [backing away from him].   You've right daring to go ask me
that, when all knows you'll be starting to some girl in your own townland, when your father's rotten in four months, or five.

CHRISTY [indignantly].   Starting from you, is it? [He follows her]. I will
not, then, and when the airs is warming in four months, or five, it's
then yourself and me should be pacing Neifin in the dews of night,
the times sweet smells do be rising, and you'd see a little shiny new
moon, maybe, sinking on the hills.

PEGEEN [looking at him playfully].   And it's that kind of a poacher's love
you'd make, Christy Mahon, on the sides of Neifin, when the night
is down?

CHRISTY.   It's little you'll think if my love's a poacher's, or an earl's
itself, when you'll feel my two hands stretched around you, and I
squeezing kisses on your puckered lips, till I'd feel a kind of pity for
the Lord God is all ages sitting lonesome in his golden chair.

PEGEEN.   That'll be right fun, Christy Mahon, and any girl would walk
her heart out before she'd meet a young man was your like for eloquence, or talk, at all.

CHRISTY [encouraged].   Let you wait, to hear me talking, till we're astray
in Erris, when Good Friday's by, drinking a sup from a well, and
making mighty kisses with our wetted mouths, or gaming in a gap or
sunshine, with yourself stretched back unto your necklace, in the flowers
of the earth.

PEGEEN [in a lower voice, moved by his tone].   I'd be nice so, is it?

CHRISTY [with rapture].   If the mitred bishops seen you that time, they'd be the like of the holy prophets, I'm thinking, do be straining the bars of Paradise to lay eyes on the Lady Helen of Troy, and she abroad, pacing back and forward, with a nosegay in her golden shawl.

PEGEEN [*with real tenderness*].   And what is it I have, Christy Mahon, to make me fitting entertainment for the like of you, that has such poet's talking, and such bravery of heart?

CHRISTY [*in a low voice*].   Isn't there the light of seven heavens in your heart alone, the way you'll be an angel's lamp to me from this out, and I abroad in the darkness, spearing salmons in the Owen, or the Carrowmore?

PEGEEN.   If I was your wife, I'd be along with you those nights, Christy Mahon, the way you'd see I was a great hand at coaxing bailiffs, or coining funny nick-names for the stars of night.

CHRISTY.   You, is it? Taking your death in the hailstones, or in the fogs of dawn.

PEGEEN.   Yourself and me would shelter easy in a narrow bush, [*with a qualm of dread*] but we're only talking, maybe, for this would be a poor, thatched place to hold a fine lad is the like of you.

CHRISTY [*putting his arm round her*].   If I wasn't a good Christian, it's on my naked knees I'd be saying my prayers and paters to every jack-straw you have roofing your head, and every stony pebble is paving the laneway to your door.

PEGEEN [*radiantly*].   If that's the truth, I'll be burning candles from this out to the miracles of God that have brought you from the south to-day, and I, with my gowns bought ready, the way that I can wed you, and not wait at all.

CHRISTY.   It's miracles, and that's the truth. Me there toiling a long while, and walking a long while, not knowing at all I was drawing all times nearer to this holy day.

PEGEEN.   And myself, a girl, was tempted often to go sailing the seas till I'd marry a Jew-man, with ten kegs of gold, and I not knowing at all there was the like of you drawing nearer, like the stars of God.

CHRISTY.   And to think I'm long years hearing women talking that talk, to all bloody fools, and this the first time I've heard the like of your voice talking sweetly for my own delight.

PEGEEN.   And to think it's me is talking sweetly, Christy Mahon, and I the fright of seven townlands for my biting tongue. Well, the heart's a wonder; and, I'm thinking, there won't be our like in Mayo, for gallant lovers, from this hour, to-day.

[*Drunken singing is heard outside.*]

There's my father coming from the wake, and when he's had his sleep we'll tell him, for he's peaceful then.

[*They separate.*]

MICHAEL [*singing outside*].

> The jailor and the turnkey
> They quickly ran us down,
> And brought us back as prisoners
> Once more to Cavan town.

[*He comes in supported by* SHAWN.]

> There we lay bewailing
> All in a prison bound. . . .

[*He sees* CHRISTY. *Goes and shakes him drunkenly by the hand, while* PEGEEN *and* SHAWN *talk on the left.*]

MICHAEL [*to* CHRISTY]. The blessing of God and the holy angels on your head, young fellow. I hear tell you're after winning all in the sports below; and wasn't it a shame I didn't bear you along with me to Kate Cassidy's wake, a fine, stout lad, the like of you, for you'd never see the match of it for flows of drink, the way when we sunk her bones at noonday in her narrow grave, there were five men, aye, and six men, stretched out retching speechless on the holy stones.

CHRISTY [*uneasily, watching* PEGEEN]. Is that the truth?

MICHAEL. It is then, and aren't you a louty schemer to go burying your poor father unbeknownst when you'd a right to throw him on the crupper of a Kerry mule and drive him westwards, like holy Joseph in the days gone by, the way we could have given him a decent burial, and not have him rotting beyond, and not a Christian drinking a smart drop to the glory of his soul?

CHRISTY [*gruffly*]. It's well enough he's lying, for the likes of him.

MICHAEL [*slapping him on the back*]. Well, aren't you a hardened slayer? It'll be a poor thing for the household man where you go sniffing for a female wife; and [*pointing to* SHAWN] look beyond at that shy and decent Christian I have chosen for my daughter's hand, and I after getting the gilded dispensation this day for to wed them now.

CHRISTY. And you'll be wedding them this day, is it?

MICHAEL [*drawing himself up.*] Aye. Are you thinking, if I'm drunk itself, I'd leave my daughter living single with a little frisky rascal is the like of you?

PEGEEN [*breaking away from* SHAWN]. Is it the truth the dispensation's come?

MICHAEL [*triumphantly*]. Father Reilly's after reading it in gallous Latin, and "It's come in the nick of time," says he; "so I'll wed them in a hurry, dreading that young gaffer who'd capsize the stars."

PEGEEN [*fiercely*]. He's missed his nick of time, for it's that lad, Christy Mahon, that I'm wedding now.

MICHAEL [*loudly with horror*]. You'd be making him a son to me, and he wet and crusted with his father's blood?

PEGEEN.   Aye. Wouldn't it be a bitter thing for a girl to go marrying the like of Shaneen, and he a middling kind of a scarecrow, with no savagery or fine words in him at all?

MICHAEL [*gasping and sinking on a chair*].   Oh, aren't you a heathen daughter to go shaking the fat of my heart, and I swamped and drownded with the weight of drink? Would you have them turning on me the way that I'd be roaring to the dawn of day with the wind upon my heart? Have you not a word to aid me, Shaneen? Are you not jealous at all?

SHANEEN [*in great misery*].   I'd be afeard to be jealous of a man did slay his da.

PEGEEN.   Well, it'd be a poor thing to go marrying your like. I'm seeing there's a world of peril for an orphan girl, and isn't it a great blessing I didn't wed you, before himself came walking from the west or south?

SHAWN.   It's a queer story you'd go picking a dirty tramp up from the highways of the world.

PEGEEN [*playfully*].   And you think you're a likely beau to go straying along with, the shiny Sundays of the opening year, when it's sooner on a bullock's liver you'd put a poor girl thinking than on the lily or the rose?

SHAWN.   And have you no mind of my weight of passion, and the holy dispensation, and the drift of heifers I am giving, and the golden ring?

PEGEEN.   I'm thinking you're too fine for the like of me, Shawn Keogh of Killakeen, and let you go off till you'd find a radiant lady with droves of bullocks on the plains of Meath, and herself bedizened in the diamond jewelleries of Paraoh's ma. That'd be your match, Shaneen. So God save you now! [*She retreats behind* CHRISTY.]

SHAWN.   Won't you hear me telling you . . . ?

CHRISTY [*with ferocity*].   Take yourself from this, young fellow, or I'll maybe add a murder to my deeds to-day.

MICHAEL [*springing up with a shriek*].   Murder is it? Is it mad yous are? Would you go making murder in this place, and it piled with poteen for our drink tonight? Go on to the foreshore if it's fighting you want, where the rising tide will wash all traces from the memory of man.

[*Pushing* SHAWN *towards* CHRISTY.]

SHAWN [*shaking himself free, and getting behind* MICHAEL].   I'll not fight him, Michael James. I'd liefer live a bachelor, simmering in passions to the end of time, than face a leaping savage the like of him has descended from the Lord knows where. Strike him yourself, Michael James, or you'll lose my drift of heifers and my blue bull from Sneem.

MICHAEL.   Is it me fight him, when it's father-slaying he's bred to now? [*Pushing* SHAWN.] Go on you fool and fight him now.

SHAWN [*coming forward a little*].   Will I strike him with my hand?

MICHAEL.   Take the loy is on your western side.

SHAWN.   I'd be afeard of the gallows if I struck him with that.

CHRISTY [*taking up the loy*].   Then I'll make you face the gallows or
   quit off from this.

   [SHAWN *flies out of the door.*]

CHRISTY.   Well, fine weather be after him, [*going to* MICHAEL, *coax-
   ingly*] and I'm thinking you wouldn't wish to have that quaking blackguard in your house at all. Let you give us your blessing and hear her
   swear her faith to me, for I'm mounted on the springtide of the stars
   of luck, the way it'll be good for any to have me in the house.

PEGEEN [*at the other side of* MICHAEL].   Bless us now, for I swear to God
   I'll wed him, and I'll not renege.

MICHAEL [*standing up in the centre, holding on to both of them*].   It's
   the will of God, I'm thinking, that all should win an easy or a cruel
   end, and it's the will of God that all should rear up lengthy families
   for the nurture of the earth. What's a single man, I ask you, eating a
   bit in one house and drinking a sup in another, and he with no place
   of his own, like an old braying jackass strayed upon the rocks? [*To*
   CHRISTY].   It's many would be in dread to bring your like into their
   house for to end them, maybe, with a sudden end; but I'm a decent
   man of Ireland, and I liefer face the grave untimely and I seeing a
   score of grandsons growing up little gallant swearers by the name of
   God, than go peopling my bedside with puny weeds the like of what
   you'd breed, I'm thinking, out of Shaneen Keogh. [*He joins their
   hands.*] A daring fellow is the jewel of the world, and a man did split
   his father's middle with a single clout, should have the bravery of ten,
   so may God and Mary and St. Patrick bless you, and increase you
   from this mortal day.

CHRISTY AND PEGEEN.   Amen, O Lord!

   [*Hubbub outside.*]
   [OLD MAHON *rushes in, followed by all the crowd, and* WIDOW
   QUIN. *He makes a rush at* CHRISTY, *knocks him down, and begins
   to beat him.*]

PEGEEN [*dragging back his arm*].   Stop that, will you. Who are you at
   all?

MAHON.   His father, God forgive me!

PEGEEN [*drawing back*].   Is it rose from the dead?

MAHON.   Do you think I look so easy quenched with the tap of a loy?
   [*Beats* CHRISTY *again.*]

PEGEEN [*glaring at* CHRISTY].   And it's lies you told, letting on you had
   him slitted, and you nothing at all.

CHRISTY [*catching* MAHON's *stick*].   He's not my father. He's a raving
   maniac would scare the world. [*Pointing to* WIDOW QUIN.] Herself
   knows it is true.

CROWD.   You're fooling Pegeen! The Widow Quin seen him this day,
   and you likely knew! You're a liar!

CHRISTY [*dumbfounded*].   It's himself was a liar, lying stretched out with an open head on him, letting on he was dead.

MAHON.   Weren't you off racing the hills before I got my breath with the start I had seeing you turn on me at all?

PEGEEN.   And to think of the coaxing glory we had given him, and he after doing nothing but hitting a soft blow and chasing northward in a sweat of fear. Quit off from this.

CHRISTY [*piteously*].   You've seen my doings this day, and let you save me from the old man; for why would you be in such a scorch of haste to spur me to destruction now?

PEGEEN.   It's there your treachery is spurring me, till I'm hard set to think you're the one I'm after lacing in my heart-strings half-an-hour gone by. [*To* MAHON.] Take him on from this, for I think bad the world should see me raging for a Munster liar, and the fool of men.

MAHON.   Rise up now to retribution, and come on with me.

CROWD [*jeeringly*].   There's the playboy! There's the lad thought he'd rule the roost in Mayo. Slate him now, mister.

CHRISTY [*getting up in shy terror*].   What is it drives you to torment me here, when I'd asked the thunders of the might of God to blast me if I ever did hurt to any saving only that one single blow.

MAHON [*loudly*].   If you didn't, you're a poor good-for-nothing, and isn't it by the like of you the sins of the whole world are committed.

CHRISTY [*raising his hands*].   In the name of the Almighty God. . . .

MAHON.   Leave troubling the Lord God. Would you have him sending down droughts, and fevers, and the old hen and the cholera morbus?

CHRISTY [*to* WIDOW QUIN].   Will you come between us and protect me now?

WIDOW QUIN.   I've tried a lot, God help me, and my share is done.

CHRISTY [*looking round in desperation*].   And I must go back into my torment is it, or run off like a vagabond straying through the Unions with the dusts of August making mudstains in the gullet of my throat, or the winds of March blowing on me till I'd take an oath I felt them making whistles of my ribs within?

SARA.   Ask Pegeen to aid you. Her like does often change.

CHRISTY.   I will not then, for there's torment in the splendour of her like, and she a girl any moon of midnight would take pride to meet, facing southwards on the heaths of Keel. But what did I want crawling forward to scorch my understanding at her flaming brow?

PEGEEN [*to* MAHON, *vehemently, fearing she will break into tears*].   Take him on from this or I'll set the young lads to destroy him here.

MAHON [*going to him, shaking his stick*].   Come on now if you wouldn't have the company to see you skelped.

PEGEEN [*half laughing, through her tears*].   That's it, now the world will see him pandied, and he an ugly liar was playing off the hero, and the fright of men.

CHRISTY [*to* MAHON, *very sharply*].   Leave me go!

CROWD. That's it. Now Christy. If them two set fighting, it will lick the world.

MAHON [*making a grab at* CHRISTY]. Come here to me.

CHRISTY [*more threateningly*]. Leave me go, I'm saying.

MAHON. I will maybe, when your legs is limping, and your back is blue.

CROWD. Keep it up, the two of you. I'll back the old one. Now the playboy.

CHRISTY [*in low and intense voice*]. Shut your yelling, for if you're after making a mighty man of me this day by the power of a lie, you're setting me now to think if it's a poor thing to be lonesome, it's worse maybe to go mixing with the fools of earth.

[MAHON *makes a movement towards him.*]

CHRISTY [*almost shouting*]. Keep off . . . lest I do show a blow unto the lot of you would set the guardian angels winking in the clouds above. [*He swings round with a sudden rapid movement and picks up a loy.*]

CROWD [*half frightened, half amused*]. He's going mad! Mind yourselves! Run from the idiot!

CHRISTY. If I am an idiot, I'm after hearing my voice this day saying words would raise the topknot on a poet in a merchant's town. I've won your racing, and your lepping, and . . .

MAHON. Shut your gullet and come on with me.

CHRISTY. I'm going, but I'll stretch you first.

[*He runs at* OLD MAHON *with the loy, chases him out of the door, followed by crowd and* WIDOW QUIN. *There is a great noise outside, then a yell, and dead silence for a moment.* CHRISTY *comes in, half dazed, and goes to fire.*]

WIDOW QUIN [*coming in, hurriedly, and going to him*]. They're turning again you. Come on, or you'll be hanged, indeed.

CHRISTY. I'm thinking, from this out, Pegeen'll be giving me praises the same as in the hours gone by.

WIDOW QUIN [*impatiently*]. Come by the back-door. I'd think bad to have you stifled on the gallows tree.

CHRISTY [*indignantly*]. I will not, then. What good'd be my life-time, if I left Pegeen?

WIDOW QUIN. Come on, and you'll be no worse than you were last night; and you with a double murder this time to be telling to the girls.

CHRISTY. I'll not leave Pegeen Mike.

WIDOW QUIN [*impatiently*]. Isn't there the match of her in every parish public, from Binghamstown unto the plain of Meath? Come on, I tell you, and I'll find you finer sweethearts at each waning moon.

CHRISTY.   It's Pegeen I'm seeking only, and what'd I care if you brought
me a drift of chosen females, standing in their shifts itself, maybe,
from this place to the Eastern World?

SARA [*runs in, pulling off one of her petticoats*].   They're going to hang
him. [*Holding out petticoat and shawl.*] Fit these upon him, and let
him run off to the east.

WIDOW QUIN.   He's raving now; but we'll fit them on him, and I'll take
him, in the ferry, to the Achill boat.

CHRISTY [*struggling feebly*].   Leave me go, will you? when I'm thinking
of my luck to-day, for she will wed me surely, and I a proven hero in
the end of all.

[*They try to fasten petticoat around him.*]

WIDOW QUIN.   Take his left hand, and we'll pull him now. Come on,
young fellow.

CHRISTY [*suddenly starting up*].   You'll be taking me from her? You're
jealous, is it, of her wedding me? Go on from this. [*He snatches up a
stool, and threatens them with it.*]

WIDOW QUIN [*going*].   It's in the mad-house they should put him, not
in jail, at all. We'll go by the back-door, to call the doctor, and we'll
save him so.

[*She goes out, with* SARA, *through inner room.* MEN *crowd in the
doorway.* CHRISTY *sits down again by the fire.*]

MICHAEL [*in a terrified whisper*].   Is the old lad killed surely?

PHILLY.   I'm after feeling the last gasps quitting his heart.

[*They peer in at* CHRISTY.]

MICHAEL [*with a rope*].   Look at the way he is. Twist a hangman's knot
on it, and slip it over his head, while he's not minding at all.

PHILLY.   Let you take it, Shaneen. You're the soberest of all that's here.

SHAWN.   Is it me to go near him, and he the wickedest and worst with
me? Let you take it, Pegeen Mike.

PEGEEN.   Come on, so.

[*She goes forward with the others, and they drop the double hitch
over his head.*]

CHRISTY.   What ails you?

SHAWN [*triumphantly, as they pull the rope tight on his arms*].   Come on
to the peelers, till they stretch you now.

CHRISTY.   Me!

MICHAEL.   If we took pity on you, the Lord God would, maybe, bring
us ruin from the law to-day, so you'd best come easy, for hanging is
an easy and a speedy end.

CHRISTY. I'll not stir. [*To* PEGEEN.] And what is it you'll say to me, and I after doing it this time in the face of all?

PEGEEN. I'll say, a strange man is a marvel, with his mighty talk; but what's a squabble in your back-yard, and the blow of a loy, have taught me that there's a great gap between a gallous story and a dirty deed. [*To* MEN.] Take him on from this, or the lot of us will be likely put on trial for his deed to-day.

CHRISTY [*with horror in his voice*]. And it's yourself will send me off, to have a horny-fingered hangman hitching his bloody slip-knots at the butt of my ear.

MEN [*pulling rope*]. Come on, will you?

[*He is pulled down on the floor.*]

CHRISTY [*twisting his legs round the table*]. Cut the rope, Pegeen, and I'll quit the lot of you, and live from this out, like the madmen of Keel, eating muck and green weeds, on the faces of the cliffs.

PEGEEN. And leave us to hang, is it, for a saucy liar, the like of you? [*To* MEN.] Take him on, out from this.

SHAWN. Pull a twist on his neck, and squeeze him so.

PHILLY. Twist yourself. Sure he cannot hurt you if you keep your distance from his teeth alone.

SHAWN. I'm afeard of him. [*To* PEGEEN.] Lift a lighted sod, will you, and scorch his leg.

PEGEEN [*blowing the fire, with a bellows*]. Leave go now, young fellow, or I'll scorch your shins.

CHRISTY. You're blowing for to torture me. [*His voice rising and growing stronger.*] That's your kind, is it? Then let the lot of you be wary, for, if I've to face the gallows, I'll have a gay march down, I tell you, and shed the blood of some of you before I die.

SHAWN [*in terror*]. Keep a good hold, Philly. Be wary, for the love of God. For I'm thinking he would liefest wreak his pains on me.

CHRISTY [*almost gaily*]. If I do lay my hands on you, it's the way you'll be at the fall of night, hanging as a scarecrow for the fowls of hell. Ah, you'll have a gallous jaunt I'm saying, coaching out through Limbo with my father's ghost.

SHAWN [*to* PEGEEN]. Make haste, will you? Oh, isn't he a holy terror, and isn't it true for Father Reilly, that all drink's a curse that has the lot of you so shaky and uncertain now?

CHRISTY. If I can wring a neck among you, I'll have a royal judgment looking on the trembling jury in the courts of law. And won't there be crying out in Mayo the day I'm stretched upon the rope with ladies in their silks and satins snivelling in their lacy kerchiefs, and they rhyming songs and ballads on the terror of my fate? [*He squirms round on the floor and bites* SHAWN's *leg.*]

SHAWN [*shrieking*].   My leg's bit on me. He's the like of a mad dog, I'm thinking, the way that I will surely die.

CHRISTY [*delighted with himself*].   You will then, the way you can shake out hell's flags of welcome for my coming in two weeks or three, for I'm thinking Satan hasn't many have killed their da in Kerry, and in Mayo too.

> [OLD MAHON *comes in behind on all fours and looks on unnoticed.*]

MEN [*to* PEGEEN].   Bring the sod, will you?

PEGEEN [*coming over*].   God help him so. [*Burns his leg.*]

CHRISTY [*kicking and screaming*].   O, glory be to God!

> [*He kicks loose from the table, and they all drag him towards the door.*]

JIMMY [*seeing* OLD MAHON].   Will you look what's come in?

> [*They all drop* CHRISTY *and run left.*]

CHRISTY [*scrambling on his knees face to face with* OLD MAHON].   Are you coming to be killed a third time, or what ails you now?

MAHON.   For what is it they have you tied?

CHRISTY.   They're taking me to the peelers to have me hanged for slaying you.

MICHAEL [*apologetically*].   It is the will of God that all should guard their little cabins from the treachery of law, and what would my daughter be doing if I was ruined or was hanged itself?

MAHON [*grimly, loosening* CHRISTY].   It's little I care if you put a bag on her back, and went picking cockles till the hour of death; but my son and myself will be going our own way, and we'll have great times from this out telling stories of the villainy of Mayo, and the fools is here. [*To* CHRISTY, *who is freed.*] Come on now.

CHRISTY.   Go with you, is it? I will then, like a gallant captain with his heathen slave. Go on now and I'll see you from this day stewing my oatmeal and washing my spuds, for I'm master of all fights from now. [*Pushing* MAHON.] Go on, I'm saying.

MAHON.   Is it me?

CHRISTY.   Not a word out of you. Go on from this.

MAHON [*walking out and looking back at* CHRISTY *over his shoulder*].   Glory be to God! [*With a broad smile.*] I am crazy again! [*Goes.*]

CHRISTY.   Ten thousand blessings upon all that's here, for you've turned me a likely gaffer in the end of all, the way I'll go romancing through a romping lifetime from this hour to the dawning of the judgment day. [*He goes out.*]

MICHAEL.   By the will of God, we'll have peace now for our drinks. Will you draw the porter, Pegeen?

SHAWN [*going up to her*].   It's a miracle Father Reilly can wed us in the end of all, and we'll have none to trouble us when his vicious bite is healed.

PEGEEN [*hitting him a box on the ear*].   Quit my sight.   [*Putting her shawl over her head and breaking out into wild lamentations.*] Oh my grief, I've lost him surely. I've lost the only Playboy of the Western World.

BERNARD SHAW

John Bull's Other Island †

Characters

BROADBENT
LARRY DOYLE
TIM HAFFIGAN
HODSON
PETER KEEGAN
PATSY FARRELL
FATHER DEMPSEY
CORNEY DOYLE
BARNEY DORAN
MATTHEW HAFFIGAN
AUNT JUDY
NORA

Period—The Present. London and Ireland

ACT ONE   *Office of Broadbent and Doyle, Civil Engineers, Great George
Street, Westminster*

ACT TWO   Scene 1: *Roscullen Hill*
Scene 2: *The Round Tower*

ACT THREE   *The Grass Plot before Corney Doyle's House*

ACT FOUR   Scene 1: *The Parlor at Corney Doyle's*
SCENE 2: *Roscullen Hill*

Act One

*Great George Street, Westminster, is the address of Doyle and Broad-
bent, civil engineers. On the threshold one reads that the firm consists of*

MR LAURENCE DOYLE *and* MR THOMAS BROADBENT, *and that their rooms are on the first floor. Most of these rooms are private; for the partners, being bachelors and bosom friends, live there; and the door marked Private, next the clerk's office, is their domestic sitting room as well as their reception room for clients. Let me describe it briefly from the point of view of a sparrow on the window sill. The outer door is in the opposite wall, close to the right hand corner. Between this door and the left hand corner is a hatstand and a table consisting of large drawing boards on trestles, with plans, rolls of tracing paper, mathematical instruments, and other draughtsman's accessories on it. In the left hand wall is the fireplace, and the door of an inner room between the fireplace and our observant sparrow. Against the right hand wall is a filing cabinet, with a cupboard on it, and, nearer, a tall office desk and stool for one person. In the middle of the room a large double writing table is set across, with a chair at each end for the two partners. It is a room which no woman would tolerate, smelling of tobacco, and much in need of repapering, repainting, and recarpeting; but this is the effect of bachelor untidiness and indifference, not want of means; for nothing that* DOYLE *and* BROADBENT *themselves have purchased is cheap; nor is anything they want lacking. On the walls hang a large map of South America, a pictorial advertisement of a steamship company, an impressive portrait of Gladstone, and several caricatures of Mr Balfour as a rabbit and Mr Chamberlain as a fox by Francis Carruthers Gould.*[1]

At twenty minutes to five o'clock on a summer afternoon in 1904, the room is empty. Presently the outer door is opened, and a VALET *comes in laden with a large Gladstone bag and a strap of rugs. He carries them into the inner room. He is a respectable valet, old enough to have lost all alacrity and acquired an air of putting up patiently with a great deal of trouble and indifferent health. The luggage belongs to* BROADBENT, *who enters after the valet. He pulls off his overcoat and hangs it with his hat on the stand. Then he comes to the writing table and looks through the letters waiting there for him. He is a robust, full-blooded, energetic man in the prime of life, sometimes eager and credulous, sometimes shrewd and roguish, sometimes portentously solemn, sometimes jolly and impetuous, always buoyant and irresistible, mostly likeable, and enormously absurd in his most earnest moments. He bursts open his letters with his thumb, and glances through them, flinging the envelopes about the floor with reckless untidiness whilst he talks to the valet.*

BROADBENT [*calling*].   Hodson.
HODSON [*in the bedroom*].   Yes sir.

---

1. W. E. Gladstone (1809–98), liberal prime minister associated with Home Rule for Ireland; Arthur James Balfour (1848–1930), conservative statesman, chief secretary for Ireland, associated with authoritarian British presence in Ireland; Joseph Chamberlain (1836–1914), MP from Birmingham opposed to Home Rule and involved in negotiation of Irish policies and treaties; Francis Carruthers Gould (1844–1925), caricaturist.

BROADBENT.   Don't unpack. Just take out the things I've worn; and put in clean things.

HODSON [*appearing at the bedroom door*].   Yes sir. [*He turns to go back into the bedroom.*]

BROADBENT.   And look here!

[*Hodson turns again.*]

Do you remember where I put my revolver?

HODSON.   Revolver, sir! Yes sir. Mr Doyle uses it as a paper-weight, sir, when he's drawing.

BROADBENT.   Well, I want it packed. Theres a packet of cartridges somewhere, I think. Find it and pack it as well.

HODSON.   Yes sir.

BROADBENT.   By the way, pack your own traps too. I shall take you with me this time.

HODSON [*hesitant*].   Is it a dangerous part youre going to, sir? Should I be expected to carry a revolver, sir?

BROADBENT.   Perhaps it might be as well. I'm going to Ireland.

HODSON [*reassured*].   Yes, sir.

BROADBENT.   You don't feel nervous about it, I suppose?

HODSON.   Not at all, sir. I'll risk it, sir.

BROADBENT.   Ever been in Ireland?

HODSON.   No sir. I understand it's a very wet climate, sir. I'd better pack your india-rubber overalls.

BROADBENT.   Do. Wheres Mr Doyle?

HODSON.   I'm expecting him at five, sir. He went out after lunch.

BROADBENT.   Anybody been looking for me?

HODSON.   A person giving the name of Haffigan has called twice today, sir.

BROADBENT.   Oh, I'm sorry. Why didnt he wait? I told him to wait if I wasnt in.

HODSON.   Well sir, I didnt know you expected him; so I thought it best to—to—not to encourage him, sir.

BROADBENT.   Oh, he's all right. He's an Irishman, and not very particular about his appearance.

HODSON.   Yes sir: I noticed that he was rather Irish.

BROADBENT.   If he calls again let him come up.

HODSON.   I think I saw him waiting about, sir, when you drove up. Shall I fetch him, sir?

BROADBENT.   Do, Hodson.

HODSON.   Yes sir. [*He makes for the outer door.*]

BROADBENT.   He'll want tea. Let us have some.

HODSON [*stopping*].   I shouldnt think he drank tea, sir.

BROADBENT.   Well, bring whatever you think he'd like.

HODSON.   Yes sir.

[*An electric bell rings.*]

Here he is, sir. Saw you arrive, sir.

BROADBENT.   Right. Shew him in.

[HODSON *goes out.* BROADBENT *gets through the rest of his letters before* HODSON *returns with the visitor.*]

HODSON.   Mr Affigan.

[HAFFIGAN *is a stunted, shortnecked, smallheaded man of about 30, with a small bullet head, a red nose, and furtive eyes. He is dressed in seedy black, almost clerically, and might be a tenth-rate schoolmaster ruined by drink. He hastens to shake* BROAD-BENT'S *hand with a show of reckless geniality and high spirits, helped out by a rollicking stage brogue. This is perhaps a comfort to himself, as he is secretly pursued by the horrors of incipient delirium tremens.*]

HAFFIGAN.   Tim Haffigan, sir, at your service. The top o the mornin to you, Misther Broadbent.

BROADBENT [*delighted with his Irish visitor*].   Good afternoon, Mr Haffigan.

TIM.   An is it the afthernoon it is already? Begorra, what I call the mornin is all the time a man fasts afther breakfast.

BROADBENT.   Havnt you lunched?

TIM.   Divil a lunch!

BROADBENT.   I'm sorry I couldnt get back from Brighton in time to offer you some; but—

TIM.   Not a word, sir, not a word. Sure itll do tomorrow. Besides, I'm Irish, sir: a poor aither, but a powerful dhrinker.

BROADBENT.   I was just about to ring for tea when you came. Sit down, Mr Haffigan.

TIM.   Tay is a good dhrink if your nerves can stand it. Mine cant.

[HAFFIGAN *sits down at the writing table, with his back to the filing cabinet.* BROADBENT *sits opposite him.* HODSON *enters empty-handed; takes two glasses, a siphon, and a tantalus from the cupboard; places them before* BROADBENT *on the writing table; looks ruthlessly at* HAFFIGAN, *who cannot meet his eye; and retires.*]

BROADBENT.   Try a whisky and soda.

TIM [*sobered*].   There you touch the national wakeness, sir. [*Piously.*] Not that I share it meself. Ive seen too much of the mischief of it.

BROADBENT [*pouring the whisky*].   Say when.

TIM.   Not too sthrong.

[BROADBENT *stops and looks inquiringly at him*].

Say half-an-half.

[BROADBENT, *somewhat startled by this demand, pours a little more, and again stops and looks*].

Just a dhrain more: the lower half o the tumbler doesnt hold a fair half. Thankya.

BROADBENT [*laughing*]. You Irishmen certainly do know how to drink. [*Pouring some whisky for himself.*] Now thats my poor English idea of a whisky and soda.

TIM. An a very good idea it is too. Dhrink is the curse o me unhappy counthry. I take it meself because Ive a wake heart and a poor digestion; but in principle I'm a tee-toatler.

BROADBENT [*suddenly solemn and strenuous*]. So am I, of course. I'm a Local Optionist[2] to the backbone. You have no idea, Mr Haffigan, of the ruin that is wrought in this country by the unholy alliance of the publicans, the bishops, the Tories, and The Times. We must close the public-houses at all costs. [*He drinks.*]

TIM. Sure I know. It's awful, [*He drinks.*] I see youre a good Liberal like meself, sir.

BROADBENT. I am a lover of liberty, like every true Englishman, Mr Haffigan. My name is Broadbent. If my name were Breitstein, and I had a hooked nose and a house in Park Lane, I should carry a Union Jack handkerchief and a penny trumpet, and tax the food of the people to support the Navy League, and clamor for the destruction of the last remnants of national liberty—

TIM. Not another word. Shake hands.

BROADBENT. But I should like to explain—

TIM. Sure I know every word youre goin to say before yev said it. *I* know the sort o man yar. An so youre thinkin o comin to Ireland for a bit?

BROADBENT. Where else can I go? I am an Englishman and a Liberal; and now that South Africa has been enslaved and destroyed, there is no country left to me to take an interest in but Ireland. Mind; I dont say that an Englishman has not other duties. He has a duty to Finland and a duty to Macedonia. But what sane man can deny that an Englishman's first duty is his duty to Ireland? Unfortunately, we have politicians here more unscrupulous than Bobrikoff,[3] more bloodthirsty than Abdul the Damned; and it is under their heel that Ireland is now writhing.

TIM. Faith, theyve reckoned up with poor oul Bobrikoff anyhow.

BROADBENT. Not that I defend assassination: God forbid! However strongly we may feel that the unfortunate and patriotic young man who avenged the wrongs of Finland on the Russian tyrant was perfectly right from his own point of view, yet every civilized man must regard murder with abhorrence. Not even in defence of Free Trade would I lift my hand against a political opponent, however richly he might deserve it.

---

2. Advocate of community right to permit or prohibit alcoholic beverages.

3. Nikolay Bobrikov (1839–1904), dictatorial Russian administrator of occupied Finland.

TIM.   I'm sure you wouldnt; and I honor you for it. Youre goin to Ireland, then, out o sympithy: is it?

BROADBENT.   I'm going to develop an estate there for the Land Development Syndicate, in which I am interested. I am convinced that all it needs to make it pay is to handle it properly, as estates are handled in England. You know the English plan, Mr Haffigan, dont you?

TIM.   Bedad I do, sir. Take all you can out of Ireland and spend it in England: thats it.

BROADBENT [not quite liking this].   My plan, sir, will be to take a little money out of England and spend it in Ireland.

TIM.   More power to your elbow! an may your shadda never be less! for youre the broth of a boy intirely. An how can I help you? Command me to the last dhrop o me blood.

BROADBENT.   Have you ever heard of Garden City?

TIM [doubtfully].   D'ye mane Heavn?

BROADBENT.   Heaven! No: it's near Hitchin. If you can spare half an hour I'll go into it with you.

TIM.   I tell you hwat. Gimme a prospectus. Lemmy take it home and reflect on it.

BROADBENT.   Youre quite right: I will. [He gives him a copy of Ebenezer Howard's book,[4] and several pamphlets.] You understand that the map of the city—the circular construction—is only a suggestion.

TIM.   I'll make a careful note o that [looking dazedly at the map].

BROADBENT.   What I say is, why not start a Garden City in Ireland?

TIM [with enthusiasm].   Thats just what was on the tip o me tongue to ask you. Why not? [Defiantly]. Tell me why not.

BROADBENT.   There are difficulties. I shall overcome them; but there are difficulties. When I first arrive in Ireland I shall be hated as an Englishman. As a Protestant, I shall be denounced from every altar. My life may be in danger. Well, I am prepared to face that.

TIM.   Never fear, sir. We know how to respict a brave innimy.

BROADBENT.   What I really dread is misunderstanding. I think you could help me to avoid that. When I heard you speak the other evening in Bermondsey at the meeting of the National League,[5] I saw at once that you were—You wont mind my speaking frankly?

TIM.   Tell me all me faults as man to man. I can stand anything but flatthery.

BROADBENT.   May I put it this way? that I saw at once that you are a thorough Irishman, with all the faults and all the qualities of your race: rash and improvident but brave and goodnatured; not likely to succeed in business on your own account perhaps, but eloquent, humorous, a lover of freedom, and a true follower of that great Englishman Gladstone.

4. Tomorrow: A Peaceful Path to Real Reform (1898).

5. Organization, founded in 1882, for the return of Irish land to Irish ownership.

TIM.   Spare me blushes. I mustnt sit here to be praised to me face. But I confess to the goodnature: it's an Irish wakeness. I'd share me last shillin with a friend.

BROADBENT.   I feel sure you would. Mr Haffigan.

TIM [impulsively].   Damn it! call me Tim. A man that talks about Ireland as you do may call me anything. Gimmy a howlt o that whisky bottle [he replenishes].

BROADBENT [smiling indulgently].   Well, Tim, will you come with me and help to break the ice between me and your warmhearted, impulsive countrymen?

TIM.   Will I come to Madagascar or Cochin China wid you? Bedad I'll come to the North Pole wid you if yll pay me fare; for the divil a shillin I have to buy a third class ticket.

BROADBENT.   Ive not forgotten that, Tim. We must put that little matter on a solid English footing, though the rest can be as Irish as you please. You must come as my—my—well, I hardly know what to call it. If we call you my agent, theyll shoot you. If we call you a bailiff, theyll duck you in the horsepond. I have a secretary already; and—

TIM.   Then we'll call him the Home Secretary and me the Irish Secretary. Eh?

BROADBENT [laughing industriously].   Capital. Your Irish wit has settled the first difficulty. Now about your salary—

TIM.   A salary, is it? Sure I'd do it for nothin, only me cloes ud disgrace you; and I'd be dhriven to borra money from your friends: a thing thats agin me nacher. But I wont take a penny more than a hundherd a year. [He looks with restless cunning at BROADBENT, trying to guess how far he may go.]

BROADBENT.   If that will satisfy you—

TIM [more than reassured].   Why shouldnt it satisfy me? A hundherd a year is twelve pound a month, isnt it?

BROADBENT.   No. Eight pound six and eightpence.

TIM.   Oh murdher! An I'll have to sind five timmy poor oul mother in Ireland. But no matther: I said a hundherd; and what I said I'll stick to, if I have to starve for it.

BROADBENT [with business caution].   Well, let us say twelve pounds for the first month. Afterwards, we shall see how we get on.

TIM.   Youre a gentleman, sir. Whin me mother turns up her toes, you shall take the five pounds off; for your expinses must be kep down wid a sthrong hand; an—[He is interrupted by the arrival of BROADBENT's partner].

[MR LAURENCE DOYLE is a man of 36, with cold grey eyes, strained nose, fine fastidious lips, critical brows, clever head, rather refined and goodlooking on the whole, but with a suggestion of thinskinnedness and dissatisfaction that contrasts strongly with BROADBENT's eupeptic jollity.

He comes in as a man at home there, but on seeing the stranger shrinks at once, and is about to withdraw when BROADBENT *reassures him. He then comes forward to the table, between the two others.*]

DOYLE [*retreating*]. Youre engaged.

BROADBENT. Not at all, not at all. Come in. [*To* TIM.] This gentleman is a friend who lives with me here: my partner, Mr DOYLE. [*To Doyle.*] This is a new Irish friend of mine, Mr Tim Haffigan.

TIM [*rising with effusion*]. Sure it's meself thats proud to meet any friend o Misther Broadbent's. The top o the mornin to you, sir! Me heart goes out teeye both. It's not often I meet two such splendid speciments iv the Anglo-Saxon race.

BROADBENT [*chuckling*]. Wrong for once, Tim. My friend Mr Doyle is a countryman of yours.

[TIM *is noticeably dashed by this announcement. He draws in his horns at once, and scowls suspicously at* DOYLE *under a vanishing mask of goodfellowship: cringing a little, too, in mere nerveless fear of him.*]

DOYLE [*with cool disgust*]. Good evening. [*He retires to the fireplace, and says to* BROADBENT *in a tone which conveys the strongest possible hint to* HAFFIGAN *that he is unwelcome.*] Will you soon be disengaged?

TIM [*his brogue decaying into a common would-be genteel accent with an unexpected strain of Glasgow in it*]. I must be going. Avnmpoartnt engeegement in the west end.

BROADBENT [*rising*]. It's settled, then, that you come with me.

TIM. Ashll be verra pleased to accompany ye, sir.

BROADBENT. But how soon? Can you start tonight? from Paddington? We go by Milford Haven.

TIM [*hesitating*]. Well—A'm afraid—A

[DOYLE *goes abruptly into the bedroom, slamming the door and shattering the last remnant of* TIM's *nerve. The poor wretch saves himself from bursting into tears by plunging again into his role of daredevil Irishman. He rushes to* BROADBENT; *plucks at his sleeve with trembling fingers; and pours forth his entreaty with all the brogue he can muster, subduing his voice lest* DOYLE *should hear and return.*]

Misther Broadbent: dont humiliate me before a fella counthryman. Look here: me cloes is up the spout. Gimmy a fypounnote—I'll pay ya nex Choosda whin me ship comes home—or you can stop it out of me month's sallery. I'll be on the platform at Paddnton punctial an ready. Gimmy it quick, before he comes back. You wont mind me axin, will ye?

BROADBENT.   Not at all. I was about to offer you an advance for travelling expenses. [*He gives him a bank note*].
TIM [*pocketing it*].   Thank you. I'll be there half an hour before the
thrain starts.

[LARRY *is heard at the bedroom door, returning.*]

Whisht: he's comin back. Goodbye an God bless ye. [*He hurries out
almost crying, the £5 note and all the drink it means to him being too
much for his empty stomach and overstrained nerves.*]
DOYLE [*returning*].   Where the devil did you pick up that seedy swin-
dler? What was he doing here? [*He goes up to the table where the plans
are, and makes a note on one of them, referring to his pocket book as
he does so.*]
BROADBENT.   There you go! Why are you so down on every Irishman
you meet, especially if he's a bit shabby? poor devil! Surely a fellow-
countryman may pass you the top of the morning without offence,
even if his coat is a bit shiny at the seams.
DOYLE [*contemptuously*].   The top of the morning! Did he call you the
broth of a boy? [*He comes to the writing table*].
BROADBENT [*triumphantly*].   Yes.
DOYLE.   And wished you more power to your elbow?
BROADBENT.   He did.
DOYLE.   And that your shadow might never be less?
BROADBENT.   Certainly.
DOYLE [*taking up the depleted whisky bottle and shaking his head at
it*].   And he got about half a pint of whisky out of you.
BROADBENT.   It did him no harm. He never turned a hair.
DOYLE.   How much money did he borrow?
BROADBENT.   It was not borrowing exactly. He shewed a very honorable
spirit about money. I believe he would share his last shilling with a
friend.
DOYLE.   No doubt he would share his friend's last shilling if his friend
was fool enough to let him. How much did he touch you for?
BROADBENT.   Oh, nothing. An advance on his salary—for travelling
expenses.
DOYLE.   Salary! In Heaven's name, what for?
BROADBENT.   For being my Home Secretary, as he very wittily called
it.
DOYLE.   I dont see the joke.
BROADBENT.   You can spoil any joke by being cold blooded about it. I
saw it all right when he said it. It was something—something really
very amusing—about the Home Secretary and the Irish Secretary. At
all events, he's evidently the very man to take with me to Ireland to
break the ice for me. He can gain the confidence of the people there,
and make them friendly to me, Eh? [*He seats himself on the office*

stool, and tilts it back so that the edge of the standing desk supports his back and prevents his toppling over.]

DOYLE.   A nice introduction, by George! Do you suppose the whole population of Ireland consists of drunken begging letter writers, or that even if it did, they would accept one another as references?

BROADBENT.   Pooh! nonsense! he's only an Irishman. Besides, you dont seriously suppose that Haffigan can humbug me, do you?

DOYLE.   No: he's too lazy to take the trouble. All he has to do is to sit there and drink your whisky while you humbug yourself. However, we neednt argue about Haffigan, for two reasons. First, with your money in his pocket he will never reach Paddington: there are too many public houses on the way. Second, he's not an Irishman at all.

BROADBENT.   Not an Irishman! [*He is so amazed by the statement that he straightens himself and brings the stool bolt upright.*]

DOYLE.   Born in Glasgow. Never was in Ireland in his life. I know all about him.

BROADBENT.   But he spoke—he behaved just like an Irishman.

DOYLE.   Like an Irishman!! Man alive, dont you know that all this top-o-the-morning and broth-of-a-boy and more-power-to-your-elbow business is got up in England to fool you, like the Albert Hall concerts of Irish music? No Irishman ever talks like that in Ireland, or ever did, or ever will. But when a thoroughly worthless Irishman comes to England, and finds the whole place full of romantic duffers like you, who will let him loaf and drink and sponge and brag as long as he flatters your sense of moral superiority by playing the fool and degrading himself and his country, he soon learns the antics that take you in. He picks them up at the theatre or the music hall. Haffigan learnt the rudiments from his father, who came from my part of Ireland. I knew his uncles, Matt and Andy Haffigan of Rosscullen.

BROADBENT [*still incredulous*].   But his brogue?

DOYLE.   His brogue! A fat lot you know about brogues! Ive heard you call a Dublin accent that you could hang your hat on, a brogue. Heaven help you! you dont know the difference between Connemara and Rathmines.[6] [*With violent irritation.*] Oh, damn Tim Haffigan! lets drop the subject: he's not worth wrangling about.

BROADBENT.   Whats wrong with you today, Larry? Why are you so bitter?

[*Doyle looks at him perplexedly; comes slowly to the writing table; and sits down at the end next to the fireplace before replying.*]

DOYLE.   Well: your letter completely upset me, for one thing.

BROADBENT.   Why?

LARRY.   Your foreclosing this Rosscullen mortgage and turning poor Nick Lestrange out of house and home has rather taken me aback; for

6. The difference between a wild, western, rural district and a Dublin suburb.

I liked the old rascal when I was a boy and had the run of his park to play in. I was brought up on the property.

BROADBENT.   But he wouldnt pay the interest. I had to foreclose on behalf of the Syndicate. So now I'm off to Rosscullen to look after the property myself. [*He sits down at the writing table opposite* LARRY, *and adds, casually, but with an anxious glance at his partner.*] Youre coming with me, of course?

DOYLE   [*rising nervously and recommencing his restless movements*].   Thats it. Thats what I dread. Thats what has upset me.

BROADBENT.   But dont you want to see your country again after 18 years absence? to see your people? to be in the old home again? to—

DOYLE [*interrupting him very impatiently*].   Yes, yes: I know all that as well as you do.

BROADBENT.   Oh well, of course [*with a shrug*] if you take it in that way, I'm sorry.

DOYLE.   Never you mind my temper: it's not meant for you, as you ought to know by this time. [*He sits down again, a little ashamed of his petulance; reflects a moment bitterly; then bursts out*] I have an instinct against going back to Ireland: an instinct so strong that I'd rather go with you to the South Pole than to Rosscullen.

BROADBENT.   What! Here you are, belonging to a nation with the strongest patriotism! the most inveterate homing instinct in the world! and you pretend youd rather go anywhere than back to Ireland. You dont suppose I believe you, do you? In your heart—

DOYLE.   Never mind my heart: an Irishman's heart is nothing but his imagination. How many of all those millions that have left Ireland have ever come back or wanted to come back? But whats the use of talking to you? Three verses of twaddle about the Irish emigrant "sitting on the stile, Mary," or three hours of Irish patriotism in Bermondsey or the Scotland Division of Liverpool, go further with you than all the facts that stare you in the face. Why, man alive, look at me! You know the way I nag, and worry, and carp, and cavil, and disparage, and am never satisfied and never quiet, and try the patience of my best friends.

BROADBENT.   Oh, come, Larry! do yourself justice. Youre very amusing and agreeable to strangers.

DOYLE.   Yes, to strangers. Perhaps if I was a bit stiffer to strangers, and a bit easier at home, like an Englishman, I'd be better company for you.

BROADBENT.   We get on well enough. Of course you have the melancholy of the Keltic race—

DOYLE [*bounding out of his chair*].   Good God!!!

BROADBENT [*slyly*].—and also its habit of using strong language when theres nothing the matter.

DOYLE.   Nothing the matter! When people talk about the Celtic race, I feel as if I could burn down London. That sort of rot does more harm than ten Coercion Acts.[7] Do you suppose a man need be a Celt to feel melancholy in Rosscullen? Why, man, Ireland was peopled just as England was; and its breed was crossed by just the same invaders.

BROADBENT.   True. All the capable people in Ireland are of English extraction. It has often struck me as a most remarkable circumstance that the only party in parliament which shews the genuine old English character and spirit is the Irish party. Look at its independence, its determination, its defiance of bad Governments, its sympathy with oppressed nationalities all the world over! How English!

DOYLE.   Not to mention the solemnity with which it talks old-fashioned nonsense which it knows perfectly well to be a century behind the times. Thats English, if you like.

BROADBENT.   No, Larry, no. You are thinking of the modern hybrids that now monopolize England. Hypocrites, humbugs, Germans, Jews, Yankees, foreigners, Park Laners, cosmopolitan riffraff. Dont call them English. They dont belong to the dear old island, but to their confounded new empire; and by George! theyre worthy of it; and I wish them joy of it.

DOYLE [unmoved by this outburst].   There! You feel better now, dont you?

BROADBENT [defiantly].   I do. Much better.

DOYLE.   My dear Tom, you only need a touch of the Irish climate to be as big a fool as I am myself. If all my Irish blood were poured into your veins, you wouldnt turn a hair of your constitution and character. Go and marry the most English Englishwoman you can find, and then bring up your son in Rosscullen; and that son's character will be so like mine and so unlike yours that everybody will accuse me of being his father. [With sudden anguish.] Rosscullen! oh, good Lord, Rosscullen! The dullness! the hopelessness! the ignorance! the bigotry!

BROADBENT [matter-of-factly].   The usual thing in the country, Larry. Just the same here.

DOYLE [hastily].   No, no: the climate is different. Here, if the life is dull, you can be dull too, and no great harm done. [Going off into a passionate dream.] But your wits cant thicken in that soft moist air, on those white springy roads, in those misty rushes and brown bogs, on those hillsides of granite rocks and magenta heather. Youve no such colors in the sky, no such lure in the distances, no such sadness in the evenings. Oh, the dreaming! the dreaming! the torturing, heartscalding, never satisfying dreaming, dreaming, dreaming, dreaming! [Savagely.] No debauchery that ever coarsened and brutalized an Englishman can take the worth and usefulness out of him like that dreaming. An Irishman's imagination never lets him alone, never convinces him, never satisfies him; but it makes him that he cant face

---

7. Introductions of martial law to suppress rebellion.

reality nor deal with it nor handle it nor conquer it: he can only sneer at them that do, and [*bitterly, at* BROADBENT] be "agreeable to strangers," like a good-for-nothing woman on the streets. [*Gabbling at* BROAD-BENT *across the table.*] It's all dreaming, all imagination. He cant be religious. The inspired Churchman that teaches him the sanctity of life and the importance of conduct is sent away empty; while the poor village priest that gives him a miracle or a sentimental story of a saint, has cathedrals built for him out of the pennies of the poor. He cant be intelligently political; he dreams of what the Shan Van Vocht said in ninetyeight.[8] If you want to interest him in Ireland youve got to call the unfortunate island Kathleen ni Hoolihan and pretend she's a little old woman. It saves thinking. It saves working. It saves everything except imagination, imagination, imagination; and imagination's such a torture that you cant bear it without whisky. [*With fierce shivering self-contempt.*] At last you get that you can bear nothing real at all: youd rather starve than cook a meal; youd rather go shabby and dirty than set your mind to take care of your clothes and wash yourself; you nag and squabble at home because your wife isnt an angel, and she despises you because youre not a hero; and you hate the whole lot round you because theyre only poor slovenly useless devils like yourself. [*Dropping his voice like a man making some shameful confidence.*] And all the while there goes on a horrible, senseless, mischievous laughter. When youre young, you exchange drinks with other young men; and you exchange vile stories with them; and as youre too futile to be able to help or cheer them, you chaff and sneer and taunt them for not doing the things you darent do yourself. And all the time you laugh! laugh! laugh! eternal derision, eternal envy, eternal folly, eternal fouling and staining and degrading, until, when you come at last to a country where men take a question seriously and give a serious answer to it, you deride them for having no sense of humor, and plume yourself on your own worthlessness as if it made you better than them.

BROADBENT [*roused to intense earnestness by* DOYLE's *eloquence*].   Never despair, Larry. There are great possibilities for Ireland. Home Rule[9] will work wonders under English guidance.

DOYLE [*pulled up short, his face twitching with a reluctant smile*].   Tom: why do you select my most tragic moments for your most irresistible strokes of humor?

BROADBENT.   Humor! I was perfectly serious. What do you mean? Do you doubt my seriousness about Home Rule?

DOYLE.   I am sure you are serious, Tom, about the English guidance.

BROADBENT [*quite reassured*].   Of course I am. Our guidance is the important thing. We English must place our capacity for government

8. The Shan Van Vocht, personification of Ireland as an old woman foretelling the arrival of the French to aid Irish rebellion.

9. Local government for Ireland by restoration of the Irish parliament.

without stint at the service of nations who are less fortunately endowed
in that respect; so as to allow them to develop in perfect freedom to
the English level of self-government, you know. You understand me?

DOYLE.   Perfectly. And Rosscullen will understand you too.

BROADBENT [*cheerfully*].   Of course it will. So thats all right. [*He pulls
up his chair and settles himself comfortably to lecture* DOYLE]. Now,
Larry, Ive listened carefully to all youve said about Ireland; and I can
see nothing whatever to prevent your coming with me. What does it
all come to? Simply that you were only a young fellow when you were
in Ireland. Youll find all that chaffing and drinking and not knowing
what to be at in Peckham just the same as in Donnybrook. You looked
at Ireland with a boy's eyes and saw only boyish things. Come back
with me and look at it with a man's; and get a better opinion of your
country.

DOYLE.   I daresay youre partly right in that: at all events I know very
well that if I had been the son of a laborer instead of the son of a
country landagent, I should have struck more grit than I did. Unfortunately I'm not going back to visit the Irish nation, but to visit my
father and Aunt Judy and Nora Reilly and Father Dempsey and the
rest of them.

BROADBENT.   Well, why not? Theyll be delighted to see you, now that
England has made a man of you.

DOYLE [*struck by this*].   Ah! you hit the mark there, Tom, with true
British inspiration.

BROADBENT.   Common sense, you mean.

DOYLE [*quickly*].   No I dont: youve no more common sense than a gan-
der. No Englishman has any common sense, or ever had, or ever will
have. Youre going on a sentimental expedition for perfectly ridiculous
reasons, with your head full of political nonsense that would not take
in any ordinarily intelligent donkey; but you can hit me in the eye
with the simple truth about myself and my father.

BROADBENT [*amazed*].   I never mentioned your father.

DOYLE [*not heeding the interruption*].   There he is in Rosscullen, a
landagent who's always been in a small way because he's a Catholic,
and the landlords are mostly Protestants. What with land courts reducing
rents and Land Purchase Acts turning big estates into little holdings,
he'd be a beggar if he hadnt taken to collecting the new purchase
instalments instead of the old rents. I doubt if he's been further from
home than Athenmullet for twenty years. And here am I, made a
man of, as you say, by England.

BROADBENT [*apologetically*].   I assure you I never meant—

DOYLE.   Oh, dont apologize: it's quite true. I daresay Ive learnt something in America and a few other remote and inferior spots; but in the
main it is by living with you and working in double harness with you
that I have learnt to live in a real world and not in an imaginary one.
I owe more to you than to any Irishman.

BROADBENT [*shaking his head with a twinkle in his eye*].   Very friendly of you, Larry, old man, but all blarney. I like blarney; but it's rot, all the same.

DOYLE.   No it's not. I should never have done anything without you; though I never stop wondering at that blessed old head of yours with all its ideas in watertight compartments, and all the compartments warranted impervious to anything it doesnt suit you to understand.

BROADBENT [*invincible*].   Unmitigated rot, Larry, I assure you.

DOYLE.   Well, at any rate you will admit that all my friends are either Englishmen or men of the big world that belongs to the big Powers. All the serious part of my life has been lived in that atmosphere: all the serious part of my work has been done with men of that sort. Just think of me as I am now going back to Rosscullen! to that hell of littleness and monotony! How am I to get on with a little country landagent that ekes out his 5 per cent with a little farming and a scrap of house property in the nearest country town? What am I to say to him? What is he to say to me?

BROADBENT [*scandalized*].   But youre father and son, man!

DOYLE.   What difference does that make? What would you say if I proposed a visit to your father?

BROADBENT [*with filial rectitude*].   I always made a point of going to see my father regularly until his mind gave way.

DOYLE [*concerned*].   Has he gone mad? You never told me.

BROADBENT.   He has joined the Tariff Reform League.[1] He would never have done that if his mind had not been weakened. [*Beginning to declaim.*] He has fallen a victim to the arts of a political charlatan who—

DOYLE [*interrupting him*].   You mean that you keep clear of your father because he differs from you about Free Trade, and you dont want to quarrel with him. Well, think of me and my father! He's a Nationalist and a Separatist. I'm a metallurgical chemist turned civil engineer. Now whatever else metallurgical chemistry may be, it's not national. It's international. And my business and yours as civil engineers is to join countries, not to separate them. The one real political conviction that our business has rubbed into us is that frontiers are hindrances and flags confounded nuisances.

BROADBENT [*still smarting under Mr Chamberlain's economic heresy*].   Only when there is a protective tariff—

DOYLE [*firmly*].   Now look here, Tom: you want to get in a speech on Free Trade; and youre not going to do it: I wont stand it. My father wants to make St George's Channel a frontier and hoist a green flag on College Green; and I want to bring Galway within 3 hours of Colchester and 24 of New York. I want Ireland to be the brains and

1. An organization for the abolition of all protective tariffs; a conservative position, associated below with Joseph Chamberlain, and antithetical to the   liberal position, associated below with Broadbent, of tariffs as beneficial economic control.

imagination of a big Commonwealth, not a Robinson Crusoe island. Then theres the religious difficulty. My Catholicism is the Catholicism of Charlemagne or Dante, qualified by a great deal of modern science and folklore which Father Dempsey would call the ravings of an Atheist. Well, my father's Catholicism is the Catholicism of Father Dempsey.

BROADBENT [*shrewdly*].   I dont want to interrupt you, Larry; but you know this is all gammon.² These differences exist in all families; but the members rub on together all right. [*Suddenly relapsing into portentousness.*] Of course there are some questions which touch the very foundations of morals; and on these I grant you even the closest relationships cannot excuse any compromise or laxity. For instance—

DOYLE [*impatiently springing up and walking about*].   For instance, Home Rule, South Africa, Free Trade, and putting the Church schools on the Education Rate. Well, I should differ from my father on every one of them, probably, just as I differ from you about them.

BROADBENT.   Yes; but you are an Irishman; and these things are not serious to you as they are to an Englishman.

DOYLE.   What! not even Home Rule!

BROADBENT [*steadfastly*].   Not even Home Rule. We owe Home Rule not to the Irish, but to our English Gladstone. No, Larry: I cant help thinking that theres something behind all this.

DOYLE [*hotly*].   What is there behind it? Do you think I'm humbugging you?

BROADBENT.   Dont fly out, old chap. I only thought—

DOYLE.   What did you think?

BROADBENT.   Well, a moment ago I caught a name which is new to me: a Miss Nora Reilly, I think.

[DOYLE *stops dead and stares at him with something like awe.*]

I don't wish to be impertinent, as you know, Larry; but are you sure she has nothing to do with your reluctance to come to Ireland with me?

DOYLE [*sitting down again, vanquished*].   Thomas Broadbent: I surrender. The poor silly-clever Irishman takes off his hat to God's Englishman. The man who could in all seriousness make that recent remark of yours about Home Rule and Gladstone must be simply the champion idiot of all the world. Yet the man who could in the very next sentence sweep away all my special pleading and go straight to the heart of my motives must be a man of genius. But that the idiot and the genius should be the same man! how is that possible? [*Springing to his feet.*] By Jove, I see it all now. I'll write an article about it, and send it to Nature.

---

2. Irrelevant and distracting chat.

BROADBENT [*staring at him*].   What on earth—
DOYLE.   It's quite simple. You know that a caterpillar—
BROADBENT.   A caterpillar!!!
DOYLE.   Yes, a caterpillar. Now give your mind to what I am going to say; for it's a new and important scientific theory of the English national character. A caterpillar—
BROADBENT.   Look here, Larry: dont be an ass.
DOYLE [*insisting*].   I say a caterpillar and I mean a caterpillar. Youll understand presently. A caterpillar

[BROADBENT *mutters a slight protest, but does not press it.*]

when it gets into a tree, instinctively makes itself look exactly like a leaf; so that both its enemies and its prey may mistake it for one and think it not worth bothering about.
BROADBENT.   Whats that got to do with our English national character?
DOYLE.   I'll tell you. The world is as full of fools as a tree is full of leaves. Well, the Englishman does what the caterpillar does. He instinctively makes himself look like a fool, and eats up all the real fools at his ease while his enemies let him alone and laugh at him for being a fool like the rest. Oh, nature is cunning! cunning! [*He sits down, lost in contemplation of his word-picture.*]
BROADBENT [*with hearty admiration*].   Now you know, Larry, that would never have occurred to me. You Irish people are amazingly clever. Of course it's all tommy rot; but it's so brilliant, you know! How the dickens do you think of such things! You really must write an article about it: theyll pay you something for it. If Nature wont have it, I can get it into Engineering for you: I know the editor.
DOYLE.   Lets get back to business. I'd better tell you about Nora Reilly.
BROADBENT.   No: never mind. I shouldnt have alluded to her.
DOYLE.   I'd rather. Nora has a fortune.
BROADBENT [*keenly interested*].   Eh? How much?
DOYLE.   Forty per annum.
BROADBENT.   Forty thousand?
DOYLE.   No, forty. Forty pounds.
BROADBENT [*much dashed*].   Thats what you call a fortune in Rosscullen, is it?
DOYLE.   A girl with a dowry of five pounds calls it a fortune in Rosscullen. Whats more, £40 a year is a fortune there; and Nora Reilly enjoys a good deal of social consideration as an heiress on the strength of it. It has helped my father's household through many a tight place. My father was her father's agent. She came on a visit to us when he died, and has lived with us ever since.
BROADBENT [*attentively, beginning to suspect* LARRY *of misconduct with* NORA, *and resolving to get to the bottom of it*].   Since when? I mean how old were you when she came?

DOYLE.   I was seventeen. So was she: if she'd been older she'd have had more sense than to stay with us. We were together for 18 months before I went up to Dublin to study. When I went home for Christmas and Easter, she was there. I suppose it used to be something of an event for her, though of course I never thought of that then.

BROADBENT.   Were you at all hard hit?

DOYLE.   Not really. I had only two ideas at that time: first, to learn to do something; and then to get out of Ireland and have a chance of doing it. She didnt count. I was romantic about her, just as I was romantic about Byron's heroines or the old Round Tower of Rosscullen; [3] but she didnt count any more than they did. Ive never crossed St George's Channel since for her sake—never even landed at Queenstown and come back to London through Ireland.

BROADBENT.   But did you ever say anything that would justify her in waiting for you?

DOYLE.   No, never. But she is waiting for me.

BROADBENT.   How do you know?

DOYLE.   She writes to me—on her birthday. She used to write on mine, and send me little things as presents; but I stopped that by pretending that it was no use when I was travelling, as they got lost in the foreign post-offices. [He pronounces post-offices with the stress on offices, instead of post.]

BROADBENT.   You answer the letters?

DOYLE.   Not very punctually. But they get acknowledged at one time or another.

BROADBENT.   How do you feel when you see her handwriting?

DOYLE.   Uneasy. I'd give £50 to escape a letter.

BROADBENT [looking grave, and throwing himself back in his chair to intimate that the cross-examination is over, and the result very damaging to the witness].   Hm!

DOYLE.   What d'ye mean by Hm!

BROADBENT.   Of course I know that the moral code is different in Ireland. But in England it's not considered fair to trifle with a woman's affections.

DOYLE.   You mean that an Englishman would get engaged to another woman and return Nora her letters and presents with a letter to say he was unworthy of her and wished her every happiness?

BROADBENT.   Well, even that would set the poor girl's mind at rest.

DOYLE.   Would it? I wonder! One thing I can tell you; and that is that Nora would wait until she died of old age sooner than ask my intentions or condescend to hint at the possibility of my having any. You

3. Ninth-century round towers, built by monastic societies, found throughout Ireland; as emblems of inspiration, they can be associated with the work of the Romantic poets such as Lord Byron (1788–1824).

dont know what Irish pride is. England may have knocked a good deal of it out of me; but she's never been in England; and if I had to choose between wounding that delicacy in her and hitting her in the face, I'd hit her in the face without a moment's hesitation.

BROADBENT [*who has been nursing his knee and reflecting, apparently rather agreeably*].   You know, all this sounds rather interesting. Theres the Irish charm about it. Thats the worst of you: the Irish charm doesnt exist for you.

DOYLE.   Oh yes it does. But it's the charm of a dream. Live in contact with dreams and you will get something of their charm: live in contact with facts and you will get something of their brutality. I wish I could find a country to live in where the facts were not brutal and the dreams not unreal.

BROADBENT [*changing his attitude and responding to* DOYLE's *earnestness with deep conviction: his elbows on the table and his hands clenched*].   Dont despair, Larry, old boy: things may look black; but there will be a great change after the next election.

DOYLE [*jumping up*].   Oh, get out, you idiot!

BROADBENT [*rising also, not a bit snubbed*].   Ha! ha! you may laugh; but we shall see. However, dont let us argue about that. Come now! you ask my advice about Miss Reilly?

DOYLE [*reddening*].   No I dont. Damn your advice! [*Softening.*] Lets have it, all the same.

BROADBENT.   Well, everything you tell me about her impresses me favorably. She seems to have the feelings of a lady; and though we must face the fact that in England her income would hardly maintain her in the lower middle class—

DOYLE [*interrupting*].   Now look here, Tom. That reminds me. When you go to Ireland, just drop talking about the middle class and bragging of belonging to it. In Ireland youre either a gentleman or youre not. If you want to be particularly offensive to Nora, you can call her a Papist; but if you call her a middle-class woman, Heaven help you!

BROADBENT [*irrepressible*].   Never fear. Youre all descended from the ancient kings: I know that. [*Complacently.*] I'm not so tactless as you think, my boy. [*Earnest again.*] I expect to find Miss Reilly a perfect lady; and I strongly advise you to come and have another look at her before you make up your mind about her. By the way, have you a photograph of her?

DOYLE.   Her photographs stopped at twenty-five.

BROADBENT [*saddened*].   Ah yes, I suppose so. [*With feeling, severely.*] Larry: youve treated that poor girl disgracefully.

DOYLE.   By George, if she only knew that two men were talking about her like this—!

BROADBENT.   She wouldnt like it, would she! Of course not. We ought to be ashamed of ourselves, Larry. [*More and more carried away by*

his new fancy]. You know, I have a sort of presentiment that Miss
Reilly is a very superior woman.
DOYLE [*staring hard at him*].   Oh! you have, have you?
BROADBENT.   Yes I have. There is something very touching about the
history of this beautiful girl.
DOYLE.   Beau—! Oho! Heres a chance for Nora! and for me! [*Calling.*]
Hodson.
HODSON [*appearing at the bedroom door*].   Did you call, sir?
DOYLE.   Pack for me too. I'm going to Ireland with Mr Broadbent.
HODSON.   Right, sir. [*He retires into the bedroom*].
BROADBENT [*clapping* DOYLE *on the shoulder*].   Thank you, old chap.
Thank you.

Act Two

*Rosscullen. Westward a hillside of granite rock and heather slopes upward
across the prospect from south to north. A huge stone stands on it in a
naturally impossible place, as if it had been tossed up there by a giant.
Over the brow, in the desolate valley beyond, is a round tower. A lonely
white high road trending away westward past the tower loses itself at the
foot of the far mountains. It is evening; and there are great breadths of
silken green in the Irish sky. The sun is setting.*

 *A man with the face of a young saint, yet with white hair and perhaps
50 years on his back, is standing near the stone in a trance of intense
melancholy, looking over the hills as if by mere intensity of gaze he could
pierce the glories of the sunset and see into the streets of heaven. He is
dressed in black, and is rather more clerical in appearance than most
English curates are nowadays; but he does not wear the collar and waistcoat of a parish priest. He is roused from his trance by the chirp of an
insect from a tuft of grass in a crevice of the stone. His face relaxes: he
turns quietly, and gravely takes off his hat to the tuft, addressing the
insect in a brogue which is the jocular assumption of a gentleman and
not in the natural speech of a peasant.*

THE MAN.   An is that yourself, Misther Grasshopper? I hope I see you
well this fine evenin.
THE GRASSHOPPER [*prompt and shrill in answer*].   X.X.
THE MAN [*encouragingly*].   Thats right. I suppose now youve come out
to make yourself miserable be admyerin the sunset?
THE GRASSHOPPER [*sadly*].   X.X.
THE MAN.   Aye, youre a true Irish grasshopper.
THE GRASSHOPPER [*loudly*].   X.X.X.
THE MAN.   Three cheers for ould Ireland, is it? That helps you to face
out the misery and the poverty and the torment, doesnt it?

THE GRASSHOPPER [*plaintively*].   X.X.

THE MAN.   Ah, it's no use, me poor little friend. If you could jump as far as a kangaroo you couldn't jump away from your own heart an its punishment. You can only look at Heaven from here: you cant reach it. There! [*pointing with his stick to the sunset*] thats the gate o glory, isnt it?

THE GRASSHOPPER [*assenting*].   X.X.

THE MAN.   Sure its the wise grasshopper yar to know that. But tell me this, Misther Unworldly Wiseman [1]: why does the sight of Heaven wring your heart an mine as the sight of holy wather wrings the heart o the divil? What wickedness have you done to bring that curse on you? Here! where are you jumpin to? Wheres your manners to go skyrocketin like that out o the box in the middle o your confession? [*He threatens it with his stick.*]

THE GRASSHOPPER [*penitently*].   X.

THE MAN [*lowering the stick*].   I accept your apology; but dont do it again. And now tell me one thing before I let you go home to bed. Which would you say this counthry was: hell or purgatory?

THE GRASSHOPPER.   X.

THE MAN.   Hell! Faith I'm afraid youre right. I wondher what you and me did when we were alive to get sent here.

THE GRASSHOPPER [*shrilly*].   X.X.

THE MAN [*nodding*].   Well, as you say, it's a delicate subject; and I wont press it on you. Now off widja.

THE GRASSHOPPER.   X.X. [*It springs away*].

THE MAN [*waving his stick*].   God speed you!

[*He walks away past the stone towards the brow of the hill. Immediately a young laborer, his face distorted with terror, slips round from behind the stone.*]

THE LABORER [*crossing himself repeatedly*].   Oh glory be to God! glory be to God! Oh Holy Mother an all the saints! Oh murdher! murdher! [*Beside himself, calling.*] Fadher Keegan! Fadher Keegan!

THE MAN [*turning*].   Who's there? Whats that?

[*He comes back and finds the laborer, who clasps his knees.*]

Patsy Farrell! What are you doing here?

PATSY.   Oh for the love o God dont lave me here wi dhe grasshopper. I hard it spakin to you. Dont let it do me any harm, Father darlint.

KEEGAN.   Get up, you foolish man, get up. Are you afraid of a poor insect because I pretended it was talking to me?

---

1. Ironic allusion to the allegory of John Bunyan (1628–88), *Pilgrim's Progress* (1678), in which a solitary wanderer named Christian encounters the character Worldly Wiseman from the town of Carnal Policy.

PATSY. Oh, it was no pretendin, Fadher dear. Didnt it give three cheers n say it was a divil out o hell? Oh say youll see me safe home, Fadher; n put a blessin on me or somethin. [*He moans with terror.*]

KEEGAN. What were you doin there, Patsy, listnin? Were you spyin on me?

PATSY. No, Fadher: on me oath an soul I wasnt: I was waitn to meet Master Larry n carry his luggage from the car; n I fell asleep on the grass; n you woke me talkin to the grasshopper; n I hard its wicked little voice. Oh, d'ye think I'll die before the year's out, Fadher?

KEEGAN. For shame, Patsy! Is that your religion, to be afraid of a little deeshy grasshopper? Suppose it was a divil, what call have you to fear it? If I could ketch it, I'd make you take it home widja in your hat for a penance.

PATSY. Sure, if you wont let it harm me, I'm not afraid, your riverence. [*He gets up, a little reassured. He is a callow, flaxen polled, smoothfaced, downy chinned lad, fully grown but not yet fully filled out, with blue eyes and an instinctively acquired air of helplessness and silliness, indicating, not his real character, but a cunning developed by his constant dread of a hostile dominance, which he habitually tries to disarm and tempt into unmasking by pretending to be a much greater fool than he really is. Englishmen think him half-witted, which is exactly what he intends them to think. He is clad in corduroy trousers, unbuttoned waistcoat, and coarse blue striped shirt.*]

KEEGAN [*admonitorily*]. Patsy: what did I tell you about callin me Father Keegan an your reverence? What did Father Dempsey tell you about it?

PATSY. Yis, Fadher.

KEEGAN. Father!

PATSY [*desperately*]. Arra, hwat am I to call you? Fadher Dempsey sez youre not a priest; n we all know youre not a man; n how do we now what ud happen to us if we shewed any disrespect to you? N sure they say wanse a priest always a priest.

KEEGAN [*sternly*]. It's not for the like of you, Patsy, to go behind the instruction of your parish priest and set yourself up to judge whether your Church is right or wrong.

PATSY. Sure I know that, sir.

KEEGAN. The Church let me be its priest as long as it thought me fit for its work. When it took away my papers it meant you to know that I was only a poor madman, unfit and unworthy to take charge of the souls of the people.

PATSY. But wasnt it only because you knew more Latn than Father Dempsey that he was jealous of you?

KEEGAN [*scolding him to keep himself from smiling*]. How dar you, Patsy Farrell, put your own wicked little spites and foolishnesses into the heart of your priest? For two pins I'd tell him what you just said.

PATSY [*coaxing*].   Sure you wouldnt—

KEEGAN.   Wouldnt I? God forgive you! youre little better than a heathen.

PATSY.   Deedn I am, Fadher: it's me bruddher the tinsmith in Dublin youre thinkin of. Sure he had to be a freethinker when he larnt a thrade and went to live in the town.

KEEGAN.   Well, he'll get to Heaven before you if youre not careful, Patsy. And now you listen to me, once and for all. Youll talk to me and pray for me by the name of Pether Keegan, so you will. And when youre angry and tempted to lift your hand agen the donkey or stamp your foot on the little grasshopper, remember that the donkey's Pether Keegan's brother, and the grasshopper Pether Keegan's friend. And when youre tempted to throw a stone at a sinner or a curse at a beggar, remember that Pether Keegan is a worse sinner and a worse beggar, and keep the stone and the curse for him the next time you meet him. Now say God bless you, Pether, to me before I go, just to practise you a bit.

PATSY.   Sure it wouldnt be right, Fadher. I cant—

KEEGAN.   Yes you can. Now out with it; or I'll put this stick into your hand an make you hit me with it.

PATSY [*throwing himself on his knees in an ecstasy of adoration*].   Sure it's your blessin I want, Fadher Keegan. I'll have no luck widhout it.

KEEGAN [*shocked*].   Get up out o that, man. Dont kneel to me: I'm not a saint.

PATSY [*with intense conviction*].   On in throth yar, sir.

> [*The grasshopper chirps.* PATSY, *terrified, clutches at* KEEGAN's *hands.*]

Dont set it on me, Fadher: I'll do anythin you bid me.

KEEGAN [*pulling him up*].   You bosthoon, you! Dont you see that it only whistled to tell me Miss Reilly's comin? There! Look at her and pull yourself together for shame. Off widja to the road: youll be late for the car if you dont make haste [*bustling him down the hill*]. I can see the dust of it in the gap already.

PATSY.   The Lord save us! [*He goes down the hill towards the road like a haunted man.*]

> [NORA REILLY *comes down the hill. A slight weak woman in a pretty muslin print gown (her best), she is a figure commonplace enough to Irish eyes; but on the inhabitants of fatter-fed, crowded, hustling and bustling modern countries she makes a very different impression. The absence of any symptoms of coarseness or hardness or appetite in her, her comparative delicacy of manner and sensibility of apprehension, her fine hands and frail figure, her novel accent, with the caressing plaintive Irish melody of her speech, give her a charm which is all the more effective because,*]

being untravelled, she is unconscious of it, and never dreams of deliberately dramatizing and exploiting it, as the Irishwomen in England do. For TOM BROADBENT *therefore, an attractive woman, whom he would even call ethereal.* To LARRY DOYLE, *an everyday woman fit only for the eighteenth century, helpless, useless, almost sexless, an invalid without the excuse of disease, an incarnation of everything in Ireland that drove him out of it. These judgements have little value and no finality; but they are the judgments on which her fate hangs just at present.* KEEGAN *touches his hat to her: he does not take it off.*]

NORA.   Mr Keegan: I want to speak to you a minute if you dont mind.

KEEGAN [*dropping the broad Irish vernacular of his speech to* PATSY].   An hour if you like, Miss Reilly: youre always welcome. Shall we sit down?

NORA.   Thank you. [*They sit on the heather. She is shy and anxious; but she comes to the point promptly because she can think of nothing else.*] They say you did a gradle[2] o travelling at one time.

KEEGAN.   Well, you see I'm not a Mnooth man [*he means that he was not a student at Maynooth College*].[3] When I was young I admired the older generation of priests that had been educated in Salamanca. So when I felt sure of my vocation I went to Salamanca. Then I walked from Salamanca to Rome, an sted in a monastery there for a year. My pilgrimage to Rome taught me that walking is a better way of travelling than the train; so I walked from Rome to the Sorbonne in Paris; and I wish I could have walked from Paris to Oxford; for I was very sick on the sea. After a year of Oxford I had to walk to Jerusalem to walk the Oxford feeling off me. From Jerusalem I came back to Patmos, and spent six months at the monastery of Mount Athos. From that I came to Ireland and settled down as a parish priest until I went mad.

NORA [*startled*].   Oh dont say that.

KEEGAN.   Why not? Dont you know the story? how I confessed a black man and gave him absolution? and how he put a spell on me and drove me mad?

NORA.   How can you talk such nonsense about yourself? For shame!

KEEGAN.   It's not nonsense at all: it's true—in a way. But never mind the black man. Now that you know what a travelled man I am, what can I do for you?

[*She hesitates and plucks nervously at the heather. He stays her hand gently.*]

Dear Miss Nora: dont pluck the little flower. If it was a pretty baby you wouldn't want to pull its head off and stick it in a vawse o water

2. A great deal.   3. Principal seminary in Ireland.

to look at. [*The grasshopper chirps:* KEEGAN *turns his head and addresses it in the vernacular.*] Be aisy, me son: she wont spoil the swing-swong in your little three. [*To* NORA, *resuming his urbane style.*] You see I'm quite cracked; but never mind: I'm harmless. Now what is it?

NORA [*embarrassed*].   Oh, only idle curiosity. I wanted to know whether you found Ireland—I mean the country part of Ireland, of course— very small and backwardlike when you came back to it from Rome and Oxford and all the great cities.

KEEGAN.   When I went to those great cities I saw wonders I had never seen in Ireland. But when I came back to Ireland I found all the wonders there waiting for me. You see they had been there all the time; but my eyes had never been opened to them. I did not know what my own house was like, because I had never been outside it.

NORA.   D'ye think thats the same with everybody?

KEEGAN.   With everybody who has eyes in his soul as well as in his head.

NORA.   But really and truly now, werent the people rather disappointing? I should think the girls must have seemed rather coarse and dowdy after the foreign princesses and people? But I suppose a priest wouldnt notice that.

KEEGAN.   It's a priest's business to notice everything. I wont tell you all I noticed about women; but I'll tell you this. The more a man knows, and the farther he travels, the more likely he is to marry a country girl afterwards.

NORA [*blushing with delight*].   Youre joking, Mr Keegan: I'm sure yar.

KEEGAN.   My way of joking is to tell the truth. It's the funniest joke in the world.

NORA [*incredulous*].   Galong with you!

KEEGAN [*springing up actively*].   Shall we go down to the road and meet the car?

[*She gives him her hand and he helps her up.*]

Patsy Farrell told me you were expecting young Doyle.

NORA [*tossing her chin up at once*].   Oh, I'm not expecting him particularly. It's a wonder he's come back at all. After staying away eighteen years he can harly expect us to be very anxious to see him: can he now?

KEEGAN.   Well, not anxious perhaps; but you will be curious to see how much he's changed in all these years.

NORA [*with a sudden bitter flush*].   I suppose thats all that brings him back to look at us, just to see how much weve changed. Well, he can wait and to see me be candlelight: I didn't come out to meet him: I'm going to walk to the Round Tower [*going west across the hill.*]

KEEGAN.   You couldnt do better this fine evening. [*Gravely.*] I'll tell him where youve gone.

[*She turns as if to forbid him; but the deep understanding in his eyes makes that impossible; and she only looks at him earnestly and goes. He watches her disappear on the other side of the hill; then says*]

Aye, he's come to torment you; and youre driven already to torment him. [*He shakes his head, and goes slowly away across the hill in the opposite direction, lost in thought.*]

[*By this time the car has arrived, and dropped three of its passengers on the high road at the foot of the hill. It is a monster jaunting car, black and dilapidated, one of the last survivors of the public vehicles known to earlier generations as Beeyankiny cars, the Irish having laid violent tongues on the name of their projector, one Bianconi, an enterprising Italian. The three passengers are the parish priest,* FATHER DEMPSEY; CORNELIUS DOYLE, LARRY's *father; and* BROADBENT, *all in overcoats and as stiff as only an Irish car could make them.*

The priest, stout and fatherly, falls far short of that finest type of countryside pastor which represents the genius of priesthood; but he is equally far above the base type in which a strongminded unscrupulous peasant uses the Church to extort money, power, and privilege. He is a priest neither by vocation nor ambition, but because the life suits him. He has boundless authority over his flock, and taxes them stiffly enough to be a rich man. The old Protestant ascendency is now too broken to gall him. On the whole, an easygoing, amiable, even modest man as long as his dues are paid and his authority and dignity fully admitted.

CORNELIUS DOYLE *is an elder of the small wiry type, with a hardskinned, rather worried face, clean shaven except for sandy whiskers blanching into a lustreless pale yellow and quite white at the roots. His dress is that of a country-town man of business: that is, an oldish shooting suit, with elastic sided boots quite unconnected with shooting. Feeling shy with* BROADBENT, *he is hasty, which is his way of trying to appear genial.*

BROADBENT, *for reasons which will appear later, has no luggage except a field glass and a guide book. The other two have left theirs to the unfortunate* PATSY FARRELL, *who struggles up the hill after them, loaded with a sack of potatoes, a hamper, a fat goose, a colossal salmon, and several paper parcels.*

CORNELIUS *leads the way up the hill, with* BROADBENT *at his heels. The priest follows.* PATSY *lags laboriously behind.*]

CORNELIUS.   This is a bit of a climb, Mr Broadbent; but it's shorter than goin round be the road.

BROADBENT [*stopping to examine the great stone*].   Just a moment, Mr

Doyle: I want to look at this stone. It must be Finian's die-cast.

CORNELIUS [*in blank bewilderment*].   Hwat?

BROADBENT.   Murray describes it. One of your great national heroes—
I cant pronounce the name—Finian Somebody, I think.

FATHER DEMPSEY [*also perplexed, and rather scandalized*].   Is it Fin
McCool you mean?

BROADBENT.   I daresay it is. [*Referring to the guide book.*] Murray says
that a huge stone, probably of Druidic origin, is still pointed out as
the die cast by Fin in his celebrated match with the devil.

CORNELIUS [*dubiously*].   Jeuce a word I ever heard of it!

FATHER DEMPSEY [*very seriously indeed, and even a little severely*].   Dont
believe any such nonsense, sir. There never was any such thing. When
people talk to you about Fin McCool and the like, take no notice of
them. It's all idle stories and superstition.

BROADBENT [*somewhat indignantly; for to be rebuked by an Irish priest
for superstition is more than he can stand*].   You dont suppose I believe
it, do you?

FATHER DEMPSEY.   Oh, I thought you did. D'ye see the top o the Roun
Tower there? thats an antiquity worth lookin at.

BROADBENT [*deeply interested*].   Have you any theory as to what the
Round Towers were for?

FATHER DEMPSEY [*a little offended*].   A theory? Me! [*Theories are connected in his mind with the late Professor Tyndall,*[4] *and with scientific
scepticism generally: also perhaps with the view that the Round Towers
are phallic symbols.*]

CORNELIUS [*remonstrating*].   Father Dempsey is the priest of the parish,
Mr Broadbent. What would he be doing with a theory?

FATHER DEMPSEY [*with gentle emphasis*].   I have a knowledge of what
the Roun Towers were, if thats what you mean. They are the forefin-
gers of the early Church, pointing us all to God.

> [PATSY, *intolerably overburdened, loses his balance, and sits down
> involuntarily. His burdens are scattered over the hillside.* COR-
> NELIUS *and* FATHER DEMPSEY *turn furiously on him, leaving*
> BROADBENT *beaming at the stone and the tower with fatuous
> interest.*]

CORNELIUS.   Oh, be the hokey, the sammin's broke in two! You schoopid
ass, what d'ye mean?

FATHER DEMPSEY.   Are you drunk, Patsy Farrell? Did I tell you to carry
that hamper carefully or did I not?

PATSY [*rubbing the back of his head, which has almost dinted a slab of
granite*].   Sure me futslipt. Howkn I carry three men's luggage at
wanst?

---

4. John Tyndall (1820–93), professor of natural history and popularizer of science in books and lectures.

FATHER DEMPSEY. You were told to leave behind what you couldnt carry, an go back for it.

PATSY. An whose things was I to lave behind? Hwat would your reverence think if I left your hamper behind in the wet grass; n hwat would the masther say if I left the sammin and the goose be the side o the road for annywan to pick up?

CORNELIUS. Oh, youve a dale to say for yourself, you butther-fingered omadhaun.[5] Waitll Ant Judy sees the state o that sammin: she'll talk to you. Here! gimmy that birdn that fish there; an take Father Dempsey's hamper to his house for him; n then come back for the rest.

FATHER DEMPSEY. Do, Patsy. And mind you dont fall down again.

PATSY. Sure I—

CORNELIUS [bustling him up the hill]. Whisht! heres Ant Judy.

> [PATSY goes grumbling in disgrace, with FATHER DEMPSEY's hamper.]
>
> [AUNT JUDY comes down the hill, a woman of 50, in no way remarkable, lively and busy without energy or grip, placid without tranquility, kindly without concern for others: indeed without much concern for herself: a contented product of a narrow, strainless life. She wears her hair parted in the middle and quite smooth, with a flattened bun at the back. Her dress is a plain brown frock, with a woollen pelerine of black and aniline mauve over her shoulders, all very trim in honor of the occasion. She looks round for LARRY; is puzzled; then stares incredulously at Broadbent.]

AUNT JUDY. Surely to goodness thats not you, Larry!

CORNELIUS. Arra how could he be Larry, woman alive? Larry's in no hurry home, it seems. I havnt set eyes on him. This is his friend, Mr Broadbent. Mr Broadbent: me sister Judy.

AUNT JUDY [hospitably: going to BROADBENT and shaking hands heartily]. Mr Broadbent! Fancy me takin you for Larry! Sure we havnt seen a sight of him for eighteen years, n he ony a lad when he left us.

BROADBENT. It's not Larry's fault: he was to have been here before me. He started in our motor an hour before Mr Doyle arrived, to meet us at Athenmullet, intending to get here long before me.

AUNT JUDY. Lord save us! do you think he's had n axidnt?

BROADBENT. No: he's wired to say he's had a breakdown and will come on as soon as he can. He expects to be here at about ten.

AUNT JUDY. There now! Fancy him trustn himself in a motor and we all expectn him! Just like him! he'd never do anything like anybody else. Well, what cant be cured must be injoored. Come on in, all of you. You must be dyin for your tea, Mr Broadbent.

5. Fool.

BROADBENT [*with a slight start*]. Oh, I'm afraid it's too late for tea. [*He looks at his watch.*]

AUNT JUDY. Not a bit: we never have it airlier than this. I hope they gave you a good dinner at Athenmullet.

BROADBENT [*trying to conceal his consternation as he realizes that he is not going to get any dinner after his drive*]. Oh—er—excellent, excellent. By the way, hadnt I better see about a room at the hotel? [*They stare at him.*]

CORNELIUS. The hotel!

FATHER DEMPSEY. Hwat hotel?

AUNT JUDY. Indeedn youre not goin to a hotel. Youll stay with us. I'd have put you into Larry's room, ony the boy's pallyass is too short for you; but we'll make a comfortable bed for you on the sofa in the parlor.

BROADBENT. Youre very kind, Miss Doyle; but really I'm ashamed to give you so much trouble unnecessarily. I shant mind the hotel in the least.

FATHER DEMPSEY. Man alive! theres no hotel in Rosscullen.

BROADBENT. No hotel! Why, the driver told me there was the finest hotel in Ireland here.

[*They regard him joylessly.*]

AUNT JUDY. Arra would you mind what the like of him would tell you? Sure he'd say hwatever was the least trouble to himself and the pleasantest to you, thinkin you might give him a thruppeny bit for himself or the like.

BROADBENT. Perhaps theres a public house.

FATHER DEMPSEY [*grimly*]. Theres seventeen.

AUNT JUDY. Ah then, how could you stay at a public house? theyd have no place to put you even if it was a right place for you to go. Come! is it the sofa youre afraid of? If it is, you can have me own bed. I can sleep with Nora.

BROADBENT. Not at all, not at all: I should be only too delighted. But to upset your arrangements in this way—

CORNELIUS [*anxious to cut short the discussion, which makes him ashamed of his house; for he guesses* BROADBENT'*s standard of comfort a little more accurately than his sister does*]. Thats all right: itll be no trouble at all. Hweres Nora?

AUNT JUDY. Oh, how do I know? She slipped out a little while ago: I thought she was goin to meet the car.

CORNELIUS [*dissatisfied*]. It's a queer thing of her to run out o the way at such a time.

AUNT JUDY. Sure she's a queer girl altogether. Come. Come in: come in.

FATHER DEMPSEY. I'll say good-night, Mr Broadbent. If theres anything I can do for you in this parish, let me know.

[*He shakes hands with* BROADBENT.]

BROADBENT [*effusively cordial*].   Thank you, Father Dempsey. Delighted to have met you, sir.

FATHER DEMPSEY [*passing on to* AUNT JUDY].   Good-night, Miss Doyle.

AUNT JUDY.   Wont you stay to tea?

FATHER DEMPSEY.   Not to-night, thank you kindly: I have business to do at home.

[*He turns to go, and meets* PATSY FARRELL *returning unloaded.*]

Have you left that hamper for me?

PATSY.   Yis, your reverence.

FATHER DEMPSEY.   Thats a good lad [*going*].

PATSY [*to* AUNT JUDY].   Fadher Keegan sez—

FATHER DEMPSEY [*turning sharply on him*].   Whats that you say?

PATSY [*frightened*].   Fadher Keegan—

FATHER DEMPSEY.   How often have you heard me bid you call Mister Keegan in his proper name, the same as I do? Father Keegan indeed! Cant you tell the difference between your priest and any ole madman in a black coat?

PATSY.   Sure I'm afraid he might put a spell on me.

FATHER DEMPSEY [*wrathfully*].   You mind what I tell you or I'll put a spell on you thatll make you lep. D'ye mind that now? [*He goes home.*]

[PATSY *goes down the hill to retrieve the fish, the bird, and the sack.*]

AUNT JUDY.   Ah, hwy cant you hold your tongue, Patsy, before Father Dempsey?

PATSY.   Well, hwat was I to do? Father Keegan bid me tell you Miss Nora was gone to the Roun Tower.

AUNT JUDY.   An hwy couldnt you wait to tell us until Father Dempsey was gone?

PATSY.   I was afeerd o forgetn it; and then may be he'd a sent the grass-hopper or the little dark looker into me at night to remind me of it. [*The dark looker is the common grey lizard, which is supposed to walk down the throats of incautious sleepers and cause them to perish in a slow decline.*]

CORNELIUS.   Yah, you great gaum,[6] you! Widjer grasshoppers and dark lookers! Here: take up them things and let me hear no more o your foolish lip.

[PATSY *obeys.*]

You can take the sammin under your oxther. [*He wedges the salmon into* PATSY's *axilla.*]

6. Buffoon.

PATSY.   I can take the goose too, sir. Put it on me back n gimmy the neck of it in me mouth.

[CORNELIUS *is about to comply thoughtlessly.*]

AUNT JUDY [*feeling that* BROADBENT'*s presence demands special puncti- liousness.*] For shame, Patsy! to offer to take the goose in your mouth that we have to eat after you! The masterll bring it in for you.

PATSY.   Arra what would a dead goose care for me mouth? [*He takes his load up the hill.*]

CORNELIUS.   Hwats Nora doin at the Roun Tower?

AUNT JUDY.   Oh, the Lord knows! Romancin, I suppose. Praps she thinks Larry would go there to look for her and see her safe home.

BROADBENT.   Miss Reilly must not be left to wait and walk home alone at night. Shall I go for her?

AUNT JUDY [*contemptuously*].   Arra hwat ud happen to her? Hurry in now, Corny. Come, Mr Broadbent: 1 left the tea on the hob to draw; and itll be black if we dont go in an drink it.

[They go up the hill. It is dusk by this time.

BROADBENT *does not fare so badly after all at* AUNT JUDY'*s board. He gets not only tea and bread-and-butter, but more mutton chops than he has ever conceived it possible to eat at one sitting. There is also a most filling substance called potato cake. Hardly have his fears of being starved been replaced by his first misgiving that he is eating too much and will be sorry for it tomorrow, when his appetite is revived by the production of a bottle of illicitly distilled whisky, called potcheen, which he has read and dreamed of (he calls it pottine) and is now at last to taste. His goodhumor rises almost to excitement before* CORNE- LIUS *shews signs of sleepiness. The contrast between* AUNT JUDY'*s table service and that of the south and east coast hotels at which he spends his Fridays-to-Tuesdays when he is in London, seems to him delightfully Irish. The almost total atrophy of any sense of enjoyment in* CORNELIUS, *or even any desire for it or toleration of the possibility of life being something better than a round of sordid worries, relieved by tobacco, punch, fine mornings, and petty successes in buying and selling, passes with his guest as the whimsical affectation of a shrewd Irish humorist and incorrigible spendthrift.* AUNT JUDY *seems to him an incarnate joke. The like- lihood that the joke will pall after a month or so, and is probably not apparent at any time to born Rossculleners, or that he him- self unconsciously entertains* AUNT JUDY *by his fantastic English personality and English mispronunciations, does not occur to him for a moment. In the end he is so charmed, and so loth to go to bed and perhaps dream of prosaic England, that he insists on going out to smoke a cigar and look for* NORA REILLY *at the Round Tower. Not that any special insistence is needed; for the English inhibitive instinct does not seem to exist in Rosscullen. Just as* NORA's *liking to miss a meal and stay out at the Round Tower is accepted as a sufficient reason for her doing it, and for the family going to bed and leaving the door open for her, so* BROADBENT's *whim to go out for a late stroll provokes neither hospitable remonstrance nor surprise. Indeed* AUNT JUDY *wants to get rid of him whilst she makes a bed for him on the sofa. So off he goes, full fed, happy and enthusiastic, to explore the valley by moonlight.*

The Round Tower stands about half an Irish mile from Rosscullen, some fifty yards south of the road on a knoll with a circle of wild greensward on it. The road once ran over this knoll; but modern engineering has tempered the level to the Beeyankiny car by carrying the road partly round the knoll and partly through a cutting; so that the way from the road to the tower is a footpath up the embankment through furze and brambles.

On the edge of this slope, at the top of the path, NORA *is straining her eyes in the moonlight, watching for* LARRY. *At last she gives it up with a sob of impatience, and retreats to the hoary foot of the tower, where she sits down discouraged and cries a little. Then she settles herself resignedly to wait, and hums a song— not an Irish melody, but a hackneyed English drawing room ballad of the season before last— until some slight noise suggests a footstep, when she springs up eagerly and runs to the edge of the slope again. Some moments of silence and suspense follow, broken by unmistakable footsteps. She gives a little gasp as she sees a man approaching.*]

NORA. Is that you, Larry? [*Frightened a little.*] Who's that?

BROADBENT's *voice from below on the path.* Dont be alarmed.

NORA. Oh, what an English accent youve got!

BROADBENT [*rising into view*]. I must introduce myself—

NORA [*violently startled, retreating*]. It's not you! Who are you? What do you want?

BROADBENT [*advancing*]. I'm really so sorry to have alarmed you, Miss Reilly. My name is Broadbent. Larry's friend, you know.

NORA [*chilled*]. And has Mr Doyle not come with you?

BROADBENT. No. Ive come instead. I hope I am not unwelcome.

NORA [*deeply mortified*]. I'm sorry Mr Doyle should have given you the trouble, I'm sure.

BROADBENT. You see, as a stranger and an Englishman, I thought it would be interesting to see the Round Tower by moonlight.

NORA. Oh, you came to see the tower. I thought—[*confused, trying to*

recover her manners]. Oh, of course. I was so startled. It's a beautiful
night, isn't it?

BROADBENT.   Lovely. I must explain why Larry has not come himself.

NORA.   Why should he come? He's seen the tower often enough: it's no
attraction to him. [*Genteelly.*] An what do you think of Ireland, Mr
Broadbent? Have you ever been here before?

BROADBENT.   Never.

NORA.   An how do you like it?

BROADBENT [*suddenly betraying a condition of extreme sentimentality*].   I can hardly trust myself to say how much I like it. The magic
of this Irish scene, and—I really dont want to be personal, Miss Reilly;
but the charm of your Irish voice—

NORA [*quite accustomed to gallantry, and attaching no seriousness whatever to it*].   Oh, get along with you, Mr Broadbent! Youre breaking
your heart about me already, I daresay, after seeing me for two minutes in the dark.

BROADBENT.   The voice is just as beautiful in the dark, you know. Besides,
Ive heard a great deal about you from Larry.

NORA [*with bitter indifference*].   Have you now? Well, thats a great honor,
I'm sure.

BROADBENT.   I have looked forward to meeting you more than to anything else in Ireland.

NORA [*ironically*].   Dear me! did you now?

BROADBENT.   I did really. I wish you had taken half as much interest in
me.

NORA.   Oh, I was dying to see you, of course. I daresay you can imagine
the sensation an Englishman like you would make among us poor
Irish people.

BROADBENT.   Ah, now youre chaffing me, Miss Reilly: you know you
are. You mustnt chaff me. I'm very much in earnest about Ireland
and everything Irish. I'm very much in earnest about you and about
Larry.

NORA.   Larry has nothing to do with me, Mr Broadbent.

BROADBENT.   If I really thought that, Miss Reilly, I should—well, I
should let myself feel that charm of which I spoke just now more
deeply than I—than I—

NORA.   Is it making love to me you are?

BROADBENT [*scared and much upset*].   On my word I believe I am, Miss
Reilly. If you say that to me again I shant answer for myself: all the
harps of Ireland are in your voice.

[*She laughs at him. He suddenly loses his head and seizes her
arms, to her great indignation.*]

Stop laughing: do you hear! I am in earnest: in English earnest. When
I say a thing like that to a woman, I mean it. [*Releasing her and trying*

to recover his ordinary manner in spite of his bewildering emotion.] I beg your pardon.

NORA. How dare you touch me?

BROADBENT. There are not many things I would not dare for you. That does not sound right perhaps; but I really—[*He stops and passes his hand over his forehead, rather lost.*]

NORA. I think you ought to be ashamed. I think if you were a gentleman, and me alone with you in this place at night, you would die rather than do such a thing.

BROADBENT. You mean that it's an act of treachery to Larry?

NORA. Deed I dont. What has Larry to do with it? It's an act of disrespect and rudeness to me: it shews what you take me for. You can go your way now; and I'll go mine. Goodnight, Mr Broadbent.

BROADBENT. No, please, Miss Reilly. One moment. Listen to me. I'm serious: I'm desperately serious. Tell me that I'm interfering with Larry; and I'll go straight from this spot back to London and never see you again. Thats on my honor: I will. Am I interfering with him?

NORA [*answering in spite of herself in a sudden spring of bitterness*]. I should think you ought to know better than me whether youre interfering with him. Youve seen him oftener than I have. You know him better than I do, by this time. Youve come to me quicker than he has, havnt you?

BROADBENT. I'm bound to tell you, Miss Reilly, that Larry has not arrived in Rosscullen yet. He meant to get here before me; but his car broke down; and he may not arrive until to-morrow.

NORA [*her face lighting up*]. Is that the truth?

BROADBENT. Yes: thats the truth.

[*She gives a sigh of relief.*]

Youre glad of that?

NORA [*up in arms at once*]. Glad indeed! Why should I be glad? As weve waited eighteen years for him we can afford to wait a day longer, I should think.

BROADBENT. If you really feel like that about him, there may be a chance for another man yet. Eh?

NORA [*deeply offended*]. I suppose people are different in England, Mr Broadbent; so perhaps you dont mean any harm. In Ireland nobody'd mind what a man'd say in fun, nor take advantage of what a woman might say in answer to it. If a woman couldnt talk to a man for two minutes at their first meeting without being treated the way youre treating me, no decent woman would ever talk to a man at all.

BROADBENT. I dont understand that. I dont admit that. I am sincere; and my intentions are perfectly honorable. I think you will accept the fact that I'm an Englishman as a guarantee that I am not a man to act hastily or romantically; though I confess that your voice had such an extraordinary effect on me just now when you asked me so quaintly whether I was making love to you—

NORA [*flushing*].   I never thought—

BROADBENT [*quickly*].   Of course you didnt: I'm not so stupid as that. But I couldnt bear your laughing at the feeling it gave me. You—[*again struggling with a surge of emotion*] you dont know what I—[*he chokes for a moment and then blurts out with unnatural steadiness*] Will you be my wife?

NORA [*promptly*].   Deed I wont. The idea! [*Looking at him more carefully.*] Arra, come home, Mr Broadbent; and get your senses back again. I think youre not accustomed to potcheen punch in the evening after your tea.

BROADBENT [*horrified*].   Do you mean to say that I—I—I—my God! that I appear drunk to you, Miss Reilly?

NORA [*compassionately*].   How many tumblers had you?

BROADBENT [*helplessly*].   Two.

NORA.   The flavor of the turf prevented you noticing the strength of it. Youd better come home to bed.

BROADBENT [*fearfully agitated*].   But this is such a horrible doubt to put into my mind—to—to—For Heaven's sake, Miss Reilly, am I really drunk?

NORA [*soothingly*].   Youll be able to judge better in the morning. Come on now back with me, an think no more about it.

[*She takes his arm with motherly solicitude and urges him gently towards the path.*]

BROADBENT [*yielding in despair*].   I must be drunk: frightfully drunk; for your voice drove me out of my senses—[*he stumbles over a stone*]. No: on my word, on my most sacred word of honor, Miss Reilly, I tripped over that stone. It was an accident: it was indeed.

NORA.   Yes, of course it was. Just take my arm, Mr Broadbent, while we're goin down the path to the road. Youll be all right then.

BROADBENT [*submissively taking it*].   I cant sufficiently apologize, Miss Reilly, or express my sense of your kindness when I am in such a disgusting state. How could I be such a bea—[*he trips again*] damn the heather! my foot caught in it.

NORA.   Steady now, steady. Come along: come.

[*He is led down to the road in the character of a convicted drunkard. To him there is something divine in the sympathetic indulgence she substitutes for the angry disgust with which one of his own countrywomen would resent his supposed condition. And he has no suspicion of the fact, or of her ignorance of it, that when an Englishman is sentimental he behaves very much as an Irishman does when he is drunk.*]

Act Three

Next morning BROADBENT *and* LARRY *are sitting at the ends of a breakfast table in the middle of a small grass plot before* CORNELIUS DOYLE's *house. They have finished their meal, and are buried in newspapers. Most of the crockery is crowded upon a large square black tray of japanned metal. The teapot is of brown delft ware. There is no silver; and the butter, on a dinner plate, is en bloc. The background to this breakfast is the house, a small white slated building, accessible by a half-glazed door. A person coming out into the garden by this door would find the table straight in front of him, and a gate leading to the road half way down the garden on his right; or, if he turned sharp to his left, he could pass round the end of the house through an unkempt shrubbery. The mutilated remnant of a huge plaster statue, nearly dissolved by the rains of a century, and vaguely resembling a majestic female in Roman draperies, with a wreath in her hand, stands neglected amid the laurels. Such statues, though apparently works of art, grow naturally in Irish gardens. Their germination is a mystery to the oldest inhabitants, to whose means and tastes they are totally foreign.*

There is a rustic bench, much soiled by the birds, and decorticated and split by the weather, near the little gate. At the opposite side, a basket lies unmolested because it might as well be there as anywhere else. An empty chair at the table was lately occupied by CORNELIUS, *who has finished his breakfast and gone in to the room in which he receives rents and keeps his books and cash, known in the household as "the office." This chair, like the two occupied by* LARRY *and* BROADBENT, *has a mahogany frame and is upholstered in black horsehair.*

LARRY *rises and goes off through the shrubbery with his newspaper.* HODSON *comes in through the garden gate, disconsolate.* BROADBENT, *who sits facing the gate, augurs the worst from his expression.*

BROADBENT.   Have you been to the village?

HODSON.   No use, sir. We'll have to get everything from London by parcel post.

BROADBENT.   I hope they made you comfortable last night.

HODSON.   I was no worse than you were on that sofa, sir. One expects to rough it here, sir.

BROADBENT.   We shall have to look out for some other arrangement. [*Cheering up irrepressibly.*] Still, it's no end of a joke. How do you like the Irish, Hodson?

HODSON.   Well, sir, theyre all right anywhere but in their own country. Ive known lots of em in England, and generally liked em. But here, sir, I seem simply to hate em. The feeling come over me the moment we landed at Cork, sir. It's no use my pretendin, sir: I cant bear em. My mind rises up agin their ways, somehow: they rub me the wrong way all over.

BROADBENT.   Oh, their faults are on the surface: at heart they are one of the finest races on earth.

> [HODSON *turns away, without affecting to respond to his enthusiasm.*]

By the way, Hodson—

HODSON [*turning*].   Yes, sir.

BROADBENT.   Did you notice anything about me last night when I came in with that lady?

HODSON [*surprised*].   No, sir.

BROADBENT.   Not any—er—? You may speak frankly.

HODSON.   I didnt notice nothing, sir. What sort of thing did you mean, sir?

BROADBENT.   Well—er—er—well, to put it plainly, was I drunk?

HODSON [*amazed*].   No, sir.

BROADBENT.   Quite sure?

HODSON.   Well, I should a said rather the opposite, sir. Usually when youve been enjoying yourself, youre a bit hearty like. Last night you seemed rather low, if anything.

BROADBENT.   I certainly have no headache. Did you try the pottine, Hodson?

HODSON.   I just took a mouthful, sir. It tasted of peat: oh! something horrid, sir. The people here call peat turf. Potcheen and strong porter is what they like, sir. I'm sure I dont know how they can stand it. Give me beer, I say.

BROADBENT.   By the way, you told me I couldnt have porridge for breakfast; but Mr Doyle had some.

HODSON.   Yes, sir. Very sorry, sir. They call it stirabout, sir: thats how it was. They know no better, sir.

BROADBENT.   All right: I'll have some tomorrow.

> [HODSON *goes to the house. When he opens the door he finds* NORA *and* AUNT JUDY *on the threshold. He stands aside to let them pass, with the air of a well trained servant oppressed by heavy trials. Then he goes in.* BROADBENT *rises.* AUNT JUDY *goes to the table and collects the plates and cups on the tray.* NORA *goes to the back of the rustic seat and looks out at the gate with the air of a woman accustomed to having nothing to do.* LARRY *returns from the shrubbery.*]

BROADBENT.   Good morning, Miss Doyle.

AUNT JUDY [*thinking it absurdly late in the day for such a salutation*].   Oh, good morning. [*Before moving his plate.*] Have you done?

BROADBENT.   Quite, thank you. You must excuse us for not waiting for you. The country air tempted us to get up early.

AUNT JUDY.   N d'ye call this airly, God help you?

LARRY.   Aunt Judy probably breakfasted about half past six.

AUNT JUDY. Whisht, you! draggin the parlor chairs out into the gardn n givin Mr Broadbent his death over his meals out here in the cold air. [*To* BROADBENT.] Why d'ye put up with his foolishness, Mr Broadbent?

BROADBENT. I assure you I like the open air.

AUNT JUDY. Ah galong! How can you like whats not natural? I hope you slept well.

NORA. Did anything wake yup with a thump at three o'clock? I thought the house was falling. But then I'm a very light sleeper.

LARRY. I seem to recollect that one of the legs of the sofa in the parlor had a way of coming out unexpectedly eighteen years ago. Was that it, Tom?

BROADBENT [*hastily*]. Oh, it doesnt matter: I was not hurt—at least—er—

AUNT JUDY. Oh now what a shame! An I told Patsy Farrll to put a nail in it.

BROADBENT. He did, Miss Doyle. There was a nail, certainly.

AUNT JUDY. Dear oh dear!

[*An oldish peasant farmer, small, leathery, peat-faced, with a deep voice and a surliness that is meant to be aggressive, and is in effect pathetic—the voice of a man of hard life and many sorrows—comes in at the gate. He is old enough to have perhaps worn a long tailed frieze coat and knee breeches in his time; but now he is dressed respectably in a black frock coat, tall hat, and pollard colored trousers; and his face is as clean as washing can make it, though that is not saying much, as the habit is recently acquired and not yet congenial.*]

THE NEW-COMER [*at the gate*]. God save all here! [*He comes a little way into the garden.*]

LARRY [*patronizingly, speaking across the garden to him*]. Is that yourself, Matt Haffigan? Do you remember me?

MATTHEW [*intentionally rude and blunt*]. No. Who are you?

NORA. Oh, I'm sure you remember him, Mr Haffigan.

MATTHEW [*grudgingly admitting it*]. I suppose he'll be young Larry Doyle that was.

LARRY. Yes.

MATTHEW [*to* LARRY]. I hear you done well in America.

LARRY. Fairly well.

MATTHEW. I suppose you saw me brother Andy out dhere.

LARRY. No. It's such a big place that looking for a man there is like looking for a needle in a bundle of hay. They tell me he's a great man out there.

MATTHEW. So he is, God be praised. Wheres your father?

AUNT JUDY. He's inside, in the office, Mr Haffigan, with Barney Doarn n Father Dempsey.

[MATTHEW, *without wasting further words on the company, goes curtly into the house.*]

LARRY [*staring after him*]. Is anything wrong with old Matt?

NORA. No. He's the same as ever. Why?

LARRY. He's not the same to me. He used to be very civil to Masther Larry: a deal too civil, I used to think. Now he's as surly and stand-off as a bear.

AUNT JUDY. Oh sure he's bought his farm in the Land Purchase. He's independent now.

NORA. It's made a great change, Larry. Youd harly know the old tenants now. Youd think it was a liberty to speak t'dhem—some o dhem.

[*She goes to the table, and helps to take off the cloth, which she and* AUNT JUDY *fold up between them.*]

AUNT JUDY. I wonder what he wants to see Corny for. He hasnt been here since he paid the last of his old rent; and then he as good as threw it in Corny's face, I thought.

LARRY. No wonder! Of course they all hated us like the devil. Ugh! [*Moodily.*] Ive seen them in that office, telling my father what a fine boy I was, and plastering him with compliments, with your honor here and your honor there, when all the time their fingers were itching to be at his throat.

AUNT JUDY. Deedn why should they want to hurt poor Corny? It was he that got Matt the lease of his farm, and stood up for him as an industrious decent man.

BROADBENT. Was he industrious? Thats remarkable, you know, in an Irishman.

LARRY. Industrious! That man's industry used to make me sick, even as a boy. I tell you, an Irish peasant's industry is not human: it's worse than the industry of a coral insect. An Englishman has some sense about working: he never does more than he can help—and hard enough to get him to do that without scamping it; but an Irishman will work as if he'd die the moment he stopped. That man Matthew Haffigan and his brother Andy made a farm out of a patch of stones on the hillside: cleared it and dug it with their own naked hands and bought their first spade out of their first crop of potatoes. Talk of making two blades of wheat grow where one grew before! those two men made a whole field of wheat grow where not even a furze bush had ever got its head up between the stones.

BROADBENT. That was magnificent, you know. Only a great race is capable of producing such men.

LARRY. Such fools, you mean! What good was it to them? The moment theyd done it, the landlord put a rent of £5 a year on them, and turned them out because they coudnt pay it.

AUNT JUDY.   Why coudnt they pay as well as Billy Byrne that took it after them?

LARRY [*angrily*].   You know very well that Billy Byrne never paid it. He only offered it to get possession. He never paid it.

AUNT JUDY.   That was because Andy Haffigan hurt him with a brick so that he was never the same again. Andy had to run away to America for it.

BROADBENT [*glowing with indignation*].   Who can blame him, Miss Doyle? Who can blame him?

LARRY [*impatiently*].   Oh, rubbish! whats the good of the man thats starved out of a farm murdering the man thats starved into it? Would you have done such a thing!

BROADBENT.   Yes. I—I—I—I—[*stammering with fury*] I should have shot the confounded landlord, and wrung the neck of the damned agent, and blown the farm up with dynamite, and Dublin Castle[1] along with it.

LARRY.   Oh yes: youd have done great things; and a fat lot of good youd have got out of it, too! Thats an Englishman all over! make bad laws and give away all the land, and then, when your economic incompetence produces its natural and inevitable results, get virtuously indignant and kill the people that carry out your laws.

AUNT JUDY.   Sure never mind him, Mr Broadbent. It doesnt matter, anyhow, because theres harly any landlords left; and therll soon be none at all.

LARRY.   On the contrary, therll soon be nothing else; and the Lord help Ireland then!

AUNT JUDY.   Ah, youre never satisfied, Larry. [*To Nora.*] Come on, alanna, an make the paste for the pie. We can leave them to their talk. They dont want us. [*She takes up the tray and goes into the house.*]

BROADBENT [*rising and gallantly protesting*].   Oh, Miss Doyle! Really, really—

> [NORA, *following* AUNT JUDY *with the rolled-up cloth in her hands, looks at him and strikes him dumb. He watches her until she disappears; then comes to* LARRY *and addresses him with sudden intensity.*]

BROADBENT.   Larry.
LARRY.   What is it?
BROADBENT.   I got drunk last night, and proposed to Miss Reilly.

---

1. Norman structure, at the time of the play the seata of British administration of Ireland.

LARRY.   You hwat??? [*He screams with laughter in the falsetto Irish register unused for that purpose in England.*]

BROADBENT.   What are you laughing at?

LARRY [*stopping dead*].   I dont know. Thats the sort of thing an Irishman laughs at. Has she accepted you?

BROADBENT.   I shall never forget that with the chivalry of her nation, though I was utterly at her mercy, she refused me.

LARRY.   That was extremely improvident of her. [*Beginning to reflect.*] But look here: when were you drunk? You were sober enough when you came back from the Round Tower with her.

BROADBENT.   No, Larry, I was drunk, I am sorry to say. I had two tumblers of punch. She had to lead me home. You must have noticed it.

LARRY.   I did not.

BROADBENT.   She did.

LARRY.   May I ask how long it took you to come to business? You can hardly have known her for more than a couple of hours.

BROADBENT.   I am afraid it was hardly a couple of minutes. She was not here when I arrived; and I saw her for the first time at the tower.

LARRY.   Well, you are a nice infant to be let loose in this country! Fancy the potcheen going to your head like that!

BROADBENT.   Not to my head, I think. I have no headache; and I could speak distinctly. No: potcheen goes to the heart, not to the head. What ought I to do?

LARRY.   Nothing. What need you do?

BROADBENT.   There is rather a delicate moral question involved. The point is, was I drunk enough not to be morally responsible for my proposal? Or was I sober enough to be bound to repeat it now that I am undoubtedly sober?

LARRY.   I should see a little more of her before deciding.

BROADBENT.   No, no. That would not be right. That would not be fair. I am either under a moral obligation or I am not. I wish I knew how drunk I was.

LARRY.   Well, you were evidently in a state of blithering sentimentality, anyhow.

BROADBENT.   That is true, Larry: I admit it. Her voice has a most extraordinary effect on me. That Irish voice!

LARRY [*sympathetically*].   Yes, I know. When I first went to London I very nearly proposed to walk out with a waitress in an Aerated Bread shop because her Whitechapel accent was so distinguished, so quaintly touching, so pretty—

BROADBENT[*angrily*].   Miss Reilly is not a waitress, is she?

LARRY.   Oh, come! The waitress was a very nice girl.

BROADBENT.   You think every Englishwoman an angel. You really have coarse tastes in that way, Larry. Miss Reilly is one of the finer types: a type rare in England, except perhaps in the best of the aristocracy.

LARRY.   Aristocracy be blowed! Do you know what Nora eats?

BROADBENT.   Eats! what do you mean?

LARRY.   Breakfast: tea and bread-and-butter, with an occasional rasher, and an egg on special occasions: say on her birthday. Dinner in the middle of the day, one course and nothing else. In the evening, tea and bread-and-butter again. You compare her with your English-women who wolf down from three to five meat meals a day; and naturally you find her a sylph. The difference is not a difference of type: it's the difference between the woman who eats not wisely but too well, and the woman who eats not wisely but too little.

BROADBENT [furious].   Larry: you—you—you disgust me. You are a damned fool. [He sits down angrily on the rustic seat, which sustains the shock with difficulty.]

LARRY.   Steady! stead-eee! [He laughs and seats himself on the table.]

[CORNELIUS DOYLE, FATHER DEMPSEY, BARNEY DORAN, AND MAT-THEW HAFFIGAN come from the house. DORAN is a stout bodied, short armed, roundheaded, red haired man on the verge of middle age, of sanguine temperament, with an enormous capacity for derisive, obscene, blasphemous, or merely cruel and senseless fun, and a violent and impetuous intolerance of other temperaments and other opinions, all this representing energy and capacity wasted and demoralized by want of sufficient training and social pressure to force it into beneficent activity and build a character with it; for BARNEY is by no means either stupid or weak. He is recklessly untidy as to his person; but the worst effects of his neglect are mitigated by a powdering of flour and mill dust; and his unbrushed clothes, made of a fashionable tailor's sackcloth, were evidently chosen regardless of expense for the sake of their appearance.

MATTHEW HAFFIGAN, ill at ease, coasts the garden shyly on the shrubbery side until he anchors near the basket, where he feels least in the way. The priest comes to the table and slaps LARRY on the shoulder. LARRY, turning quickly, and recognizing FATHER DEMPSEY, alights from the table and shakes the priest's hand warmly. DORAN comes down the garden between FATHER DEMP-SEY and MATT; and CORNELIUS, on the other side of the table, turns to BROADBENT, who rises genially.]

CORNELIUS.   I think we all met las night.

DORAN.   I hadnt that pleasure.

CORNELIUS.   To be sure, Barney: I forgot. [To BROADBENT, introducing BARNEY.] Mr Doran. He owns that fine mill you noticed from the car.

BROADBENT [delighted with them all].   Most happy, Mr Doran. Very pleased indeed.

[DORAN, *not quite sure whether he is being courted or patronized,
nods independently.*]

DORAN.   Hows yourself, Larry?
LARRY.   Finely, thank you. No need to ask you.

DORAN *grins; and they shake hands.*]

CORNELIUS.   Give Father Dempsey a chair, Larry.

[MATTHEW HAFFIGAN *runs to the nearest end of the table and
takes the chair from it, placing it near the basket; but* LARRY *has
already taken the chair from the other end and placed it in front
of the table.* FATHER DEMPSEY *accepts that more central position.*]

CORNELIUS.   Sit down, Barney, will you; and you, Matt.

[DORAN *takes the chair* MATT *is still offering to the priest; and
poor* MATTHEW, *outfaced by the miller, humbly turns the basket
upside down and sits on it.* CORNELIUS *brings his own breakfast
chair from the table and sits down on* FATHER DEMPSEY's *right.*
BROADBENT *resumes his seat on the rustic bench.* LARRY *crosses
to the bench and is about to sit down beside him when* BROAD-
BENT *holds him off nervously.*]

BROADBENT.   Do you think it will bear two, Larry?
LARRY.   Perhaps not. Dont move. I'll stand [*He posts himself behind the
bench.*]

[*They are all now seated, except* LARRY; *and the session assumes
a portentous air, as if something important were coming.*]

CORNELIUS.   Praps youll explain, Father Dempsey.
FATHER DEMPSEY.   No, no: go on, you: the Church has no politics.
CORNELIUS.   Were yever thinkin o goin into parliament at all, Larry?
LARRY.   Me!
FATHER DEMPSEY [*encouragingly*].   Yes, you. Hwy not?
LARRY.   I'm afraid my ideas would not be popular enough.
CORNELIUS.   I dont know that. Do you, Barney?
DORAN.   Theres too much blatherumskite in Irish politics: a dale too
much.
LARRY.   But what about your present member? Is he going to retire?
CORNELIUS.   No: I dont know that he is.
LARRY [*interrogatively*].   Well? then?
MATTHEW [*breaking out with surly bitterness*].   Weve had enough of his
foolish talk agen lanlords. Hwat call has he to talk about the lan, that
never was outside of a city office in his life?
CORNELIUS.   We're tired of him. He doesn't know hwere to stop. Every

man cant own land; and some men must own it to employ them. It was all very well when solid men like Doran an Matt were kep from ownin land. But hwat man in his senses ever wanted to give land to Patsy Farrll an dhe like o him?

BROADBENT.   But surely Irish landlordism was accountable for what Mr Haffigan suffered.

MATTHEW   Never mind hwat I suffered. I know what I suffered adhout you tellin me. But did I ever ask for more dhan the farm I made wid me own hans? tell me that, Corny Doyle, and you that knows. Was I fit for the responsibility or was I not? [*Snarling angrily at* CORNELIUS.] Am I to be compared to Patsy Farrll, that doesnt harly know his right hand from his left? What did he ever suffer, I'd like to know?

CORNELIUS.   Thats just what I say. I wasnt comparin you to your disadvantage.

MATTHEW [*implacable*].   Then hwat did you mane be talkin about givin him lan?

DORAN.   Aisy, Matt, aisy. Youre like a bear with a sore back.

MATTHEW [*trembling with rage*].   An who are you, to offer to taitch me manners?

FATHER DEMPSEY [*admonitorily*].   Now, now, now, Matt! none o dhat. How often have I told you youre too ready to take offence where none is meant? You dont understand: Corny Doyle is saying just what you want to have said. [*To* CORNELIUS.] Go on, Mr Doyle; and never mind him.

MATTHEW [*rising*].   Well, if me lan is to be given to Patsy and his like, I'm goin oura dhis. I—

DORAN [*with violent impatience*].   Arra who's goin to give your lan to Patsy, yowl fool ye?

FATHER DEMPSEY.   Aisy, Barney, aisy. [*Sternly, to* MATT.] I told you, Matthew Haffigan, that Corny Doyle was sayin nothin against you. I'm sorry your priest's word is not good enough for you. I'll go, sooner than stay to make you commit a sin against the Church. Good morning, gentlemen.

[*He rises. They all rise, except* BROADBENT.]

DORAN [*to Matt*].   There Sarve you dam well right, you cantankerous oul noodle.

MATTHEW [*appalled*].   Dont say dhat, Fadher Dempsey. I never had a thought agen you or the Holy Church. I know I'm a bit hasty when I think about the lan. I ax your pardon for it.

FATHER DEMPSEY [*resuming his seat with dignified reserve*].   Very well: I'll overlook it this time.

[*He sits down. The others sit down, except* MATTHEW. FATHER DEMPSEY, *about to ask* CORNY *to proceed, remembers* MATTHEW *and turns to him, giving him just a crumb of graciousness.*]

Sit down, Matt

[MATTHEW, *crushed, sits down in disgrace, and is silent, his eyes shifting piteously from one speaker to another in an intensely mistrustful effort to understand them.*]

Go on, Mr Doyle. We can make allowances. Go on.

CORNELIUS.   Well, you see how it is, Larry. Round about here, weve got the land at last; and we want no more Goverment meddlin. We want a new class o man in parliament: one dhat knows dhat the farmer's the real backbone o the country, n doesnt care a snap of his fingers for the shoutn o the riff-raff in the towns, or for the foolishness of the laborers.

DORAN.   Aye; an dhat can afford to live in London and pay his own way until Home Rule comes, instead o wantin subscriptions and the like.

FATHER DEMPSEY.   Yes: thats a good point, Barney. When too much money goes to politics, it's the Church that has to starve for it. A member of parliament ought to be a help to the Church instead of a burden on it.

LARRY.   Heres a chance for you, Tom. What do you say?

BROADBENT [*deprecatory, but important and smiling*].   Oh, I have no claim whatever to the seat. Besides, I'm a Saxon.

DORAN.   A hwat?

BROADBENT.   A Saxon. An Englishman.

DORAN.   An Englishman. Bedad I never heard it called dhat before.

MATTHEW [*cunningly*].   If I might make so bould, Fadher, I woudnt say but an English Prodestn mightnt have a more indepindent mind about the lan, an be less afeerd to spake out about it, dhan an Irish Catholic.

CORNELIUS.   But sure Larry's as good as English: arnt you, Larry?

LARRY.   You may put me out of your head, father, once for all.

CORNELIUS.   Arra why?

LARRY.   I have strong opinions which wouldnt suit you.

DORAN [*rallying him blatantly*].   Is it still Larry the bould Fenian?

LARRY.   No: the bold Fenian is now an older and possibly foolisher man.

CORNELIUS.   Hwat does it matter to us hwat your opinions are? You know that your father's bought his place here, just the same as Matt's farm n Barney's mill. All we ask now is to be let alone. Youve nothin against that, have you?

LARRY.   Certainly I have. I dont believe in letting anybody or anything alone.

CORNELIUS [*losing his temper*].   Arra what d'ye mean, you young fool? Here Ive got you the offer of a good seat in parliament; n you think yourself mighty smart to stand there and talk foolishness to me. Will you take it or leave it?

LARRY.   Very well: I'll take it with pleasure if youll give it to me.

CORNELIUS [*subsiding sulkily*].   Well, why couldnt you say so at once? It's a good job youve made up your mind at last.

DORAN [*suspiciously*].   Stop a bit: stop a bit.

MATTHEW [*writhing between his dissatisfaction and his fear of the priest*].   It's not because he's your son that he's to get the sate. Fadher Dempsey: wouldnt you think well to ask him what he manes about the lan?

LARRY [*coming down on* MATT *promptly*].   I'll tell you, Matt. I always thought it was a stupid, lazy, good-for-nothing sort of thing to leave the land in the hands of the old landlords without calling them to a strict account for the use they made of it, and the condition of the people on it. I could see for myself that they thought of nothing but what they could get out of it to spend in England; and that they mortgaged and mortgaged until hardly one of them owned his own property or could have afforded to keep it up decently if he'd wanted to. But I tell you plump and plain, Matt, that if anybody thinks things will be any better now that the land is handed over to a lot of little men like you, without calling you to account either, theyre mistaken.

MATTHEW [*sullenly*].   What call have you to look down on me? I suppose you think youre everybody because your father was a land agent.

LARRY.   What call have you to look down on Patsy Farrell? I suppose you think youre everybody because you own a few fields.

MATTHEW   Was Patsy Farrll ever ever ill used as I was ill used? tell me dhat.

LARRY.   He will be, if ever he gets into your power as you were in the power of your old landlord. Do you think, because youre poor and ignorant and half-crazy with toiling and moiling morning noon and night, that youll be any less greedy and oppressive to them that have no land at all than old Nick Lestrange, who was an educated travelled gentleman that would not have been tempted as hard by a hundred pounds as youd be by five shillings? Nick was too high above Patsy Farrell to be jealous of him; but you, that are only one little step above him, would die sooner than let him come up that step; and well you know it.

MATTHEW [*black with rage, in a low growl*].   Lemmy oura *dhis*.

[He tries to rise; but DORAN *catches his coat and drags him down again*.]

I'm goin, I say. [*Raising his voice.*] Leggo me coat, Barney Doran.

DORAN.   Sit down, yowl omadhaun, you. [*Whispering.*] Dont you want to stay an vote agen him?

FATHER DEMPSEY [*holding up his finger*].   Matt!

[MATT *subsides.*]

Now, now, now! come, come! Hwats all dhis about Patsy Farrll? Hwy need you fall out about him?

LARRY.   Because it was by using Patsy's poverty to undersell England in the markets of the world that we drove England to ruin Ireland. And she'll ruin us again the moment we lift our heads from the dust if we trade in cheap labor; and serve us right too! If I get into parliament, I'll try to get an Act to prevent any of you from giving Patsy less than a pound a week [*they all start, hardly able to believe their ears*] or working him harder than youd work a horse that cost you fifty guineas.

DORAN.   Hwat!!!

CORNELIUS [*aghast*].   A pound a—God save us! the boy's mad.

[MATTHEW, *feeling that here is something quite beyond his powers, turns openmouthed to the priest, as if looking for nothing less than the summary excommunication of* LARRY.]

LARRY.   How is the man to marry and live a decent life on less?

FATHER DEMPSEY.   Man alive, hwere have you been living all these years? and hwat have you been dreaming of? Why, some o dhese honest men here cant make that much out o the land for dhemselves, much less give it to a laborer.

LARRY [*now thoroughly roused*].   Then let them make room for those who can. Is Ireland never to have a chance? First she was given to the rich; and now that they have gorged on her flesh, her bones are to be flung to the poor, that can do nothing but suck the marrow out of her. If we cant have men of honor own the land, lets have men of ability. If we cant have men with ability, let us at least have men with capital. Anybody's better than Matt, who has neither honor, nor ability, nor capital, nor anything but mere brute labor and greed in him, Heaven help him!

DORAN.   Well, we're not all foostherin oul doddherers like Matt. [*Pleasantly, to the subject of this description.*] Are we, Matt?

LARRY.   For modern industrial purposes you might just as well be, Barney. Youre all children: the big world that I belong to has gone past you and left you. Anyhow, we Irishmen were never made to be farmers; and we'll never do any good at it. We're like the Jews: the Almighty gave us brains, and bid us farm them, and leave the clay and the worms alone.

FATHER DEMPSEY [*with gentle irony*].   Oh! is it Jews you want to make of us? I must catechize you a bit meself, I think. The next thing youll be proposing is to repeal the disestablishment of the so-called Irish Church.[2]

LARRY   Yes: why not?

[*Sensation.*]

2. The Church of Ireland, Protestant and Anglican; in 1869 it was disestablished, or stripped of a privileged connection with government.

MATTHEW [*rancorously*].   He's a turncoat.

LARRY.   St Peter, the rock on which our Church was built, was crucified head downwards for being a turncoat.

FATHER DEMPSEY [*with a quiet authoritative dignity which checks* DORAN,
who is on the point of breaking out].   Thats true. You hold your
tongue as befits your ignorance, Matthew Haffigan; and trust your
priest to deal with this young man. Now, Larry Doyle, whatever the
blessed St Peter was crucified for, it was not for being a Prodestan.
Are you one?

LARRY.   No. I am a Catholic intelligent enough to see that the Protestants are never more dangerous to us than when they are free from all
alliances with the State. The so-called Irish Church is stronger today
that ever it was.

MATTHEW.   Fadher Dempsey: will you tell him dhat me mother's ant
was shot and kilt dead in the sthreet o Rosscullen be a soljer in the
tithe war? [*Frantically.*] He wants to put the tithes on us again. He—

LARRY [*interrupting him with overbearing contempt*].   Put the tithes on
you again! Did the tithes ever come off you? Was your land any dearer
when you paid the tithe to the parson than it was when you paid the
same money to Nick Lestrange as rent, and he handed it over to the
Church Sustentation Fund? Will you always be duped by Acts of
Parliament that change nothing but the necktie of the man that picks
your pocket? I'll tell you what I'd do with you, Matt Haffigan: I'd
make you pay tithes to your own Church. I want the Catholic Church
established in Ireland: thats what I want. Do you think that I, brought
up to regard myself as the son of a great and holy Church, can bear
to see her begging her bread from the ignorance and superstition of
men like you? I would have her as high above worldly want as I would
have her above worldly pride or ambition. Aye; and I would have
Ireland compete with Rome itself for the chair of St Peter and the
citadel of the Church; for Rome, in spite of all the blood of the martyrs, is pagan at heart to this day, while in Ireland the people is the
Church and the Church the people.

FATHER DEMPSEY [*startled, but not at all displeased*].   Whisht, man!
youre worse than mad Pether Keegan himself.

BROADBENT [*who has listened in the greatest astonishment*].   You amaze
me, Larry. Who would have thought of your coming out like this!
[*Solemnly.*] But much as I appreciate your really brilliant eloquence,
I implore you not to desert the great Liberal principle of Disestablishment.

LARRY.   I am not a Liberal: Heaven forbid! A disestablished Church is
the worst tyranny a nation can groan under.

BROADBENT [*making a wry face*].   Dont be paradoxical, Larry. It really
gives me a pain in my stomach.

LARRY.   Youll soon find out the truth of it here. Look at Father Dempsey! he is disestablished: he has nothing to hope or fear from the State; and the result is that he's the most powerful man in Rosscullen. The member for Rosscullen would shake in his shoes if Father Dempsey looked crooked at him.

[FATHER DEMPSEY *smiles, by no means averse to this acknowledgment of his authority.*]

Look at yourself! you would defy the established Archbishop of Canterbury ten times a day; but catch you daring to say a word that would shock a Nonconformist! not you. The Conservative party today is the only one thats not priestridden—excuse the expression, Father

[FATHER DEMPSEY *nods tolerantly*].

—because it's the only one that has established its Church and can prevent a clergyman becoming a bishop if he's not a Statesman as well as a Churchman.

[*He stops. They stare at him dumbfounded, and leave it to the priest to answer him.*]

FATHER DEMPSEY [*judicially*].   Young man; youll not be the member for Roscullen; but dheres more in your head than the comb will take out.

LARRY.   I'm sorry to disappoint you, father; but I told you it would be no use. And now I think the candidate had better retire and leave you to discuss his successor.

[*He takes a newspaper from the table and goes away through the shrubbery amid dead silence, all turning to watch him until he passes out of sight round the corner of the house.*]

DORAN [*dazed*].   Hwat sort of a fella is he at all at all?

FATHER DEMPSEY.   He's a clever lad: dheres the making of a man in him yet.

MATTHEW [*in consternation*].   D'ye mane to say dhat yll put him into parliament to bring back Nick Lesthrange on me, and to put tithes on me, and to rob me for the like o Patsy Farrll, because he's Corny Doyle's son?

DORAN [*brutally*].   Arra hould your whist: who's goin to send him into parliament? Maybe youd like us to send you dhere to thrate dhem to a little o your anxiety about dhat dirty little podato patch o yours.

MATTHEW [*plaintively*].   Am I to be towld dhis afther all me sufferins?

DORAN.   Och, I'm tired o your sufferins. Weve been hearin nothin else ever since we was childher but sufferins. Hwen it wasnt yours it was somebody else's; and hwen it was nobody else's it was ould Irelan's. How the divil are we to live on wan anodher's sufferins?

FATHER DEMPSEY.   Thats a thrue word, Barney Doarn; only your tongue's
a little too familiar wi dhe divil. [*To* MATT.] If youd think a little more
o the sufferins of the blessed saints, Matt, an a little less o your own,
youd find the way shorter from your farm to heaven.

>   [MATT *is about to reply.*]

Dhere now! dhats enough! we know you mean well; an I'm not angry
with you.
BROADBENT.   Surely, Mr Haffigan, you can see the simple explanation
of all this. My friend Larry Doyle is a most brilliant speaker; but he's
a Tory: an ingrained old-fashioned Tory.
CORNELIUS.   N how d'ye make dhat out, if I might ask you, Mr Broadbent?
BROADBENT [*collecting himself for a political deliverance*].   Well, you
know, Mr Doyle, theres a strong dash of Toryism in the Irish character. Larry himself says that the great Duke of Wellington was the
most typical Irishman that ever lived. Of course thats an absurd paradox; but still theres a great deal of truth in it. Now I am a Liberal.
You know the great principles of the Liberal Party. Peace—
FATHER DEMPSEY [*piously*].   Hear! hear!
BROADBENT [*encouraged*].   Thank you. Retrenchment—[*he waits for
further applause*].
MATTHEW [*timidly*].   What might rethrenchment mane now?
BROADBENT.   It means an immense reduction in the burden of the rates
and taxes.
MATTHEW [*respectfully approving*].   Dhats right. Dhats right, sir.
BROADBENT [*perfunctorily*].   And, of course, Reform.
CORNELIUS ⎫
FATHER DEMPSEY ⎬ [*conventionally*].   Of course.
DORAN ⎭
MATTHEW [*still suspicious*].   Hwat does Reform mane, sir? Does it mane
altherin annythin dhats as it is now?
BROADBENT [*impressively*].   It means, Mr Haffigan, maintaining those
reforms which have already been conferred on humanity by the Lib-
eral Party, and trusting for future developments to the free activity of
a free people on the basis of those reforms.
DORAN.   Dhats right. No more meddlin. We're all right now: all we
want is to be let alone.
CORNELIUS.   Hwat about Home Rule?
BROADBENT [*rising so as to address them more imposingly*].   I really cannot tell you what I feel about Home Rule without using the language
of hyperbole.
DORAN.   Savin Fadher Dempsey's presence, eh?
BROADBENT [*not understanding him*].   Quite so—er—oh yes. All I can

say is that as an Englishman I blush for the Union.[3] It is the blackest
stain on our national history. I look forward to the time—and it cannot be far distant, gentlemen, because Humanity is looking forward
to it too, and insisting on it with no uncertain voice—I look forward
to the time when an Irish legislature shall arise once more on the
emerald pasture of College Green, and the Union Jack—that detestable symbol of a decadent Imperialism—be replaced by a flag as green
as the island over which it waves: a flag on which we shall ask for
England only a modest quartering in memory of our great party and
of the immortal name of our grand old leader.

DORAN [*enthusiastically*].   Dhats the style, begob! [*He smites his knee,
and winks at* MATT.]

MATTHEW.   More power to you, sir!

BROADBENT.   I shall leave you now, gentlemen, to your deliberations.
I should like to have enlarged on the services rendered by the Liberal
Party to the religious faith of the great majority of the people of Ireland; but I shall content myself with saying that in my opinion you
should choose no representative who—no matter what his personal
creed may be—is not an ardent supporter of freedom of conscience,
and is not prepared to prove it by contributions, as lavish as his means
will allow, to the great and beneficent work which you, Father Dempsey

[FATHER DEMPSEY *bows*],

are doing for the people of Rosscullen. Nor should the lighter, but
still most important question of the sports of the people be forgotten.
The local cricket club—

CORNELIUS.   The hwat!

DORAN.   Nobody plays bat n ball here, if dhats what you mane.

BROADBENT.   Well, let us say quoits. I saw two men, I think, last night—
but after all, these are questions of detail. The main thing is that your
candidate, whoever he may be, shall be a man of some means, able
to help the locality instead of burdening it. And if he were a countryman of my own, the moral effect on the House of Commons would
be immense! tremendous! Pardon my saying these few words: nobody
feels their impertinence more than I do. Good morning, gentlemen.
[*He turns impressively to the gate, and trots away, congratulating
himself, with a little twist of his head and cock of his eye, on having
done a good stroke of political business.*]

HAFFIGAN [*awestruck*].   Good morning, sir.

THE REST.   Good morning. [*They watch him vacantly until he is out of
earshot.*]

3. The Act of Union, absorption of the Irish parliament by the British parliament on January 1, 1801.

CORNELIUS.   Hwat d'ye think, Father Dempsey?

FATHER DEMPSEY [*indulgently*].   Well, he hasnt much sense, God help him; but for the matter o that, neether has our present member.

DORAN.   Arra musha he's good enough for parliament: what is there to do there but gas a bit, an chivy the Goverment, an vote wi dh Irish party?

CORNELIUS [*ruminatively*].   He's the queerest Englishman I ever met. When he opened the paper dhis mornin the first thing he saw was that an English expedition had been bet in a battle in Inja somewhere; an he was as pleased as Punch! Larry told him that if he'd been alive when the news o Waterloo[4] came, he'd a died o grief over it. Bedad I dont think he's quite right in his head.

DORAN.   Divil a matther if he has plenty o money. He'll do for us right enough.

MATTHEW [*deeply impressed by* BROADBENT, *and unable to understand their levity concerning him*].   Did you mind what he said about rethrenchment? That was very good, I thought.

FATHER DEMPSEY.   You might find out from Larry, Corny, what his means are. God forgive us all! it's poor work spoiling the Egyptians, though we have good warrant for it; so I'd like to know how much spoil there is before I commit meself.

[*He rises. They all rise respectfully.*]

CORNELIUS [*ruefully*].   I'd set me mind on Larry himself for the seat; but I suppose it cant be helped.

FATHER DEMPSEY [*consoling him*].   Well, the boy's young yet; an he had a head on him. Goodbye, all. [*He goes out through the gate.*]

DORAN.   I must be goin, too. [*He directs* CORNELIUS's *attention to what is passing in the road.*] Look at me bould Englishman shaking hans wid Fadher Dempsey for all the world like a candidate on election day. And look at Fadher Dempsey givin him a squeeze an a wink as much as to say It's all right, me boy. You watch him shakin hans with me too: he's waitn for me. I'll tell him he's as good as elected. [*He goes, chuckling mischievously.*]

CORNELIUS.   Come in with me, Matt. I think I'll sell you the pig after all. Come in an wet the bargain.

MATTHEW [*instantly dropping into the old whine of the tenant*].   I'm afeerd I can't afford the price, sir. [*He follows* CORNELIUS *into the house.*]

[LARRY, *newspaper still in hand, comes back through the shrubbery.* BROADBENT *returns through the gate.*]

LARRY.   Well? What has happened?

BROADBENT [*hugely self-satisfied*].   I think Ive done the trick this time.

4. Defeat of Napoleon on June 18, 1815, by the British commanded by the Dublin-born duke of Wellington (1769–1852).

I just gave them a bit of straight talk; and it went home. They were greatly impressed: everyone of those men believes in me and will vote for me when the question of selecting a candidate comes up. After all, whatever you say, Larry, they like an Englishman. They feel they can trust him, I suppose.

LARRY.   Oh! theyve transferred the honor to you, have they?

BROADBENT [*complacently*].   Well, it was a pretty obvious move, I should think. You know, these fellows have plenty of shrewdness in spite of their Irish oddity.

[HODSON *comes from the house.* LARRY *sits in* DORAN's *chair and reads.*]

Oh, by the way, Hodson—

HODSON [*coming between* BROADBENT *and* LARRY].   Yes, sir?

BROADBENT.   I want you to be rather particular as to how you treat the people here.

HODSON.   I havnt treated any of em yet, sir. If I was to accept all the treats they offer me I shouldnt be able to stand at this present moment, sir.

BROADBENT.   Oh well, dont be too stand-offish, you know, Hodson. I should like you to be popular. If it costs anything I'll make it up to you. It doesnt matter if you get a bit upset at first: theyll like you all the better for it.

HODSON.   I'm sure youre very kind, sir; but it dont seem to matter to me whether they like me or not. I'm not going to stand for parliament here, sir.

BROADBENT.   Well, I am. Now do you understand?

HODSON [*waking up at once*].   Oh, I beg your pardon, sir, I'm sure. I understand, sir.

CORNELIUS [*appearing at the house door with* MATT].   Patsy'll drive the pig over this evenin, Matt. Goodbye.

[*He goes back into the house.* MATT *makes for the gate.* BROADBENT *stops him.* HODSON, *pained by the derelict basket, picks it up and carries it away behind the house.*]

BROADBENT [*beaming candidatorially*].   I must thank you very particularly, Mr Haffigan, for your support this morning. I value it because I know that the real heart of a nation is the class you represent, the yeomanry.

MATTHEW [*aghast*].   The yeomanry!!!

LARRY [*looking up from his paper*].   Take care, Tom! In Rosscullen a yeoman means a sort of Orange Bashi-Bazouk.[5] In England, Matt, they call a freehold farmer a yeoman.

MATTHEW [*huffily*].   I dont need to be insthructed be you, Larry Doyle.

5. Protestant mercenary soldier.

Some people think no one knows anythin but dhemselves. [*To* BROAD-
BENT, *deferentially.*] Of course I know a gentleman like you would
not compare me to the yeomanry. Me own granfather was flogged in
the sthreets of Athenmullet be them when they put a gun in the thatch
of his house an then went and found it there, bad cess to them!

BROADBENT [*with sympathetic interest*].   Then you are not the first martyr of your family, Mr. Haffigan?

MATTHEW.   They turned me out o the farm I made out of the stones o
Little Rosscullen hill wid me own hans.

BROADBENT.   I have heard about it; and my blood still boils at the thought.
[*Calling.*] Hodson—

HODSON [*behind the corner of the house*].   Yes, sir. [*He hurries forward.*]

BROADBENT.   Hodson: this gentleman's sufferings should make every
Englishman think. It is want of thought rather than want of heart that
allows such iniquities to disgrace society.

HODSON [*prosaically*].   Yes, sir.

MÁTTHEW.   Well, I'll be goin. Good mornin to you kindly, sir.

BROADBENT.   You have some distance to go, Mr Haffigan: will you allow
me to drive you home?

MATTHEW.   Oh sure it'd be throublin your honor.

BROADBENT.   I insist: it will give me the greatest pleasure, I assure you.
My car is in the stable: I can get it round in five minutes.

MATTHEW.   Well, sir, if you wouldnt mind, we could bring the pig Ive
just bought from Corny—

BROADBENT [*with enthusiasm*].   Certainly, Mr Haffigan: it will be quite
delightful to drive with a pig in the car: I shall feel quite like an Irishman. Hodson: stay with Mr Haffigan; and give him a hand with the
pig if necessary. Come, Larry; and help me. [*He rushes away through
the shrubbery.*]

LARRY [*throwing the paper ill-humoredly on the chair*].   Look here, Tom!
here, I saw! counfound it!—[*he runs after him*].

MATTHEW [*glowering disdainfully at* HODSON, *and sitting down on* COR-
NELIUS's *chair as an act of social self-assertion*].   N are you the valley?

HODSON.   The valley? Oh, I follow you: yes: I'm Mr Broadbent's valet.

MATTHEW.   Ye have an aisy time of it: you look purty sleek. [*With suppressed ferocity.*] Look at me! Do I look sleek?

HODSON [*sadly*].   I wish I ad your ealth: you look as ard as nails. I suffer
from an excess of uric acid.

MATTHEW.   Musha what sort o disease is zhouragassid? Didjever suffer
from injustice and starvation? Dhats the Irish disease. It's aisy for you
to talk o sufferin, an you livin on the fat o the land wid money wrung
from us.

HODSON [*suddenly dropping the well-spoken valet, and breaking out in
his native cockney*].   Wots wrong with you, aold chep? Ez ennybody
been doin ennythink to you?

MATTHEW.   Anythin timmy! Didnt your English masther say that the blood biled in him to hear the way they put a rint on me for the farm I made wid me own hans, and turned me out of it to give it to Billy Byrne?

HODSON.   Ow, Tom Broadbent's blad boils pretty easy over ennything that eppens aht of his aown cantry. Downt you be tiken in by my aowl men, Peddy.

MATTHEW [*indignantly*].   Paddy yourself! How dar you call me Paddy?

HODSON [*unmoved*].   You jast keep your air on and listen to me. You Awrish people are too well off: thets wots the metter with you. [*With sudden passion.*] You talk of your rotten little fawm cause you mide it by chackin a few stowns dahn a ill! Well, wot prawce maw gren-fawther, Oi should lawk to knaow, that fitted up a fust clawss shop and built ap a fust clawss dripery business in Landon by sixty years work, and then was chacked aht of it on is ed at the end of is lease withaht a penny for his goodwill. You talk of evictions! you that cawnt be moved until youve ran ap ighteen months rent. Oi once ran ap four weeks in Lembeth wen Oi was aht of a job in winter. They took the door off its inges and the winder aht of its seshes on me, and gev maw wawf pnoomownia. Oi'm a widower nah. [*Between his teeth.*] Gawd! when Oi think of the things we Englishmen as to pat ap with, and eah you Awrish ahlin abaht your silly little grievances, and see the wy you mike it worse for haz by the rotten wiges youll cam over and tike and the rotten plices youll sleep in, I jast feel that I could tike the aowl bloomin British awland and mike you a present of it, jast to let you fawnd aht wot reel awdship's lawk.

MATTHEW [*starting up, more in scandalized incredulity than in anger*].   D'ye have the face to set up England agen Ireland for injustices an wrongs an disthress an sufferin?

HODSON [*with intense disgust and contempt*].   Ow, chack it, Paddy. Cheese it. You danno wot awdship is owver eah: all you knaow is ah to ahl abaht it. You tike the biscuit at thet, you do. Oi'm a Owm Ruler, Oi em. Do you knaow woy?

MATTHEW [*equally contemptuous*].   D'ye know, yourself?

HODSON.   Yus Oido. It's because Oi want a little attention pide to my aown cantry; and thetll never be as long as your cheps are ollerin at Wesminister as if nowbody mettered but your own bloomin selves. Send em beck to ell or C'naught, as good aowld English Cramwell[6] said. I'm jast sick of Awrland. Let it gow. Cat the caible. Mike it a present to Germany to keep the aowl Kyzer[7] busy for a wawl; and give poor aowld England a chawnce: thets wot Oi sy.

---

6. Oliver Cromwell (1599–1658) brutally conquered Ireland in 1649 and transferred Irish landholders to the west, thus condemning them "to Hell or Connacht."

7. Kaiser Wilhelm (1859–1941), king of Prussia, emperor of Germany, and antagonist of Britain until World War I.

MATTHEW [*full of scorn for a man so ignorant as to be unable to pronounce the word Connaught, which practically rhymes with bonnet in
Ireland, though in* HODSON'*s dialect it rhymes with untaught*].   Take
care we dont cut the cable ourselves some day, bad scran [8] to you! An
tell me dhis: have yanny Coercion Acs in England? Have yanny
Removable magisthruts? [9] Have you Dublin Castle to suppress every
newspaper dhat takes the part o your own counthry?

HODSON.   We can beyive ahrselves withaht sich things.

MATTHEW.   Bedad youre right. It'd ony be waste o time to muzzle a
sheep. Here! wheres me pig? God forgimmy for talkin to a poor ignorant craycher like you!

HODSON [*grinning with good-humored malice, too convinced of his own
superiority to feel his withers wrung*].   Your pig'll ev a rare doin in
that car, Peddy. Forty mawl an ahr dahn that rocky line will strawk it
pretty pink, you bet.

MATTHEW [*scornfully*].   Hwy cant you tell a raisonable lie when youre
about it? What horse can go forty mile an hour?

HODSON.   Orse! Wy, you silly aowl rotter, it's not a orse: it's a mowtor.
Do you spowse Tom Broadbent ud gow himself to fetch a orse?

MATTHEW [*in consternation*].   Holy Moses! dont tell me it's the ingine
he wants to take me on.

HODSON.   Wot else?

MATTHEW.   Your sowl to Morris Kelly! why didnt you tell me that before?
The divil an ingine he'll get me on this day. [*His ear catches an
approaching teuf-teuf.*] Oh murdher! It's comin afther me: I hear the
puff-puff of it.

> [*He runs away through the gate, much to* HODSON'*s amusement.
> The noise of the motor ceases; and* HODSON, *anticipating* BROAD-
> BENT'*s return, throws off the cockney and recomposes himself as
> a valet.* BROADBENT *and* LARRY *come through the shrubbery* HOD-
> SON *moves aside to the gate.*]

BROADBENT.   Where is Mr Haffigan? Has he gone for the pig?

HODSON.   Bolted, sir? Afraid of the motor, sir.

BROADBENT [*much disappointed*].   Oh, thats very tiresome. Did he leave
any message?

HODSON.   He was in too great a hurry, sir. Started to run home, sir,
and left his pig behind him.

BROADBENT [*eagerly*].   Left the pig! Then it's all right. The pig's the
thing: the pig will win over every Irish heart to me. We'll take the pig
home to Haffigan's farm in the motor: it will have a tremendous effect.
Hodson!

8. Bad luck.
9. Appointed magistrates subject to removal from

office and so, in Ireland, eager to please colonial
authorities.

HODSON.   Yes, sir?

BROADBENT.   Do you think you could collect a crowd to see the motor?

HODSON.   Well, I'll try, sir.

BROADBENT.   Thank you, Hodson: do.

[HODSON *goes out through the gate.*]

LARRY [*desperately*].   Once more, Tom, will you listen to me?

BROADBENT.   Rubbish! I tell you it will be all right.

LARRY.   Only this morning you confessed how surprised you were to find that the people here shewed no sense of humor.

BROADBENT [*suddenly very solemn*].   Yes: their sense of humor is in abeyance: I noticed it the moment we landed. Think of that in a country where every man is a born humorist! Think of what it means! [*Impressively.*] Larry: we are in the presence of a great national grief.

LARRY.   Whats to grieve them?

BROADBENT.   I divined it, Larry: I saw it in their faces. Ireland has never smiled since her hopes were buried in the grave of Gladstone.

LARRY.   Oh, whats the use of talking to such a man? Now look here, Tom. Be serious for a moment if you can.

BROADBENT[*stupent*].   Serious! I!!!

LARRY.   Yes, you. You say the Irish sense of humor is in abeyance. Well, if you drive through Rosscullen in a motor car with Haffigan's pig, it wont stay in abeyance. Now I warn you.

BRAODBENT [*breezily*].   Why, so much the better! I shall enjoy the joke myself more than any of them. [*Shouting.*] Hallo, Patsy Farrell, where are you?

PATSY [*appearing in the shrubbery*].   Here I am, your honor.

BROADBENT.   Go and catch the pig and put into the car: we're going to take it to Mr Haffigan's. [*He gives* LARRY *a slap on the shoulders that sends him staggering off through the gate, and follows him buoyantly, exclaiming*] Come on, you old croaker! I'll shew you how to win an Irish seat.

PATSY [*meditatively*].   Bedad, if dhat pig gets a howlt o the handle o the machine—[*He shakes his head ominously and drifts away to the pigsty.*]

Act Four

The parlor in CORNELIUS DOYLE's *house. It communicates with the garden by a half glazed door. The fireplace is at the other side of the room, opposite the door and windows, the architect not having been sensitive to draughts. The table, rescued from the garden, is in the middle; and at it sits* KEEGAN, *the central figure in a rather crowded apartment.* NORA, *sitting with her back to the fire at the end of the table, is playing backgammon across its corner with him, on his left hand.* AUNT JUDY, *a little further back, sits facing the fire knitting, with her feet on the fender. A little to* KEEGAN's *right, in front of the table, and almost sitting on it, is* BARNEY DORAN. *Half a dozen friends of his, all men, are between him and the open door, supported by others outside. In the corner behind them is the sofa, of mahogany and horsehair, made up as a bed for* BROADBENT. *Against the wall behind* KEEGAN *stands a mahogany sideboard. A door leading to the interior of the house is near the fireplace, behind* AUNT JUDY. *There are chairs against the wall, one at each end of the sideboard.* KEEGAN's *hat is on the one nearest the inner door; and his stick is leaning against it. A third chair, also against the wall, is near the garden door.*

There is a strong contrast of emotional atmosphere between the two sides of the room. KEEGAN *is extraordinarily stern: no game of backgammon could possibly make a man's face so grim.* AUNT JUDY *is quietly busy.* NORA *is trying to ignore* DORAN *and attend to her game.*

On the other hand DORAN *is reeling in an ecstasy of mischievous mirth which has infected all his friends. They are screaming with laughter, doubled up, leaning on the furniture and against the walls, shouting, screeching, crying.*

AUNT JUDY [*as the noise lulls for a moment*].   Arra hold your noise, Barney. What is there to laugh at?
DORAN.   It got its fut into the little hweel—[*he is overcome afresh; and the rest collapse again*].
AUNT JUDY.   Ah, have some sense: youre like a parcel o childher. Nora: hit him a thump on the back: he'll have a fit.
DORAN[*with squeezed eyes, exsufflicate with cachinnation*].   Frens, he sez to dhem outside Doolan's: I'm takin the gintleman that pays the rint for a dhrive.
AUNT JUDY.   Who did he mean be that?
DORAN.   They call a pig that in England. Thats their notion of a joke.
AUNT JUDY.   Musha God help them if they can joke no better than that!
DORAN [*with renewed symptoms*].   Thin—
AUNT JUDY.   Ah now dont be tellin it all over and settin yourself off again, Barney.
NORA.   Youve told us three times, Mr Doran.
DORAN.   Well but whin I think of it—!
AUNT JUDY.   Then dont think of it, alanna.
DORAN.   Dhere was Patsy Farrll in the back sate wi dhe pig between his knees, n me bould English boyoh in front at the machinery, n Larry Doyle in the road startin the injine wid a bed winch. At the first puff of it the pig lep out of its skin and bled Patsy's nose wi dhe ring in its snout.

[*Roars of laughter:* KEEGAN *glares at them*].

Before Broadbint knew hwere he was, the pig was up his back and over into his lap; and bedad the poor baste did credit to Corny's thrainin of it; for it put in the fourth speed wid its right crubeen as if it was enthered for the Gordn Bennett.[1]

NORA [reproachfully]. And Larry in front of it and all! It's nothin to laugh at, Mr Doran.

DORAN. Bedad, Miss Reilly, Larry cleared six yards sideways at wan jump if he cleared an inch; and he'd a cleared seven if Doolan's granmother hadnt cotch him in her apern widout intindin to.

[Immense merriment.]

AUNT JUDY. Ah, for shame, Barney! the poor old woman! An she was hurt before, too, when she slipped on the stairs.

DORAN. Bedad, maam, she's hurt behind now; for Larry bouled her over like a skittle.

[General delight at this typical stroke of Irish Rabelaisianism.]

NORA. It's well Mr Doyle wasnt killed.

DORAN. Faith it wasnt o Larry we were thinkin jus dhen, wi dhe pig takin the main sthreet o Rosscullen on market day at a mile a minnit. Dh ony thing Broadbint could get at wi dhe pig in front of him was a fut brake; n the pig's tail was undher dhat; so that whin he thought he was putn non the brake he was ony squeezin the life out of the pig's tail. The more he put the brake on the more the pig squealed n the fasther he dhruv.

AUNT JUDY. Why couldnt he throw the pig out into the road?

DORAN. Sure he couldnt stand up to it, because he was spanchelledlike between his seat and dhat thing like a wheel on top of a stick between his knees.

AUNT JUDY. Lord have mercy on us!

NORA. I dont know how you can laugh. Do you, Mr Keegan?

KEEGAN [grimly]. Why not? There is danger, destruction, torment! What more do we need to make us merry? Go on, Barney: the last drops of joy are not squeezed from the story yet. Tell us again how our brother was torn asunder.

DORAN [puzzled]. Whose bruddher?

KEEGAN. Mine.

NORA. He means the pig, Mr Doran. You know his way.

DORAN [rising gallantly to the occasion]. Bedad I'm sorry for your poor bruddher, Misther Keegan; but I recommend you to try him wid a couple of fried eggs for your breakfast tomorrow. It was a case of Excelsior wi dhat ambitious baste; for not content wid jumpin from the back seat into the front wan, he jumped from the front wan into the road in front of the car. And—

KEEGAN. And everybody laughed!

NORA. Dont go over that again, please, Mr Doran.

1. Annual international automobile race.

DORAN.   Faith be the time the car went over the poor pig dhere was little left for me or anywan else to go over except wid a knife an fork.

AUNT JUDY.   Why didnt Mr Broadbent stop the car when the pig was gone?

DORAN.   Stop the car! He might as well ha thried to stop a mad bull. First it went wan way an made fireworks o Molly Ryan's crockery stall, an dhen it slewed round an ripped ten fut o wall out o the corner o the pound. [*With enormous enjoyment.*] Begob, it just tore the town in two and sent the whole dam market to blazes.

> [NORA *offended, rises.*]

KEEGAN [*indignantly*].   Sir!

DORAN [*quickly*].   Savin your presence, Miss Reilly, and Misther Keegan's. Dhere! I wont say anuddher word.

NORA.   I'm surprised at you, Mr Doran. [*She sits down again.*]

DORAN [*reflectively*].   He has the divil's own luck, that Englishman, annyway; for hwen they picked him up he hadnt a scratch on him, barrn hwat the pig did to his cloes. Patsy had two fingers out of jynt; but the smith pulled them sthraight for him. Oh, you never heard such a hullaballoo as there was. There was Molly cryin Me chaney, me beautyful chaney! n oul Matt shoutin Me pig, me pig! n the polus takin the number o the car, n not a man in the town able to speak for laughin—

KEEGAN [*with intense emphasis*].   It is hell: it is hell. Nowhere else coud such a scene be a burst of happiness for the people.

> [CORNELIUS *comes in hastily from the garden, pushing his way through the little crowd.*]

CORNELIUS.   Whisht your laughin, boys! Here he is. [*He puts his hat on the sideboard, and goes to the fireplace, where he posts himself with his back to the chimneypiece.*]

AUNT JUDY.   Remember your behavior, now.

> [*Everybody becomes silent, solemn, concerned, sympathetic.* BROADBENT *enters, soiled and disordered as to his motoring coat: immensely important and serious as to himself. He makes his way to the end of the table nearest the garden door, whilst* LARRY, *who accompanies him, throws his motoring coat on the sofa bed, and sits down, watching the proceedings.*]

BROADBENT [*taking off his leather cap with dignity and placing it on the table*].   I hope you have not been anxious about me.

AUNT JUDY.   Deedn we have, Mr Broadbent. It's a mercy you werent killed.

DORAN.   Kilt! It's a mercy dheres two bones of you left houldin together.

How dijjescape at all at all? Well, I never thought I'd be so glad to see you safe and sound again. Not a man in the town would say less.

[*Murmurs of kindly assent.*]

Wont you come down to Doolan's and have a dhrop o brandy to take the shock off?

BROADBENT. Youre all really too kind; but the shock has quite passed off.

DORAN [*jovially*]. Never mind. Come along all the same and tell us about it over a frenly glass.

BROADBENT. May I say how deeply I feel the kindness with which I have been overwhelmed since my accident? I can truthfully declare that I am glad it happened, because it has brought out the kindness and sympathy of the Irish character to an extent I had no conception of.

SEVERAL { Oh, sure youre welcome!
PRESENT { Sure it's only natural.
{ Sure you might have been kilt.

[*A young man, feeling that he must laugh or burst, hurries out. BARNEY puts an iron constraint on his features.*]

BROADBENT. All I can say is that I wish I could drink the health of everyone of you.

DORAN. Dhen come an do it.

BROADBENT [*very solemnly*]. No: I am a teetotaller.

AUNT JUDY [*incredulously*]. Arra since when?

BROADBENT. Since this morning, Miss Doyle. I have had a lesson [*he looks at NORA significantly*] that I shall not forget. It may be that total abstinence has already saved my life; for I was astonished at the steadiness of my nerves when death stared me in the face today. So I will ask you to excuse me. [*He collects himself for a speech.*] Gentlemen: I hope the gravity of the peril through which we have all passed—for I know that the danger to the bystanders was as great as to the occupants of the car—will prove an earnest of closer and more serious relations between us in the future. We have had a somewhat agitating day: a valuable and innocent animal has lost its life: a public building has been wrecked: an aged and infirm lady has suffered an impact for which I feel personally responsible, though my old friend Mr Laurence Doyle unfortunately incurred the first effects of her very natural resentment. I greatly regret the damage to Mr Patrick Farrell's fingers; and I have of course taken care that he shall not suffer pecuniarily by his mishap.

[*Murmurs of admiration at his magnanimity, and A Voice "Youre a gentleman, sir".*]

I am glad to say that Patsy took it like an Irishman, and, far from expressing any vindictive feeling, declared his willingness to break all his fingers and toes for me on the same terms.

[*Subdued applause, and* "More power to Patsy!"]

Gentlemen: I felt at home in Ireland from the first.

[*Rising excitement among his hearers.*]

In every Irish breast I have found that spirit of liberty,

[*A cheery voice* "Hear Hear."]

that instinctive mistrust of the Government,

[*A small pious voice, with intense expression,* "God bless you, sir!"]

that . love of independence [A *defiant voice,* "Thats it! Independence!"], that indignant sympathy with the cause of oppressed nationalities abroad

[*A threatening growl from all: the ground-swell of patriotic passion.*]

and with the resolute assertion of personal rights at home, which is all but extinct in my own country. If it were legally possible I should become a naturalized Irishman; and if ever it be my good fortune to represent an Irish constituency in parliament, it shall be my first care to introduce a Bill legalizing such an operation. I believe a large secton of the Liberal party would avail themselves of it.

[*Momentary scepticism.*]

I do.

[*Convulsive cheering.*]

Gentlemen: I have said enough.

[*Cries of* "Go on."]

No: I have as yet no right to address you at all on political subjects; and we must not abuse the warmhearted Irish hospitality of Miss Doyle by turning her sitting room into a public meeting.

DORAN [*energetically*].   Three cheers for Tom Broadbent, the future member for Rosscullen!

AUNT JUDY [*waving a half knitted sock*].   Hip hip hurray!

[*The cheers are given with great heartiness, as it is by this time, for the more humorous spirits present, a question of vociferation of internal rupture.*]

BROADBENT. Thank you from the bottom of my heart, friends.

NORA [whispering to DORAN]. Take them away, Mr Doran.

[They shake hands.]

Good evenin, Miss Doyle.

[General handshaking, BROADBENT shaking hands with everybody effusively. He accompanies them to the garden and can be heard outside saying Goodnight in every inflexion known to parliamentary candidates. NORA, AUNT JUDY, KEEGAN, LARRY, and CORNELIUS are left in the parlor. LARRY goes to the threshold and watches the scene in the garden.]

NORA. It's a shame to make game of him like that. He's a gradle more good in him than Barney Doran.

CORNELIUS. It's all up with his candidature. He'll be laughed out o the town.

LARRY [turning quickly from the doorway]. Oh no he wont: he's not an Irishman. He'll never know theyre laughing at him; and while theyre laughing he'll win the scat.

CORNELIUS. But he cant prevent the story getting about.

LARRY. He wont want to. He'll tell it himself as one of the most providential episodes in the history of England and Ireland.

AUNT JUDY. Sure he wouldn't make a fool of himself like that.

LARRY. Are you sure he's such a fool after all, Aunt Judy? Suppose you had a vote! which would you rather give it to? the man that told the story of Haffigan's pig Barney Doran's way or Broadbent's way?

AUNT JUDY. Faith I wouldnt give it to a man at all. It's a few women they want in parliament to stop their foolish blather.

BROADBENT [bustling into the room, and taking off his damaged motoring overcoat, which he puts down on the sofa]. Well, thats over. I must apologize for making a speech, Miss Doyle; but they like it, you know. Everything helps in electioneering.

[LARRY takes the chair near the door; draws it near the table; and sits astride it, with his elbows folded on the back.]

AUNT JUDY. I'd no notion you were such an orator, Mr Broadbent.

BROADBENT. Oh, it's only a knack. One picks it up on the platform. It stokes up their enthusiasm.

AUNT JUDY. Oh, I forgot. Youve not met Mr Keegan. Let me introjoosha.

BROADBENT [shaking hands effusively]. Most happy to meet you, Mr Keegan. I have heard of you, though I have not had the pleasure of shaking your hand before. And now may I ask you—for I value no man's opinion more—what you think of my chances here.

KEEGAN [*coldly*]. Your chances, sir, are excellent. You will get into parliament.

BROADBENT [*delighted*]. I hope so. I think so. [*Fluctuating.*] You really think so? You are sure you are not allowing your enthusiasm for our principles to get the better of your judgment?

KEEGAN. I have no enthusiasm for your principles, sir. You will get into parliament because you want to get into it enough to be prepared to take the necessary steps to induce the people to vote for you. That is how people usually get into that fantastic assembly.

BROADBENT [*puzzled*]. Of course. [*Pause.*] Quite so. [*Pause.*] Er—yes. [*Buoyant again.*] I think they will vote for me. Eh? Yes?

AUNT JUDY. Arra why shouldnt they? Look at the people they do vote for!

BROADBENT [*encouraged*]. Thats true: thats very true. When I see the windbags, the carpet-baggers, the charlatans, the—the—the fools and ignoramuses who corrupt the multitude by their wealth, or seduce them by spouting balderdash to them, I cannot help thinking that an Englishman with no humbug about him, who will talk straight common sense and take his stand on the solid ground of principle and public duty, must win his way with men of all classes.

KEEGAN [*quietly*]. Sir: there was a time, in my ignorant youth, when I should have called you a hypocrite.

BROADBENT [*reddening*]. A hypocrite!

NORA [*hastily*]. Oh I'm sure you dont think anything of the sort, Mr Keegan.

BROADBENT [*emphatically*]. Thank you, Miss Reilly: thank you.

CORNELIUS [*gloomily*]. We all have to stretch it a bit in politics: hwats the use o pretendin we dont?

BROADBENT [*stiffly*]. I hope I have said or done nothing that calls for any such observation, Mr Doyle. If there is a vice I detest—or against which my whole public life has been a protest—it is the vice of hypocrisy. I would almost rather be inconsistent than insincere.

KEEGAN. Do not be offended, sir: I know that you are quite sincere. There is a saying in the Scripture which runs—so far as the memory of an oldish man can carry the words—Let not the right side of your brain know what the left side doeth. I learnt at Oxford that this is the secret of the Englishman's strange power of making the best of both worlds.

BROADBENT. Surely the text refers to our right and left hands. I am somewhat surprised to hear a member of your Church quote so essentially Protestant a document as the Bible; but at least you might quote it accurately.

LARRY. Tom: with the best intentions youre making an ass of yourself. You dont understand Mr Keegan's peculiar vein of humor.

BROADBENT [*instantly recovering his confidence*]. Ah! it was only your

delightful Irish humor, Mr Keegan. Of course, of course. How stupid
of me! I'm so sorry. [*He pats* KEEGAN *consolingly on the back.*] John
Bull's wits are still slow, you see. Besides, calling me a hypocrite was
too big a joke to swallow all at once, you know.

KEEGAN.   You must also allow for the fact that I am mad.

NORA.   Ah, dont talk like that, Mr Keegan.

BROADBENT [*encouragingly*].   Not at all, not at all. Only a whimsical
Irishman, eh?

LARRY.   Are you really mad, Mr Keegan?

AUNT JUDY [*shocked*].   Oh, Larry, how could you ask him such a thing?

LARRY.   I dont think Mr Keegan minds. [*To* KEEGAN.] Whats the true
version of the story of that black man you confessed on his deathbed?

KEEGAN.   What story have you heard about that?

LARRY.   I am informed that when the devil came for the black heathen,
he took off your head and turned it three times round before putting
it on again; and that your head's been turned ever since.

NORA [*reproachfully*].   Larry!

KEEGAN [*blandly*].   That is not quite what occurred. [*He collects himself
for a serious utterance: they attend involuntarily.*] I heard that a black
man was dying, and that the people were afraid to go near him. When
I went to the place I found an elderly Hindoo, who told me one of
those tales of unmerited misfortune, of cruel ill luck, of relentless
persecution by destiny, which sometimes wither the commonplaces
of consolation on the lips of a priest. But this man did not complain
of his misfortunes. They were brought upon him, he said, by sins
committed in a former existence. Then, without a word of comfort
from me, he died with a cleareyed resignation that my most earnest
exhortations have rarely produced in a Christian, and left me sitting
there by his bedside with the mystery of this world suddenly revealed
to me.

BROADBENT.   That is a remarkable tribute to the liberty of conscience
enjoyed by the subjects of our Indian Empire.

LARRY.   No doubt; but may we venture to ask what is the mystery of
this world?

KEEGAN.   This world, sir, is very clearly a place of torment and penance,
a place where the fool flourishes and the good and wise are hated and
persecuted, a place where men and women torture one another in the
name of love; where children are scourged and enslaved in the name
of parental duty and education; where the weak in body are poisoned
and mutilated in the name of healing, and the weak in character are
put to the horrible torture of imprisonment, not for hours but for
years, in the name of justice. It is a place where the hardest toil is a
welcome refuge from the horror and tedium of pleasure, and where
charity and good works are done only for hire to ransom the souls of
the spoiler and the sybarite. Now, sir, there is only one place of horror

and torment known to my religion; and that place is hell. Therefore it is plain to me that this earth of ours must be hell, and that we are all here, as the Indian, revealed to me—perhaps he was sent to reveal it to me—to expiate crimes committed by us in as former existence.

AUNT JUDY [*awestruck*].   Heaven save us, what a thing to say!

CORNELIUS [*sighing*].   It's a queer world: thats certain.

BROADBENT.   Your idea is a very clever one, Mr Keegan: really most brilliant: I should never have thought of it. But it seems to me—if I may say so—that you are overlooking the fact that, of the evils you describe, some are absolutely necessary for the preservation of society, and others are encouraged only when the Tories are in office.

LARRY.   I expect you were a Tory in a former existence; and that is why you are here.

BROADBENT [*with conviction*].   Never, Larry, never. But leaving politics out of the question, I find the world quite good enough for me: rather a jolly place, in fact.

KEEGAN [*looking at him with quiet wonder*].   You are satisfied?

BROADBENT.   As a reasonable man, yes. I see no evils in the world— except, of course, natural evils—that cannot be remedied by freedom, self-government, and English institutions. I think so, not because I am an Englishman, but as a matter of common sense.

KEEGAN.   You feel at home in the world, then?

BROADBENT.   Of course. Dont you?

KEEGAN [*from the very depths of his nature*].   No.

BROADBENT [*breezily*].   Try phosphorus pills. I always take them when my brain is overworked. I'll give you the address in Oxford Street.

KEEGAN [*enigmatically: rising*].   Miss Doyle: my wandering fit has come on me: will you excuse me?

AUNT JUDY.   To be sure: you know you can come in n nout as you like.

KEEGAN.   We can finish the game some other time, Miss Reilly. [*He goes for his hat and stick.*]

NORA.   No: I'm out with you [*she disarranges the pieces and rises*]. I was too wicked in a former existence to play backgammon with a good man like you.

AUNT JUDY [*whispering to her*].   Whisht, whisht, child! Dont set him back on that again.

KEEGAN [*to* NORA].   When I look at you, I think that perhaps Ireland is only purgatory, after all. [*He passes on to the garden door.*]

NORA.   Galong with you!

BROADBENT [*whispering to Cornelius*].   Has he a vote?

CORNELIUS [*nodding*].   Yes. An theres lotsle vote the way he tells them.

KEEGAN [*at the garden door, with gentle gravity*].   Good evening, Mr Broadbent. You have set me thinking. Thank you.

BROADBENT [*delighted, hurrying across to him to shake hands*].   No, really? You find that contact with English ideas is stimulating, eh?

KEEGAN. I am never tired of hearing you talk, Mr Broadbent.

BROADBENT [*modestly remonstrating*]. Oh come! come!

KEEGAN. Yes, I assure you. You are an extremely interesting man. [*He goes out.*]

BROADBENT [*enthusiastically*].   What a nice chap! What an intelligent, broadminded character, considering his cloth! By the way, I'd better have a wash. [*He takes up his coat and cap, and leaves the room through the inner door.*]

[NORA *returns to her chair and shuts up the backgammon board.*]

AUNT JUDY. Keegan's very queer today. He has his mad fit on him.

CORNELIUS [*worried and bitter*].   I wouldn't say but he's right after all. It's a contrairy world. [*To* LARRY.] Why would you be such a fool as to let Broadbent take the seat in parliament from you?

LARRY [*glancing at* NORA].   He will take more than that from me before he's done here.

CORNELIUS. I wish he'd never set foot in my house, bad luck to his fat face! D'ye think he'd lend me £300 on the farm, Larry? When I'm so hard up, it seems a waste o money not to mortgage it now it's me own.

LARRY. I can lend you £300 on it.

CORNELIUS. No, no; I wasnt putn in for that. When I die and leave you the farm I should like to be able to feel that it was all me own, and not half yours to start with. Now I'll take me oath Barney Doarn's going to ask Broadbent to lend him £500 on the mill to put in a new hweel; for the old one'll harly hol together. An Haffigan cant sleep with covetn that corner o land at the foot of his medda that belongs to Doolan. He'll have to mortgage to buy it. I may as well be first as last. D'ye think Broadbent'd len me a little?

LARRY. I'm quite sure he will.

CORNELIUS. Is he as ready as that? Would he len me five hunderd, d'ye think?

LARRY. He'll lend you more than the landll ever be worth to you; so for Heaven's sake be prudent.

CORNELIUS [*judicially*].   All right, all right, me son: I'll be careful. I'm goin into the office for a bit. [*He withdraws through the inner door, obviously to prepare his application to* BROADBENT.]

AUNT JUDY [*indignantly*].   As if he hadnt seen enough o borryin when he was an agent without beginning borryin himself! [*She rises.*] I'll borry him, so I will. [*She puts her knitting on the table and follows him out, with a resolute air that bodes trouble for* CORNELIUS.]

[LARRY *and* NORA *are left together for the first time since his arrival. She looks at him with a smile that perishes as she sees him aimlessly rocking his chair, and reflecting, evidently not about her, with his lips pursed as if he were whistling. With a catch in her throat she takes up* AUNT JUDY's *knitting, and makes a pretence of going on with it.*]

NORA.　I suppose it didnt seem very long to you.

LARRY [*starting*].　Eh? What didnt?

NORA.　The eighteen years youve been away.

LARRY.　Oh, that! No: it seems hardly more than a week. I've been so busy—had so little time to think.

NORA.　Ive had nothin else to do but think.

LARRY.　That was very bad for you. Why didnt you give it up? Why did you stay here?

NORA.　Because nobody sent for me to go anywhere else, I suppose. Thats why.

LARRY.　Yes: one does stick frightfully in the same place, unless some external force comes and routs one out.

[*He yawns slightly; but as she looks up quickly at him, he pulls himself together and rises with an air of waking up and setting to work cheerfully to make himself agreeable.*]

And how have you been all this time?

NORA.　Quite well, thank you.

LARRY.　Thats right. [*Suddenly finding that he has nothing else to say, and being ill at ease in consequence, he strolls about the room humming distractedly.*]

NORA [*struggling with her tears*].　Is that all you have to say to me, Larry?

LARRY.　Well, what is there to say? You see, we know each other so well.

NORA [*a little consoled*].　Yes: of course we do.

[*He does not reply.*]

I wonder you came back at all.

LARRY.　I couldnt help it.

[*She looks up affectionately.*]

Tom made me.

[*She looks down again quickly to conceal the effect of this blow. He whistles another stave; then resumes.*]

I had a sort of dread of returning to Ireland. I felt somehow that my luck would turn if I came back. And now here I am, none the worse.

NORA.　Praps it's a little dull for you.

LARRY.　No: I havnt exhausted the interest of strolling about the old places and remembering and romancing about them.

NORA [*hopefully*].   Oh! You do remember the places, then?

LARRY.   Of course. They have associations.

NORA [*not doubting that the associations are with her*].   I suppose so.

LARRY.   M'yes. I can remember particular spots where I had long fits of thinking about the countries I meant to get to when I escaped from Ireland. America and London, and sometimes Rome and the east.

NORA [*deeply mortified*].   Was that all you used to be thinking about?

LARRY.   Well, there was precious little else to think about here, my dear Nora, except sometimes at sunset, when one got maudlin and called Ireland Erin, and imagined one was remembering the days of old, and so forth. [*He whistles Let Erin Remember.*]

NORA.   Did jever get a letter I wrote you last February?

LARRY.   Oh yes; and I really intended to answer it. But I havnt had a moment; and I knew you wouldnt mind. You see, I am so afraid of boring you by writing about affairs you dont understand and people you dont know! And yet what else have I to write about? I begin a letter; and then I tear it up again. The fact is, fond as we are of one another, Nora, we have so little in common—I mean of course the things one can put in a letter—that correspondence is apt to become the hardest of hard work.

NORA.   Yes: it's hard for me to know anything about you if you never tell me anything.

LARRY [*pettishly*].   Nora: a man cant sit down and write his life day by day when he's tired enough with having lived it.

NORA.   I'm not blaming you.

LARRY [*looking at her with some concern*].   You seem rather out of spirits. [*Going closer to her, anxiously and tenderly.*] You havnt got neuralgia, have you?

NORA.   No.

LARRY [*reassured*].   I get a touch of it sometimes when I am below par. [*Absently, again strolling about.*] Yes, yes. [*He gazes through the doorway at the Irish landscape, and sings, almost unconsciously, but very expressively, an air from Offenbach's Whittington.*][2]

Though sum-mer smiles on here for e-ver, And though full sweet the charm may

be,   Tell Eng-land I'll for-get her ne-ver,

_____

2. Jacques Offenbach (1819–80); "Whittington and His Cat" (1874), operetta based on folktale.

[NORA, *who has been at first touched by the tenderness of his singing, puts down her knitting at this very unexpected sentiment, and stares at him. He continues until the melody soars out of his range, when he trails off into whistling* Let Erin Remember.]

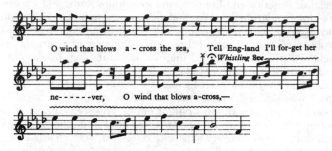

O wind that blows a - cross the sea, Tell Eng-land I'll for-get her ne- - - - - -ver, O wind that blows a-cross,—

I'm afraid I'm boring you, Nora, though youre too kind to say so.

NORA.   Are you wanting to get back to England already?

LARRY.   Not at all. Not at all.

NORA.   Thats a queer song to sing to me if youre not.

LARRY.   The song! Oh, it doesnt mean anything: it's by a German Jew, like most English patriotic sentiment. Never mind me, my dear: go on with your work; and dont let me bore you.

NORA [*bitterly*].   Rosscullen isnt such a lively place that I am likely to be bored by you at our first talk together after eighteen years, though you dont seem to have much to say to me after all.

LARRY.   Eighteen years is a devilish long time, Nora. Now if it had been eighteen minutes, or even eighteen months, we should be able to pick up the interrupted thread, and chatter like two magpies. But as it is, I have simply nothing to say; and you seem to have less.

NORA.   I—[*her tears choke her; but she keeps up appearances desperately*].

LARRY [*quite unconscious of his cruelty*].   In a week or so we shall be quite old friends again. Meanwhile, as I feel that I am not making myself particularly entertaining, I'll take myself off. Tell Tom Ive gone for a stroll over the hill.

NORA.   You seem very fond of Tom, as you call him.

LARRY [*the triviality going suddenly out of his voice*].   Yes: I'm fond of Tom.

NORA.   Oh, well, dont let me keep you from him.

LARRY.   I know quite well that my departure will be a relief. Rather a failure, this first meeting after eighteen years, eh? Well, never mind: these great sentimental events always are failures; and now the worst of it's over anyhow. [*He goes out through the garden door.*]

[NORA, *left alone, struggles wildly to save herself from breaking down, and then drops her face on the table and gives way to a convulsion of crying. Her sobs shake her so that she can hear nothing; and she has no suspicion that she is no longer alone until her head and breast are raised by* BROADBENT, *who, returning newly washed and combed through the inner door, has seen her condition, first with surprise and concern, and then with an emotional disturbance that quite upsets him.*]

BROADBENT.   Miss Reilly. Miss Reilly. Whats the matter? Dont cry: I cant stand it: you musnt cry.

[*She makes a choked effort to speak, so painful that he continues with impulsive sympathy.*]

No: dont try to speak: it's all right now. Have your cry out: never mind me: trust me. [*Gathering her to him, and babbling consolatorily.*] Cry on my chest: the only really comfortable place for a woman to cry is a man's chest: a real man, a real friend. A good broad chest, eh? not less than forty-two inches—no: dont fuss: never mind the conventions: we're two friends, arnt we? Come now, come, come! It's all right and comfortable and happy now, isnt it?

NORA [*through her tears*].   Let me go. I want me handkerchief.

BROADBENT [*holding her with one arm and producing a large silk handkerchief from his breast pocket*].   Heres a handkerchief. Let me [*he dabs her tears dry with it*]. Never mind your own: it's too small: it's one of those wretched little cambric handkerchiefs—

NORA [*sobbing*].   Indeed it's a common cotton one.

BROADBENT.   Of course it's a common cotton one—silly little cotton one—not good enough for the dear eyes of Nora Cryna—

NORA [*spluttering into a hysterical laugh and clutching him convulsively with her fingers while she tries to stifle her laughter against his collar bone*].   Oh dont make me laugh: please dont make me laugh.

BROADBENT [*terrified*].   I didnt mean to, on my soul. What is it? What is it?

NORA.   Nora Creena, Nora Creena.

BROADBENT [*patting her*].   Yes, yes, of course, Nora Creena, Nora acushla[3] [*he makes cush rhyme to plush*]—

NORA.   Acushla [*she makes cush rhyme to bush*].

BROADBENT.   Oh, confound the language! Nora darling—my Nora—the Nora I love—

NORA [*shocked into propriety*].   You musnt talk like that to me.

BROADBENT [*suddenly becoming prodigiously solemn and letting her go*].   No, of course not. I dont mean it. At least I do mean it; but I

3. Gaelic endearment: Nora of my heart.

know it's premature. I had no right to take advantage of your being a little upset; but I lost my self-control for a moment.

NORA [*wondering at him*].   I think youre a very kindhearted man, Mr Broadbent; but you seem to me to have no self-control at all [*she turns her face away with a keen pang of shame and adds*] no more than myself.

BROADBENT [*resolutely*].   Oh yes, I have: you should see me when I am really roused: then I have TREMENDOUS self-control. Remember: we have been alone together only once before; and then, I regret to say, I was in a disgusting state.

NORA.   Ah no, Mr Broadbent: you wernt disgusting.

BROADBENT [*mercilessly*].   Yes I was: nothing can excuse it: perfectly beastly. It must have made a most unfavorable impression on you.

NORA.   Oh, sure it's all right. Say no more about that.

BROADBENT.   I must, Miss Reilly: it is my duty. I shall not detain you long. May I ask you to sit down.

[*He indicates her chair with oppressive solemnity. She sits down wondering. He then, with the same portentous gravity, places a chair for himself near her; sits down; and proceeds to explain.*]

First, Miss Reilly, may I say that I have tasted nothing of an alcoholic nature today.

NORA.   It doesnt seem to make as much difference in you as it would in an Irishman, somehow.

BROADBENT.   Perhaps not. Perhaps not. I never quite lose myself.

NORA [*consolingly*].   Well, anyhow, youre all right now.

BROADBENT [*fervently*].   Thank you, Miss Reilly: I am. Now we shall get along. [*Tenderly, lowering his voice.*] Nora: I was in earnest last night.

[NORA *moves as if to rise.*]

No: one moment. You must not think I am going to press you for an answer before you have known me for 24 hours. I am a reasonable man, I hope; and I am prepared to wait as long as you like, provided you will give me some small assurance that the answer will not be unfavorable.

NORA.   How could I go back from it if I did? I sometimes think youre not quite right in your head, Mr Broadbent, you say such funny things.

BROADBENT.   Yes: I know I have a strong sense of humor which sometimes makes people doubt whether I am quite serious. That is why I have always thought I should like to marry an Irishwoman. She would always understand my jokes. For instance, you would understand them, eh?

NORA [*uneasily*].   Mr Broadbent: I couldnt.

BROADBENT [*soothingly*].   Wait: let me break this to you gently, Miss

Reilly: hear me out. I daresay you have noticed that in speaking to you I have been putting a very strong constraint on myself, so as to avoid wounding your delicacy by too abrupt an avowal of my feelings. Well, I feel now that the time has come to be open, to be frank, to be explicit. Miss Reilly: you have inspired in me a very strong attachment. Perhaps, with a woman's intuition, you have already guessed that.

NORA [rising distractedly].   Why do you talk to me in that unfeeling nonsensical way?

BROADBENT [rising also, much astonished].   Unfeeling! Nonsensical!

NORA.   Dont you know that you have said things to me that no man ought to say unless—unless—[she suddenly breaks down again and hides her face on the table as before]. Oh, go away from me: I wont get married at all: what is it but heartbreak and disappointment?

BROADBENT [developing the most formidable symptoms of rage and grief].   Do you mean to say that you are going to refuse me: that you dont care for me?

NORA [looking at him in consternation].   Oh, dont take it to heart, Mr Br—

BROADBENT [flushed and almost choking].   I dont want to be petted and blarneyed. [With childish rage.] I love you. I want you for my wife. [In despair] I cant help your refusing. I'm helpless: I can do nothing. You have no right to ruin my whole life. You—[a hysterical convulsion stops him].

NORA [almost awestruck].   Youre not going to cry, are you? I never thought a man could cry. Dont.

BROADBENT.   I'm not crying. I—I—I leave that sort of thing to your damned sentimental Irishmen. You think I have no feeling because I am a plain unemotional Englishman, with no powers of expression.

NORA.   I dont think you know the sort of man you are at all. Whatever may be the matter with you, it's not want of feeling.

BROADBENT [hurt and petulant].   It's you who have no feeling. Youre as heartless as Larry.

NORA.   What do you expect me to do? Is it to throw meself at your head the minute the word is out o your mouth?

BROADBENT [striking his silly head with his fists].   Oh, what a fool! what a brute I am! It's only your Irish delicacy: of course, of course. You mean Yes. Eh? What? Yes? yes? yes?

NORA.   I think you might understand that though I might choose to be an old maid, I could never marry anybody but you now.

BROADBENT [clasping her violently to his breast, with a crow of immense relief and triumph].   Ah, thats right, thats right: thats magnificent. I knew you would see what a first-rate thing this will be for both of us.

NORA [incommoded and not at all enraptured by his ardor].   Youre dreadfully strong, an a gradle too free with your strength. An I never thought o whether it'd be a good thing for us or not. But when you found me here that time, I let you be kind to me, and cried in your arms, because I was too wretched to think of anything but the comfort of it. An how could I let any other man touch me after that?

BROADBENT [*moved*].   Now thats very nice of you, Nora: thats really most delicately womanly. [*He kisses her hand chivalrously.*]

NORA [*looking earnestly and a little doubtfully at him*].   Surely if you let one woman cry on you like that youd never let another touch you.

BROADBENT [*conscientiously*].   One should not. One ought not, my dear girl. But the honest truth is, if a chap is at all a pleasant sort of chap, his chest becomes a fortification that has to stand many assaults: at least it is so in England.

NORA [*curtly, much disgusted*].   Then youd better marry an English-woman.

BROADBENT [*making a wry face*].   No, no: the Englishwoman is too prosaic for my taste, too material, too much of the animated beefsteak about her. The ideal is what I like. Now Larry's taste is just the oppo-site: he likes em solid and bouncing and rather keen about him. It's a very convenient difference; for weve never been in love with the same woman.

NORA.   An d'ye mean to tell me to me face that youve ever been in love before?

BROADBENT.   Lord! yes.

NORA.   I'm not your first love!

BROADBENT.   First love is only a little foolishness and a lot of curiosity: no really self-respecting woman would take advantage of it. No, my dear Nora: Ive done with all that long ago. Love affairs always end in rows. We're not going to have any rows: we're going to have a solid four-square home: man and wife: comfort and common sense. And plenty of affection, eh [*he puts his arm round her with confident pro-prietorship*]?

NORA [*coldly, trying to get away*].   I dont want any other woman's leav-ings.

BROADBENT [*holding her*].   Nobody asked you to, maam. I never asked any woman to marry me before.

NORA [*severely*].   Then why didnt you if youre an honorable man?

BROADBENT.   Well, to tell you the truth, they were mostly married already. But never mind! there was nothing wrong. Come! dont take a mean advantage of me. After all, you must have had a fancy or two yourself, eh?

NORA [*conscience-stricken*].   Yes. I suppose Ive no right to be particular.

BROADBENT [*humbly*].   I know I'm not good enough for you, Nora. But no man is, you know, when the woman is a really nice woman.

NORA.   Oh, I'm no better than yourself. I may as well tell you about it.

BROADBENT.   No, no: lets have no telling: much better not. *I* shant tell you anything: dont you tell me anything. Perfect confidence in one another and no tellings: thats the way to avoid rows.

NORA.   Dont think it was anything I need be ashamed of.

BROADBENT.   I dont.

NORA.   It was only that I'd never known anybody else that I could care for; and I was foolish enough once to think that Larry—

BROADBENT [*disposing of the idea at once*].   Larry! Oh, that wouldnt have done at all, not at all. You dont know Larry as I do, my dear. He has absolutely no capacity for enjoyment: he couldnt make any woman happy. He's as clever as beblowed; but life's too earthly for him: he doesnt really care for anything or anybody.

NORA.   Ive found that out.

BROADBENT.   Of course you have. No, my dear: take my word for it, youre jolly well out of that. There! [*swinging her round against his breast*] thats much more comfortable for you.

NORA [*with Irish peevishness*].   Ah, you mustnt go on like that. I dont like it.

BROADBENT [*unabashed*].   Youll acquire the taste by degrees. You mustnt mind me: it's an absolute necessity of my nature that I should have somebody to hug occasionally. Besides, it's food for you: itll plump out your muscles and make em elastic and set up your figure.

NORA.   Well, I'm sure! if this is English manners! Arnt you ashamed to talk about such things?

BROADBENT [*in the highest feather*].   Not a bit. By George, Nora, it's a tremendous thing to be able to enjoy oneself. Lets go off for a walk out of this stuffy little room. I want the open air to expand in, Come along. Co-o-ome along.

> [*He puts her arm into his and sweeps her out into the garden as an equinoctial gale might sweep a dry leaf.*
>
> *Later in the evening, the grasshopper is again enjoying the sunset by the great stone on the hill; but this time he enjoys neither the stimulus of* KEEGAN's *conversation nor the pleasure of terrifying* PATSY FARRELL. *He is alone until* NORA *and* BROAD-BENT *come up the hill arm in arm.* BROADBENT *is still breezy and confident; but she has her head averted from him and is almost in tears.*]

BROADBENT [*stopping to snuff up the hillside air*].   Ah! I like this spot. I like this view. This would be a jolly good place for a hotel and a golf links. Friday to Tuesday, railway ticket and hotel all inclusive. I tell you, Nora, I'm going to develop this place. [*Looking at her.*] Hallo! Whats the matter? Tired?

NORA [*unable to restrain her tears*].   I'm ashamed out o me life.

BROADBENT [*astonished*].   Ashamed! What of?

NORA.   Oh, how could you drag me all round the place like that, telling everybody that we're going to be married, and introjoocing me to the lowest of the low, and letting them shake hans with me, and encouraging them to make free with us? I little thought I should live to be shaken hans with be Doolan in broad daylight in the public street of Rosscullen.

BROADBENT.   But, my dear, Doolan's a publican: a most influential man. By the way, I asked him if his wife would be at home tomorrow. He said she would; so you must take the motor car round and call on her.

NORA [aghast].   Is it me call on Doolan's wife!

BROADBENT.   Yes, of course: call on all their wives. We must get a copy of the register and a supply of canvassing cards. No use calling on people who havnt votes. Youll be a great success as a canvasser, Nora: they call you the heiress; and theyll be flattered no end by your calling, especially as youve never cheapened yourself by speaking to them before—have you?

NORA [indignantly].   Not likely, indeed.

BROADBENT.   Well, we musnt be stiff and stand-off, you know. We must be thoroughly democratic, and patronize everybody without distinction of class. I tell you I'm a jolly lucky man, Nora Cryna. I get engaged to the most delightful woman in Ireland; and it turns out that I couldnt have done a smarter stroke of electioneering.

NORA.   An would you let me demean meself like that, just to get yourself into parliament?

BROADBENT [buoyantly].   Aha! Wait til you find out what an exciting game electioneering is: youll be mad to get me in. Besides, youd like people to say that Tom Broadbent's wife had been the making of him? that she got him into parliament? into the Cabinet, perhaps, eh?

NORA.   God knows I dont grudge you me money! But to lower meself to the level of common people—

BROADBENT.   To a member's wife, Nora, nobody is common provided he's on the register. Come, my dear! it's all right: do you think I'd let you do it if it wasnt? The best people do it. Everybody does it.

NORA [who has been biting her lip and looking over the hill, disconsolate and unconvinced].   Well, praps you know best what they do in England. They must have very little respect for themselves. I think I'll go in now. I see Larry and Mr Keegan coming up the hill; and I'm not fit to talk to them.

BROADBENT.   Just wait and say something nice to Keegan. They tell me he controls nearly as many votes as Father Dempsey himself.

NORA.   You little know Peter Keegan. He'd see through me as if I was a pane o glass.

BROADBENT.   Oh, he wont like it any the less for that. What really flatters a man is that you think him worth flattering. Not that I would flatter any man: dont think that. I'll just go and meet him.

[*He goes down the hill with the eager forward look of a man about to greet a valued acquaintance.* NORA *dries her eyes, and turns to go as* LARRY *strolls up the hill to her.*]

LARRY. Nora.

[*She turns and looks at him hardly, without a word. He continues anxiously, in his most conciliatory tone.*]

When I left you that time, I was just as wretched as you. I didnt rightly know what I wanted to say; and my tongue kept clacking to cover the loss I was at. Well, Ive been thinking ever since; and now I know what I ought to have said. Ive come back to say it.

NORA. Youve come too late, then. You thought eighteen years was not long enough, and that you might keep me waiting a day longer. Well, you were mistaken. I'm engaged to your friend Mr Broadbent; and I'm done with you.

LARRY [*naïvely*]. But that was the very thing I was going to advise you to do.

NORA [*involuntarily*]. Oh you brute! to tell me that to me face!

LARRY [*nervously relapsing into his most Irish manner*]. Nora, dear, dont you understand that I'm an Irishman, and he's an Englishman. He wants you; and he grabs you. *I* want you; and I quarrel with you and have to go on wanting you.

NORA. So you may. Youd better go back to England to the animated beefsteaks youre so fond of.

LARRY [*amazed*]. Nora! [*Guessing where she got the metaphor.*] He's been talking about me, I see. Well, never mind: we must be friends, you and I. I dont want his marriage to you to be his divorce from me.

NORA. You care more for him than you ever did for me.

LARRY [*with curt sincerity*]. Yes of course I do: why should I tell you lies about it? Nora Reilly was a person of very little consequence to me or anyone else outside this miserable little hole. But Mrs Tom Broadbent will be a person of very considerable consequence indeed. Play your new part well, and there will be no more neglect, no more loneliness, no more idle regrettings and vain-hopings in the evenings by the Round Tower, but real life and real work and real cares and real joys among real people: solid English life in London, the very centre of the world. You will find your work cut out for you keeping Tom's house and entertaining Tom's friends and getting Tom into parliament; but it will be worth the effort.

NORA. You talk as if I was under an obligation to him for marrying me.

LARRY. I talk as I think. Youve made a very good match, let me tell you.

NORA. Indeed! Well, some people might say he's not done so badly himself.

LARRY. If you mean that you will be a treasure to him, he thinks so now; and you can keep him thinking so if you like.

NORA. I wasnt thinking o meself at all.

LARRY. Were you thinking of your money, Nora?

NORA. I didnt say so.

LARRY. Your money will not pay your cook's wages in London.

NORA [*flaming up*]. If thats true—and the more shame for you to throw it in me face if it is true—at all events itll make us independent; for if the worst comes to the worst, we can always come back here an live on it. An if I have to keep his house for him, at all events I can keep you out of it; for Ive done with you; and I wish I'd never seen you. So goodbye to you, Mister Larry Doyle. [*She turns her back on him and goes home.*]

LARRY [*watching her as she goes*]. Goodbye. Goodbye, Oh, thats so Irish! Irish both of us to the backbone: Irish! Irish! Iri—

[BROADBENT *arrives, conversing energetically with* KEEGAN.]

BROADBENT. Nothing pays like a golfing hotel, if you hold the land instead of the shares, and if the furniture people stand in with you, and if you are a good man of business.

LARRY. Nora's gone home.

BROADBENT [*with conviction*]. You were right this morning, Larry. I must feed up Nora. She's weak; and it makes her fanciful. Oh, by the way, did I tell you that we're engaged?

LARRY. She told me herself.

BROADBENT [*complacently*]. She's rather full of it, as you may imagine. Poor Nora! Well, Mr Keegan, as I said, I begin to see my way here. I begin to see my way.

KEEGAN [*with a courteous inclination*]. The conquering Englishman, sir. Within 24 hours of your arrival you have carried off our only heiress, and practically secured the parliamentary seat. And you have promised me that when I come here in the evenings to meditate on my madness; to watch the shadow of the Round Tower lengthening in the sunset; to break my heart uselessly in the curtained gloaming over the dead heart and blinded soul of the island of the saints, you will comfort me with the bustle of a great hotel, and the sight of the little children carrying the golf clubs of your tourists as a preparation for the life to come.

BROADBENT [*quite touched, mutely offering him a cigar to console him, at which he smiles and shakes his head*]. Yes, Mr Keegan: youre quite right. Theres poetry in everything, even [*looking absently into the cigar case*] in the most modern prosaic things, if you know how to extract it [*he extracts a cigar for himself and offers one to* LARRY, *who takes it*]. If I was to be shot for it I couldnt extract it myself; but thats where you come in, you see. [*Roguishly, waking up from his reverie and bustling* KEEGAN *goodhumoredly.*] And then I shall wake you up a bit. Thats where I come in: eh? d'ye see? Eh? eh? [*He pats him very pleasantly on the shoulder, half admiringly, half pityingly.*] Just so, just so. [*Coming back to business.*] By the way, I believe I can do better than a light railway here. There seems to be no question now that the motor boat has come to stay. Well, look at your magnificent river there, going to waste.

KEEGAN [*closing his eyes*]. "Silent, O Moyle, be the roar of thy waters."[4]

BROADBENT. You know, the roar of a motor boat is quite pretty.

KEEGAN. Provided it does not drown the Angelus.

BROADBENT [*reassuringly*]. Oh no: it wont do that: not the least danger. You know, a church bell can make a devil of a noise when it likes.

KEEGAN. You have an answer for everything, sir. But your plans leave one question still unanswered: how to get butter out of a dog's throat.

BROADBENT. Eh?

KEEGAN. You cannot build your golf links and hotels in the air. For that you must own our land. And how will you drag our acres from the ferret's grip of Matthew Haffigan? How will you persuade Cornelius Doyle to forgo the pride of being a small landowner? How will Barney Doran's millrace agree with your motor boats? Will Doolan help you to get a license for your hotel?

BROADBENT. My dear sir: to all intents and purposes the syndicate I represent already owns half Rosscullen. Doolan's is a tied house; and the brewers are in the syndicate. As to Haffigan's farm and Doran's mill and Mr Doyle's place and half a dozen others, they will be mortgaged to me before a month is out.

KEEGAN. But pardon me, you will not lend them more on their land than the land is worth; so they will be able to pay you the interest.

BROADBENT. Ah, you are a poet, Mr Keegan, not a man of business.

LARRY. We will lend everyone of these men half as much again on their land as it is worth, or ever can be worth, to them.

BROADBENT. You forget, sir, that we, with our capital, our knowledge, our organization, and may I say our English business habits, can make or lose ten pounds out of land that Haffigan, with all his industry, could not make or lose ten shillings out of. Doran's mill is a superannuated folly: I shall want it for electric lighting.

LARRY. What is the use of giving land to such men? they are too small, too poor, too ignorant, too simpleminded to hold it against us: you might as well give a dukedom to a crossing sweeper.

BROADBENT. Yes, Mr Keegan: this place may have an industrial future, or it may have a residential future: I cant tell yet; but it's not going to be a future in the hands of your Dorans and Haffigans, poor devils!

KEEGAN. It may have no future at all. Have you thought of that?

4. "The Song of Fionnuala," by Irish poet Thomas Moore (1779–1852).

BROADBENT.   Oh, I'm not afraid of that. I have faith in Ireland. Great faith, Mr Keegan.

KEEGAN.   And we have none: only empty enthusiasms and patriotisms, and emptier memories and regrets. Ah yes: you have some excuse for believing that if there be any future, it will be yours; for our faith seems dead, and our hearts cold and cowed. An island of dreamers who wake up in your jails, of critics and cowards whom you buy and tame for your own service, of bold rogues who help you to plunder us that they may plunder you afterwards.

BROADBENT [*a little impatient of this unbusinesslike view*].   Yes, yes; but you know you might say that of any country. The fact is, there are only two qualities in the world: efficiency and inefficiency, and only two sorts of people: the efficient and the inefficient. It dont matter whether theyre English or Irish. I shall collar this place, not because I'm an Englishman and Haffigan and Co are Irishmen, but because theyre duffers, and I know my way about.

KEEGAN.   Have you considered what is to become of Haffigan?

LARRY.   Oh, we'll employ him in some capacity or other, and probably pay him more than he makes for himself now.

BROADBENT [*dubiously*].   Do you think so? No no: Haffigan's too old. It really doesnt pay now to take on men over forty even for unskilled labor, which I suppose is all Haffigan would be good for. No: Haffigan had better go to America, or into the Union,[5] poor old chap! He's worked out, you know: you can see it.

KEEGAN.   Poor lost soul, so cunningly fenced in with invisible bars!

LARRY.   Haffigan doesnt matter much. He'll die presently.

BROADBENT [*shocked*].   Oh come, Larry! Don't be unfeeling. It's hard on Haffigan. It's always hard on the inefficient.

LARRY.   Pah! what does it matter where an old and broken man spends his last days, or whether he has a million at the bank or only the workhouse dole? It's the young men, the able men, that matter. The real tragedy of Haffigan is the tragedy of his wasted youth, his stunted mind, his drudging over his clods and pigs until he has become a clod and a pig himself—until the soul within him has smouldered into nothing but a dull temper that hurts himself and all around him. I say let him die, and let us have no more of his like. And let young Ireland take care that it doesnt share his fate, instead of making another empty grievance of it. Let your syndicate come—

BROADBENT.   Your syndicate too, old chap. You have your bit of the stock.

LARRY.   Yes: mine if you like. Well, our syndicate has no conscience: it has no more regard for your Haffigans and Doolans and Dorans than it has for a gang of Chinese coolies. It will use your patriotic

5. Public-assistance workhouse.

blatherskite and balderdash to get parliamentary powers over you as cynically as it would bait a mousetrap with toasted cheese. It will plan, and organize, and find capital while you slave like bees for it and revenge yourselves by paying politicians and penny newspapers out of your small wages to write articles and report speeches against its wickedness and tyranny, and to crack up your own Irish heroism, just as Haffigan once paid a witch a penny to put a spell on Billy Byrne's cow. In the end it will grind the nonsense out of you, and grind strength and sense into you.

BROADBENT [*out of patience*]. Why cant you say a simple thing simply, Larry, without all that Irish exaggeration and talky-talky? The syndicate is a perfectly respectable body of responsible men of good position. We'll take Ireland in hand, and by straightforward business habits teach it efficiency and self-help on sound Liberal principles. You agree with me, Mr Keegan, dont you?

KEEGAN. Sir: I may even vote for you.

BROADBENT [*sincerely moved, shaking his hand warmly*]. You shall never regret it, Mr Keegan: I give you my word for that. I shall bring money here: I shall raise wages: I shall found public institutions: a library, Polytechnic (undenominational, of course), a gymnasium, a cricket club, perhaps an art school. I shall make a Garden city of Rosscullen: the round tower shall be thoroughly repaired and restored.

KEEGAN. And our place of torment shall be as clean and orderly as the cleanest and most orderly place I know in Ireland, which is our poetically named Mountjoy prison.[6] Well, perhaps I had better vote for an efficient devil that knows his own mind and his own business than for a foolish patriot who has no mind and no business.

BROADBENT [*stiffly*]. Devil is rather a strong expression in that connexion, Mr Keegan.

KEEGAN. Not from a man who knows that this world is hell. But since the word offends you, let me soften it, and compare you simply to an ass.

[LARRY *whitens with anger.*]

BROADBENT [*reddening*]. An ass!

KEEGAN [*gently*]. You may take it without offence from a madman who calls the ass his brother—and a very honest, useful and faithful brother too. The ass, sir, is the most efficient of beasts, matter-of-fact, hardy, friendly when you treat him as a fellow-creature, stubborn when you abuse him, ridiculous only in love, which sets him braying, and in politics, which move him to roll about in the public road and raise a dust about nothing. Can you deny these qualities and habits in yourself, sir?

6. Prison in Dublin.

BROADBENT [*goodhumoredly*].   Well, yes, I'm afraid I do, you know.

KEEGAN.   Then perhaps you will confess to the ass's one fault.

BROADBENT.   Perhaps so: what is it?

KEEGAN.   That he wastes all his virtues—his efficiency, as you call it—
in doing the will of his greedy masters instead of doing the will of
Heaven that is in himself. He is efficient in the service of Mammon,
mighty in mischief, skilful in ruin, heroic in destruction. But he comes
to browse here without knowing that the soil his hoof touches is holy
ground. Ireland, sir, for good or evil, is like no other place under
heaven; and no man can touch its sod or breathe its air without
becoming better or worse. It produces two kinds of men in strange
perfection: saints and traitors. It is called the island of the saints; but
indeed in these later years it might be more fitly called the island of
the traitors; for our harvest of these is the fine flower of the world's
crop of infamy. But the day may come when these islands shall live
by the quality of their men rather than by the abundance of their
minerals; and then we shall see.

LARRY.   Mr Keegan: if you are going to be sentimental about Ireland, I
shall bid you good evening. We have had enough of that, and more
than enough of cleverly proving that everybody who is not an Irishman is an ass. It is neither good sense nor good manners. It will not
stop the syndicate; and it will not interest young Ireland so much as
my friend's gospel of efficiency.

BROADBENT.   An, yes, yes: efficiency is the thing. I dont in the least
mind your chaff, Mr Keegan; but Larry's right on the main point.
The world belongs to the efficient.

KEEGAN [*with polished irony*].   I stand rebuked, gentlemen. But believe
me, I do every justice to the efficiency of you and your syndicate. You
are both, I am told, thoroughly efficient civil engineers; and I have
no doubt the golf links will be a triumph of your art. Mr. Broadbent
will get into parliament most efficiently, which is more than St Patrick
could do if he were alive now. You may even build the hotel efficiently if you can find enough efficient masons, carpenters, and
plumbers, which I rather doubt. [*Dropping his irony, and beginning
to fall into the attitude of the priest rebuking sin.*] When the hotel
becomes insolvent

> [BROADBENT *takes his cigar out of his mouth, a little taken aback.*]

your English business habits will secure the thorough efficiency of the
liquidation. You will reorganize the scheme efficiently; you will liq-
uidate its second bankruptcy efficiently;

> [BROADBENT *and* LARRY *look quickly at one another; for this,
> unless the priest is an old financial hand, must be inspiration.*]

you will get rid of its original shareholders efficiently after efficiently
ruining them; and you will finally profit very efficiently by getting that

hotel for a few shillings on the pound. [*More and more sternly.*] Besides these efficient operations, you will foreclose your mortgages most efficiently [*his rebuking forefinger goes up in spite of himself*]; you will drive Haffigan to America very efficiently; you will find a use for Barney Doran's foul mouth and bullying temper by employing him to slavedrive your laborers very efficiently; and [*low and bitter*] when at last this poor desolate countryside becomes a busy mint in which we shall all slave to make money for you, with our Polytechnic to teach us how to do it efficiently, and our library to fuddle the few imaginations your distilleries will spare, and our repaired Round Tower with admission sixpence, and refreshments and penny-in-the-slot mutoscopes to make it interesting, then no doubt your English and American shareholders will spend all the money we make for them very efficiently in shooting and hunting, in operations for cancer and appendicitis, in gluttony and gambling; and you will devote what they save to fresh land development schemes. For four wicked centuries the world has dreamed this foolish dream of efficiency; and the end is not yet. But the end will come.

BROADBENT [*seriously*].   Too true, Mr Keegan, only too true. And most eloquently put. It reminds me of poor Ruskin: a great man, you know. I sympathize. Believe me, I'm on your side. Dont sneer, Larry: I used to read a lot of Shelley [7] years ago. Let us be faithful to the dreams of our youth [*he wafts a wreath of cigar smoke at large across the hill*].

KEEGAN.   Come, Mr Doyle! is this English sentiment so much more efficient than our Irish sentiment, after all? Mr Broadbent spends his life inefficiently admiring the thoughts of great men, and efficiently serving the cupidity of base money hunters. We spend our lives efficiently sneering at him and doing nothing. Which of us has any right to reproach the other?

BROADBENT [*coming down the hill again to* KEEGAN's *right hand*].   But you know, something must be done.

KEEGAN.   Yes: when we cease to do, we cease to live. Well, what shall we do?

BROADBENT.   Why, what lies to our hand.

KEEGAN.   Which is the making of golf links and hotels to bring idlers to a country which workers have left in millions because it is a hungry land, a naked land, an ignorant and oppressed land.

BROADBENT.   But, hang it all, the idlers will bring money from England to Ireland!

KEEGAN.   Just as our idlers have for so many generations taken money from Ireland to England. Has that saved England from poverty and degradation more horrible than we have ever dreamed of? When I went to England, sir, I hated England. Now I pity it.

---

7. John Ruskin (1819–1900), art critic and social commentator; Percy Bysshe Shelley (1792–1822), English Romantic poet: both critical of commercial progress.

[BROADBENT *can hardly conceive an Irishman pitying England;
but as* LARRY *intervenes angrily, he gives it up and takes to the
hill and his cigar again.*]

LARRY. Much good your pity will do it!

KEEGAN. In the accounts kept in heaven, Mr Doyle, a heart purified
of hatred may be worth more than even a Land Development Syndicate of Anglicized Irishmen and Gladstonized Englishmen.

LARRY. Oh, in heaven, no doubt. I have never been there. Can you
tell me where it is?

KEEGAN. Could you have told me this morning where hell is? Yet you
know now that it is here. Do not despair of finding heaven: it may be
no farther off.

LARRY [*ironically*]. On this holy ground, as you call it, eh?

KEEGAN [*with fierce intensity*]. Yes, perhaps, even on this holy ground
which such Irishmen as you have turned into a Land of Derision.

BROADBENT [*coming between them*]. Take care! you will be quarrelling
presently. Oh, you Irishmen, you Irishmen! Toujours Ballyhooly, eh?

[LARRY, *with a shrug, half comic, half impatient, turns away up
the hill, but presently strolls back on* KEEGAN'S *right.* BROADBENT
adds, confidentially to KEEGAN.]

Stick to the Englishman, Mr Keegan: he has a bad name here; but at
least he can forgive you for being an Irishman.

KEEGAN. Sir: when you speak to me of English and Irish you forget
that I am a Catholic. My country is not Ireland nor England, but the
whole mighty realm of my Church. For me there are but two countries: heaven and hell; but two conditions of men: salvation and damnation. Standing here between you the Englishman, so clever in your
foolishness, and this Irishman, so foolish in his cleverness, I cannot
in my ignorance be sure which of you is the more deeply damned;
but I should be unfaithful to my calling if I opened the gates of my
heart less widely to one than to the other.

LARRY. In either case it would be an impertinence, Mr Keegan, as your
approval is not of the slightest consequence to us. What use do you
suppose all this drivel is to men with serious practical business in
hand?

BROADBENT. I dont agree with that, Larry. I think these things cannot
be said too often: they keep up the moral tone of the community. As
you know, I claim the right to think for myself in religious matters: in
fact, I am ready to avow myself a bit of a—of a—well, I dont care
who knows it—a bit of a Unitarian; but if the Church of England
contained a few men like Mr Keegan, I should certainly join it.

KEEGAN. You do me too much honor, sir. [*With priestly humility to*
LARRY.] Mr. Doyle: I am to blame for having unintentionally set your
mind somewhat on edge against me. I beg your pardon.

LARRY [*unimpressed and hostile*].   I didnt stand on ceremony with you: you neednt stand on it with me. Fine manners and fine words are cheap in Ireland: you can keep both for my friend here, who is still imposed on by them. *I* know their value.

KEEGAN.   You mean you dont know their value.

LARRY [*angrily*].   I mean what I say.

KEEGAN [*turning quietly to the Englishman*].   You see, Mr Broadbent, I only make the hearts of my countrymen harder when I preach to them: the gates of hell still prevail against me. I shall wish you good evening. I am better alone, at the Round Tower, dreaming of heaven. [*He goes up the hill.*]

LARRY.   Aye, thats it! there you are! dreaming! dreaming! dreaming! dreaming!

KEEGAN [*halting and turning to them for the last time*].   Every dream is a prophecy: every jest is an earnest in the womb of Time.

BROADBENT [*reflectively*].   Once, when I was a small kid, I dreamt I was in heaven.

[*They both stare at him.*]

It was a sort of pale blue satin place, with all the pious old ladies in our congregation sitting as if they were at a service; and there was some awful person in the study at the other side of the hall. I didnt enjoy it, you know. What is it like in your dreams?

KEEGAN.   In my dreams it is a country where the State is the Church and the Church the people: three in one and one in three. It is a commonwealth in which work is play and play is life: three in one and one in three. It is a temple in which the priest is the worshipper and the worshipper the worshipped: three in one and one in three. It is a godhead in which all life is human and all humanity divine: three in one and one in three. It is, in short, the dream of a madman. [*He goes away across the hill.*]

BROADBENT [*looking after him affectionately*].   What a regular old Church and State Tory he is! He's a character: he'll be an attraction here. Really almost equal to Ruskin and Carlyle.[8]

LARRY.   Yes; and much good they did with all their talk!

BROADBENT.   Oh tut, tut, Larry! They improved my mind: they raised my tone enormously. I feel sincerely obliged to Keegan: he has made me feel a better man: distinctly better. [*With sincere elevation.*] I feel now as I never did before that I am right in devoting my life to the cause of Ireland. Come along and help me to choose the site for the hotel.

---

8. Thomas Carlyle (1795–1881), historian, novelist, lecturer, who was "Tory," or conservative, in opposition to modernization.

SEAN O'CASEY

Juno and the Paycock†

A Tragedy in Three Acts

Characters

'CAPTAIN' JACK BOYLE
JUNE BOYLE, *his wife*
JOHNNY BOYLE ⎫ *their children*
MARY BOYLE ⎭
'JOXER' DALY
MRS MAISIE MADIGAN
'NEEDLE' NUGENT, A TAILOR
MRS TANCRED
JERRY DEVINE

⎫
⎬ *residents in*
⎪ *the tenement*
⎪
⎭

CHARLES BENTHAM, *a schoolteacher*
AN IRREGULAR MOBILISER
TWO IRREGULARS
A COAL-BLOCK VENDOR
A SEWING-MACHINE MAN
TWO FURNITURE-REMOVAL MEN
TWO NEIGHBOURS

Place and Time

Act One. The living apartment of a two-roomed tenancy of the Boyle family, in a tenement house in Dublin.
Act Two. The same.
Act Three. The same.

A few days elapse between Acts ONE and TWO, and two months between Acts TWO and THREE.

From *Seven Plays by Sean O'Casey* (New York: St. Martin's Press, 1985). Copyright © Sean O'Casey 1925, published by Macmillan, London and Basingstoke. Reprinted by permission.

During Act III the curtain is lowered for a few minutes to denote the lapse of one hour. Period of the play, 1922.[1]

Act One

The living-room of a two-room tenancy occupied by the Boyle family in a tenement house in Dublin. Left, a door leading to another part of the house; left of door a window looking into the street; at back a dresser; farther to right at back, a window looking into the back of the house. Between the window and the dresser is a picture of the Virgin; below the picture, on a bracket, is a crimson bowl in which a floating votive light is burning. Farther to the right is a small bed partly concealed by cretonne hangings strung on a twine. To the right is the fireplace; near the fireplace is a door leading to the other room. Beside the fireplace is a box containing coal. On the mantelshelf is an alarm clock lying on its face. In a corner near the window looking into the back is a galvanised bath. A table and some chairs. On the table are breakfast things for one. A teapot is on the hob and a frying-pan stands inside the fender. There are a few books on the dresser and one on the table. Leaning against the dresser is a long-handled shovel—the kind invariably used by labourers when turning concrete or mixing mortar. JOHNNY BOYLE *is sitting crouched beside the fire.* MARY *with her jumper off—it is lying on the back of a chair—is arranging her hair before a tiny mirror perched on the table. Beside the mirror is stretched out the morning paper, which she looks at when she isn't gazing into the mirror. She is a well-made and good-looking girl of twenty-two. Two forces are working in her mind—one, through the circumstances of her life, pulling her back; the other, through the influence of books she has read, pushing her forward. The opposing forces are apparent in her speech and her manners, both of which are degraded by her environment, and improved by her acquaintance—slight though it be—with literature. The time is early forenoon.*

MARY [*looking at the paper*].   On a little by-road, out beyant Finglas, he was found.

> [MRS BOYLE *enters by door on right; she has been shopping and carries a small parcel in her hand. She is forty-five years of age, and twenty years ago she must have been a pretty woman; but her face has now assumed that look which ultimately settles down upon the faces of the women of the working-class; a look of listless monotony and harassed anxiety, blending with an expression of*

---

1. The Anglo-Irish Treaty of 1921 granted Ireland some degree of political autonomy; disagreement between those satisfied with the treaty (Free Sta- ters) and those dissatisfied with it (Republicans, or "Diehards") led to the Irish Civil War, 1922–23.

mechanical resistance. Were circumstances favourable, she would probably be a handsome, active and clever woman.]

MRS BOYLE.   Isn't he come in yet?

MARY.   No, mother.

MRS BOYLE.   Oh, he'll come in when he likes; struttin' about the town like a paycock with Joxer, I suppose. I hear all about Mrs Tancred's son is in this mornin's paper.

MARY.   The full details are in it this mornin'; seven wounds he had—one entherin' the neck, with an exit wound beneath the left shoulder-blade; another in the left breast penethratin' the heart, an' . . .

JOHNNY [*springing up from the fire*].   Oh, quit readin' for God's sake! Are yous losin' all your feelin's? It'll soon be that none of you'll read anythin' that's not about butcherin'! [*He goes quickly into the room on the left.*]

MARY.   He's gettin' very sensitive, all of a sudden!

MRS BOYLE.   I'll read it myself, Mary, by an' by, when I come home. Everybody's sayin' that he was a Diehard—thanks be to God that Johnny had nothin' to do with him this long time. . . . [*Opening the parcel and taking out some sausages, which she places on a plate.*] Ah, then, if that father o' yours doesn't come in soon for his breakfast, he may go without any; I'll not wait much longer for him.

MARY.   Can't you let him get it himself when he comes in?

MRS BOYLE.   Yes, an' let him bring in Joxer Daly along with him? Ay, that's what he'd like an' that's what he's waitin' for—till he thinks I'm gone to work, an' then sail in with the boul' Joxer, to burn all the coal an' dhrink all the tea in the place, to show them what a good Samaritan he is! But I'll stop here till he comes in, if I have to wait till tomorrow mornin'.

VOICE OF JOHNNY INSIDE.   Mother!

MRS BOYLE.   Yis?

VOICE OF JOHNNY.   Bring us in a dhrink o' wather.

MRS BOYLE.   Bring in that fella a dhrink o' wather, for God's sake, Mary.

MARY.   Isn't he big an' able enough to come out an' get it himself?

MRS BOYLE.   If you weren't well yourself you'd like somebody to bring you in a dhrink o' wather. [*She brings in drink and returns.*] Isn't it terrible to have to be waitin' this way! You'd think he was bringin' twenty poun's a week into the house the way he's going on. He wore out the Health Insurance long ago, he's afther wearin' out the unemployment dole, an', now he's thryin' to wear out me! An' constantly singin', no less, when he ought always to be on his knees offerin' up a Novena for a job!

MARY [*tying a ribbon fillet-wise around her head*].   I don't like this ribbon, Ma; I think I'll wear the green—it looks better than the blue.

MRS BOYLE.   Ah, wear whatever ribbon you like, girl, only don't be botherin' me. I don't know what a girl on strike wants to be wearin' a ribbon round her head for, or silk stockin's on her legs either; it's wearin' them things that make the employers think they're givin' yous too much money.

MARY. The hour is past now when we'll ask the employers' permission to wear what we like.

MRS BOYLE. I don't know why you wanted to walk out for Jennie Claffey; up to this you never had a good word for her.

MARY. What's the use of belongin' to a Trades Union if you won't stand up for your principles? Why did they sack her? It was a clear case of victimisation. We couldn't let her walk the streets, could we?

MRS BOYLE. No, of course yous couldn't—yous wanted to keep her company. Wan victim wasn't enough. When the employers sacrifice wan victim, the Trades Unions go wan betther be sacrificin' a hundred.

MARY. It doesn't matter what you say, Ma—a principle's a principle.

MRS BOYLE. Yis; an' when I go into oul' Murphy's tomorrow, an' he gets to know that, instead o' payin' all, I'm goin' to borry more, what'll he say when I tell him a principle's a principle? What'll we do if he refuses to give us any more on tick?

MARY. He daren't refuse—if he does, can't you tell him he's paid?

MRS BOYLE. It's lookin' as if he was paid, whether he refuses or no.

[JOHNNY *appears at the door on left. He can be plainly seen now; he is a thin, delicate fellow, something younger than* MARY. *He has evidently gone through a rough time. His face is pale and drawn; there is a tremulous look of indefinite fear in his eyes. The left sleeve of his coat is empty, and he walks with a slight halt.*]

JOHNNY. I was lyin' down; I thought yous were gone. Oul' Simon Mackay is thrampin' about like a horse over me head, an' I can't sleep with him—they're like thunder-claps in me brain! The curse o'—God forgive me for goin' to curse!

MRS BOYLE. There, now; go back an' lie down again an' I'll bring you in a nice cup o' tay.

JOHNNY. Tay, tay, tay! You're always thinkin' o' tay. If a man was dyin', you'd thry to make him swally a cup o' tay! [*He goes back.*]

MRS BOYLE. I don't know what's goin' to be done with him. The bullet he got in the hip in Easter Week was bad enough; but the bomb that shatthered his arm in the fight in O'Connell Street put the finishin' touch on him. I knew he was makin' a fool of himself. God knows I went down on me bended knees to him not to go agen the Free State. [2]

---

2. The Irish Free State created in 1921 was the result of a rebellion launched by Republicans during Easter Week 1916 with violence centered along O'Connell Street, the central boulevard of Dublin.

MARY.   He stuck to his principles, an', no matter how you may argue, ma, a principle's a principle.

VOICE OF JOHNNY.   Is Mary goin' to stay here?

MARY.   No, I'm not goin' to stay here; you can't expect me to be always at your beck an' call, can you?

VOICE OF JOHNNY.   I won't stop here be meself!

MRS BOYLE.   Amn't I nicely handicapped with the whole o' yous! I don't know what any o' yous ud do without your ma. [*To* JOHNNY.] Your father'll be here in a minute, an' if you want anythin',' he'll get it for you.

JOHNNY.   I hate assin' him for anythin' . . . He hates to be assed to stir. . . . Is the light lightin' before the picture o' the Virgin?

MRS BOYLE.   Yis, yis! The wan inside to St Anthony isn't enough, but he must have another wan to the Virgin here!

> [JERRY DEVINE *enters hastily. He is about twenty-five, well set, active and earnest. He is a type, becoming very common now in the Labour Movement, of a mind knowing enough to make the mass of his associates, who know less, a power, and too little to broaden that power for the benefit of all.* MARY *seizes her jumper and runs hastily into room left.*]

JERRY [*breathless*].   Where's the Captain, Mrs Boyle, where's the Captain?

MRS BOYLE.   You may well ass a body that: he's wherever Joxer Daly is—dhrinkin' in some snug[3] or another.

JERRY.   Father Farrell is just afther stoppin' to tell me to run up an' get him to go to the new job that's goin' on in Rathmines; his cousin is foreman o' the job, an' Father Farrell was speakin' to him about poor Johnny an' his father bein' so idle so long, an' the foreman told Father Farrell to send the Captain up an' he'd give him a start—I wondher where I'd find him?

MRS BOYLE.   You'll find he's ayther in Ryan's or Foley's.

JERRY.   I'll run round to Ryan's—I know it's a great house o' Joxer's. [*He rushes out.*]

MRS BOYLE [*piteously*].   There now, he'll miss that job, or I know for what! If he gets win' o' the word, he'll not come back till evenin', so that it'll be too late. There'll never be any good got out o' him so long as he goes with that shouldher-shruggin' Joxer. I killin' meself workin', an' he sthruttin' about from mornin' till night like a paycock!

> [The steps of two persons are heard coming up a flight of stairs. They are the footsteps of CAPTAIN BOYLE *and* JOXER. CAPTAIN BOYLE *is singing in a deep, sonorous, self-honouring voice.*]

---

3. Small, comfortable side-room of a pub, or tavern.

THE CAPTAIN. Sweet Spirit, hear me prayer! Hear . . . oh . . . hear
. . . me prayer . . . hear, oh, hear . . . Oh, he . . . ar . . . oh,
he . . . ar . . . me . . . pray . . . er!

JOXER [outside]. Ah, that's a darlin' song, a daaarlin' song!

MRS BOYLE [viciously]. Sweet spirit hear his prayer! Ah, then, I'll take
me solemn affeydavey[4], it's not for a job he's prayin'! [She sits down
on the bed so that the cretomne hangings hide her from the view of
those entering.]

> [The CAPTAIN comes in. He is a man of about sixty; stout, grey-
> haired and stocky. His neck is short, and his head looks like a
> stone ball that one sometimes sees on top of a gate-post. His
> cheeks, reddish-purple, are puffed out, as if he were always
> repressing an almost irrepressible ejaculation. On his upper lip
> is a crisp, tightly cropped moustache; he carries himself with the
> upper part of his body slightly thrown back, and his stomach
> slightly thrust forward. His walk is a slow, consequential strut.
> His clothes are dingy, and he wears a faded seaman's-cap with a
> glazed peak.]

BOYLE [to JOXER, who is still outside]. Come on, come on in, Joxer;
she's gone out long ago, man. If there's nothing else to be got, we'll
furrage out a cup o' tay, anyway. It's the only bit I get in comfort
when she's away. 'Tisn't Juno should be her pet name at all, but
Deirdre of the Sorras[5], for she's always grousin'.

> [JOXER steps cautiously into the room. He may be younger than
> the CAPTAIN but he looks a lot older. His face is like a bundle of
> crinkled paper; his eyes have a cunning twinkle; he is spare and
> loosely built; he has a habit of constantly shrugging his shoulders
> with a peculiar twitching movement, meant to be ingratiating.
> His face is invariably ornamented with a grin.]

JOXER. It's a terrible thing to be tied to a woman that's always grousin'.
I don't know how you stick it—it ud put years on me. It's a good job
she has to be so ofen away, for [with a shrug] when the cat's away, the
mice can play!

BOYLE [with a commanding and complacent gesture]. Pull over to the
fire, Joxer, an' we'll have a cup o' tay in a minute.

JOXER. Ah, a cup o' tay's a darlin' thing, a daaarlin' thing—the cup
that cheers but doesn't . . .

> [JOXER's rhapsody is cut short by the sight of MRS BOYLE coming
> forward and confronting the two cronies. Both are stupefied.]

---

4. Affidavit, sworn statement.
5. Heroine of Celtic mythology sorrowful for
doomed flight with a true love from an arranged
marriage; a number of modern versions of the story
were written during the Irish literary revival.

MRS BOYLE [*with sweet irony—poking the fire, and turning her head to glare at* JOXER]. Pull over to the fire, Joxer Daly, an' we'll have a cup o' tay in a minute! Are you sure, now, you wouldn't like an egg?

JOXER. I can't stop, Mrs Boyle; I'm in a desperate hurry, a desperate hurry.

MRS BOYLE. Pull over to the fire, Joxer Daly; people is always far more comfortabler here than they are in their own place.

[JOXER *makes hastily for the door.*]

BOYLE [*stirs to follow him; thinks of something to relieve the situation— stops, and says suddenly*] Joxer!

JOXER [*at door ready to bolt*]. Yis?

BOYLE. You know the foreman o' that job that's goin' on down in Killesther, don't you, Joxer?

JOXER [*puzzled*]. Foreman—Killesther?

BOYLE [*with a meaning look*]. He's a butty o' yours, isn't he?

JOXER [*the truth dawning on him*]. The foreman at Killesther—oh yis, yis. He's an oul' butty o' mine—oh, he's a darlin' man, a daarlin' man.

BOYLE. Oh, then, it's a sure thing. It's a pity we didn't go down at breakfast first thing this mornin'—we might ha' been working now; but you didn't know it then.

JOXER [*with a shrug*]. It's better late then never.

BOYLE. It's nearly time we got a start, anyhow; I'm fed up knockin' round, doin' nothin'. He promised you—gave you the straight tip?

JOXER. Yis. 'Come down on the blow o' dinner', says he, 'an' I'll start you, an' any friend you like to brin' with you.' 'Ah,' says I, 'you're a darlin' man, a daaarlin' man.'

BOYLE. Well, it couldn't come at a betther time—we're a long time waitin' for it.

JOXER. Indeed we were; but it's a long lane that has no turnin'.

BOYLE. The blow-up for dinner is at one—wait till I see what time it 'tis. [*He goes over to the mantelpiece, and gingerly lifts the clock.*]

MRS BOYLE. Min' now, how you go on fiddlin' with that clock—you know the least little thing sets it asthray.

BOYLE. The job couldn't come at a betther time; I'm feelin' in great fettle, Joxer. I'd hardly believe I ever had a pain in me legs, an' last week I was nearly crippled with them.

JOXER. That's betther an' betther; ah, God never shut wan door but He opened another!

BOYLE. It's only eleven o'clock; we've lashins o' time. I'll slip on me oul' moleskins afther breakfast, an' we can saunther down at our ayse. [*Putting his hand on the shovel.*] I think, Joxer, we'd betther bring our shovels?

JOXER. Yis, Captain, yis; it's betther to go fully prepared an' ready for all eventualities. You bring your long-tailed shovel, an' I'll bring me navvy. We mighten' want them, an', then agen, we might: for want of a nail the shoe was lost, for want of a shoe the horse was lost, an' for want of a horse the man was lost—aw, that's a darlin' proverb, a daaarlin' . . .

[As JOXER *is finishing his sentence,* MRS BOYLE *approaches the door and* JOXER *retreats hurriedly. She shuts the door with a bang.*]

BOYLE [*suggestively*].   We won't be long pullin' ourselves together agen when I'm working for a few weeks.

[MRS BOYLE *takes no notice.*]

The foreman on the job is an oul' butty o' Joxer's; I have an idea that I know him meself. [*Silence.*] . . . There's a button off the back o' me moleskin trousers. . . . If you leave out a needle an' thread I'll sew it on meself. . . . Thanks be to God, the pains in me legs is gone, anyhow!

MRS BOYLE [*with a burst*].   Look here, Mr Jackie Boyle, them yarns won't go down with Juno. I know you an' Joxer Daly of an oul' date, an' if you think you're able to come it over me with them fairy tales, you're in the wrong shop.

BOYLE [*coughing subduedly to relieve the tenseness of the situation*]. U-u-u-ugh!

MRS BOYLE.   Butty o' Joxer's! Oh, you'll do a lot o' good as long as you continue to be a butty o' Joxer's!

BOYLE.   U-u-u-ugh!

MRS BOYLE.   Shovel! Ah, then, me boyo, you'd do far more work with a knife an' fork than ever you'll do with a shovel! If there was e'er a genuine job goin' you'd be dh'other way about—not able to lift your arms with the pains in your legs! Your poor wife slavin' to keep the bit in your mouth, an' you gallivantin' about all the day like a paycock!

BOYLE.   It ud be betther for a man to be dead, betther for a man to be dead.

MRS BOYLE [*ignoring the interruption*].   Everybody callin' you 'Captain', an' you only wanst on the wather, in an oul' collier from here to Liverpool, when anybody, to listen or look at you, ud take you for a second Christo For Columbus!

BOYLE.   Are you never goin' to give us a rest?

MRS BOYLE.   Oh, you're never tired o' lookin' for a rest.

BOYLE.   D'ye want to dhrive me out o' the house?

MRS BOYLE.   It ud be easier to dhrive you out o' the house than to dhrive you into a job. Here, sit down an' take your breakfast—it may be the last you'll get, for I don't know where the next is goin' to come from.

BOYLE.   If I get this job we'll be all right.

MRS BOYLE.   Did ye see Jerry Devine?

BOYLE [*testily*].   No, I didn't see him.

MRS BOYLE.   No, but you seen Joxer. Well, he was here lookin' for you.

BOYLE.   Well, let him look!

MRS BOYLE.   Oh, indeed, he may well look, for it ud be hard for him to see you, an' you stuck in Ryan's snug.

BOYLE.   I wasn't in Ryan's snug—I don't go into Ryan's.

MRS BOYLE.   Oh, is there a mad dog there? Well, if you weren't in Ryan's you were in Foley's.

BOYLE.   I'm telling you for the last three weeks I haven't tasted a dhrop of intoxicatin' liquor. I wasn't in ayther wan snug or dh'other—I could swear that on a prayer-book—I'm as innocent as the child unborn!

MRS BOYLE.   Well, if you'd been in for your breakfast you'd ha' seen him.

BOYLE [*suspiciously*].   What does he want me for?

MRS BOYLE.   He'll be back any minute an' then you'll soon know.

BOYLE.   I'll dhrop out an' see if I can meet him.

MRS BOYLE.   You'll sit down an' take your breakfast, an' let me go to me work, for I'm an hour late already waitin' for you.

BOYLE.   You needn't ha' waited, for I'll take no breakfast—I've a little spirit left in me still!

MRS BOYLE.   Are you goin' to have your breakfast—yes or no?

BOYLE [*too proud to yield*].   I'll have no breakfast—yous can keep your breakfast. [*Plaintively.*] I'll knock out a bit somewhere, never fear.

MRS BOYLE.   Nobody's goin' to coax you—don't think that. [*She vigorously replaces the pan and the sausages in the press.*]

BOYLE.   I've a little spirit left in me still.

[JERRY DEVINE *enters hastily.*]

JERRY.   Oh, here you are at last! I've been searchin' for you everywhere. The foreman in Foley's told me you hadn't left the snug with Joxer ten minutes before I went in.

MRS BOYLE.   An' he swearin' on the holy prayer-book that he wasn't in no snug!

BOYLE [*to* JERRY].   What business is it o' yours whether I was in a snug or no? What do you want to be gallopin' about afther me for? Is a man not allowed to leave his house for a minute without havin' a pack o' spies, pimps an' informers cantherin' at his heels?

JERRY.   Oh, you're takin' a wrong view of it, Mr Boyle; I simply was anxious to do you a good turn. I have a message for you from Father Farrell: he says that if you go to the job that's on in Rathmines, an' ask for Foreman Mangan, you'll get a start.

BOYLE.   That's all right, but I don't want the motions of me body to be watched the way an ashtronomer ud watch a star. If you're folleyin' Mary aself, you've no pereeogative to be folleyin' me. [*Suddenly catching his thigh.*] U-ugh, I'm afther gettin' a terrible twinge in me right leg!

MRS BOYLE.   Oh, it won't be very long now till it travels into your left wan. It's miraculous that whenever he scents a job in front of him, his legs begin to fail him! Then, me bucko, if you lose this chance, you may go an' furrage for yourself!

JERRY.   This job'll last for some time too, Captain, an' as soon as the foundations are in, it'll be cushy enough.

BOYLE.   Won't it be a climbin' job? How d'ye expect me to be able to go up a ladder with these legs? An', if I get up aself, how am I goin to get down agen?

MRS BOYLE [*viciously*].   Get wan o' the labourers to carry you down in a hod! You can't climb a laddher, but you can skip like a goat into a snug!

JERRY.   I wouldn't let myself be let down that easy, Mr Boyle; a little exercise, now, might do you all the good in the world.

BOYLE.   It's a docthor you should have been, Devine—maybe you know more about the pains in me legs than meself that has them?

JERRY [*irritated*].   Oh, I know nothin' about the pains in your legs; I've brought the message that Father Farrell gave me, an' that's all I can do.

MRS BOYLE.   Here, sit down an' take your breakfast, an' go an' get ready; an' don't be actin' as if you couldn't pull a wing out of a dead bee.

BOYLE.   I want no breakfast, I tell you; it ud choke me afther all that's been said. I've a little spirit left in me still.

MRS BOYLE.   Well, let's see your spirit, then, an' go in at wanst an' put on your moleskin trousers!

BOYLE [*moving towards the door on left*].   It ud be betther for a man to be dead! U-ugh! There's another twinge in me other leg! Nobody but meself knows the sufferin' I'm goin' through with the pains in these legs o' mine!

[*He goes into the room on left as* MARY *comes out with her hat in her hand.*]

MRS BOYLE.   I'll have to push off now, for I'm terrible late already, but I was determined to stay an' hunt that Joxer this time. [*She goes off.*]

JERRY.   Are you going out, Mary?

MARY.   It looks like it when I'm putting on my hat, doesn't it?

JERRY.   The bitther word agen, Mary.

MARY.   You won't allow me to be friendly with you; if I thry, you deliberately misundherstand it.

JERRY.   I didn't always misundherstand it; you were often delighted to have the arms of Jerry around you.

MARY.   If you go on talkin' like this, Jerry Devine, you'll make me hate you!

JERRY.   Well, let it be either a weddin' or a wake! Listen, Mary, I'm

standin' for the Secretaryship of our Union. There's only one opposin'
me; I'm popular with all the men, an' a good speaker—all are sayin'
that I'll get elected.

MARY. Well?

JERRY. The job's worth three hundred an' fifty pounds a year, Mary.
You an' I could live nice an' cosily on that; it would lift you out o'
this place an' . . .

MARY. I haven't time to listen to you now—I have to go.

[*She is going out, when* JERRY *bars the way.*]

JERRY [*appealingly*]. Mary, what's come over you with me for the last
few weeks? You hardly speak to me, an' then only a word with a face
o' bitherness on it. Have you forgotten, Mary, all the happy evenins
that were as sweet as the scented hawthorn that sheltered the sides o'
the road as we saunthered through the country?

MARY. That's all over now. When you get your new job, Jerry, you
won't be long findin' a girl far betther than I am for your sweetheart.

JERRY. Never, never, Mary! No matther what happens, you'll always
be the same to me.

MARY. I must be off; please let me go, Jerry.

JERRY. I'll go a bit o' the way with you.

MARY. You needn't, thanks; I want to be by meself.

JERRY [*catching her arm*]. You're goin' to meet another fella; you've
clicked with someone else, me lady!

MARY. That's no concern o' yours, Jerry Devine; let me go!

JERRY. I saw yous comin' out o' the Cornflower Dance class, an' you
hangin' on his arm—a thin, lanky strip of a Micky Dazzler, with a
walkin' stick an' gloves!

VOICE OF JOHNNY [*loudly*]. What are you doin' there—pullin' about
everything!

VOICE OF BOYLE [*loudly and viciously*]. I'm puttin' on me moleskin
trousers!

MARY. You're hurtin' me arm! Let me go, or I'll scream, an' then
you'll have the oul' fella out on top of us!

JERRY. Don't be so hard on a fella, Mary, don't be so hard.

BOYLE [*appearing at the door*]. What's the meanin' of all this hillabaloo?

MARY. Let me go, let me go!

BOYLE. D'ye hear me—what's all this hillabaloo about?

JERRY [*plaintively.*] Will you not give us one kind word, one kind word,
Mary?

BOYLE. D'ye hear me talkin' to yous? What's all this hillabaloo for?

JERRY. Let me kiss your hand, your little, tiny, white hand!

BOYLE. Your little, tiny, white hand—are you takin' leave o' your senses,
man?

[MARY *breaks away and rushes out.*]

This is a nice goin's on in front of her father!

JERRY.   Ah, dhry up, for God's sake! [*He follows* MARY.]

BOYLE.   Chiselurs[6] don't care a damn now about their parents, they're bringin' their father's grey hairs down with sorra to the grave, an' laughin' at it. Ah, I suppose it's just the same everywhere—the whole worl's in a state o' chassis![7] [*He sits by the fire.*] Breakfast! Well, they can keep their breakfast for me. Not if they went down on their bended knees would I take it—I'll show them I've a little spirit in me still! [*He goes over to the press, takes out a plate and looks at it.*] Sassige! Well, let her keep her sassige. [*He returns to the fire, takes up the teapot and gives it a gentle shake.*] The tea's wet right enough. [*A pause; he rises, goes to the press, takes out the sausage, puts it on the pan, and puts both on the fire. He attends the sausage with a fork. Singing*]

> When the robins nest agen,
> And the flowers are in bloom,
> When the Springtime's sunny smile seems to banish all
>   sorrow an' gloom;
> Then me bonny blue-ey'd lad, if me heart be true till then—
> He's promised he'll come back to me,
> When the robins nest agen!

> [*He lifts his head at the high note, and then drops his eyes to the pan. Singing*]

> When the . . .

> [*Steps are heard approaching; he whips the pan off the fire and puts it under the bed, then sits down at the fire. The door opens and a bearded man looking in says*]

You don't happen to want a sewin' machine?

BOYLE [*furiously*].   No, I don't want e'er a sewin' machine! [*He returns the pan to the fire, and commences to sing again. Singing*]

> When the robins nest asgen,
> And the flowers they are in bloom,
> He's . . .

> [*A thundering knock is heard at the street door.*]

There's a terrible tatheraraa—that's a stranger—that's nobody belongin' to the house.

> [*Another loud knock.*]

6. Youths.   7. Chaos, in Boyle's own malapropism.

JOXER [*sticking his head in at the door*].   Did ye hear them tatherarahs?
BOYLE.   Well, Joxer, I'm not deaf.
JOHNNY [*appearing in his shirt and trousers at the door on left; his face is
    anxious and his voice is tremulous*].   Who's that at the door; who's
    that at the door? Who gave that knock—d'ye yous hear me—are yous
    deaf or dhrunk or what?
BOYLE [*to* JOHNNY].   How the hell do I know who 'tis? Joxer, stick your
    head out o' the window an' see.
JOXER.   An' mebbe get a bullet in the kisser? Ah, none o' them thricks
    for Joxer! It's betther to be a coward than a corpse!
BOYLE [*looking cautiously out of the window*].   It's a fella in a thrench
    coat.
JOHNNY.   Holy Mary, Mother o' God, I . . .
BOYLE.   He's goin' away—he must ha' got tired knockin'.

        [JOHNNY *returns to the room on left.*]

BOYLE.   Sit down an' have a cup o' tay, Joxer.
JOXER.   I'm afraid the missus ud pop in on us agen before we'd know
    where we are. Somethin's tellin' me to go at wanst.
BOYLE.   Don't be superstitious, man; we're Dublin men, an' not boyos
    that's only afther comin' up from the bog o' Allen[8]—though if she did
    come in, right enough, we'd be caught like rats in a thrap.
JOXER.   An' you know the sort she is—she wouldn't listen to reason—
    an' wanse bitten twice shy.
BOYLE [*going over to the window at back*].   If the worst came to the
    worst, you could dart out here, Joxer; it's only a dhrop of a few feet to
    the roof of the return room[9], an' the first minute she goes into dh'other
    room I'll give you the bend, an' you can slip in an' away.
JOXER [*yielding to the temptation*].   Ah, I won't stop very long anyhow.
    [*Picking up a book from the table.*] Whose is the buk?
BOYLE.   Aw, one o' Mary's; she's always readin' lately—nothin' but thrash,
    too. There's one I was lookin' at dh'other day: three stories, *The Doll's
    House, Ghosts,* an' *The Wild Duck*[1]—buks only fit for chiselurs!
JOXER.   Didja ever rade *Elizabeth,* or *Th' Exile o' Sibayria?* . . . Ah,
    it's a darlin' story, a daarlin' story!
BOYLE.   You eat your sassige, an' never min' *Th' Exile o' Sibayria.*

        [Both sit down; BOYLE *fills out tea, pours gravy on* JOXER's *plate,
        and keeps the sausage for himself.*]

JOXER.   What are you wearin' your moleskin trousers for?
BOYLE.   I have to go to a job, Joxer. Just afther you'd gone, Devine kem

---

8. Great central bog of Ireland, associated by Boyle
with primitive life and premodern society.
9. Building extension.

1. Plays by Norwegian playwright Henrik Ibsen
(1828–1906) about oppressive family life.

runnin' in to tell us that Father Farrell said if I went down to the job that's goin' on in Rathmines I'd get a start.

JOXER.   Be the holy, that's good news!

BOYLE.   How is it good news? I wondher if you were in my condition, would you call it good news?

JOXER.   I thought . . .

BOYLE.   You thought! You think too sudden sometimes, Joxer. D'ye know, I'm hardly able to crawl with the pains in me legs!

JOXER.   Yis, yis; I forgot the pains in your legs. I know you can do nothin' while they're at you.

BOYLE.   You forget; I don't think any of yous realise the state I'm in with the pains in my legs. What ud happen if I had to carry a bag o' cement?

JOXER.   Ah, any man havin' the like of them pains id be down an' out, down an' out.

BOYLE.   I wouldn't mind if he had said it to meself; but, no, oh no, he rushes in an' shouts it out in front o' Juno, an' you know what Juno is, Joxer. We all know Devine knows a little more than the rest of us, but he doesn't act as if he did; he's a good boy, sober, able to talk an' all that, but still . . .

JOXER.   Oh ay; able to argufy, but still . . .

BOYLE.   If he's runnin' afther Mary, aself, he's not goin' to be runnin' afther me. Captain Boyle's able to take care of himself. Afther all, I'm not gettin' brought up on Virol.[2] I never heard him usin' a curse; I don't believe he was ever dhrunk in his life—sure he's not like a Christian at all!

JOXER.   You're afther takin' the word out o' me mouth—afther all, a Christian's natural, but he's unnatural.

BOYLE.   His oul' fella was just the same—a Wicklow man.

JOXER.   A Wicklow man! That explains the whole thing. I've met many a Wicklow man in me time, but I never met wan that was any good.

BOYLE.   'Father Farrell', says he, 'sent me down to tell you.' Father Farrell! . . . D'ye know, Joxer, I never like to be beholden to any o' the clergy.

JOXER.   It's dangerous, right enough.

BOYLE.   If they do anything for you, they'd want you to be livin' in the Chapel . . . I'm goin' to tell you somethin', Joxer, that I wouldn't tell to anybody else—the clergy always had too much power over the people in this unfortunate country.

JOXER.   You could sing that if you had an air to it!

BOYLE [becoming enthusiastic].   Didn't they prevent the people in '47 from seizin' the corn, an' they starvin'; didn't they down Parnell; didn't they say that hell wasn't hot enough nor eternity long enough to pun-

2. Baby food.

ish the Fenians?[3] We don't forget, we don't forget them things, Joxer. If they've taken everything else from us, Joxer, they've left us our memory.

JOXER [*emotionally*].   For mem'ry's the only friend that grief can call its own, that grief . . . can . . . call . . . its own!

BOYLE.   Father Farrell's beginnin' to take a great intherest in Captain Boyle; because of what Johnny did for his country, says he to me wan day. It's a curious way to reward Johnny be makin' his poor oul' father work. But that's what the clergy want, Joxer—work, work, work for me an' you; havin' us mulin' from mornin' till night, so that they may be in betther fettle when they come hoppin' round for their dues! Job! Well, let him give his job to wan of his hymn-singin', prayer-spoutin', craw-thumpin' Confraternity[4] men!

[*The voice of a* COAL-BLOCK VENDOR *is heard chanting in the street.*]

VOICE OF THE COAL VENDOR.   Blocks . . . coal-blocks! Blocks . . . coal-blocks!

JOXER.   God be with the young days when you were steppin' the deck of a manly ship, with the win' blowin' a hurricane through the masts, an' the only sound you'd hear was 'Port your helm!' an' the only answer, 'Port it is, sir!'

BOYLE.   Them was days, Joxer, them was days. Nothin' was too hot or too heavy for me then. Sailin' from the Gulf o' Mexico to the Antanartic Ocean. I seen things, I seen things, Joxer, that no mortal man should speak about that knows his Catechism. Ofen, an' ofen, when I was fixed to the wheel with a marlin-spike, an' the win's blowin' fierce an' the waves lashin' an' lashin', till you'd think every minute was goin' to be your last, an' it blowed—blew is the right word, Joxer, but blowed is what the sailors use. . . .

JOXER.   Aw, it's a darlin' word, a daarlin' word.

BOYLE.   An', as it blowed, I ofen looked up at the sky an' assed meself the question—what is the stars, what is the stars?

VOICE OF THE COAL VENDOR.   Any blocks, coal-blocks; blocks, coal-blocks!

JOXER.   Ah, that's the question, that's the question—what is the stars?

BOYLE.   An' then, I'd have another look, an' I'd ass meself—what is the moon?

JOXER.   Ah, that's the question—what is the moon, what is the moon?

[*Rapid steps are heard coming towards the door.* BOYLE *makes desperate efforts to hide everything;* JOXER *rushes to the window*

3. Corn, or grain, was exported from Ireland during the famine in the years around 1847; Charles Stewart Parnell (1846–91), parliamentarian agitator for Home Rule for Ireland until undone by the scandal of an extramarital affair; Fenians, or members of the Irish Republican Brotherhood, a late nineteenth-century secret society for military overthrow of British government.
4. The Confraternity of the Sacred Heart.

in a frantic effort to get out; BOYLE *begins to innocently lilt 'Oh, me darlin' Jennie, I will be thrue to thee', when the door is opened, and the black face of the* COAL VENDOR *appears.*]

THE COAL VENDOR. D'yez want any blocks?

BOYLE [*with a roar*]. No, we don't want any blocks!

JOXER [*coming back with a sigh of relief*]. That's afther puttin' the heart across me—I could ha' sworn it was Juno. I'd betther be goin', Captain; you couldn't tell the minute Juno'd hop in on us.

BOYLE. Let her hop in; we may as well have it out first as at last. I've made up me mind—I'm not goin' to do only what she damn well likes.

JOXER. Them sentiments does you credit, Captain; I don't like to say anything as between man an' wife, but I say as a butty, as a butty, Captain, that you've stuck it too long, an' that it's about time you showed a little spunk.

How can a man die betther than facin' fearful odds,
For th' ashes of his fathers an' the temples of his gods?[5]

BOYLE. She has her rights—there's no denyin' it, but haven't I me rights too?

JOXER. Of course you have—the sacred rights o' man!

BOYLE. Today, Joxer, there's goin' to be issued a proclamation be me, establishin' an independent Republic, an' Juno'll have to take an oath of allegiance.

JOXER. Be firm, be firm, Captain; the first few minutes'll be the worst: if you gently touch a nettle it'll sting you for your pains; grasp it like a lad of mettle, an' as soft as silk remains!

VOICE OF MRS BOYLE OUTSIDE. Can't stop, Mrs Madigan—I haven't a minute!

JOXER [*flying out of the window*]. Holy God, here she is!

BOYLE [*packing the things away with a rush in the press*]. I knew that fella ud stop till she was in on top of us! [*He sits down by the fire.*]

MRS BOYLE [*enters hastily; she is flurried and excited*]. Oh, you're in—you must have been only afther comin' in?

BOYLE. No, I never went out.

MRS BOYLE. It's curious, then, you never heard the knockin'. [*She puts her coat and hat on bed.*]

BOYLE. Knockin'? Of course I heard the knockin'.

MRS BOYLE. An' why didn't you open the door, then? I suppose you were so busy with Joxer that you hadn't time.

BOYLE. I haven't seen Joxer since I seen him before. Joxer! What ud bring Joxer here?

MRS BOYLE. D'ye mean to tell me that the pair of yous wasn't collogin' together here when me back was turned?

5. Thomas Babington Macaulay (1800–59), "Horatius," from *Lays of Ancient Rome* (1842).

BOYLE.   What ud we be collogin' together about? I have somethin' else
to think of besides collogin' with Joxer. I can swear on all the holy
prayer-books . . .

MRS BOYLE.   That you weren't in no snug! Go on in at wanst now, an'
take off that moleskin trousers o' yours, an' put on a collar an' tie to
smarten yourself up a bit. There's a visitor comin' with Mary in a
minute, an' he has great news for you.

BOYLE.   A job, I suppose; let us get wan first before we start lookin' for
another.

MRS BOYLE.   That's the thing that's able to put the win' up you. Well,
it's no job, but news that'll give you the chance o' your life.

BOYLE.   What's all the mystery about?

MRS BOYLE.   G'win an' take off the moleskin trousers when you're told!

[BOYLE *goes into room on left.* MRS BOYLE *tidies up the room,
puts the shovel under the bed, and goes to the press.*]

Oh, God bless us, looka the way everything's thrun about! Oh, Joxer
was here, Joxer was here!

[MARY *enters with* CHARLIE BENTHAM; *he is a young man of twenty-
five, tall, good-looking, with a very high opinion of himself generally. He is dressed in a brown coat, brown knee-breeches, grey
stockings, a brown sweater, with a deep blue tie; he carries gloves
and a walking-stick.*]

MRS BOYLE [*fussing round*].   Come in, Mr Bentham; sit down, Mr Bentham, in this chair; it's more comfortabler than that, Mr Bentham.
Himself'll be here in a minute; he's just takin' off his trousers.

MARY.   Mother!

BENTHAM.   Please don't put yourself to any trouble, Mrs Boyle—I'm
quite all right here, thank you.

MRS BOYLE.   An' to think of you knowin' Mary, an' she knowin' the
news you had for us, an' wouldn't let on; but it's all the more wel-
comer now, for we were on our last lap!

VOICE OF JOHNNY INSIDE.   What are you kickin' up all the racket for?

BOYLE [*roughly*].   I'm takin' off me moleskin trousers!

JOHNNY.   Can't you do it, then, without lettin' th' whole house know
you're takin' off your trousers? What d'ye want puttin' them on an'
takin' them off again?

BOYLE.   Will you let me alone, will you let me alone? Am I never goin'
to be done thryin' to please th' whole o' yous?

MRS BOYLE [*to* BENTHAM].   You must excuse th' state o' th' place, Mr
Bentham; th' minute I turn me back that man o' mine always makes
a litther o' th' place.

BENTHAM.   Don't worry, Mrs Boyle; it's all right, I assure . . .

BOYLE [*inside*].   Where's me braces; where in th' name o' God did I leave me braces? . . . Ay, did you see where I put me braces?

JOHNNY [*inside, calling out*]. Ma, will you come in here an' take da away ou' o' this or he'll dhrive me mad.

MRS BOYLE [*going towards the door*]. Dear, dear, dear, that man'll be lookin' for somethin' on th' day o' Judgement. [*Looking into room and calling to* BOYLE] Look at your braces, man, hangin' round your neck!

BOYLE [*inside*]. Aw, Holy God!

MRS BOYLE [*calling*]. Johnny, Johnny, come out here for a minute.

JOHNNY. Ah, leave Johnny alone, an' don't be annoyin' him!

MRS BOYLE. Come on, Johnny, till I inthroduce you to Mr Bentham. [*To* BENTHAM.] My son, Mr Bentham; he's after goin' through the mill. He was only a chiselur of a Boy Scout in Easter Week, when he got hit in the hip; and his arm was blew off in the fight in O'Connell Street.

[JOHNNY *comes in.*]

Here he is, Mr Bentham; Mr Bentham, Johnny. None can deny he done his bit for Irelan', if that's goin' to do him any good.

JOHNNY [*boastfully*]. I'd do it agen, ma, I'd do it agen; for a principle's a principle.

MRS BOYLE. Ah, you lost your best principle, me boy, when you lost your arm; them's the only sort o' principles that's any good to a workin' man.

JOHNNY. Ireland only half free'll never be at peace while she has a son left to pull a trigger.

MRS BOYLE. To be sure, to be sure—no bread's a lot betther than half a loaf. [*Calling loudly in to* BOYLE.] Will you hurry up there?

[BOYLE *enters in his best trousers, which aren't too good, and looks very uncomfortable in his collar and tie.*]

MRS BOYLE. This is my husband; Mr Boyle, Mr Bentham.

BENTHAM. Ah, very glad to know you, Mr Boyle. How are you?

MRS BOYLE. Ah, I'm not too well at all; I suffer terrible with pains in me legs. Juno can tell you there what . . .

MRS BOYLE. You won't have many pains in your legs when you hear what Mr Bentham has to tell you.

BENTHAM. Juno! What an interesting name! It reminds one of Homer's glorious story of ancient gods and heroes.

BOYLE. Yis, doesn't it? You see, Juno was born an' christened in June; I met her in June; we were married in June, an' Johnny was born in June, so wan day I says to her, 'You should ha' been called Juno', an' the name stuck to her ever since.[6]

6. To most the name would suggest the Juno of Roman mythology, jealous wife of Jupiter and keeper of peacocks.

MRS BOYLE.   Here, we can talk o' them things agen; let Mr Bentham
   say what he has to say now.
BENTHAM.   Well, Mr Boyle, I suppose you'll remember a Mr Ellison
   of Santry—he's a relative of yours, I think.
BOYLE [*viciously*].   Is it that prognosticator an' procrastinator! Of course
   I remember him.
BENTHAM.   Well, he's dead, Mr Boyle . . .
BOYLE.   Sorra many'll go into mournin' for him.
MRS BOYLE.   Wait till you hear what Mr Bentham has to say, an' then,
   maybe, you'll change your opinion.
BENTHAM.   A week before he died he sent for me to write his will for
   him. He told me that there were two only that he wished to leave his
   property to: his second cousin, Michael Finnegan of Santry, and John
   Boyle, his first cousin, of Dublin.
BOYLE [*excitedly*].   Me, is it me, me?
BENTHAM.   You, Mr Boyle; I'll read a copy of the will that I have here
   with me, which has been duly filed in the Court of Probate. [*He takes
   a paper from his pocket and reads.*]

6th February 1922

This is the last Will and Testament of William Ellison, of Santry, in
the County of Dublin. I hereby order and wish my property to be sold
and divided as follows:
   £20 to the St Vincent de Paul Society.
   £60 for Masses for the repose of my soul (5s. for each Mass).
   The rest of my property to be divided between my first and second
cousins.
   I hereby appoint Timothy Buckly, of Santry, and Hugh Brierly, of
Coolock, to be my Executors.

(SIGNED)   WILLIAM ELLISON
               HUGH BRIERLY
               TIMOTHY BUCKLY
               CHARLES BENTHAM, NT[7]

BOYLE [*eagerly*].   An' how much'll be comin' out of it, Mr Bentham?
BENTHAM.   The Executors told me that half of the property would be
   anything between £1500 and £2000.
MARY.   A fortune, father, a fortune!
JOHNNY.   We'll be able to get out o' this place now, an' go somewhere
   we're not known.
MRS BOYLE.   You won't have to trouble about a job for awhile, Jack.

---

7. National Teacher, a certification, but not as a lawyer.

BOYLE [*fervently*].   I'll never doubt the goodness o' God agen.
BENTHAM.   I congratulate you, Mr Boyle.

[*They shake hands.*]

BOYLE.   An' now, Mr Bentham, you'll have to have a wet.
BENTHAM.   A wet?
BOYLE.   A wet—a jar—a boul!
MRS BOYLE.   Jack, you're speakin' to Mr Bentham, an' not to Joxer.
BOYLE [*solemnly*].   Juno . . . Mary . . . Johnny . . . we'll have to go
into mournin' at wanst. . . . I never expected that poor Bill ud die so
sudden. . . . Well, we all have to die some day . . . you, Juno, today
. . . an' me, maybe, tomorrow. . . . It's sad, but it can't be helped. . . .
Requiescat in pace . . . or, usin' our oul' tongue like
St Patrick or St Bridget, *Guh sayeree jeea ayera*!
MARY.   Oh, father, that's not Rest in Peace; that's God save Ireland.
BOYLE.   U-u-ugh, it's all the same—isn't it a prayer? . . . Juno, I'm
done with Joxer; he's nothin' but a prognosticator an' a . . .
JOXER [*climbing angrily through the window and bounding into the
room*].   You're done with Joxer, are you? Maybe you thought I'd stop
on the roof all the night for you! Joxer out on the roof with the win'
blowin' through him was nothin' to you an' your friend with the collar
an' tie!
MRS BOYLE.   What in the name o' God brought you out on the roof;
what were you doin' there?
JOXER [*ironically*].   I was dhreamin' I was standin' on the bridge of a
ship, an' she sailin' the Antartic Ocean, an' it blowed, an' blowed, an'
I lookin' up at the sky an' saying', what is the stars, what is the stars?
MRS BOYLE [*opening the door and standing at it*].   Here, get ou' o' this,
Joxer Daly; I was always thinkin' you had a slate off.
JOXER [*moving to the door*].   I have to laugh every time I look at the
deep-sea sailor; an' a row on a river ud make him sea-sick!
BOYLE.   Get ou' o' this before I take the law into me own hands!
JOXER [*going out*].   Say aw rewaeawr, but not goodbye. Lookin' for work,
an' prayin' to God he won't get it! [*He goes.*]
MRS BOYLE.   I'm tired tellin' you what Joxer was; maybe now you see
yourself the kind he is.
BOYLE.   He'll never blow the froth off a pint o' mine agen, that's a sure
thing. Johnny . . . Mary . . . you're to keep yourselves to yourselves
for the future. Juno, I'm done with Joxer. . . . I'm a new man from
this out. . . . [*Clasping* MRS BOYLE's *hand, and singing emotionally.*]
      O, me darlin' Juno, I will be thrue to thee;
      Me own, me darlin' Juno, you're all the world to me.

Act Two

The same, but the furniture is more plentiful, and of a vulgar nature. A glaringly upholstered armchair and lounge; cheap pictures and photos everywhere. Every available spot is ornamented with huge vases filled with artificial flowers. Crossed festoons of coloured paper chains stretch from end to end of ceiling. On the table is an old attaché case. It is about six in the evening, and two days after the First Act. BOYLE, *in his shirt-sleeves, is voluptuously stretched on the sofa; he is smoking a clay pipe. He is half asleep. A lamp is lighting on the table. After a few moments' pause the voice of* JOXER *is heard singing softly outside at the door—'Me pipe I'll smoke, as I dhrive me moke—are you there, Mor . . . ee . . . ar . . . i . . . teee!'*

BOYLE [*leaping up, takes a pen in his hand and busies himself with papers*]. Come along, Joxer, me son, come along.
JOXER [*putting his head in*]. Are you be yourself?
BOYLE. Come on, come on; that doesn't matther; I'm masther now, an' I'm goin' to remain masther.

[JOXER *comes in.*]

JOXER. How d'ye feel now, as a man o' money?
BOYLE [*solemnly*]. It's a responsibility, Joxer, a great responsibility.
JOXER. I suppose 'tis now, though you wouldn't think it.
BOYLE. Joxer, han' me over that attackey case on the table there.

[JOXER *hands the case.*]

Ever since the Will was passed I've run hundreds o' dockyments through me han's—I tell you, you have to keep your wits about you. [*He busies himself with papers.*]
JOXER. Well, I won't disturb you; I'll dhrop in when . . .
BOYLE [*hastily*]. It's all right, Joxer, this is the last one to be signed today. [*He signs a paper, puts it into the case, which he shuts with a snap, and sits back pompously in the chair.*] Now, Joxer, you want to see me; I'm at your service—what can I do for you, me man?
JOXER. I've just dhropped in with the three pouns five shillings that Mrs Madigan riz on the blankets an' table for you, an' she says you're to be in no hurry payin' it back.
BOYLE. She won't be long without it; I expect the first cheque for a couple o' hundhred any day. There's the five bob for yourself—go on, take it, man; it'll not be the last you'll get from the Captain. Now an' agen we have our differ, but we're there together all the time.
JOXER. Me for you, an' you for me, like the two Musketeers.
BOYLE. Father Farrell stopped me today an' tole me how glad he was I fell in for the money.

JOXER.   He'll be stoppin' you ofen enough now; I suppose it was 'Mr'
Boyle with him?

BOYLE.   He shuk me be the han' . . .

JOXER [*ironically*].   I met with Napper Tandy, an' he shuk me be the
han'![1]

BOYLE.   You're seldom asthray, Joxer, but you're wrong shipped this
time. What you're sayin' of Father Farrell is very near to blasfeemey.
I don't like anyone to talk disrespectful of Father Farrell.

JOXER.   You're takin' me up wrong, Captain; I wouldn't let a word be
said agen Father Farrell—the heart o' the rowl, that's what he is; I
always said he was a darlin' man, a daarlin' man.

BOYLE.   Comin' up the stairs who did I meet but that bummer, Nugent.
'I seen you talkin' to Father Farrell', says he, with a grin on him.
'He'll be folleyin' you,' says he, 'like a Guardian Angel from this out'—
all the time the oul' grin on him, Joxer.

JOXER.   I never seen him yet but he had the oul' grin on him!

BOYLE.   'Mr Nugent,' says I, 'Father Farrell is a man o' the people, an',
as far as I know the History o' me country, the priests was always in
the van of the fight for Irelan's freedom.'

JOXER [*fervently*].
        Who was it led the van, Soggart Aroon?[2]
        Since the fight first began, Soggart Aroon?

BOYLE.   'Who are you tellin'?' says he. 'Didn't they let down the Fenians, an' didn't they do in Parnell? An' now . . .' 'You ought to be
ashamed o' yourself,' says I, interruptin' him, 'not to know the History
o' your country.' An' I left him gawkin' where he was.

JOXER.   Where ignorance's bliss 'tis folly to be wise; I wondher did he
ever read *The Story o' Ireland*.[3]

BOYLE.   Be J. L. Sullivan? Don't you know he didn't.

JOXER.   Ah, it's a darlin' buk, a daarlin' buk!

BOYLE.   You'd betther be goin', now, Joxer; his Majesty, Bentham'll be
here any minute, now.

JOXER.   Be the way things is lookin', it'll be a match between him an'
Mary. She's thrun over Jerry altogether. Well, I hope it will, for he's
a darlin' man.

BOYLE.   I'm glad you think so—I don't. [*Irritably.*] What's darlin' about
him?

JOXER [*nonplussed*].   I only seen him twiced; if you want to know me,
come an' live with me.

BOYLE.   He's too dignified for me—to hear him talk you'd think he

1. Line from the song "The Wearing of the Green"
about James Napper Tandy (1740–1803), who
attempted to instigate a rebellion in Ireland in 1798.
2. Irish for "dear priest."
3. Joxer quotes the English poet Thomas Gray

(1716–71); he refers to A. M. Sullivan's *The Story
of Ireland* (1883), a nationalist, notoriously
romanticized, and extremely popular history; John
L. Sullivan was the American prizefighter.

knew as much as a Boney's Oraculum.[4] He's given up his job as teacher, an' is goin' to become a solicitor in Dublin—he's been studyin' law. I suppose he thinks I'll set him up, but he's wrong shipped. An' th' other fella—Jerry's as bad. The two o' them ud give you a pain in your face, listenin' to them; Jerry believin' in nothin', an' Bentham believin' in everythin'. One that says all is God an' no man; an' th' other that says all is man an' no God!

JOXER.   Well, I'll be off now.

BOYLE.   Don't forget to dhrop down afther awhile; we'll have a quiet jar, an' a song or two.

JOXER.   Never fear.

BOYLE.   An' tell Mrs Madigan that I hope we'll have the pleasure of her organisation at our little enthertainment.

JOXER.   Righto; we'll come down together. [*He goes out.*]

[JOHNNY *comes from room on left, and sits down moodily at the fire.* BOYLE *looks at him for a few moments, and shakes his head. He fills his pipe.*]

VOICE OF MRS BOYLE AT THE DOOR.   Open the door, Jack; this thing has me nearly kilt with the weight.

[BOYLE *opens the door.* MRS BOYLE *enters carrying the box of a gramophone, followed by* MARY *carrying the horn and some parcels.* MRS BOYLE *leaves the box on the table and flops into a chair.*]

MRS BOYLE.   Carryin' that from Henry Street was no joke.

BOYLE.   U-u-ugh, that's a grand-lookin' insthrument—how much was it?

MRS BOYLE.   Pound down, an' five to be paid at two shillin's a week.

BOYLE.   That's reasonable enough.

MRS BOYLE.   I'm afraid we're runnin' into too much debt; first the furniture, an' now this.

BOYLE.   The whole lot won't be much out of £2000.

MARY.   I don't know what you wanted a gramophone for—I know Charlie hates them; he says they're destructive of real music.

BOYLE.   Desthructive of music—that fella ud give you a pain in your face. All a gramophone wants is to be properly played; its thrue wondher is only felt when everythin's quiet—what a gramophone wants is dead silence!

MARY.   But, father, Jerry says the same; afther all, you can only appreciate music when your ear is properly trained.

BOYLE.   That's another fella ud give you a pain in your face. Properly thrained! I suppose you couldn't appreciate football unless your fut was properly thrained.

4. A cheap and unreliable compendium of "improving" knowledge.

MRS BOYLE [*to* MARY].   Go on in ower that an' dress or Charlie'll be in on you, an' tea nor nothin'll be ready.

[MARY *goes into room left.*]

MRS BOYLE [*arranging table for tea*].   You didn't look at your new gramophone, Johnny?

JOHNNY.   'Tisn't gramophones I'm thinking of.

MRS BOYLE.   An' what is it you're thinkin' of, allanna?[5]

JOHNNY.   Nothin', nothin', nothin'.

MRS BOYLE.   Sure, you must be thinkin' of somethin'; it's yourself that has yourself the way y'are; sleepin' wan night in me sisther's, an' the nex' in your father's brother's—you'll get no rest goin' on that way.

JOHNNY.   I can rest nowhere, nowhere, nowhere.

MRS BOYLE.   Sure, you're not thryin' to rest anywhere.

JOHNNY.   Let me alone, let me alone, let me alone, for God's sake.

[*A knock at street door.*]

MRS BOYLE [*in a flutter*].   Here he is; here's Mr Bentham!

BOYLE.   Well, there's room for him; it's a pity there's not a brass band to play him in.

MRS BOYLE.   We'll han' the tea round, an' not be clusthered round the table, as if we never seen nothin'.

[*Steps are heard approaching, and* MRS BOYLE, *opening the door, allows* BENTHAM *to enter.*]

Give your hat an' stick to Jack, there . . . sit down, Mr Bentham . . . no, not there . . . in th' easy chair be the fire . . . there, that's betther. Mary'll be out to you in a minute.

BOYLE [*solemnly*].   I seen be the paper this mornin' that Consols[6] was down half per cent. That's serious, min' you, an' shows the whole counthry's in a state o' chassis.

MRS BOYLE.   What's Consols, Jack?

BOYLE.   Consols? Oh, Consols is—oh, there's no use tellin' women what Consols is—th' wouldn't undherstand.

BENTHAM.   It's just as you were saying, Mrs Boyle.

[MARY *enters, charmingly dressed.*]

Oh, good evening, Mary; how pretty you're looking!

MARY [*archly*].   Am I?

BOYLE.   We were just talkin' when you kem in, Mary; I was tellin' Mr Bentham that the whole counthry's in a state o' chassis.

MARY [*to* BENTHAM].   Would you prefer the green or the blue ribbon round me hair, Charlie?

MRS BOYLE.   Mary, your father's speakin'.

---

5. Irish *an leanbh*, "O child."   6. Securities traded on the stock market.

BOYLE [*rapidly*].   I was jus' tellin' Mr Bentham that the whole country's
in a state o' chassis.

MARY.   I'm sure you're frettin', da, whether it is or no.

MRS BOYLE.   With all our churches an' religions, the worl's not a bit
the betther.

BOYLE [*with a commanding gesture*].   Tay!

[MARY *and* MRS BOYLE *dispense the tea.*]

MRS BOYLE.   An' Irelan's takin' a leaf out o' the worl's buk; when we got
the makin' of our own laws I thought we'd never stop to look behind
us, but instead of that we never stopped to look before us! If the people
ud folley up their religion betther there'd be a betther chance for us—
what do you think, Mr Bentham?

BENTHAM.   I'm afraid I can't venture to express an opinion on that point,
Mrs Boyle; dogma has no attraction for me.

MRS BOYLE.   I forgot you didn't hold with us: what's this you said you
were?

BENTHAM.   A Theosophist, Mrs Boyle.

MRS BOYLE.   An' what in the name o' God's a Theosophist?

BOYLE.   A Theosophist, Juno, 's a—tell her, Mr Bentham, tell her.

BENTHAM.   It's hard to explain in a few words: Theosophy's founded on
the Vedas, the religious books of the East. Its central theme is the
existence of an all-pervading Spirit—the Life-Breath. Nothing really
exists but this one Universal Life-Breath. And whatever even seems
to exist separately from this Life-Breath, doesn't really exist at all. It is
all vital force in man, in all animals, and in all vegetation. This Life-
Breath is called the Prawna.

MRS BOYLE.   The Prawna! What a comical name.

BOYLE.   Prawna; yis, the Prawna. [*Blowing gently through his lips.*] That's
the Prawna!

MRS BOYLE.   Whist, whist, Jack.

BENTHAM.   The happiness of man depends upon his sympathy with this
Spirit. Men who have reached a high state of excellence are called
Yogi. Some men become Yogi in a short time, it may take others
millions of years.

BOYLE.   Yogi! I seen hundhreds of them in the streets o' San Francisco.

BENTHAM.   It is said by these Yogi that if we practise certain mental
exercises we would have powers denied to others—for instance, the
faculty of seeing things that happen miles and miles away.

MRS BOYLE.   I wouldn't care to meddle with that sort o' belief; it's a very
curious religion, altogether.

BOYLE.   What's curious about it? Isn't all religions curious?—if
they weren't, you wouldn't get any one to believe them. But religions
is passin' away—they've had their day like everything else. Take the
real Dublin people, f'rinstance: they know more about Charlie

Chaplin an' Tommy Mix[7] than they do about SS. Peter an' Paul!

MRS BOYLE.   You don't believe in ghosts, Mr Bentham?

MARY.   Don't you know he doesn't, mother?

BENTHAM.   I don't know that, Mary. Scientists are beginning to think that what we call ghosts are sometimes seen by persons of a certain nature. They say that sensational actions, such as the killing of a person, demand great energy, and that energy lingers in the place where the action occurred. People may live in the place and see nothing, when someone may come along whose personality has some peculiar connection with the energy of the place, and, in a flash, the person sees the whole affair.

JOHNNY [rising swiftly, pale and affected].   What sort o' talk is this to be goin' on with? Is there nothin' betther to be talkin' about but the killin' o' people? My God, isn't it bad enough for these things to happen without talkin' about them! [He hurriedly goes into the room on left.]

BENTHAM.   Oh, I'm very sorry, Mrs Boyle; I never thought . . .

MRS BOYLE [apologetically].   Never mind, Mr Bentham, he's very touchy.

[A frightened scream is heard from JOHNNY inside.]

Mother of God, what's that?

[He rushes out again, his face pale, his lips twitching, his limbs trembling.]

JOHNNY.   Shut the door, shut the door, quick, for God's sake! Great God, have mercy on me! Blessed Mother o' God, shelter me, shelter your son!

MRS BOYLE [catching him in her arms].   What's wrong with you? What ails you? Sit down, sit down, here, no the bed . . . there now . . . there now.

MARY.   Johnny, Johnny, what ails you?

JOHNNY.   I seen him, I seen him . . . kneelin' in front o' the statue . . . merciful Jesus, have pity on me!

MRS BOYLE [to BOYLE].   Get him a glass o' whisky . . . quick, man, an' don't stand gawkin'.

[BOYLE gets the whisky.]

JOHNNY.   Sit here, sit here, mother . . . between me an' the door.

MRS BOYLE.   I'll sit beside you as long as you like, only tell me what was it came across you at all?

JOHNNY [after taking some drink].   I seen him. . . . I seen Robbie Tancred kneelin' down before the statue . . . an' the red light shinin' on him . . . an' when I went in . . . he turned an' looked at me . . . an' I seen the woun's bleedin' in his breast. . . . Oh, why did he look at

7. Film stars.

me like that? . . . it wasn't my fault that he was done in. . . . Mother
o' God, keep him away from me!

MRS BOYLE.   There, there, child, you've imagined it all. There was
nothin' there at all—it was the red light you seen, an' the talk we had
put all the rest into your head. Here, dhrink more o' this—it'll do you
good. . . . An', now, stretch yourself down on the bed for a little. [*To*
BOYLE.] Go in, Jack, an' show him it was only in his own head it was.

BOYLE [*making no move*].   E-e-e-e-eh; it's all nonsense; it was only a
shadda he saw.

MARY.   Mother o' God, he made me heart lep!

BENTHAM.   It was simply due to an overwrought imagination—we all
get that way at times.

MRS BOYLE.   There, dear, lie down in the bed, an' I'll put the quilt
across you . . . e-e-e-eh, that's it . . . you'll be as right as the mail in
a few minutes.

JOHNNY.   Mother, go into the room an' see if the light's lightin' before
the statue.

MRS BOYLE [*to* BOYLE].   Jack, run in an' see if the light's lightin' before
the statue.

BOYLE [*to* MARY].   Mary, slip in an' see if the light's lightin' before the
statue.

> [MARY *hesitates to go in.*]

BENTHAM.   It's all right; Mary, I'll go. [*He goes into the room; remains*
for a few moments, and returns.] Everything's just as it was—the light
burning bravely before the statue.

BOYLE.   Of course; I knew it was all nonsense. [*A knock at the door.*
Going to open the door] E-e-e-e-eh.

> [*He opens it, and* JOXER, *followed by* MRS MADIGAN, *enters.* MRS
> MADIGAN *is a strong, dapper little woman of about forty-five; her*
> *face is almost always a widespread smile of complacency. She is*
> *a woman who, in manner at least, can mourn with them that*
> *mourn, and rejoice with them that do rejoice. When she is feeling*
> *comfortable, she is inclined to be reminiscent; when others say*
> *anything, or following a statement made by herself, she has a*
> *habit of putting her head a little to one side, and nodding it*
> *rapidly several times in succession, like a bird pecking at a hard*
> *berry. Indeed, she has a good deal of the bird in her, but the bird*
> *instinct is by no means a melodious one. She is ignorant, vulgar*
> *and forward, but her heart is generous withal. For instance, she*
> *would help a neighbour's sick child; she would probably kill the*
> *child, but her intention would be to cure it; she would be more*
> *at home helping a drayman to lift a fallen horse. She is dressed*
> *in a rather soiled grey dress and a vivid purple blouse; in her hair*

is a huge comb, ornamented with huge coloured beads. She enters
with a gliding step, beaming smile and nodding head. BOYLE
receives them effusively.]

BOYLE. Come on in, Mrs Madigan; come on in; I was afraid you weren't
comin'. . . . [*Slyly.*] There's some people able to dhress, ay, Joxer?

JOXER. Fair as the blossoms that bloom in the May, an' sweet as the
scent of the new-mown hay. . . . Ah, well she may wear them.

MRS MADIGAN [*looking at* MARY]. I know some as are as sweet as the
blossoms that bloom in the May—oh, no names, no pack dhrill.

BOYLE. An' now I'll inthroduce the pair o' yous to Mary's intended: Mr
Bentham, this is Mrs Madigan, an oul' back-parlour neighbour, that,
if she could help it at all, ud never see a body shuk!

BENTHAM [*rising, and tentatively shaking the hand of* MRS MADI-
GAN]. I'm sure, it's a great pleasure to know you, Mrs Madigan.

MRS MADIGAN. An, I'm goin' to tell you, Mr Bentham, you're goin' to
get as nice a bit o' skirt in Mary, there, as ever you seen in your puff.
Not like some of the dhressed-up dolls that's knockin' about lookin'
for men when it's a skelpin[8] they want. I remember, as well as I
remember yestherday, the day she was born—of a Tuesday, the 25th
o' June, in the year 1901, at thirty-three minutes past wan in the day
by Foley's clock, the pub at the corner o' the street. A cowld day it
was too, for the season o' the year, an' I remember sayin' to Joxer,
there, who I met comin' up th' stairs, that the new arrival in Boyle's
ud grow up a hardy chiselur if it lived, an' that she'd be somethin' one
o' these days that nobody suspected, an' so signs on it, here she is
today, goin' to be married to a young man lookin' as if he'd be fit to
commensurate in any position in life it ud please God to call him!

BOYLE [*effusively*]. Sit down, Mrs Madigan, sit down, me oul' sport.
[*To* BENTHAM.] This is Joxer Daly, Past Chief Ranger of the Dear
Little Shamrock Branch of the Irish National Foresters, an oul' front-
top neighbour, that never despaired, even in the darkest days of Ireland's sorra.

JOXER. *Nil desperandum*, Captain, *nil desperandum.*[9]

BOYLE. Sit down, Joxer, sit down. The two of us was ofen in a tight
corner.

MRS BOYLE. Ay, in Foley's snug!

JOXER. An' we kem out of it flyin', we kem out of it flyin', Captain.

BOYLE. An' now for a dhrink—I know yous won't refuse an oul' friend.

MRS MADIGAN [*to* MRS BOYLE]. Is Johnny not well, Mrs . . . .

MRS BOYLE [*warningly*]. S-s-s-sh.

MRS MADIGAN. Oh, the poor darlin'.

BOYLE. Well, Mrs Madigan, is it tea or what?

MRS MADIGAN. Well, speakin' for meself, I jus' had me tea a minute

---

8. Spanking.   9. Do not despair.

ago, an' I'm afraid to dhrink any more—I'm never the same when I
dhrink too much tay. Thanks, all the same, Mr Boyle.
BOYLE.   Well, what about a bottle o' stout or a dhrop o' whisky?
MRS MADIGAN.   A bottle o' stout ud be a little too heavy for me stum-
mock afther me tay. . . . A-a-ah, I'll thry the ball o' malt.

[BOYLE *prepares the whisky.*]

There's nothin' like a ball o' malt occasional like—too much of it isn't
good. [*To* BOYLE, *who is adding water.*] Ah, God, Johnny, don't put
too much wather on it! [*She drinks.*] I suppose yous'll be lavin' this
place.
BOYLE.   I'm looking for a place near the sea; I'd like the place that you
might say was me cradle, to be me grave as well. The sea is always
callin' me.
JOXER.   She is callin', callin', callin', in the win' an' on the sea.
BOYLE.   Another dhrop o' whisky, Mrs Madigan?
MRS MADIGAN.   Well, now, it ud be hard to refuse seein' the suspicious
times that's in it.
BOYLE [*with a commanding gesture*].   Song! . . . Juno . . . Mary . . .
'Home to our Mountains'!
MRS MADIGAN [*enthusiastically*].   Hear, hear!
JOXER.   Oh, tha's a darlin' song, a daarlin' song!
MARY [*bashfully*].   Ah no, da; I'm not in a singin' humour.
MRS MADIGAN.   Gawn with you, child, an' you only goin' to be marrid;
I remember as well as I remember yestherday—it was on a lovely
August evenin', exactly, accordin' to date, fifteen years ago, come the
Tuesday folleyin' the nex' that's comin' on, when me own man—*the
Lord be good to him*—an' me was sittin' shy together in a doty little
nook on a counthry road, adjacent to The Stiles.[1] 'That'll scratch
your lovely, little white neck', says he, ketchin' hould of a danglin'
bramble branch, holdin' clusters of the loveliest flowers you ever seen,
an' breakin' if off, so that his arm fell, accidental like, roun' me waist,
an' as I felt it tightenin', an tightenin', an' tightenin', I thought me
buzzom was every minute goin' to burst out into a roystherin' song
about

> The little green leaves that were shakin' on the threes,
> The gallivantin' buttherflies, an' buzzin' o' the bees!

BOYLE.   Ordher for the song!
MRS BOYLE.   Come on, Mary—we'll do our best.

[MRS BOYLE *and* MARY *stand up, and choosing a suitable position, sing simply* 'Home to our Mountains'. *They bow to the
company, and return to their places.*]

---

1. Place by the northern side of Dublin Bay.

BOYLE [*emotionally, at the end of the song*].   'Lull . . . me . . . to . . .
   rest!'
JOXER [*clapping his hands*].   Bravo, bravo! Darlin' girulls, darlin' girulls!
MRS MADIGAN.   Juno, I never seen you in better form.
BENTHAM.   Very nicely rendered indeed.
MRS MADIGAN.   A noble call, a noble call!
MRS BOYLE.   What about yourself, Mrs Madigan?

[*After some coaxing,* MRS MADIGAN *rises, and in a quavering voice
sings the following verse:*]

If I were a blackbird I'd whistle and sing;
I'd follow the ship that my thrue love was in;
An' on the top riggin', I'd there build me nest,
An' at night I would sleep on me Willie's white breast!

[*Becoming husky, amid applause, she sits down.*]

MRS MADIGAN.   Ah, me voice is too husky now, Juno; though I remember the time when Maisie Madigan could sing like a nightingale at
   matin' time. I remember as well as I remember yestherday, at a party
   given to celebrate the comin' of the first chiselur to Annie an' Benny
   Jimeson—who was the barber, yous may remember, in Henrietta Street,
   that, afther Easter Week, hung out a green, white an' orange pole,
   an' then, when the Tans[2] started their jazz dancin', whipped it in
   agen, an' stuck out a red, white an' blue wan instead, givin' as an
   excuse that a barber's pole was strictly non-political—singin' 'An' You'll
   Remember Me' with the top notes quiverin' in a dead hush of peth-
   rified attention, folleyed be a clappin' o' han's that shuk the tumblers
   on the table, an' capped by Jimeson, the barber, sayin' that it was the
   best rendherin' of 'You'll Remember Me' he ever heard in his natural!
BOYLE [*peremptorily*].   Ordher for Joxer's song!
JOXER.   Ah no, I couldn't; don't ass me, Captain.
BOYLE.   Joxer's song, Joxer's song—give us wan of your shut-eyed wans.
JOXER [*settles himself in his chair; takes a drink; clears his throat; solemnly closes his eyes, and begins to sing in a very querulous voice*].

She is far from the lan' where her young hero sleeps,[3]
An' lovers around her are sighing [*He hesitates.*]
An' lovers around her are sighin' . . . sighin' . . .
   sighin' . . . [*A pause.*]

BOYLE [*imitating* JOXER].
      And lovers around her are sighing!
What's the use of you thryin' to sing the song if you don't know it?

---

2. The Black and Tans, so-called for uniform colors, a brutal auxiliary police force employed in
Dublin by the British.

3. One of the poet Thomas Moore's *Irish Melo-
dies* (1808).

MARY.   Thry another one, Mr Daly—maybe you'd be more fortunate.
MRS MADIGAN.   Gawn, Joxer; thry another wan.
JOXER [*starting again*].

I have heard the mavis singin' his love song to the morn;[4]
I have seen the dew-dhrop clingin' to the rose jus' newly born;
    but . . . but . . . [*frantically*] To the rose jus' newly born . . .
    newly born . . . born.

JOHNNY.   Mother, put on the gramophone, for God's sake, an' stop
Joxer's bawlin'.
BOYLE [*commandingly*].   Gramophone! . . . I hate to see fellas thryin'
to do what they're not able to do. [BOYLE *arranges the gramophone,
and is about to start it, when voices are heard of persons descending
the stairs.*]
MRS BOYLE [*warningly*].   Whisht, Jack, don't put it on, don't put it on
yet; this must be poor Mrs Tancred comin' down to go to the hospital—I forgot all about them bringin' the body to the church tonight.
Open the door, Mary, an' give them a bit o' light.

[MARY *opens the door, and* MRS TANCRED—*a very old woman,
obviously shaken by the death of her son—appears, accompanied
by several* NEIGHBOURS. *The first few phrases are spoken before
they appear.*]

FIRST NEIGHBOUR.   It's a sad journey we're goin' on, but God's good,
an' the Republicans won't be always down.
MRS TANCRED.   Ah, what good is that to me now? Whether they're up
or down—it won't bring me darlin' boy from the grave.
MRS BOYLE.   Come in an' have a hot cup o' tay, Mrs Tancred, before
you go.
MRS TANCRED.   Ah, I can take nothin' now, Mrs Boyle—I won't be long
afther him.
FIRST NEIGHBOUR.   Still an' all, he died a noble death, an' we'll bury
him like a king.
MRS TANCRED.   An' I'll go on livin' like a pauper. Ah, what's the pains
I suffered bringin' him into the world to carry him to his cradle, to
the pains I'm sufferin' now, carryin' him out o' the world to bring him
to his grave!
MARY.   It would be better for you not to go at all, Mrs Tancred, but to
stay at home beside the fire with some o' the neighbours.
MRS TANCRED.   I seen the first of him, an' I'll see the last of him.
MRS BOYLE.   You'd want a shawl, Mrs Tancred; it's a cowld night, an'
the win's blowin' sharp.
MRS MADIGAN [*rushing out*].   I've a shawl above.

4. "Mary of Argyle," by Charles Jefferys (1807–65).

MRS TANCRED. Me home is gone now; he was me only child, an' to think that he was lyin' for a whole night stretched out on the side of a lonely counthry lane, with his head, his darlin' head, that I ofen kissed an' fondled, half hidden in the wather of a runnin' brook. An' I'm told he was the leadher of the ambush where me nex' door neighbour, Mrs Mannin', lost her Free State soldier son. An' now here's the two of us oul' women, standin' one on each side of a scales o' sorra, balanced be the bodies of our two dead darlin' sons.

[MRS MADIGAN *returns, and wraps a shawl around her.*]

God bless you, Mrs Madigan. . . . [*She moves slowly towards the door.*] Mother o' God, Mother o' God, have pity on the pair of us! . . . O Blessed Virgin, where were you when me darlin' son was riddled with bullets, when me darlin' son was riddled with bullets! . . . Sacred Heart of the Crucified Jesus, take away our hearts o' stone . . . an' give us hearts o' flesh![5] . . . Take away this murdherin' hate . . . an' give us Thine own eternal love!

[*They pass out of the room.*]

MRS BOYLE [*explanatorily to* BENTHAM]. That was Mrs Tancred of the two-pair back; her son was found, e'er yestherday, lyin' out beyant Finglas riddled with bullets. A Diehard he was, be all accounts. He was a nice quiet boy, but lattherly he went to hell, with his Republic first, an' Republic last an' Republic over all. He often took tea with us here, in the oul' days, an' Johnny, there, an' him used to be always together.

JOHNNY. Am I always to be havin' to tell you that he was no friend o' mine? I never cared for him, an' he could never stick me. It's not because he was Commandant of the Battalion that I was Quarther-Masther of, that we were friends.

MRS BOYLE. He's gone now—the Lord be good to him! God help his poor oul' creature of a mother, for no matther whose friend or enemy he was, he was her poor son.

BENTHAM. The whole thing is terrible, Mrs Boyle; but the only way to deal with a mad dog is to destroy him.

MRS BOYLE. An' to think of me forgettin' about him bein' brought to the church tonight, an' we singin' an' all, but it was well we hadn't the gramophone goin', anyhow.

BOYLE. Even if we had aself. We've nothin' to do with these things, one way or t'other. That's the Government's business, an' let them do what we're payin' them for doin'.

MRS BOYLE. I'd like to know how a body's not to mind these things; look at the way they're afther leavin' the people in this very house.

5. Ezekiel 36.26.

Hasn't the whole house, nearly, been massacreed? There's young Dougherty's husband with his leg off; Mrs Travers that had her son blew up be a mine in Inchegeela, in County Cork; Mrs Mannin' that lost wan of her sons in an ambush a few weeks ago, an' now, poor Mrs Tancred's only child gone west with his body made a collandher of. Sure, if it's not our business, I don't know whose business it is.

BOYLE.　Here, there, that's enough about them things; they don't affect us, an' we needn't give a damn. If they want a wake, well, let them have a wake. When I was a sailor, I was always resigned to meet with a wathery grave; an' if they want to be soldiers, well, there's no use o' them squealin' when they meet a soldier's fate.

JOXER.　Let me like a soldier fall—me breast expandin' to th' ball![6]

MRS BOYLE.　In wan way, she deserves all she got; for lately, she let th' Diehards make an open house of th' place; an' for th' last couple of months, either when th' sun was risin' or when th' sun was settin', you had CID[7] men burstin' into your room, assin' you where were you born, where were you christened, where were you married, an' where would you be buried!

JOHNNY.　For God's sake, let us have no more o' this talk.

MRS MADIGAN.　What about Mr Boyle's song before we start th' gramophone?

MARY [getting her hat, and putting it on].　Mother, Charlie and I are goin' out for a little sthroll.

MRS BOYLE.　All right, darlin'.

BENTHAM [going out with MARY].　We won't be long away, Mrs Boyle.

MRS MADIGAN.　Gwan, Captain, gwan.

BOYLE.　E-e-e-e-eh, I'd want to have a few more jars in me, before I'd be in fettle for singin'.

JOXER.　Give us that poem you writ t'other day. [To the rest.] Aw, it's a darlin' poem, a daarlin' poem.

MRS BOYLE.　God bless us, is he startin' to write poetry!

BOYLE [rising to his feet].　E-e-e-e-eh. [He recites in an emotional, consequential manner the following verses.]

Shawn an' I were friends, sir, to me he was all in all.
His work was very heavy and his wages were very small.
None betther on th' beach as Docker, I'll go bail,
'Tis now I'm feelin' lonely, for today he lies in jail.
He was not what some call pious—seldom at church or prayer;
For the greatest scoundrels I know, sir, goes every Sunday there.
Fond of his pint—well, rather, but hated the Boss by creed
But never refused a copper to comfort a pal in need.
E-e-e-e-eh. [He sits down.]

6. From the opera Maritana (1845) by W. V.　7. Criminal Investigation Department
Wallace (1812–65).

MRS MADIGAN.   Grand, grand; you should folly that up, you should folly that up.

JOXER.   It's a daarlin' poem!

BOYLE [*delightedlyi*].   E-e-e-e-eh.

JOHNNY.   Are yous goin' to put on th' gramophone tonight, or are yous not?

MRS BOYLE.   Gwan, Jack, put on a record.

MRS MADIGAN.   Gwan, Captain, gwan.

BOYLE.   Well, yous'll want to keep a dead silence.

> [*He sets a record, starts the machine, and it begins to play 'If You're Irish Come into the Parlour'. As the tune is in full blare, the door is suddenly opened by a brisk, little bald-headed man, dressed circumspectly in a black suit; he glares fiercely at all in the room; he is* 'NEEDLE' NUGENT, *a tailor. He carries his hat in his hand.*]

NUGENT [*loudly, above the noise of the gramophone*].   Are yous goin' to have that thing bawlin' an' the funeral of Mrs Tancred's son passin' the house? Have none of yous any respect for the Irish people's National regard for the dead?

> [BOYLE *stops the gramophone.*]

MRS BOYLE.   Maybe, Needle Nugent, it's nearly time we had a little less respect for the dead, an' a little more regard for the livin'.

MRS MADIGAN.   We don't want you, Mr Nugent, to teach us what we learned at our mother's knee. You don't look yourself as if you were dyin' of grief; if y'ass Maisie Madigan anything, I'd call you a real thrue Diehard an' live-soft Republican, attendin' Republican funerals in the day, an' stoppin' up half the night makin' suits for the Civic Guards!

> [*Persons are heard running down the street, some saying 'Here it is, here it is.'* NUGENT *withdraws, and the rest, except* JOHNNY, *go to the window looking into the street, and look out. Sounds of a crowd coming nearer are heard; portions are singing*]

> To Jesus' Heart all burning
> With fervent love for men,
> My heart with fondest yearning
> Shall raise its joyful strain.
> While ages course along,
> Blest be with loudest song
> The Sacred Heart of Jesus
> By every heart and tongue.

MRS BOYLE.   Here's the hearse, here's the hearse!
BOYLE.   There's t' oul' mother walkin' behin' the coffin.
MRS MADIGAN.   You can hardly see the coffin with the wreaths.
JOXER.   Oh, it's a darlin' funeral, a daarlin' funeral!
MRS MADIGAN.   We'd have a betther view from the street.
BOYLE.   Yes—this place ud give you a crick in your neck.

> [*They leave the room, and go down.* JOHNNY *sits moodily by the fire. A* YOUNG MAN *enters; he looks at* JOHNNY *for a moment.*]

YOUNG MAN.   Quarther-Masther Boyle.
JOHNNY [*with a start*].   The Mobiliser!
YOUNG MAN.   You're not at the funeral?
JOHNNY.   I'm not well.
YOUNG MAN.   I'm glad I've found you; you were stoppin' at your aunt's;
   I called there but you'd gone. I've to give you an ordher to attend a
   Battalion Staff meetin' the night afther tomorrow.
JOHNNY.   Where?
YOUNG MAN.   I don't know; you're to meet me at the Pillar[8] at eight
   o'clock; then we're to go to a place I'll be told of tonight; there we'll
   meet a mothor that'll bring us to the meeting. They think you might
   be able to know somethin' about them that gave the bend where Com-
   mandant Tancred was shelterin'.
JOHNNY.   I'm not goin', then. I know nothing about Tancred.
YOUNG MAN [*at the door*].   You'd better come for you own sake—
   remember your oath.
JOHNNY [*passionately*].   I won't go! Haven't I done enough for Ireland!
   I've lost me arm, an' me hip's desthroyed so that I'll never be able to
   walk right agen! Good God, haven't I done enough for Ireland?
YOUNG MAN.   Boyle, no man can do enough for Ireland! [*He goes.*]

> [*Faintly in the distance the crowd is heard saying*]

> Hail, Mary, full of grace, the Lord is with Thee;
> Blessed art Thou amongst women, and blessed [*etc.*]

Act Three

*The same as Act Three. It is about half-past six on a November evening;
a bright fire burns in the grate;* MARY, *dressed to go out, is sitting on a
chair by the fire, leaning forward, her hands under her chin, her elbows
on her knees. A look of dejection, mingled with uncertain anxiety, is on*

---

8. O'Connell Street monument to Admiral Lord
Nelson (1758–1805); it was destroyed by the Irish
Republican Army in 1966, fiftieth anniversary of
Easter Week 1916, for symbolizing British influ-
ence.

*her face. A lamp, turned low, is lighting on the table. The votive light
under the picture of the Virgin gleams more redly than ever.* MRS BOYLE
is putting on her hat and coat. It is two months later.

MRS BOYLE.   An' has Bentham never even written to you since—not
   one line for the past month?
MARY [*tonelessly*].   Not even a line, mother.
MRS BOYLE.   That's very curious. . . . What came between the two of
   yous at all? To leave you so sudden, an' yous so great together. . . .
   To go away t' England, an' not to even leave you his address. . . .
   The way he was always bringin' you to dances, I thought he was mad
   afther you. Are you sure you said nothin' to him?
MARY.   No, mother—at least nothing that could possibly explain his
   givin' me up.
MRS BOYLE.   You know you're a bit hasty at times, Mary, an' say things
   you shouldn't say.
MARY.   I never said to him what I shouldn't say, I'm sure of that.
MRS BOYLE.   How are you sure of it?
MARY.   Because I love him with all my heart and soul, mother. Why,
   I don't know; I often thought to myself that he wasn't the man poor
   Jerry was, but I couldn't help loving him, all the same.
MRS BOYLE.   But you shouldn't be frettin' the way you are; when a woman
   loses a man, she never knows what she's afther losin', to be sure, but,
   then, she never knows what she's afther gainin', either. You're not
   the one girl of a month ago—you look like one pinin' away. It's long
   ago I had a right to bring you to the doctor, instead of waitin' till
   tonight.
MARY.   There's no necessity, really, mother, to go to the doctor; nothing serious is wrong with me—I'm run down and disappointed, that's
   all.
MRS BOYLE.   I'll not wait another minute; I don't like the look of you at
   all. . . . I'm afraid we made a mistake in throwin' over poor Jerry.
   . . . He'd have been betther for you than that Bentham.
MARY.   Mother, the best man for a woman is the one for whom she has
   the most love, and Charlic had it all.
MRS BOYLE.   Well, there's one thing to be said for him—he couldn't
   have been thinkin' of the money, or he wouldn't ha' left you . . . it
   must ha' been somethin' else.
MARY [*wearily*].   I don't know, mother . . . only I think . . .
MRS BOYLE.   What d'ye think?
MARY.   I imagine . . . he thought . . . we weren't . . . good enough
   for him.
MRS BOYLE.   An' what was he himself, only a school teacher? Though
   I don't blame him for fightin' shy of people like that Joxer fella an'
   that oul' Madigan wan—nice sort o' people for your father to inthro-

duce to a man like Mr Bentham. You might have told me all about this before now, Mary; I don't know why you like to hide everything from your mother; you knew Bentham, an' I'd ha' known nothin' about it if it hadn't bin for the Will; an' it was only today, afther long coaxin', that you let out that he's left you.

MARY. It would have been useless to tell you—you wouldn't understand.

MRS BOYLE [*hurt*]. Maybe not. . . . Maybe I wouldn't understand. . . . Well, we'll be off now. [*She goes over to door left, and speaks to* BOYLE *inside.*] We're goin' now to the doctor's. Are you goin' to get up this evenin'?

BOYLE [*from inside*]. The pains in me legs is terrible! It's me should be poppin' off to the doctor instead o' Mary, the way I feel.

MRS BOYLE. Sorra mend you! A nice way you were in last night—carried in in a frog's march, dead to the world. If that's the way you'll go on when you get the money it'll be the grave for you, an asylum for me and the Poorhouse for Johnny.

BOYLE. I thought you were goin'?

MRS BOYLE. That's what has you as you are—you can't bear to be spoken to. Knowin' the way we are, up to our ears in debt, it's a wondher you wouldn't ha' got up to go to th' solicitor's an' see if we could ha' gotten a little o' the money even.

BOYLE [*shouting*]. I can't be goin' up there night, noon an' mornin', can I? He can't give the money till he gets it, can he? I can't get blood out of a turnip, can I?

MRS BOYLE. It's nearly two months since we heard of the Will, an' the money seems as far off as ever. . . . I suppose you know we owe twenty pouns to oul' Murphy?

BOYLE. I've a faint recollection of you tellin' me that before.

MRS BOYLE. Well, you'll go over to the shop yourself for the things in future—I'll face him no more.

BOYLE. I thought you said you were goin'?

MRS BOYLE. I'm goin' now; come on, Mary.

BOYLE. Ey, Juno, ey!

MRS BOYLE. Well, what d'ye want now?

BOYLE. Is there e're a bottle o' stout left?

MRS BOYLE. There's two o' them here still.

BOYLE. Show us in one o' them an' leave t'other there till I get up. An' throw us in the paper that's on the table, an' the bottle o' Sloan's Liniment that's in th' drawer.

MRS BOYLE [*getting the liniment and the stout*]. What paper is it you want—the *Messenger?*

BOYLE. *Messenger!* The *News o' the World!* [1]

[MRS BOYLE *brings in the things asked for, and comes out again.*]

1. *Messenger,* a pious, Catholic, and Irish newspaper; the *News,* a sensational British tabloid.

MRS BOYLE [*at door*]. Mind the candle, now, an' don't burn the house over our heads. I left t'other bottle o' stout on the table.

[*She puts bottle of stout on table. She goes out with* MARY. *A cork is heard popping inside.*]

[*A pause; then outside the door is heard the voice of* JOXER *lilting softly:* 'Me pipe I'll smoke, as I dhrive me moke . . . are you . . . there . . . Mor . . . ee . . . ar . . . i . . . teee!' *A gentle knock is heard, and after a pause the door opens and* JOXER, *followed by* NUGENT, *enters.*]

JOXER. Be God, they must be all out; I was thinkin' there was somethin' up when he didn't answer the signal. We seen Juno an' Mary goin', but I didn't see him, an' it's very seldom he escapes me.

NUGENT. He's not goin' to escape me—he's not goin' to be let go to the fair altogether.

JOXER. Sure, the house couldn't hould them lately; an' he goin' about like a mastherpiece of the Free State counthry; forgettin' their friends; forgettin' God—wouldn't even lift his hat passin' a chapel! Sure they were bound to get a dhrop! An' you really think there's no money comin' to him afther all?

NUGENT. Not as much as a red rex, man; I've been a bit anxious this long time over me money, an' I went up to the solicitor's to find out all I could—ah, man, they were goin' to throw me down the stairs. They toul' me that the·oul' cock himself had the stairs worn away comin' up afther it, an' they black in the face tellin' him he'd get nothin'. Some way or another that the Will is writ he won't be entitled to get as much as a make!

JOXER. Ah, I thought there was somethin' curious about the whole thing; I've bin havin' sthrange dhreams for the last couple o' weeks. An' I notice that that Bentham fella doesn't be comin' here now— there must be somethin' on the mat there too. Anyhow, who, in the name o' God, ud leave anythin' to that oul' bummer? Sure it ud be unnatural. An' the way Juno an' him's been throwin' their weight about for the last few months! Ah, him that goes a borrowin' goes a sorrowin'!

NUGENT. Well, he's not goin' to throw his weight about in the suit I made for him much longer. I'm tellin' you seven pouns aren't to be found growin' on the bushes these days.

JOXER. An' there isn't hardly a neighbour in the whole street that hasn't lent him money on the strength of what he was goin' to get, but they're after backing the wrong horse. Wasn't it a mercy o' God that I'd nothin' to give him! The softy I am, you know, I'd ha' lent him me last juice! I must have had somebody's good prayers. Ah, afther all, an honest man's the noblest work o' God!

[BOYLE *coughs inside.*]

Whisht, damn it, he must be inside in bed.

NUGENT.   Inside o' bed or outside of it, he's goin' to pay me for that suit, or give it back—he'll not climb up my back as easily as he thinks.

JOXER.   Gwan in at wanst, man, an' get it off him, an' don't be a fool.

NUGENT [*going to door left, opening it and looking in*].   Ah, don't disturb yourself, Mr Boyle; I hope you're not sick?

BOYLE.   Th' oul' legs, Mr Nugent, the oul' legs.

NUGENT.   I just called over to see if you could let me have anything off the suit?

BOYLE.   E-e-e-eh, how much is this it is?

NUGENT.   It's the same as it was at the start—seven pouns.

BOYLE.   I'm glad you kem, Mr Nugent; I want a good heavy topcoat— Irish frieze, if you have it. How much would a topcoat like that be, now?

NUGENT.   About six pouns.

BOYLE.   Six pouns—six an' seven, six an' seven is thirteen—that'll be thirteen pounds I'll owe you.

> [JOXER *slips the bottle of stout that is on the table into his pocket.* NUGENT *rushes into the room, and returns with suit on his arm; he pauses by the door.*

NUGENT.   You'll owe me no thirteen pouns. Maybe you think you're betther able to owe it than pay it!

BOYLE [*frantically*].   Here, come back to hell ower that—where're you goin' with them clothes o' mine?

NUGENT.   Where am I goin' with them clothes o' yours? Well, I like your damn cheek!

BOYLE.   Here, what am I going' to dhress meself in when I'm goin' out?

NUGENT.   What do I care what you dhress yourself in! You can put yourself in a bolsther cover,[2] if you like.

> [*He goes towards the other door, followed by* JOXER.]

JOXER.   What'll he dhress himself in! Gentleman Jack an' his frieze coat!

> [*They go out.*]

BOYLE [*inside.*]   Ey, Nugent; ey, Mr Nugent, Mr Nugent! [*After a pause* BOYLE *enters hastily, buttoning the braces of his moleskin trousers; his coat and vest are on his arm; he throws these on a chair and hurries to the door on right.*] Ey, Mr Nugent, Mr Nugent!

JOXER [*meeting him at the door*].   What's up, what's wrong, Captain?

BOYLE.   Nugent's been here an' took away me suit—the only things I had to go out in!

---

2. Pillowcase.

JOXER.   Tuk your suit—for God's sake! An' what were you doin' while he was takin' them?

BOYLE.   I was in bed when he stole in like a thief in the night, an' before I knew even what he was thinkin' of, he whipped them from the chair an' was off like a redshank! [3]

JOXER.   An' what, in the name o' God, did he do that for?

BOYLE.   What did he do it for? How the hell do I know what he done it for?—jealousy an' spite, I suppose.

JOXER.   Did he not say what he done it for?

BOYLE.   Amn't I afther tellin' you that he had them whipped up an' was gone before I could open me mouth?

JOXER.   That was a very sudden thing to do; there mus' be somethin' behin' it. Did he hear anythin', I wondher?

BOYLE.   Did he hear anythin'?—you talk very queer, Joxer—what could he hear?

JOXER.   About you not gettin' the money, in some way or t'other?

BOYLE.   An' what ud prevent me from gettin' th' money?

JOXER.   That's jus' what I was thinkin'—what ud prevent you from gettin' the money—nothin', as far as I can see.

BOYLE [*looking round for bottle of stout, with an exclamation*].   Aw, holy God!

JOXER.   What's up, Jack?

BOYLE.   He must have afther lifted the bottle o' stout that Juno left on the table!

JOXER [*horrified*].   Ah no, ah no; he wouldn't be afther doin' that now.

BOYLE.   An' who done it then? Juno left a bottle o' stout here, an' it's gone—it didn't walk, did it?

JOXER.   Oh, that's shockin'; ah, man's inhumanity to man makes countless thousands mourn! [4]

MRS MADIGAN [*appearing at the door*].   I hope I'm not disturbin' you in any discussion on your forthcomin' legacy—if I may use the word—an' that you'll let me have a barny [5] for a minute or two with you, Mr Boyle.

BOYLE [*uneasily*].   To be sure, Mrs Madigan—an oul' friend's always welcome.

JOXER.   Come in the evenin', come in th' mornin'; come when your assed, or come without warnin', Mrs Madigan.

BOYLE.   Sit down, Mrs Madigan.

MRS MADIGAN [*ominously*].   Th' few words I have to say can be said standin'. Puttin' aside all formularies, I suppose you remember me lendin' you some time ago three pouns that I raised on blankets an' furniture in me uncle's?

---

3. Swift wading bird, and also an archaic, derogatory term for the Irish or Scottish as red-legged because of wearing kilts.

4. From "Man Was Made to Mourn," by Robert Burns (1759–96).

5. Brief word.

BOYLE.   I remember it well. I have it recorded in me book—three pouns five shillings from Maisie Madigan, raised on articles pawned; an' item: fourpence, given to make up the price of a pint, on th' principle that no bird ever flew on wan wing; all to be repaid at par, when the ship comes home.

MRS MADIGAN.   Well, ever since I shoved in the blankets I've been perishing with th' cowld, an' I've decided, if I'll be too hot in th' next' world aself, I'm not goin' to be too cowld in this wan; an' consequently, I want me three pouns if you please.

BOYLE.   This is a very sudden demand, Mrs Madigan, an' can't be met; but I'm willin' to give you a receipt in full, in full.

MRS MADIGAN.   Come on, out with th' money, an' don't be jack-actin'.

BOYLE.   You can't get blood out of a turnip, can you?

MRS MADIGAN [*rushing over and shaking him*].   Gimme me money, y'oul' reprobate, or I'll shake the worth of it out of you!

BOYLE.   Ey, houl' on, there; houl' on, there! You'll wait for your money now, me lassie!

MRS MADIGAN [*looking around the room and seeing the gramophone*].   I'll wait for it, will I? Well, I'll not wait long; if I can't get th' cash, I'll get th' worth of it. [*She snatches up the gramophone.*]

BOYLE.   Ey, ey, there, wher'r you goin' with that?

MRS MADIGAN.   I'm goin' to th' pawn to get me three quid five shillins'; I'll brin' you th' ticket, an' then you can do what you like, me bucko.

BOYLE.   You can't touch that, you can't touch that! It's not my property, an' it's not ped for yet!

MRS MADIGAN.   So much th' better. It'll be an ayse to me conscience, for I'm takin' what doesn't belong to you. You're not goin' to be swankin' it like a paycock with Maisie Madigan's money—I'll pull some o' th' gorgeous feathers out o' your tail! [*She goes off with the gramophone.*]

BOYLE.   What's th' world comin' to at all? I ass you, Joxer Daly, is there any morality left anywhere?

JOXER.   I wouldn't ha' believed it, only I see it with me own two eyes. I didn't think Maisie Madigan was that sort of woman; she has either a sup taken, or she's heard somethin'.

BOYLE.   Heard somethin'—about what, if it's not any harm to ass you?

JOXER.   She must ha' heard some rumour or other that you weren't goin' to get th' money.

BOYLE.   Who says I'm not goin' to get th' money?

JOXER.   Sure, I don't know—I was only sayin'.

BOYLE.   Only sayin' what?

JOXER.   Nothin'.

BOYLE.   You were goin' to say somethin'—don't be a twisther.

JOXER [*angrily*].   Who's a twisther?

BOYLE.   Why don't you speak your mind, then?

JOXER. You never twisted yourself—no, you wouldn't know how!

BOYLE. Did you ever know me to twist; did you ever know me to twist?

JOXER [*fiercely*]. Did you ever do anythin' else! Sure, you can't believe a word that comes out o' your mouth.

BOYLE. Here, get out, ower o' this; I always knew you were a prognosticator an' a procrastinator!

JOXER [*going out as* JOHNNY *comes in*]. The anchor's weighed, farewell, ree . . . mem . . . me. Jacky Boyle, Esquire, infernal rogue an' damned liar.

JOHNNY. Joxer an' you at it agen?—when are you goin' to have a little respect for yourself, an' not be always makin' a show of us all?

BOYLE. Are you goin' to lecture me now?

JOHNNY. Is mother back from the doctor yet, with Mary?

> [MRS BOYLE *enters; it is apparent from the serious look on her face that something has happened. She takes off her hat and coat without a word and puts them by. She then sits down near the fire, and there is a few moments' pause.*]

BOYLE. Well, what did the doctor say about Mary?

MRS BOYLE [*in an earnest manner and with suppressed agitation*]. Sit down here, Jack; I've something to say to you . . . about Mary.

BOYLE [*awed by her manner*]. About . . . Mary?

MRS BOYLE. Close that door there and sit down here.

BOYLE [*closing the door*]. More throuble in our native land, is it? [*He sits down.*] Well, what is it?

MRS BOYLE. It's about Mary.

BOYLE. Well, what about Mary—there's nothin' wrong with her, is there?

MRS BOYLE. I'm sorry to say there's a gradle[6] wrong with her.

BOYLE. A gradle wrong with her! [*Peevishly.*] First Johnny an' now Mary; is the whole house goin' to become an hospital! It's not consumption, is it?

MRS BOYLE. No . . . it's not consumption . . . it's worse.

JOHNNY. Worse! Well, we'll have to get her into some place ower this, there's no one here to mind her.

MRS BOYLE. We'll all have to mind her now. You might as well know now, Johnny, as another time. [*To* BOYLE.] D'ye know what the doctor said to me about her, Jack?

BOYLE. How ud I know—I wasn't there, was I?

MRS BOYLE. He told me to get her married at wanst.

BOYLE. Married at wanst! An' why did he say the like o' that?

MRS BOYLE. Because Mary's goin' to have a baby in a short time.

6. Great deal.

BOYLE. Goin' to have a baby!—my God, what'll Bentham say when he hears that?

MRS BOYLE. Are you blind, man, that you can't see that it was Bentham that has done this wrong to her?

BOYLE [*passionately*]. Then he'll marry her, he'll have to marry her!

MRS BOYLE. You know he's gone to England, an' God knows where he is now.

BOYLE. I'll folly him, I'll folly him, an' bring him back, an' make him do her justice. The scoundrel, I might ha' known what he was, with his Yogees an' his Prawna!

MRS BOYLE. We'll have to keep it quiet till we see what we can do.

BOYLE. Oh, isn't this a nice thing to come on top o' me, an' the state I'm in! A pretty show I'll be to Joxer an' to that oul' wan, Madigan! Amn't I afther goin' through enough without havin' to go through this!

MRS BOYLE. What you an' I'll have to go through'll be nothin' to what poor Mary'll have to go through; for you an' me is middlin' old, an' most of our years is spent; but Mary'll have maybe forty years to face an' handle, an' every wan of them'll be tainted with a bitther memory.

BOYLE. Where is she? Where is she till I tell her off? I'm tellin' you when I'm done with her she'll be a sorry girl!

MRS BOYLE. I left her in me sister's till I came to speak to you. You'll say nothin' to her, Jack; ever since she left school she's earned her livin', an' your fatherly care never throubled the poor girl.

BOYLE. Gwan, take her part agen her father! But I'll let you see whether I'll say nothin' to her or no! Her an' her readin'! That's more o' th' blasted nonsense that has the house fallin' on top of us! What did th' likes of her, born in a tenement house, want with readin'? Her readin's afther bringin' her to a nice pass—oh, it's madnin', madnin', madnin'!

MRS BOYLE. When she comes back say nothin' to her, Jack, or she'll leave this place.

BOYLE. Leave this place! Ay, she'll leave this place, an' quick too!

MRS BOYLE. If Mary goes, I'll go with her.

BOYLE. Well, go with her! Well, go, th' pair o' yous! I lived before I seen yous, an' I can live when yous are gone. Isn't this a nice thing to come rollin' in on top o' me afther all your prayin' to St Anthony an' the Little Flower! An' she's a Child o' Mary, too—I wonder what'll the nuns think of her now? An' it'll be bellows'd all over th' disthrict before you could say Jack Robinson; an' whenever I'm seen they'll whisper, 'That's th' father of Mary Boyle that had th' kid be th' swank she used to go with; d'ye know?' To be sure they'll know—more about it than I will meself!

JOHNNY. She should be dhriven out o' th' house she's brought disgrace on!

MRS BOYLE. Hush, you, Johnny. We needn't let it be bellows'd all over

the place; all we've got to do is to leave this place quietly an' go somewhere where we're not known an' nobody'll be th' wiser.

BOYLE.   You're talkin' like a two-year-oul', woman. Where'll we get a
place ou' o' this—places aren't that easily got.

MRS BOYLE.   But, Jack, when we get the money . . .

BOYLE.   Money—what money?

MRS BOYLE.   Why, oul' Ellison's money, of course.

BOYLE.   There's no money comin' from oul' Ellison, or any one else.
Since you've heard of wan throuble, you might as well hear of another.
There's no money comin' to us at all—the Will's a wash-out!

MRS BOYLE.   What are you sayin', man—no money?

JOHNNY.   How could it be a wash-out?

BOYLE.   The boyo that's afther doin' it to Mary done it to me as well.
The thick made out the Will wrong; he said in th' Will, only first
cousin an' second cousin, instead of mentionin' our names, an' now
any one that thinks he's a first cousin or second cousin t'oul Ellison
can claim the money as well as me, an' they're springin' up in hundreds,
an' comin' from America an' Australia, thinkin' to get their whack out
of it, while all the time the lawyers is gobblin' it up, till there's not as
much as ud buy a stockin' for your lovely daughter's baby!

MRS BOYLE.   I don't believe it, I don't believe it, I don't believe it!

JOHNNY.   Why did you say nothin' about this before?

MRS BOYLE.   You're not serious, Jack; you're not serious!

BOYLE.   I'm tellin' you the scholar, Bentham, made a banjax o' th'
Will; instead o' sayin', 'th' rest o' me property to be divided between
me first cousin, Jack Boyle, an' me second cousin Mick Finnegan, o'
Santhry', he writ down only, 'me first an' second cousins', an' the
world an' his wife are afther th' property now.

MRS BOYLE.   Now I know why Bentham left poor Mary in th' lurch; I
can see it all now—oh, is there not even a middlin' honest man left
in th' world?

JOHNNY [to BOYLE].   An' you let us run into debt, an' you borreyed money
from everybody to fill yourself with beer! An' now you tell us the
whole thing's a washout! Oh, if it's thrue, I'm done with you, for
you're worse than me sisther Mary!

BOYLE.   You hole your tongue, d'ye hear? I'll not take any lip from you.
Go an' get Bentham if you want satisfaction for all that's afther hap-
penin' us.

JOHNNY.   I won't hole me tongue, I won't hole me tongue! I'll tell you
what I think of you, father an' all as you are . . . you . . .

MRS BOYLE.   Johnny, Johnny, Johnny, for God's sake, be quiet!

JOHNNY.   I'll not be quiet, I'll not be quiet; he's a nice father, isn't he?
is it any wondher Mary went asthray, when . . .

MRS BOYLE.   Johnny, Johnny, for my sake be quiet—for your mother's
sake!

BOYLE.   I'm goin' out now to have a few dhrinks with th' last few makes

I have, an' tell that lassie o' yours not to be here when I come back;
for if I lay me eyes on her, I'll lay me hans on her, an' if I lay me
hans on her, I won't be accountable for me actions!

JOHNNY. Take care somebody doesn't lay his hans on you—y'oul' . . .

MRS BOYLE. Johnny, Johnny!

BOYLE [*at door, about to go out*]. Oh, a nice son, an' a nicer daughter,
I have. [*Calling loudly upstairs.*] Joxer, Joxer, are you there?

JOXER [*from a distance*]. I'm here, More . . . ee . . . aar . . . i . . .
tee!

BOYLE. I'm goin' down to Foley's—are you comin'?

JOXER. Come with you? With that sweet call me heart is stirred; I'm
only waiting for the word, an' I'll be with you, like a bird!

[BOYLE *and* JOXER *pass the door going out.*]

JOHNNY [*throwing himself on the bed*]. I've a nice sisther, an' a nice
father, there's no bettin' on it. I wish to God a bullet or a bomb had
whipped me ou' o' this long ago! Not one o' yous, have any thought
for me!

MRS BOYLE [*with passionate remonstrance*]. If you don't whisht, Johnny,
you'll drive me mad. Who has kep' th' home together for the past few
years—only me? An' who'll have to bear th' biggest part o' this throuble but me?—but whinin' an' whingin' isn't goin' to do any good.

JOHNNY. You're to blame yourself for a gradle of it—givin' him his own
way in everything, an' never assin' to check him, no matther what he
done. Why didn't you look afther th' money? why . . .

[There is a knock at the door; MRS BOYLE *opens it;* JOHNNY *rises
on his elbow to look and listen; two men enter.*]

FIRST MAN. We've been sent up be th' Manager of the Hibernian Fur-
nishing Company, Mrs Boyle, to take back the furniture that was got
a while ago.

MRS BOYLE. Yous'll touch nothin' here—how do I know who yous are?

FIRST MAN [*showing a paper*]. There's the ordher, ma'am. [*Reading.*] A
chest o' drawers, a table, wan easy an' two ordinary chairs; wan mirror;
wan chesterfield divan, an' a wardrobe an' two vases. [*To his comrade.*]
Come on, Bill, it's afther knockin-off time already.

JOHNNY. For God's sake, mother, run down to Foley's an' bring father
back, or we'll be left without a stick.

[*The men carry out the table.*]

MRS BOYLE. What good would it be?—you heard what he said before
he went out.

JOHNNY. Can't you thry? He ought to be here, an' the like of this goin'
on.

[MRS BOYLE *puts a shawl around her, as* MARY *enters.*]

MARY.   What's up, mother? I met a man carryin' away the table, an' everybody's talking about us not gettin' the money after all.

MRS BOYLE.   Everythin's gone wrong, Mary, everythin'. We're not gettin' a penny out o' the Will, not a penny—I'll tell you all when I come back; I'm goin' for your father. [*She runs out.*]

JOHNNY [*to* MARY, *who has sat down by the fire*].   It's a wondher you're not ashamed to show your face here, afther what has happened.

[JERRY *enters slowly; there is a look of earnest hope on his face. He looks at* MARY *for a few moments.*]

JERRY [*softly*].   Mary! [MARY *does not answer.*] Mary, I want to speak to you for a few moments, may I? [MARY *remains silent;* JOHNNY *goes slowly into room on left.*] Your mother has told me everything, Mary, and I have come to you. . . . I have come to tell you, Mary, that my love for you is greater and deeper than ever. . . .

MARY [*with a sob*].   Oh, Jerry, Jerry, say no more; all that is over now; anything like that is impossible now!

JERRY.   Impossible? Why do you talk like that, Mary?

MARY.   After all that has happened.

JERRY.   What does it matter what has happened? We are young enough to be able to forget all those things. [*He catches her hand.*] Mary, Mary, I am pleading for your love. With Labour, Mary, humanity is above everything; we are the Leaders in the fight for a new life. I want to forget Bentham, I want to forget that you left me—even for a while.

MARY.   Oh, Jerry, Jerry, you haven't the bitter word of scorn for me after all.

JERRY [*passionately*].   Scorn! I love you, love you, Mary!

MARY [*rising, and looking him in the eyes*].   Even though . . .

JERRY.   Even though you threw me over for another man; even though you gave me many a bitter word!

MARY.   Yes, yes, I know; but you love me, even though . . . even though . . . I'm . . . goin' . . . goin' . . .

[*He looks at her questioningly, and fear gathers in his eyes.*]

Ah, I was thinkin' so. . . . You don't know everything!

JERRY [*poignantly*].   Surely to God, Mary, you don't mean that . . . that . . . that . . .

MARY.   Now you know all, Jerry; now you know all!

JERRY.   My God, Mary, have you fallen as low as that?

MARY.   Yes, Jerry, as you say, I have fallen as low as that.

JERRY.   I didn't mean it that way, Mary . . . it came on me so sudden, that I didn't mind what I was sayin'. . . . I never expected this—your mother never told me. . . . I'm sorry . . . God knows, I'm sorry for you, Mary.

MARY.   Let us say no more, Jerry; I don't blame you for thinkin' it's terrible. . . . I suppose it is. . . . Everybody'll think the same . . . it's only as I expected—your humanity is just as narrow as the humanity of the others.

JERRY. I'm sorry, all the same . . . I shouldn't have troubled you. . . . I wouldn't if I'd known. . . . If I can do anything for you . . . Mary . . . I will. [*He turns to go, and halts at the door.*]

MARY. Do you remember, Jerry, the verses you read when you gave the lecture in the Socialist Rooms some time ago, on Humanity's Strife with Nature?

JERRY. The verses—no; I don't remember them.

MARY. I do. They're runnin' in me head now—

> An' we felt the power that fashion'd
> All the lovely things we saw,
> That created all the murmur
> Of an everlasting law,
> Was a hand of force an' beauty,
> With an eagle's tearin' claw.
>
> Then we saw our globe of beauty
> Was an ugly thing as well,
> A hymn divine whose chorus
> Was an agonisin' yell;
> Like the story of a demon,
> That an angel had to tell;
>
> Like a glowin' picture by a
> Hand unsteady, brought to ruin;
> Like her craters, if their deadness
> Could give life unto the moon;
> Like the agonising horror
> Of a violin out of tune.

[*There is a pause, and* JERRY *goes slowly out.*]

JOHNNY [*returning*]. Is he gone?

MARY. Yes.

[*The two men re-enter.*]

FIRST MAN. We can't wait any longer for t'oul' fella—sorry, Miss, but we have to live as well as th' nex' man. [*They carry out some things.*]

JOHNNY. Oh, isn't this terrible! . . . I suppose you told him everything . . . couldn't you have waited for a few days? . . . he'd have stopped th' takin' of the things, if you'd kep' your mouth shut. Are you burnin' to tell every one of the shame you've brought on us?

MARY [*snatching up her hat and coat.*] Oh, this is unbearable! [*She rushes out.*]

FIRST MAN [re-entering].   We'll take the chest o' drawers next—it's the heaviest.

[The votive light flickers for a moment, and goes out.]

JOHNNY [in a cry of fear].   Mother o' God, the light's afther goin' out!

FIRST MAN.   You put the win' up me the way you bawled that time. The oil's all gone, that's all.

JOHNNY [with an agonising cry].   Mother o' God, there's a shot I'm afther gettin'!

FIRST MAN.   What's wrong with you, man? Is it a fit you're takin'?

JOHNNY.   I'm afther feelin' a pain in me breast, like the tearin' by of a bullet!

FIRST MAN.   He's goin' mad—it's a wondher they'd leave a chap like that here by myself.

[Two IRREGULARS enter swiftly; they carry revolvers; one goes over to JOHNNY; the other covers the two furniture men.]

FIRST IRREGULAR [to the men, quietly and incisively].   Who are you?— what are yous doin' here?—quick!

FIRST MAN.   Removin' furniture that's not paid for.

IRREGULAR.   Get over to the other end of the room an' turn your faces to the wall—quick!   [The two men turn their faces to the wall, with their hands up.]

SECOND IRREGULAR [to JOHNNY]   Come on, Sean Boyle, you're wanted; some of us have a word to say to you.

JOHNNY.   I'm sick, I can't—what do you want with me?

SECOND IRREGULAR.   Come on, come on; we've a distance to go an' haven't much time—come on.

JOHNNY.   I'm an oul' comrade—yous wouldn't shoot an oul' comrade.

SECOND IRREGULAR.   Poor Tancred was an oul' comrade o' yours, but you didn't think o' that when you gave him away to the gang that sent him to his grave. But we've no time to waste; come on—here, Dermot, ketch his arm. [To JOHNNY.] Have you your beads?

JOHNNY.   Me beads! Why do you ass me that, why do you ass me that?

SECOND IRREGULAR.   Go on, go on, march!

JOHNNY.   Are yous goin' to do in a comrade?—look at me arm, I lost it for Ireland.

SECOND IRREGULAR.   Commandant Tancred lost his life for Ireland.

JOHNNY.   Sacred Heart of Jesus, have mercy on me! Mother o' God pray for me—be with me now in the agonies o' death! . . . Hail, Mary, full o' grace . . . the Lord is . . . with Thee.

[They drag out JOHNNY BOYLE, and the curtain falls. When it rises again the most of the furniture is gone. MARY and MRS BOYLE, one on each side, are sitting in a darkened room, by the fire; it is an hour later.]

MRS BOYLE.   I'll not wait much longer . . . what did they bring him
away in the mothor for? Nugent says he thinks they had guns . . . is
me throubles never goin' to be over? . . . If anything ud happen to
poor Johnny, I think I'd lose me mind. . . . I'll go to the Police Station, surely they ought to be able to do somethin'.

[*Below is heard the sound of voices.*]

Whisht, is that something? Maybe, it's your father, though when I
left him in Foley's he was hardly able to lift his head. Whisht!

[A *knock at the door, and the voice of* MRS MADIGAN, *speaking
very softly:*]

Mrs Boyle, Mrs Boyle. [MRS BOYLE *opens the door.*]   Oh, Mrs Boyle,
God an' His Blessed Mother be with you this night!
MRS BOYLE [*calmly*].   What is it, Mrs Madigan? It's Johnny—something
about Johnny.
MRS MADIGAN.   God send it's not, God send it's not Johnny!
MRS BOYLE.   Don't keep me waitin', Mrs Madigan; I've gone through
so much lately that I feel able for anything.
MRS MADIGAN.   Two polismen below wantin' you.
MRS BOYLE.   Wantin' me; an' why do they want me?
MRS MADIGAN.   Some poor fella's been found, an' they think it's, it's . . .
MRS BOYLE.   Johnny, Johnny!
MARY [*with her arms round her mother*].   Oh, mother, mother, me poor,
darlin' mother.
MRS BOYLE.   Hush, hush, darlin'; you'll shortly have your own throuble
to bear. [*To* MRS MADIGAN.]   An' why do the polis think it's Johnny,
Mrs Madigan?
MRS MADIGAN.   Because one o' the doctors knew him when he was
attendin' with his poor arm.
MRS BOYLE.   Oh, it's thrue, then; it's Johnny, it's me son, me own son!
MARY.   Oh, it's thrue, it's thrue what Jerry Devine says—there isn't a
God, there isn't a God; if there was He wouldn't let these things happen!
MRS BOYLE.   Mary, you mustn't say them things. We'll want all the
help we can get from God an' His Blessed Mother now! These things
have nothin' to do with the Will o' God. Ah, what can God do agen
the stupidity o' men!
MRS MADIGAN.   The polis want you to go with them to the hospital to
see the poor body—they're waitin' below.
MRS BOYLE.   We'll go. Come, Mary, an' we'll never come back here
agen. Let your father furrage for himself now; I've done all I could
an' it was all no use—he'll be hopeless till the end of his days. I've got
a little room in me sisther's where we'll stop till your throuble is over,
an' then we'll work together for the sake of the baby.

MARY.   My poor little child that'll have no father!

MRS BOYLE.   It'll have what's far betther—it'll have two mothers.

A ROUGH VOICE SHOUTING FROM BELOW.   Are yous goin' to keep us waitin' for yous all night?

MRS MADIGAN [*going to the door, and shouting down*].   Take your hour, there, take your hour! If yous are in such a hurry, skip off, then, for nobody wants you here—if they did yous wouldn't be found. For you're the same as yous were undher the British Government—never where yous are wanted! As far as I can see, the Polis as Polis, in this city, is Null an' Void!

MRS BOYLE.   We'll go, Mary, we'll go; you to see your poor dead brother, an' me to see me poor dead son!

MARY.   I dhread it, mother, I dhread it!

MRS BOYLE.   I forgot, Mary, I forgot; your poor oul' selfish mother was only thinkin' of herself. No, no, you mustn't come—it wouldn't be good for you. You go on to me sisther's an' I'll face th' ordeal meself. Maybe I didn't feel sorry enough for Mrs Tancred when her poor son was found as Johnny's been found now—because he was a Diehard! Ah, why didn't I remember that then he wasn't a Diehard or a Stater, but only a poor dead son! It's well I remember all that she said—an' it's my turn to say it now: What was the pain I suffered, Johnny, bringin' you into the world to carry you to your cradle, to the pains I'll suffer carryin' you out o' the world to bring you to your grave! Mother o' God, Mother o' God, have pity on us all! Blessed Virgin, where were you when me darlin' son was riddled with bullets, when me darlin' son was riddled with bullets? Sacred Heart o' Jesus, take away our hearts o' stone, and give us hearts o' flesh! Take away this murdherin' hate, an' give us Thine own eternal love!

[*They all go slowly out.*]

[*There is a pause; then a sound of shuffling steps on the stairs outside. The door opens and* BOYLE *and* JOXER, *both of them very drunk, enter.*]

BOYLE.   I'm able to go no farther. . . . Two polis, ey . . . what were they doin' here, I wondher? . . . Up to no good, anyhow . . . an' Juno an' that lovely daughter o' mine with them. [*Taking a sixpence from his pocket and looking at it.*] Wan single, solitary tanner left out of all I borreyed . . . [*He lets it fall.*] The last o' the Mohecans. . . . The blinds is down, Joxer, the blinds is down!

JOXER [*walking unsteadily across the room, and anchoring at the bed*]. Put all . . . your throubles . . . in your oul' kit-bag . . . an' smile . . . smile . . . smile!

BOYLE.   The counthry'll have to steady itself . . . it's goin' . . . to hell. . . . Where'r all . . . the chairs . . . gone to . . . steady itself, Joxer.

. . . Chairs'll . . . have to . . . steady themselves. . . . No matther . . . what any one may . . . say. . . . Irelan' sober . . . is Irelan' . . . free.

JOXER [*stretching himself on the bed*].   Chains . . . an' . . . slaveree . . . that's a darlin' motto . . . a daaarlin' . . . motto!

BOYLE.   If th' worst comes . . . to th' worse . . . I can join a . . . flyin' . . . column . . . I done . . . me bit . . . in Easther Week . . . had no business . . . to . . . be . . . there . . . but Captain Boyle's Captain Boyle!

JOXER.   Breathes there a man with soul . . . so . . . de . . . ad . . . this . . . me . . . o . . . wn, me nat . . . ive l . . . an'!

BOYLE [*subsiding into a sitting posture on the floor*].   Commandant Kelly died . . . in them . . . arms . . . Joxer. . . . Tell me Volunteer butties . . . says he . . . that . . . I died for . . . Irelan'!

JOXER.   D'jever rade 'Willie . . . Reilly . . . an' His Own . . . Colleen . . . Bawn?[7] It's a darlin' story, a daarlin' story!

BOYLE.   I'm telling you . . . Joxer . . . th' whole worl's . . . in a terr . . . ible state o' . . . chassis!

---

7. Traditional Irish ballad; "colleen bawn," Irish for a blond-haired young woman.

BRENDAN BEHAN

The Quare Fellow†

Persons in the Play

WARDER DONELLY
PRISONER A.
PRISONER B.
DUNLAVIN
SCHOLARA ⎫
SHAYBO ⎭ *juvenile prisoners*
THE LIFER, *a reprieved murderer*
THE OTHER FELLOW
NEIGHBOUR
A MEDICAL ORDERLY
MR HEALEY, *an official of the department*
WARDER REGAN
THE CHAPLAIN
PRISONER C., *a young Kerry boy*
MICKSER
THE VOICE OF AN ENGLISHMAN ON REMAND
A COOK FROM THE HOSPITAL
THE CHIEF WARDER
A PRINCIPAL WARDER
THE SPEAKING VOICE OF A PRISONER IN THE PUNISHMENT CELLS
PRISONER D., *a middle-aged bourgeois*
WARDER CRINNIN
A HANGMAN
FIRST WARDER
SECOND WARDER
THE GOVERNOR
ASSISTANT HANGMAN, ENOCH JENKINSON
ASSISTANT HANGMAN, CHRISTMAS HALLIWELL
SINGING VOICE OF THE PRISONER IN THE PUNISHMENT CELLS

† From *Brendan Behan: The Complete Plays* (New York: Grove Press; London: Eyre Methuen, 1978). Reprinted by permission of Grove Press, a division of Wheatland Corporation, and Tessa Sayle Agency. Copyright © 1956 by Brendan Behan and Theatre Workshop.

Act One

[A PRISONER *sings: he is in one of the punishment cells.*]

A hungry feeling came o'er me stealing
And the mice were squealing in my prison cell,
And that old triangle
Went jingle jangle,
Along the banks of the Royal Canal.

The curtain rises.

[*The scene is the bottom floor or landing of a wing in a city prison, "B.1". The cell doors are of metal with a card giving the name, age and religion of the occupant. Two of the cells have no cards. The left of the stage leads to the circle, the administrative heart of the prison, and on the right, in the wall and at right angles to the audience, is a window, from which a view may be had of the laundry yard of the women's prison. On the wall and facing the audience is printed in large block shaded Victorian lettering the word "SILENCE".*]

PRISONER.

To begin the morning
The warder bawling
Get out of bed and clean up your cell,
And that old triangle
Went jingle jangle,
Along the banks of the Royal Canal.

[*A triangle is beaten, loudly and raucously. A* WARDER *comes briskly and, swinging a bunch of keys, goes to the vacant cells, looks in the spyholes, takes two white cards from his pocket, and puts one on each door. Then he goes to the other doors, looks in the spyholes and unlocks them.*]
[*Meanwhile the singer in the base punishment cells is on his third verse:*]

The screw was peeping
And the lag was weeping . . .

[*But this only gets as far as the second line, for the* WARDER *leans over the stairs and shouts down . . .*]

WARDER.   The screw is listening as well as peeping, and you'll be bloody well weeping if you don't give over your moaning. We might go down there and give you something to moan about. [*The singing stops and he turns and shouts up and down the landing.*] B. Wings: two, three and one. Stand to your doors. Come on, clean up your cells there. [*He goes off* R.]

> [PRISONERS A. *and* B. *come out of their cells, collect buckets and brushes, and start the morning's chores.* A. *is a man of 40, he has done two "laggings", a sentence of five years or more, and some preventive detention.* B. *is a gentle-looking man and easy-going.*]

PRISONER A.   Nice day for the races.

PRISONER B.   Don't think I can make it today. Too much to do in the office. Did you hear the commotion last night round in D. Wing? A reprieve must have come through.

PRISONER A.   Aye, but there's two for a haircut and shave, I wonder which one's been chucked?

PRISONER B.   Dunlavin might know; give him a call there.

PRISONER A.   Dunlavin!

VOICE [*from cell*].

> There are hands that will welcome you in
> There are lips that I am burning to kiss
> There are two eyes that shine . . .

PRISONER A.   Hey, Dunlavin, are you going to scrub that place of yours away?

VOICE.

> Far away where the blue shadows fall
> I will come to contentment and rest,
> And the toils of the day
> Will be all charmed away . . .

PRISONER A.   Hey, Dunlavin.

> [DUNLAVIN *appears in the door of the cell polishing a large enamel chamber pot with a cloth. An old man, he has spent most of his life in jail. Unlike most old lags he has not become absolutely dulled from imprisonment.*]

DUNLAVIN.   . . . In my little grey home in the West.

PRISONER A.   What do you think that is you're polishing—the Railway Cup?

DUNLAVIN.   I'm shining this up for a special visitor. Healey of the Department of Justice is coming up today to inspect the cells.

PRISONER A.   Will he be round again so soon?

DUNLAVIN.   He's always round the day before an execution. I think he must be in the hanging and flogging section.

PRISONER B.   Dunlavin, there you are, at the corner of the wing, with
the joints in the hot-water pipes bringing you news from every art and
part, any time you put your ear to it.

DUNLAVIN.   Well? Well?

PRISONER B.   Well, what was the commotion last night round in D.
Wing? Did the quare fellow get a reprieve?

DUNLAVIN.   Just a minute till I put back me little bit of china, and I'll
return and tell all. Now which quare fellow do you mean? The fellow
beat his wife to death with the silver-topped cane, that was a presentation to him from the Combined Staffs, Excess and Refunds branch
of the late Great Southern Railways, was reprieved, though why him
any more than the other fellow is more nor I can tell.

PRISONER A.   Well, I suppose they looked at it, he only killed her and
left it at that. He didn't cut the corpse up afterwards with a butcher's
knife.

DUNLAVIN.   Yes, and then of course the other fellow used a meat-chop-
per. Real bog-man[1] act. Nearly as bad as a shotgun, or getting the
weed-killer mixed up in the stir-about. But a man with a silver-topped
cane, that's a man that's a cut above meat-choppers whichever way
you look at it.

PRISONER A.   Well, I suppose we can expect Silver-top round soon to
start his life.

PRISONER B.   Aye, we've a couple of vacancies.

PRISONER A.   There's a new card up here already.

DUNLAVIN.   I declare to God you're right. [*Goes to read one of the cards.*]
It's not him at all, it's another fellow, doing two year, for . . . oh, the
dirty beast, look what the dirty man-beast is in for. 'Clare to God,
putting the likes of that beside me. They must think this is the bloody
sloblands.[2]

PRISONER B.   There's another fellow here.

DUNLAVIN.   I hope it's not another of that persuasion. [*Reads the card.*]
Ah, no, it's only the murderer, thanks be to God.

> [*The others have a read of the card and skip back to their own
> cells.*]

DUNLAVIN.   You wouldn't mind old Silver-top. Killing your wife is a
natural class of a thing could happen to the best of us. But this other
dirty animal on me left . . .

PRISONER B.   Ah well, now he's here he'll just have to do his birdlime
like anyone else.

DUNLAVIN.   That doesn't say that he should do it in the next flowery
dell to me. Robbers, thieves and murderers I can abide, but when it
comes to that class of carry-on—Good night, Joe Doyle.

---

1. Primitive, as in the prehistoric relics found pre-   2. Muddy, marginal land reclaimed from water.
served in Ireland's bogs.

PRISONER A. [*indicates* 22]. This fellow was dead lucky.

PRISONER B.   Live lucky.

PRISONER A.   Two fellows waiting to be topped and he's the one that gets away. As a general rule they don't like reprieving one and topping the other.

DUNLAVIN.   So as to be on the safe side, and not to be making fish of one and flesh of the other, they usually top both. Then, of course, the Minister might have said, enough is as good as a feast.

[*They rest on their brooms.*]

PRISONER B.   It must be a great thing to be told at the last minute that you're not going to be topped after all. To be lying there sweating and watching. The two screws for the death watch coming on at twelve o'clock and the two going off shaking hands with you, and you go to bed, and stare up at the ceiling.

DUNLAVIN.   And the two screws nod to each other across the fire to make a sup of tea, but to do it easy in case they wake you, and you turn round in the bed towards the fire and you say "I'll take a sup as you're at it" and one of the screws says "Ah, so you're awake, Mick. We were just wetting it; isn't it a good job you spoke up in time."

PRISONER A.   And after that, the tea is drunk and they offer you cigarettes, though the mouth is burned off you from smoking and anyway you've more than they have, you've got that many you'll be leaving them after you, and you lie down and get up, and get up and lie down, and the two screws not letting on to be minding you and not taking their eyes off you for one half-minute, and you walk up and down a little bit more . . .

PRISONER B.   And they ask you would you like another game of draughts or would you sooner write a letter, and getting on to morning you hear a bell out in the city, and you ask them the time, but they won't tell you.

DUNLAVIN.   But they put a good face on it, and one says "There's that old watch stopped again" and he says to the other screw "Have you your watch, Jack?" and the other fellow makes a great joke of it, "I'll have to take a run up as far as the North City Pawn shop and ask them to let me have a look at it." And then the door is unlocked and everyone sweats blood, and they come in and ask your man to stand up a minute, that's if he's able, while they read him something: "I am instructed to inform you that the Minister has, he hasn't, he has, he hasn't recommended to the President, that . . ."

PRISONER A.   And the quare fellow says "Did you say 'has recommended or has not recommended . . . ?' I didn't quite catch that."

DUNLAVIN.   My bloody oath but he catches it. Although I remember once in a case like now when there were two fellows to be topped over two different jobs, didn't the bloody fellow from the Prison Board, as it was then, in old Max Greeb's time, didn't he tell the wrong man he was reprieved? Your man was delighted for a few hours and then they had to go back and tell him "Sorry, my mistake, but you're to be topped after all"?

PRISONER B.   And the fellow that was reprieved, I bet he was glad.

DUNLAVIN.   Of course he was glad, anyone that says that a condemned man would be better off hung than doing life, let them leave it to his own discretion. Do you know who feels it worse going out to be topped?

PRISONER A.   Corkmen and Northerners . . . they've such bloody hard necks.

DUNLAVIN.   I have to do me funny half-hour for Holy Healey. I'm talking serious now.

PRISONER A.   All right, come on, let's have it—

DUNLAVIN.   The man that feels it worst, going into that little house with the red door and the silver painted gates at the bottom of D. Wing, is a man that has been in the nick before, when some other merchant was topped; or he's heard screws or old lags in the bag shop or at exercise talking about it. A new chap that's never done anything but murder, and that only once, is usually a respectable man, such as this Silver-top here. He knows nothing about it, except the few lines that he'd see in the papers. "Condemned man entered the hang-house at seven fifty-nine. At eight three the doctor pronounced life extinct."

PRISONER B.   That's a lot of mullarkey. In the first place the doctor has his back turned after the trap goes down, and doesn't turn and face it until a screw has caught the rope and stopped it wriggling. Then they go out and lock up the shop and have their breakfast and don't come back for an hour. Then they cut your man down and the doctor slits the back of his neck to see if the bones are broken. Who's to know what happens in the hour your man is swinging there, maybe wriggling to himself in the pit.

PRISONER A.   You're right there. When I was in the nick in England, there was a screw doing time, he'd been smuggling out medical reports on hangings and selling them to the Sunday papers, and he told me that one bloke had lived seventeen minutes at the end of a rope.

DUNLAVIN.   I don't believe that! Seventeen minutes is a bloody long time to be hanging on the end of a rope.

PRISONER A.   It was their own medical report.

PRISONER B.   I'll lay odds to a make that Silver-top isn't half charmed with himself he's not going with the meatchopper in the morning.

DUNLAVIN.   You could sing that if you had an air to it.

PRISONER A.   They'll have him down to reception, changed into Fry's and over here any time now.

DUNLAVIN.   Him and this other jewel here. Bad an' all as Silver-top was to beat his wife's brains out, I'd as lief have him near to me as this article. Dirty beast! I won't have an hour's luck for the rest of me six months, and me hoping to touch Uncle Healey today for a letter to the Room-Keepers for when I'd go out.

PRISONER B.   Eh, Dunlavin, is the Department trying to reform, recon-
struct and rehabilitate you in your old age?

DUNLAVIN.   Ah no, it's nothing to do with the Department. Outside his
job in the Department, Uncle Healey's in some holy crowd, that does
good be stealth. They never let the right hand know what the left hand
doeth, as the man said. Of course they never put either hand in their
pocket, so you'd never get money off them, but they can give letters
to the Prisoners' Aid and the Room-Keepers. Mind you. Healey's not
here today as a holy man. He'll just be fixing up the man that's getting
hung in the morning, but if I can get on the right side of him, he
might mix business with pleasure and give me a letter for when I get
out.

PRISONER B.   Now we know the cause of all the spring-cleaning.

DUNLAVIN.   And a fellow in the kitchen told us they're doing a special
dinner for us on account of Uncle Healey's visit.

PRISONER A.   Do you mean we're getting food with our meals today?

DUNLAVIN.   That's right, and I can't be standing yapping to youse. I've
to hang up my holy pictures and think up a few funny remarks for
him. God, what Jimmie O'Dea[3] is getting thousands for I've to do for
a pair of old socks and a ticket for the Prisoners' Aid.

> [DUNLAVIN goes into his cell. Two YOUNG PRISONERS aged about
> seventeen go past with sweeping brushes in front of them, singing
> softly and in unison.]

YOUNG PRISONERS.

> Only one more cell inspection
> We go out next Saturday,
> Only one more cell inspection
> And we go far, far away.

PRISONER A.   What brings you fellows round here this morning?

YOUNG PRISONER 1.   Our screw told us to sweep all round the Juvenile
Wing and then to come round here and give it a bit of a going over.

PRISONER B.   And have you your own wing done?

YOUNG PRISONER 2.   No, but if we did our wing first, we'd miss the
mots hanging out the laundry. You can't see them from our wing.

PRISONER A.   Just as well, maybe; you're bad enough as it is.

YOUNG PRISONER 1.   But I tell you what you will see from our wing this
morning. It's the carpenter bringing up the coffin for the quare fellow
and leaving it over in the mortuary to have it handy for the morning.
There's two orderlies besides us over in the Juveniles, and we were
going to toss up who'd come over here, but they're country fellows
and they'd said they'd sooner see the coffin. I'd sooner a pike at a
good-looking mot than the best coffin in Ireland, wouldn't you, Shaybo?

3. Irish comedian (1899–1965).

YOUNG PRISONER 2. Certainly I would, and outside that, when you're over here, there's always a chance of getting a bit of education about screwing jobs, and suchlike, from experienced men. Do you think Triplex or celluloid is the best for Yale locks, sir?

YOUNG PRISONER 1. Do you carry the stick all the time, sir?

PRISONER A. If I had a stick I'd know where to put it, across your bloody . . .

YOUNG PRISONER 2. Scholara, get sweeping, here's the screw.

[*They drift off sweeping and singing softly.*]

PRISONER B. He's bringing one of 'em. Is it Silver-top or the other fellow?

PRISONER A. Silver-top. I remember him being half carried into the circle the night he was sentenced to death.

PRISONER B. He has a right spring in his step this morning then.

PRISONER A. He's not looking all that happy. Still, I suppose he hasn't got over the shock yet.

[WARDER *and a* PRISONER *come on* L. *The* PRISONER *is in early middle age; when he speaks he has a "good accent". He is carrying a pillow slip which contains his sheets and other kit. The* WARDER *halts him.*]

WARDER REGAN. Stand by the door with your name on it. Later on when you've seen the doctor these fellows will show you how to lay your kit. Stand there now, till the doctor is ready to see you. [*He goes. There is a pause, while the* PRISONERS *survey the newcomer.*]

PRISONER B. He'll bloody well cheer the place up, won't he?

LIFER. Have any of you got a cigarette?

PRISONER A. That's a good one. You're not in the condemned cell now, you know. No snout allowed here.

PRISONER B. Unless you manage to scrounge a dog-end off the remands.

PRISONER A. Or pick one up in the exercise yard after a man the like of yourself that's allowed them as a special concession. Not, by God, that we picked up much after you. What did you do with your dog-ends?

LIFER. Threw them in the fire.

PRISONER B. You what!

PRISONER A. How was it the other poor bastard, that's got no reprieve and is to be topped in the morning—how was it he was always able to leave a trail of butts behind him when he went off exercise?

LIFER. I've never been in prison before; how was I to know?

PRISONER A. You're a curse of God liar, my friend, you did know; for it was whispered to him by the fellows from the hospital bringing over the grub to the condemned cell. He never gave them as much as a match! And he couldn't even bring his dog-ends to the exercise yard and drop them behind for us to pick up when we came out later.

PRISONER B.   I bet you're charmed with yourself that you're not going through the iron door tomorrow morning.

[*The* LIFER *doesn't speak, but looks down at his suit.*]

PRISONER A.   Aye, you're better off in that old suit, bad as it is, than the wooden overcoat the quare fellow is going to get tomorrow morning.

PRISONER B.   The longest you could do would be twenty years. More than likely you'll get out in half of that. Last man to finish up in the Bog,[4] he done eleven.

LIFER.   Eleven. How do you live through it?

PRISONER A.   A minute at a time.

PRISONER B.   You haven't got a bit of snout for him, have you?

[PRISONER A. *shakes his head.*]

Maybe Dunlavin has. Hey, Dunlavin, have you e'er a smoke you'd give this chap? Hey, Dunlavin.

DUNLAVIN [*coming from his cell*].   Yes, what is it? Anyone there the name of headache?

PRISONER B.   Could you manage to give this chap something to smoke? E'er a bit of snout at all.

DUNLAVIN.   There's only one brand of tobacco allowed here—"Three Nuns". None today, none tomorrow, and none the day after. [*He goes back into his cell.*]

PRISONER B.   Eh, Dunlavin, come back to hell out of that.

DUNLAVIN.   Well, what?

PRISONER B.   This poor chap after being smoking about sixty a day . . .

DUNLAVIN.   Where?

PRISONER B.   In the condemned cell—where else?

DUNLAVIN.   Now I have you. Sure I thought you were the other fellow, and you're not, you're only the murderer. God comfort you. [*Shakes hands.*] Certainly so. [*Takes off his jacket, looks up and down the wing, undoes his trousers and from the depths of his combinations he produces a cigarette end, and a match, and presents them to the* LIFER.] Reprieved in the small hours of this morning. Certainly so. The dead arose and appeared to many, as the man said, but you'll be getting yourself a bad name standing near that other fellow's door. This is your flowery dell, see? It has your name there on that little card. And all your particulars. Age forty-three. Religion R.C.[5]

LIFER [*reads*].   Life.

DUNLAVIN.   And a bloody sight better than death any day of the week.

PRISONER B.   It always says that. The Governor will explain it all to you later this morning.

4. To finish a penal sentence in the ward.   5. Roman Catholic

DUNLAVIN. Or maybe they'll get holy Uncle Healey to do it.

PRISONER B. Go into your cell and have a smoke for yourself. Bring your kit bag. [*Passes in kit to* LIFER.] Have a quiet burn there before the screw comes round; we'll keep nick.

[LIFER *closes the door of his cell.*]

DUNLAVIN. God knows I got the pick of good neighbours. Lovely people. Give me a decent murderer though, rather than the likes of this other fellow. Well, I'll go into me little place and get on with me bit of dobying so as to have it all nice for Healey when he comes round. [HE *goes back to his cell.*]

PRISONER B. [*to* LIFER]. Don't light up yet! Here's the screw coming.

PRISONER A. With the other fellow.

[WARDER REGAN *and another prisoner, "the* OTHER FELLOW*", an anxious-faced man, wearing prison clothes and carrying a kit bag, come on* L.]

WARDER REGAN. Yes, this is your flowery dell. Leave in your kitbag and stand at your door and wait for the doctor. These other fellows will show you where to go when he comes.

OTHER FELLOW. Right, sir. Very good, sir.

[WARDER REGAN *goes, the* OTHER FELLOW *has a look round.*]

PRISONER B. There's a bloke in the end cell getting himself a quiet burn. Why don't you join him before the screws get back?

[*The* OTHER FELLOW *notices the card on* LIFER's *cell.*]

OTHER FELLOW. My God! Is this what I've come to, mixing with murderers! I'd rather not, thank you, though I could do with a smoke. I'll have to spend long months here, even if I get my remission, with murderers and thieves and God knows what! You're not all murderers are you? You haven't killed anyone, have you?

PRISONER B. Not for a while, I haven't.

OTHER FELLOW. I cannot imagine any worse crime than taking a life, can you?

PRISONER B. It'd depend whose life.

OTHER FELLOW. Of course. I mean, a murderer would be justified in taking his own life, wouldn't he? "We send him forth" says Carlisle— you've heard of Carlisle haven't you?—"We send him forth, back to the void, back to the darkness, far out beyond the stars. Let him go from us."[6]

DUNLAVIN [*head out of door of cell*]. Oh. [*Looks at* OTHER FELLOW]. I

6. Frederick Howard, fifth earl of Carlisle (1748–1825), playwright, poet, lord lieutenant of Ireland (1780–82).

thought it was Healey from the Department or someone giving it out of them.

PRISONER A.   Looks like this man is a bit of an intellectual.

DUNLAVIN.   Is that what they call it now?

LIFER.   Thanks for the smoke, Mr. Dunlavin.

DUNLAVIN.   Not at all, sure, you're welcome, call again when you're passing. But remember the next wife you kill and you getting forty fags a day in the condemned cell, think of them as is not so fortunate as yourself and leave a few dog-ends around the exercise yard after you. Here's these noisy little gets again.

[*The two* YOUNG PRISONERS *come round from the left, their sweeping brushes in front of them and singing their song. The* OTHER FELLOW *stands quite still at his door.*]

YOUNG PRISONERS.

> Only one more cell inspection
> We go out next Saturday
> Only one more cell inspection
> Then we go far far away.

[*They are sweeping near the* LIFER.]

> Only one more cell inspection
> We go out next Saturday
> Only one more cell . . .

LIFER.   For God's sake shut up that squeaking . . .

YOUNG PRISONER 1.   We've as much right to open our mouth as what you have, and you only a wet day in the place.

PRISONER B.   Leave the kids alone. You don't own the place, you know. They're doing no harm. [*To the* YOUNG PRISONERS.] You want to sweep this bit of floor away?

DUNLAVIN.   What brings you round here so often? If you went over to the remand wings[7] you might pick up a bit of snout or a look at the paper.

YOUNG PRISONER 1.   We get a smoke and the *Mail* every day off a limey on our road that's on remand. He's in over the car smuggling. But round here this morning you can see the mots from the laundry over on the female side hanging out the washing in the exercise yard. Do youse look at them? I suppose when you get old, though, you don't much bother about women.

PRISONER B.   I'm thirty, mac.

YOUNG PRISONER 1.   Ah, I thought that. Don't suppose you care if you

---

7. Where accused await trial.

never see a mot. There's Shaybo there and he never thinks of anything else. Do you think of anything else but women, Shaybo?

YOUNG PRISONER 2.   Yes. Robbing and stealing, Scholara. You go to the window and keep an eye out for them and I'll sweep on round here till you give us a call.

YOUNG PRISONER 1.   Right, Shaybo, they should be nearly out now. [*Goes up and stands by window.*]

PRISONER B.   I forgot about the women.

DUNLAVIN.   I didn't. It's a great bit of a treat today—that and having me leg rubbed. Neighbour and I wait in for it.

YOUNG PRISONER 1 [*from the window, in a coarse whisper*]. Shaybo, you can see them now.

YOUNG PRISONER 2.   The blondy one from North Crumlin?

YOUNG PRISONER 1.   Yes, and there's another one with her. I don't know her.

YOUNG PRISONER 2.   Must be a country mot. Scholara doesn't know her. Women

DUNLAVIN.   Women.

PRISONER A.   I see the blondy one waving.

YOUNG PRISONER 1.   If it's all the one to you, I'd like you to know that's my mot and it's me she's waving at.

PRISONER A.   I'll wave you a thick ear.

DUNLAVIN.   Hey, Neighbour! Where the hell is he this morning? Neighbour!

AN OLD MAN'S CREAKING VOICE.   Here I am, Neighbour, here I am.

[NEIGHBOUR, *a bent old man, comes on from* L., *hobbling as quickly as he can on a stick.*]

DUNLAVIN.   Ah, you lost mass.

NEIGHBOUR.   What, are they gone in already?

DUNLAVIN.   No, but they're finished hanging up the top row of clothes. There'll be no stretching or reaching off chairs.

NEIGHBOUR.   Still, thanks be to God for small mercies. They'll be out again this day week.

PRISONER A.   If you lives to see it.

NEIGHBOUR.   Why wouldn't I live to see it as well as what you would? This is not the nearest I was to fine women, nor are they the first good-looking ones I saw.

PRISONER A.   With that old cough of yours they could easy be the last.

NEIGHBOUR.   God, you're a desperate old gas bag. We remember better-looking women than ever they were, don't we, Dunlavin? Meena La Bloom, do you remember her?

DUNLAVIN.   Indeed and I do; many's the seaman myself and Meena gave the hey and a do, and Mickey Finn to.

NEIGHBOUR.   And poor May Oblong.

DUNLAVIN.   Ah, where do you leave poor May? The Lord have mercy
on her, wasn't I with her one night in the digs, and there was a Member of Parliament there, and May after locking him in the back room
and taking away his trousers, with him going over the north wall that
morning to vote for Home Rule. [8] "For the love of your country and
mine," he shouts under the door to May, "give me back me trousers."
"So I will," says May, "if you shove a fiver out under the door."

NEIGHBOUR.   He had the wad hid? Dirty suspicious old beast.

DUNLAVIN.   That's right. He was cute enough to hide his wad somewhere, drunk and all as he was the previous night. All we got in his
trousers was a locket of hair of the patriotic plumber of Dolphin's Barn
that swore to let his hair grow till Ireland was free.

NEIGHBOUR.   Ah, poor May, God help her, she was the heart of the
roll.

DUNLAVIN.   And when she was arrested for carrying on after the curfew,
the time of the trouble, she was fined for having concealed about her
person two Thompson submachine guns, 1921 pattern, three Mills
bombs, and a stick of dynamite.

NEIGHBOUR.   And will you ever forget poor Lottie L'Estrange, that got
had up for pushing the soldier into Spencer Dock?

DUNLAVIN.   Ah, God be with the youth of us.

NEIGHBOUR.   And Cork Annie, and Lady Limerick.

DUNLAVIN.   And Julia Rice and the Goofy One.

NEIGHBOUR [turns towards window].   Hey, you, move out of the way
there and give us a look. Dunlavin, come up here before they go, and
have a look at the blondy one.

YOUNG PRISONER 1.   Go 'long, you dirty old dog. That's my mot you're
speaking about. [Shoves NEIGHBOUR.]   You old heap of dirt, to wave
at a decent girl.

PRISONER A.   Hey, snots, d'you think you won the bloody place?

YOUNG PRISONER 1.   Would you like it, to have that dirty old eyebox
looking at your mot?

PRISONER B.   He's not going to eat her.

DUNLAVIN [from behind].   No, but he'd like to.

YOUNG PRISONER 2.   That's right and Scholara is nearly married to her.
At least she had a squealer for him and he has to pay her money every
week. Any week he's outside like, to give it, or her to get it.

YOUNG PRISONER 1 [blows a kiss].   That's right, and I have him putting
his rotten old eye on her.

OTHER FELLOW [at his doorway].   God preserve us.

PRISONER A.   Well, you don't own the bloody window.

---

8. The Member of Parliament in London was to vote for an independent Irish parliament, or Home
Rule, a principal issue during "the troubles," mentioned below, early in the twentieth century.

[*Shoves* YOUNG PRISONER 1 *out of way and brings over* NEIGH-BOUR.]

Come on, you, if you want to see the May procession.

NEIGHBOUR. Ah, thanks, butty, your blood's worth bottling.

PRISONER A. I didn't do it on account of you, but if you let them young pups get away with too much they'd be running the place.

YOUNG PRISONER 2. Come on Scholara, we'll mosey back. The screw will think we're lost.

[*They go back down the stairs, pick up their brushes, and start sweeping again and singing . . .*]

YOUNG PRISONER 1.

> Only one more cell inspection
> We go out next Saturday

YOUNG PRISONER 2.

> Only one more cell inspection . . .

LIFER. Shut your bloody row, can't you?

DUNLAVIN. Shut up yourself; you're making more noise than any of them.

YOUNG PRISONER 1. Don't tell us to shut up, you bastard.

PRISONER B. Ah, leave him alone; he started life this morning.

YOUNG PRISONER 1. Ah, we're sorry, mister, ain't we, Shaybo?

YOUNG PRISONER 2. God, we are. Go over and take a pike at the female yard. They hang up the clothes now and Scholara's mot is over there. You can have a look at her. Scholara won't mind, will you, Schol?

YOUNG PRISONER 1. Certainly and I won't. Not with you going to the Bog to start life in a couple of days, where you won't see a woman.

YOUNG PRISONER 2. A child.

YOUNG PRISONER 1. A dog.

YOUNG PRISONER 2. A fire.

PRISONER 1. Get to hell out of that round to your own wing. Wouldn't you think a man would know all that forbye you telling it to him?

YOUNG PRISONER 2. We were going anyway. We've seen all we wanted to see. It wasn't to look at a lot of old men we came here, but to see mots hanging out the washing.

YOUNG PRISONER 1. And eitherways, we'll be a lot nearer the women than you'll be next Saturday night. Think of us when you're sitting locked up in the old flowery, studying the Bible, Chapter 1, verse 2, and we trucking round in chase of charver.

[*They samba out with their brushes for partners, humming the Wedding Samba.*]

PRISONER A. Them young gets have too much old gab out of them altogether. I was a Y.P.[9] in Walton before the war and I can tell you they'd be quiet boys if they got the larrying we used to get.

OTHER FELLOW. And talking so disrespectfully about the Bible.

NEIGHBOUR. Belied and they needn't; many's the time the Bible was a consolation to a fellow all alone in the old cell. The lovely thin paper with a bit of mattress coir in it, if you could get a match or a bit of tinder or any class of light, was as good a smoke as ever I tasted. Am I right, Dunlavin?

DUNLAVIN. Damn the lie, Neighbour. The first twelve months I done, I smoked my way half-way through the book of Genesis and three inches of my mattress. When the Free State[1] came in we were afraid of our life they were going to change the mattresses for feather beds. And you couldn't smoke feathers, not, be God, if they were rolled in the Song of Solomon itself. But sure, thanks to God, the Free State didn't change anything more than the badge on the warders' caps.

OTHER FELLOW. Can I be into my cell for a while?

PRISONER B. Until the doctor calls you. [*Goes into his cell.*]

PRISONER A. Well, I'm going to have a rest. It's hard work doing a lagging.

LIFER. A lagging? That's penal servitude, isn't it?

DUNLAVIN. Three years or anything over.

LIFER. Three years is a long time.

DUNLAVIN. I wouldn't like to be that long hanging.

NEIGHBOUR. Is he the . . .

DUNLAVIN [*sotto voce*]. Silver-top! [*Aloud.*] Started life this morning.

NEIGHBOUR. So they're not going to top you after all? Well, you're a lucky man. I worked one time in the hospital, helping the screw there, and the morning of the execution he gave me two bottles of stout to take the hood off the fellow was after being topped. I wouldn't have done it a second time for two glasses of malt, no, nor a bottle of it. I cut the hood away; his head was all twisted and his face black, but the two eyes were the worst; like a rabbit's; it was fear that had done it.

LIFER. Perhaps he didn't feel anything. How do you know?

NEIGHBOUR. I only seen him. I never had a chance of asking him. [NEIGHBOUR *goes to the murderer's door.*] Date of expiration of sentence, life. In some ways I wouldn't mind if that was my lot. What do you say?

DUNLAVIN. I don't know; it's true we're too old and bet for lobbywatching and shaking down anywhere, so that you'd fall down and sleep on the pavement of a winter's night and not know but you were lying snug and comfortable in the Shelbourne.

NEIGHBOUR. Only then to wake up on some lobby and the hard floor-

9. Young prisoner.   1. 1921, first outcome of "the troubles."

boards under you, and a lump of hard filth for your pillow, and the cold and the drink shaking you, wishing it was morning for the market pubs to open, where if you had the price of a drink you could sit in the warm anyway. Except, God look down on you, if it was Sunday.

DUNLAVIN.　Ah, there's the agony. No pub open, but the bells battering your bared nerves and all you could do with the cold and the sickness was to lean over on your side and wish that God would call you.

LIFER.　If I was outside my life wouldn't be like that.

NEIGHBOUR.　No, but ours would.

DUNLAVIN [quietly].　See, we're selfish, mister, like everyone else.

WARDER [shouts off].　Medical applications and receptions. Fall in for the doctor. [LIFER looks lost.]

DUNLAVIN.　Yes, that's you. Go up there to the top of the wing and wait there till the screw tells you to go in. Neighbour, call them other fellows.

[Exit LIFER.]

NEIGHBOUR.　Come on—the vet's here.

DUNLAVIN [calling in to the OTHER FELLOW].　Hey, come out and get gelded.

[OTHER FELLOW and PRISONERS A. and B. come out of cells.]

NEIGHBOUR.　You're for the doctor. Go on up there with the rest of them. Me and Dunlavin don't go up. We only wait to be rubbed.

DUNLAVIN.　Don't have any chat at all with that fellow. D'you see what he's in for?

[NEIGHBOUR goes and looks. Exit OTHER FELLOW and PRISONERS A. and B.]

NEIGHBOUR.　What the hell does that mean?

DUNLAVIN.　A bloody sex mechanic.

NEIGHBOUR.　I didn't know.

DUNLAVIN.　Well, you know now. I'll go in and get me chair. You can sit on it after me. It'll save you bringing yours out.

NEIGHBOUR.　Well, if you go first and you have a chance of a go at the spirit bottle, don't swig the bloody lot. Remember I'm for treatment too.

DUNLAVIN.　Don't be such an old begrudger. He'll bring a quart bottle of it, and who could swallow that much methylated spirit in the few drops you'd get at it?

NEIGHBOUR.　You could, or a bucket of it, if it was lying anywhere handy. I seen you do it, bluestone and all, only buns to a bear as far as you were concerned.

DUNLAVIN.　Do you remember the old doctor they had here years ago?

NEIGHBOUR.　The one they used to call Crippen.

DUNLAVIN. The very man. There was one day I was brought in for drinking the chat and I went to court that morning and was here in the afternoon still as drunk as Pontius Pilate. Crippen was examining me. "When I put me hand there you cough," and all to that effect. "Did you ever have V.D.?" says he. "I haven't got your habits," says I to him. These fellows weren't long.

[*Re-enter* PRISONERS A. *and* B.]

NEIGHBOUR. What did he give youse?

PRISONER B. [*passing into cell*]. Extra six ounces of bread. Says we're undernourished.

PRISONER A. Is the bar open yet?

NEIGHBOUR. Never you mind the bar. I've cruel pains in my leg that I want rubbed to take out the rheumatics, not to be jeered at, and I've had them genuine since the war.

PRISONER A. What war? The economic war?

NEIGHBOUR. Ah, you maggot. It's all your fault, Dunlavin, telling them fellows we do get an odd sup out of the spirit bottle. Letting everyone know our business.

[PRISONERS A. *and* B. *go into cells and shut the doors.*]

DUNLAVIN. No sign of Holy Healey yet.

NEIGHBOUR. You're wasting your time chasing after old Healey. He told me here one day, and I trying to get myself an old overcoat out of him, that he was here only as a head man of the Department of Justice, and he couldn't do other business of any other sort or size whatever, good, bad or indifferent. It's my opinion that old Healey does be half-jarred a deal of the time anyway.

DUNLAVIN. The likes of Healey would take a sup all right, but being a high-up civil servant, he wouldn't drink under his own name. You'd see the likes of Healey nourishing themselves with balls of malt, at eleven in the morning, in little black snugs round Merrion Row. The barman would lose his job if he so much as breathed their name. It'd be "Mr. H. wants a drop of water but not too much." "Yes, Mr. O." "No, sir, Mr. Mac wasn't in this morning." "Yes, Mr. D. Fine morning; it will be a lovely day if it doesn't snow." Educated drinking, you know. Even a bit of chat about God at an odd time, so as you'd think God was in another department, but not long off the Bog, and they was doing Him a good turn to be talking well about Him.

NEIGHBOUR. Here's the other two back. The M.O.[2] will be down to us soon.

[LIFER *and* OTHER FELLOW *go into cells and shut the doors.*]

_____

2. Medical orderly.

DUNLAVIN.   That other fellow's not looking as if this place is agreeing with him.

NEIGHBOUR.   You told me a minute ago that I wasn't even to speak to him.

DUNLAVIN.   Ah, when all is said and done, he's someone's rearing after all, he could be worse, he could be a screw or an official from the Department.

> [WARDER REGAN *comes on with a bottle marked "methylated spirit".*]

WARDER REGAN.   You're the two for rubs, for your rheumatism.

DUNLAVIN.   That's right, Mr. Regan sir, old and bet, sir, that's us. And the old pains is very bad with us these times, sir.

WARDER REGAN.   Not so much lip, and sit down whoever is first for treatment.

DUNLAVIN.   That's me, sir. Age before ignorance, as the man said. [*Sits in the chair.*]

WARDER REGAN.   Rise the leg of your trousers. Which leg is it?

DUNLAVIN.   The left, sir.

WARDER REGAN.   That's the right leg you're showing me.

DUNLAVIN.   That's what I was saying, sir. The left is worst one day and the right is bad the next. To be on the safe side, you'd have to do two of them. It's only the mercy of God I'm not a centipede, sir, with the weather that's in it.

WARDER REGAN.   Is that where the pain is?

DUNLAVIN [*bending down slowly towards the bottle*].   A little lower down, sir, if you please. [*Grabs the bottle and raises it to his mouth.*] Just a little lower down, sir, if it's all equal to you.

> [REGAN *rubs, head well bent, and* DUNLAVIN *drinks long and deeply and as quickly lowers the bottle on to the floor again, wiping his mouth and making the most frightful grimaces, for the stuff doesn't go down easy at first. He goes through the pantomime of being burnt inside for* NEIGHBOUR'S *benefit and rubs his mouth with the back of his hand.*]

DUNLAVIN.   Ah, that's massive, sir. 'Tis you that has the healing hand. You must have desperate luck at the horses; I'd only love to be with you copying your dockets.

> [REGAN *turns and pours more spirit on his hands.*]

Ah, that's it, sir, well into me I can feel it going. [*Reaches forward towards the bottle again, drinks.*] Ah, that's it, I can feel it going right into me. And doing me all the good in the world.

> [REGAN *reaches and puts more spirit on his hand and sets to rubbing again.*]

That's it, sir, thorough does it; if you're going to do a thing at all you might as well do it well.

[*Reaches forward for the bottle again and raises it.* NEIGHBOUR *looks across in piteous appeal to him not to drink so much, but he merely waves the bottle in elegant salute, as if to wish him good health, and takes another drink.*]

May God reward you, sir, you must be the seventh son of the seventh son or one of the Lees from Limerick on your mother's side maybe. [*Drinks again.*] Ah, that's the cure for the cold of the wind and the world's neglectment.

WARDER REGAN.   Right, now you.

[NEIGHBOUR *comes forward.*]

WARDER DONELLY [*offstage*].   All present and correct, Mr. Healey, sir.
DUNLAVIN.   Holy Healey!

[*Enter* WARDER DONELLY].

WARDER DONELLY.   This way, Mr. Healey.
WARDER REGAN.   Attention! Stand by your doors.
DUNLAVIN.   By the left, laugh.
WARDER DONELLY.   This way.

[*Enter* MR. HEALEY, *an elegantly dressed gentleman.*]

HEALEY.   Good morning.
WARDER DONELLY.   Any complaints?
PRISONER A.   No, sir.
HEALEY.   Good morning!
WARDER DONELLY.   Any complaints?
OTHER FELLOW.   ⎫
PRISONER B.   ⎬No, sir.
HEALEY.   Good morning all! Well, now, I'm here representing the Department of Justice, if there are any complaints now is the time to make them.
SEVERAL PRISONERS.   No complaints, sir.
WARDER REGAN.   All correct, sir. Two receiving medical treatment here, sir.
DUNLAVIN.   Just getting the old leg rubbed, sir, Mr. Healey.
HEALEY.   Well, well, it almost smells like a bar.
DUNLAVIN.   I'm near drunk myself on the smell of it, sir.
HEALEY.   Don't let me interrupt the good work.
DUNLAVIN.   Ah, the old legs. It's being out in all weathers that does it, sir. Of course we don't have that to contend with while we're here, sir.
HEALEY.   Out in all weathers, I should think not indeed. Well, my man, I will be inspecting your cell amongst others in due course.

DUNLAVIN.   Yes, sir.
HEALEY.   It's always a credit to you, I must say that. [*He turns to* REGAN.]
Incorrigible, some of these old fellows, but rather amusing.
WARDER REGAN.   Yes, sir.
HEALEY.   It's Regan, isn't it?
WARDER REGAN.   Yes, sir.
HEALEY.   Ah yes, you're helping the Canon at the execution tomorrow
morning, I understand.
WARDER REGAN.   Well, I shall be with the condemned man sir, seeing
that he doesn't do away with himself during the night and that he goes
down the hole with his neck properly broken in the morning, without
making too much fuss about it.
HEALEY.   A sad duty.
WARDER REGAN.   Neck breaking and throttling, sir?

[HEALEY *gives him a sharp look.*]

You must excuse me, sir. I've seen rather a lot of it. They say familiarity breeds contempt.
HEALEY.   Well, we have one consolation, Regan, the condemned man
gets the priest and the sacraments, more than his victim got maybe. I
venture to suggest that some of them die holier deaths than if they
had finished their natural span.
WARDER REGAN.   We can't advertise "Commit a murder and die a happy
death," sir. We'd have them all at it. They take religion very seriously
in this country.
HEALEY.   Quite, quite so! Now, I understand you have the reprieved
man over here, Regan.
WARDER REGAN.   No. Twenty-six sir.
DUNLAVIN.   Just beside me, sir.
HEALEY.   Ah, yes! So here we are! Here's the lucky man, eh? Well,
now, the Governor will explain your position to you later in the day.
Your case will be examined every five years. Meanwhile I thought
you might like a holy picture to hang up in your cell. Keep a cheerful
countenance, my friend. God gave you back your life and the least
you can do is to thank him with every breath you draw! Right? Well,
be of good heart. I will call in and see you again, that is, if duty
permits. [*He moves to* DUNLAVIN's *cell.*]
HEALEY [*at* DUNLAVIN's *cell*].   Very creditable. Hm.
DUNLAVIN.   Well, to tell you the truth, sir, it's a bit extra special today.
You see, we heard you was here.
HEALEY.   Very nice.
DUNLAVIN.   Of course I do like to keep my little place as homely
as I can with the little holy pictures you gave me of Blessed Martin,
sir.
HEALEY.   I see you don't recognize the colour bar.

DUNLAVIN.   The only bar I recognize, sir, is the Bridge Bar or the Beamish House the corner of Thomas Street.

HEALEY.   Well, I must be off now, and I'm glad to see you're being well looked after.

DUNLAVIN.   It's neither this nor that, but if you could spare a minute, sir?

HEALEY.   Yes, what is it? But hurry; remember I've a lot to do today.

DUNLAVIN.   It's like this, sir. I won't always be here, sir, having me leg rubbed and me bit of grub brought to me. As it says in the Bible, sir, have it yourself or be without it and put ye by for the rainy day, for thou knowest not the night thou mayest be sleeping in a lobby.

HEALEY.   Yes, yes, but what is it you want?

DUNLAVIN.   I've the chance of a little room up round Buckingham Street, sir, if you could only give me a letter to the Room-Keepers after I go out, for a bit of help with the rent.

HEALEY.   Well, you know, when I visit the prison, I'm not here as a member of any outside organization of which I may be a member but simply as an official of the Department of Justice.

DUNLAVIN.   Yes, but where else would I be likely to meet you, sir? I'd hardly bump into you in the Bridge Bar when I'd be outside, would I, sir?

HEALEY.   No, no, certainly not. But you know the Society offices in the Square. See me there any Friday night, between eight and nine.

DUNLAVIN.   Thank you, sir, and a bed in heaven to you, sir.

HEALEY.   And the same to you. [*Goes to next cell.*]

DUNLAVIN.   And many of them, and I hope we're all here this time next year [*venomously after* MR. HEALEY] that it may choke you.

[WARDER DONELLY *bangs on* LIFER'S *closed door, then looks in.*]

WARDER DONELLY.   Jesus Christ, sir. He's put the sheet up! Quick.

[REGAN *and* DONELLY *go into* LIFER'S *cell. He is hanging. They cut him down.*]

WARDER REGAN.   Gently does it.

[*They lay him down in the passage and try to restore him.*]

HEALEY.   What a dreadful business, and with this other coming off tomorrow.

[THE PRISONERS *crowd out of line.*]

WARDER DONELLY.   Get back to your cells!

HEALEY.   Is he still with us?

WARDER REGAN.   He'll be all right in an hour or two. Better get the M.O., Mr. Donelly.

[*The triangle sounds.*]

WARDER DONELLY. B. Wing, two, three and one. Stand by your doors. Right, lead on. Now come on, come on, this is no holiday. Right sir, over to you. Lead on, B.1.

[WARDER REGAN *and* HEALEY *are left with the unconscious* LIFER.]

HEALEY. Dear, dear. The Canon will be very upset about this.

WARDER REGAN. There's not much harm done, thank God. They don't have to put a death certificate against the receipt for his live body.

HEALEY. That doesn't seem a very nice way of looking at it, Regan.

WARDER REGAN. A lot of people mightn't consider ours a very nice job, sir.

HEALEY. Ours?

WARDER REGAN. Yes, ours, sir. Mine, the Canon's, the hangman's, and if you don't mind my saying so, yours, sir.

HEALEY. Society cannot exist without prisons, Regan. My job is to bring what help and comfort I can to these unfortunates. Really, a man with your outlook, I cannot see why you stay in the service.

WARDER REGAN. It's a soft job, sir, between hangings.

[*The triangle is heard. The* M.O. *comes on with two stretcher-bearers.*]

Act Two

The prison yard, a fine evening.

VOICE OF PRISONER [*off-stage, singing*].

> A hungry feeling came o'er me stealing
> And the mice were squealing in my prison cell
> And the old triangle
> Went jingle jangle
> Along the banks of the Royal Canal.

WARDER DONELLY. B.1. B.2. B.3. Head on for exercise, right! Lead on, B.1. All one, away to exercise.

[*The* PRISONERS *file out,* WARDER DONELLY *with them.*]

> On a fine spring evening,
> The lag lay dreaming
> The seagulls wheeling high above the wall.
> And the old triangle
> Went jingle jangle
> Along the banks of the Royal Canal.

The screw was peeping
The lag was sleeping,

[*The* PRISONERS *wander where they will; most go and take a glance at the half-dug grave.*]

While he lay weeping for the girl Sal,

WARDER DONELLY.   Who's the bloody baritone? Shut up that noise, you. Where do you think you are?

NEIGHBOUR.   It's not up here, sir; it's one of the fellows in the basement, sir, in the solitary.

WARDER DONELLY.   He must be getting birdseed with his bread and water. I'll bloody well show him he's not in a singing house.

[*Song is still going on.*]

Hey, shut up that noise! Shut up there or I'll leave you weeping. Where do you think you are?

[*Song stops.*]

You can get sitting down any of you that wants it.

[DUNLAVIN *sits.*]

NEIGHBOUR [*at the grave*].   They'll have to bottom out another couple of feet before morning.

PRISONER B.   They! Us you mean; they've got four of us in a working party after tea.

NEIGHBOUR.   You want to get that clay nice and neat for filling in. [*He spits and wanders away.*]

PRISONER B.   We'll get a couple of smokes for the job at least.

[*They wander.*]

NEIGHBOUR.   How are you, Neighbour?

DUNLAVIN.   Dying.

NEIGHBOUR.   If you are itself, it's greed that's killing you. I only got a sup of what was left.

DUNLAVIN.   I saved your life then; it was very bad meths.

PRISONER B.   What did Regan say when he caught youse lying in the cell?

NEIGHBOUR.   He wanted to take us up for drinking it on him, but Dunlavin said we were distracted with the events of the morning and didn't know what we were doing. So he just told us to get to hell out of it and he hoped it would destroy us for life.

DUNLAVIN.   May God forgive him.

NEIGHBOUR.   I thought it was as good a drop of meths as ever I tasted. It would never come up to the prewar article, but between the springtime and the warmth of it, it would put new life into you. Oh, it's a grand evening and another day's work behind us.

PRISONER B. With the winter over, Neighbour, I suppose you don't feel a day over ninety.

NEIGHBOUR. If you'd have done all the time I have you wouldn't look so young.

PRISONER A. What time? Sure, you never done a lagging in your life. A month here and a week there for lifting the collection box out of a chapel or running out of a chemist's with a bottle of cheap wine. Anything over six months would be the death of you.

NEIGHBOUR. Oh, you're the hard chaw.

PRISONER A. Two laggings, I've done. Five year and seven, and a bit of Preventive Detention, on the Moor and at Parkhurst.

NEIGHBOUR. What for? Ferocious begging?

PRISONER A. I've never been a grasshopper or a nark for the screws anyway, wherever I was; and if you were in a lagging station I know what they'd give you, shopping the poor bastard that was singing in the chokey. He was only trying to be company for himself down there all alone and not knowing whether it was day or night.

NEIGHBOUR. I only did it for his own good. If the screw hadn't checked him the Principal might have been coming out and giving him an extra few days down there.

DUNLAVIN. Will youse give over the pair of youse for God's sake. The noise of youse battering me bared nerves is unhuman. Begod, an Englishman would have more nature to a fellow lying with a sick head. A methylated martyr, that's what I am.

NEIGHBOUR [to PRISONER A.]. Meself and that man sitting there, we done time before you came up. In Kilmainham,[1] and that's where you never were. First fourteen days without a mattress, skilly three times a day. None of your sitting out in the yard like nowadays. I got my toe amputated by one of the old lags so I could get into hospital for a feed.

DUNLAVIN [looks up and feebly moans]. A pity you didn't get your head amputated as you were at it. It would have kept you quiet for a bit.

NEIGHBOUR. I got me mouth to talk, the same as the next man. Maybe we're not all that well up, that we get up at the Christmas concert and do the electrocutionist performance, like some I could mention.

DUNLAVIN. It's neither this nor that, Neighbour, but if you would only give over arguing the toss about nothing and change over to a friendly subject of mutual interest—like the quare fellow that's to be topped in the morning.

NEIGHBOUR. True, true, Dunlavin, and a comfortable old flowery dell he'll have down there. [He prods the grave with his stick.] We'll be eating the cabbages off that one in a month or two.

---

1. Old Dublin jail associated with imprisonment of patriots.

PRISONER A.   You're in a terrible hurry to get the poor scut under the cabbages. How do you know he won't get a reprieve, like old Silvertop?

LIFER.   Jesus, Mary and Joseph, you'd like to see me in there, wouldn't you! [*He moves violently away from them.*]

NEIGHBOUR.   Your man doesn't like any talk about hanging.

PRISONER A.   No more would you, if you'd tried to top yourself this morning.

NEIGHBOUR.   Anyway he's gone now and we can have a chat about it in peace. Sure we must be saying something and it's better than scandalizing our neighbours.

PRISONER B.   You never know what might happen to the quare fellow. God is good.

PRISONER C.   And has a good mother.

[*They look in surprise at the young person who has quietly joined them.*]

DUNLAVIN.   No, no, it's too late now for him to be chucked.

PRISONER A.   It has been known, a last-minute reprieve, you know.

NEIGHBOUR.   He bled his brother into a crock, didn't he, that had been set aside for the pig-slaughtering and mangled the remains beyond all hope of identification.

PRISONER C.   Go bfoiridh Dia reinn. [2]

NEIGHBOUR.   He hasn't got a chance, never in a race of cats. He'll be hung as high as Guilderoy.

PRISONER A.   You're the life of the party, aren't you? You put me in mind of the little girl who was sent in to cheer her father up. She was so good at it that he cut his throat.

PRISONER E.   Ah, sure he was only computing the odds to it. He'll be topped.

NEIGHBOUR.   I'd lay me Sunday bacon on it if anyone would be idiot enough to take me up.

[PRISONER E., *a bookie, has been listening.*]

PRISONER E.   I wouldn't take your bacon, but I'll lay it off for you if you like.

[*Another prisoner watches for the screws.* PRISONER E. *acts as if he were a tick-tack man at the races.*]

PRISONER E.   The old firm. Here we are again. Neighbour lays his Sunday bacon the quare fellow will be topped tomorrow morning. Any takers?

PRISONER D.   Five snout.

PRISONER E.   Away home to your mother.

2. God look down on us.

MICKSER. Half a bacon.

PRISONER E. Half a . . .

NEIGHBOUR. Even bacons.

PRISONER E. Even bacons. Even bacons any takers? Yourself, sir, come on now, you look like a sportsman.

PRISONER A. I wouldn't eat anything after he'd touched it, not if I were starving.

NEIGHBOUR. Is that so . . .

PRISONER E. Now, now, now, don't interrupt the betting. Any takers?

DUNLAVIN. I'll take him up if only to shut his greedy gob.

NEIGHBOUR. You won't! You're having me on!

DUNLAVIN. No, I'll bet you my Sunday bacon that a reprieve will come through before morning. I feel it in my bones.

NEIGHBOUR. That's the rheumatics.

PRISONER E. Is he on, Neighbour?

NEIGHBOUR. He is.

PRISONER E. Shake on it, the two of youse!

DUNLAVIN. How d'ye do, Lord Lonsdale!

NEIGHBOUR. Never mind all that. The minute the trap goes down tomorrow morning your Sunday bacon is mine.

PRISONER A. God leave you health to enjoy it.

NEIGHBOUR. He'll be topped all right.

PRISONER A. And if he isn't, I'm the very man will tell him you bet your bacon on his life.

NEIGHBOUR. You never would.

PRISONER A. Wouldn't I?

NEIGHBOUR. You'd never be bad enough.

PRISONER A. And what would be bad about it?

NEIGHBOUR. Causing a dissension and a disturbance.

[*The two* YOUNG PRISONERS *enter.*]

PRISONER A. You mean he mightn't take it for a joke.

PRISONER B. Here's them two young prisoners; they've the life of Reilly, rambling round the place. Where youse wandering off to now?

SCHOLARA. We came over here to see a chiner of ours. He turned twenty the day before yesterday, so they shifted him away from the Juveniles to here. [*He sees* PRISONER C.] Ah, there you are. We were over in the hospital being examined for going out on Saturday and we had a bit of snout to give you.

[*Takes out a Woodbine package, extracts a cigarette from it and gives it to* PRISONER C., *who shyly stands and takes it.*]

PRISONER C. [*quietly*]. Thanks.

SCHOLARA. Gurra morra gut, you mean.

PRISONER C. [*smiles faintly*]. Go raibh maith agat.

SCHOLARA [*grandly*].   Na bac leis. [*To the other prisoners.*] Talks Irish to beat the band. Comes from an island between here and America. And Shaybo will give you a couple of strikers.

SHAYBO [*reaches in the seams of his coat and takes out a match which he presents to* PRISONER C.].   Here you are. It's a bloody shame to shove you over here among all these old men even if you are twenty itself, but maybe you won't be long after us, and you going home.

PRISONER C. [*Kerry accent*].   I will, please God. It will be summer-time and where I come from is lovely when the sun is shining.

[*They stand there, looking embarrassed for a moment.*]

DUNLAVIN.   Go on, why don't you kiss him good-bye.

SHAYBO.   Eh, Schol, let's have a pike at the grave before the screw comes out.

SCHOLARA.   Ah, yes, we must have a look at the grave.

[*They dive into the grave, the old men shout at them, but* WAR-DER DONELLY *comes to the door of the hospital.*]

WARDER DONELLY.   Get up to hell out of that and back to your own wing, youse two. [*Shouts to the warders in the prison wing.*] Two on you there, pass them fellows into the Juveniles. Get to hell out of that!

[SCHOLARA *and* SHAYBO *samba off, give the so-called V-sign, slap the right biceps with the left palm, and turning lightly, run in through the door.*]

NEIGHBOUR.   Aren't they the impudent pups? Too easy a time they have of it. I'd tan their pink backsides for them. That'd leave them fresh and easy. Impudent young curs is going these days. No respect for God nor man, pinch anything that wasn't nailed down.

PRISONER B.   Neighbour, the meths is rising in you.

DUNLAVIN.   He might as well rave there as in bed.

ENGLISH VOICE [*from one of the cell windows*].   I say, I say, down there in the yard.

DUNLAVIN.   The voice of the Lord!

PRISONER A.   That's the geezer from London that's in over the car smuggling.

ENGLISH VOICE.   I say, down there.

PRISONER B.   Hello, up there.

NEIGHBOUR.   How are you fixed for fillet?

PRISONER B.   Shut up a minute. Wait till we hear what is it he wants.

ENGLISH VOICE.   Is there any bloke down there going out this week?

PRISONER B.   Mickser is going out tomorrow. He's on this exercise. [*Shouts.*] Hold on a minute. [*Looks round.*] Hey, Mickser.

MICKSER.   What's up?

PRISONER B. That English fellow that's on remand over the cars, he wants to know if there's anyone going out this week. You're going out tomorrow, ain't you?

MICKSER. Yes, I am. I'm going out in the morning. [*To* ENGLISH PRISONER.] What do you want?

ENGLISH VOICE. I want you to go up and contact my mate. He's in Dublin. It's about bail for me. I can write his name and address here and let it down to you on my string. I didn't want the law to get his address in Dublin, so I can't write to him. I got a quid in with me, without the screw finding it, and I'll let it down with the address if you'll do it.

MICKSER. Good enough. Let down the address and the quid.

ENGLISH VOICE. My mate will give you some more when you see him.

MICKSER. That's all right. Let the quid down now and the address before the screw comes out of the hospital. I'm going out tomorrow and I'll see him for you, soon as we get out of the market pubs at half two.

PRISONER B. He's letting it down now.

MICKSER. There's the quid anyway.

> [*Reading the note.* NEIGHBOUR *gets to his feet and goes behind and peers over his shoulder.* MICKSER *sees him.*]

Get to hell out of it, you.

NEIGHBOUR. I only just wanted to have a look at what he wrote.

MICKSER. And have his mate in the Bridewell, before the day was out. I know you, you bloody old stag.

NEIGHBOUR. I saw the day you wouldn't say the like of that.

MICKSER [*proffering him the pound*]. Here, get a mass said for yourself.

NEIGHBOUR. It wouldn't do you much harm to put yourself under the hand of a priest either.

MICKSER [*laughs at him*]. That's for sinners. Only dirty people has to wash.

NEIGHBOUR. A man of your talent and wasting your time here.

MICKSER [*going back to walk with the* PRISONERS *behind*]. Good luck now, Neighbour. I'll call up and see you in the hospice for the dying.

NEIGHBOUR [*stands and calls loudly after him*]. You watch yourself. I saw the quare fellow in here a couple of years ago. He was a young hard chaw like you in all the pride of his strength and impudence. He was kicking a ball about over in A yard and I was walking around with poor old Mockridge, neither of us minding no one. All of a sudden I gets such a wallop on the head it knocks the legs from under me and very nigh cuts off my ear. "You headed that well," says he, and I deaf for three days after it! Who's got the best of it now, young as he is and strong as he is? How will his own ear feel tomorrow morning, with the washer under it, and whose legs will be the weakest when the trap goes down and he's slung into the pit? And what use is the young heart?

[*Some of the* PRISONERS *walking round stop and listen to him,
but* MICKSER *gives him a contemptuous look and walks on,
shouting at him in passing.*]

MICKSER. Get along with you, you dirty half animal.

[A WARDER *passes, sounds of the town heard, factory sirens, distant ships. Some of the* PRISONERS *pace up and down liked caged
animals.*]

NEIGHBOUR. Dunlavin, have you the loan of a pencil for a minute?

DUNLAVIN. What do you want it for?

NEIGHBOUR. I just want to write something to that English fellow about
his bail.

DUNLAVIN. You'd better hurry, before the screw comes back out.

[NEIGHBOUR *writes.*]

NEIGHBOUR. Hey, you up there that's looking for the bail.

ENGLISH VOICE. Hello, you got the quid and the address?

PRISONER A. What's the old dog up to?

DUNLAVIN. Ah, leave him alone. He's a bit hasty, but poor old Neighbour has good turns in him.

PRISONER A. So has a corkscrew.

NEIGHBOUR. Let down your string and I'll send you up this bit of a
message.

ENGLISH VOICE [*his hands can be seen at the window holding the
note*]. "Get a bucket and bail yourself out." [*Shouts in rage.*] You
dirty bastard bleeder to take my quid and I'll tell the bloody screw I
will; I'll shop you, you bleeding . . .

MICKSER. What's up with you?

NEIGHBOUR. Get a bucket and bail yourself out. [*Laughing an old man's
cackle.*]

ENGLISH VOICE. You told me to get a bucket and bail my bleeding self
out, but I'll tell the screw; I'll shop you about that quid.

MICKSER [*shouts up to the window*]. Shut your bloody big mouth for a
minute. I told you nothing.

PRISONER A. It was this old get here.

MICKSER. I sent you no message; it was this old pox bottle.

NEIGHBOUR [*ceases to laugh, is alarmed at the approach of* MICK-
SER]. Now, now, Mickser, take a joke, can't you, it was only a bit
of gas.

MICKSER [*advancing*]. I'll give you gas.

[MICKSER *advances on* NEIGHBOUR. *The lags stop and look—suddenly* MICKSER *seizes the old man and, yelling with delight, carries* NEIGHBOUR *over to the grave and thrusts him into it. The
prisoners all crowd around kicking dirt on to the old man and
shouting "Get a bucket and bail yourself out".*]

PRISONER B.   Nick, Mickser, nick, nick here's the screw.

PRISONER A.   It's only the cook with the quare fellow's tea.

> [A PRISONER *comes through the hospital gate and down the steps.*
> *He wears a white apron, carries a tray and is surrounded by an*
> *interested band, except for the* LIFER *who stands apart, and* DUN-
> LAVIN, *who lies prone on the front asleep. From the* PRISONERS
> *around the food rises an excited chorus:*]

PRISONER A.   Rashers and eggs.

PRISONER B.   He got that last night.

MICKSER.   Chicken.

NEIGHBOUR.   He had that for dinner.

PRISONER B.   Sweet cake.

PRISONER A.   It's getting hung he is, not married.

NEIGHBOUR.   Steak and onions.

MICKSER.   Sausages and bacon.

PRISONER B.   And liver.

PRISONER A.   Pork chops.

PRISONER B.   Pig's feet.

PRISONER A.   Salmon.

NEIGHBOUR.   Fish and chips.

MICKSER.   Jelly and custard.

NEIGHBOUR.   Roast lamb.

PRISONER A.   Plum pudding.

PRISONER B.   Turkey.

NEIGHBOUR.   Goose.

PRISONERS A., B., AND NEIGHBOUR.   Rashers and eggs.

ALL.   Rashers and eggs, rashers and eggs, and eggs and rashers and eggs and rashers it is.

COOK [*desperate*].   Ah, here, lads.

PRISONERS.   Here, give us a look, lift up the lid, eh, here, I never seen it.

> [*The* COOK *struggles to protect his cargo, the* PRISONERS *mill round*
> *in a loose scrum of excitement and greed, their nostrils mad almost*
> *to the point of snatching a bit. There is a roar from the gate.*]

WARDER DONELLY [*from inside the hospital gate*].   Get to hell out of that. What do youse think you are on?

> [*The* PRISONERS *scatter in a rush.*]

> [*The* COOK *with great dignity carries on.*]

NEIGHBOUR [*sitting down*].   Oh, the two eggs, the yolk in the middle like . . . a bride's eye under a pink veil, and the grease of the rashers . . . pale and pure like melted gold.

DUNLAVIN.   Oh, may God forgive you, as if a body wasn't sick enough as it is.

NEIGHBOUR.   And the two big back rashers.

PRISONER A.   Go along, you begrudging old dog. Maybe when you go back the standard of living in your town residence, No. 1 St. James Street,[3] might be gone up. And they'll be serving rashers and eggs. You'd do a lot for them, when you'd begrudge them to a man for his last meal on this earth.

NEIGHBOUR.   Well, it's not his last meal if you want to know. He'll get a supper tonight and a breakfast in the morning, and I don't begrudge him the little he'll eat of that, seeing the rope stew to follow, and lever pudding and trap door doddle for desert. And anyway didn't you run over the same as the rest of us to see what he was getting?

PRISONER A.   And if I did, it wasn't to begrudge it to the man.

PRISONER B.   Sure we all ran over, anything to break the monotony in a kip like this.

[The triangle is heard.]

PRISONER A. [gloomily].   I suppose you're right. In Strangeways, Manchester, and I in it during the war, we used to wish for an air-raid. We had one and we were left locked up in our cells. We stood up on our tables and took the blackouts off the windows and had a grandstand view of the whole city burning away under us. The screws were running round shouting in the spy-holes at us to get down from the windows, but they soon ran off down the shelters. We had a great view of the whole thing till a bomb landed on the Assize Court next door, and the blast killed twenty of the lags. They were left standing on their tables without a mark on them, stone dead. Sure anyway, we all agreed it broke the monotony.

[Enter WARDER DONELLY.]

WARDER DONELLY.   Right, fall in there!

PRISONER B.   Don't forget the bet, Neighbour.

WARDER DONELLY.   Come on, get in line there.

PRISONER A.   And don't forget what I'm going to tell the quare fellow.

WARDER DONELLY.   Silence there. [Search begins.] What's this you've got in your pocket? A file? Scissors out of the bag shop? No? A bit of rope? Oh, your handkerchief, so it is. [Searching next PRISONER.] You, here, what's this? A bit of wax end, you forgot to leave in the bag shop? Well, don't forget the next time. What's this?

[MAN takes out two inches of rope.]

3. A fashionable London address.

What's this for? You were roping mail bags today, and after all they don't rope themselves. Ah, you forgot to leave it behind? Well, go easy, save as much as that each time and in five years' time you'd have enough to make a rope ladder. Oh, you're only doing six months? Well maybe you want to save the taxpayers a few quid and hang yourself. Sorrow the loss if you did, but they'd want to know where you got the rope from.

[PRISONERS *laugh as they are expected to do.*]

Come on, next man. [*He hurries along now.*] Come along now, no mailbags, needles, knives, razor blades, guns, hatchets or empty porter bottles. No? [*To the last* PRISONER.] Well, will you buy a ticket to the Police Ball?

[PRISONERS *laugh dutifully.*]

WARDER REGAN [*voice from prison wing*].　All done, sir?
PRISONER A.　Don't forget, Neighbour.
WARDER DONELLY.　Right, sir, on to you, sir.

[*Gate swings open.*]

Right, lead on, B.1.
NEIGHBOUR.　Anyway, his grave's dug and the hangman's on his way.
PRISONER A.　That doesn't mean a thing, they always dig the grave, just to put the wind up them—
WARDER DONELLY.　Silence!

[*The* PRISONERS *march, the gate clangs behind them; the tramp of their feet is heard as they mark time inside.*]

WARDER REGAN [*voice from the prison wing*].　Right, B. Wing, bang out your doors. B.1, get in off your steps and bang out your doors, into your cells and bang out your doors. Get locked up. BANG THEM DOORS! GET INSIDE AND BANG OUT THEM DOORS!

[*The last door bangs lonely on its own and then there is silence.*]

VOICE FROM BELOW [*singing*].

> The wind was rising,
> And the day declining
> As I lay pining in my prison cell
> And that old triangle
> Went jingle jangle

[*The triangle is beaten, the gate of the prison wing opens and the* CHIEF *and* WARDER DONELLY *come down the steps and approach the grave.*]

Along the banks of the Royal Canal.

CHIEF [*resplendent in silver braid*].   Who's that singing?
WARDER DONELLY.   I think it's one of the prisoners in the chokey, sir.
CHIEF.   Where?
WARDER DONELLY.   In the punishment cells, sir.
CHIEF.   That's more like it. Well, tell him to cut it out.
SONG.

> In the female prison
> There are seventy women . . .

WARDER DONELLY [*goes down to the area and leans and shouts*].   Hey,
you down there, cut it out, or I'll give you jingle jangle.

[*The song stops.* WARDER DONELLY *walks back.*]

CHIEF.   Is the quare fellow finished his tea?
WARDER DONELLY.   He is. He is just ready to come out for exercise,
now. The wings are all clear. They're locked up having their tea. He'll
be along any minute.
CHIEF.   He's coming out here?
WARDER DONELLY.   Yes, sir.
CHIEF [*exasperated*].   Do you want him to see his grave, bloody well
half dug? Run in quick and tell those bloody idiots to take him out
the side door, and exercise him over the far side of the stokehold, and
tell them to keep him well into the wall where he'll be out of sight of
the cell windows. Hurry and don't let him hear you. Let on it's something about another duty. Warders! You'd get better in Woolworths.

[*He goes to the area and shouts down.*]

Hey, you down there. You in the cell under the steps. You do be
singing there to keep yourself company? You needn't be afraid, it's
only the Chief. How long you doing down there? Seven days No. 1
and twenty-one days No. 2. God bless us and love us, you must have
done something desperate. I may be able to do something for you,
though God knows you needn't count on it, I don't own the place.
You what? With who? Ah sure, I often have a bit of a tiff with the
same man myself. We'll see what we can do for you. It's a long time
to be stuck down there, no matter who you had the tiff with.

[*Enter* WARDER DONELLY.]

CHIEF.   Well?
WARDER DONELLY.   It's all right, they've brought him out the other way.

[*They look out beyond the stage.*]

CHIEF.   Looks as if they're arguing the toss about something.
WARDER DONELLY.   Football.
CHIEF.   Begod, look at them stopping while the quare fellow hammers
his point home.

WARDER DONELLY.   I was down in the condemned cell while he was getting his tea. I asked him if it was all right. He said it was, and "Aren't the evenings getting a grand stretch?" he says.

CHIEF.   Look at him now, putting his nose to the air.

WARDER DONELLY.   He's a grand evening for his last.

CHIEF.   I took the name of the fellow giving the concert in the punishment cells. In the morning when we get this over, see he's shifted to Hell's gates over the far side. He can serenade the stokehold wall for a change if he's light enough to make out his music.

[WARDER DONELLY *copies the name and number.*]

CHIEF.   I have to attend to every mortal thing in this place. None of youse seem to want to do a hand's turn, bar draw your money—you're quick enough at that. Well, come on, let's get down to business.

[WARDER DONELLY *goes and uncovers the grave.*]

CHIEF [*looking off*].   Just a minute. It's all right. They've taken him round the back of the stokehold. [*Looking at the grave.*] Not so bad, another couple of feet out of the bottom and we're elected. Regan should be down with the working party any minute, as soon as the quare fellow's finished his exercise.

WARDER DONELLY.   There, he's away in now, sir. See him looking at the sky?

CHIEF.   You'd think he was trying to kiss it good-bye. Well, that's the last he'll see of it.

WARDER DONELLY.   No chance of a reprieve, sir?

CHIEF.   Not a chance. Healey never even mentioned fixing up a line with the Post Office. If there'd been any chance of developments he'd have asked us to put a man on all night. All he said was "The Governor will get the last word before the night's out." That means only one thing. Go ahead.

[WARDERS REGAN *and* CRIMMIN *come out with* PRISONERS A. B. C. *and* D.]

WARDER REGAN.   Working party all correct, sir. Come on, get those boards off. Bottom out a couple more feet and leave the clay at the top, nice and neat.

CHIEF.   Oh, Mr. Regan.

WARDER REGAN.   Take over, Mr. Crimmin.

CHIEF.   Mr. Regan. All I was going to say was—why don't you take yourself a bit of a rest while these fellows are at work on the grave. It's a long old pull till eight tomorrow morning.

WARDER REGAN.   Thank you, sir.

CHIEF.   Don't mention it. I'll see you before you go down to the cell. Get yourself a bit of a smoke, in the hospital. Don't forget now.

[He *and* WARDER DONELLY *go back in.*]

WARDER REGAN.   Mr. Crimmin. The Chief, a decent man, he's after giving us his kind permission to go into hospital and have a sit down and a smoke for ourselves when these fellows have the work started. He knew we'd go in anyway, so he saw the chance of being floochalach, at no expense to the management. Here [*takes out a packet of cigarettes, and takes some from it*], here's a few fags for the lads.

CRIMMIN.   I'll give them some of mine too.

WARDER REGAN.   Don't do anything of the sort. One each is enough, you can slip them a couple when they're going to be locked up, if you like, but if these fellows had two fags each, they'd not work at all but spend the time out here blowing smoke rings in the evening air like lords. I'll slip in now, you come in after me. Tell them not to have them in their mouths if the Chief or the Governor comes out. [*He goes up the steps to the hospital.*]

CRIMMIN [*calls* PRISONER C.].   Hey!

PRISONER C. [*comes to him*].   Seadh a Thomais? [4]

CRIMMIN [*gives him cigarettes and matches*].   Seo, cupla toitin. Taim fhcin is an scew eile ag dul isteach chuig an cispeadeal, noimeat. Roinn amach na toitini siud, is glacfhaidh sibh gal. Mathagann an Governor no'n Chief no an Principal, na biodh in bhur moeil agaibh iad. A' tuigeann tu?

PRISONER C.   Tuigim, a Thomais, go raibh maith agat.

CRIMMIN [*officially*].   Right, now get back to your work.

PRISONER C.   Yes, sir.

[CRIMMIN *goes up the hospital steps.*]

PRISONER C.   He gave me some cigarettes.

[PRISONER D. *has gone straight to the grave*, PRISONER B. *is near it.*]

PRISONER A.   May I never dig a grave for less! You two get on and do a bit of digging while we have a quiet burn, then we'll take over.

PRISONER C.   He said to watch out for the chief and them.

PRISONER B.   Pass down a light to your man. He says he'd enjoy it better down there, where he can't be seen! Decent of him and Regan wasn't it?

PRISONER A.   They'd have you dead from decency. That same Regan was like a savage in the bag shop today, you couldn't get a word to the fellow next to you.

---

4. PRISONER C. [*comes to him*].   Yes, Thomas? CRIMMIN [*gives him cigarettes and matches*].   Here, a couple of cigarettes. Myself and the other screw are going into the hospital for a moment. Divide these cigarettes and let you take a smoke. If the Governor or the Chief or the Principal come, let you not have them in your mouths. Do you understand? PRISONER A.   I understand, Thomas, thanks.

PRISONER C. I never saw him like that before.

PRISONER B. He's always the same at a time like this, hanging seems to get on his nerves.

PRISONER A. Why should he worry, he won't feel it.

PRISONER B. He's on the last watch. Twelve till eight.

PRISONER A. Till death do us part.

PRISONER C. The quare fellow asked for him, didn't he?

PRISONER A. They all do.

PRISONER C. He asked to have Mr. Crimmin too.

PRISONER A. It'll break that young screw up, and him only a wet day in the place.

PRISONER B. Funny the way they all ask for Regan..Perhaps they think he'll bring them good luck, him being good living.

PRISONER A. Good living! Whoever heard of a good living screw? Did you never hear of the screw, married the prostitute?

PRISONER B. No, what happened to him?

PRISONER A. He dragged her down to his own level.

PRISONER B. He told me once that if I kept off the beer I need never come back here. I asked him what about himself, and he told me he was terrible hardened to it and would I pray for him.

PRISONER C. When I was over in the Juveniles he used to talk like that to us. He said that the Blessed Virgin knew us better than the police or the judges—or ourselves even. We might think we were terrible sinners but she knew we were good boys only a bit wild . . .

PRISONER A. Bloody mad he is.

PRISONER C. And that we were doing penance here for the men who took us up, especially the judges, they being mostly rich old men with great opportunity for vice.

[PRISONER D. *appears from the grave.*]

PRISONER A. The dead arose and appeared to many.

[PRISONER A. *goes and rearranges the work which* PRISONER D. *has upset.*]

PRISONER B. What's brought you out of your fox hole?

PRISONER D. I thought it more discreet to remain in concealment while I smoked but I could not stop down there listening to talk like that, as a ratepayer, I couldn't stand for it, especially those libellous remarks about the judiciary. [*He looks accusingly at the boy.*]

PRISONER C. I was only repeating what Mr. Regan said, sir.

PRISONER D. He could be taken up for it. According to that man, there should be no such thing as law and order. We could all be murdered in our beds, the innocent prey of every ruffian that took it into his head to appropriate our goods, our lives even. Property must have security! What do you think society would come to without police

and judges and suitable punishments? Chaos! In my opinion hanging's too good for 'em.

PRISONER C.   Oh, Mr. Regan doesn't believe in capital punishment, sir.

PRISONER D.   My God, the man's an atheist! He should be dismissed
from the public service. I shall take it up with the Minister when I get
out of here. I went to school with his cousin.

PRISONER A.   Who the hell does he think he is, a bloody high court
judge?

PRISONER D.   Chaos!

PRISONER B.   He's in for embezzlement, there were two suicides and a
bye-election [5] over him.

PRISONER D.   There are still a few of us who care about the state of the
country, you know. My family's national tradition goes back to the
Land War.[6] Grandfather did four weeks for incitement to mutiny—
and we've never looked back since. One of my young nephews, as a
matter of fact, has just gone over to Sandhurst.

PRISONER B.   Isn't that where you done your four years?

PRISONER A.   No, that was Parkhurst.

PRISONER C.   [to others].   A college educated man in here, funny, isn't
it?

PRISONER D.   I shall certainly bring all my influence to bear to settle
this Regan fellow.

PRISONER C.   You must be a very important man, sir.

PRISONER D.   I am one of the Cashel Carrolls, my boy, related on my
mother's side to the Killens of Killcock.

PRISONER B.   Used to wash for our family.

PRISONER C.   Go bhfoiridh Dia 'rainn.[7]

PRISONER D.   Irish speaking?

PRISONER D.   Yes, sir.

PRISONER D.   Then it might interest you to know that I took my gold
medal in Irish.

PRISONER C.   Does that mean he speaks Irish?

PRISONER D.   Of course.

PRISONER C.   Oh sir. Ta Gaeilge go leor agamsa. O'n gcliabhain amach,
sir.[8]

PRISONER B.   That's fixed you.

PRISONER D.   Quite. Tuigim tu.[9]

PRISONER B.   The young lad's from Kerry, from an island where they
don't speak much else.

PRISONER D.   Kerry? Well of course you speak with a different dialect to
the one I was taught.

---

5. Special election held to replace an office holder.
6. Agitation in the late nineteenth century for Irish
ownership of Irish farmland.
7. God look down on us.

8. Oh sir. I have Irish galore. From the cradle up,
sir.
9. Quite. I understand you.

PRISONER B.   The young screw Crimmin's from the same place. He sneaks up to the landing sometimes when the other screws aren't watching and there they are for hours talking through the spy hole, all in Irish.

PRISONER D.   Most irregular.

PRISONER B.   There's not much harm in it.

PRISONER D.   How can there be proper discipline between warder and prisoner with that kind of familiarity?

PRISONER C.   He does only be giving me the news from home and who's gone to America or England; he's not long up here and neither am I . . . the two of us do each be as lonely as the other.

PRISONER B.   The lad here sings an old song betimes. It's very nice. It makes the night less lonely, each man alone and sad maybe in the old cell. The quare fellow heard him singing and after he was sentenced to death he sent over word he'd be listening every night around midnight for him.

PRISONER A.   You'd better make a bit effort tonight, kid, for his last concert.

PRISONER C.   Ah, God help him! Sure, you'd pity him all the same. It must be awful to die at the end of a swinging rope and a black hood over his poor face.

PRISONER A.   Begod, he's not being topped for nothing—to cut his own brother up and butcher him like a pig.

PRISONER D.   I must heartily agree with you sir, a barbarian if ever there was one.

PRISONER C.   Maybe he did those things, but God help him this minute and he knowing this night his last on earth. Waiting over there he is, to be shaken out of his sleep and rushed to the rope.

PRISONER A.   What sleep will he take? They won't have to set the alarm clock for a quarter to eight, you can bet your life on that.

PRISONER C.   May he find peace on the other side.

PRISONER A.   Or his brother waiting to have a word with him about being quartered in such an unmannerly fashion.

PRISONER C.   None of us can know for certain.

PRISONER D.   It was proved in a court of law that this man had experience as a pork butcher and put his expert knowledge to use by killing his brother with an axe and dismembering the body, the better to dispose of it.

PRISONER C.   Go bfoiridh. Dia rainn.

PRISONER A.   I wouldn't put much to the court of law part of it, but I heard about it myself from a fellow in from his part of the country. He said he had the brother strung up in an outhouse like a pig.

PRISONER D.   Actually he was bleeding him into a farmhouse vessel according to the evidence. He should be hung three or four times over.

PRISONER A.   Seeing your uncle was at school with the President's granny, perhaps he could fix it up for you.

PRISONER C.   I don't believe he is a bad man. When I was on remand he used to walk around with me at exercise every day and he was sad when I told him about my brother, who died in the Yank's army, and my father, who was buried alive at the demolition of Manchester . . . He was great company for me who knew no one, only jackeens would be making game of me, and I'm sorry for him.

PRISONER A.   Sure, it's a terrible pity about you and him. Maybe the jackeens[1] should spread out the red carpet for you and every other bog barbarian that comes into the place. [*He moves away irritably.*] Let's get a bit more off his bloody hole.

PRISONER B.   Nick. Nick.

WARDER REGAN [*entering with* CRIMMIN].   I've been watching you for the last ten minutes and damn the thing you've done except yap, yap, yap the whole time. The Chief or the Governor or any of them could have been watching you. They'd have thought it was a bloody mother's meeting. What with you and my other bald mahogany gas pipe here.

PRISONER D.   We were merely exchanging a few comments, sir.

WARDER REGAN.   That's a lie and it's not worth a lie.

PRISONER A.   All right! So we were caught talking at labour. I didn't ask to be an undertaker's assistant. Go on, bang me inside and case me in the morning! Let the Governor give me three days of No. 1.

WARDER REGAN.   Much that'd worry you.

PRISONER A.   You're dead right.

WARDER REGAN.   Don't be such a bloody big baby. We all know you're a hard case. Where did you do your lagging? On the bog?

PRISONER A.   I did not. Two laggings I done! At Parkhurst and on the Moor.

WARDER REGAN.   There's the national inferiority complex for you. Our own Irish cat-o'-nine-tails and the batons of the warders loaded with lead from Carrick mines aren't good enough for him. He has to go Dartmooring and Parkhursting it. It's a wonder you didn't go further while you were at it, to Sing Sing or Devil's Island.

PRISONER A. [*stung*].   I'm not here to be made a mock of, whether I done a lagging in England or not.

WARDER REGAN.   Who said a word about it, only yourself—doing the returned Yank in front of these other fellows? Look, the quare fellow's got to be buried in the morning, whether we like it or not, so cut the mullarkey and get back to work.

PRISONER A.   I don't let anyone make game of me!

WARDER REGAN.   Well, what are you going to do about it? Complain to

1. Irish slang for "city boys."

Holy Healey's department? He's a fine bloody imposter, isn't he? Like an old I.R.A. man with a good agency in the Sweep now. Recommend me to the respectable people! Drop it for Christ's sake, man. It's a bad night for all of us. Fine job, isn't it, for a young fellow like him, fresh from his mother's apron strings. You haven't forgotten what it's like to come from a decent home, have you, with the family rosary said every night?

PRISONER A.   I haven't any time for that kind of gab. I never saw religion do anything but back up the screws. I was in Walton last Christmas Eve, when the clergyman came to visit a young lad that had been given eighteen strokes of the cat that morning. When the kid stopped moaning long enough to hear what he had to say, he was told to think on the Lord's sufferings, then the cell door closed with a bang, leaving a smell of booze that would have tripped you up. [He takes a look at the quare fellow's side of the stage and, muttering to himself, goes back to work.]

WARDER REGAN.   You should pray for a man hardened in drink. Get back to it, all of you, and get that work a bit more advanced. Myself and Crimmin here have a long night ahead of us; we don't want to be finishing off your jobs for you.

[They get into the grave.]

PRISONER A.   I never seen a screw like that before.
PRISONER B.   Neither did anyone else.

[They work.]

CRIMMIN.   What time is it, sir?
WARDER REGAN.   Ten to seven.
CRIMMIN.   Is himself here yet?
WARDER REGAN.   Yes, he came by last night's boat. He's nervous of the 'plane, says it isn't natural. He'll be about soon. He's been having a sleep after the trip. We'll have to wait till he's measured the quare fellow for the drop, then we can go off till twelve.
CRIMMIN.   Good.
WARDER REGAN.   And for Christ's sake try to look a bit more cheerful when you come back on.
CRIMMIN.   I've never seen anyone die, Mr. Regan.
WARDER REGAN.   Of course, I'm a callous savage that's used to it.
CRIMMIN.   I didn't mean that.
WARDER REGAN.   I don't like it now any more than I did the first time.
CRIMMIN.   No sir.
WARDER REGAN.   It was a little Protestant lad, the first time; he asked if he could be walked backwards into the hanghouse so as he wouldn't see the rope.
CRIMMIN.   God forgive them.

WARDER REGAN.   May He forgive us all. The young clergyman that was
on asked if the prison chaplain could accompany him; it was his first
hanging too. I went to the Canon to ask him, a fine big man he was.
"Regan," he says, "I thought I was going to escape it this time, but
you never escape. I don't suppose neither of us ever will. Ah well,"
he says, "maybe being hung twenty times will get me out of purgatory
a minute or two sooner."

CRIMMIN.   Amen, a Thighearna Dhia.

WARDER REGAN.   The young clergyman was great; he read a bit of the
Bible to the little Protestant lad while they waited and he came in
with him, holding his hand and telling him, in their way, to lean on
God's mercy that was stronger than the power of men. I walked beside
them and guided the boy on to the trap and under the beam. The
rope was put round him and the washer under his ear and the hood
pulled over his face. And still the young clergyman called out to him,
in a grand steady voice, in through the hood: "I declare to you, my
living Christ this night . . ." and he stroked his head till he went
down. Then he fainted; the Canon and myself had to carry him out
to the Governor's office.

[*A pause. We are aware of the men working at the grave.*]

WARDER REGAN.   The quare fellow asked for you especially, Crimmin;
he wanted you because you're a young lad, not yet practised in bad-
ness. You'll be a consolation to him in the morning when he's surrounded by a crowd of bigger bloody ruffians than himself, if the truth
were but told. He's depending on you, and you're going to do your
best for him.

CRIMMIN.   Yes, Mr. Regan.

[REGAN *walks to the grave.*]

WARDER REGAN.   How's it going?

PRISONER A.   Just about done, sir.

WARDER REGAN.   All right, you can leave it.

[*They get up.*]

WARDER REGAN.   Leave your shovels; you'll be wanting them in the
morning. Go and tell the warder they've finished, Mr. Crimmin. I'll
turn them over.

[*He searches the* PRISONERS, *finds a cigarette end on* A. *and sniffs
it.*]

Coffin nail. Most appropriate. [*He goes towards exit and calls.*] You
needn't bother searching them, sir. I've turned them over.

PRISONER A. [*aside*].   He's as mad as a coot.

PRISONER C.   But charitable.

WARDER REGAN.   Right, lead on there!

PRISONER D.   This is no place for charity, on the taxpayers' money.

PRISONER A.   Take it up with your uncle when you get back into your stockbroker's trousers.

WARDER REGAN.   Silence. Right, sir, working party off.

[*As the* PRISONERS *march off, the* HANGMAN *comes slowly down the steps.*]

CRIMMIN.   Is this . . .

WARDER REGAN.   Himself.

HANGMAN.   It's Mr. Regan, isn't it? Well, as the girl said to the soldier "Here we are again."

WARDER REGAN.   Nice evening. I hope you had a good crossing.

HANGMAN.   Not bad. It's nice to get over to old Ireland you know, a nice bit of steak and a couple of pints as soon as you get off the boat. Well, you'll be wanting to knock off, won't you? I'll just pop down and have a look, then you can knock off.

WARDER REGAN.   We were just waiting for you.

HANGMAN.   This young man coming with us in the morning?

CRIMMIN.   Yes, sir.

HANGMAN.   Lend us your cap a minute, lad.

CRIMMIN.   I don't think it would fit you, sir.

HANGMAN.   We don't have to be so particular. Mr. Regan's will do. It ought to fit me by this time, and he won't catch cold the time I'll be away. [*He goes out.*]

CRIMMIN.   What does he want the cap for?

WARDER REGAN.   He gets the quare fellow's weight from the doctor so as he'll know what drop to give him, but he likes to have a look at him as well, to see what build he is, how thick his neck is, and so on. He says he can judge better with the eye. If he gave him too much one way he'd strangle him instead of breaking his neck, and too much the other way he'd pull the head clean off his shoulders.

CRIMMIN.   Go bhfoiridh Dia 'rainn.[2]

WARDER REGAN.   You should have lent him your cap. When he lifts the corner of the spy-hole all the quare fellow can see is the peak of a warder's cap. It could be you or me or anyone looking at him. Himself has no more to do with it than you or I or the people that pay us, and that's every man or woman that pays taxes or votes in elections. If they don't like it, they needn't have it.

[*The* HANGMAN *comes back.*]

HANGMAN.   Well set up lad. Twelve stone, fine pair of shoulders on him. Well, I expect you'll give us a call this evening over at the hos-

2. God look down on us.

pital. I'm in my usual apartments. This young man is very welcome, too, if he wants to join the company.

WARDER REGAN.   Right, sir.

HANGMAN.   See you later. [*He goes out.*]

WARDER REGAN.   Right, Crimmin. Twelve o'clock and look lively. The quare fellow's got enough on his plate without putting him in the blue jigs altogether. As the old Home Office memorandum says "An air of cheerful decorum is indicated, as a readiness to play such games as draughts, ludo, or snakes and ladders; a readiness to enter into conversations on sporting topics will also be appreciated."

CRIMMIN.   Yes, sir.

WARDER REGAN [*as they go*].   And, Crimmin, . . .

CRIMMIN.   Yes, sir?

WARDER REGAN.   Take off your watch.

[*They go out.*]

NEIGHBOUR [*from his cell*].   Hey, Dunlavin. Don't forget that Sunday bacon. The bet stands. They're after being at the grave. I just heard them. Dunlavin, do you hear me?

PRISONER A.   Get down on your bed, you old Anti-Christ. You sound like something in a week-end pass out of Hell.

ENGLISH PRISONER.   Hey, you bloke that's going out in the morning. Don't forget to see my chiner and get him to bail me out.

NEIGHBOUR.   Get a bucket and bail yourself out.

SONG.   The day was dying and the wind was sighing,
    As I lay crying in my prison cell,
    And the old triangle
    Went jingle jangle
    Along the banks of the Royal Canal.

Act Three

Scene One

Later the same night. Cell windows lit. A blue lamp in the courtyard. A faint tapping is heard intermittently.

As the curtain rises, two WARDERS *are seen. One is* DONELLY, *the other a fellow new to the job.*

WARDER 1.   Watch the match.

WARDER 2.   Sorry.

WARDER 1.   We're all right for a couple of minutes, the Chief'll have plenty to worry him tonight; he's not likely to be prowling about.

WARDER 2.   Hell of a job, night patrol, at any time.

WARDER 1.   We're supposed to pass each cell every half-hour tonight, but what's the use? Listen to 'em.

[*The tapping can be distinctly heard.*]

WARDER 2.   Yap, yap, yap. It's a wonder the bloody old hot-water pipes aren't worn through.

[*Tapping.*]

WARDER 1.   Damn it all, they've been yapping in association since seven o'clock.

[*Tapping.*]

WARDER 2.   Will I go round the landings and see who it is?

WARDER 1.   See who it is? Listen!

WARDER 2.   Do you think I should go?

WARDER 1.   Stay where you are and get yourself a bit of a burn. Devil a bit of use it'd be anyway. As soon as you lifted the first spy-hole, the next fellow would have heard you and passed it on to the whole landing. Mind the cigarette, keep it covered. Have you ever been in one of these before?

WARDER 2.   No.

WARDER 1.   They'll be at it from six o'clock tomorrow morning, and when it comes a quarter to eight it'll be like a running commentary in the Grand National.

[*Tapping.*]

WARDER 1 [*quietly*].   Shut your bloody row! And then the screeches and roars of them when his time comes. They say it's the last thing the fellow hears.

[*Tapping dies down.*]

WARDER 2.   Talk about something else.

[*Tapping.*]

WARDER 1.   They're quietening down a bit. You'd think they'd be in the humour for a read or a sleep wouldn't you?

WARDER 2.   It's a hell of a job.

WARDER 1.   We're in it for the three P's, boy, pay, promotion and pension, that's all that should bother civil servants like us.

WARDER 2.   You're quite right.

WARDER 1.   And without doing the sergeant major on you, I'm senior man of us two, isn't that right, now?

WARDER 2.   I know what you mean.

WARDER 1.   Well, neither bragging nor boasting—God gives us the brains and no credit to ourselves—I think I might speak to you as a senior man, if you didn't mind.

WARDER 2.   Not at all. Any tip you could give me I'd be only too grateful for it. Sure it'd only be a thick wouldn't improve his knowledge when an older man would be willing to tell him something that would be of benefit to him in his career.

WARDER 1.   Well now, would I be right in saying that you've no landing of your own?

WARDER 2.   Quite right, quite right. I'm only on here, there or any old where when you or any other senior man is wanting me.

WARDER 1.   Well, facts is facts and must be faced. We must all creep before we can walk, as the man said; but I may as well tell you straight, what I told the Principal about you.

WARDER 2.   Tell me face to face. If it's fault you found in me I'd as lief hear it from me friend as from me enemy.

WARDER 1.   It was no fault I found in you. If I couldn't do a man a good turn—I'd be sorry to do him a bad one.

WARDER 2.   Ah, sure I know that.

WARDER 1.   What I said to the Principal about you was: that you could easily handle a landing of your own. If it happened that one was left vacant. And I don't think I'm giving official information away, when I say that such a vacancy may occur in the near future. Before the month is out. Have you me?

WARDER 2.   I have you, and I'm more than grateful to you. But sure I'd expect no less from you. You're all nature.

WARDER 1.   It might happen that our Principal was going to the Bog on promotion, and it might happen that a certain senior officer would be promoted in his place.

WARDER 2.   Ah, no.

WARDER 1.   But ah, yes.

WARDER 2.   But there's no one in the prison but'd be delighted to serve under you. You've such a way with you. Even with the prisoners.

WARDER 1.   Well, I hope I can do my best by me fellow men, and that's the most any can hope to do, barring a double-dyed bloody hypocrite like a certain party we needn't mention. Well, him and me have equal service and it's only the one of us can be made Principal, and I'm damn sure they're not going to appoint a half-lunatic that goes round asking murderers to pray for him.

WARDER 2.   Certainly they're not, unless they're bloody-well half-mad themselves.

WARDER 1.   And I think they know him as well as we do.

WARDER 2.   Except the Canon, poor man; he has him well recommended.

WARDER 1.   You can leave out the "poor man" part of it. God forgive me and I renounce the sin of it, the Lord says "touch not my anointed", but the Canon is a bloody sight worse than himself, if you knew only the half of it.

WARDER 2.   Go to God.

WARDER 1.   Right, I'll tell you now. He was silenced for something before he came here and this is the *only* job he can get. Something terrible he did, though God forgive us, maybe it's not right to talk of it.

WARDER 2.   You might sing it.

WARDER 1.   I hear it was the way that he made the housekeeper take a girl into the house, the priest's house, to have a baby, an illegitimate!

WARDER 2.   And could a man like that be fit to be a priest!

WARDER 1.   He'd hardly be fit to be a prison chaplain, even. Here's the Chief or one of them coming. Get inside quick and let on you're looking for them fellows talking on the hot-water pipes, and not a word about what I said. That's between ourselves.

WARDER 2.   Ah sure I know that's under foot. Thanks anyway.

WARDER 1.   You're more than welcome. Don't be surprised if you get your landing sooner than you expected. Thirty cells all to yourself before you're fifty.

WARDER 2.   I'll have the sister's children pray for you.

[*Enter* CHIEF WARDER.]

WARDER 1.   All correct, sir.

CHIEF.   What the hell do you mean, "All correct, sir"? I've been watching you this half-hour yapping away to that other fellow.

WARDER 1.   There were men communicating on the hot-water pipes, sir, and I told him ten times if I told him once to go inside the landing and see who it was; it's my opinion, sir, the man is a bit thick.

CHIEF.   It's your opinion. Well, you're that thick yourself you ought to be a fair judge. And who the bloody hell are you to tell anyone to do anything? You're on night patrol the same as what he is.

WARDER 1.   I thought, sir, on account of the night that's in it.

CHIEF.   Why, is it Christmas? Listen here, that there is an execution in the morning is nothing to do with you. It's not your job to care, and a good job too, or you'd probably trip over the rope and fall through the bloody trap. What business have you out here, anyway?

WARDER 1.   I thought I had to patrol by the grave, sir.

CHIEF.   Afraid somebody might pinch it? True enough, this place is that full of thieves, you can leave nothing out of your hand. Get inside and resume your patrol. If you weren't one of the old hands I'd report you to the Governor. Get along with you and we'll forget about it.

WARDER 1.   Very good, sir, and thank you, sir.

[*Tapping.*]

CHIEF.   And stop that tapping on the pipes.

WARDER 1.   I will, sir, and thanks again, sir.

[FIRST WARDER *salutes, goes up the steps to the prison gates, which open. The* GOVERNOR *comes in in evening dress. The* FIRST WARDER *comes sharply to attention, salutes and goes off. The* GOVERNOR *continues down the steps and over to the* CHIEF WARDER.]

CHIEF.   All correct, sir.

GOVERNOR.   Good. We had final word about the reprieve this after-noon. But you know how these things are, Chief, hoping for last-minute developments. I must say I should have been more than sur-prised had the Minister made a recommendation. I'll go down and see him before the Canon comes in. It makes them more settled for confession when they know there is absolutely no hope. How is he?

CHIEF.   Very well, sir. Sitting by the fire and chatting to the warders. He says he might go to bed after he sees the priest.

GOVERNOR.   You'll see that there's a good breakfast for himself and the two assistants?

CHIEF.   Oh, yes, sir, he's very particular about having two rashers and eggs. Last time they were here, some hungry pig ate half his breakfast and he kicked up murder.

GOVERNOR.   See it doesn't happen this time.

CHIEF.   No indeed. There's a fellow under sentence of death next week in the Crumlin; we don't want him going up to Belfast and saying we starved him.

GOVERNOR.   Have they come back from town yet?

CHIEF [*looks at his watch*].   It's after closing time. I don't expect they'll be long now. I put Clancy on the side gate to let them in. After he took the quare fellow's measurements he went over to the place he drinks in. Some pub at the top of Grafton Street. I believe he's the life of the bar there, sir; the customers think he's an English traveller. The publican knows who he is, but then they're both in the pub business, and sure that's as tight a trade as hanging.

GOVERNOR.   I suppose his work here makes him philosophical, and they say that drink is the comfort of the philosophers.

CHIEF.   I wouldn't doubt but you'd be right there, sir. But he told me himself he only takes a drink when he's on a job. The rest of the time he's serving behind his own bar.

GOVERNOR.   Is Jenkinson with him?

CHIEF.   Yes, sir. He likes to have him with him, in case he gets a bit jarred. Once he went straight from the boat to the pubs and spent the day in them, and when he got here wasn't he after leaving the black box with his rope and his washers and his other little odds and ends behind him in a pub and forgot which one it was he left them in.

GOVERNOR.   Really.

CHIEF. You could sing it. You were in Limerick at the time, sir, but here we were, in a desperate state. An execution coming off in the morning and we without the black box that had all his tools in it. The Governor we had then, he promised a novena to St. Anthony and two insertions in the *Messenger* if they were found in time. And sure enough after squad cars were all over in the city, the box was got in a pub down the North Wall, the first one he went into. It shows you the power of prayer, sir.

GOVERNOR. Yes, I see what you mean.

CHIEF. So now he always brings Jenkinson with him. You see, Jenkinson takes nothing, begin very good living. A street preacher he is, for the Methodists or something. Himself prefers T.T.s.[1] He had an Irishman from Clare helping one time, but he sacked him over the drink. In this Circus, he said, there's only one allowed to drink and that's the Ringmaster.

GOVERNOR. We advertised for a native hangman during the Economic War. Must be fluent Irish speaker. Cailioctai de reir Meamram V. a seacht.[2] There were no suitable applicants.

CHIEF. By the way, sir, I must tell you that the warders on night patrol were out here conversing, instead of going round the landings.

GOVERNOR. Remind me to make a note of it tomorrow.

CHIEF. I will, sir, and I think I ought to tell you that I heard the principal warder make a joke about the execution.

GOVERNOR. Good God, this sort of thing is getting out of hand. I was at my School Union this evening. I had to leave in sheer embarrassment; supposedly witty remarks made to me at my own table. My eldest son was furious with me for going at all. He was at a table with a crowd from the University. They were even worse. One young pup went so far as to ask him if he thought I would oblige with a rendering of "The night before Larry was stretched". I shall certainly tell the Principal that there's at least one place in this city where an execution is taken very seriously indeed. Good night to you.

CHIEF. Good night, sir.

[*Tapping. The* CHIEF WARDER *walks up and down.* REGAN *enters.*]

Ah, Mr. Regan, the other man coming along?

WARDER REGAN. He'll be along in a minute.

CHIEF. I don't know what we'd do without you, Regan, on these jobs. Is there anything the Governor or I could do to make things easier?

WARDER REGAN. You could say a decade of the rosary.

CHIEF. I could hardly ask the Governor to do that.

WARDER REGAN. His prayers would be as good as anyone else's.

---

1. T-total, for total temperance, abstinence from alcohol.

2. Qualifications in accordance with Memorandum Seven . . .

CHIEF.   Is there anything on the practical side we could send down?

WARDER REGAN.   A bottle of malt.

CHIEF.   Do you think he'd drink it?

WARDER REGAN.   No, but I would.

CHIEF.   Regan, I'm surprised at you.

WARDER REGAN.   I was reared among people that drank at a death or prayed. Some did both. You think the law makes this man's death someway different, not like anyone else's. Your own, for instance.

CHIEF.   I wasn't found guilty of murder.

WARDER REGAN.   No, nor no one is going to jump on you in the morning and throttle the life out of you, but it's not him I'm thinking of. It's myself. And you're not going to give me that stuff about just shoving over the lever and bob's your uncle. You forget the times the fellow gets caught and has to be kicked off the edge of the trap hole. You never heard of the warders down below swinging on his legs the better to break his neck, or jumping on his back when the drop was too short.

CHIEF.   Mr. Regan, I'm surprised at you.

WARDER REGAN.   That's the second time tonight.

[*Tapping. Enter* CRIMMIN.]

CRIMMIN.   All correct, sir.

CHIEF.   Regan, I hope you'll forget those things you mentioned just now. If talk the like of that got outside the prison . . .

WARDER REGAN [*almost shouts*].   I think the whole show should be put on in Croke Park; after all, it's at the public expense and they let it go on. They should have something more for their money than a bit of paper stuck up on the gate.

CHIEF.   Good night, Regan. If I didn't know you, I'd report what you said to the Governor.

WARDER REGAN.   You will anyway.

CHIEF.   Good night, Regan.

WARDER REGAN [*to* CRIMMIN].   Crimmin, there you are. I'm going into the hospital to fix up some supper for us. An empty sack won't stand, as the man said, nor a full one won't bend.

[*He goes.* CRIMMIN *strolls. Traffic is heard in the distance, drowning the tapping. A drunken crowd are heard singing.* DONELLY *and the* NEW WARDER *appear in the darkness.*]

WARDER 1.   Is that young Mr. Crimmin?

CRIMMIN.   Yes, it's me.

WARDER 1.   You've a desperate job for a young warder this night. But I'll tell you one thing, you've a great man with you. Myself and this other man here are only after being talking about him.

WARDER 2.   That's right, so we were. A grand man and very good liv-
ing.
WARDER 1.   There's someone coming. Too fine a night to be indoors.
Good night, Mr. Crimmin.
CRIMMIN.   Good night, sir.
WARDER 1 [as they go off].   Come on, let's get a sup of tea.

[CRIMMIN waits. Tapping heard. WARDER REGAN reenters.]

WARDER REGAN.   Supper's fixed. It's a fine clear night. Do you hear the
buses? Fellows leaving their mot's home, after the pictures or coming
from dances, and a few old fellows well jarred but half sober for fear
of what herself will say when they get in the door. Only a hundred
yards up there on the bridge, and it might as well be a hundred miles
away. Here they are back from the pub.

[Voices are heard in the dark approaching. Enter HANGMAN and
JENKINSON.]

HANGMAN [sings].

"She was lovely and fair like the rose of the summer,
Though 'twas not her beauty alone that won me,
Oh, no, 'twas the truth in her eyes ever shining,
That made love Mary the Rose of Tralee."

Don't see any signs of Regan.
JENKINSON.   He's probably had to go on duty. You've left it too late.
HANGMAN.   Well, if the mountain won't come to M'ammed then the
M'ammed must go to the mountain.
WARDER REGAN [from the darkness].   As the girl said to the soldier.
HANGMAN.   As the girl said to the soldier, Oh, it's you, Regan. Will
you have a drink?
WARDER REGAN.   I'm afraid we've got to be off now.
HANGMAN.   Never mind off now. Have one with me. It's a pleasure to
see you again. We meet all too seldom. You have one with me. Adam,
give him a bottle of stout. [He sings again.]

"Oh, no, 'twas the truth in her eyes ever shining,
That made me love Mary the Rose of Tralee."

Not bad for an old 'un. Lovely song, in't it? Very religious though.
"The Poor Christian Fountain." I'm very fond of the old Irish songs;
we get a lot of Irish in our place on a Saturday night, you know.
WARDER REGAN.   Is it what they call a sporting pub?
HANGMAN.   That's just what it is, and an old sport behind the bar counter
an' all. All the Irish come in, don't they, Adam?
JENKINSON [gloomily].   Reckon they do. Perhaps because no one else
would go in it.

HANGMAN. What do you mean? It's best beer in the district. Not that you could tell the difference.

WARDER REGAN. Good health.

HANGMAN. May we never do worse. [To JENKINSON.] You're in a right cut, aren't you, making out there's nobody but Irish coming into my pub? I've never wanted for friends. Do you know why? Because I'd go a 'undred mile to do a man a good turn. I've always tried to do my duty.

JENKINSON. And so have I.

HANGMAN. Do you remember the time I got out from a sickbed to 'ang a soldier at Strangeways, when I thought you and Christmas 'adn't had enough experience?

JENKINSON. Aye, that's right enough.

HANGMAN. I'm not going to quarrel with you. Here, go and fetch your concertina and sing 'em that hymn you composed.

[JENKINSON *hesitates*.]

HANGMAN. Go on. It's a grand tune, a real credit to you. Go on, lad.

JENKINSON. Well, only for the hymn, mind. [*He goes off to fetch it.*]

WARDER REGAN. Sure, that's right.

HANGMAN. 'E's a good lad is our Adam, but 'e's down in the dumps at the moment. 'Im and Christmas, they used to sing on street corners with the Band of Holy Joy, every Saturday night, concertina and all. But some of the lads found out who they were and started putting bits of rope in collection boxes; it's put them off outdoor testimony. But this 'ymn's very moving about hanging and mercy and so forth. Brings tears to your eyes to 'ear Adam and Christmas singing it.

[JENKINSON *returns*.]

JENKINSON. Right?

HANGMAN. Right!

JENKINSON [*sings*].

> My brother, sit and think.
> While yet some time is left to thee
> Kneel to thy God who from thee does not shrink
> And lay thy sins on Him who died for thee.

HANGMAN. Take a fourteen-stone man as a basis and giving him a drop of eight foot . . .

JENKINSON.

> Men shrink from thee but not I,
> Come close to me I love my erring sheep.
> My blood can cleanse thy sins of blackest dye,
> I understand if thou canst only weep.

HANGMAN.   Every half-stone lighter would require a two-inch longer drop, so for weight thirteen and a half stone—drop eight feet two inches, and for weight thirteen stone—drop eight feet four inches.

JENKINSON.

> Though thou hast grieved me sore,
> My arms of mercy still are open wide,
> I still hold open Heaven's shining door
> Come then, take refuge in my wounded side.

HANGMAN.   Now he's only twelve stone so he should have eight foot eight, but he's got a thick neck on him so I'd better give him another couple of inches. Yes, eight foot ten.

JENKINSON.

> Come now, the time is short.
> Longing to pardon and bless I wait.
> Look up to me, my sheep so dearly bought
> And say, forgive me, ere it is too late.

HANGMAN.   Divide 412 by the weight of the body in stones, multiply by two gives the length of the drop in inches. [*He looks up and seems sobered.*] 'E's an R.C., I suppose, Mr. Regan? [*Puts book in his pocket.*]

WARDER REGAN.   That's right.

HANGMAN.   That's all, then. Good night.

JENKINSON.   Good night.

WARDER REGAN.   Good night.

[*The* HANGMAN *and* JENKINSON *go off.*]

Thanks for the hymn. Great night for stars. If there's life on any of them, I wonder do the same things happen up there? Maybe some warders on a planet are walking across a prison yard this minute and some fellow up there waiting on the rope in the morning, and looking out through the bars, for a last look at our earth and the moon for the last time. Though I never saw them to bother much about things like that. It's nearly always letters to their wives or mothers, and then we don't send them—only throw them into the grave after them. What'd be the sense of broadcasting such distressful rubbish?

PRISONER C [*sings from his cell window*].   Is e fath mo bhuartha na bhfhaghaim cead chuarta. [3]

WARDER REGAN.   Regular choir practice going on round here tonight.

CRIMMIN.   He's singing for . . . for . . .

WARDER REGAN.   For the quare fellow.

CRIMMIN.   Yes. Why did the Englishman ask if he was a Catholic?

---

3. It is the cause of my sorrow that I have not permission to visit.

WARDER REGAN.   So as they'd know to have the hood slit to anoint him on the rope, and so as the fellows below would know to take off his boots and socks for the holy oil on his feet when he goes down.

PRISONER C [*sings*].   Ni'l gaoth adthuaidh ann. ni'l sneachta cruaidh ann . . .[4]

WARDER REGAN.   We'd better be getting in. The other screws will be hopping mad to get out; they've been there since four o'clock today.

PRISONER C [*sings*].   Mo mhuirnin bhan . . .[5]

[*His song dies away and the empty stage is gradually lightened for*]

Scene Two

The prison yard. It is morning.

WARDER 1.   How's the time?

WARDER 2.   Seven minutes.

WARDER 1.   As soon as it goes five to eight they'll start. You'd think they were working with stop watches. I wish I was at home having my breakfast. How's the time?

WARDER 2.   Just past six minutes.

MICKSER'S VOICE.   Bail o dhis orribh go leir a chairdre.

WARDER 1.   I knew it. That's that bloody Mickser. I'll fix him this time.

MICKSER'S VOICE.   And we take you to the bottom of D. Wing.

WARDER 1.   You bastard, I'll give you D. Wing.

MICKSER'S VOICE.   We're ready for the start, and in good time, and who do I see lined up for the off but the High Sheriff of this ancient city of ours, famous in song and story as the place where the pig ate the whitewash brushes and—[*The* WARDERS *remove their caps.*] We're off, in this order: the Governor, the Chief, two screws Regan and Crimmin, the quare fellow between them, two more screws and three runners from across the Channel, getting well in front, now the Canon. He's making a big effort for the last two furlongs. He's got the white pudding bag on his head, just a short distance to go. He's in. [*A clock begins to chime the hour. Each quarter sounds louder.*] His feet to the chalk line. He'll be pinioned, his feet together. The bag will be pulled down over his face. The screws come off the trap and steady him. Himself goes to the lever and . . .

[*The hour strikes. The* WARDERS *cross themselves and put on their caps. From the* PRISONERS *comes a ferocious howling.*]

---

4. There is no north wind there, there is no hard   5. My white darling mavourneen . . .
snow there . . .

PRISONERS.   One off, one away, one off, one away.
WARDER 1.   Shut up there.
WARDER 2.   Shut up, shut up.
WARDER 1.   I know your windows, I'll get you. Shut up.

[*The noise dies down and at last ceases altogether.*]

Now we'll go in and get that Mickser. [*Grimly.*] *I'll* soften his cough.
Come on . . .

[WARDER REGAN *comes out.*]

WARDER REGAN.   Give us a hand with this fellow.
WARDER 1.   We're going after that Mickser.
WARDER REGAN.   Never mind that now, give us a hand. He fainted
when the trap was sprung.
WARDER 1.   These young screws, not worth a light.

[*They carry* CRIMMIN *across the yard.*]

NEIGHBOUR'S VOICE.   Dunlavin, that's a Sunday bacon you owe me.
Your man was topped, wasn't he?
PRISONER A'S VOICE.   You won't be long after him.
DUNLAVIN'S VOICE.   Don't mind him, Neighbour.
NEIGHBOUR'S VOICE.   Don't you forget that bacon, Dunlavin.
DUNLAVIN'S VOICE.   I forgot to tell you, Neighbour.
NEIGHBOUR'S VOICE.   What did you forget to tell me?
ENGLISH VOICE.   Where's the bloke what's going out this morning?
NEIGHBOUR'S VOICE.   He's up in Nelly's room behind the clock. What
about that bacon, Dunlavin?
ENGLISH VOICE.   You bloke that's going out this morning, remember to
see my chiner and tell him to 'ave me bailed out.
NEIGHBOUR'S VOICE.   Get a bucket and bail yourself out. What about
me bacon, Dunlavin?
ENGLISH VOICE.   Sod you and your bleeding bacon.
DUNLAVIN'S VOICE.   Shut up a minute about your bail, till I tell Neigh-
bour about his bet.
NEIGHBOUR'S VOICE.   You lost it, that's all I know.
DUNLAVIN'S VOICE.   Yes, but the doctor told me that me stomach was
out of order; he's put me on a milk diet.
CHIEF [*comes through prison gates and looks up*].   Get down from those
windows. Get down at once.

[*He beckons inside and* PRISONERS A., B., C., *and* D. *file past him
and go down on the steps.* PRISONER B. *is carrying a cold hammer
and chisel.*]

Hey, you there in front, have you the cold chisel and hammer?
PRISONER B.   Yes, sir.

CHIEF.   You other three, the shovels are where you left them; get to work there and clear the top and have it ready for filling in.

[*They go on to the canvas, take up the shovels from behind and begin work.* PRISONER B. *stands on the foot of the steps with his cold chisel while the* CHIEF *studies his paper to give final instructions.*]

CHIEF.   Yes, that's it. You're to carve E.777. Got that?
PRISONER B.   Yes, sir. E.777.
CHIEF.   That's it. It should be E.779 according to the book, but a "7" is easier for you to do than a "9". Right, the stone in the wall that's nearest to the spot. Go ahead now. [*Raising his voice.*] There's the usual two bottles of stout a man, but only if you work fast.
WARDER 1.   I know the worst fellow was making this noise, sir. It was Mickser, sir. I'm going in to case him now. I'll take an hour's overtime to do it, sir.
CHIEF.   You're a bit late. He was going out this morning and had his civilian clothing on in the cell. We were only waiting for this to be over to let him out.
WARDER 1.   But . . . Sir, he was the whole cause.
CHIEF.   Well, what do you want me to do, run down the Circular Road after him? He went out on remission. We could have stopped him. But you were too bloody slow for that.
WARDER 1.   I was helping to carry . . .
CHIEF.   You were helping to carry . . . Warders! I'd get better in Woolworths.
WARDER 2.   To think of that dirty savage getting away like that. Shouting and a man going to his God.
WARDER 1.   Never mind that part of it. He gave me lip in the woodyard in '42 and I couldn't do anything because he was only on remand. I've been waiting years to get that fellow.
WARDER 2.   Ah, well, you've one consolation. He'll be back.

[*At the grave* PRISONER A. *is the only one visible over the canvas.*]

PRISONER B.   Would you say that this was the stone in the wall nearest to it?
PRISONER A.   It'll do well enough. It's only for the records.
They're not likely to be digging him up to canonize him.
PRISONER B.   Fair enough. E.777.

[REGAN *drops the letters into the grave, and goes*].

PRISONER A.   Give us them bloody letters. They're worth money to one of the Sunday papers.
PRISONER B.   So I understood you to say yesterday.
PRISONER A.   Well, give us them.

PRISONER D. They're not exclusively your property any more than anyone else's.

PRISONER B. There's no need to have a battle over them. Divide them.
Anyone that likes can have my share and I suppose the same goes for
the kid.

PRISONER D. Yes, we can act like businessmen. There are three. One
each and toss for the third. I'm a businessman.

PRISONER A. Fair enough. Amn't I a businessman myself? For what's
a crook, only a businessman without a shop.

PRISONER D. What side are you on? The blank side or the side with the
address?

VOICE OF PRISONER BELOW [*singing*].

> In the female prison
> There are seventy women
> I wish it was with them that I did dwell,
> Then that old triangle
> Could jingle jangle
> Along the banks of the Royal Canal.

SAMUEL BECKETT

Krapp's
Last
Tape †

A *late evening in the future.*

KRAPP's *den.*

Front centre a small table, the two drawers of which open towards audience.

Sitting at the table, facing front, i.e. across from the drawers, a wearish old man:
KRAPP.

Rusty black narrow trousers too short for him. Rusty black sleeveless waistcoat, four capacious pockets. Heavy silver watch and chain. Grimy white shirt open at neck, no collar. Surprising pair of dirty white boots, size ten at least, very narrow and pointed.

White face. Purple nose. Disordered grey hair. Unshaven.

Very near-sighted (but unspectacled). Hard of hearing.
Cracked voice. Distinctive intonation.

Laborious walk.

On the table a tape-recorder with microphone and a number of cardboard boxes containing reels of recorded tapes.

† Reprinted by permission of Grove Press, a division of Wheatland Corporation. Copyright © 1958 by Grove Press, Inc. Also reprinted by permission of Faber and Faber Ltd.

Table and immediately adjacent area in strong white light. Rest of stage in darkness.

KRAPP *remains a moment motionless, heaves a great sigh, looks at his watch, fumbles in his pockets, takes out an envelope, puts it back, fumbles, takes out a small bunch of keys, raises it to his eyes, chooses a key, gets up and moves to front of table. He stoops, unlocks first drawer, peers into it, feels about inside it, takes out a reel of tape, peers at it, puts it back, locks drawer, unlocks second drawer, peers into it, feels about inside it, takes out a large banana, peers at it, locks drawer, puts keys back in his pocket. He turns, advances to edge of stage, halts, strokes banana, peels it, drops skin at his feet, puts end of banana in his mouth and remains motionless, staring vacuously before him. Finally he bites off the end, turns aside and begins pacing to and fro at edge of stage, in the light, i.e. not more than four or five paces either way, meditatively eating banana. He treads on skin, slips, nearly falls, recovers himself, stoops and peers at skin and finally pushes it, still stooping, with his foot over the edge of stage into pit. He resumes his pacing, finishes banana, returns to table, sits down, remains a moment motionless, heaves a great sigh, takes keys from his pockets, raises them to his eyes, chooses key, gets up and moves to front of table, unlocks second drawer, takes out a second large banana, peers at it, locks drawer, puts back keys in his pocket, turns, advances to edge of stage, halts, strokes banana, peels it, tosses skin into pit, puts end of banana in his mouth and remains motionless, staring vacuously before him. Finally he has an idea, puts banana in his waistcoat pocket, the end emerging, and goes with all the speed he can muster backstage into darkness. Ten seconds. Loud pop of cork. Fifteen seconds. He comes back into light carrying an old ledger and sits down at table. He lays ledger on table, wipes his mouth, wipes his hands on the front of his waistcoat, brings them smartly together and rubs them.*

KRAPP [*briskly*]. Ah! [*He bends over ledger, turns the pages, finds the entry he wants, reads.*] Box . . . thrree . . . spool . . . five. [*He raises his head and stares front. With relish.*] Spool! [*Pause.*] Spooool! [*Happy smile. Pause. He bends over table, starts peering and poking at the boxes.*] Box . . . thrree . . . thrree . . . four . . . two . . . [*with surprise*] nine! good God! . . . seven . . . ah! the little rascal! [*He takes up box, peers at it.*] Box thrree. [*He lays it on table, opens it and peers at spools inside.*] Spool . . . [*he peers at ledger*] . . . five . . . [*he peers at spools*] . . . five . . . five . . . ah! the little scoundrel! [*He takes out a spool, peers at it.*] Spool five. [*He lays it on table, closes box three, puts it back with the others, takes up the spool.*] Box thrree, spool five. [*He bends over the machine, looks up. With relish.*] Spooool! [*Happy smile. He bends, loads spool on machine, rubs his hands.*] Ah! [*He peers at ledger, reads entry at foot of page.*] Mother at rest at last . . .

Hm . . . The black ball . . . [*He raises his head, stares blankly front.*
Puzzled.] Black ball? . . . [*He peers again at ledger, reads.*] The dark
nurse . . . [*He raises his head, broods, peers again at ledger, reads.*]
Sight improvement in bowel condition . . . Hm . . . Memorable . . .
what? [*He peers closer.*] Equinox, memorable equinox. [*He raises his
head, stares blankly front. Puzzled.*] Memorable equinox? . . . [*Pause.
He shrugs his shoulders, peers again at ledger, reads.*] Farewell to—[*he
turns the page*]—love.

[*He raises his head, broods, bends over machine, switches on and
assumes listening posture, i.e. leaning forward, elbows on table,
hand cupping ear towards machine, face front.*]

TAPE [*strong voice, rather pompous, clearly* KRAPP'*s at a much earlier
time*].   Thirty-nine today, sound as a—[*settling himself more comfortably he knocks one of the boxes off the table, curses, switches off,
sweeps boxes and ledger violently to the ground, winds tape back to
beginning, switches on, resumes posture*]. Thirty-nine today, sound as
a bell, apart from my old weakness, and intellectually I have now
every reason to suspect at the . . . [*hesitates*] . . . crest of the wave—
or thereabouts. Celebrated the awful occasion, as in recent years, quietly at the Winehouse. Not a soul. Sat before the fire with closed eyes,
separating the grain from the husks. Jotted down a few notes, on the
back of an envelope. Good to be back in my den, in my old rags.
Have just eaten I regret to say three bananas and only with difficulty
refrained from a fourth. Fatal things for a man with my condition.
[*Vehemently.*] Cut 'em out! [*Pause.*] The new light above my table is
a great improvement. With all this darkness round me I feel less alone.
[*Pause.*] In a way. [*Pause.*] I love to get up and move about in it, then
back here to . . . [*hesitates*] . . . me. [*Pause.*] Krapp.

[*Pause.*]

The grain, now what I wonder do I mean by that, I mean . . . [*hesitates*] . . . I suppose I mean those things worth having when all the
dust has—when all *my* dust has settled. I close my eyes and try and
imagine them.

[*Pause.* KRAPP *closes his eyes briefly.*]

Extraordinary silence this evening, I strain my ears and do not hear a
sound. Old Miss McGlome always sings at this hour. But not tonight.
Songs of her girlhood, she says. Hard to think of her as a girl. Won-
derful woman though. Connaught, I fancy. [*Pause.*] Shall I sing when
I am her age, if I ever am? No. [*Pause.*] Did I sing as a boy? No.
[*Pause.*] Did I ever sing? No.

[*Pause.*]

Just been listening to an old year, passages at random. I did not check in the book, but it must be at least ten or twelve years ago. At that time I was still living on and off with Bianca in Kedar Street. Well out of that, Jesus yes! Hopeless business. [*Pause.*] Not much about her, apart from a tribute to her eyes. Very warm. I suddenly saw them again. [*Pause.*] Incomparable! [*Pause.*] Ah well . . . [*Pause.*] These old P.M.s[1] are gruesome, but I often find them—[KRAPP *switches off, broods, switches on*]—a help before embarking on a new . . . [*hesitates*] . . . retrospect. Hard to believe I was ever that young whelp. The voice! Jesus! And the aspirations! [*Brief laugh in which* KRAPP *joins.*] And the resolutions! [*Brief laugh in which* KRAPP *joins.*] To drink less, in particular. [*Brief laugh of* KRAPP *alone.*] Statistics. Seventeen hundred hours, out of the preceding eight thousand odd, consumed on licensed premises alone. More than 20%, say 40% of his waking life. [*Pause.*] Plans for a less . . . [*hesitates*] . . . engrossing sexual life. Last illness of his father. Flagging pursuit of happiness. Unattainable laxation. Sneers at what he calls his youth and thanks to God that it's over. [*Pause.*] False ring there. [*Pause.*] Shadows of the opus . . . magnum. Closing with a—[*brief laugh*]—yelp to Providence. [*Prolonged laugh in which* KRAPP *joins.*] What remains of all that misery? A girl in a shabby green coat, on a railway-station platform? No?

[*Pause.*]

When I look—

[KRAPP *switches off, broods, looks at his watch, gets up, goes backstage into darkness. Ten seconds. Pop of cork. Ten seconds. Second cork. Ten seconds. Third cork. Ten seconds. Brief burst of quavering song.*]

KRAPP [*sings*].   Now the day is over,
                    Night is drawing nigh-igh,
                    Shadows—[2]

[*Fit of coughing. He comes back into light, sits down, wipes his mouth, switches on, resumes his listening posture.*]

TAPE.   —back on the year that is gone, with what I hope is perhaps a glint of the old eye to come, there is of course the house on the canal where mother lay a-dying, in the late autumn, after her long viduity [KRAPP *gives a start*], and the—[KRAPP *switches off, winds back tape a little, bends his ear closer to machine, switches on*]—a-dying, in the late autumn, after her long viduity, and the—

1. Postmortems.
2. "Now the Day is Over," a hymn; the first verse continues: "Shadows of the evening / Steal across the sky."

[KRAPP *switches off, raises his head, stares blankly before him. His lips move in the syllables of "viduity." No sound. He gets up, goes backstage into darkness, comes back with an enormous dictionary, lays it on table, sits down and looks up the word.*]

KRAPP [*reading from dictionary*]. State—or condition of being—or remaining—a widow—or widower. [*Looks up. Puzzled.*] Being—or remaining? . . . [*Pause. He peers again at dictionary. Reading.*] "Deep weeds of viduity" . . . Also of an animal, especially a bird . . . the vidua or weaver-bird . . . Black plumage of male . . . [*He looks up. With relish.*] The vidua-bird!

[*Pause. He closes dictionary, switches on, resumes listening posture.*]

TAPE. —bench by the weir from where I could see her window. There I sat, in the biting wind, wishing she were gone. [*Pause.*] Hardly a soul, just a few regulars, nursemaids, infants, old men, dogs. I got to know them quite well—on by appearance of course I mean! One dark young beauty I recollect particularly, all white and starch, incomparable bosom, with a big black hooded perambulator, most funereal thing. Whenever I looked in her direction she had her eyes on me. And yet when I was bold enough to speak to her—not having been introduced—she threatened to call a policeman. As if I had designs on her virtue! [*Laugh. Pause.*] The face she had! The eyes! Like . . . [*hesitates*] . . . chrysolite! [*Pause.*] Ah well . . . [*Pause.*] I was there when—[KRAPP *switches off, broods, switches on again*]—the blind went down, one of those dirty brown roller affairs, throwing a ball for a little white dog, as chance would have it. I happened to look up and there it was. All over and done with, at last. I sat on for a few moments with the ball in my hand and the dog yelping and pawing at me. [*Pause.*] Moments. Her moments, my moments. [*Pause.*] The dog's moments. [*Pause.*] In the end I held it out to him and he took it in his mouth, gently, gently. A small, old, black, hard, solid rubber ball. [*Pause.*] I shall feel it, in my hand, until my dying day. [*Pause.*] I might have kept it. [*Pause.*] But I gave it to the dog.

[*Pause.*]

Ah well . . .

[*Pause.*]

Spiritually a year of profound gloom and indigence until that memorable night in March, at the end of the jetty, in the howling wind, never to be forgotten, when suddenly I saw the whole thing. The vision, at last. This I fancy is what I have chiefly to record this evening, against the day when my work will be done and perhaps no place left in my memory, warm or cold, for the miracle that . . .

[*hesitates*] . . . for the fire that set it alight. What I suddenly saw then
was this, that the belief I had been going on all my life, namely—
[KRAPP *switches off impatiently, winds tape forward, switches on again*]—
great granite rocks the foam flying up in the light of the lighthouse
and the wind-gauge spinning like a propellor, clear to me at last that
the dark I have always struggled to keep under is in reality my most—
[KRAPP *curses, switches off, winds tape forward, switches on again*]—
unshatterable association until my dissolution of storm and night with
the light of the understanding and the fire—[KRAPP *curses louder,
switches off, winds tape forward, switches on again*]—my face in her
breasts and my hand on her. We lay there without moving. But under
us all moved, and moved us, gently, up and down, and from side to
side.

[*Pause.*]

Past midnight. Never knew such silence. The earth might be uninhabited.

[*Pause.*]

Here I end—

[KRAPP *switches off, winds tape back, switches on again.*]

—upper lake, with the punt, bathed off the bank, then pushed out
into the stream and drifted. She lay stretched out on the floorboards
with her hands under her head and her eyes closed. Sun blazing down,
bit of a breeze, water nice and lively. I noticed a scratch on her thigh
and asked her how she came by it. Picking gooseberries, she said. I
said again I thought it was hopeless and no good going on, and she
agreed, without opening her eyes. [*Pause.*] I asked her to look at me
and after a few moments—[*Pause.*]—after a few moments she did,
but the eyes just slits, because of the glare. I bent over her to get them
in the shadow and they opened. [*Pause. Low.*] Let me in. [*Pause.*]
We drifted in among the flags and stuck. The way they went down,
sighing, before the stem! [*Pause.*] I lay down across her with my face
in her breasts and my hand on her. We lay there without moving.
But under us all moved, and moved us, gently, up and down, and
from side to side.

[*Pause.*]

Past midnight. Never knew—

[KRAPP *switches off, broods. Finally he fumbles in his pockets,
encounters the banana, takes it out, peers at it, puts it back,
fumbles, brings out the envelope, fumbles, puts back envelope,
looks at his watch, gets up and goes backstage into darkness. Ten*

*seconds. Sound of bottle against glass, then brief siphon. Ten
seconds. Bottle against glass alone. Ten seconds. He comes back
a little unsteadily into light, goes to front of table, takes out
keys, raises them to his eyes, chooses key, unlocks first drawer,
peers into it, feels about inside, takes out reel, peers at it, locks
drawer, puts keys back in his pocket, goes and sits down, takes
reel off machine, lays it on dictionary, loads virgin reel on machine,
takes envelope from his pocket, consults back of it, lays it on
table, switches on, clears his throat and begins to record.]*

KRAPP.   Just been listening to that stupid bastard I took myself for thirty
years ago, hard to believe I was ever as bad as that. Thank God that's
all done with anyway. [*Pause.*] The eyes she had! [*Broods, realizes he
is recording silence, switches off, broods. Finally.*] Everything there,
everything, all the—[*Realizes this is not being recorded, switches on.*]
Everything there, everything on this old muckball, all the light and
dark and famine and feasting of . . . [*hesitates*] . . . the ages! [*In a
shout.*] Yes! [*Pause.*] Let that go! Jesus! Take his mind off his home-
work! Jesus! [*Pause. Weary.*] Ah well, maybe he was right. [*Pause.*]
Maybe he was right. [*Broods. Realizes. Switches off. Consults envelope.*] Pah! [*Crumples it and throws it away. Broods. Switches on.*]
Nothing to say, not a squeak. What's a year now? The sour cud and
the iron stool. [*Pause.*] Revelled in the word spool. [*With relish.*]
Spooool! Happiest moment of the past half million. [*Pause.*] Seventeen copies sold, of which eleven at trade price to free circulating
libraries beyond the seas. Getting known. [*Pause.*] One pound six and
something, eight I have little doubt. [*Pause.*] Crawled out once or
twice, before the summer was cold. Sat shivering in the park, drowned
in dreams and burning to be gone. Not a soul. [*Pause.*] Last fancies.
[*Vehemently.*] Keep 'em under! [*Pause.*] Scalded the eyes out of me
reading *Effie* again, a page a day, with tears again. Effie[3] . . . [*Pause.*]
Could have been happy with her, up there on the Baltic, and the
pines, and the dunes. [*Pause.*] Could I? [*Pause.*] And she? [*Pause.*]
Pah! [*Pause.*] Fanny came in a couple of times. Bony old ghost of a
whore. Couldn't do much, but I suppose better than a kick in the
crutch. The last time wasn't so bad. How do you manage it, she said,
at your age? I told her I'd been saving up for her all my life. [*Pause.*]
Went to Vespers once, like when I was in short trousers. [*Pause. Sings.*]

> Now the day is over,
> Night is drawing nigh-igh,
> Shadows—[*coughing, then almost
>   inaudible*]—of the evening
> Steal across the sky.

3. *Effi Briest* (1895), by German novelist Theodor Fontane (1819–98).

[*Gasping.*] Went to sleep and fell off the pew. [*Pause.*] Sometimes wondered in the night if a last effort mightn't—[*Pause.*] Ah finish your booze now and get to your bed. Go on with this drivel in the morning. Or leave it at that. [*Pause.*] Leave it at that. [*Pause.*] Lie propped up in the dark—and wander. Be again in the dingle on a Christmas Eve, gathering holly, the red-berried. [*Pause.*] Be again on Croghan[4] on a Sunday morning, in the haze, with the bitch, stop and listen to the bells. [*Pause.*] And so on. [*Pause.*] Be again, be again. [*Pause.*] All that old misery. [*Pause.*] Once wasn't enough for you. [*Pause.*] Lie down across her.

> [*Long pause. He suddenly bends over machine, switches off, wrenches off tape, throws it away, puts on the other, winds it forward to the passage he wants, switches on, listens staring front.*]

TAPE.   —gooseberries, she said. I said again I thought it was hopeless and no good going on, and she agreed, without opening her eyes. [*Pause.*] I asked her to look at me and after a few moments—[*pause*]—after a few moments she did, but the eyes just slits, because of the glare. I bent over her to get them in the shadow and they opened. [*Pause. Low.*] Let me in. [*Pause.*] We drifted in among the flags and stuck. The way they went down, sighing, before the stem! [*Pause.*] I lay down across her with my face in her breasts and my hand on her. We lay there without moving. But under us all moved, and moved us, gently, up and down, and from side to side.

> [*Pause.* KRAPP's *lips move. No sound.*]

Past midnight. Never knew such silence. The earth might be uninhabited.

> [*Pause.*]

Here I end this reel. Box—[*pause*]—three, spool—[*pause*]—five. [*Pause.*] Perhaps my best years are gone. When there was a chance of happiness. But I wouldn't want them back. Not with the fire in me now. No, I wouldn't want them back.

> [KRAPP *motionless staring before him. The tape runs on in silence.*]

4. Mountain south of Dublin.

BRIAN FRIEL

Translations †

Persons in the Play

MANUS
SARAH
JIMMY JACK
MAIRE
DOALTY
BRIDGET
HUGH
OWEN
CAPTAIN LANCEY
LIEUTENANT HOLLAND

The action takes place in a hedge-school in the townland of Baile Beag/
Ballybeg, an Irish-speaking community in County Donegal.

ACT ONE An afternoon in late August 1833.
ACT TWO A few days later.
ACT THREE The evening of the following day.
One-interval—between the two scenes in Act Two.

Act One

*The hedge-school is held in a disused barn or hay-shed or byre. Along the
back wall are the remains of five or six stalls—wooden posts and chains—
where cows were once milked and bedded. A double door left, large enough
to allow a cart to enter. A window right. A wooden stairway without a
banister leads to the upstairs living-quarters (off) of the schoolmaster and
his son. Around the room are broken and forgotten implements: a cart-
wheel, some lobster-pots, farming tools, a battle of hay, a churn, etc.*

† Reprinted by permission of Faber and Faber Ltd. and by permission of the Catholic University Press of
America.

*There are also the stools and bench-seats which the pupils use and a table
and chair for the master. At the door a pail of water and a soiled towel.
The room is comfortless and dusty and functional—there is no trace of a
woman's hand.*

When the play opens, MANUS *is teaching* SARAH *to speak. He kneels
beside her. She is sitting on a low stool, her head down, very tense, clutching a slate on her knees. He is coaxing her gently and firmly and—as
with everything he does—with a kind of zeal.*

MANUS *is in his late twenties/early thirties; the master's older son. He
is pale-faced, lightly built, intense, and works as an unpaid assistant—
a monitor—to his father. His clothes are shabby; and when he moves we
see that he is lame.*

SARAH's *speech is so bad that all her life she has been considered locally
to be dumb and she has accepted this: when she wishes to communicate,
she grunts and makes unintelligible nasal sounds. She has a waiflike
appearance and could be any age from seventeen to thirty-five.*

JIMMY JACK CASSIE—*known as the Infant Prodigy—sits by himself,
contentedly reading Homer in Greek and smiling to himself. He is a
bachelor in his sixties, lives alone, and comes to these evening classes
partly for the company and partly for the intellectual stimulation. He is
fluent in Latin and Greek but is in no way pedantic—to him it is perfectly normal to speak these tongues. He never washes. His clothes—
heavy top coat, hat, mittens, which he wears now—are filthy and he lives
in them summer and winter, day and night. He now reads in a quiet
voice and smiles in profound satisfaction. For* JIMMY *the world of the gods
and the ancient myths is as real and as immediate as everyday life in the
townland of Baile Beag.*

MANUS *holds* SARAH's *hands in his and he articulates slowly and distinctly into her face.*

MANUS.   We're doing very well. And we're going to try it once more—
just once more. Now—relax and breathe in . . . deep . . . and out
. . . in . . . and out . . .

[SARAH *shakes her head vigorously and stubbornly.*]

MANUS.   Come on, Sarah. This is our secret.

[*Again vigorous and stubborn shaking of* SARAH's *head.*]

MANUS.   Nobody's listening. Nobody hears you.
JIMMY.   'Ton d'emeibet epeita thea glaukopis Athene . . .'[1]
MANUS.   Get your tongue and your lips working. 'My name—' Come
on. One more try. 'My name is—' Good girl.

---

1. But the grey-eyed goddess Athene then replied to him (Homer, *Odyssey* 13.420).

SARAH. My . . .
MANUS. Great. 'My name—'
SARAH. My . . . my . . .
MANUS. Raise your head. Shout it out. Nobody's listening.
JIMMY. '. . . alla hekelos estai en Atreidao domois . . .'[2]
MANUS. Jimmy, please! Once more—just once more—'My name—'
Good girl. Come on now. Head up. Mouth open.
SARAH. My . . .
MANUS. Good.
SARAH. My . . .
MANUS. Great.
SARAH. My name . . .
MANUS. Yes?
SARAH. My name is . . .
MANUS. Yes?

[SARAH *pauses. Then in a rush.*]

SARAH. My name is Sarah.
MANUS. Marvellous! Bloody marvellous!

[MANUS *hugs* SARAH. *She smiles in shy, embarrassed pleasure.*]

Did you hear that, Jimmy?—'My name is Sarah'—clear as a bell.
[*To* SARAH] The Infant Prodigy doesn't know what we're at.

[SARAH *laughs at this.* MANUS *hugs her again and stands up.*]

Now we're really started! Nothing'll stop us now! Nothing in the wide
world!
[JIMMY, *chuckling at his text, comes over to them.*]
JIMMY. Listen to this, Manus.
MANUS. Soon you'll be telling me all the secrets that have been in that
head of yours all these years. Certainly, James—what is it? [*To*
SARAH.] Maybe you'd set out the stools? [MANUS *runs up the stairs.*]
JIMMY. Wait till you hear this, Manus.
MANUS. Go ahead. I'll be straight down.
JIMMY. 'Hos ara min phamene rabdo epemassat Athene—' 'After Ath-
ene had said this, she touched Ulysses with her wand. She withered
the fair skin of his supple limbs and destroyed the flaxen hair from off
his head and about his limbs she put the skin of an old man . . .'!
The divil! The divil!

[MANUS *has emerged again with a bowl of milk and a piece of
bread.*]

JIMMY. And wait till you hear! She's not finished with him yet!

2. . . . but he sits at ease in the halls of the Sons of Athens . . . (Homer, *Odyssey* 13.423–4).

[As MANUS *descends the stairs he toasts* SARAH *with his bowl.*]

JIMMY. '*Knuzosen de oi osse*—' 'She dimmed his two eyes that were so beautiful and clothed him in a vile ragged cloak begrimed with filthy smoke . . .'! D'you see! Smoke! Smoke! D'you see! Sure look at what the same turf-smoke has done to myself! [*He rapidly removes his hat to display his bald head.*] Would you call that flaxen hair?

MANUS. Of course I would.

JIMMY. 'And about him she cast the great skin of a filthy hind, stripped of the hair, and into his hand she thrust a staff and a wallet'! Ha-ha-ha! Athene did that to Ulysses! Made him into a tramp! Isn't she the tight one?

MANUS. You couldn't watch her, Jimmy.

JIMMY. You know what they call her?

MANUS. '*Glaukopis Athene.*'

JIMMY. That's it! The flashing-eyed Athene! By God, Manus, sir, if you had a woman like that about the house, it's not stripping a turf-bank you'd be thinking about—eh?

MANUS. She was a goddess, Jimmy.

JIMMY. Better still. Sure isn't our own Grania a class of a goddess and—

MANUS. Who?

JIMMY. Grania—Grania—Diarmuid's Grania.

MANUS. Ah.

JIMMY. And sure she can't get her fill of men.

MANUS. Jimmy, you're impossible.

JIMMY. I was just thinking to myself last night: if you had the choosing between Athene and Artemis and Helen of Troy—all three of them Zeus's girls—imagine three powerful-looking daughters like that all in the one parish of Athens!—now, if you had the picking between them, which would you take?

MANUS [*to* SARAH]. Which should I take, Sarah?

JIMMY. No harm to Helen; and no harm to Artemis; and indeed no harm to our own Grania, Manus. But I think I've no choice but to go bull-straight for Athene. By God, sir, them flashing eyes would fair keep a man jigged up constant!

[*Suddenly and momentarily, as if in spasm,* JIMMY *stands to attention and salutes, his face raised in pained ecstasy.* MANUS *laughs. So does* SARAH. JIMMY *goes back to his seat, and his reading.*]

MANUS. You're a dangerous bloody man, Jimmy Jack.

JIMMY. 'Flashing-eyed'! Hah! Sure Homer knows it all, boy. Homer knows it all.

[MANUS *goes to the window and looks out.*]

MANUS. Where the hell has he got to?

[SARAH *goes to* MANUS *and touches his elbow. She mimes rocking a baby.*]

MANUS. Yes, I know he's at the christening; but it doesn't take them all day to put a name on a baby, does it?

[SARAH *mimes pouring drinks and tossing them back quickly.*]

MANUS. You may be sure. Which pub?

[SARAH *indicates.*]

MANUS. Gracie's?

[*No. Further away.*]

MANUS. Con Connie Tim's?

[*No. To the right of there.*]

MANUS. Anna na mBreag's?

[*Yes. That's it.*]

MANUS. Great. She'll fill him up. I suppose I may take the class then.

[MANUS *begins to distribute some books, slates and chalk, texts, etc., beside the seats.* SARAH *goes over to the straw and produces a bunch of flowers she has hidden there. During this:*]

JIMMY. '*Autar o ek limenos prosebe*—' 'But Ulysses went forth from the harbour and through the woodland to the place where Athene had shown him he could find the good swineherd who—'*o oi biotoio malista kedeto*'—what's that, Manus?

MANUS. 'Who cared most for his substance.'

JIMMY. That's it! 'The good swineherd who cared most for his substance above all the slaves that Ulysses possessed . . .'

[SARAH *presents the flowers to* MANUS.]

MANUS. Those are lovely, Sarah.

[*But* SARAH *has fled in embarrassment to her seat and has her head buried in a book.* MANUS *goes to her.*]

MANUS. Flow-ers.

[*Pause.* SARAH *does not look up.*]

MANUS. Say the word: flow-ers. Come on—flow-ers.

SARAH. Flowers.

MANUS. You see?—you're off!

[MANUS *leans down and kisses the top of* SARAH'*s head.*]

MANUS. And they're beautiful flowers. Thank you.

[MAIRE *enters, a strong-minded, strong-bodied woman in her twenties with a head of curly hair. She is carrying a small can of milk.*]

MAIRE.   Is this all's here? Is there no school this evening?

MANUS.   If my father's not back, I'll take it. [MANUS *stands awkwardly, having been caught kissing* SARAH *and with the flowers almost formally at his chest.*]

MAIRE.   Well now, isn't that a pretty sight. There's your milk. How's Sarah?

[SARAH *grunts a reply.*]

MANUS.   I saw you out at the hay.

[MAIRE *ignores this and goes to* JIMMY.]

MAIRE.   And how's Jimmy Jack Cassie?

JIMMY.   Sit down beside me, Maire.

MAIRE.   Would I be safe?

JIMMY.   No safer man in Donegal.

[MAIRE *flops on a stool beside* JIMMY.]

MAIRE.   Ooooh. The best harvest in living memory, they say; but I don't want to see another like it. [*Showing* JIMMY *her hands.*] Look at the blisters.

JIMMY.   *Esne fatigata?* [3]

MAIRE.   *Sum fatigatissima.*

JIMMY.   *Bene! Optime!*

MAIRE.   That's the height of my Latin. Fit me better if I had even that much English.

JIMMY.   English? I thought you had some English?

MAIRE.   Three words. Wait—there was a spake I used to have off by heart. What's this it was? [*Her accent is strange because she is speaking a foreign language and because she does not understand what she is saying.*] 'In Norfolk we besport ourselves around the maypoll.' What about that!

MANUS.   Maypole.

[*Again* MAIRE *ignores* MANUS.]

MAIRE.   God have mercy on my Aunt Mary—she taught me that when I was about four, whatever it means. Do you know what it means, Jimmy?

JIMMY.   Sure you know I have only Irish like yourself.

MAIRE.   And Latin. And Greek.

3. Are you tired? / I am very tired / Good! Excellent!

JIMMY. I'm telling you a lie: I know one English word.
MAIRE. What?
JIMMY. Bo-som.
MAIRE. What's a bo-som?
JIMMY. You know—[*he illustrates with his hands*]—bo-som—bo-som— you know—Diana, the huntress, she has two powerful bosom.
MAIRE. You may be sure that's the one English word you would know. [*Rises.*] Is there a drop of water about?

[MANUS *gives* MAIRE *his bowl of milk.*]

MANUS. I'm sorry I couldn't get up last night.
MAIRE. Doesn't matter.
MANUS. Biddy Hanna sent for me to write a letter to her sister in Nova Scotia. All the gossip of the parish. 'I brought the cow to the bull three times last week but no good. There's nothing for it now but Big Ned Frank.'
MAIRE [*drinking*]. That's better.
MANUS. And she got so engrossed in that she forgot who she was dictating to: 'The aul drunken schoolmaster and that lame son of his are still footering about in the hedge-school, wasting people's good time and money.'

[MAIRE *has to laugh at this.*]

MAIRE. She did not!
MANUS. And me taking it all down. 'Thank God one of them new national schools is being built above at Poll na gCaorach.' It was after midnight by the time I got back.
MAIRE. Great to be a busy man.

[MAIRE *moves away.* MANUS *follows.*]

MANUS. I could hear music on my way past but I thought it was too late to call.
MAIRE. [*to* SARAH]. Wasn't your father in great voice last night?

[SARAH *nods and smiles.*]

MAIRE. It must have been near three o'clock by the time you got home?

[SARAH *holds up four fingers.*]

MAIRE. Was it four? No wonder we're in pieces.
MANUS. I can give you a hand at the hay tomorrow.
MAIRE. That's the name of a hornpipe, isn't it?—'The Scholar In The Hayfield'—or is it a reel?
MANUS. If the day's good.
MAIRE. Suit yourself. The English soldiers below in the tents, them sapper fellas, they're coming up to give us a hand. I don't know a

word they're saying, nor they me; but sure that doesn't matter, does it?

MANUS.   What the hell are you so crabbed about?!

[DOALTY *and* BRIDGET *enter noisily. Both are in their twenties.* DOALTY *is brandishing a surveyor's pole. He is an open-minded, open-hearted, generous and slightly thick young man.* BRIDGET *is a plump, fresh young girl, ready to laugh, vain, and with a countrywoman's instinctive cunning.* DOALTY *enters doing his imitation of the master.*]

DOALTY.   Vesperal salutations to you all.

BRIDGET.   He's coming down past Carraig na Ri and he's as full as a pig!

DOALTY.   *Ignari, stuli, rustici*—pot-boys and peasant whelps—semi-literates and illegitimates.

BRIDGET.   He's been on the batter since this morning; he sent the wee ones home at eleven o'clock.

DOALTY.   Three questions. Question A—Am I drunk? Question B—Am I sober? [*Into* MAIRE'*s face.*]—*Responde—responde!*

BRIDGET.   Question C, Master—When were you last sober?

MAIRE.   What's the weapon, Doalty?

BRIDGET.   I warned him. He'll be arrested one of these days.

DOALTY.   Up in the bog with Bridget and her aul fella, and the Red Coats were just across at the foot of Croc na Mona, dragging them aul chains and peeping through that big machine they lug about everywhere with them—you know the name of it, Manus?

MAIRE.   Theodolite. [4]

BRIDGET.   How do you know?

MAIRE.   They leave it in our byre at night sometimes if it's raining.

JIMMY.   Theodolite—what's the etymology of that word, Manus?

MANUS.   No idea.

BRIDGET.   Get on with the story.

JIMMY.   *Theo-theos*—something to do with a god. Maybe *thea*—a goddess! What shape's the yoke?

DOALTY.   'Shape!' Will you shut up, you aul eejit you! Anyway, every time they'd stick one of these poles into the ground and move across the bog, I'd creep up and shift it twenty or thirty paces to the side.

BRIDGET.   God!

DOALTY.   Then they'd come back and stare at it and look at their calculations and stare at it again and scratch their heads. And cripes, d'you know what they ended up doing?

4. "A portable surveying instrument, originally for measuring horizontal angles, and consisting essentially of a planisphere or horizontal graduated circular plate, with an alidad or index bearing sights." *OED*.

BRIDGET. Wait till you hear!

DOALTY. They took the bloody machine apart! [*And immediately he speaks in gibberish—an imitation of two very agitated and confused sappers in rapid conversation.*]

BRIDGET. That's the image of them!

MAIRE. You must be proud of yourself, Doalty.

DOALTY. What d'you mean?

MAIRE. That was a very clever piece of work.

MANUS. It was a gesture.

MAIRE. What sort of gesture?

MANUS. Just to indicate . . . a presence.

MAIRE. Hah!

BRIDGET. I'm telling you—you'll be arrested.

[*When* DOALTY *is embarrassed—or pleased—he reacts physically. He now grabs* BRIDGET *around the waist.*]

DOALTY. What d'you make of that for an implement, Bridget? Wouldn't that make a great aul shaft for your churn?

BRIDGET. Let go of me, you dirty brute! I've a headline to do before Big Hughie comes.

MANUS. I don't think we'll wait for him. Let's get started.

[*Slowly, reluctantly they begin to move to their seats and specific tasks.* DOALTY *goes to the bucket of water at the door and washes his hands.* BRIDGET *sets up a hand-mirror and combs her hair.*]

BRIDGET. Nellie Ruadh's baby was to be christened this morning. Did any of yous hear what she called it? Did you, Sarah?

[SARAH *grunts: No.*]

BRIDGET. Did you, Maire?

MAIRE. No.

BRIDGET. Our Seamus says she was threatening she was going to call it after its father.

DOALTY. Who's the father?

BRIDGET. That's the point, you donkey you!

DOALTY. Ah.

BRIDGET. So there's a lot of uneasy bucks about Baile Beag this day.

DOALTY. She told me last Sunday she was going to call it Jimmy.

BRIDGET. You're a liar, Doalty.

DOALTY. Would I tell you a lie? Hi, Jimmy, Nellie Ruadh's aul fella's looking for you.

JIMMY. For me?

MAIRE. Come on, Doalty.

DOALTY. Someone told him . . .

MAIRE. Doalty!

DOALTY.　He heard you know the first book of the Satires of Horace off by heart . . .

JIMMY.　That's true.

DOALTY.　. . . and he wants you to recite it for him.

JIMMY.　I'll do that for him certainly, certainly.

DOALTY.　He's busting to hear it.

> [JIMMY *fumbles in his pockets.*]

JIMMY.　I came across this last night—this'll interest you—in Book Two of Virgil's *Georgics.*

DOALTY.　Be God, that's my territory alright.

BRIDGET.　You clown you. [*To* SARAH.] Hold this for me, would you? [*Her mirror.*]

JIMMY.　Listen to this, Manus. '*Nigra fere et presso pinguis sub vomere terra . . .*'

DOALTY.　Steady on now—easy, boys, easy—don't rush me, boys—[*He mimes great concentration.*]

JIMMY.　Manus?

MANUS.　'Land that is black and rich beneath the pressure of the plough . . .'

DOALTY.　Give *me* a chance!

JIMMY.　'And with *cui putre*—with crumbly soil—is in the main best for corn.' There you are!

DOALTY.　There you are.

JIMMY.　'From no other land will you see more wagons wending home-ward behind slow bullocks.' Virgil! There!

DOALTY.　'Slow bullocks'!

JIMMY.　Isn't that what I'm always telling you? Black soil for corn. *That's* what you should have in that upper field of yours—corn, not spuds.

DOALTY.　Would you listen to that fella! Too lazy be Jasus to wash himself and he's lecturing me on agriculture! Would you go and take a running race at yourself, Jimmy Jack Cassie! [*Grabs* SARAH.] Come away out of this with me, Sarah, and we'll plant some corn together.

MANUS.　All right—all right. Let's settle down and get some work done. I know Sean Beag isn't coming—he's at the salmon. What about the Donnelly twins? [*To* DOALTY.] Are the Donnelly twins not coming any more?

> [DOALTY *shrugs and turns away.*]

Did you ask them?

DOALTY.　Haven't seen them. Not about these days.

> [DOALTY *begins whistling through his teeth. Suddenly the atmo-sphere is silent and alert.*]

MANUS.　Aren't they at home?

DOALTY.　No.

MANUS.   Where are they then?

DOALTY.   How would I know?

BRIDGET.   Our Seamus says two of the soldiers' horses were found last night at the foot of the cliffs at Machaire Buidhe and . . . [*She stops suddenly and begins writing with chalk on her slate.*] D'you hear the whistles of this aul slate? Sure nobody could write on an aul slippery thing like that.

MANUS.   What headline did my father set you?

BRIDGET.   'It's easier to stamp out learning than to recall it.'

JIMMY.   Book Three, the *Agricola* of Tacitus.

BRIDGET.   God but you're a dose.

MANUS.   Can you do it?

BRIDGET.   There. Is it bad? Will he ate me?

MANUS.   It's very good. Keep your elbow in closer to your side. Doalty?

DOALTY.   I'm at the seven-times table. I'm perfect, skipper.

[MANUS *moves to* SARAH.]

MANUS.   Do you understand those sums?

[SARAH *nods: Yes.* MANUS *leans down to her ear.*]

MANUS.   My name is Sarah.

[MANUS *goes to* MAIRE. *While he is talking to her the others swop books, talk quietly, etc.*]

MANUS.   Can I help you? What are you at?

MAIRE.   Map of America. [*Pause.*] The passage money came last Friday.

MANUS.   You never told me that.

MAIRE.   Because I haven't seen you since, have I?

MANUS.   You don't want to go. You said that yourself.

MAIRE.   There's ten below me to be raised and no man in the house. What do you suggest?

MANUS.   Do you want to go?

MAIRE.   Did you apply for that job in the new national school?

MANUS.   No.

MAIRE.   You said you would.

MANUS.   I said I might.

MAIRE.   When it opens, this is finished: nobody's going to pay to go to a hedge-school.

MANUS.   I know that and I . . .

[*He breaks off because he sees* SARAH, *obviously listening at his shoulder. She moves away again.*]

I was thinking that maybe I could . . .

MAIRE.   It's £56 a year you're throwing away.

MANUS.   I can't apply for it.
MAIRE.   You *promised* me you would.
MANUS.   My father has applied for it.
MAIRE.   He has not!
MANUS.   Day before yesterday.
MAIRE.   For God's sake, sure you know he'd never—
MANUS.   I couldn't—I can't go in against him.

[MAIRE *looks at him for a second. Then:*]

MAIRE.   Suit yourself. [*To* BRIDGET.] I saw your Seamus heading off to
the Port fair early this morning.
BRIDGET.   And wait till you hear this—I forgot to tell you this. He said
that as soon as he crossed over the gap at Cnoc na Mona—just beyond
where the soldiers are making the maps—the sweet smell was every-
where.
DOALTY.   You never told me that.
BRIDGET.   It went out of my head.
DOALTY.   He saw the crops in Port?
BRIDGET.   Some.
MANUS.   How did the tops look?
BRIDGET.   Fine—I think.
DOALTY.   In flower?
BRIDGET.   I don't know. I think so. He didn't say.
MANUS.   Just the sweet smell—that's all?
BRIDGET.   They say that's the way it snakes in, don't they? First the
smell; and then one morning the stalks are all black and limp.
DOALTY.   Are you stupid? It's the rotting stalks makes the sweet smell
for God's sake. That's what the smell is—rotting stalks.
MAIRE.   Sweet smell! Sweet smell! Every year at this time somebody
comes back with stories of the sweet smell. Sweet God, did the potatoes ever fail in Baile Beag? Well, did they ever—ever? Never! There
was never blight here. Never. Never. But we're always sniffing about
for it, aren't we?—looking for disaster. The rents are going to go up
again—the harvest's going to be lost—the herring have gone away for
ever—there's going to be evictions. Honest to God, some of you people aren't happy unless you're miserable and you'll not be right content until you're dead!
DOALTY.   Bloody right, Maire. And sure St Colmcille prophesied there'd
never be blight here. He said:

The spuds will bloom in Baile Beag
Till rabbits grow an extra lug. [5]

5. St. Colmcille (also St. Columba) (521–97), founder of churches in Ireland and in Scotland; a "lug" is
an ear.

And sure that'll never be. So we're all right. Seven threes are twenty-one; seven fours are twenty-eight; seven fives are forty-nine—Hi, Jimmy, do you fancy my chances as boss of the new national school?

JIMMY.   What's that?—what's that?

DOALTY.   Agh, g'way back home to Greece, son.

MAIRE.   You ought to apply, Doalty.

DOALTY.   D'you think so? Cripes, maybe I will. Hah!

BRIDGET.   Did you know that you start at the age of six and you have to stick at it until you're twelve at least—no matter how smart you are or how much you know.

DOALTY.   Who told you that yarn?

BRIDGET.   And every child from every house has to go all day, every day, summer or winter. That's the law.

DOALTY.   I'll tell you something—nobody's going to go near them—they're not going to take on—law or no law.

BRIDGET.   And everything's free in them. You pay for nothing except the books you use; that's what our Seamus says.

DOALTY.   'Our Seamus'. Sure your Seamus wouldn't pay anyway. She's making this all up.

BRIDGET.   Isn't that right, Manus?

MANUS.   I think so.

BRIDGET.   And from the very first day you go, you'll not hear one word of Irish spoken. You'll be taught to speak English and every subject will be taught through English and everyone'll end up as cute as the Buncrana people.

[SARAH *suddenly grunts and mimes a warning that the master is coming. The atmosphere changes. Sudden business. Heads down.*]

DOALTY.   He's here, boys. Cripes, he'll make yella meal out of me for those bloody tables.

BRIDGET.   Have you any extra chalk, Manus?

MAIRE.   And the atlas for me.

[DOALTY *goes to* MAIRE *who is sitting on a stool at the back.*]

DOALTY.   Swop you seats.

MAIRE.   Why?

DOALTY.   There's an empty one beside the Infant Prodigy.

MAIRE.   I'm fine here.

DOALTY.   Please, Maire. I want to jouk in the back here.

[MAIRE *rises.*]

God love you. [*Aloud.*] Anyone got a bloody table-book? Cripes, I'm wrecked.

[SARAH *gives him one.*]

God, I'm dying about you.

> [*In his haste to get to the back seat,* DOALTY *bumps into* BRIDGET
> *who is kneeling on the floor and writing laboriously on a slate
> resting on top of a bench-seat.*]

BRIDGET.   Watch where you're going, Doalty!

> [DOALTY *gooses* BRIDGET. *She squeals. Now the quiet hum of
> work:* JIMMY *reading Homer in a low voice;* BRIDGET *copying her
> headline;* MAIRE *studying the atlas;* DOALTY, *his eyes shut tight,
> mouthing his tables;* SARAH *doing sums. After a few seconds:—*]

BRIDGET.   Is this 'g' right, Manus? How do you put a tail on it?
DOALTY.   Will you shut up! I can't concentrate!

> [*A few more seconds of work. Then* DOALTY *opens his eyes and
> looks around.*]

False alarm, boys. The bugger's not coming at all. Sure the bugger's
hardly fit to walk.

> [*And immediately* HUGH *enters. A large man, with residual dig-
> nity, shabbily dressed, carrying a stick. He has, as always, a
> large quantity of drink taken, but he is by no means drunk. He
> is in his early sixties.*]

HUGH.   *Adsum,*[6] Doalty, *adsum.* Perhaps not in *sobrietate perfecta*[7] but
adequately *sobrius* to overhear your quip. Vesperal salutations to you
all.

> [*Various responses.*]

JIMMY.   *Ave,* Hugh.
HUGH.   James.

> [*He moves his hat and coat and hands them and his stick to*
> MANUS, *as if to a footman.*]

Apologies for my late arrival: we were celebrating the baptism of Nel-
lie Ruadh's baby.
BRIDGET [*innocently*].   What name did she put on it, Master?
HUGH.   Was it Eamon? Yes, it was Eamon.
BRIDGET.   Eamon Donal from Tor! Cripes!
HUGH.   And after the *caerimonia nominations*—Maire?
MAIRE.   The ritual of naming.
HUGH.   Indeed—we then had a few libations to mark the occasion.
Altogether very pleasant. The derivation of the word 'baptize'?—where
are my Greek scholars? Doalty?

6. I am present   7. with complete sobriety

DOALTY. Would it be—ah—ah—

HUGH. Too slow. James?

JIMMY. '*Baptizein*'—to dip or immerse.

HUGH. Indeed—our friend Pliny Minor speaks of the '*baptisterium*'—the cold bath.

DOALTY. Master.

HUGH. Doalty?

DOALTY. I suppose you could talk then about baptizing a sheep at sheep-dipping, could you?

[*Laughter. Comments.*]

HUGH. Indeed—the precedent is there—the day you were appropriately named Doalty—seven nines?

DOALTY. What's that, Master?

HUGH. Seven times nine?

DOALTY. Seven nines—seven nines—seven times nine—seven times nine are—cripes, it's on the tip of my tongue, Master—I knew it for sure this morning—funny that's the only one that foxes me—

BRIDGET [*prompt*]. Sixty-three.

DOALTY. What's wrong with me: sure seven nines are fifty-three, Master.

HUGH. Sophocles from Colonus would agree with Doalty Dan Doalty from Tulach Alainn: 'To know nothing is the sweetest life.' Where's Sean Beag?

MANUS. He's at the salmon.

HUGH. And Nora Dan?

MAIRE. She says she's not coming back any more.

HUGH. Ah. Nora Dan can now write her name—Nora Dan's education is complete. And the Donnelly twins?

[*Brief pause. Then:—*]

BRIDGET. They're probably at the turf. [*She goes to* HUGH.] There's the one-and-eight I owe you for last quarter's arithmetic and there's my one-and-six for this quarter's writing.

HUGH. *Gratias tibi ago.*[8] [*He sits at his table.*] Before we commence our *studia* I have three items of information to impart to you—[*to* MANUS] a bowl of tea, strong tea, black—

[MANUS *leaves.*]

Item A: on my perambulations today—Bridget? Too slow. Maire?

MAIRE. Perambulare—to walk about.

HUGH. Indeed—I encountered Captain Lancey of the Royal Engineers who is engaged in the ordnance survey of this area. He tells me that

8. I thank you

in the past few days two of his horses have strayed and some of his equipment seems to be mislaid. I expressed my regret and suggested he address you himself on these matters. He then explained that he does not speak Irish. Latin? I asked. None. Greek? Not a syllable. He speaks—on his own admission—only English; and to his credit he seemed suitably verecund—James?

JIMMY. *Verecundus*—humble.

HUGH. Indeed—he voiced some surprise that we did not speak his language. I explained that a few of us did, on occasion—outside the parish of course—and then usually for the purposes of commerce, a use to which his tongue seemed particularly suited—[*shouts*] and a slice of soda bread—and I went on to propose that our own culture and the classical tongues made a happier conjugation—Doalty?

DOALTY. *Conjugo*—I join together.

[DOALTY *is so pleased with himself that he prods and winks at* BRIDGET]

HUGH. Indeed—English, I suggested, couldn't really express us.　And again to his credit he acquiesced to my logic. Acquiesced—Maire?

[MAIRE *turns away impatiently.* HUGH *is unaware of the gesture.*]

Too slow. Bridget?

BRIDGET. *Acquiesco.*[9]

HUGH. *Procede.*

BRIDGET. *Acquiesco, acquiescere, acquievi, acquietum.*

HUGH. Indeed—and Item B . . .

MAIRE. Master.

HUGH. Yes?

[MAIRE *gets to her feet uneasily but determinedly. Pause.*]

Well, girl?

MAIRE. We should all be learning to speak English. That's what my mother says. That's what I say. That's what Dan O'Connell[1] said last month in Ennis. He said the sooner we all learn to speak English the better.

[*Suddenly several speak together.*]

JIMMY. What's she saying? What? What?

DOALTY, It's Irish he uses when he's travelling around scrounging votes.

BRIDGET. And sleeping with married women. Sure no woman's safe from that fella.

9. *acquiesco, acquiescere:* to rest, to find comfort in

1. "The Liberator" (1775–1847) and organizer of Catholic, Gaelic Ireland in mass meetings that helped achieve Catholic Emancipation; his reformist compromises, such as encouraging English, have long been subject to debate.

JIMMY.   Who-who-who? Who's this? Who's this
HUGH.   *Silentium!* [*Pause.*] Who is she talking about?
MAIRE.   I'm talking about Daniel O'Connell.
HUGH.   Does she mean that little Kerry politician?
MAIRE.   I'm talking about the Liberator, Master, as you well know. And
what he said was this: 'The old language is a barrier to modern prog-
ress.' He said that last month. And he's right. I don't want Greek. I
don't want Latin. I want English.

[MANUS *reappears on the platform above.*]

I want to be able to speak English because I'm going to America as
soon as the harvest's all saved.

[MAIRE *remains standing.* HUGH *puts his hand into his pocket
and produces a flask of whiskey. He removes the cap, pours a
drink into it, tosses it back, replaces the cap, puts the flask back
into his pocket. Then:—*]

HUGH.   We have been diverted—*diverto*—*divertere*—Where were we?
DOALTY.   Three items of information, Master. You're at Item B.
HUGH.   Indeed—Item B—Item B—yes—On my way to the christening
this morning I chanced to meet Mr George Alexander, Justice of the
Peace. We discussed the new national school. Mr Alexander invited
me to take charge of it when it opens. I thanked him and explained
that I could do that only if I were free to run it as I have run this
hedge-school for the past thirty-five years—filling what our friend
Euripides calls the '*aplestos pithos*'—James?
JIMMY.   'The cask that cannot be filled'.
HUGH.   Indeed—and Mr Alexander retorted courteously and emphatically that he hopes that is how it will be run.

[MAIRE *now sits.*]

Indeed. I have had a strenuous day and I am weary of you all. [*He
rises.*] Manus will take care of you.

[HUGH *goes towards the steps.* OWEN *enters.* OWEN *is the younger
son, a handsome, attractive young man in his twenties. He is
dressed smartly—a city man. His manner is easy and charming:
everything he does is invested with consideration and enthusiasm. He now stands framed in the doorway, a traveling bag
across his shoulder.*]

OWEN.   Could anybody tell me is this where Hugh Mor O'Donnell
holds his hedge-school?
DOALTY.   It's Owen—Owen Hugh! Look, boys—it's Owen Hugh!

[OWEN *enters. As he crosses the room he touches and has a word
for each person.*]

OWEN.   Doalty! [*Playful punch.*] How are you, boy? *Jacobe, quid agis?*[2]
Are you well?

JIMMY.   Fine. Fine.

OWEN.   And Bridget! Give us a kiss. Aaaaaah!

BRIDGET.   You're welcome, Owen.

OWEN.   It's not—Yes, it *is* Maire Chatach! God! A young woman!

MAIRE.   How are you, Owen?

[OWEN *is now in front of* HUGH. *He puts his two hands on his*
FATHER's *shoulders.*]

OWEN.   And how's the old man himself?

HUGH.   Fair—fair.

OWEN.   Fair? For God's sake you never looked better! Come here to
me. [*He embraces* HUGH *warmly and genuinely.*] Great to see you,
Father. Great to be back.

[HUGH's *eyes are moist—partly joy, partly the drink.*]

HUGH.   I—I'm—I'm—pay no attention to—

OWEN.   Come on—come one—come on—[*He gives* HUGH *his handkerchief.*] Do you know what you and I are going to do tonight? We are
going to go up to Anna na mBreag's . . .

DOALTY.   Not there, Owen.

OWEN.   Why not?

DOALTY.   Her poteen's worse than ever.

BRIDGET.   They say she puts frogs in it!

OWEN.   All the better. [*To* HUGH.] And you and I are going to get footless drunk. That's arranged.

[OWEN *sees* MANUS *coming down the steps with tea and soda
bread. They meet at the bottom.*]

And Manus!

MANUS.   You're welcome, Owen.

OWEN.   I know I am. And it's great to be here. [*He turns round, arms
outstretched.*] I can't believe it. I come back after six years and everything's just as it was! Nothing's changed! Not a thing! [*Sniffs.*] Even
that smell—that's the same smell this place always had. What is it
anyway? Is it the straw?

DOALTY.   Jimmy Jack's feet.

[*General laughter. It opens little pockets of conversation round
the room.*]

OWEN.   And Doalty Dan Doalty hasn't changed either!

DOALTY.   Bloody right, Owen.

2. James, how are you?

OWEN.   Jimmy, are you well?

JIMMY.   Dodging about.

OWEN.   Any word of the big day?

[*This is greeted with 'ohs' and 'ahs'.*]

Time enough, Jimmy. Homer's easier to live with, isn't he?

MAIRE.   We heard stories that you own ten big shops in Dublin—is it true?

OWEN.   Only nine.

BRIDGET.   And you've twelve horses and six servants.

OWEN.   Yes—that's true. God Almighty, would you listen to them—taking a hand at me!

MANUS.   When did you arrive?

OWEN.   We left Dublin yesterday morning, spent last night in Omagh and got here half an hour ago.

MANUS.   You're hungry then.

HUGH.   Indeed—get him food—get him a drink.

OWEN.   Not now, thanks; later. Listen—am I interrupting you all?

HUGH.   By no means. We're finished for the day.

OWEN.   Wonderful. I'll tell you why. Two friends of mine are waiting outside the door. They'd like to meet you and I'd like you to meet them. May I bring them in?

HUGH.   Certainly. You'll all eat and have . . .

OWEN.   Not just yet, Father. You've seen the sappers working in this area for the past fortnight, haven't you? Well, the older man is Captain Lancey . . .

HUGH.   I've met Captain Lancey.

OWEN.   Great. He's the cartographer in charge of this whole area. Cartographer—James? [OWEN *begins to play this game—his father's game—partly to involve his classroom audience, partly to show he has not forgotten it, and indeed partly because he enjoys it.*]

JIMMY.   A maker of maps.

OWEN.   Indeed—and the younger man that I traveled with from Dublin, his name is Lieutenant Yolland and he is attached to the toponymic department—Father?—*responde—responde!*

HUGH.   He gives names to places.

OWEN.   Indeed—although he is in fact an orthographer—Doalty?—too slow—Manus?

MANUS.   The correct spelling of those names.

OWEN.   Indeed—indeed!

[OWEN *laughs and claps his hands. Some of the others join in.*]

Beautiful! Beautiful! Honest to God, it's such a delight to be back here with you all again—'civilized' people. Anyhow—may I bring them in?

HUGH.   Your friends are our friends.
OWEN.   I'll be straight back.

> [*There is general talk as* OWEN *goes towards the door. He stops beside* SARAH.]

OWEN.   That's a new face. Who are you?

> [*A very brief hesitation. Then?—*]

SARAH.   My name is Sarah.
OWEN.   Sarah who?
SARAH.   Sarah Johnny Sally.
OWEN.   Of course! From Bun na hAbhann! I'm Owen—Owen Hugh Mor. From Baile Beag. Good to see you.

> [*During this* OWEN–SARAH *exchange.*]

HUGH.   Come on now. Let's tidy this place up. [*He rubs the top of his table with his sleeve.*] Move, Doalty—lift those books off the floor.
DOALTY.   Right, Master; certainly, Master; I'm doing my best, Master.

> [OWEN *stops at the door.*]

OWEN.   One small thing, Father.
HUGH.   *Silentium!*
OWEN.   I'm on their pay-roll.

> [SARAH, *very elated at her success, is beside* MANUS.]

SARAH.   I said it, Manus!

> [MANUS *ignores* SARAH. *He is much more interested in* OWEN *now.*]

MANUS.   You haven't enlisted, have you?!

> [SARAH *moves away.*]

OWEN.   Me a soldier? I'm employed as a part-time, underpaid, civilian interpreter. My job is to translate the quaint, archaic tongue you people persist in speaking into the King's good English. [*He goes out.*]
HUGH.   Move—move—move! Put some order on things! Come on, Sarah—hide that bucket. Whose are these slates? Somebody takes these dishes away. *Festinate! Festinate!*[3]

> [MANUS *goes to* MAIRE *who is busy tidying.*]

MANUS.   You didn't tell me you were definitely leaving.
MAIRE.   Not now.
HUGH.   Good girl, Bridget. That's the style.
MANUS.   You might at least have told me.

3. Hurry!

HUGH.   Are these your books, James?
JIMMY.   Thank you.
MANUS.   Fine! Fine! Go ahead! Go ahead!
MAIRE.   You talk to me about getting married—with neither a roof over
your head nor a sod of ground under your foot. I suggest you go for
the new school; but no—'My father's in for that.' Well now he's got
it and now this is finished and now you've nothing.
MANUS.   I can always . . .
MAIRE.   What? Teach classics to the cows? Agh—

> [MAIRE *moves away from* MANUS. OWEN *enters with* LANCEY *and*
> YOLLAND. CAPTAIN LANCEY *is middle-aged; a small, crisp officer,*
> *expert in his field as cartographer but uneasy with people—espe-*
> *cially civilians, especially these foreign civilians. His skill is with*
> *deeds, not words.* LIEUTENANT YOLLAND *is in his late twenties /*
> *early thirties. He is tall and thin and gangling, blond hair, a*
> *shy, awkward manner. A soldier by accident.*]

OWEN.   Here we are. Captain Lancey—my father.
LANCEY.   Good evening.

> [HUGH *becomes expansive, almost courtly, with his visitors.*]

HUGH.   You and I have already met, sir.
LANCEY.   Yes.
OWEN.   And Lieutenant Yolland—both Royal Engineers—my father.
HUGH.   You're very welcome, gentlemen.
YOLLAND.   How do you do.
HUGH.   *Gaudeo vos hic adesse.*[4]
OWEN.   And I'll make no other introductions except that these are some
of the people of Baile Beag and—what?—well you're among the best
people in Ireland now. [*He pauses to allow* LANCEY *to speak.* LANCEY
does not.] Would you like to say a few words, Captain.
HUGH.   What about a drop, sir?
LANCEY.   A what?
HUGH.   Perhaps a modest refreshment? A little sampling of our *aqua
vitae?*
LANCEY.   No, no.
HUGH.   Later perhaps when—
LANCEY.   I'll say what I have to say, if I may, and as briefly as possible.
Do they speak *any* English, Roland?
OWEN.   Don't worry. I'll translate.
LANCEY.   I see. [*He clears his throat. He speaks as if he were addressing
children—a shade too loudly and enunciating excessively.*] You may
have seen me—seen me—working in this section—section?—work-

4. Welcome

ing. We are here—here—in this place—you understand?—to make a
map—a map—a map and—

JIMMY.   *Nonne Latine loquitur?*[5]

[HUGH *holds up a restraining hand.*]

HUGH.   James.

LANCEY [*to* JIMMY].   I do not speak Gaelic, sir. [*He looks at* OWEN.]

OWEN.   Carry on.

LANCEY.   A map is a representation on paper—a picture—you understand picture?—a paper picture—showing, representing this country—yes?—showing your country in miniature—a scaled drawing on
paper of—of—of—

[*Suddenly* DOALTY *sniggers. Then* BRIDGET. *Then* SARAH. OWEN
leaps in quickly.]

OWEN.   It might be better if you *assume* they understand you—

LANCEY.   Yes?

OWEN.   And I'll translate as you go along.

LANCEY.   I see. Yes. Very well. Perhaps you're right. Well. What we
are doing is this.

[*He looks at* OWEN. OWEN *nods reassuringly.*]

His Majesty's government has ordered the first ever comprehensive
survey of this entire country—a general triangulation which will
embrace detailed hydrographic and topographic information and which
will be executed to a scale of six inches to the English mile.

HUGH [*pouring a drink*].   Excellent—excellent.

[LANCEY *looks at* OWEN.]

OWEN.   A new map is being made of the whole country.

[LANCEY *looks to* OWEN: *Is that all?* OWEN *smiles reassuringly
and indicates to proceed.*]

LANCEY.   This enormous task has been embarked on so that the military
authorities will be equipped with up-to-date and accurate information
on every corner of this part of the Empire.

OWEN.   The job is being done by soldiers because they are skilled in
this work.

LANCEY.   And also so that the entire basis of land valuation can be
reassessed for purposes of more equitable taxation.

OWEN.   This new map will take the place of the estate agent's map so
that from now on you will know exactly what is yours in law.

LANCEY.   In conclusion I wish to quote two brief extracts from the white
paper which is our governing charter: [*Reads*] 'All former surveys of

5. Does he not speak Latin?

Ireland originated in forfeiture and violent transfer of property; the present survey has for its object the relief which can be afforded to the proprietors and occupiers of land from unequal taxation.'

OWEN. The captain hopes that the public will cooperate with the sappers and that the new map will mean that taxes are reduced.

HUGH. A worthy enterprise—*opus honestrum!* And Extract B?

LANCEY. 'Ireland is privileged. No such survey is being undertaken in England. So this survey cannot but be received as proof of the disposition of this government to advance the interests of Ireland.' My sentiments, too.

OWEN. This survey demonstrates the government's interest in Ireland and the captain thanks you for listening so attentively to him.

HUGH. Our pleasure, Captain.

LANCEY. Lieutenant Yolland?

YOLLAND. I—I—I've nothing to say—really—

OWEN. The captain is the man who actually makes the new map. George's task is to see that the place-names on this map are . . . correct. [*To* YOLLAND.] Just a few words—they'd like to hear you. [*To class.*] Don't you want to hear George, too?

MAIRE. Has he anything to say?

YOLLAND [*to* MAIRE]. Sorry—sorry?

OWEN. She says she's dying to hear you.

YOLLAND [*to* MAIRE]. Very kind of you—thank you . . . [*To class.*] I can only say that I feel—I feel very foolish to—to—to be working here and not to speak your language. But I intend to rectify that—with Roland's help—indeed I do.

OWEN. He wants me to teach him Irish!

HUGH. You are doubly welcome, sir.

YOLLAND. I think your countryside is—is—is—is very beautiful. I've fallen in love with it already. I hope we're not too—too crude an intrusion on your lives. And I know that I'm going to be happy, very happy, here.

OWEN. He is already a committed Hibernophile—

JIMMY. He loves—

OWEN. All right, Jimmy—we know—he loves Baile Beag; and he loves you all.

HUGH. Please . . . May I . . . ? [HUGH *is now drunk. He holds on to the edge of the table.*]

OWEN. Go ahead, Father. [*Hands up for quiet.*] Please—please.

HUGH. And we, gentlemen, we in turn are happy to offer you our friendship, our hospitality, and every assistance that you may require. Gentlemen—welcome!

[*A few desultory claps. The formalities are over. General conversation. The soldiers meet the locals.* MANUS *and* OWEN *meet down stage.*]

OWEN.   Lancey's a bloody ramrod but George's all right. How are you
    anyway?
MANUS.   What sort of translation was that, Owen?
OWEN.   Did I make a mess of it?
MANUS.   You weren't saying what Lancey was saying!
OWEN.   'Uncertainty in meaning is incipient poetry'—who said that?
MANUS.   There was nothing uncertain about what Lancey said: it's a
    bloody military operation, Owen! And what's Yolland's function?
    What's 'incorrect' about the place-names we have here?
OWEN.   Nothing at all. They're just going to be standardized.
MANUS.   You mean changed into English?
OWEN.   Where there's ambiguity, they'll be Anglicized.
MANUS.   And they call you Roland! They both call you Roland!
OWEN.   Shhhhh. Isn't it ridiculous? They seemed to get it wrong from
    the very beginning—or else they can't pronounce Owen. I was afraid
    some of you bastards would laugh.
MANUS.   Aren't you going to tell them?
OWEN.   Yes—yes—soon—soon.
MANUS.   But they . . .
OWEN.   Easy, man, easy. Owen—Roland—what the hell. It's only a
    name. It's the same me, isn't it? Well, isn't it?
MANUS.   Indeed it is. It's the same Owen.
OWEN.   And the same Manus. And in a way we complement each other.
    [He punches MANUS lightly, playfully and turns to join the others. As
    he goes.] All right—who has met whom? Isn't this a job for the go-
    between?

    [MANUS watches OWEN move confidently across the floor, taking
    MAIRE by the hand and introducing her to YOLLAND. HUGH is
    trying to negotiate the steps. JIMMY is lost in a text. DOALTY and
    BRIDGET are reliving their giggling. SARAH is staring at MANUS.]

Act Two

Scene I

The sappers have already mapped most of the area. YOLLAND's *official
task, which* OWEN *is now doing, is to take each of the Gaelic names—
every hill, stream, rock, even every patch of ground which possessed its
own distinctive Irish name—and Anglicize it, either by changing it into
its approximate English sound or by translating it into English words.
For example, a Gaelic name like Cnoc Ban could become Knockban or—
directly translated—Fair Hill. These new standardized names were entered
into the Name-Book, and when the new maps appeared they contained*

all these new Anglicized names. OWEN's *official function as translator is to pronounce each name in Irish and then provide the English translation.*

The hot weather continues. It is late afternoon some days later.

Stage right: an improvised clothes-line strung between the shafts of the cart and a nail in the wall; on it are some shirts and socks.

A large map—one of the new blank maps—is spread out on the floor. OWEN *is on his hands and knees, consulting it. He is totally engrossed in his task which he pursues with great energy and efficiency.*

YOLLAND's *hesitancy has vanished—he is at home here now. He is sitting on the floor, his long legs stretched out before him, his back resting against a creel, his eyes closed. His mind is elsewhere. One of the reference books—a church registry—lies open on his lap.*

Around them are various reference books, the Name-Book, a bottle of poteen, some cups, etc.

OWEN *completes an entry in the Name-Book and returns to the map on the floor.*

OWEN. Now. Where have we got to? Yes—the point where that stream enters the sea—that tiny little beach there. George!

YOLLAND. Yes. I'm listening. What do you call it? Say the Irish name again?

OWEN. Bun na hAbhann.

YOLLAND. Again.

OWEN. Bun na hAbhann.

YOLLAND. Bun na hAbhann.

OWEN. That's terrible, George.

YOLLAND. I know. I'm sorry. Say it again.

OWEN. Bun na hAbbann.

YOLLAND. Bun na hAbbann.

OWEN. That's better. Bun is the Irish word for bottom. And Abha means river. So it's literally the mouth of the river.

YOLLAND. Let's leave it alone. There's no English equivalent for a sound like that.

OWEN. What is it called in the church registry?

[*Only now does* YOLLAND *open his eyes.*]

YOLLAND. Let's see . . . Banowen.

OWEN. That's wrong. [*Consults text.*] The list of freeholders calls it Owenmore—that's completely wrong: Owenmore's the big river at the west end of the parish. [*Another text.*] And in the grand jury lists it's called—God!—Binhone!—wherever they got that. I suppose we could Anglicize it to Bunowen; but somehow that's neither fish nor flesh.

[YOLLAND *closes his eyes again.*]

YOLLAND. I give up.
OWEN [*at map*]. Back to first principles. What are we trying to do?
YOLLAND. Good question.
OWEN. We are trying to denominate and at the same time describe that tiny area of soggy, rocky, sandy ground where that little stream enters the sea, an area known locally as Bun na hAbhann . . . Burnfoot! What about Burnfoot?
YOLLAND [*indifferently*]. Good, Roland, Burnfoot's good.
OWEN. George, my name isn't . . .
YOLLAND. B-u-r-n-f-o-o-t?
OWEN. Are you happy with that?
YOLLAND. Yes.
OWEN. Burnfoot it is then. [*He makes the entry into the Name-Book.*] Bun na hAbhann—B-u-r-n-
YOLLAND. You're becoming very skilled at this.
OWEN. We're not moving fast enough.
YOLLAND [*opens eyes again*]. Lancey lectured me again last night.
OWEN. When does he finish here?
YOLLAND. The sappers are pulling out at the end of the week. The trouble is, the maps they've completed can't be printed without these names. So London screams at Lancey and Lancey screams at me. But I wasn't intimidated.

[MANUS *emerges from upstairs and descends.*]

'I'm sorry, sir,' I said, 'But certain tasks demand their own tempo. You cannot rename a whole country overnight.' Your Irish air has made me bold. [*To* MANUS.] Do you want us to leave?
MANUS. Time enough. Class won't begin for another half-hour.
YOLLAND. Sorry—sorry?
OWEN. Can't you speak English?

[MANUS *gathers the things off the clothes-line.* OWEN *returns to the map.*]

OWEN. We now come across that beach . . .
YOLLAND. Tra—that's the Irish for beach. [*To* MANUS.] I'm picking up the odd word, Manus.
MANUS. So.
OWEN. . . . on past Burnfoot; and there's nothing around here that has any name that I know of until we come down here to the south end, just about here . . . and there should be a ridge of rocks there . . . Have the sappers marked it? They have. Look, George.
YOLLAND. Where are we?
OWEN. There.
YOLLAND. I'm lost.
OWEN. Here. And the name of that ridge is Druim Dubh. Put English on that, Lieutenant.

YOLLAND. Say it again.

OWEN. Druim Dubh.

YOLLAND. Dubh means black.

OWEN. Yes.

YOLLAND. And Druim means . . . what? a fort?

OWEN. We met it yesterday in Druim Luachra.

YOLLAND. A ridge! The Black Ridge! [*To* MANUS.] You see, Manus?

OWEN. We'll have you fluent at the Irish before the summer's over.

YOLLAND. Oh, I wish I were.

[*To* MANUS *as he crosses to go back upstairs.*]

We got a crate of oranges from Dublin today. I'll send some up to you.

MANUS. Thanks. [*To* OWEN.] Better hide that bottle. Father's just up and he'd be better without it.

OWEN. Can't you speak English before your man?

MANUS. Why?

OWEN. Out of courtesy.

MANUS. Doesn't he want to learn Irish? [*To* YOLLAND.] Don't you want to learn Irish?

YOLLAND. Sorry—sorry? I—I—

MANUS. I understand the Lancey's perfectly but people like you puzzle me.

OWEN. Manus, for God's sake!

MANUS [*still to* YOLLAND]. How's the work going?

YOLLAND. The work?—the work? Oh, it's—it's staggering along—I think—[*to* OWEN]—isn't it? But we'd be lost without Roland.

MANUS [*leaving*]. I'm sure. But there are always the Rolands, aren't there? [*He goes upstairs and exits.*]

YOLLAND. What was that he said?—something about Lancey, was it?

OWEN. He said we should hide that bottle before Father gets his hands on it.

YOLLAND. Ah.

OWEN. He's always trying to protect him.

YOLLAND. Was he lame from birth?

OWEN. An accident when he was a baby: Father fell across his cradle. That's why Manus feels so responsible for him.

YOLLAND. Why doesn't he marry?

OWEN. Can't afford to, I suppose.

YOLLAND. Hasn't he a salary?

OWEN. What salary? All he gets is the odd shilling Father throws him— and that's seldom enough. I got out in time, didn't I?

[YOLLAND *is pouring a drink.*]

Easy with that stuff—it'll hit you suddenly.

YOLLAND. I like it.

OWEN. Let's get back to the job. Druim Dubh—what's it called in the jury lists? [*Consults texts.*]

YOLLAND. Some people here resent us.

OWEN. Dramduff—wrong as usual.

YOLLAND. I was passing a little girl yesterday and she spat at me.

OWEN. And it's Drimdoo here. What's it called in the registry?

YOLLAND. Do you know the Donnelly twins?

OWEN. Who?

YOLLAND. The Donnelly twins.

OWEN. Yes. Best fishermen about here. What about them?

YOLLAND. Lancey's looking for them.

OWEN. What for?

YOLLAND. He wants them for questioning.

OWEN. Probably stolen somebody's nets. Dramduffy! Nobody ever called it Dramduffy. Take your pick of those three.

YOLLAND. My head's addled. Let's take a rest. Do you want a drink?

OWEN. Thanks. Now, every Dubh we've come across we've changed to Duff. So if we're to be consistent, I suppose Druim Dubh has to become Dromduff.

[YOLLAND *is now looking out the window.*]

You can see the end of the ridge from where you're standing. But D-r-u-m- or D-r-o-m-? [*Name-Book.*] Do you remember—which did we agree on for Druim Luachra?

YOLLAND. That house immediately above where we're camped—

OWEN. Mm?

YOLLAND. The house where Maire lives.

OWEN. Maire? Oh, Maire Chatach.

YOLLAND. What does that mean?

OWEN. Curly-haired; the whole family are called the Catachs. What about it?

YOLLAND. I hear music coming from that house almost every night.

OWEN. Why don't you drop in?

YOLLAND. Could I?

OWEN. Why not? We used D-r-o-m then. So we've got to call it D-r-o-m-d-u-f-f—all right?

YOLLAND. Go back up to where the new school is being built and just say the names again for me, would you?

OWEN. That's a good idea. Poolkerry, Ballybeg—

YOLLAND. No, no; as they still are—in your own language.

OWEN. Poll na gCaorach,

[YOLLAND *repeats the names silently after him.*]

Baile Beag, Ceann Balor, Lis Maol, Machaire Buidhe, Baile na gGall, Carraig na Ri, Mullach Dearg—

YOLLAND. Do you think I could live here?
OWEN. What are you talking about?
YOLLAND. Settle down here—live here.
OWEN. Come on, George.
YOLLAND. I mean it.
OWEN. Live on what? Potatoes? Buttermilk?
YOLLAND. It's really heavenly.
OWEN. For God's sake! The first hot summer in fifty years and you think it's Eden. Don't be such a bloody romantic. You wouldn't survive a mild winter here.
YOLLAND. Do you think not? Maybe you're right.

[DOALTY *enters in a rush.*]

DOALTY. Hi, boys, is Manus about?
OWEN. He's upstairs. Give him a shout.
DOALTY. Manus! The cattle's going mad in that heat—Cripes, running wild all over the place. [*To* YOLLAND.] How are you doing, skipper?

[MANUS *appears.*]

YOLLAND. Thank you for—I—I'm very grateful to you for—
DOALTY. Wasting your time. I don't know a word you're saying. Hi, Manus, there's two bucks down the road there asking for you.
MANUS [*descending*]. Who are they?
DOALTY. Never clapped eyes on them. They want to talk to you.
MANUS. What about?
DOALTY. They wouldn't say. Come on. The bloody beasts'll end up in Loch an Iubhair if they're not capped. Good luck, boys!

[DOALTY *rushes off.* MANUS *follows him.*]

OWEN. Good luck! What were you thanking Doalty for?
YOLLAND. I was washing outside my tent this morning and he was passing with a scythe across his shoulder and he came up to me and pointed to the long grass and then cut a pathway round my tent and from the tent down to the road—so that my feet won't get wet with the dew. Wasn't that kind of him? And I have no words to thank him . . . I suppose you're right: I suppose I couldn't live here . . . Just before Doalty came up to me this morning, I was thinking that at that moment I might have been in Bombay instead of Ballybeg. You see, my father was at his wits end with me and finally he got me a job with the East India Company—some kind of clerkship. This was ten, eleven months ago. So I set off for London. Unfortunately I—I—I missed the boat. Literally. And since I couldn't face Father and hadn't enough money to hang about until the next sailing, I joined the army. And they stuck me into the Engineers and posted me to Dublin. And Dub-

lin sent me here. And while I was washing this morning and looking across the Tra Bhan, I was thinking how very, very lucky I am to be here and not in Bombay.

OWEN.   Do you believe in fate?

YOLLAND.   Lancey's so like my father. I was watching him last night. He met every group of sappers as they reported in. He checked the field kitchens. He examined the horses. He inspected every single report—even examining the texture of the paper and commenting on the neatness of the handwriting. The perfect colonial servant: not only must the job be done—it must be done with excellence. Father has that drive, too; that dedication; that indefatigable energy. He builds roads—hopping from one end of the Empire to the other. Can't sit still for five minutes. He says himself the longest time he ever sat still was the night before Waterloo when they were waiting for Wellington to make up his mind to attack.[1]

OWEN.   What age is he?

YOLLAND.   Born in 1789—the very day the Bastille[2] fell. I've often thought maybe that gave his whole life its character. Do you think it could? He inherited a new world the day he was born—The Year One. Ancient time was at an end. The world had cast off its old skin. There were no longer any frontiers to man's potential. Possibilities were endless and exciting. He still believes that. The Apocalypse is just about to happen . . . I'm afraid I'm a great disappointment to him. I've neither his energy, nor his coherence, nor his belief. Do I believe in fate? The day I arrived in Ballybeg—no, Baile Beag—the moment you brought me in here, I had a curious sensation. It's difficult to describe. It was a momentary sense of discovery; no—not quite a sense of discovery—a sense of recognition, of confirmation of something I half knew instinctively; as if I had stepped . . .

OWEN.   Back into ancient time?

YOLLAND.   No, no. It wasn't an awareness of *direction* being changed but of experience being of a totally different order. I had moved into a consciousness that wasn't striving nor agitated, but at its ease and with its own conviction and assurance. And when I heard Jimmy Jack and your father swapping stories about Apollo and Cuchulainn and Paris and Ferdia[3]—as if they lived down the road—it was then that I thought—I knew—perhaps I could live here . . . [*Now embarrassed.*] Where's the pot-een?

OWEN.   Poteen.

YOLLAND.   Poteen—poteen—poteen. Even if I did speak Irish I'd always be an outsider here, wouldn't I? I may learn the password but the

---

1. The duke of Wellington defeated Napoleon at Waterloo, in Belgium, on June 18, 1815.
2. The Paris jail destroyed on July 14, the onset of the French Revolution.
3. Figures of classical and Celtic mythology.

language of the tribe will always elude me, won't it? The private core
will always be . . . hermetic, won't it?

OWEN.   You can learn to decode us.

[HUGH *emerges from upstairs and descends. He is dressed for the
road. Today he is physically and mentally jaunty and alert—
almost self-consciously jaunty and alert. Indeed, as the scene
progresses, one has the sense that he is deliberately parodying
himself. The moment* HUGH *gets to the bottom of the steps* YOL-
LAND *leaps respectfully to his feet.*]

HUGH [*as he descends*].

> *Quantumvis cursum longum fessumque moratur*
> *Sol, sacro tandem carmine vesper adest.*

I dabble in verse, Lieutenant, after the style of Ovid. [*To* OWEN.] A
drop of that to fortify me.

YOLLAND.   You'll have to translate it for me.

HUGH.   Let's see—

No matter how long the sun may linger on his long and weary journey
At length evening comes with its sacred song.

YOLLAND.   Very nice, sir.

HUGH.   English succeeds in making it sound . . . plebeian.

OWEN.   Where are you off to, Father?

HUGH.   An *expeditio* with three purposes. Purpose A: to acquire a testi-
monial from our parish priest—[*to* YOLLAND.] a worthy man but barely
literate; and since he'll ask me to write it myself, how in all modesty
can I do myself justice? [*To* OWEN.] Where did this [*drink*] come from?

OWEN.   Anna na mBreag's.

HUGH [*to* YOLLAND].   In that case address yourself to it with circumspec-
tion. [*And* HUGH *instantly tosses the drink back in one gulp and gri-
maces.*] Aaaaaaagh! [*Holds out his glass for a refill.*] Anna na mBreag
means Anna of the Lies. And Purpose B: to talk to the builders of the
new school about the kind of living accommodation I will require
there. I have lived too long like a journeyman tailor.

YOLLAND.   Some years ago we lived fairly close to a poet—well, about
three miles away.

HUGH.   His name?

YOLLAND.   Wordsworth—William Wordsworth.[4]

HUGH.   Did he speak of me to you?

YOLLAND.   Actually I never talked to him. I just saw him out walking—
in the distance.

---

4. The English Romantic poet (1770–1850).

HUGH.　Wordsworth? . . . No. I'm afraid we're not familiar with your literature, Lieutenant. We feel closer to the warm Mediterranean. We tend to overlook your island.

YOLLAND.　I'm learning to speak Irish, sir.

HUGH.　Good.

YOLLAND.　Roland's teaching me.

HUGH.　Splendid.

YOLLAND.　I mean—I feel so cut off from the people here. And I was trying to explain a few minutes ago how remarkable a community this is. To meet people like yourself and Jimmy Jack who actually converse in Greek in Latin. And your place names—what was the one we came across this morning?—Termon, from Terminus, the god of boundaries. It—it—it's really astonishing.

HUGH.　We like to think we endure around truths immemorially posited.

YOLLAND.　And your Gaelic literature—you're a poet yourself—

HUGH.　Only in Latin, I'm afraid.

YOLLAND.　I understand it's enormously rich and ornate.

HUGH.　Indeed, Lieutenant. A rich language. A rich literature. You'll find, sir, that certain cultures expend on their vocabularies and syntax acquisitive energies and ostentations entirely lacking in their material lives. I suppose you could call us a spiritual people.

OWEN [not unkindly; more out of embarrassment before YOLLAND].　Will you stop that nonsense, Father.

HUGH.　Nonsense? What nonsense?

OWEN.　Do you know where the priest lives?

HUGH.　At Lis na Muc, over near . . .

OWEN.　No, he doesn't. Lis na Muc, the Fort of the Pigs, has become Swinefort. [Now turning the pages of the Name-Book—a page per name.] And to get to Swinefort you pass through Greencastle and Fair Head and Strandhill and Gort and Whiteplains. And the new school isn't at Poll na gCaorach—it's at Sheepsrock. Will you be able to find your way?

[HUGH pours himself another drink. Then:—]

HUGH.　Yes, it is a rich language, Lieutenant, full of the mythologies of fantasy and hope and self-deception—a syntax opulent with tomorrows. It is our response to mud cabins and a diet of potatoes; our only method of replying to . . . inevitabilities. [To OWEN.] Can you give me the loan of half-a-crown? I'll repay you out of the subscriptions I'm collecting for the publication of my new book. [To YOLLAND.] It is entitled: 'The Pentaglot Preceptor or Elementary Institute of the English, Greek, Hebrew, Latin and Irish Languages; Particularly Calculated for the Instruction of such Ladies and Gentlemen as may Wish to Learn without the Help of a Master'.

YOLLAND [*laughs*].   That's a wonderful title!

HUGH.   Between ourselves—the best part of the enterprise. Nor do I, in fact, speak Hebrew. And that last phrase—'without the Help of a Master'—that was written before the new national school was thrust upon me—do you think I ought to drop it now? After all you don't dispose of the cow just because it has produced a magnificent calf, do you?

YOLLAND.   You certainly do not.

HUGH.   The phrase goes. And I'm interrupting work of moment. [*He goes to the door and stops there.*] To return briefly to that other matter, Lieutenant. I understand your sense of exclusion, of being cut off from a life here; and I trust you will find access to us with my son's help. But remember that words are signals, counters. They are not immortal. And it can happen—to use an image you'll understand—it can happen that a civilization can be imprisoned in a linguistic contour which no longer matches the landscape of . . . fact. Gentlemen. [*He leaves.*]

OWEN.   'An *expeditio* with three purposes': the children laugh at him: he always promises three points and he never gets beyond A and B.

MANUS.   He's an astute man.

OWEN.   He's bloody pompous.

YOLLAND.   But so astute.

OWEN.   And he drinks too much. Is it astute not to be able to adjust for survival? Enduring around truths immemorially posited—hah!

YOLLAND.   He knows what's happening.

OWEN.   What is happening?

YOLLAND.   I'm not sure. But I'm concerned about my part in it. It's an eviction of sorts.

OWEN.   We're making a six-inch map of the country. Is there something sinister in that?

YOLLAND.   Not in—

OWEN.   And we're taking place-names that are riddled with confusion and—

YOLLAND.   Who's confused? Are the people confused?

OWEN.   —and we're standardizing those names as accurately and as sensitively as we can.

YOLLAND.   Something is being eroded.

OWEN.   Back to the romance again. All right! Fine! Fine! Look where we've got to. [*He drops on his hands and knees and stabs a finger at the map.*] We've come to this crossroads. Come here and look at it, man! Look at it! And we call that crossroads Tobair Vree. And why do we call it Tobair Vree? I'll tell you why. Tobair means a well. But what does Vree mean? It's a corruption of Brian—[*Gaelic pronunciation*] Brian—an erosion of Tobair Bhriain. Because a hundred-and-fifty years ago there used to be a well there, not at the crossroads, mind you—that would be too simple—but in a field close to the crossroads. And an old man called Brian, whose face was disfigured by an enormous growth, got it into his head that the water in that well was blessed; and every day for seven months he went there and bathed his face in it. But the growth didn't go away; and one morning Brian was found drowned in that well. And ever since that crossroads is known as Tobair Vree—even though that well has long since dried up. I know the story because my grandfather told it to me. But ask Doalty—or Maire—or Bridget—even my father—even Manus—why it's called Tobair Vree; and do you think they'll know? I know they don't know. So the question I put to you, Lieutenant, is this: what do we do with a name like that? Do we scrap Tobair Vree altogether and call it—what?—The Cross? Crossroads? Or do we keep piety with a man long dead, long forgotten, his name 'eroded' beyond recognition, whose trivial little story nobody in the parish remembers?

YOLLAND. Except you.

OWEN. I've left here.

YOLLAND. You remember it.

OWEN. I'm asking you: what do we write in the Name-Book?

YOLLAND. Tobair Vree.

OWEN. Even though the well is a hundred yards from the actual cross-roads—and there's no well anyway—and what the hell does Vree mean?

YOLLAND. Tobair Vree.

OWEN. That's what you want?

YOLLAND. Yes.

OWEN. You're certain?

YOLLAND. Yes.

OWEN. Fine. Fine. That's what you'll get.

YOLLAND. That's what you want, too, Roland.

[*Pause.*]

OWEN [*explodes*]. George! For God's sake! *My name is not Roland!*

YOLLAND. What?

OWEN [*softly*]. My name is Owen.

[*Pause.*]

YOLLAND. Not Roland?

OWEN. Owen.

YOLLAND. You mean to say—?

OWEN. Owen.

YOLLAND. But I've been—

OWEN. O-w-e-n.

YOLLAND. Where did Roland come from?

OWEN. I don't know.

YOLLAND. It was never Roland?

OWEN.   Never.
YOLLAND.   O my God!

[*Pause. They stare at one another. Then the absurdity of the situation strikes them suddenly. They explode with laughter.* OWEN *pours drinks. As they roll about, their lines overlap.*]

YOLLAND.   Why didn't you tell me?
OWEN.   Do I look like a Roland?
YOLLAND.   Spell Owen again.
OWEN.   I was getting fond of Roland.
YOLLAND.   O my God!
OWEN.   O-w-e-n.
YOLLAND.   What'll we write—
OWEN.   —in the Name-Book?!
YOLLAND.   R-o-w-e-n!
OWEN.   Or what about Ol-
YOLLAND.   Ol- what?
OWEN.   Oland!

[*And again they explode.* MANUS *enters. He is very elated.*]

MANUS.   What's the celebration?
OWEN.   A christening!
YOLLAND.   A baptism!
OWEN.   A hundred christenings!
YOLLAND.   A thousand baptisms! Welcome to Eden!
OWEN.   Eden's right! We name a thing and—bang!—it leaps into existence!
YOLLAND.   Each name a perfect equation with its roots.
OWEN.   A perfect congruence with its reality. [*To* MANUS.] Take a drink.
YOLLAND.   Poteen—beautiful.
OWEN.   Lying Anna's poteen.
YOLLAND.   Anna na mBreag's poteen.
OWEN.   Excellent, George.
YOLLAND.   I'll decode you yet.
OWEN [*offers drink*].   Manus?
MANUS.   Not if that's what it does you you.
OWEN.   You're right. Steady—steady—sober up—sober up.
YOLLAND.   Sober as a judge, Owen.

[MANUS *moves beside* OWEN.]

MANUS.   I've got good news! Where's Father?
OWEN.   He's gone out. What's the good news?
MANUS.   I've been offered a job.
OWEN.   Where? [*Now aware of* YOLLAND.] Come on, man—speak in English.

MANUS. For the benefit of the colonist?
OWEN. He's a decent man.
MANUS. Aren't they all at some level?
OWEN. Please.

[MANUS *shrugs.*]

He's been offered a job.
YOLLAND. Where?
OWEN. Well—tell us!
MANUS. I've just had a meeting with two men from Inis Meadhon. They want me to go there and start a hedge-school. They're giving me a free house, free turf, and free milk; a rood of standing corn; twelve drills of potatoes; and—[*He stops.*]
OWEN. And what?
MANUS. A salary of £42 a year!
OWEN. Manus, that's wonderful!
MANUS. You're talking to a man of substance.
OWEN. I'm delighted.
YOLLAND. Where's Inis Meadhon?
OWEN. An island south of here. And they came looking for you?
MANUS. Well, I mean to say . . .

[OWEN *punches* MANUS.]

OWEN. Aaaaagh! This calls for a real celebration.
YOLLAND. Congratulations.
MANUS. Thank you.
OWEN. Where are you, Anna?
YOLLAND. When do you start?
MANUS. Next Monday.
OWEN. We'll stay with you when we're there. [*To* YOLLAND.] How long will it be before we reach Inis Meadhon?
YOLLAND. How far south is it?
MANUS. About fifty miles.
YOLLAND. Could we make it by December?
OWEN. We'll have Christmas together. [*Sings.*] 'Christmas Day on Inis Meadhon . . .'
YOLLAND [*toast*]. I hope you're very content there, Manus.
MANUS. Thank you.

[YOLLAND *holds out his hand.* MANUS *takes it. They shake warmly.*]

OWEN [*toast*]. Manus.
MANUS [*toast*]. To Inis Meadhon. [*He drinks quickly and turns to leave.*]
OWEN. Hold on—hold on—refills coming up.
MANUS. I've got to go.
OWEN. Come on, man; this is an occasion. Where are you rushing to?
MANUS. I've got to tell Maire.

[MAIRE *enters with her can of milk.*]

MAIRE.   You've got to tell Maire what?
OWEN.   He's got a job!
MAIRE.   Manus?
OWEN.   He's been invited to start a hedge-school in Inis Meadhon.
MAIRE.   Where?
MANUS.   Inis Meadhon—the island! They're giving me £42 a year
and . . .
OWEN.   A house, fuel, milk, potatoes, corn, pupils, what-not!
MANUS.   I start on Monday.
OWEN.   You'll take a drink. Isn't it great?
MANUS.   I want to talk to you for—
MAIRE.   There's your milk. I need the can back.

[MANUS *takes the can and runs up the steps.*]

MANUS [*as he goes*].   How will you like living on an island?
OWEN.   You know George, don't you?
MAIRE.   We wave to each other across the fields.
YOLLAND.   Sorry-sorry?
OWEN.   She says you wave to each other across the fields.
YOLLAND.   Yes, we do; oh, yes; indeed we do.
MAIRE.   What's he saying?
OWEN.   He says you wave to each other across the fields.
MAIRE.   That's right. So we do.
YOLLAND.   What's she saying?
OWEN.   Nothing—nothing—nothing. [*To* MAIRE.] What's the news?

[MAIRE *moves away, touching the text books with her toe.*]

MAIRE.   Not a thing. You're busy, the two of you.
OWEN.   We think we are.
MAIRE.   I hear the Fiddler O'Shea's about. There's some talk of a dance
tomorrow night.
OWEN.   Where will it be?
MAIRE.   Maybe over the road. Maybe at Tobair Vree.
YOLLAND.   Tobair Vree!
MAIRE.   Yes.
YOLLAND.   Tobair Vree! Tobair Vree!
MAIRE.   Does he know what I'm saying?
OWEN.   Not a word.
MAIRE.   Tell him then.
OWEN.   Tell him what?
MAIRE.   About the dance.
OWEN.   Maire says there may be a dance tomorrow night.
YOLLAND [*to* OWEN].   Yes? May I come? [*To* MAIRE.] Would anybody
object if I came?

MAIRE [*to* OWEN].   What's he saying?
OWEN [*to* YOLLAND].   Who would object?
MAIRE [*to* OWEN].   Did you tell him?
YOLLAND [*to* MAIRE].   Sorry-sorry?
OWEN [*to* MAIRE].   He says may he come?
MAIRE [*to* YOLLAND].   That's up to you.
YOLLAND [*to* OWEN].   What does she say?
OWEN [*to* YOLLAND].   She says—
YOLLAND [*to* MAIRE].   What-what?
MAIRE [*to* OWEN].   Well?
YOLLAND [*to* OWEN].   Sorry-sorry?
OWEN [*to* YOLLAND].   Will you go?
YOLLAND [*to* MAIRE].   Yes, yes, if I may.
MAIRE [*to* OWEN].   What does he say?
YOLLAND [*to* OWEN].   What is she saying?
OWEN.   Oh for God's sake! [*To* MANUS, *who is descending with the empty can.*] You take on this job, Manus.
MANUS.   I'll walk you up to the house. Is your mother at home? I want to talk to her.
MAIRE.   What's the rush? [*To* OWEN.] Didn't you offer me a drink?
OWEN.   Will you risk Anna na mBreag?
MAIRE.   Why not.

> [YOLLAND *is suddenly intoxicated. He leaps up on a stool, raises his glass and shouts.*]

YOLLAND.   Anna na mBreag! Baile Beag! Inis Meadhon! Bombay! Tobair Vree! Eden! And poteen—correct, Owen?
OWEN.   Perfect.
YOLLAND.   And bloody marvellous stuff it is, too. I love it! Bloody, bloody, bloody marvellous!

> [*Simultaneously with his final 'bloody marvellous' bring up very loud the introductory music of the reel. Then immediately go to black. Retain the music throughout the very brief interval.*]

Scene II

The following night.
   This scene may be played in the schoolroom, but it would be preferable to lose—by lighting—as much of the schoolroom as possible, and to play the scene down front in a vaguely 'outside' area.
   The music rises to a crescendo. Then in the distance we hear MAIRE *and* YOLLAND *approach—laughing and running. They run on, hand-in-hand. They have just left the dance. Fade the music to distant back-*

ground. Then after a time it is lost and replaced by guitar music. MAIRE *and* YOLLAND *are now down front, still holding hands and excited by their sudden and impetuous escape from the dance.*

MAIRE.   O my God, that leap across the ditch nearly killed me.
YOLLAND.   I could scarcely keep up with you.
MAIRE.   Wait till I get my breath back.
YOLLAND.   We must have looked as if we were being chased.

[*They now realize they are alone and holding hands—the beginnings of embarrassment. The hands disengage. They begin to drift apart. Pause.*]

MAIRE.   Manus'll wonder where I've got to.
YOLLAND.   I wonder did anyone notice us leave.

[*Pause. Slightly further apart.*]

MAIRE.   The grass must be wet. My feet are soaking.

[*Another pause. Another few paces apart. They are now a long distance from one another.*]

YOLLAND [*indicating himself*].   George.

[MAIRE *nods: Yes-yes. Then:—*]

MAIRE.   Lieutenant George.
YOLLAND.   Don't call me that. I never think of myself as Lieutenant.
MAIRE.   What-what?
YOLLAND.   Sorry-sorry. [*He points to himself again.*] George.

[MAIRE *nods: Yes-yes. Then points to herself.*]

MAIRE.   Maire.
YOLLAND.   Yes, I know you're Maire. Of course I know you're Maire. I mean I've been watching you night and day for the past—
MAIRE [*eagerly*].   What-what?
YOLLAND [*points*].   Maire. [*Points.*] George. [*Points both.*] Maire and George.

[MAIRE *nods: Yes-yes-yes.*]

I—I—I—
MAIRE.   Say anything at all. I love the sound of your speech.
YOLLAND [*eagerly*].   Sorry-sorry? [*In acute frustration he looks around, hoping for some inspiration that will provide him with communicative means. Now he has a thought: he tries raising his voice and articulating in a staccato style and with equal and absurd emphasis on each word.*] Every-morning-I-see-you-feeding-brown-hens-and-giving-meal-to-black-calf—[*the futility of it.*]—O my God.

[MAIRE *smiles. She moves towards him. She will try to commu-nicate in Latin.*]

MAIRE.   *Tu es centurio in—in—in exercitu Britannico—*[5]
YOLLAND.   Yes-yes? Go on—go on—say anything at all—I love the sound of your speech.
MAIRE.   *—et es in castris quae—quae—quae sunt in agro—*[6] [*the futility of it.*]—O my God.

[YOLLAND *smiles. He moves towards her. Now for her English words.*]

George—water.
YOLLAND.   'Water'? Water! Oh yes—water—water—very good—water—good—good.
MAIRE.   Fire.
YOLLAND.   Fire—indeed — wonderful — fire, fire, fire — splendid — splendid!
MAIRE.   Ah . . . ah . . .
YOLLAND.   Yes? Go on.
MAIRE.   Earth.
YOLLAND.   'Earth'?
MAIRE.   Earth. Earth.

[YOLLAND *still does not understand.* MAIRE *stoops down and picks up a handful of clay. Holding it out.*]

Earth.
YOLLAND.   Earth! Of course—earth! Earth. Earth. Good Lord, Maire, your English is perfect!
MAIRE [*eagerly*].   What-what?
YOLLAND.   Perfect English. English perfect.
MAIRE.   George—
YOLLAND.   That's beautiful—oh, that's really beautiful.
MAIRE.   George—
YOLLAND.   Say it again—say it again—
MAIRE.   Shhh. [*She holds her hand up for silence—she is trying to remember her one line of English. Now she remembers it and she delivers the line as if English were her language—easily, fluidly, conversationally.*] George, 'In Norfolk we besport ourselves around the maypoll.'
YOLLAND.   Good God, do you? That's where my mother comes from—Norfolk. Norwich actually. Not exactly Norwich town but a small village called Little Walsingham close beside it. But in our own village of Winfarthing we have a maypole too and every year on the first

5. You are a centurion in the British Army   6. And you are in the camp in the field

of May—[*He stops abruptly, only now realizing. He stares at her. She in turn misunderstands his excitement.*]

MAIRE [*to herself*].   Mother of God, my Aunt Mary wouldn't have taught me something dirty, would she?

[*Pause.* YOLLAND *extends his hand to* MAIRE. *She turns away from him and moves slowly across the stage.*]

YOLLAND.   Maire.

[*She still moves away.*]

Maire Chatach.

[*She still moves away.*]

Bun na hAbhann? [*He says the name softly, almost privately, very tentatively, as if he were searching for a sound she might respond to. He tries again.*] Druim Dubh?

[MAIRE *stops. She is listening.* YOLLAND *is encouraged.*]

Poll na gCaorach. Lis Maol.

[MAIRE *turns towards him.*]

Lis na nGall.

MAIRE.   Lis na nGradh.

[*They are now facing each other and begin moving—almost imperceptibly—towards one another.*]

MAIRE.   Carraig an Phoill.
YOLLAND.   Carraig na Ri. Loch na nEan.
MAIRE.   Loch an Iubhair. Machaire Buidhe.
YOLLAND.   Machaire Mor. Cnoc na Mona.
MAIRE.   Cnoc na nGabhar.
YOLLAND.   Mullach.
MAIRE.   Port.
YOLLAND.   Tor.
YOLLAND.   Lag.

[*She holds out her hands to* YOLLAND. *He takes them. Each now speaks almost to himself / herself.*]

YOLLAND.   I wish to God you could understand me.
MAIRE.   Soft hands; a gentleman's hands.
YOLLAND.   Because if you could understand me I could tell you how I spend my days either thinking of you or gazing up at your house in the hope that you'll appear even for a second.
MAIRE.   Every evening you walk by yourself along the Tra Bhan and every morning you wash yourself in front of your tent.

YOLLAND.   I would tell you how beautiful you are, curly-headed Maire.
I would so like to tell you how beautiful you are.
MAIRE.   Your arms are long and thin and the skin on your shoulders is
very white.
YOLLAND.   I would tell you . . .
MAIRE.   Don't stop—I know what you're saying.
YOLLAND.   I would tell you how I want to be here—to live here—always—
with you—always, always.
MAIRE.   'Always'? What is that word—'always'?
YOLLAND.   Yes-yes; always.
MAIRE.   You're trembling.
YOLLAND.   Yes, I'm trembling because of you.
MAIRE.   I'm trembling, too.

[*She holds his face in her hand.*]

YOLLAND.   I've made up my mind . . .
MAIRE.   Shhhh.
YOLLAND.   I'm not going to leave here . . .
MAIRE.   Shhh—listen to me. I want you, too, soldier.
YOLLAND.   Don't stop—I know what you're saying.
MAIRE.   I want to live with you—anywhere—anywhere at all—always—
always.
YOLLAND.   'Always'? What is that word—'always'?
MAIRE.   Take me away with you, George.

[*Pause. Suddenly they kiss.* SARAH *enters. She sees them. She
stands shocked, staring at them. Her mouth works. Then almost
to herself.*]

SARAH.   Manus . . . Manus!

[SARAH *runs off. Music to crescendo.*]

Act Three

The following evening. It is raining.
    SARAH *and* OWEN *alone in the schoolroom.* SARAH, *more waiflike than
ever, is sitting very still on a stool, an open book across her knee. She is
pretending to read but her eyes keep going up to the room upstairs.* OWEN
*is working on the floor as before, surrounded by his reference books, map,
Name-Book, etc. But he has neither concentration nor interest; and like*
SARAH *he glances up at the upstairs room.*
    After a few seconds MANUS *emerges and descends, carrying a large paper
bag which already contains his clothes. His movements are determined*

and urgent. He moves around the classroom, picking up books, examining each title carefully, and choosing about six of them which he puts into his bag. As he selects these books:—

OWEN.   You know that old limekiln beyond Con Connie Tim's pub, the place we call The Murren?—do you know why it's called The Murren?

> [MANUS *does not answer.*]

I've only just discovered: it's a corruption of Saint Muranus. It seems Saint Muranus had a monastery somewhere about there at the beginning of the seventh century. And over the years the name became shortened to the Murren. Very unattractive name, isn't it? I think we should go back to the original—Saint Muranus. What do you think? The original's Saint Muranus. Don't you think we should go back to that?

> [*No response.* OWEN *begins writing the name into the Name-Book.* MANUS *is now rooting about among the forgotten imple-. ments for a piece of rope. He finds a piece. He begins to tie the mouth of the flimsy, overloaded bag—and it bursts, the contents spilling out on the floor.*]

MANUS.   Bloody, bloody, bloody hell!

> [*His voice breaks in exasperation: he is about to cry.* OWEN *leaps to his feet.*]

OWEN.   Hold on. I've a bag upstairs.

> [*He runs upstairs.* SARAH *waits until* OWEN *is off. Then:—*]

SARAH.   Manus . . . Manus, I . . .

> [MANUS *hears* SARAH *but makes no acknowledgement. He gathers up his belongings.* OWEN *reappears with the bag he had on his arrival.*]

OWEN.   Take this one—I'm finished with it anyway. And it's supposed to keep out the rain.

> [MANUS *transfers his few belongings.* OWEN *drifts back to his task. The packing is now complete.*]

MANUS.   You'll be here for a while? For a week or two anyhow?
OWEN.   Yes.
MANUS.   You're not leaving with the army?
OWEN.   I haven't made up my mind. Why?
MANUS.   Those Inis Meadhon men will be back to see why I haven't turned up. Tell them—tell them I'll write to them as soon as I can.

Tell them I still want the job but that it might be three or four months
before I'm free to go.

OWEN.   You're being damned stupid, Manus.

MANUS.   Will you do that for me?

OWEN.   Clear out now and Lancey'll think you're involved somehow.

MANUS.   Will you do that for me?

OWEN.   Wait a couple of days even. You know George—he's a bloody
romantic—maybe he's gone out to one of the islands and he'll suddenly reappear tomorrow morning. Or maybe the search party'll find
him this evening lying drunk somewhere in the sandhills. You've seen
him drinking that poteen—doesn't know how to handle it. Had he
drink on him last night at the dance?

MANUS.   I had a stone in my hand when I went out looking for him—I
was going to fell him. The lame scholar turned violent.

OWEN.   Did anybody see you?

MANUS [again close to tears].   But when I saw him standing there at the
side of the road—smiling—and her face buried in his shoulder—I
couldn't even go close to them. I just shouted something stupid—
something like, 'You're a bastard, Yolland.' If I'd even said it in English
. . . 'cos he kept saying 'Sorry-sorry?' The wrong gesture in the wrong
language.

OWEN.   And you didn't see him again?

MANUS.   'Sorry?'

OWEN.   Before you leave tell Lancey that—just to clear yourself.

MANUS.   What have I to say to Lancey? You'll give that message to the
islandmen?

OWEN.   I'm warning you: run away now and you're bound to be—

MANUS [to SARAH].   Will you give that message to the Inis Meadhon
men?

SARAH.   I will.

[MANUS picks up an old sack and throws it across his shoulders.]

OWEN.   Have you any idea where you're going?

MANUS.   Mayo, maybe. I remember Mother saying she had cousins
somewhere away out in the Erris Peninsula. [He picks up his bag.]
Tell Father I took only the Virgil and the Caesar and the Aeschylus
because they're mine anyway—I bought them with the money I got
for that pet lamb I reared—do you remember that pet lamb? And tell
him that Nora Dan never returned the dictionary and that she still
owes him two-and-six for last quarter's reading—he always forgets those
things.

OWEN.   Yes.

MANUS.   And his good shirt's ironed and hanging up in the press and
his clean socks are in the butter-box under the bed.

OWEN.   All right.

MANUS. And tell him I'll write.

OWEN. If Maire asks where you've gone . . . ?

MANUS. He'll need only half the amount of milk now, won't he? Even less than half—he usually takes his tea black. [*Pause.*] And when he comes in at night—you'll hear him; he makes a lot of noise—I usually come down and give him a hand up. Those stairs are dangerous without a banister. Maybe before you leave you'd get Big Ned Frank to put up some sort of a handrail. [*Pause.*] And if you can bake, he's very fond of soda bread.

OWEN. I can give you money. I'm wealthy. Do you know what they pay me? Two shillings a day for this—this—this—

[MANUS *rejects the offer by holding out his hand.*]

Goodbye, Manus.

[MANUS *and* OWEN *shake hands. Then* MANUS *picks up his bag briskly and goes towards the door. He stops a few paces beyond* SARAH, *turns, comes back to her. He addresses her as he did in Act One but now without warmth or concern for her.*]

MANUS. What is your name? [*Pause.*] Come on. What is your name?

SARAH. My name is Sarah.

MANUS. Just Sarah? Sarah what? [*Pause.*] Well?

SARAH. Sarah Johnny Sally.

MANUS. And where do you live? Come on.

SARAH. I live in Bun na hAbhann. [*She is now crying quietly.*]

MANUS. Very good, Sarah Johnny Sally. There's nothing to stop you now—nothing in the wide world. [*Pause. He looks down at her.*] It's all right—it's all right—you did no harm—you did no harm at all. [*He stoops over her and kisses the top of her head—as if in absolution. Then briskly to the door and off.*]

OWEN. Good luck, Manus!

SARAH [*quietly*]. I'm sorry . . . I'm sorry . . . I'm so sorry, Manus . . .

[OWEN *tries to work but cannot concentrate. He begins folding up the map. As he does:—*]

OWEN. Is there a class this evening?

[SARAH *nods: yes.*]

I suppose Father knows. Where is he anyhow?

[SARAH *points.*]

Where?

[SARAH *mimes rocking a baby.*]   .

I don't understand—where?

[SARAH *repeats the mime and wipes away tears.* OWEN *is still puzzled.*]

It doesn't matter. He'll probably turn up.

[BRIDGET *and* DOALTY *enter, sacks over their heads against the rain. They are self-consciously noisier, more ebullient, more garrulous than ever—brimming over with excitement and gossip and brio.*]

DOALTY.   You're missing the crack, boys! Cripes, you're missing the crack! Fifty more soldiers arrived an hour ago!

BRIDGET.   And they're spread out in a big line from Sean Neal's over to Lag and they're moving straight across the fields towards Cnoc na nGabhar!

DOALTY.   Prodding every inch of the ground in front of them with their bayonets and scattering animals and hens in all directions!

BRIDGET.   And tumbling everything before them—fences, ditches, haystacks, turf-stacks!

DOALTY.   They came to Barney Petey's field of corn—straight through it be God as if it was heather!

BRIDGET.   Not a blade of it left standing!

DOALTY.   And Barney Petey just out of his bed and running after them in his drawers: 'You hoors you! Get out of my corn, you hoors you!'

BRIDGET.   First time he ever ran in his life.

DOALTY.   Too lazy, the wee get, to cut it when the weather was good.

[SARAH *begins putting out the seats.*]

BRIDGET.   Tell them about Big Hughie.

DOALTY.   Cripes, if you'd seen your aul fella, Owen.

BRIDGET.   They were all inside in Anna na mBreag's pub—all the crowd from the wake—

DOALTY.   And they hear the commotion and they all come out to the street—

BRIDGET.   Your father in front; the Infant Prodigy footless behind him!

DOALTY.   And your aul fella, he sees the army stretched across the countryside—

BRIDGET.   O my God!

DOALTY.   And Cripes he starts roaring at them!

BRIDGET.   'Visigoths! Huns! Vandals!'

DOALTY.   *'Ignari! Stulti! Rustici!'* [1]

BRIDGET.   And wee Jimmy Jack jumping up and down and shouting, 'Thermopylae! Thermopylae!' [2]

---

1. Ignoramuses! Fools! Peasants!
2. Gap between mountain and sea defended by

Greeks for three days in 480 B.C. against a far larger Persian force.

DOALTY.   You never saw crack like it in your life, boys. Come away on out with me, Sarah, and you'll see it all.

BRIDGET.   Big Hughie's fit to take no class. Is Manus about?

OWEN.   Manus is gone.

BRIDGET.   Gone where?

OWEN.   He's left—gone away.

DOALTY.   Where to?

OWEN.   He doesn't know. Mayo, maybe.

DOALTY.   What's on in Mayo?

OWEN [to BRIDGET].   Did you see George and Maire Chatach leave the dance last night?

BRIDGET.   We did. Didn't we, Doalty?

OWEN.   Did you see Manus following them out?

BRIDGET.   I didn't see him going out but I saw him coming in by himself later.

OWEN.   Did George and Maire come back to the dance?

BRIDGET.   No.

OWEN.   Did you see them again?

BRIDGET.   He left her home. We passed them going up the back road—didn't we, Doalty?

OWEN.   And Manus stayed till the end of the dance?

DOALTY.   We know nothing. What are you asking us for?

OWEN.   Because Lancey'll question me when he hears Manus's gone. [Back to BRIDGET.] That's the way George went home? By the back road? That's where you saw him?

BRIDGET.   Leave me alone, Owen. I know nothing about Yolland. If you want to know about Yolland, ask the Donnelly twins.

[Silence. DOALTY moves over to the window.]

[To SARAH.] He's a powerful fiddler, O'Shea, isn't he? He told our Seamus he'll come back for a night at Hallowe'en.

[OWEN goes to DOALTY who looks resolutely out the window.]

OWEN.   What's this about the Donnellys? [Pause.] Were they about last night?

DOALTY.   Didn't see them if they were. [Begins whistling through his teeth.]

OWEN.   George is a friend of mine.

DOALTY.   So.

OWEN.   I want to know what's happened to him.

DOALTY.   Couldn't tell you.

OWEN.   What have the Donnelly twins to do with it? [Pause.] Doalty!

DOALTY.   I know nothing, Owen—nothing at all—I swear to God. All I know is this: on my way to the dance I saw their boat beached at Port. It wasn't there on my way home, after I left Bridget. And that's

all I know. As God's my judge. The half-dozen times I met him I
didn't know a word he said to me; but he seemed a right enough sort
. . . [*With sudden excessive interest in the scene outside.*] Cripes, they're
crawling all over the place! Cripes, there's millions of them! Cripes,
they're levelling the whole land!

> [OWEN *moves away.* MAIRE *enters. She is bareheaded and wet
> from the rain; her hair in disarray. She attempts to appear nor-
> mal but she is in acute distress, on the verge of being distraught.
> She is carrying the milk-can.*]

MAIRE.   Honest to God, I must be going off my head. I'm halfway here
and I think to myself, 'Isn't this can very light?' and I look into it and
isn't it empty.
OWEN.   It doesn't matter.
MAIRE.   How will you manage for tonight?
OWEN.   We have enough.
MAIRE.   Are you sure?
OWEN.   Plenty, thanks.
MAIRE.   It'll take me no time at all to go back up for some.
OWEN.   Honestly, Maire.
MAIRE.   Sure it's better you have it than that black calf that's . . . that
. . . [*She looks around.*] Have you heard anything?
OWEN.   Nothing.
MAIRE.   What does Lancey say?
OWEN.   I haven't seen him since this morning.
MAIRE.   What does he *think*?
OWEN.   We really didn't talk. He was here for only a few seconds.
MAIRE.   He left me home, Owen. And the last thing he said to me—
he tried to speak in Irish—he said, 'I'll see you yesterday'—he meant
to say 'I'll see you tomorrow.' And I laughed that much he pretended
to get cross and he said 'Maypoll! Maypoll!' because I said that word
wrong. And off he went, laughing—laughing, Owen! Do you think
he's all right? What do *you* think?
OWEN.   I'm sure he'll turn up. Maire.
MAIRE.   He comes from a tiny wee place called Winfarthing. [*She suddenly drops on her hands and knees on the floor—where* OWEN *had his
map a few minutes ago—and with her finger traces out an outline
map.*] Come here till you see. Look. There's Winfarthing. And there's
two other wee villages right beside it; one of them's called Barton
Bendish—it's there; and the other's called Saxingham Nethergate—
it's about there. And there's Little Walsingham—that's his mother's
townland. Aren't they odd names? Sure they make no sense to me at
all. And Winfarthing's near a big town called Norwich. And Norwich
is in a county called Norfolk. And Norfolk is in the east of England.
He drew a map for me on the wet strand and wrote the names on it.

I have it all in my head now: Winfarthing—Barton Bendish—Saxingham Nethergate—Little Walsingham—Norwich—Norfolk. Strange
sounds, aren't they? But nice sounds; like Jimmy Jack reciting his
Homer. [*She gets to her feet and looks around; she is almost serene
now. To* SARAH.] You were looking lovely last night, Sarah. Is that the
dress you got from Boston? Green suits you. [*To* OWEN.] Something
very bad's happened to him, Owen. I know. He wouldn't go away
without telling me. Where is he, Owen? You're his friend—where is
he? [*Again she looks around the room; then sits on a stool.*] I didn't get
a chance to do my geography last night. The master'll be angry with
me. [*She rises again.*] I think I'll go home now. The wee ones have
to be washed and put to bed and that black calf has to be fed . . . My
hands are that rough; they're still blistered from the hay. I'm ashamed
of them. I hope to God there's no hay to be saved in Brooklyn. [*She
stops at the door.*] Did you hear? Nellie Ruadh's baby died in the
middle of the night. I must go up to the wake. It didn't last long, did
it?

[MAIRE *leaves. Silence. Then.*]

OWEN.   I don't think there'll be any class. Maybe you should . . .

[OWEN *begins picking up his texts.* DOALTY *goes to him.*]

DOALTY.   Is he long gone?—Manus.
OWEN.   Half an hour.
DOALTY.   Stupid bloody fool.
OWEN.   I told him that.
DOALTY.   Do they know he's gone?
OWEN.   Who?
DOALTY.   The army.
OWEN.   Not yet.
DOALTY.   They'll be after him like bloody beagles. Bloody, bloody fool,
limping along the coast. They'll overtake him before night for Christ's
sake.

[DOALTY *returns to the window.* LANCEY *enters—now the commanding officer.*]

OWEN.   Any news? Any word?

[LANCEY *moves into the centre of the room, looking around as he
does.*]

LANCEY.   I understood there was a class. Where are the others?
OWEN.   There was to be a class but my father—
LANCEY.   This will suffice. I will address them and it will be their
responsibility to pass on what I have to say to every family in this
section.

[LANCEY *indicates to* OWEN *to translate.* OWEN *hesitates, trying to assess the change in* LANCEY'*s manner and attitude.*]

I'm in a hurry, O'Donnell.

OWEN.   The captain has an announcement to make.

LANCEY.   Lieutenant Yolland is missing. We are searching for him. If we don't find him, or if we receive no information as to where he is to be found, I will pursue the following course of action. [*He indicates to* OWEN *to translate.*]

OWEN.   They are searching for George. If they don't find him—

LANCEY.   Commencing twenty-four hours from now we will shoot all livestock in Ballybeg.

[OWEN *stares at* LANCEY.]

At once.

OWEN.   Beginning this time tomorrow they'll kill every animal in Baile Beag—unless they're told where George is.

LANCEY.   If that doesn't bear results, commencing forty-eight hours from now we will embark on a series of evictions and levelling of every abode in the following selected areas—

OWEN.   You're not—!

LANCEY.   Do your job. Translate.

OWEN.   If they still haven't found him in two days time they'll begin evicting and levelling every house starting with these townlands.

[LANCEY *reads from his list.*]

LANCEY.   Swinefort.

OWEN.   Lis na Muc.

LANCEY.   Burnfoot.

OWEN.   Bun na hAbhann.

LANCEY.   Dromduff.

OWEN.   Druim Dubh.

LANCEY.   Whiteplains.

OWEN.   Machaire Ban.

LANCEY.   Kings Head.

OWEN.   Cnoc na Ri.

LANCEY.   If by then the lieutenant hasn't been found, we will proceed until a complete clearance is made of this entire section.

OWEN.   If Yolland hasn't been got by then, they will ravish the whole parish.

LANCEY.   I trust they know exactly what they've got to do. [*Pointing to* BRIDGET.] I know you. I know where you live. [*Pointing to* SARAH.] Who are you? Name!

[SARAH'*s mouth opens and shuts, opens and shuts. Her face becomes contorted.*]

What's your name?

[*Again* SARAH tries frantically.]

OWEN.   Go on, Sarah. You can tell him.

[*But* SARAH *cannot. And she knows she cannot. She closes her mouth. Her head goes down.*]

OWEN.   Her name is Sarah Johnny Sally.
LANCEY.   Where does she live?
OWEN.   Bun na hAbhann.
LANCEY.   Where?
OWEN.   Burnfoot.
LANCEY.   I want to talk to your brother—is he here?
OWEN.   Not at the moment.
LANCEY.   Where is he?
OWEN.   He's at a wake.
LANCEY.   What wake?

[DOALTY, *who has been looking out the window all through* LAN-CEY's *announcements, now speaks—calmly, almost casually.*]

DOALTY.   Tell him his whole camp's on fire.
LANCEY.   What's your name? [*To* OWEN.] Who's that lout?
OWEN.   Doalty Dan Doalty.
LANCEY.   Where does he live?
OWEN.   Tulach Alainn.
LANCEY.   What do we call it?
OWEN.   Fair Hill. He says your whole camp is on fire.

[LANCEY *rushes to the window and looks out. Then he wheels on* DOALTY.]

LANCEY.   I'll remember you, Mr Doalty. [*To* OWEN.] You carry a big responsibility in all this. [*He goes off.*]
BRIDGET. Mother of God, does he mean it, Owen?
OWEN.   Yes, he does.
BRIDGET. We'll have to hide the beasts somewhere—our Seamus'll know where. Maybe at the back of Lis na nGradh—or in the caves at the far end of the Tra Bhan. Come on, Doalty! Come on! Don't be standing about there!

[DOALTY *does not move.* BRIDGET *runs to the door and stops suddenly. She sniffs the air. Panic.*]

The sweet smell! Smell it! It's the sweet smell! Jesus, it's the potato blight!
DOALTY.   It's the army tents burning, Bridget.

BRIDGET.   Is it? Are you sure? Is that what it is? God, I thought we were destroyed altogether. Come on! Come on!

[*She runs off.* OWEN *goes to* SARAH *who is preparing to leave.*]

OWEN.   How are you? Are you all right?

[SARAH *nods: Yes.*]

OWEN.   Don't worry. It will come back to you again.

[SARAH *shakes her head.*]

OWEN.   It will. You're upset now. He frightened you. That's all's wrong.

[*Again* SARAH *shakes her head, slowly, emphatically, and smiles at* OWEN. *Then she leaves.* OWEN *busies himself gathering his belongings.* DOALTY *leaves the window and goes to him.*]

DOALTY.   He'll do it, too.
OWEN.   Unless Yolland's found.
DOALTY.   Hah!
OWEN.   Then he'll certainly do it.
DOALTY.   When my grandfather was a boy they did the same thing. [*Simply, altogether without irony.*] And after all the trouble you went to, mapping the place and thinking up new names for it.

[OWEN *busies himself. Pause.* DOALTY *almost dreamily.*]

I've damned little to defend but he'll not put me out without a fight. And there'll be others who think the same as me.
OWEN.   That's a matter for you.
DOALTY.   If we'd all stick together. If we knew how to defend ourselves.
OWEN.   Against a trained army.
DOALTY.   The Donnelly twins know how.
OWEN.   If they could be found.
DOALTY.   If they could be found. [*He goes to the door.*] Give me a shout after you've finished with Lancey. I might know something then. [*He leaves.*]

[OWEN *picks up the Name-Book. He looks at it momentarily, then puts it on top of the pile he is carrying. It falls to the floor. He stoops to pick it up—hesitates—leaves it. He goes upstairs. As* OWEN *ascends,* HUGH *and* JIMMY JACK *enter. Both wet and drunk.* JIMMY *is very unsteady. He is trotting behind* HUGH, *trying to break in on* HUGH's *declamation.* HUGH *is equally drunk but more experienced in drunkenness: there is a portion of his mind which retains its clarity.*]

HUGH.   There I was, appropriately dispositioned to proffer my condolences to the bereaved mother . . .

JIMMY.   Hugh—

HUGH.   . . . and about to enter the *domus lugubris*—Maire Chatach?

JIMMY.   The wake house.

HUGH.   Indeed—when I experience a plucking at my elbow: Mister George Alexander, Justice of the Peace. 'My tidings are infelicitious,' said he—Bridget? Too slow. Doalty?

JIMMY.   *Infelix*—unhappy.

HUGH.   Unhappy indeed. 'Master Bartley Timlin has been appointed to the new national school.' 'Timlin? Who is Timlin?' 'A schoolmaster from Cork. And he will be a major asset to the community: he is also a very skilled bacon-curer!'

JIMMY.   Hugh—

HUGH.   Ha-ha-ha-ha-ha! The Cork bacon-curer! *Barbarus hic ego sum quia non intelligor ulli*—James?

JIMMY.   Ovid.

HUGH.   *Procede.*

JIMMY.   'I am a barbarian in this place because I am not understood by anyone.'

HUGH.   Indeed—[*Shouts.*] Manus! Tea! I will compose a satire on Master Bartley Timlin, schoolmaster and bacon-curer. But it will be too easy, won't it? [*Shouts.*] Strong tea! Black!

> [*The only way* JIMMY *can get* HUGH's *attention is by standing in front of him and holding his arms.*]

JIMMY.   Will you listen to me, Hugh!

HUGH.   James. [*Shouts.*] And a slice of soda bread.

JIMMY.   I'm going to get married.

HUGH.   Well!

JIMMY.   At Christmas.

HUGH.   Splendid.

JIMMY.   To Athene.

HUGH.   Who?

JIMMY.   Pallas Athene.

HUGH.   *Glaukopis Athene?*

JIMMY.   Flashing-eyed, Hugh, flashing-eyed! [*He attempts the gesture he has made before: standing to attention, the momentary spasm, the salute, the face raised in pained ecstasy—but the body does not respond efficiently this time. The gesture is grotesque.*]

HUGH.   The lady has assented?

JIMMY.   She asked *me*—I assented.

HUGH.   Ah. When was this?

JIMMY.   Last night.

HUGH.   What does her mother say?

JIMMY.   Metis from Hellespont? Decent people—good stock.

HUGH.   And her father?

JIMMY. I'm meeting Zeus tomorrow. Hugh, will you be my best man?
HUGH. Honoured, James; profoundly honoured.
JIMMY. You know what I'm looking for, Hugh, don't you? I mean to say—you know—I—I—I joke like the rest of them—you know?— [*Again he attempts the pathetic routine but abandons it instantly.*] You know yourself, Hugh—don't you?—you know all that. But what I'm really looking for, Hugh—what I really want—companionship, Hugh—at my time of life, companionship, company, someone to talk to. Away up in Beann na Gaoithe—you've no idea how lonely it is. Companionship—correct, Hugh? Correct?
HUGH. Correct.
JIMMY. And I always liked her, Hugh. Correct?
HUGH. Correct, James.
JIMMY. Someone to talk to.
HUGH. Indeed.
JIMMY. That's all, Hugh. The whole story. You know it all now, Hugh. You know it all.

[As JIMMY *says those last lines he is crying, shaking his head, trying to keep his balance, and holding a finger up to his lips in absurd gestures of secrecy and intimacy. Now he staggers away, tries to sit on a stool, misses it, slides to the floor, his feet in front of him, his back against the broken cart. Almost at once he is asleep.* HUGH *watches all of this. Then he produces his flask and is about to pour a drink when he sees the Name-Book on the floor. He picks it up and leafs through it, pronouncing the strange names as he does. Just as he begins,* OWEN *emerges and descends with two bowls of tea.*]

HUGH. Ballybeg. Burnfoot. King's Head. Whiteplains. Fair Hill. Dunboy. Green Bank.

[OWEN *snatches the book from* HUGH.]

OWEN. I'll take that. [*In apology.*] It's only a catalogue of names.
HUGH. I know what it is.
OWEN. A mistake—my mistake—nothing to do with us. I hope that's strong enough [*tea*]. [*He throws the book on the table and crosses over to* JIMMY.] Jimmy. Wake up, Jimmy. Wake up, man.
JIMMY. What—what-what?
OWEN. Here. Drink this. Then go on away home. There may be trouble. Do you hear me, Jimmy? There may be trouble.
HUGH [*indicating Name-Book*]. We must learn those new names.
OWEN [*searching around*]. Did you see a sack lying about?
HUGH. We must learn where we live. We must learn to make them our own. We must make them our new home.

[OWEN *finds a sack and throws it across his shoulders.*]

OWEN.   I know where I live.

HUGH.   James thinks he knows, too. I look at James and three thoughts occur to me: A—that it is not the literal past, the 'facts' of history, that shape us, but images of the past embodied in language. James has ceased to make that discrimination.

OWEN.   Don't lecture me, Father.

HUGH.   B—we must never cease renewing those images; because once we do, we fossilize. Is there no soda bread?

OWEN.   And C, Father—one single, unalterable 'fact': if Yolland is not found, we are all going to be evicted. Lancey has issued the order.

HUGH.   Ah. *Edictum imperatoris.*[3]

OWEN.   You should change out of those wet clothes. I've got to go. I've got to see Doalty Dan Doalty.

HUGH.   What about?

OWEN.   I'll be back soon.

[As OWEN *exits.*]

HUGH.   Take care, Owen. To remember everything is a form of madness. [*He looks around the room, carefully, as if he were about to leave it forever. Then he looks at* JIMMY, *sleep again.*] The road to Sligo. A spring morning. 1798.[4] Going into battle. Do you remember, James? Two young gallants with pikes across their shoulders and the *Aeneid* in their pockets. Everything seemed to find definition that spring—a congruence, a miraculous matching of hope and past and present and possibility. Striding across the fresh, green land. The rhythms of perception heightened. The whole enterprise of consciousness accelerated. We were gods that morning, James; and I had recently married *my* goddess, Caitlin Dubh Nic Reactainn, may she rest in peace. And to leave her and my infant son in his cradle—that was heroic, too. By God, sir, we were magnificent. We marched as far as—where was it?—Glenties! All of twenty-three miles in one day. And it was there, in Phelan's pub, that we got homesick for Athens, just like Ulysses. The *desiderium nostrorum*—the need for our own. Our *pietas*,[5] James, was for older, quieter things. And that was the longest twenty-three miles back I ever made. [*Toasts* JIMMY.] My friend, confusion is not an ignoble condition.

[MAIRE *enters.*]

MAIRE.   I'm back again. I set out for somewhere but I couldn't remember where. So I came back here.

HUGH.   Yes, I will teach you English, Maire Chatach.

MAIRE.   Will you, Master? I must learn it. I need to learn it.

---

3. The decree of the commander
4. A year of rebellious outbreaks leading to the landing of French supporters in August and quick

British suppression of insurrection.
5. piety

HUGH.   Indeed you may well be my only pupil. [*He goes towards the steps and begins to ascend.*]

MAIRE.   When can we start?

HUGH.   Not today. Tomorrow, perhaps. After the funeral. We'll begin tomorrow. [*Ascending.*] But don't expect too much. I will provide you with the available words and the available grammar. But will that help you to interpret between privacies? I have no idea. But it's all we have. I have no idea at all. [*He is now at the top.*]

MAIRE.   Master, what does the English word 'always' mean?

HUGH.   *Semper—per omnia saecula.*[6] The Greeks called it '*aei*'. It's not a word I'd start with. It's a silly word, girl.

> [*He sits.* JIMMY *is awake. He gets to his feet.* MAIRE *sees the Name-Book, picks it up, and sits with it on her knee.*]

MAIRE.   When he comes back, this is where he'll come to. He told me this is where he was happiest.

> [JIMMY *sits beside* MAIRE.]

JIMMY.   Do you know the Greek word *endogamein?* It means to marry within the tribe. And the word *exogamein* means to marry outside the tribe. And you don't cross those borders casually—both sides get very angry. Now, the problem is this: Is Athene sufficiently mortal or am I sufficiently godlike for the marriage to be acceptable to her people and to my people? You think about that.

HUGH.   *Urbs antiqua fuit*—there was an ancient city which, 'tis said, Juno loved above all the lands. And it was the goddess's aim and cherished hope that here should be the capital of all nations—should the fates perchance allow that. Yet in truth she discovered that a race was springing from Trojan blood to overthrow some day these Tyrian towers—a people *late regem belloque superbum*—kings of broad realms and proud in war who would come forth for Lybia's downfall—such was—such was the course—such was the course ordained—ordained by fate . . . What the hell's wrong with me? Sure I know it backwards. I'll begin again. *Urbs antiqua fuit*—there was an ancient city which, 'tis said, Juno loved above all the lands.

> [*Begin to bring down the lights.*]

And it was the goddess's aim and cherished hope that here should be the capital of nations—should the fates perchance allow that. Yet in truth she discovered that a race was springing from Trojan blood to overthrow some day these Tyrian towers—a people kings of broad realms and proud in war who would come forth for Lybia's downfall . . .

Black

---

6. Always—for all time.

BACKGROUNDS
AND CRITICISM

Irish Drama

LADY GREGORY

Our Irish Theatre †

* * *

On one of those days at Duras in 1898,[1] Mr. Edward Martyn, my neighbour, came to see the Count, bringing with him Mr. Yeats, whom I did not then know very well, though I cared for his work very much and had already, through his directions, been gathering folk-lore. They had lunch with us, but it was a wet day, and we could not go out. After a while I thought the Count wanted to talk to Mr. Martyn alone; so I took Mr. Yeats to the office where the steward used to come to talk,—less about business I think than of the Land War or the state of the country, or the last year's deaths and marriages from Kinvara to the headland of Aughanish. We sat there through that wet afternoon, and though I had never been at all interested in theatres, our talk turned on plays. Mr. Martyn had written two, *The Heather Field* and *Maeve*. They had been offered to London managers, and now he thought of trying to have them produced in Germany where there seemed to be more room for new drama than in England. I said it was a pity we had no Irish theatre where such plays could be given. Mr. Yeats said that had always been a dream of his, but he had of late thought it an impossible one, for it could not at first pay its way, and there was no money to be found for such a thing in Ireland.

We went on talking about it, and things seemed to grow possible as we talked, and before the end of the afternoon we had made our plan. We said we would collect money, or rather ask to have a certain sum of money guaranteed. We would then take a Dublin theatre and give a

† From *Our Irish Theatre: A Chapter of Autobiography* (New York: Oxford University Press; Bucks: Colin Smythe Ltd., 1972). 1. In fact 1897.

performance of Mr. Martyn's *Heather Field* and one of Mr. Yeats's own plays, *The Countess Cathleen*. I offered the first guarantee of £25.

A few days after that I was back at Coole,[2] and Mr. Yeats came over from Mr. Martyn's home, Tillyra, and we wrote a formal letter to send out. We neither of us write a very clear hand, but a friend had just given me a Remington typewriter and I was learning to use it, and I wrote out the letter with its help. That typewriter has done a great deal of work since that day, making it easy for the printers to read my plays and translations, and Mr. Yeats's plays and essays, and sometimes his poems. I have used it also for many, many hundreds of letters that have had to be written about theatre business in each of these last fifteen years. It has gone with me very often up and down to Dublin and back again, and it went with me even to America last year that I might write my letters home. And while I am writing the leaves are falling, and since I have written those last words on its keys, she who had given it to me has gone. She gave me also the great gift of her friendship through more than half my lifetime, Enid, Lady Layard, Ambassadress at Constantinople and Madrid, helper of the miserable and the wounded in the Turkish-Russian war; helper of the sick in the hospital she founded at Venice, friend and hostess and guest of queens in England and Germany and Rome. She was her husband's good helpmate while he lived—is not the Cyprus treaty set down in that clear handwriting I shall never see coming in here again? And widowed, she kept his name in honour, living after him for fifteen years, and herself leaving a noble memory in all places where she had stayed, and in Venice where her home was and where she died.

Our statement—it seems now a little pompous—began:

"We propose to have performed in Dublin in the spring of every year certain Celtic and Irish plays, which whatever be their degree of excellence will be written with a high ambition, and so to build up a Celtic and Irish school of dramatic literature. We hope to find in Ireland an uncorrupted and imaginative audience trained to listen by its passion for oratory, and believe that our desire to bring upon the stage the deeper thoughts and emotions of Ireland will ensure for us a tolerant welcome, and that freedom to experiment which is not found in theatres of England, and without which no new movement in art or literature can succeed. We will show that Ireland is not the home of buffoonery and of easy sentiment, as it has been represented, but the home of an ancient idealism. We are confident of the support of all Irish people, who are

2. Coole Park, county Galway, her home and the subject of several Yeats poems [*Editor*].

weary of misrepresentation, in carrying out a work that is outside all the political questions that divide us."

I think the word "Celtic" was put in for the sake of Fiona Macleod, whose plays however we never acted, though we used to amuse ourselves by thinking of the call for "author" that might follow one, and the possible appearance of William Sharp in place of the beautiful woman he had given her out to be, for even then we had little doubt they were one and the same person. I myself never quite understood the meaning of the "Celtic Movement," which we were said to belong to. When I was asked about it, I used to say it was a movement meant to persuade the Scotch to begin buying our books, while we continued not to buy theirs.

We asked for a guarantee fund of £300 to make the experiment, which we hoped to carry on during three years. The first person I wrote to was the old poet, Aubrey de Vere. He answered very kindly, saying, "Whatever develops the genius of Ireland, must in the most effectual way benefit her; and in Ireland's genius I have long been a strong believer. Circumstances of very various sorts have hitherto tended much to retard the development of that genius; but it cannot fail to make itself recognised before very long, and Ireland will have cause for gratitude to all those who have hastened the coming of that day."

I am glad we had this letter, carrying as it were the blessing of the generation passing away to that which was taking its place. He was the first poet I had ever met and spoken with; he had come in my girlhood to a neighbour's house. He was so gentle, so fragile, he seemed to have been wafted in by that "wind from the plains of Athenry" of which he wrote in one of his most charming little poems. He was of the Lake School, and talked of Wordsworth, and I think it was a sort of courtesy or deference to him that I determined to finish reading The Excursion, which though a reader of poetry it had failed me, as we say, to get through. At last one morning I climbed up to a wide wood, Grobawn, on one of the hillsides of Slieve Echtge, determined not to come down again until I had honestly read every line. I think I saw the sun set behind the far-off Connemara hills before I came home, exhausted but triumphant! I have a charming picture of Aubrey de Vere in my mind as I last saw him, at a garden party in London. He was walking about, having on his arm, in the old-world style, the beautiful Lady Somers, lovely to the last as in Thackeray's day, and as I had heard of her from many of that time, and as she had been painted by [George Frederick] Watts.

Some gave us their promise with enthusiasm but some from good will only, without much faith that an Irish Theatre would ever come to success. One friend, a writer of historical romance, wrote: "October 15th. I enclose a cheque for £1, but confess it is more as a proof of regard for *you* than a belief in the drama, for I cannot with the best wish in the world to do so, feel hopeful on that subject. My experience has been that any attempt at treating Irish history is a fatal handicap, not to say absolute *bar*, to anything in the shape of popularity, and I cannot see how any drama can flourish which is not to some degree supported by the public, as it is even more dependent on it than literature is. There *are* popular Irish dramatists, of course, and *very* popular ones, but then unhappily they did not treat of Irish subjects, and *The School for Scandal* and *She Stoops to Conquer*[3] would hardly come under your category. You will think me very discouraging, but I cannot help it, and I am also afraid that putting plays experimentally on the boards is a very costly entertainment. Where will they be acted in the first instance? And has any stage manager undertaken to produce them? Forgive my tiresomeness; it does not come from want of sympathy, only from a little want of hope, the result of experience."

"October 19th: I seize the opportunity of writing again as I am afraid you will have thought I wrote such a unsympathetic letter. It is not, believe me, that I would not give anything to see Irish literature and Irish drama taking a good place, as it ought to do, and several of the authors you name I admire extremely. It is only from the practical and *paying* point of view that I feel it to be rather rash. Plays cost more, I take it, to produce than novels, and one would feel rather rash if one brought out a novel at one's own risk."

I think the only actual refusals I had were from three members of the Upper House. I may give their words as types of the discouragement which we have often met with from friends: "I need not, I am sure, tell you how I gladly would take part in anything for the honour of Old Ireland and especially anything of the kind in which you feel an interest; but I must tell you frankly that I do not much believe in the movement about which you have written to me. I have no sympathy, you will be horrified to hear, with the 'London Independent Theatre', and I am sure that if Ibsen and Co. could know what is in my mind, they would regard me as a 'Philistine' of the coarsest class! Alas! so far from wishing to see the Irish characters of Charles Lever[4] supplanted by more refined types, they have always been the delight of my heart, and there is no author in whose healthy, rollicking company, even nowadays, I spend a spare hour

3. By Irish-born playwrights, respectively, Richard Brinsley Sheridan (1751–1816) and Oliver Goldsmith (1730–74) [Editor].

4. Irish novelist (1806–72) whose characters were by many Irish considered gross caricatures [Editor].

with more thorough enjoyment. I am very sorry that I cannot agree with you in these matters, and I am irreclaimable; but all the same I remain with many pleasant remembrances and good wishes for you and yours, Yours very truly——"

Another, the late Lord Ashbourne, wrote: "I know too little of the matter or the practicability of the idea to be able to give my name to your list, but I shall watch the experiment with interest and be glad to attend. The idea is novel and curious and how far it is capable of real-isation I am not at all in a position to judge. Some of the names you mention are well known in literature but not as dramatists or playwriters, and therefore the public will be one to be worked up by enthusiasm and love of country. The existing class of actors will not, of course, be avail-able, and the existing playgoers are satisfied with their present attrac-tions. Whether 'houses' can be got to attend the new plays, founded on new ideas and played by new actors, no one can foretell."

One, who curiously has since then become an almost too zealous supporter of our theatre, says: "I fear I am not too sanguine about the success in a pecuniary way of a 'Celtic Theatre' nor am I familiar with the works, dramatic or otherwise, of Mr. Yeats or of Mr. Martyn. There-fore, at the risk of branding myself in your estimation as a hopeless Saxon and Philistine, I regret I cannot see my way to giving my name to the enterprise or joining in the guarantee." On the other hand, Pro-fessor [John Pentland] Mahaffy says, rather unexpectedly, writing from Trinity College: "I am ready to risk £5 for your scheme and hope they may yet play their drama in Irish. It will be as intelligible to the nation as Italian, which we so often hear upon our stage."

And many joined who had seemed too far apart to join in any scheme. Mr. William Hartpole Lecky sent a promise of £5 instead of the £1 I had asked. Lord Dufferin, Viceroy of India and Canada, Ambassador at Paris, Constantinople, St. Petersburg, and Rome, not only promised but sent his guarantee in advance. I returned it later, for the sums guaran-teed were never called for, Mr. Martyn very generously making up all loss. Miss Jane Barlow, Miss Emily Lawless, the Lord Chancellor of Ireland ("Peter the Packer" as he was called by Nationalists), John O'Leary, Mr. T. M. Healy, Lord and Lady Ardilaun, the Duchess of St. Albans, Doctor Douglas Hyde, the Rt. Hon. Horace Plunkett, Mr. John Dillon, M.P., all joined. Mr. John Redmond supported us, and afterwards wrote me a letter of commendation with leave to use it. Mr. William O'Brien was another supporter. I did not know him personally but I remember one day long ago going to tea at the Speaker's house, after I had heard him in a debate, and saying I thought him the most stirring speaker of all the Irish party, and I was amused when my gentle and dignified hostess, Mrs. Peel, said, "I quite agree with you. When I hear William O'Brien make a speech, I feel that if I were an Irishwoman, I should like to go and break windows."

Then Mr. Yeats and Mr. Martyn went to Dublin to make preparations, but the way was unexpectedly blocked by the impossibility of getting a theatre. The only Dublin theatres, the Gaiety, the Royal, and the Queen's, were engaged far ahead, and in any case we could not have given them their price. Then we thought of taking a hall or a concert room, but there again we met with disappointment. We found there was an old Act in existence, passed just before the Union, putting a fine of £300 upon any one who should give a performance for money in any unlicensed building. As the three large theatres were the only buildings licensed, a claim for a special license would have to be argued by lawyers, charging lawyer's fees, before the Privy Council. We found that even amateurs who acted for charities were forced to take one of the licensed theatres, so leaving but little profit for the charity. There were suggestions made of forming a society like the Stage Society in London, to give performances to its members only, but this would not have been a fit beginning for the National Theatre of our dreams. I wrote in a letter at that time: "I am all for having the Act repealed or a Bill brought in, empowering the Municipality to license halls when desirable." And although this was looked on as a counsel of perfection, it was actually done within the year. I wrote to Mr. [W. E. H.] Lecky for advice and help, and he told me there was a Bill actually going through the House of Commons, the Local Government (Ireland) Bill, in which he thought it possible a clause might be inserted that would meet our case. Mr John Redmond and Mr. Dillon promised their help; so did Mr. T. M. Healy, who wrote to Mr. Yeats: "I am acquainted with the state of the law in Dublin which I should gladly assist to alter as proposed. Whether the Government are equally well disposed may be doubted, as the subject is a little outside their Bill, and no adequate time exists for discussing it and many other important questions. They will come up about midnight or later and will be yawned out of hearing by our masters."

A Clause was drawn up by a Nationalist member, Mr. Clancy, but in July, 1898, Mr. Lecky writes from the House of Commons: "I have not been forgetting the Celtic Theatre and I think the enclosed Clause, with the Government have brought forward, will practically meet its requirements. The Attorney-General objected to Mr. Clancy's Clause as too wide and as interfering with existing patent rights, but promised a Clause authorising amateur acting. I wrote to him, however, stating the Celtic case, and urging that writers should be able, like those who got up the Ibsen plays in London, to get regular actors to play for them, and I think this Clause will allow it. . . . After Clause 59 insert the following Clause: (1) Notwithstanding anything in the Act of Parliament of Ireland of the twenty-sixth year of King George the Third, Chapter fifty-seven, intituled an Act for regulating the stage in the city and county of Dublin, the Lord Lieutenant may on the application of the council for the county of Dublin or the county borough of Dublin grant an occasional license for the performance of any stage play or other dramatic entertainment in any theatre, room or building where the profits arising therefrom are to be applied for charitable purpose or in aid of funds of any society instituted for the purpose of science, literature, or the fine arts exclusively. (2) The license may contain such conditions and regulations as appear fit to the Lord Lieutenant, and may be revoked by him."

This Clause was passed but we are independent now of it,—the Abbey Theatre holds its own Patent. But the many amateur societies which play so often here and there in Dublin may well call for a blessing sometimes on the names of those by whom their charter was won.

We announced our first performance for May 8, 1899, nearly a year after that talk on the Galway coast, at the Ancient Concert Rooms. Mr. Yeats's *Countess Cathleen* and Mr. Martyn's *Heather Field* were the plays chosen, as we had planned at the first. Mr. George Moore gave excellent help in finding actors, and the plays were rehearsed in London. But then something unexpected happened. A writer who had a political quarrel with Mr. Yeats sent out a pamphlet in which he attacked *The Countess Cathleen*, on the ground of religious unorthodoxy.[5] The plot of the play, taken from an old legend, is this: during a famine in Ireland some starving country people, having been tempted by demons dressed as merchants to sell their souls for money that their bodies may be saved from perishing, the Countess Cathleen sells her own soul to redeem theirs, and dies. The accusation made was that it was a libel on the people of Ireland to say that they could under any circumstances consent to sell their souls and that it was a libel on the demons that they counted the soul of a countess of more worth than those of the poor. At Cathleen's death, the play tells us, "God looks on the intention, not the deed," and so she is forgiven at the last and taken into Heaven; and this it was said is against the teaching of the Church.

Mr. Martyn is an orthodox Catholic, and to quiet his mind, the play

5. Frank Hugh O'Donnell (1848–1916) and his pamphlet *Souls for Gold! Pseudo-Celtic Drama in Dublin* (1899) [*Editor*].

was submitted to two good Churchmen. Neither found heresy enough in it to call for its withdrawal. One of them, the Rev. Dr. Barry, the author of *The New Antigone*, wrote:

> "BRIDGE HOUSE, WALLINGFORD,
> March 26, 1899

DEAR MR. YEATS,

"I read your *Countess Cathleen* as soon as possible after seeing you. It is beautiful and touching. I hope you will not be kept back from giving it by foolish talk. Obviously, from the literal point of view theologians, Catholic or other, would object that no one is free to sell his soul in order to buy bread even for the starving. But St. Paul says, 'I wish to be anathema for my brethren'; which is another way of expressing what you have put into a story. I would give the play first and explanations afterwards.

"Sometimes perhaps you will come and spend a night here and I shall be charmed. But don't take a superfluous journey now. It is an awkward place to get at. I could only tell you, as I am doing, that if people will not read or look at a play of this kind in the spirit which dictated it, no change you might make would satisfy them. You have given us what is really an Auto,[6] in the manner of Calderon, with the old Irish folk-lore as a perceptive; and to measure it by the iron rule of experts and schoolmen would be most unfair to it. Some one else will say that you have learned from the Jesuits to make the end justify the means—and much that man will know of you or the Jesuits. With many kind wishes for your success, and fraternal greetings in the name of Ireland,

> Ever yours,
> "WILLIAM BARRY.

So our preparations went on. Mr. Yeats wrote a little time before the first performance: "Everybody tells me we are going to have good audiences. My play, too, in acting goes wonderfully well. The actors are all pretty sound. The first Demon is a little over-violent and restless but he will improve. Lionel Johnson has done a prologue which I enclose."

That prologue, written by so Catholic and orthodox a poet, was spoken before the plays at the Ancient Concert Rooms on May 8, 1899:

> The May fire once on every dreaming hill
> All the fair land with burning bloom would fill;
> All the fair land, at visionary night,
> Gave loving glory to the Lord of Light.

6. A play [*Editor*].

Have we no leaping flames of Beltaine[7] praise
To kindle in the joyous ancient ways;
No fire of song, of vision, of white dream,
Fit for the Master of the Heavenly Gleam;
For him who first made Ireland move in chime
Musical from the misty dawn of time?

Ah, yes; for sacrifice this night we bring
The passion of a lost soul's triumphing;
All rich with faery airs that, wandering long,
Uncaught, here gather into Irish song;
Sweet as the old remembering winds that wail,
From hill to hill of gracious Inisfail;
Sad as the unforgetting winds that pass
Over her children in her holy grass
At home, and sleeping well upon her breast,
Where snowy Deirdre and her sorrows rest.

Come, then, and keep with us an Irish feast,
Wherein the Lord of Light and Song is priest;
Now, at this opening of the gentle May,
Watch warring passions at their storm and play;
Wrought with the flaming ecstasy of art,
Sprung from the dreaming of an Irish heart.

But alas! His call to "watch warring passions at their storm and play,"
was no vain one. The pamphlet, *Souls for Gold*, had been sent about,
and sentences spoken by the demons in the play and given detached
from it were quoted as Mr. Yeats' own unholy beliefs. A Cardinal who
confessed he had read none of the play outside these sentences condemned it. Young men from the Catholic University were roused to
come and make a protest against this "insult to their faith." There was
hooting and booing in the gallery. In the end the gallery was lined with
police, for an attack on the actors was feared. They, being English and
ignorant of Ireland, found it hard to understand the excitement, but they
went through their parts very well. There was enthusiasm for both plays,
and after the first night London critics were sent over, Mr. Max Beer-
bohm among them, and gave a good report. Yet it was a stormy beginning for our enterprise, and a rough reception for a poetic play. The
only moment, I think, at which I saw Mr. Yeats really angry was at the
last performance. I was sitting next him, and the play had reached

7. Gaelic for the festival of May 1 and the beginning of summer [*Editor*].

the point where the stage direction says, "The Second Merchant goes out through the door and returns with the hen strangled. He flings it on the floor." The merchant came in indeed, but without the strangled hen. Mr. Yeats got up, filled with suspicions that it also might have been objected to on some unknown ground, and went round to the back of the stage. But he was given a simple explanation. The chief Demon said he had been given charge of the hen, and had hung it out of a window every night, "And this morning," he said, "when I pulled up the string, there was nothing on it at all."

But that battle was not a very real one. We have put on *Countess Cathleen* a good many times of late with no one speaking against it at all. And some of those young men who hissed it then are our good supporters now.

* * *

JOHN EGLINTON

What Should Be the Subjects of National Drama? †

Supposing a writer of dramatic genius were to appear in Ireland, where would he look for the subject of a national drama? This question might serve as a test of what nationality really amounts to in Ireland—a somewhat trying one, perhaps, yet it is scarcely unfair to put the question to those who speak of our national literature with hardly less satisfaction in the present than confidence in the future. Would he look for it in the Irish legends, or in the life of the peasantry and folk-lore, or in Irish history and patriotism, or in life at large as reflected in his own consciousness? There are several reasons for thinking that the growing hopes of something in store for national life in this country are likely to come to something. In the great countries of Europe, although literature is apparently as prosperous as ever and is maintained with a circumstance which would seem to ensure it eternal honour, yet the springs from which the modern literary movements have been fed are probably dried up—the springs of simplicity, hope, belief, and an absolute originality like that of Wordsworth. If also, as seems likely, the approaching ages

---

† From *Literary Ideals in Ireland*, a collection of essays by Eglinton, W. B. Yeats, and others, published in 1899.

on the Continent are to be filled with great social and political questions and events which can hardly have immediate expression in literature, it is quite conceivable that literature, as it did once before, would migrate to a quiet country like Ireland, where there is no great tradition to be upset or much social sediment to be stirred up, and where the spectacle of such changes might afford a purely intellectual impulse. More important, of course, and certain than any such chances from without, is the positive feeling of encouragement which is now taking the place of the hatreds and despondencies of the past. We may think that the peasantry are outside the reach of culture, that the gentry exhaust their function in contributing able officers to the British army, and that, frankly, there is nothing going on in the political or ecclesiastical or social life of Ireland on which to rest any but the most sober hopes for the future, still no one can say that political feebleness or stagnation might not be actually favourable to some original manifestation in the world of ideas. What [Ernest] Renan says, in speaking of the Jews, that "a nation whose mission it is to revolve in its bosom spiritual truths is often weak politically," may be used with regard to Ireland as an argument that at least nothing stands in its way in this direction.

The ancient legends of Ireland undoubtedly contain situations and characters as well suited for drama as most of those used in the Greek tragedies which have come down to us. It is, nevertheless, a question whether the mere fact of Ireland having been the scene of these stories is enough to give an Irish writer much advantage over anyone else who is attracted by them, or whether anything but belles lettres, as distinguished from a national literature, is likely to spring from a determined pre-occupation with them. Belles lettres seek a subject outside experience, while a national literature, or any literature of a genuine kind, is simply the outcome and expression of a strong interest in life itself. The truth is, these subjects, much as we may admire them and regret that we have nothing equivalent to them in the modern world, obstinately refuse to be taken up out of their old environment and be transplanted into the world of modern sympathies. The proper mode of treating them is a secret lost with the subjects themselves. It is clear that if Celtic traditions are to be an active influence in future Irish literature they must seem to us worthy of the same compliment as that paid by Europe to the Greeks; we must go to them rather than expect them to come to us, studying them as closely as possible, and allowing them to influence us as they may. The significance of that interest in folklore and antiquities, which is so strong in this country, can hardly be different from that of the writings of [Johann Gottfried] Herder and others in German literature, and may lie in this, that some hint is caught in such studies of the forgotten mythopoetic secret.

As to Irish history and the subjects which it offers—a well-known Scotch Professor once said that Ireland was not a nation because it had never had a Burns nor a Bannockburn.[1] It is, however, as reasonable to think that these glorious memories of Scottish nationality will form a drag on its further evolution as that the want of a peasant poet, or of a recollection of having at least once given the Saxons a drubbing, will be fatal to an attempt to raise people above themselves in this country by giving expression to latent ideals. Ireland must exchange the patriotism which looks back for the patriotism which looks forward. The Jews had this kind of patriotism, and it came to something, and the Celtic peoples have been remarkable for it. The Saxon believes in the present, and, indeed, it belongs to him. The Romance nations, from whose hold the world has been slipping, can hardly be expected just yet to give up the consolations of history.

In short, we need to realise in Ireland that a national drama or litera- ture must spring from a native interest in life and its problems and a strong capacity for life among the people. If these do not, or cannot exist, there cannot exist a national drama or literature. In London and Paris they seem to believe in theories and "movements," and to regard individuality as a noble but "impossible" savage; and we are in some danger of being absorbed into their error. Some of our disadvantages are our safeguards. In all ages poets and thinkers have owed far less to their countries than their countries have owed to them.

W. B. YEATS

An Irish National Theatre †

[The performance of Mr. Synge's *Shadow of the Glen* started a quarrel with the extreme National party, and the following paragraphs are from letters written in the play's defence. The organ of the party was at the time *The United Irishman*, but the first serious attack began in *The Independent*. *The United Irishman*, however, took up the quarrel, and from that on has attacked almost every play produced at our theatre, and the suspicion it managed to arouse among the political clubs against

---

1. Scottish poet Robert Burns (1759–96); the bat- tle, described in Burns's "Lord of the Isles," in which in 1314 the Scots under Robert Bruce defeated the English under Edward II [*Editor*]. † From *Explorations* by W. B. Yeats (New York: Macmillan/Collier Books, 1973).

Mr. Synge especially led a few years later to the organised attempt to drive *The Playboy of the Western World* from the stage.—1908.]

When we were all fighting about the selection of books for the New Irish Library some ten years ago, we had to discuss the question, What is National Poetry? In those days a patriotic young man would have thought but poorly of himself if he did not believe that *The Spirit of the Nation*[1] was great lyric poetry, and a much finer kind of poetry than Shelley's *Ode to the West Wind*, or Keats's *Ode on a Grecian Urn*. When two or three of us denied this, we were told that we had effeminate tastes or that we were putting Ireland in a bad light before her enemies. If one said that *The Spirit of the Nation* was but salutary rhetoric, England might overhear us and take up the cry. We said it, and who will say that Irish literature has not a greater name in the world to-day than it had ten years ago?

To-day there is another question that we must make up our minds about, and an even more pressing one, What is a National Theatre? A man may write a book of lyrics if he have but a friend or two that will care for them, but he cannot write a good play if there are not audiences to listen to it. If we think that a national play must be as near as possible a page out of *The Spirit of the Nation* put into dramatic form, and mean to go on thinking it to the end, then we may be sure that this generation will not see the rise in Ireland of a theatre that will reflect the life of Ireland as the Scandinavian theatre reflects the Scandinavian life. The brazen head has an unexpected way of falling to pieces. We have a company of admirable and disinterested players, and the next few months will, in all likelihood, decide whether a great work for this country is to be accomplished. The poetry of Young Ireland,[2] when it was an attempt to change or strengthen opinion, was rhetoric; but it became poetry when patriotism was transformed into a personal emotion by the events of life, as in that lamentation written by Doheny 'on his keeping' among the hills. Literature is always personal, always one man's vision of the world, one man's experience, and it can only be popular when men are ready to welcome the visions of others. A community that is opinion-ridden, even when those opinions are in themselves noble, is likely to put its creative minds into some sort of a prison. If creative minds preoccupy themselves with incidents from the political history of Ireland, so much the better, but we must not enforce them to select those incidents. If, in

---

1. An anthology of patriotic verse compiled by Sir Charles Gavan Duffy (1816–1903) [*Editor*].
2. Mid-nineteenth-century nationalistic movement led by writers and editors of the journal *The*

Nation, especially Charles Gavan Duffy, Thomas Davis (1814–45), and, named below, Michael Doheny (1805–63), who wrote a rebel's autobiography, *The Felon's Track* (1849) [*Editor*].

the sincere working-out of their plot, they alight on a moral that is obviously and directly serviceable to the National cause, so much the better, but we must not force that moral upon them. I am a Nationalist, and certain of my intimate friends have made Irish politics the business of their lives, and this made certain thoughts habitual with me, and an accident made these thoughts take fire in such a way that I could give them dramatic expression. I had a very vivid dream one night, and I made *Cathleen ni Houlihan* out of this dream. But if some external necessity had forced me to write nothing but drama with an obviously patriotic intention, instead of letting my work shape itself under the casual impulses of dreams and daily thoughts, I would have lost, in a short time, the power to write movingly upon any theme. I could have aroused opinions; but I could not have touched the heart, for I would have been busy at the oakum-picking that is not the less mere journalism for being in dramatic form. Above all, we must not say that certain incidents which have been a part of literature in all other lands are forbidden to us. It may be our duty, as it has been the duty of many dramatic move-ments, to bring new kinds of subjects into the theatre, but it cannot be our duty to make the bounds of drama narrower. For instance, we are told that the English theatre is immoral, because it is preoccupied with the husband, the wife, and the lover. It is, perhaps, too exclusively preoccupied with that subject, and it is certain it has not shed any new light upon it for a considerable time, but a subject that inspired Homer and about half the great literature of the world will, one doubts not, be a necessity to our National Theatre also. Literature is, to my mind, the great teaching power of the world, the ultimate creator of all values, and it is this, not only in the sacred books whose power everybody acknowl-edges, but by every movement of imagination in song or story or drama that height of intensity and sincerity has made literature at all. Literature must take the responsibility of its power, and keep all its freedom: it must be like the spirit and like the wind that blows where it listeth; it must claim its right to pierce through every crevice of human nature, and to describe the relation of the soul and the heart to the facts of life and of law, and to describe that relation as it is, not as we would have it be; and in so far as it fails to do this it fails to give us that foundation of under-standing and charity for whose lack our moral sense can be but cruelty. It must be as incapable of telling a lie as Nature, and it must sometimes say before all the virtues, 'The greatest of these is charity'. Sometimes the patriot will have to falter and the wife to desert her home, and nei-ther be followed by divine vengeance or man's judgment. At other moments it must be content to judge without remorse, compelled by nothing but its own capricious spirit that has yet its message from the foundation of the world. Aristophanes held up the people of Athens to ridicule, and even prouder of that spirit than of themselves, they invited the foreign ambassadors to the spectacle.

I would sooner our theatre failed through the indifference or hostility of our audiences than gained an immense popularity by any loss of freedom. I ask nothing that my masters have not asked for, but I ask all that they were given. I ask no help that would limit our freedom from either official or patriotic hands, though I am glad of the help of any who love the arts so dearly that they would not bring them into even honourable captivity. A good Nationalist is, I suppose, one who is ready to give up a great deal that he may preserve to his country whatever part of her possessions he is best fitted to guard, and that theatre where the capricious spirit that bloweth as it listeth has for a moment found a dwelling-place, has good right to call itself a National Theatre.

FRANK J. FAY

An Irish National Theatre †

In a well-meaning, but cocky, contemporary of ours, there appeared a couple of weeks ago an article headed 'An Irish National Theatre,' the writer of which suggests that we in Ireland should emulate the example of the Tyrolese, who, it appears, annually represent in dramatic form, 'the exploits of their heroes in the struggle against the Napoleonic invasion of 1809.' While the suggestion is quite feasible, and might be productive of no small amount of good, an Irish National Theatre could never be treated from such a basis.

My notion of an Irish National Theatre is that it ought to be the nursery of an Irish dramatic literature which, while making a world-wide appeal, would see life through Irish eyes. For myself, I must say that I cannot conceive it possible to achieve this except through the medium of the Irish language. English as spoken by educated Irishmen differs from that spoken by Englishmen chiefly by reason of the difference in quality of voice between the two countries; in difference in inflexion or intonation and accentuation; in the use of expressions which show the subtle Gaelic mind vainly struggling for expression through an unsym-

† From *Towards a National Theatre: The Dramatic Criticism of Frank J. Fay*, edited by Robert Hogan (Dublin: Dolmen Press, 1970).

pathetic medium. I have read and seen many plays purporting to be Irish written in English, but save that they told an Irish story, the only real distinction was in the employment of a dialect more or less accurate, generally less. It is the old saying over again: No language, no nation, and consequently no drama. English is not our language; it is foreign to our nature, and weighs us down. If we must speak a foreign tongue, French is nearer to us; indeed the Irish voice is very like the French. But if happily, and the splendid success of the Gaelic movement would seem to point to it, the Irish nature is determined to assert its individuality, our old tongue will be found an ideal one for dramatic utterance, and I am convinced that plays given in it would not only be an invaluable boon to students, but would win us converts, and become a powerful weapon with which to fight the spread of Saxonism in this country. Certainly plays in English dealing with Irish heroic, legendary, or historical subjects cannot be written in dialect; instinctively, they will be written in as pure English as an Irishman can command, and so the national note will not be struck. Now that the Gaelic movement is so large, the time is ripe, if not for an Irish National Theatre, at least for the nucleus of one in the shape of the frequent performance of plays in the Irish language.

We have now several very capable Anglo-Irish dramatists, but the Irish Literary Theatre is their proper place, unless they will take the trouble, as many people of much less eminence have done, of learning to express themselves in Irish.

There have also been published recently several plays in Irish, and it is with these that an Irish National Theatre should begin its work. And here it may be well to remind those who write plays in Irish to aim at simplicity both as regards plot and scenery. We must creep before we walk. There will be no Coquelins, or Mounet Sullys, or Irvings on our Irish boards for many years to come.

The modern drama owes its origin largely to the old mystery plays, which used to be acted by amateur actors, and these becoming enamoured of the pursuit or of their own real or fancied ability, gradually turned a pastime into a profession. In the same way, the first actors of an Irish National Theatre must be amateurs and there is plenty of talent to be had by those who choose to seek for it. Acting is a matter of temperament; constant practice before an audience and unremitting rehearsal will do the rest. Annual performances are all but useless. It would be well if in our Irish National Theatre we could have for our first actors well-educated native Irish speakers, and if possible, they should speak Connaught Irish. In this way an Irish National Theatre would be able to set a standard diction before its audiences. I fear, however, we shall not be so lucky as to get people of this sort, firstly because they have other things to do and could not devote the time and attention and study which go to making actors, and secondly, because side by side with the histrionic temperament and delight in dramatic display which is very common in Ireland, there exists a scathing contempt for the 'play-actor'; he is not considered respectable, and we have been long suffering from an acute attack of respectability. Our actors would have to be got from the advanced pupils of the Gaelic classes, now happily spread over the land, who show ability as reciters in Irish. I, myself, had the pleasure of hearing a number of boys recite in Irish at the recent Leinster Feis,[1] most of whom would have been able to give a very creditable account of themselves in a play, and nearly all of whom were gifted with splendid voices. The Irish language is a fine voice producer. They had, to be sure, been trained after the methods of the conventional reciter, so far as gesture was concerned, but that could easily be remedied.

The article in our contemporary to which I allude has been followed by a letter from a gentleman who strongly advocates the formation of a National Theatre, either through the medium of subscription, by which means a wonderfully successful People's Theatre has been working for some years in Berlin, or by floating a company. The last suggestion makes one boil with rage. We don't want any of the financial gang, who would run the Universe, Limited, if they could, in connection with an Irish National Theatre. Those who have lately been abusing the English stage should abuse the syndicates who are running it, and who are the real authors of the vulgarity now rampant there. Only the other day, at a meeting of the Lyceum Theatre, Limited, or whatever they call it, one of these money-grubbers, who are making earth hideous, suggested turning that theatre into a variety show. Let us keep cursed commercialism at arm's length. It pollutes everything it touches. The writer of this letter gives the names of several people whom he would constitute patrons. You see there's no getting over the Irish nature, or perhaps, one should say, the Anglo-Irish nature—we must have patrons. It is, of course, characteristic of the paper to which this correspondent writes that Mr. Yeats's name should be omitted from the list of proposed patrons, although he is better entitled to be mentioned than Mr. George Moore. But, stay, perhaps the pious editor's hidebound prejudice moved him to expunge Mr. Yeats's name, which may, after all, have been in the original letter.

Personally, I see the way clear before me to a National Theatre. I do

---

1. Gaelic word for festival.

not think we need financial bounders or aristocratic patrons. The people who support the Gaelic movement will support a Gaelic Theatre. We would have a very, very small beginning, but many great things have started from less promising surroundings than an Irish National Theatre such as I conceive would have to encounter.

I will next week give a very short description of what Norway has done in this direction. The only superiority she had to Ireland was that she stuck to her own language.

ERNEST BOYD

The Dramatic Movement †

It is rather generally believed that the present National Theatre Society developed out of the Irish Literary Theatre, although a strong effort of imagination is demanded to connect the two. How can a theatre justly famous for its school of folk-drama and peculiarly appropriate tradition of acting represent the further evolution of an institution which contained no trace of either, and ceased to exist because of its supposed inability to admit them? The truth is, it does not. The National Theatre Society traces its origins to an entirely different source, which existed prior to the separation of the founders of the Irish Literary Theatre. The brothers, W. G. and F. J. Fay, were responsible for bringing together the company of Irish actors which grew into what is now called the Irish Theatre. They had a native genius for acting which they imperfectly satisfied by giving amateur performances in different places throughout Dublin and its neighbourhood, but on coming into contact with A. E., [1] through the intermediary of James H. Cousins, the Fays were encouraged to lay the foundations of the Irish National Theatre. A. E. had written that delicate prose poem, *Deirdre*, which was published five years later, in 1907, as his only contribution to our dramatic literature. This play at once appealed to Frank Fay and his brother, who recognised in it the sort of work which they had sought, and partially found, in Alice Milligan's *Deliverance of Red Hugh*, their performance of which had interested A. E. The desire of the Fays was all for purely national drama,

† From Ernest Boyd, *Ireland's Literary Renaissance*, rev. ed. Copyright 1916, 1922 by Alfred A. Knopf, Inc. Reprinted by permission of Little, Brown and Company.

1. Pen name of George Russell (1867–1935), poet, painter, editor, agriculturalist, central figure in the Irish literary revival [Editor].

acted by Irish players, and interpreted in the native tradition, far removed from that of the English stage, commercial or otherwise. Obviously, here were the collaborators required by Yeats, in his dissatisfaction with the English actors and the divergent aims of the Irish Literary Theatre. In a short time he, too, had made the acquaintance of this new company, which had independently been working along the lines he himself had wished the Literary Theatre to follow. Most conveniently he found an instrument ready to carry on the work which had not recommended itself to his original collaborators.

On the 2nd of April, 1902, A.E.'s *Deirdre*, for which he himself designed the costumes and scenery, was produced by the Fays and their group of actors, now styled the "Irish National Dramatic Company." On the same programme appeared *Cathleen Ni Houlihan* by W. B. Yeats. The charm of the acting, into which the Fays infused that fine spirit whose service to the Theatre can never be overestimated, enhanced the success of these two beautiful little plays, and determined the fate of the Irish Theatre. There was now no doubt that native Irish drama could be developed with the assistance of this group of enthusiasts, whose energies were controlled by two actors of genius. Later on in the same year they moved to the Antient Concert Rooms, and on the scene of the Literary Theatre's *début*, repeated their initial triumph, in addition to producing four new plays: *The Sleep of the King* and *The Racing Lug*, by James H. Cousins; *A Pot of Broth*, by W. B. Yeats; and *The Laying of the Foundations*, by Frederick Ryan. With the exception of the last-mentioned, a satirical comedy of municipal life, recalling Edward Martyn's similar attempts, all these plays were definitely of the then new school, now so familiar. *The Sleep of the King* was a minor essay in the *genre* which Yeats's poetic dramas of ancient legend alone have illustrated successfully during the later years of the Irish Theatre. *The Racing Lug*, a peasant tragedy of the sea, foreshadowed Synge's little masterpiece, while *A Pot of Broth* was the legitimate ancestor of those comedies and farces which Lady Gregory has made especially her own, having been, in fact, largely written by her.

Thus, at the close of its second season the Irish National Dramatic Company, under the influence and direction of the brothers Fay, had traced, as it were, the boundaries of the domain in which the Irish Theatre was to become master. They had prepared the ground, collected the company and created the tradition of acting which was to give the fullest play to the peculiar quality of our national folk and poetic drama. Once they had the collaboration of playwrights whose work corresponded to their histrionic genius, the framework of a National Theatre was rapidly constructed. But this framework was essentially determined by the Fays, inasmuch as their limitations imposed the lines within which the drama was enclosed. We can now see why the second phase of the Dramatic Movement was dominated by that element which is at once its strength and its weakness. When W. B. Yeats and Lady Gregory turned to the Irish National Dramatic Company they had not the freedom enjoyed by the Literary Theatre. They had to accept, for the furtherance of their purpose, a medium already formed, and with certain pronounced characteristics. It so happened that these characteristics harmonised almost miraculously with their own conception of what the greater part of Irish drama should be. But a limit was necessarily imposed upon the development of the drama, outside of which failure was obvious. It became, therefore, the duty of Yeats to explain why the limitations of a theatre where only subjects drawn from legend and peasant life could be treated, were preferable to those of the theatre which Edward Martyn desired. To this question Yeats as editor of the Theatre's organ, *Samhain*, devoted many eloquent pages, to which we shall return.

In 1903 control passed out of the hands of W. G. and F. J. Fay, when the Irish National Theatre Society was formed, with W. B. Yeats as president. In a prospectus the Society claimed "to continue on a more permanent basis the work of the Irish Literary Theatre," whereas its real purpose was to carry on the work of the Fays, who remained in the Theatre until 1908, giving the best of themselves and helping it to distinction in a measure only surpassed by J. M. Synge. Indeed, the latter's stage success, as distinct from the recognition accorded to his published work, was due to them; to W. G. Fay for his wonderful interpretation of the title role in *The Playboy of the Western World*, and his creation of the chief male part in every other play of Synge's previously performed in Ireland; to Frank Fay for the training of a company, without which the Irish Theatre would have been deprived of its most valuable asset. It is noteworthy that its decline dates from their departure, when the spirit which made the tradition upon which the Theatre now lives began to fade. But at this time there could be no question of decline, for the Dramatic Movement was surely approaching its apogee. The year 1903 saw not only the production of Yeats's admirable poetic plays, *The King's Threshold* and *The Shadowy Waters*, but also J. M. Synge's *In the Shadow of the Glen* and Padraic Colum's *Broken Soil*, with which the two most notable of the new dramatists introduced themselves as remarkable, but totally dissimilar, exponents of peasant drama. Then the Irish Literary Society invited the players to London, where the appreciation of disinterested critics confirmed the wisdom of the enterprise, the more so as it took, in one instance, the form of a substantial deed. Miss A. E. F. Horniman was so favourably impressed that she granted the Irish National Theatre Society an annual subsidy, provided the Abbey Theatre, and leased it to them rent free for a term of six years. From 1904 on we have been possessed of a National Theatre, in the material as well as the literary sense of the world. The fact was signalised by the adoption in 1905 of the title, The National Theatre Society, the ultimate metamorphosis of W. G. Fay's Irish National Dramatic Company, and the final variation of its nomenclature.

Perhaps the most succinct statement of the conception of national drama which separated W. B. Yeats from Edward Martyn was that made by the former in the 1902 issue of *Samhain:* "Our movement is a return to the people . . . and the drama of society would but magnify a condition of life which the countryman and the artisan could but copy to their hurt. The play that is to give them a quite natural pleasure should either tell them of their own life, or of that life of poetry where every man can see his own image, because there alone does human nature escape from arbitrary conditions." Written at the beginning of the National Theatre's career, these words forecast definitely the nature of its work, and show precisely on what grounds Yeats preferred the limitations of the second to those of the first phase of the Dramatic Movement. The imaginative re-creation of history and legend, coupled with the study of life amongst those classes whose national characteristics are most marked, seemed to Yeats the best foundation upon which to build an Irish Theatre. Arguing before events had come to prove the truth of his assertions, he was obliged to refer to classical literature, English and foreign, for support of his contention. He knew, however, that the facts of Irish life would ultimately furnish contemporary evidence in his favour. The countryside still preserved that unwritten literature, poetic and legendary, whose exploitation in the theatre would at once create the bond of personal sympathy and interest which united the mind of the dramatist with that of the simple people in Elizabethan England. In another issue of *Samhain* he illustrates this advantage of the Irish writer, contrasting the absence of a common ground between the poet and the people in England, with the contrary condition in Ireland. "Milton set the story of Sampson into the form of a Greek play, because he knew that Sampson was, in the English imagination, what Herakles was in the imagination of Greece." But a censorship deprives the dramatist of such subjects nowadays, although the Bible stories occupy the same place in the popular mind of England as the tales of Finn and Ossian in Ireland.

If we add to this the closely related fact of Gaelic speech, we have all the circumstances that have helped to give substance to the theory from which Yeats started. The Anglo-Irish idiom, uncontaminated by cheap journalistic influences, full of vigorous archaisms, and coloured by the poetic energy of Gaelic, has done more than anything else to raise the peasant drama to the level of literature. This factor enters, of course, into the belief expressed by Yeats that a return to the people is necessary to the creation of national drama, but he was singularly fortunate in finding a dramatist who was to make of the popular idiom the most powerful vehicle of literary expression in modern times. It cannot be denied that he was, in any case, entirely justified in holding romantic, historical and peasant plays to be the true basis of our national dramatic art. The essence of nationality could be extracted from such material, and, although Yeats's plays have had no important successors, the folk-drama has flourished, with the help of a few original, and a host of imitative, dramatists. It is the latter, numerously present and to the exclusion of all others, who enable us to sympathise with Edward Martyn's plea for another class of play. Once the peasant convention had been reduced to a formula, it was natural to turn away impatiently in the hope of seeing some innovator prepared to renounce the assured success of repetition. In recent years there has been a noticeable decline in the quality of the plays produced in obedience to the principle, sound as it was, which Yeats invoked against Edward Martyn more than a decade ago. If the drama of peasant life had not transcended the limits of success which might, at the outset, have been assigned to it, the Irish Theatre would not find itself dominated by one particular *genre*. But the domination is largely the result of an unforeseen circumstance, the transfiguration of the peasant play by a writer [Synge] of such genius that his work is already classic.

DAVID KRAUSE

The Hagiography of Cathleen Ni Houlihan †

The rebirth of a nation's literature, to extend the irony of Denis Johnston, is not an immaculate conception. It is a process of renewal that often grows out of tragic attrition and comic desecration, a civil strife of violent words and conflicting aspirations. The Irish literary renaissance

† Reprinted from David Krause: *The Profane Book of Irish Comedy*. Copyright © 1982 by Cornell University Press. Used by permission of the publisher, Cornell University Press.

that developed at the turn of the twentieth century was not the result of a predestined revelation of the Celtic mystique, whatever that sacred vision might be; it evolved against the grain of patriotic fervor as the nation's new literature arose from a seemingly irreconcilable struggle between political necessity and creative imagination.

Paradoxically, though Irish nationalism and literature had an urgent need of each other's vitality and vision, their leaders were from the start suspicious of their respective values and methods; they were sharply divided by the common goal of seeking to reassert the country's heritage and pride. On the nationalist side, the political spokesmen tried to establish a public cult to idealize and purify the national life; and on the literary side, the creative artists tried to express their personal views of the ideals and ironies of the national life. It was therefore inevitable that the artists would question and even mock many of the nationalist dogmas. Militant nationalism often seems at the point of winning the struggle, especially during a revolutionary period, when in the cause of national honor all the writers are urged celebrate the proposition that every Irishman is a courageous patriot, every Irishwoman is a paragon of virtue, and an unquestioning love of country is the greatest glory. But even when they have been inspired by unimpeachable principles of revolutionary justice, such unalloyed attempts to canonize the national character in the name of the sanctified Cathleen Ni Houlihan ironically threaten to become the occasion of national hypocrisy. They also become the obvious target of those uncompromising writers who gain the final victory because they owe their Irish allegiance to what might be called the higher nationalism—the search for the truth about the people and the nation, the quintessential nature of their character and their world. What Yeats and Lady Gregory had in mind for their new theater movement was a cultural nationalism, not the chauvinistic nationalism that was to become one of the chief opponents of that theater.

After the death of Parnell in 1891 the movement for national independence and the literary renaissance naturally but only temporarily coincided, each force guiding and inspiring the other in the early days as they worked toward the liberation of the country from British domination. Nevertheless, it soon became evident that nationalism and literature were destined to collide with each other when they weren't colliding with Britain. The record of that internal collision can be found in the life and work of Ireland's major writers, Yeats and Joyce, Synge and O'Casey, four Irishmen who felt they had to desecrate the pieties of Cathleen Ni Houlihan in order to be truthfully Irish. They maintained their loyalty to the higher nationalism of artistic integrity. Perhaps what

W. R. Rodgers once wrote about Synge effectively expresses the writer's responsibility to his nation: "A writer's first duty to his country is disloyalty, and Synge did his duty in Ireland in presenting her as he found her and not as she wished to be found." [1] Synge is one of the seminal figures, and this view of his constructive disloyalty no doubt has its roots in Yeats's comment on the genius of Synge and the way it exposed the gap that often exists between the artist and the nation: "When a country produces a man of genius he is never what it wants or believes it wants; he is always unlike its idea of itself." [2]

Synge had raised the whole issue in 1903 with his first play, *In the Shadow of the Glen*, an irreverent lampoon of idyllic peasant life that was completely at odds with the country's sentimental idea of itself. And Yeats was also early in the field. On the controversial occasion of that first performance of Synge's play, presented by Yeats's Irish National Theatre Society at Molesworth Hall on October 8, 1903, the company also performed the premiere of Yeats's new play, *The King's Threshold*, which could be described as an ironic comment on, perhaps even a recantation of his highly nationalistic play of the previous year, *Cathleen Ni Houlihan*. It was no surprise, then, that Synge and Yeats were accused of slandering Ireland by the nationalist critics, the self-appointed guardians of the country's honor, and were vehemently attacked by Arthur Griffith, one of the leading apostles of the new nationalism. Founder of Sinn Fein and later president of the Irish Free State government, the formidable Griffith launched the first of his unrelenting assaults against Synge and Yeats and the new theater movement. About Synge's play he wrote the following comment:

> The Irish National Theatre Society was ill-advised when it decided to give its imprimatur to such a play as "In a Wicklow Glen" [*In the Shadow of the Glen*]. The play has an Irish name, but it is no more Irish than the Decameron. It is a staging of a corrupt version of that world-wide libel on womankind—the "Widow of Ephesus," which was made current in Ireland by the hedge-schoolmaster. . . . Mr. Synge's play purports to attack "our Irish institution, the loveless marriage"—a reprehensible institution but not one peculiar to Ireland. We believe the loveless marriage is something of an institution in France and Germany and even in the superior country across the way, and, if we recollect our books, it was something of

1. *Sunday Times*, June 7, 1959. This was Rodgers' review of David H. Greene and Edward M. Stephens, *J. M. Synge* (New York: Macmillan, 1959).

2. W. B. Yeats, "The Death of Synge" (1928), in *The Autobiographies of W. B. Yeats* (London: Macmillan, 1953), p. 316.

an institution in that nursery of the arts—ancient Greece. . . . Man
and woman in rural Ireland, according to Mr. Synge, marry lacking love, and, as a consequence, the woman proves unfaithful. Mr.
Synge never found that in Irish life.[3]

Well, hardly ever. There is unintentional humor in this quixotic defense
of the purity of Irish womanhood, but Griffith was unable to see the
humor in the play and disinclined to judge it as a work of art. According
to his nationalistic idealism, the play was a profane and foreign influence, a dangerous libel against Irish women, and therefore false. Nor
was he alone in holding this chauvinistic view, for the performance of
the play was greeted by some hissing and a minor disturbance when
three prominent members of the Theatre Society who were in the audience walked out in protest and resigned from the company. Dr. James
H. Cousins, the Irish poet and critic who was present at the time, has
described the motive for the walkout: "Maud Gonne, Maire Quinn and
Dudley Digges left the hall in protest against what they regarded as a
decadent intrusion where the inspiration of idealism rather than the down
pull of realism was needed."[4] The Irish artist, therefore, was now a
decadent intruder in his native land, and by these pure standards of
uplifting behavior, a fabricated idealism was more palatable than the
ironic realities of Irish life.

If the three protesters had remained in the hall to see the following
performance of Yeats's new play, they would have been exposed to another
shock. They had all acted in his *Cathleen Ni Houlihan* in 1902, with
Maud Gonne in the title role of the regal Old Woman who exhorts the
patriots of the 1798 Rising to die a martyr's death for Ireland—"They
shall be remembered for ever." But now in *The King's Threshold* Yeats
turned away from the sacred symbolism of Cathleen Ni Houlihan and
created a martyred poet as "the inspiration of idealism," the higher idealism of art. Now the poet, not the patriot, was to be remembered for
ever. The Celtic parable in this play is Yeats's manifesto in defense of
the poet's great gift of lyric power and his ancient right of high honor in
the state. When King Guaire, following the advice of his national coun-
cillors, the bishops and judges and soldiers, insults the poet Seanchan
(Shanahan) by dismissing him from the state council—"it is against their
dignity / For a mere man of words to sit amongst them"—Seanchan acts

3. *United Irishman*, October 17, 1903.
4. Quoted in Lennox Robinson, *Ireland's Abbey
Theatre: A History, 1899–1951* (London: Sidgwick
and Jackson, 1951), p. 36. Robinson had para-
phrased Cousins' account of the reaction to *In the*

Shadow of the Glen, and the original account
appeared in the memoirs Cousins wrote with his
wife: James H. and Margaret E. Cousins, *We Two
Together* (Mardas: Ganesh, 1950).

to uphold his traditional position by going on a hunger strike on the palace steps. Rejecting all attempts at compromise, he sacrifices his life for the belief that the arts must never be controlled or diminished by the state. At one point Seanchan offers his disciples a Dionysian vision of the poet's great gift of tragic joy, a vision that owes more to Nietzsche than to nationalism:

> And I would have all know that when all falls
> In ruin, poetry calls out in joy,
> Being the scattering hand, the bursting pod,
> The victim's joy among the holy flame,
> God's laughter at the shattering of the world. [5]

The later and major Yeats is prefigured in these apocalyptic lines. Only poetry—and, one might add, comedy—can transform the tragic patterns of life and triumph over them; it is a mythic process of aesthetic joy that Yeats later embodied in such poems as "Sailing to Byzantium" and "Lapis Lazuli," and in such a symbolic comedy as *The Player Queen*; it is a mythic process of aesthetic joy that Synge and O'Casey embodied in all their dark comedies. Perhaps, in an analogous burst of comic joy, God's laughter can be approximated by human laughter, particularly at the shattering of romantic or nationalistic illusions of the world.

Seanchan's fight for the absolute supremacy of poetry led Una Ellis-Fermor to make the following comment on Yeats's aesthetic: "It is a flaming exaltation of that vision which is the symbol of all spiritual knowledge and the gift of the spirit beside which all other values are disvalued. Poetry is either the root of life or it is nothing. . . . Even Brand himself never proclaimed more unflinchingly the doctrine of 'all or nothing.' " [6] It is only surprising that Ellis-Fermor, instead of looking to Ibsen's Brand for a parallel to Yeats's Seanchan, did not more appropriately turn to Ibsen's great Irish disciple, James Joyce; for Seanchan is a blood brother of Joyce and surely anticipates his martyred high priest and jester of art, Stephen Dedalus. More precisely, perhaps, the priority of kinship between Yeats and Joyce on the absolute supremacy of art should be reversed, with Joyce as the initiator of the principle. It was the young Joyce, disdainfully aloof from both the literary and the national movements in Ireland at the turn of the century, who, in "The Day of the Rabblement" in 1901, had warned Yeats not to allow the Irish the-

5. W. B. Yeats, *The King's Threshold* (1903), in *Plays in Prose and Verse* (London: Macmillan, 1922), p. 75. In a note on the play, Yeats made a relevant comment: "It was written when our Society was beginning its fight for the recognition of true art in a community of which one half is buried in the practical affairs of life, and the other half in politics and a propagandist patriotism" (p. 423).
6. Una Ellis-Fermor, *The Irish Dramatic Movement* (London: Methuen, 1954), p. 93.

ater to become corrupted by the new nationalism. In that prophetic essay the nineteen-year-old Joyce had written with his characteristic arrogance that "Mr. Yeats's treacherous instinct of adaptability must be blamed for his recent association with a platform from which even self-respect should have urged him to refrain." [7] By 1903, however, the disenchanted Yeats had finally abandoned the nationalist platform, cut himself off from Edward Martyn and George Moore, who were grinding different axes, and as if in reply to Joyce, created his apocalyptic and Joycean Seanchan. In retrospect, it should be clear that Joyce in his "all or nothing" essay had defined the crux of the creative issue for all Irish artists, not only for a Seanchan and a Dedalus, who were destined to collide with the sacred Cathleen Ni Houlihan:

> If an artist courts the favor of the multitude he cannot escape the contagion of its fetichism and deliberate self-deception, and if he joined in a popular movement he does so at his own risk. Therefore, the Irish Literary Theatre by its surrender to the trolls has cut itself adrift from the line of advancement. Until he has freed himself from the mean influences about him—sodden enthusiasm and clever insinuation and every flattering influence of vanity and low ambition—no man is an artist at all. [8]

Fortunately, Yeats did not surrender to the fetichism of the nationalist trolls, who, if they had their way, would have fulfilled the symbolism of The King's Threshold by placing literature in a subordinate and probably suppressed position in the new Sinn Fein Ireland. No less than Joyce or O'Casey, Yeats spent the rest of his life fighting for the freedom of the artist, rejecting the favor of the multitude, defending his independent theater from nationalist attacks and riots. Predictably, Arthur Griffith did not like The King's Threshold, mainly because his sympathies were with the villain of the piece, the autocratic King Guaire, and because he had no use for what he called the "selfish" poet who ridiculously and unreasonably was fighting the wrong battle against the wrong enemy. Yeats wrote a formal reply, "An Irish National Theater and Three Sorts of Ignorance," which Griffith printed in the October 24, 1903, issue of his United Irishman, defending his theater, his play, and Synge. In this article Yeats identified his version of Irish trollism as the "obscurantist" attitude of the three main pressure groups in the country that had made it their mission to protect the national honor against the profane artist:

7. The Critical Writings of James Joyce, ed. Ellsworth Mason and Richard Ellmann (London: Faber and Faber, 1959), p. 71.
8. Ibid., pp. 71–72.

the political, religious, and Gaelic language propagandists.[9] This time
Yeats had anticipated Joyce and initiated the principle, for there is a
similar manifesto in A *Portrait of the Artist as a Young Man* (1916),
when Stephen Dedalus, in rejecting the arguments of the nationalistic
Davin, also identifies the triple enemy of the artist: "When the soul of a
man is born in this country there are nets flung at it to hold it back from
flight. You talk to me of nationality, language, religion. I shall try to fly
by those nets." [1]

So Griffith had flung up his nationalistic net, and he was joined by
Maud Gonne, who, in the same issue of the *United Irishman* in which
Yeats's article had appeared, issued her own warning to the poet. From
the time she had played the role of Cathleen Ni Houlihan in his play
she behaved as if she were Cathleen incarnate, and she now wrote: "Mr.
Yeats asks for freedom for the theatre, freedom even from patriotic captivity. I would ask for freedom for it from one thing more deadly than
all else—freedom from the insidious and destructive tyranny of foreign
influence." [2] But for Yeats and the major writers of Ireland, all of whom
were at various times accused of bringing foreign or pagan influences
into Irish literature, and later had their works banned on this account by
the Censorship of Publications Board, the most insidious and destructive
tyranny for the artist was "patriotic captivity," or any form of captivity
that restricted artistic expression.

Several months after Yeats's article appeared, in a letter of January 2,
1904, to Lady Gregory, he wrote: "Did I tell you of my idea of challenging Griffith to debate with me in public our two policies—his that literature should be subordinate to nationalism, and mine that it must have
its own ideal." [3] Unfortunately that public debate never materialized;
nevertheless, the substance of the issue, literature vs. nationalism, runs
throughout modern Irish literature, not only in the heroic stance of Yeats's
Seanchan and Joyce's Dedalus but also in the mock-heroic antics of
barbarous Irish comedy, particularly in the mendacious strutting of Synge's
"playboys" and O'Casey's "paycocks," who in their irreverent behavior

9. W. B. Yeats, "An Irish National Theatre and
Three Sorts of Ignorance," *United Irishman*,
October 24, 1903: "1st. There is the hatred of ideas
of the more ignorant sort of Gaelic propagandist,
who would have nothing said or thought that is not
in country Gaelic. One knows him without trouble. He writes the worst English, and would have
us give up Plato and all the sages for a grammar.
2nd. There is the obscurantism of the more ignorant sort of priest, who, forgetful of the great traditions of his Church, would deny all ideas that

might perplex a parish of farmers or artisans or half-
educated shop-keepers. 3rd. There is the obscurantism of the politician and not always of the more
ignorant sort, who would reject every idea which
is not of immediate service to his cause."
1. James Joyce, *A Portrait of the Artist as a Young
Man* (1916), in *The Essential James Joyce*, ed. Harry
Levin (Harmondsworth: Penguin, 1963), p. 211.
2. *United Irishman*, October 24, 1903.
3. *The Letters of W. B. Yeats*, ed. Alan Wade
(London: Macmillan, 1954), pp. 421–22.

mock the hagiography of Cathleen Ni Houlihan. As a result Synge and O'Casey were more visibly controversial figures than Yeats and Joyce, and their works touched off violent demonstrations of protest in the Abbey Theatre; though this violence was probably due to the fact that the theater is a more public and more immediately provocative art than poetry and fiction, and comic desecration is a more openly recognizable sign of "disloyalty" than literary martyrdom. This is in no way meant to belittle the massive influence of Yeats as a chastizer of the Irish philistines, or the versatile power of the apostate Joyce. Far from being limited to the arrogant aesthetics of Stephen Dedalus, Joyce was a master of comic irreverence in all his works and took satiric pleasure in exposing the nationalistic follies of his countrymen; for example, in the Cyclops chapter of *Ulysses*, where Leopold Bloom plays the sensitive mock hero as farcical scapegoat tormented by the patriotic ranting of the boorish Citizen. But few Irishmen had the opportunity to read Joyce during his lifetime, when the unofficial censorship kept his books hidden from most of the people; and Yeats's unpopular verse plays, seldom produced at the Abbey, never achieved notoriety, since they were actually written to be performed in private drawing rooms for carefully chosen audiences of no more than fifty sympathetic listeners.

Although the British tyranny had over many centuries created the need for Irish nationalism, and by its harsh Penal Laws forbidding all written references to Ireland had forced the poets to invent such allegorical names as Cathleen Ni Houlihan, the Dark Rosaleen, and the Shan Van Vocht (the Poor Old Woman), the insidious pressure of British domination was replaced by the sentimental piety of Irish chauvinism. To such moralistic guardians of the household gods as Arthur Griffith and Maud Gonne, and their more militant counterparts now out in force across the land, Synge and O'Casey were guilty of slandering Ireland; but in the hindsight of history and the assessment of literary value, it is apparent that the two dramatists, though they are still regarded with suspicion or enmity by some of their diehard countrymen, were guilty only of presenting Ireland "as they found her and not as she wished to be found."

*   *   *

W. B. Yeats

An Introduction for My Plays †

I

The theatre for which these plays were written was the creation of seven people: four players, Sara Allgood, her sister Maire O'Neill, girls in a blind factory who joined a patriotic society; William Fay, Frank Fay, an electric light fitter and an accountant's clerk who got up plays at a coffee-house; three writers, Lady Gregory, John Synge, and I. If we all told the story we would all tell it differently. Somewhere among my printed diaries is a note describing how on the same night my two sisters and their servant dreamt the same dream in three different grotesque forms. Once I was in meditation with three students of the supernormal faculties; our instructor had given us the same theme, what, I have forgotten; one saw a ripe fruit, one an unripe, one a lit torch, one an unlit. Science has never thought about the subject and so has no explanation of those parallel streams that make up a great part of history. When I follow back my stream to its source I find two dominant desires: I wanted to get rid of irrelevant movement—the stage must become still that words might keep all their vividness—and I wanted vivid words. When I saw a London play, I saw actors crossing the stage not because the play compelled them, but because a producer said they must do so to keep the attention of the audience; and I heard words that had no vividness except what they borrowed from the situation. It seems that I was confirmed in this idea or I found it when I first saw Sarah Bernhardt play in *Phèdre*, [1] and that it was I who converted the players, but I am old, I must have many false memories; perhaps I was Synge's convert. It was certainly a day of triumph when the first act of *The Well of the Saints* held its audience, though the two chief persons sat side by side under a stone cross from start to finish. This rejection of all needless movement first drew the

---

† Reprinted with permission of Macmillan Publishing Company from *Essays and Introductions* by W. B. Yeats. Copyright © Mrs. W. B. Yeats

1961.
1. By the French playwright Jean Racine (1639–99) [*Editor*].

attention of critics. The players still try to preserve it, though audiences accustomed to the cinema expect constant change; perhaps it was most necessary in that first period when the comedies of Lady Gregory, the tragi-comedies of Synge, my own blank-verse plays, made up our repertory, all needing whether in verse or prose an ear attentive to every rhythm.

I hated the existing conventions of the theatre, not because conventions are wrong but because soliloquies and players who must always face the audience and stand far apart when they speak—'dressing the stage' it was called—had been mixed up with too many bad plays to be endurable. Frank Fay agreed, yet he knew the history of all the conventions and sometimes loved them. I would put into his hands a spear instead of a sword because I knew that he would flourish a sword in imitation of an actor in an eighteenth-century engraving. He knew everything, even that Racine at rehearsal made his leading lady speak on musical notes and that Ireland had preserved longer than England the rhythmical utterance of the Shakespearean stage. He was openly, dogmatically, of that school of Talma[2] which permits an actor, as Gordon Craig[3] has said, to throw up an arm calling down the thunderbolts of Heaven, instead of seeming to pick up pins from the floor. Were he living now and both of us young, I would ask his help to elaborate new conventions in writing and representation; for Synge, Lady Gregory, and I were all instinctively of the school of Talma. Do not those tragic sentences, 'shivering into seventy winters,' 'a starved ass braying in the yard,' require convention as much as a blank-verse line? And there are scenes in *The Well of the Saints* which seem to me over-rich in words because the realistic action does not permit that stilling and slowing which turns the imagination in upon itself.

II

I wanted all my poetry to be spoken on a stage or sung and, because I did not understand my own instincts, gave half a dozen wrong or secondary reasons; but a month ago I understood my reasons. I have spent my life in clearing out of poetry every phrase written for the eye, and bringing all back to syntax that is for ear alone. Let the eye take delight in the form of the singer and in the panorama of the stage and be content with that. Charles Ricketts[4] once designed for me a black jester costume for the singer, and both he and Craig helped with the panorama, but

2. Francis Joseph Talma (1763–1826), French actor [Editor].
3. Edward Gordon Craig (1872–1966), stage

designer and theorist of modern drama [Editor].
4. Charles Ricketts (1866–1931), designer and editor [Editor].

my audience was for comedy—for Synge, for Lady Gregory, for O'Casey—not for me. I was content, for I knew that comedy was the modern art.

As I altered my syntax I altered my intellect. Browning said that he could not write a successful play because interested not in character in action but in action in character. I had begun to get rid of everything that is not, whether in lyric or dramatic poetry, in some sense character in action; a pause in the midst of action perhaps, but action always its end and theme. 'Write for the ear,' I thought, so that you may be instantly understood as when actor or folk singer stands before an audience. I delight in active men, taking the same delight in soldier and craftsman; I would have poetry turn its back upon all that modish curiosity, psychology—the poetic theme has always been present. I recall an Indian tale: certain men said to the greatest of the sages, 'Who are your Masters?' And he replied, 'The wind and the harlot, the virgin and the child, the lion and the eagle.'

PHILLIP L. MARCUS

[Yeats and the Irish Renaissance] †

Yeats's role in the beginning of the literary renaissance was indeed decisive. Some of his ideals had been entertained by others, and there was considerable latent talent; but it was primarily he who, by giving those ideals form and life and propagandizing vigorously for them, as well as by the compelling example of his own outstanding creative work and his interaction with contemporary Irish writers, initiated the actual movement. The extent of his influence was certainly * * *[great]* * * for beyond the area of immediate contacts there was a periphery in which connections appear without any evidence of direct communication. The case of Edith Somerville and Violet Martin is illustrative in this regard. Their literary collaboration began in 1889 with *An Irish Cousin* and soon produced two of the finest Irish novels of the nineteenth century, *Naboth's Vineyard* (1891) and *The Real Charlotte* (1894). Both of these books were penetrating, realistic studies of the seamier side of Irish life, the first dealing with a "gombeen man" (a usurer who lends money at ruinous interest to peasants and small farmers) and the second with ruth-

† From *Yeats and the Beginning of the Irish Renaissance* (Ithaca: Cornell University Press, 1970).

less economic and social behavior among the middle class. The authors were isolated both geographically and by their ties with the Anglo-Irish upper class from the current center of Irish literary activity; at this period Yeats and his associates knew little or nothing about them, and there is no specific proof of greater awareness in the opposite direction. (After the turn of the century Somerville and Ross did come into direct contact with Yeats and many of his colleagues.) Nevertheless, the treatment of Ireland in their next novel, *The Silver Fox* (1897), differs in an important way from anything in their previous works. The silver fox of the title is believed by the Irish peasants to be a witch, and they predict bad luck to anyone who harms it. While the authors clearly feel that the peasants are dirty, ignorant and superstitious, the fact that misfortune does pursue the various hunters and other people involved suggests that some credence is to be given to the validity of the preternatural in the book. One of the characters even sees a vision of a dead man, easily enough explicable as a hallucination, but the decision is left up to the reader. Furthermore, the main spokesman for reason and common sense is the villain of the story, the railway contractor Mr. Glasgow. That this novel appeared during the very period at which Yeats was proclaiming the wisdom of the peasants, the closeness in Ireland of the spiritual world, and contrasting this situation with English materialism probably does not represent a direct influence, but it may be that the climate of opinion he was creating touched even the two fox-hunting cousins.

Nor was Yeats content with merely initiating: he worked diligently to insure that Irish literature would continue to develop along the lines he had conceived for it. * * * [H]is main vehicle was the Irish Theatre. A passage from the preliminary manifesto sent to various people who the founders hoped would guarantee the project financially very plainly reveals his design:

> We propose to have performed in Dublin in the spring of every year certain Celtic and Irish plays, which whatever be their degree of excellence will be written with a high ambition, and so to build up a Celtic and Irish school of dramatic literature. We hope to find in Ireland an uncorrupted and imaginative audience trained to listen by its passion for oratory, and believe that our desire to bring upon the stage the deeper thoughts and emotions of Ireland will insure for us a tolerant welcome, and that freedom to experiment which is not found in theatres of England, and without which no new movement in art or literature can succeed. We will show that Ireland is not the home of buffoonery and of easy sentiment, as it

has been represented, but the home of an ancient idealism. We are confident of the support of all Irish people, who are weary of misrepresentation, in carrying out a work that is outside all the political questions that divide us.[1]

The provision that the work of the theater movement would be "outside all the political questions that divide us" is obviously intended to deal with the problem of national literature. At the time this manifesto was written there was, in addition to the old opposition of Nationalist and Unionist, the new bitterness left by the split within the Nationalist Party following the fall of Parnell. Consequently, the position that political relevance was not an essential requirement for national literature was particularly useful in providing a sufficiently broad basis of appeal for what was intended to be a national theater. Of course political plays—ranging from the transparent Nationalist allegory of *Cathleen Ni Houlihan* to the satire of *The Bending of the Bough*, which contained hits at all factions—were produced, but they were put on for their artistic, not their political, merits, and not to the exclusion of apolitical works.

The call for "freedom to experiment" as a necessary condition for the future success of Irish literature perpetuated another of Yeats's early concerns. The theater project itself, in a country with no viable dramatic tradition, was an experiment; and once in existence the theater became the trying ground for many specific dramatic experiments, in subject-matter, style, staging, and acting.

Also significant was the promise to "show that Ireland is not the home of buffoonery and of easy sentiment, as it has been represented, but the home of an ancient idealism." Until the beginning of the theater movement, Ireland had been depicted in drama primarily by the stage Irishman. While that figure did have a basis in fact in relation to one segment of the population, he was nevertheless an exaggeration; furthermore, his "buffoonery and easy sentiment" greatly impeded recognition of higher qualities of Irish life, the "ancient idealism" and the "deeper thoughts and emotions." Consequently, Yeats and his associates substituted subjects drawn from Irish folklore and mythology. Admittedly, much of the idealism attributed at this time to the ancient Irish was a misinterpretation arising from romanticized texts like those of [Standish Hayes] O'Grady; and folk and mythological themes were before long somewhat displaced by realistic studies of contemporary life. But the later work would not have had a hearing if the earlier had not made serious Irish drama respectable.

1. Quoted in Lady Gregory, *Our Irish Theater*, pp. 8–9 [also pp. 378–79 above in this volume—*Editor*].

Yeats's desire to spread a sense of group effort is discernible in this passage, and his rhetorical intimations were in fact valid, for the theater movement, despite serious internal dissensions, *was* a group effort and was conceived within the context of a living movement. Consequently it became for a period so much the center of Irish literary activity that even the young Joyce, who found it hard to curb his pride enough to associate with any group, is believed to have planned to submit a play for consideration.[2]

Finally, the manifesto exudes ambition and confidence. The attempt to inaugurate a theater movement was in itself most ambitious, and the response of the Irish people to the literary activities of the 1890's had been far from enthusiastic. Yeats had been discouraged about the possibility of a popular audience after the book-scheme fiasco,[3] but now he hoped that if the people could not be made to read good literature, they might at least be persuaded to see and hear it. In this hope he was not entirely wrong: people did come to the theater. The audiences were not, needless to say, uniformly "uncorrupted and imaginative": the heirs of Yeats's opponents in the controversy over national literature made their presence felt from the beginning of the actual performances, and disturbances like those over *The Countess Cathleen* were repeated periodically, *The Playboy of the Western World* and *The Plough and the Stars* being notable examples. But there was enough support so that the idea of a theater in Dublin became a permanent reality.

Similarly, Yeats's confidence that the movement could write, cast, and stage plays was based upon the general confidence he had developed during the nineties about the solid literary beginnings made at that period rather than upon any specific evidence of dramatic talent among the early workers in the field. He himself had already written *The Countess Cathleen* and *The Land of Heart's Desire*, and Edward Martyn had some work in hand, but they were virtually alone as playwrights, and neither had any substantial practical knowledge of the theater. The addition of George Moore was a help, because he had not only written plays, but also had had experience with the stage in London. And the very existence of confidence helped produce the event that justified it. It led to the establishment of the theater; the theater offered a chance to write for performance; and given that chance Yeats became a master of the craft; Synge, Padraic Colum, and the Fay brothers were able to reveal their great talent; and Lady Gregory, who would otherwise probably never

2. *The Critical Writings of James Joyce*, ed. Ellsworth Mason and Richard Ellmann (New York: Viking Press, 1959), p. 68.

3. See the opening of Yeats's "An Irish National Theatre," p. 389 above [*Editor*].

even have written a play, soon learned to produce very competent work. Other, lesser names were drawn into the movement in the same way, and the result was that "Irish school of dramatic literature," rich and diverse, which the preliminary manifesto had promised. And the drama movement in turn served to perpetuate its inheritance * * *.

Yeats's anticosmopolitan stance, implicit in the reference to "Celtic and Irish plays," emerged explicitly in other pieces of theater propaganda, in which he declared that at first only plays specifically Irish in content would be put on, with the range of subjects gradually being expanded once the national character of the drama movement was firmly established. So too he envisioned that the Irish writers upon whom the theater would principally depend would be those "who wrote as men should write who have never doubted that all things are shadows of spiritual things."[4]

During the post-1900 years of the literary renaissance Yeats remained faithful to all of his early literary ideals, though the emphasis upon the spiritual did undergo an important modification. Soon after the turn of the century Yeats felt that a change had taken place in the world: "The close of the last century was full of a strange desire to get out of form, to get to some kind of disembodied beauty, and now it seems to me the contrary impulse has come. I feel about me and in me an impulse to create form, to carry the realization of beauty as far as possible" (*Letters*, 402). Hereafter, while the spiritual world remained one of his primary concerns, he no longer consistently felt that he must completely devaluate the concrete, and thus gave full expression in his work to mundane as well as supernatural life.

The mature phase of the movement also saw his ideals become firmly established among virtually all the better writers. For example, while there were quarters in which Nationalistic work continued to be written and championed, verse in the manner of Young Ireland[5] scarcely represented a temptation to young poets who had in Yeats the example he himself had lacked: a great national poet who did not feel compelled to write political propaganda. The dominance of Yeats's principle was of particular importance when between 1916 and 1922 Nationalist politics became the central fact of Irish life. Yeats and AE [George Russell] both praised the Uprising in their poetry but preserved certain reservations about it and did not celebrate it to aid the cause, while O'Casey was severely critical. After the Civil War the problem took on a new dimen-

4. "The Irish Literary Theatre," *Daily Express* (Dublin), January 14, 1899.
5. Mid-nineteenth-century nationalistic move-

ment, known for patriotic poetry, led by writers and editors of the Irish journal *The Nation* [Editor].

sion as the internal concessions required to establish the Free State added
to the already great power of the Church, which in turn produced per-
vasive, often tasteless shows of piety, a repressive sexual code, literary
censorship, and a tremendous loss of "life" and vitality. Irish society
became antipathetic to many Irish writers, and their works often reveal
extreme antagonism towards it. Yeats placed more and more positive
emphasis on the vanishing Anglo-Irish tradition, and AE compared the
country to "a lout I knew in boyhood who had become a hero and then
subsided into a lout again."[6] O'Casey attacked the current situation in
his later plays, offering in its place a natural and exuberant sensuality;
and Austin Clarke emerged as an excellent poetic satirist, sharpening his
wits upon the latest examples of folly and narrow-mindedness. Frank
O'Connor and Liam O'Flaherty were others who found themselves violently opposed to much of contemporary Irish life. All of these writers
accepted the position that an Irish artist has the right to include in his
art criticism of his country's faults.

Yeats's *dictum* that "a writer is not the less national because he shows
the influence of other countries and of the great writers of the world"
also found wide acceptance. James Stephens followed the lead of Yeats
and AE in turning to Eastern thought. Joyce decided early that there
was virtually nothing in past Irish literature that could be of use to the
supreme artist and turned abroad for inspiration, yet was careful to anchor
all his major works from *Dubliners* through *Finnegans Wake* in the life
of his nation. Even writers such as O'Casey, O'Connor, O'Flaherty and
Sean O'Faolain, who *had* found good local models when they began to
write, would not cut themselves off from the best foreign traditions:
O'Casey drew upon the Expressionist playwrights, and the fiction writers
were attracted to the works of such figures as Dostoevski, Chekhov, Tur-
genev, and Maupassant.

The particular sources of subject-matter that Yeats had stressed continued to arouse interest, and gradually Irish literature expanded to
embrace *all* aspects of Irish life, temptation-ridden priests and the broth-
els of Nighttown as well as the fairy mounds and the hovels of the peasants. Virtually every possible theme and technique found exploiters, and
craftsmanship, so widely suspect during the eighties and nineties, became
a matter for pride among many Irish writers. (Concerned with this problem till the very end of his life, Yeats in "Under Ben Bulben" had extorted:
"Irish poets, learn your trade.")

In sum, while during the twentieth century Ireland itself actually

6. Letter to Yeats of March 6, 1932 (Alan Denson manuscript).

became *less* receptive to the burgeoning of a native artistic movement, that burgeoning did take place, largely as a result of a liberation of the minds of the Irish writers from restricting conceptions of literature, and it was Yeats who through means direct and indirect had been the primary liberator.

G. J. WATSON

[Cathleen Ni Houlihan] †

From an early age Yeats was conscious of the anomalous status of the Protestant middle and professional class of Ireland into which he had been born. Of his childhood he wrote:

> Everyone I knew well in Sligo despised Nationalists and Catholics, but all disliked England with a prejudice that had come down perhaps from the days of the Irish Parliament.
>
> (*Autobiographies*, pp. 33–4)

There was a double aspect to this sense of not quite belonging anywhere in Yeats's case, since he goes on to record how, as a young man, he felt ill at ease even inside his own background:

> I had noticed that Irish Catholics among whom had been born so many political martyrs had not the good taste, the household courtesy and decency of the Protestant Ireland I had known, yet Protestant Ireland seemed to think of nothing but getting on in the world.
>
> (*Autobiographies*, pp. 101–2)

Here lay the seeds of that 'Anglo-Irish solitude', as he was later to call it,[1] which moulded and shaped both his whole life and his art.

How did the man brought up in that nationalist-despising Sligo come to write *Cathleen ni Houlihan* for the Irish National Theatre Society,

---

† From G. J. Watson, *Irish Identity and the Literary Revival: Synge, Yeats, Joyce and O'Casey* (London: Croom Helm, 1979).
1. [*Autobiographies*, London: Macmillan, 1961—Editor.] In "Pages from a Diary in 1930," Yeats writes of his reactions to the portrait of him by Augustus John, that at first he (Yeats) saw the portrait as that of "an unshaven, drunken bartender, and then I began to feel John had found something that he liked in me, something closer than character, and by that very transformation made it visible. He had found Anglo-Irish solitude, a solitude I have made for myself, an outlawed solitude" (*Explorations*, London: Macmillan, 1962, p. 308).

which first performed the little play in 1902 (and regularly afterwards)? For, with the possible exceptions of the poem 'September, 1913' and some of the late ballads on Parnell and Casement, this is the most intensely and narrowly nationalist of all Yeats's writings. It was of this play that Yeats was thinking when he wrote, near the end of his life:

> All that I have said and done,
> Now that I am old and ill,
> Turns into a question till
> I lie awake night after night
> And never get the answers right.
> Did that play of mine send out
> Certain men the English shot?
> ('The Man and the Echo')

The answer to the poet's question must be 'No', but it is a question he can ask without fatuity.[2] The play, set in the revolutionary year of 1798 ('Who fears to speak of '98?' is the title of one of Ireland's most famous republican anthems), tells with ballad-like speed, economy and force, of the arrival in a peasant cottage in the west of a Poor Old Woman (one of the many personifications in tradition for Ireland herself). Sustained by hopes of getting her 'four beautiful green fields' back, and 'putting the strangers out of my house', she contemptuously rejects the peasants' offer of money—'If any one would give me help he must give me himself, he must give me all', and goes off to join the friends who are gathering to help her ('If they are put down today they will get the upper hand to-morrow'), with these ringing words:

> It is a hard service they take that help me. Many that are red-cheeked now will be pale-cheeked; many that have been free to walk the hills and the bogs and the rushes will be sent to walk hard streets in far countries; many a good plan will be broken; many that have gathered money will not stay to spend it; many a child will be born and there will be no father at its christening to give it a name. They that have red cheeks will have pale cheeks for my sake, and for all that, they will think they are well paid.

2. Stephen Gwynn wrote: "The effect of *Cathleen Ni Houlihan* on me was that I went home asking myself if such plays should be produced unless one was prepared for people to go out to shoot and be shot" (cited A. N. Jeffares, *A Commentary on the Collected Poems of W. B. Yeats*, Macmillan, London, 1968, p. 512). For the Republican revolutionary P. S. O'Hegarty, the play was "a sort of sacrament," and, writes Conor Cruise O'Brien, Constance Markievicz, sentenced to death for her part in the 1916 rising, recalled in prison that for her the play had been "a sort of gospel" (*States of Ireland*, p. 70).

[She goes out; her voice is heard outside singing.]
They shall be remembered for ever,
They shall be alive for ever,
They shall be speaking for ever,
The people shall hear them for ever.

Responding to the latent symbolism and the appeal of the Old Woman's words, Michael, the elder son of the cottage, rushes out after her voice away from his family and the girl he is to marry the following day. When the younger son comes in, his father asks him 'Did you see an old woman going down the path?', and he replies 'I did not, but I saw a young girl, and she had the walk of a queen.'

In this short play Yeats has embodied and unleashed, in an extraordinarily powerful way, the definitive myths of the republican nationalist movement. There is the binding nature of the call of total sacrifice of all merely personal ties and interests to the service of Ireland; the emphasis on the need for blood-sacrifice; the emphasis on the gloriousness of the heroic gesture, a glory which makes failure irrelevant, or indeed can make failure a kind of triumph; the transmutation of the individual caught in history into a legendary being ('They shall be remembered for ever'), made possible by the sacrificial act; the belief in the power of the heroic sacrifice to work its own miraculous, quasi-religious transubstantiation on Ireland herself—the poor old woman becomes, at the moment of commitment to her, a young girl with the walk of a queen. It is historical fact that such emotions and ideas filled the minds and informed the deeds of the leaders of the Rising which took place fourteen years after the first performance of Yeats's play, especially in the case of the romantic [Padraig] Pearse.[3] And such emotions and ideas, further validated, as it were, by the (partial) success of that Rising—itself so much a romantic-heroic gesture—continue to play a large part in the mythology of republican nationalism in Ireland to this very day.

Many factors were at work in the young Yeats's alignment of himself with the nationalist *credo* of which *Cathleen ni Houlihan* is such a passionate expression.[4] In the first place, it is an indication of that cultural

3. See Nicholas Mansergh, *The Irish Question 1840–1921*, esp. ch. 8. "The Influence of the Romantic Idea in Irish Politics," and W. I. Thompson, *The Imagination of an Insurrection: Dublin, Easter 1916*.
4. Probably the fullest, and certainly the most stimulating and provocative, account of Yeats's relationship to Irish politics is given by Conor Cruise

O'Brien, "Passion and Cunning; Notes on the Politics of Yeats," in A. N. Jeffares and K. G. W. Cross, eds., *In Excited Reverie: Centenary Tribute to W. B. Yeats* (Macmillan, London, 1965), pp. 207–278. As will be seen, however, I do not agree with the overall tone of Dr. O'Brien's hugely entertaining essay.

or racial loneliness discussed above—Yeats did not feel English, despite the traditional Unionism of his class, and further felt that his membership of that class cut him off from the majority of his fellow countrymen. As he wrote in 1901:

> Moses was little good to his people until he had killed an Egyptian; and for the most part a writer or public man of the upper classes is useless to this country till he has done something that separates him from his class.
>
> (*Explorations*, p. 83)

Cathleen is very much an act of severance, and an attempt to assert a sense of identity with an uncompromised 'Irishness'.

Yeats might have achieved this more simply by becoming a Catholic, of course, the whimsical could argue. But the silly point serves to indicate a special appeal of radical republicanism to him; it had been, from its origins, anti-clerical, a regular recipient of episcopal condemnations, and hence—in Yeats's early years, and especially after the fall of Parnell, which did much to fan anti-clericalism in the country—could meet his desire for identity without making him feel swamped by the vulgarity of Catholicism (the lack of 'good taste,' of 'household courtesy and decency').

It would be very wrong to suggest, naturally, that sociological factors alone motivated Yeats's nationalist tendencies. There was a genuine idealism in the romantic republican tradition which meshed with a genuine romantic idealism in Yeats himself. The revulsion from the comic stereotypical Irish man of *Punch* with his 'amusing' tipsiness, unreliability, inability to speak proper English and farcical indifference to tomorrow, underlay much of the idealisation in the writings of the literary revival. Both Yeats and Lady Gregory saw the prime aim of their work at the outset as the necessity to bring back dignity to the image of Ireland, both at home and abroad. The intransigence of the republican tradition, the persistence of the ideal of selfless service to a romantic vision of Ireland through fair times and foul, the self-perpetuating legendary quality of this romantic nationalism which could invest the present and the future with the glamour of a glorious past ('They shall be remembered for ever,' says the Old Woman, and proves it by citing her own litany of the glorious dead)—all of this certainly suggests and supplies images and symbols of more 'dignity' than anything in the Paddy-with-the-pig-in-his-kitchen-and-the-caubeen-in-his-gob, stage-Irish stereotype. Yeats was to change his mind about the virtues of intransigence, of 'hearts with one purpose alone'; but at this early stage, he found it necessary, as well as congenial, to present Ireland in his art as tragic heroine rather than comic ape.[5]

Also, the record of the extreme nationalist movement, like the record of Irish history at large, is one of failure (on a fairy spectacular scale). This made it profoundly appealing to Yeats. One does not say this cynically, implying that Yeats could quite happily throw in his emotional lot with 'the irreconcilable temper' (as Joyce called it), in the satisfying knowledge that there would be no danger of having to take practical steps to mount, or consolidate, a revolution. Rather, the tradition of heroic defeat stirred something in the deepest sources of Yeats's poetic personality, creating or finding there the emotional and spiritual commitment to lost causes which can be traced through all of Yeats's life,[6] and which gives so much of his art its profound elegiac or even eschatological tone. For Yeats identified failure—the failure of his country politically and economically—with spirituality and a higher kind of power than the merely material, the power of poetry and romance and idealism. Thus he writes in 1897:

> It is hardly an exaggeration to say that the spiritual history of the world has been the history of conquered races. Those learned in the traditions of many lands, understand that it is almost always some defeated or perhaps dwindling tribe hidden among the hills or in the forests, that is most famous for the understanding of charms and the reading of dreams, and the seeing of visions. And has not our Christianity come to us from defeated and captive Judea?
>
> (*Uncollected Prose*, vol. 2, p. 70)

Failure and poetry went together, then, and Yeats feared success if the price to be paid was prose.[7] Ireland's attainment of her political ends was

5. In his essay of 1886, on Ferguson's poetry, Yeats writes: "In these poems and the legends they contain lies the refutation of the calumnies of England and those amongst us who are false to their country. We are often told that we are men of infirm will and lavish lips, planning one thing and doing another, seeking this today and that tomorrow. But a widely different story do these legends tell. The mind of the Celt loves to linger on images of persistence; implacable hate, implacable love, on Conor and Deirdre, and Setanta watching by the door of Cullan" (*Uncollected Prose*, London: Macmillan, 1970, vol. 1, p. 104).
6. A particularly clear example of Yeats's attitude is given in this passage, written in 1934: "Even our best histories treat men as function. Why must I think the victorious cause the better? Why should

Mommsen think the less of Cicero because Caesar beat him? . . . I prefer that the defeated cause should be more vividly described than that which has the advertisement of victory" (*Explorations*, p. 398).
7. "When I was a young lad all Ireland was organised under Parnell. Ireland then had great political power; she seemed on the verge of attaining great amelioration, and yet when we regret the breaking up of that power . . . we must remember that we paid for that power . . . on a very great price. The intellect of Ireland died under its shadow. Every other interest had to be put aside to attain it. I remember the *Freeman's Journal* publishing an article which contrasted the Parnell movement with the movement that had gone before it by saying: 'The last movement was poetry plus cabbage gar-

not worth the loss of her soul. It is a very characteristic Yeatsian stance, in that it casts doubt on the political struggle *as worthy in itself*; but it is not quietist, since the heroic reassertion of nationalism in revolutionary gesture, from generation to generation, is necessary to, and proof of, the vitality of that idealism of those who are only undefeated because they have kept on trying.

For both 'sociological' and idealistic reasons, then, Yeats found the ethos of romantic nationalism congenial. One must also say that the adherence of Maud Gonne and John O'Leary to the republican ideal played a major part in swaying Yeats towards the frame of mind out of which he could create *Cathleen ni Houlihan*. For they were two of his 'beautiful lofty things', and had the power to make him feel, against any personal reservations, the dignity of passionate commitment to a cause. As he says in his *Memoirs* of Maud and O'Leary at this time:

> We were seeking different things: she, some memorable action for final consecration of her youth, and I, after all, but to discover and communicate a state of being. Perhaps even in politics it would in the end be enough to have lived and thought passionately and have, like O'Leary, a head worthy of a Roman coin.

Romantic nationalism involves 'passion', then—always a good for Yeats. One can see here, however, the beginnings of that tendency in Yeats to subordinate political and historical reality to the demands of his aesthetic sense. Thus, the aims of nationalist struggle are less important than the motive and the cue it provides for 'passionate' living and thinking, and heroism becomes itself aesthetic, divorced from purposeful action, frozen and static, a head on a coin. Years later, Yeats was to write, characteristically, of the culminating deed in the long saga of nationalist endeavour: 'A terrible *beauty* is born'[8] (my italics).

Nevertheless, it is important to begin a discussion of Yeats by asserting that an idealism in him met and understood an idealism in the romantic nationalism of the republican school, and that this enabled him to express memorably a major aspect of Irish life in those troubled years. Yeats's art, ironically enough, displays more genuine innerness with this powerful force than the art of the Catholic Joyce for whom 'romantic Ire-

---

den' (meaning poetry and the failure of Smith O'Brien), 'but this movement is going to be prose plus success.' When that was written Ireland was ceasing to read her own poetry. Ireland was putting aside everything to attain her own poetry. Ireland was putting aside everything to attain her one political end." From a speech on Robert Emmet—

a spectacular example of heroic failure—in New York in 1904 (*Uncollected Prose*, vol. 2, p. 320).
8. See Donald Davie, "The Young Yeats," in Conor Cruise O'Brien, ed., *The Shaping of Modern Ireland* (Routledge and Kegan Paul, London, 1960), p. 143.

land' does not exist except as a joke, or than the art of O'Casey who was actually a founder-member of the Irish Citizen Army.

Cathleen ni Houlihan is, however, as I hinted earlier, unusual among Yeats's nationalist writings for the directness and uncompromising clarity with which it articulates the mythology which inspired the republican movement. More frequently, Yeats is more oblique, his interest in the occult, in the epic Ireland of ancient myth and legend, and in the folk and 'fairy' Ireland, blurring the stark outline of the simple recurrent drama in which Cathleen calls her sons to heroic martyrdom.

* * *

JAMES W. FLANNERY

[On Baile's Strand] †

Yeats employed many * * * dramaturgical techniques in the revisions of *On Baile's Strand*, which he undertook just three days after its first production on December 27, 1904.[1] By utilizing a double plot that involved two pairs of antithetical characters, Yeats had two purposes in mind. One was to reflect the dialectical theme of the play by contrasting the relationship between the Fool and the Blind Man with that of the heroic characters, Cuchulain and Conchubar.[2] His other purpose was to break the logical rigidity of the one-act form by evoking an almost Elizabethan multilayered response that he termed "emotion of multitude".[3] On seeing the play performed, however, Yeats discovered that his problem was again one of imposing "abstract ideas" upon flesh-and-blood characters.[4]

As with his revisions of *The King's Threshold*, Yeats was aided in overcoming his problems with language, structure, and characterization by Lady Gregory. This is particularly evident in his reworking of the characters of the Fool and the Blind Man. In the initial version of *On Baile's Strand*, the exposition of the play was handled by means of an opening

---

† From W. B. *Yeats and the Idea of a Theatre: The Early Abbey Theatre in Theory and Practice* (New Haven: Yale University Press, 1976, 1989).

1. *Vide* unpublished letter to Lady Gregory (December 30, 1904) quoted by Brigit Bjersby, *The Interpretations of the Cuchulain Legend in the Works of W. B. Yeats* (Uppsala: Lundequistska Bokhanden, 1950), p. 75. *On Baile's Strand* was first published in *In the Seven Woods* (Dundrum:

Dun Emer Press, 1903), pp. 26–66.
2. *Vide* letter to Frank Fay (January 20, 1904), in which Yeats analyses the characters in terms of these antitheses, *Letters*, ed. Alan Wade (London: Hart-Davis, 1954), p. 425.
3. *Essays and Introductions*, (London: Macmillan, 1961), p. 215.
4. *Explorations*, (London: Macmillan, 1962), p. 393.

dialogue between the Fool and the Blind Man in which they blatantly provided the audience with background information. The scene was not helped by the fact that the characters possessed neither charm no individuality, but instead were close to being "stage Irish" farcical types. In the revision of the play published in 1906,[5] however, the background information concerning Cuchulain's relationship with his former mistress, Aoife, her subsequent enmity for him, and the existence of an unknown son, who has vowed to kill him, is skilfully introduced by the Blind Man in the form of a story to divert the attention of the Fool from his hunger. Then Yeats—and Lady Gregory—pull the threads of the plot together, delineate the main character relationships, and deepen the audience's interest by the clever device of having the Fool puzzle out the story again, this time in strikingly histrionic terms appropriate to his own character:

> FOOL. What a mix-up you make of everything, Blind Man! You were telling me one story, and now you tell me another story. . . . How can I get the hang of it at the end if you mix everything at the beginning? Wait till I settle it out. There now, there's Cuchulain (he points to one foot), and there is the young man (he points to the other foot) that is coming to kill him, and Cuchulain doesn't know. But where's Conchubar? (Takes bag from side.) That's Conchubar with all his riches—Cuchulain, young man, Conchubar.—And where's Aoife, high up on the mountains in high hungry Scotland. Maybe it's not true after all. Maybe it was your own making up. It's many a time you cheated me before with your lies. Come to the cooking-pot, my stomach is pinched and rusty. Would you have it to be creaking like a gate?[6]

Perhaps the most important difference between the expositionary scenes in the 1903 and 1906 versions is that in the latter version the Blind Man withholds from the Fool (and the audience) the dreadful knowledge that the Young Man is none other than Cuchulain's own son. Thus, as S. B. Bushrui points out, the audience is absorbed by the tale of the Blind Man, but does not fully discover its tragic implications until later in the play.[7]

Yeats's second major change in the 1906 version of On Baile's Strand

5. Poems 1899–1905, (London: Bullen, 1906), pp. 73–138.
6. Ibid., p. 78. The fact that Lady Gregory aided Yeats in rewriting this scene is evident from an unpublished letter of January 14, 1905, in possession of Michael Yeats.
7. S. B. Bushrui, Yeats's Verse-Plays (London: Oxford, 1965), p. 58.

was in vastly enriching the characters of Cuchulain and Conchubar. In the 1903 version of the play, Cuchulain appears to be almost petty in his opposition to Conchubar's order that the must take an oath of obedience to him. His only expression of rebellion consisted of a few mild expletives muttered form the far end of the Council Chamber, like a naughty schoolboy. For the revised version Yeats created a confrontation scene between the two characters that allows each to plumb the full range of the conflict between them. As with the scene between Aibric and Forgael in *The Shadowy Waters*, the philosophic issues at stake—Conchubar's desire for a rational social order versus Cuchulain's will to retain his personal sense of freedom—are eloquently debated. But the most striking element in the scene is that, in the course of their debate, the characters move far beyond mere argument and take on a passionate life of their own. It is the sheer humanity of Cuchulain and Conchubar that ultimately touches the heart and engages the mind: Cuchulain's disdain for Conchubar's life of settled ease is mingled with his longing for a son; Conchubar's arrogant awareness of his power is mingled with his envy of Cuchulain's wild abandon. Neither point of view is absolutely right or wrong, and thereby we perceive the tragic dilemma inherent in Yeats's dialectical philosophy.

At length, the other Kings, who have already submitted to Conchubar, persuade Cuchulain that he, too, must obey. Cuchulain agrees to take the oath, but only in defiance of them and of whatever fate may have in store for himself:

> I'll take what oath you will
> The moon, the sun, the water, light or air
> I do not care how binding. [8]

This scene is followed by another new interpolation—the ritual enactment of Cuchulain's oath of obedience. The hypnotic rhythm of the swaying bodies, the flames burning with "fragrant herbs", and the chanted lyrics of the "Singing Women" carry the action far beyond the Council Room and into the mythic realm of the supernatural. Suddenly, the mood is broken and the Young Man is at the door. The dreadful knowledge of the Blind Man is suddenly upon us: Cuchulain's fate—that he must kill his own son—is tied with mortal and immortal bonds that he is powerless to break.

---

8. *Poems 1899–1905*, p. 101. Reg Skene brilliantly relates the natural imagery employed by Yeats throughout the Cuchulain cycle to the doctrine of elementals taught by Madame Blaatsky and by the Order of the Golden Dawn. Vide *The Cuchulain Plays of W. B. Yeats*, (London: Macmillan, 1974), pp. 125–27.

On *Baile's Strand* is possibly the finest of all Yeats's plays. Certainly it is the most perfect early realization of his ideal of a dialectical drama.

* * *

DONALD T. TORCHIANA

[*Purgatory*] †

The best way to open discussion of the play is to review Yeats's remarks prompted by its first performance. Strangely enough, those who have written with such confidence on *Purgatory* have paid no attention to these remarks. At the conclusion of the first Abbey performance on Wednesday night, August 10, 1938, Yeats had said, when called to the stage, that *Purgatory* contained his beliefs about this world and the next.[1] The next evening at a lecture on Yeats by F. R. Higgins during the Abbey Theatre Festival, the Rev. Terence L. Connolly, head of the English department at Boston College, asked the meaning of the play's symbolism and, amazingly, got no answer. On the 12th, Yeats was interviewed by a reporter from the *Irish Independent* on the puzzle. In this interview, Yeats elaborated on his original remarks:

Father Connolly said that my plot is perfectly clear but that he does not understand my meaning. My plot is my meaning. I think the dead suffer and re-create their old lives just as I have described. There are mediaeval Japanese plays about it, and much in the folk-lore of all countries.

In my play, a spirit suffers because of its share, when alive, in the destruction of an honoured house; that destruction is taking place all over Ireland to-day. Sometimes it is the result of poverty, *but more often because a new individualistic generation has lost interest in the ancient sanctities.*

I know of old houses, old pictures, old furniture that have been sold without apparent regret. In some few cases a house has been destroyed by a mesalliance. I have founded my play on this exceptional case, partly because of my interest in certain problems of

† From W. B. *Yeats and Georgian Ireland* (Evanston: Northwestern University Press, 1966). Copyright © 1966 by Donald T. Torchiana.

1. "Mr. W. B. Yeats's New Play," *Evening Mail,* 11 August 1938.

eugenics, partly because it enables me to depict more vividly than would otherwise be possible the tragedy of the house.

In Germany there is special legislation to enable old families to go on living where their fathers lived. The problem is not Irish, but European, though it is perhaps more acute here than elsewhere. [2]

Quite clearly, then, it is life in this individualistic world that Yeats symbolizes. The relevance of the prose parts of *On the Boiler* decrying the loss of ancient wisdom must be evident. So too are those two prose tracts from these years, one a lecture, the other part of a book, in which Yeats theorizes on the development of modern Ireland after the flight of the Wild Geese. Both the lecture "Modern Ireland" and its ultimate form, the prose of Yeats's *Commentary on "A Parnellite at Parnell's Funeral,"* stress four periods, * * * each going to the toll of a tragic bell: the Flight of the Earls; the Battle of the Boyne; the influence of the French Revolution; and the death of Parnell. Yeats claimed some knowledge of the last three. In the next to the last section of the lecture, Section VIII, Yeats sums up his meaning to that point and also helps us see how the main characters are meant to be taken in *Purgatory*:

> I have spoken of the three periods which have made the Irish nation. When a period is over, what it has created remains in the national character. The eighteenth-century governing class is still with us, though it [is] now Catholic and sometimes can speak Gaelic, and the second period still fights against it in our blood and against the third period with its bitter national self-knowledge and self-absorption. [3]

And at the end of this section, Yeats focuses on what he takes to be the most widespread view of Ireland held by modern Irish writers:

> Though I have classed Mr. Bernard Shaw with the writers of an earlier period, he has in the one play he wrote for the Abbey Theatre, *John Bull's Other Island*, displayed in the character of the spoilt priest Ireland as it appears to the Irish novelists and dramatists of today, and summed up what might be their final thought. Four years [ago], while ill in Italy, and not sure I would know active life again, I wrote in my diary the events of life and art that had most [moved] me, and I numbered the moralizing of the spoilt priest: [. . . There is only one place of horror and torment known to my

2. "Dramatist's Answer to U.S. Priest's Query," *Irish Independent*, 13 August 1938. The italics are mine.

3. "Modern Ireland," *Massachusetts Review*, V, 267.

religion; and that place is hell. Therefore it is plain to me that this earth of ours must be hell, and that we are all here, as the Indian revealed to me—perhaps he was sent to reveal it to me—to expiate crimes committed by us in a former existence.][4]

These comments and preoccupations, beyond the evidence of prose and poetry in *On the Boiler*, are added because modern Ireland, its past and future, is the essential material for *Purgatory*. From the destruction of a house, we see the decline of the family and the individual into the final spiritual anguish of souls in purgatory, while the Old Man lives in virtual hell on earth. Clearly I cannot agree with those who find the subject of Ireland somewhat beneath Yeats's talent. Equally obvious must be my indebtedness to interpretations of the play offered by Donald Pearce and John Heath-Stubbs.[5]

The action, immediately perceived, is curiously timeless. Yet if one contemplates it as present action, he can be said to meet an old pedlar—who had "lived among great houses"—and his son before the ruins of an ancient house. The Old Man had seen the house and the bare tree a year before. We are also told on the first page that he had seen it fifty years earlier, "before the thunderbolt had riven it." Presumably he would have seen it just before Parnell was rejected by his party in 1889, an act that split the nation. The scenario has the Old Man begotten some sixty-three years earlier than the time of the play. As I speculate, the scenario was written in early 1938. Thus the destruction of the house by his drunken father, when the Old Man was sixteen, would have occurred close to the death of Parnell in October 1891. If we continue to believe the play contemporary, the Boy was born near August 10, 1922, by his own words: ". . . my age, sixteen years old/At the Puck Fair." One need not elaborate on the Saturnalia of those three days (9, 10, 11 August). The Fair, the beginning of the Free State, and the opening day of the play, August 10, 1938, all seem tied together. There is no reason to review the action that brings the Old Man to kill his son. However, as the Old Man discovers, that killing has not stopped his mother's purgatorial dream, for the consequences of her transgressions rest upon herself and her husband; thus "There is no help but in themselves/And in the mercy of God." She remains in her purgatory, her son the Old Man in his hell on earth. This double state is summed up in his final cry:

4. Ibid., pp. 267–68. The bracketed material is Shaw's, added by Curtis Bradford, the editor of Yeats's piece.
5. Donald R. Pearce, "Yeats's Last Plays: An Interpretation," *ELH*, XVIII (March 1951), 71–

75; and John Heath-Stubbs, *On a Darkling Plain* (London, 1950), p. 205. Those who deny the importance of Ireland to the play may also be denying Yeats's intention of placing *Purgatory* at the end of *On the Boiler*.

O God
Release my mother's soul from its dream!
Mankind can do no more. Appease
The misery of the living and the remorse of the dead.

Without turning the play into an allegory, which those with an historical interest like mine may tend to do, one can nevertheless see how the characters are nationally symbolic. Yeats himself had insisted in his statement to the Irish press that the play was to be read symbolically, not allegorically. Hence it does seem that Yeats's three periods of modern Irish history are dramatized in the characters.

Symbolically, the mother represents the second period, from the Battle of the Boyne to the French Revolution. As heir to the culture of that Protestant Ireland, she turned irresponsible to her tradition and married a groom. Seduced by his looks, she had married him and died in childbirth. These events seem to be shadowy parallels to the democratic seductions of the French Revolution and even to the popular seductions of schoolmaster and journalist that Yeats felt had turned "the English mind into a bed-hot harlot." In any case, Ireland's espousing the democratic politics of O'Connell—"the smile through the horse-collar"— seems perfectly symbolized in her choice of a groom.

Her son, the Old Man, is more complicated. He is the first consequence. His career appears representative of nineteenth-century Ireland under O'Connell, a nation in Yeats's eyes given to huckstering, denying its origins, hampered by ignorance, at best mourning over its lost heritage. The Old Man is close to being a very complete member of the Garrison, whose Catholic father later, drunk on piety and politics, burned the house down and destroyed the last vestige of that Protestant past in denying Parnell. To intrude on this neat scheme for a moment, one is also reminded of the equally relevant fanatic burning of Big Houses in 1922–23. As Yeats discovered many times from the *Playboy* days on, O'Connell's Ireland had lived on into the twentieth century and begot the Free State and those who fought it. But the difficulty—and it probably saves the Old Man from being considered allegorically—is that he suggests so much more. For one thing—and this is an important point— he is linked to both the second and the fourth periods, and seems to have all three warring within his blood. For another, as an Old Man, he also comes close to dramatizing many sides of Yeats himself: his love of the eighteenth century, his origins in the nineteenth, his helping establish an art and public opinion favorable to an independent Ireland, his increased hatred of O'Connell and those he took to be his heirs. Nor is there need to stop here. For many events of Yeats's life and memory crowd in and intensify the historical symbolism, not the least among them being Coole House itself, already marked for destruction in his mind. In fact, lines are actually used to describe the ruined house on the stage which he and Lady Gregory had used to describe Coole House:

> Great people lived and died in this house;
> Magistrates, colonels, members of Parliament,
> Captains and Governors, and long ago
> Men that had fought at Aughrim and the Boyne.
> Some that had gone on government work
> To London or to India came home to die,
> Or came from London every spring
> To look at the May-blossom in the park.

And then, in what is certainly Yeats' own voice:

> . . . to kill a house
> Where great men grew up, married, died,
> I here declare a capital offence.[6]

Yet there is also much more of him in the play. After his death, Yeats felt, the woods of Coole would have his longest visits.[7] There was the ghost story he had heard in 1916 about a crime, a consequent haunting, and the degeneration of a family.[8] The fact of Edward Martyn's peasant background and the coarsening of George Moore's blood had not escaped his notice.[9] There is an accursed, ruined house and a pear tree that bears no fruit in *John Sherman*.[1] Yeats had also carefully noted that statement an old man once made to Synge: "The young people are of no use. . . . I am not as good a man as my father was and my son is growing up worse than I am."[2] Then, too, Yeats had written an early story, ghostly and cataclysmic, of Oona Hearne, a woman who had fallen in love with a rascal, Michael Creed, "through that love of strength which is deep in the heart of even the subtlest among them [women]."[3] Nor may the symbolic overtones of one more ruined house, empty at the top and

6. Lady Gregory had written, and Yeats had read and remembered, this passage in her *Journals* for June 1922: "I have been out till after 9 o'c. Everything is beatiful, one must stand to look at blossoming tree after tree; the thorns in the Park that William used to come over from London to see at this time of the year best of all" (p. 22). According to Mrs. Yeats, W. B. thought such trips all too typical of Garrison responsibility to Ireland. See also Russell K. Alspach, *Variorum Edition of the Plays of W. B. Yeats* (London, 1966), pp. 833–34.

7. *Autobiographies* (London, 1961), pp. 377–78.
8. Joseph Hone, *W. B. Yeats* (London, 1943), pp. 284, 472.
9. *Autobiographies*, pp. 388, 402.
1. *Collected Works*, (Stratford, 1908), VII, 208, 279.
2. "The Great Blasket," *Spectator*, 2 June 1933, p. 798.
3. "Those Who Live in the Storm," *The Speaker*, 21 July 1894, pp. 74–75.

marked with a bit of shell from a daw's nest, remain very far from the powerful images in poems like "The Stare's Nest by my Window" and "Blood and the Moon."

Perhaps the bastard Boy needs little comment at all. His few actions show him to be a sensation-seeking thief, a potential killer, and a dull, embittered individualist. He refuses his father's wisdom, considers killing him, and openly admires his drunken forefather's success. How else consider right and wrong? Only before his death does he begin to see the light of his grandmother's purgatorial dream. Does Yeats hope that the sixteen-year-old Eire will also see its light? Yet the ignorant Boy helps *us* see how opposites meet in time, how dying is but a moving from one room to another, how we may embody truth without knowing it.

The stage settings intimate another dimension to the symbolism. The ruined great house offers to Ireland, Europe, and the world the ironic triumph of romantic individualism. That house, with its traveled men, library, administrators, and soldiers, is a memorial to what Swift, Berkeley, Burke, and Goldsmith had offered Ireland and, by 1938, Ireland had rejected. The Old Man's first words in the play are "Study that house." His next speech continues to claim our attention:

> The moonlight falls upon the path,
> The shadow of a cloud upon the house
> And that's symbolic; study that tree,
> What is it like?

And the Boy answers, "A silly old man." The meanings of the tree have been discussed previously. But now, seen together, the moonlight, path, cloud, and house—they remain unchanged throughout the play—are a composite image of eighteenth-century excellence fallen on evil days. A ruined house, ruined family, and ruined tree suggest individual, familial, and national failures. The house—"Its threshold gone to patch a pigstye"—empty at the top, dark beneath a cloud or curse of vaporous patriotism from a "century disastrous to national intellect," flanked by a tree bathed in the light of hatred, symbolized the haunted remains of Georgian Ireland. Other witnesses hover about in grim association. Specifically, there is Swift cursed with sibylline foresight and glaring over the wreckage to come; Burke in the tree stripped of its leaves and riven by the thunderbolt, and Burke who had fought the materialistic anarchy voiced by the Boy and the leveling democracy that had seduced his grandmother; Berkeley who had proved the world of pigsties but a dream had man's imagination and intellect enough to see everything in God's eye, and Berkeley who declared the subjectivity of space and time and so the uniqueness of all men whatever station they graced; and Goldsmith—yes, perhaps the path and the journey of the Old Man would have been otherwise in his company. Yet the Boy is also right. The tree *is* like a silly old man, his father, the Old Man, and, in the light of hatred, like Yeats. He rages under the cloud of emotional, Gaelic, Catholic, middle-class patriotism everywhere triumphant.

Tragic irony also gleams from this Georgian memorial. For the heart of this symbol of purpose and co-ordination, to re-echo Yeats's definitions of mother-wit, has at its center the Old Man's mother. The consequence of her act has been family degeneration, truly national degeneration, if we take her to symbolize that period beginning modern Ireland. Her transgression was to marry and pass on coarsened blood, a curse. Her crime, however, was really one of intellect, a wrong choice, a refusal of traditional sanctities, perhaps something like that of her original in paradise. But this fall is not fortunate, it is tragic. She had been seduced by commonness. In the face of destruction and murder the consequences must yet be played out. Hearing those eighteenth-century hoof beats on the drive of the house, must we not wonder at Yeats's words in *On the Boiler*,

> A woman's face, though she be lost or childless, may foretell a transformation of the people, be a more dire or beneficent omen than those trumpets heard by Etruscan seers in middle air,

especially since they explain a phrase describing the tragic complement of generations: ". . . each living the other's death, dying the other's life." The woman and her house had, for Yeats, the virtually sacred task of education Swift had assigned himself in *The Words Upon the Windowpane*. But here the scene of passion and the scene of remorse come together in one scene of tragic ecstasy for our edification.

Is this possible? I think so, for *Purgatory* points to the actual hell of the present. All is done. There is none to turn to except God. The limit has been reached: murder cannot dislodge historical consequence, though the Old Man mourns his lost mother and stretches his arms in supplication to God. Yeats has depicted a national genealogical tragedy in a manner that stresses action. He has recognized the awesome power of the body. His drama is based on what he takes to be true history. The end, however murderous, is not vulgar or morbid. The wicked are punished and the blame is fixed. One may imagine Yeats smiling joyously.

He may be terribly wrong, just as *On the Boiler* as a whole can be viewed as preposterous. But there is a truth expressed in the pamphlet and the play which all must feel even though it is felt in different ways. It is the truth of the purgatory all men experience from the errors inherent in the flesh during their strivings as individuals, members of families, and spirits in mortal coils. Like Swift, Yeats, and the mother of the Old Man, we are dragged down into mankind. Hence this inevitable tragedy may yet provide—and this is the great power of *Purgatory*—an aimless joy in allowing us to be the spectators of the ages. Yeats never forgot the story told him by Paddy Flynn of God's smiling at the last day both on those he rewards and those he sends to everlasting flames. One may imagine Yeats and those Augustan spirits—who shared his timeless indignation against the weaknesses of the flesh, the mind, and the society that might wreck a house or a country—happy, especially since reality was "a timeless and spaceless community of Spirits which perceive each other," and the pure joy of election still remained theirs.

Lady Gregory

Spreading the News †

The idea of this play first came to me as a tragedy. I kept seeing as in a picture people sitting by the roadside, and a girl passing to the market, gay and fearless. And then I saw her passing by the same place at evening, her head hanging, the heads of others turned from her, because of some sudden story that had risen out of a chance word, and had snatched away her good name.

But comedy and not tragedy was wanted at our theatre to put beside the high poetic work, [Yeats's] *The King's Threshold, The Shadowy Waters, On Baile's Strand,* [and Synge's] *The Well of the Saints;* and I let laughter have its way with the little play. I was delayed in beginning it for a while, because I could only think of Bartley Fallon as dull-witted or silly or ignorant, and the handcuffs seemed too harsh a punishment. But one day by the sea at Duras a melancholy man who was telling me of the crosses he had gone through at home said—"But I'm thinking if I went to America, its long ago to-day I'd be dead. And it's a great expense for a poor man to be buried in America." Bartley was born at that moment, and, far from harshness, I felt I was providing him with a happy old age in giving him the lasting glory of that great and crowning day of misfortune.

It has been acted very often by other companies as well as our own, and the Boers [1] have done me the honour of translating and pirating it.

---

† This and the next two "notes" are from *The Comedies of Lady Gregory, Being the First Volume of The Collected Plays,* ed. Ann Saddlemyer (New York: Oxford University Press; Bucks: Colin Smythe Ltd., 1970).

1. Dutch settlers of South Africa at odds with Britain, especially in the Boer War (1899–1902), in which Britain reasserted its colonial control [*Editor*].

A Note on *Spreading the News*

Some time ago at a debate in Dublin a speaker complained that the Irish peasantry were slandered in *Spreading the News,* because nowhere in Ireland would so improbable a story grow out of so little; and in the same speech he said our Theatre was not worthy of support, because we "had given our first performance at the Castle."[1] Another speaker pointed to this fiction as a very Spreading of the News. Since that day it has been said of us that we never play but in Irish, that our Theatre is "something done for the Roman Catholics," that it has been "got up by the Irish Parliamentary Party with Mr. Healy at the head of them," that we have a special fee of fifty pounds a performance for anybody from Trinity College who wishes to hire the Theatre, that our "attitude to the Irish peasant arises out of class prejudice which keeps us from seeing anything that is good in him," that we encourage agrarian outrage by the performance of "Cathleeen Ni Houlihan," that through fear of offending the English we will not play anything founded upon events that happened since their arrival under Strongbow, that we are neglecting Dublin for England, that we are "a Fenian lot," and that we give ourselves airs. Some at least of these accusations must be founded on evidence as airy as that given in the case of the murder of Jack Smith.

The Rising of the Moon

When I was a child and came with my elders to Galway for their salmon fishing in the river that rushes past the gaol, I used to look with awe at the window where men were hung, and the dark, closed gate. I used to wonder if ever a prisoner might by some means climb the high, buttressed wall and slip away in the darkness by the canal to the quays and find friends to hide him under a load of kelp in a fishing boat, as happens to my ballad-singing man. The play was considered offensive to some extreme Nationalists before it was acted, because it showed the police in too favourable a light, and a Unionist paper attacked it after it was acted because the policeman was represented "as a coward and a traitor"; but

1. Dublin Castle, at the time seat of British administration of Ireland. The references that follow include: Timothy Healy (1855–1931) MP, advocate of several and occasionally conflicting causes; Richard FitzGilbert, "Strongbow," leader of Normans from Wales to Ireland in 1170; and "Fenians," both the Irish Republican Brotherhood founded in 1858 and the nationalist tradition in Ireland [*Editor*].

after the Belfast police strike that same paper praised its "insight into Irish character." After all these ups and downs it passes unchallenged on both sides of the Irish Sea.

ANN SADDLEMYER

Image-Maker for Ireland: Augusta, Lady Gregory †

> . . . but we are "image-makers," and must carry out our dreams.
> (Letter to Sir Hugh Lane)

> Ups and downs, ups and downs; and we know nothing till all is over.
> . . . I would like my name set in clean letters in the book of the people.
> (Sarsfield in *The White Cockade*)

Throughout Lady Gregory's work and constant in her collaborations with Yeats is a delight in what she called "our incorrigible genius for myth-making," and despite the courage with which she struggled to keep the Abbey Theatre going for so many years, it is perhaps as myth-maker and mythologizer that she can best be recognized in "the book of the people." For even in her dream of an Irish theatre, Lady Gregory's main ambition was to restore once again to Ireland her native dignity:

> I had had from the beginning a vision of historical plays being sent by us through all the countries of Ireland. For to have a real success and to come into the life of the country, one must touch a real and eternal emotion, and history comes only next to religion in our country. And although the realism of our young writers is taking the place of fantasy and romance in the cities, I still hope to see a little season given up every year to plays on history and in sequence at the Abbey, and I think schools and colleges may ask to have them sent and played in their halls, as a part of the day's lesson.

Her first play, *Colman and Guaire*, was written not with stage production in mind, but as a play in rhyme which "might perhaps be learned and acted by Kiltartan school-children." Consistently she saw the theatre as part of the same movement which had earlier given impetus to the Gaelic League:

† From *The World of W. B. Yeats*, ed. Robin Skelton and Ann Saddlemyer (Seattle: University of Washington Press, 1965). Copyright © 1965 Robin Skelton and Ann Saddlemyer.

It was a movement for keeping the Irish language a spoken one, with, as a chief end, the preserving of our own nationality. That does not sound like the beginning of a revolution, yet it was one. It was the discovery, the disclosure of the folk-learning, the folk-poetry, the folk-tradition. Our Theatre was caught into that current, and it is that current, as I believe, that has brought it on its triumphant way. It is chiefly known now as a folk-theatre. It has not only the great mass of primitive material and legend to draw on, but it has been made a living thing by the excitement of that discovery.

Twenty years after she wrote these passages in *Our Irish Theatre* she was still writing plays that children as well as adults could enjoy. Unlike Yeats's, her dream of an Irish theatre was fulfilled, with her own work playing a far more important part than she had ever dreamed possible. In 1934 Yeats wrote that her plays were "constantly acted, not only in Dublin but by little companies in village halls. Their names are as familiar as old proverbs." [1] A visitor to Ireland will still find her work popular, both in English and in Irish, at the Abbey and in the provinces. Always she wrote for Ireland: writing of her people as she had observed them during her childhood and widowhood in Galway; of Irish history and folklore as she had collected it for her books; for the children and countryfolk of her nation.

Patriotism for Lady Gregory was a simpler ideal, founded on a much smaller scale than the literary nationalism of her colleagues. Descendant of the Persses of Roxborough who arrived in Ireland with Cromwell, and of the O'Gradys of literary and legal fame, until her marriage with Sir William Gregory of Coole she had seen little of Ireland beyond her own county, Galway. But the west of Ireland she did know well; as a young girl she had eagerly observed the great working-estate, and as a young widow she capably managed the Coole property for her son Robert, later for her grandson Richard. Yeats had memories of tales told by Mary Battle in the kitchen at Sligo; Lady Gregory heard tales of the faery— even more stirring, of the rebellion of '98—from her old nurse Mary Sheridan. Later she herself participated in the foundation of village libraries, visited the cottages on the estate, acted as secretary to the families of American immigrants. Her marriage for some years interrupted her firm relationship with the peasantry but did not dissolve it, and after her husband died she once more picked up the threads of her friendship with those who still hold her memory dear in Ireland. "She has been like a serving-maid among us," said an old peasant to Yeats.

1. *The Irish National Theatre* (Roma: Reale Accademia D'Italia, 1935), 6.

Patriotic she had always been, ever since the first Fenian pamphlet she bought as a child in the small village of Loughrea:

> For a romantic love of country had awakened in me, perhaps through the wide beauty of my home . . . or it may be through the half revealed sympathy of my old nurse for the rebels whose cheering she remembered when the French landed at Killala in '98; or perhaps but through the natural breaking of a younger child of the house from the conservatism of her elders.[2]

However, it was not until she found herself turning against England that she became intensely nationalistic. In 1898 her edition of her husband's grandfather's papers was published, and when questioned concerning the Home Rule sentiments that crept into her comments, she replied: "I defy anyone to study Irish History without getting a dislike and distrust of England." (At the unexpected success of Martyn's re-written play, *The Bending of the Bough*, she assured the bewildered authors, "We are not working for Home Rule; we are preparing for it.") It was not, in fact, until after she had become involved with the Irish Literary Theatre that she met John O'Leary and the other political rebels who had influenced Yeats. Through her husband, one-time Member of Parliament and Governor of Ceylon, she had made many friends among English Unionists, but at all times she managed to reconcile, if at times uneasily, the friendships formed during Sir William's work for England and those she herself made in her work for Ireland. In this sense alone, she was invaluable to Yeats; he was willing to accept "the baptism of the gutter" for the sake of his national dream, but she preferred "the baptism of clean water."[3] Involvement in the idea of a national theatre, however, increased her nationalism still more, and where Yeats subordinated his ideals of art to no nation, she avowed her determination to work principally for "the dignity of Ireland." As her interest in art increased, so too did her love for her country. The one inspiration fed on the other.

As she herself sought for the dignity her nationalism demanded for her country, so she also demanded it of others. The patriotic verses in *The Spirit of the Nation* appealed to her because of "a certain dignity, an intensity born of continuity of purpose; they are roughly hammered links in a chain of unequal workmanship, but stretching back through the centuries to the Munster poets of the days of Elizabeth." In her own work she strove for this same dignity and "continuity of purpose." (Many

2. Introduction to *The Kiltartan Poetry Book* (London: Putnam's Sons, 1919), 3–4.

3. *Our Irish Theatre* (London: Putnam's Sons, 1913), 71.

years later Yeats was to place her—along with Queen Victoria—in Phase
Twenty-four of *A Vision* in which the true mask is self-reliance and
organization.) She, like Yeats, was moved by the death of Parnell, not
realizing until later, however, that by tearing from the corner of a newspaper Katharine Tynan's lament she had

> unwittingly taken note of almost the moment of a new impulse in
> literature, in poetry. For with that death, the loss of that dominant
> personality, and in the quarrel that followed, came the disbanding
> of an army, the unloosing of forces, the setting free of the imagi-
> nation of Ireland.

Always her nationalism retained this strong desire to win once more the
dignity of Ireland, and like Yeats, she believed it possible through the
arts. One day while collecting folk tales on Aran, she happened to glance
through a volume of *Don Quixote*, and the thought of England's false
half-vision of Ireland crossed her mind:

> They see in us one part boastful quarrelsome adventurer, one part
> vulgar rollicking buffoon. . . . But we begin to think after all that
> truth is best, that we have worn the mask thrust upon us too long,
> and that we are more likely to win at least respect when we appear
> in our own form. . . . Poetry and pathos may be granted to us, but
> when we claim dignity, those who see only the sham fights of West-
> minister shake their heads. But here, in real Ireland, dignity can
> live side by side with the strongest political feeling.[4]

The words re-echo through the Irish Literary Theatre's manifesto of 1897:
"We will show that Ireland is not the home of buffoonery and easy
sentiment . . . but of ancient idealism."

*   *   *

DANIEL J. MURPHY

Lady Gregory, Co-Author and Sometimes Author of the Plays of W. B. Yeats [†]

When the Irish National Theatre Society began producing plays in 1899,
it soon became apparent that many new plays would be needed if the

4. "Ireland, Real and Ideal," *Nineteenth Century* 1898, 769–782.
† From *Modern Irish Literature: Essays in Honor* *of William York Tindall*, ed. Raymond J. Porter and James D. Brophy (New York: Iona College Press, 1972). Reprinted by permission.

theatre were to survive, for the patent limited the theatre to plays by Irish authors or foreign masterpieces. Given the limited audience available in Dublin for serious drama, new plays were constantly needed to attract the same audience to the theatre. Indeed, as Lady Gregory notes, audiences could be so painfully thin at times that she would go out the stage door and in the front to give passersby the impression that the theatre was doing some business. Since the principal architect of the theatre was W. B. Yeats, he was expected to supply poetic drama, while George Moore and Edward Martyn supplied prose. Of the first eight plays produced in English by the company, these three accounted for six. Obviously, new authors were needed, and Lady Gregory decided to fill that need.

While Lady Gregory had no background as a playwright, she was not without literary credentials. She had edited her husband's *Autobiography* in 1894 and his father's letters in 1898. But her principal works were her translations of the major Irish sagas, *Cuchulain of Muirthemne* (1902) and *Gods and Fighting Men* (1904). At some point during this period, Lady Gregory began to help Yeats with the dialogue for his plays.[1] She began to write, she explains in *Our Irish Theatre* (80), because the audience sometimes tired of verse plays, for the "ear and mind crave ease and unbending, and so comedies are needed to give this rest." Her contribution originally was slight. She began, she writes on the same page, by suggesting a sentence or two to Yeats when he began dictating *Diarmuid and Grania* to her, a play on which Yeats and Moore were collaborating: "Mr. Yeats used to dictate parts of *Diarmuid and Grania* to me, and I would suggest a sentence here and there." Her contribution may be more than a sentence here or there, for Yeats, writing to Lady Gregory on December 31, 1909, suggests a list of plays that would suit Gordon Craig's "invention"—his new design for staging plays—including "your Diarmuid and Grania." There can be no doubt that she prepared the original synopsis of the Diarmuid and Grania legend.[2]

Lady Gregory next helped Yeats with *Where There Is Nothing*, a debt which Yeats acknowledged in his dedication:

> I offer you a book which is in part your own. . . . You said I might dictate to you, and we worked in the mornings at Coole, and

---

1. The order of the plays in this essay is based on the order in which Yeats placed them in the 1922 edition of *Plays in Prose and Verse*, except for *Unicorn* and *Where There is Nothing*, which are treated together.

2. William Becker, in his introductory notes to *Diarmuid and Grania, Dublin Magazine* (April–

June, 1951), writes: ". . . there is every possibility that Lady Gregory and Arthur Symons had their fingers in the pie in a small way. Lady Gregory, at least, prepared the original synopsis of the Diarmuid and Grania legend, from which Yeats and Moore worked, and seems to have referred a good many of their quarrels."

> I never did anything that went so easily and quickly; for when I hesitated you had the right thought ready and it was almost always you who gave the right turn to the phrase and gave it the ring of daily life.[3]

Some of the characters in the play speak in a dialect that Lady Gregory later called Kiltartan, after the name of a town near her home; a dialect that Yeats, by his own admission, could not master. Some examples of this dialect can be found throughout the play—the dialogue of Sabina Silver and Colman, for example, are in this idiom:

> Sabina Silver: Oh! Paul, Paul, is it to leave you we must? And you never once struck a kick or a blow on me this time, not even and you in pain with the rheumatism. (76)

> Colman: What can poor people that have their own troubles on them get from a few words like that they hear at a cross road or a market, and the wind maybe blowing them away? (107)

Since Lady Gregory did not usefully develop Kiltartan dialogue in a play until her *Spreading the News* was performed at the Abbey in 1904, it would be difficult to establish that this idiom is Lady Gregory's but for the existence of a pamphlet, *A Phantom's Pilgrimage; or Home Ruin* (London, 1893), published anonymously in 1893. In this pamphlet, written to support the retention of English rule in Ireland, Lady Gregory returns the ghost of Charles Stewart Parnell to Ireland to discover the imaginary result of his Home Rule movement. As he wanders through the Irish countryside, he encounters peasants who speak in an early version of Kiltartan:

> It's walkin' the roads I am this fortnight, lookin for work, an' none to give it. An' me poor wife, I'm after leavin' her dead by the roadside. . . ."
> "Take this, an' welcome," he said, kindly enough; "but sure you wouldn't break your fast of a Friday with all I have in the house, these times. Sure we thought we'd be made when we got rid o' the landlords; an' sorra much luck we had ever since. It's taxes an' taxes till we're payin' more that we ever did in rint; an' the shops 'll give no credit so much as for a ha'porth o' salt; an' no sale for oats or chickens, or any earthly thing. . . . As for meself, indeed, since I

---

3. William Butler Yeats, *Where There is Nothing* (London, 1903), pp. ix–x.

gave some offence to the corner boys by wishin' the old times back, it's me haystack that was burned down o' Sunday night last. . . ."

Variations of the speech patterns, which Lady Gregory discovered among the Irish workers on her estate, occur in Lady Gregory's first plays. For example, in *Spreading the News*, the most successful comedy in the early days of the Abbey, Mrs. Tarpey answers a question of another character in the play: "No trade at all but to be talking." The use of the reflexive pronoun is also a stylistic characteristic prevalent in the plays: "Maybe it's yourself will be buried in the graveyard of Cloonmara before me, Mary Fallon, and I myself that will be dying unbeknownst some night, and no one a-near me." Frequently the subject and the verb are placed at the end of the sentence or clause: "bleaching the clothes on the hedge she is. . . ."

In these and other adaptations of peasant dialogue, Yeats found a dramatic language he could admire but could not imitate. He makes this clear when he began to change *Where There Is Nothing* into *Unicorn from the Stars*:

> That I might free myself from what seemed a contamination, I asked Lady Gregory to help me turn my old plot into *The Unicorn from the Stars*. I began to dictate, but since I had last worked with her, her mastery of the stage and her knowledge of dialect had so increased that my imagination could not go neck and neck with hers. I found myself, too, stopped by an old difficulty, that my words never flow freely but when people speak in verse; and so after an attempt to work alone I gave up my scheme to her. The result is a play almost wholly hers in handiwork, which is so much mine in thought that she does not wish to include it in her own works. She has enabled me to carry out an old thought for which my own knowledge is insufficient, and to commingle the ancient phantasies of poetry with the rough, vivid, ever-contemporaneous tumult of the roadside; to share in the creation of a form that otherwise I could but dream of . . . an art that murmured, though with worn and failing verse, of the day when Quixote and Sancho Panza, long estranged, may once again go out gaily into the bleak air.[4]

The authorship of *Cathleen ni Houlihan* has been a subject of controversy for years. Lennox Robinson, associated with the Abbey for many years as a producer and playwright, wrote that Lady Gregory "had a big

---

4. Yeats, "Unicorn from the Stars," *Plays in Prose and Verse* (London, 1922), pp. 246–47.

share of Kathleen ni Houlihan."[5] George Moore also wrote that Lady
Gregory had some share in both *Cathleen ni Houlihan* and *Pot of Broth*.[6]
Yeats, addressing himself to the problems of the authorship of the play,
spoke of Lady Gregory's role in its creation:

> One night I had a dream almost as distinct as a vision, of a cot-
> tage where there was well-being and firelight and talk of a marriage,
> and into the midst of that cottage there came an old woman in a
> long cloak. She was Ireland herself, that Cathleen ni Houlihan for
> whom so many songs have been sung and about whom so many
> stories have been told and for whose sake so many have gone to
> their death. I thought if I could write this out as a little play I could
> make others see my dream as I had seen it, but I could not get
> down out of that high window of dramatic verse, and in spite of all
> you had done for me I had not the country speech. One has to live
> among the people, like you, of whom an old man said in my hear-
> ing, 'she has been a serving-maid among us,' before one can think
> the thoughts of the people and speak with their tongue. We turned
> my dream into the little play, *Cathleen ni Houlihan*, and when we
> gave it to the little theatre in Dublin and found that the working-
> people, liked it, you helped me to put my other dramatic fables into
> speech.[7]

Lady Gregory never spoke publicly of the authorship of the play, but
she did record in her "Journal" that she was the sole author of the play:
"I see in a list of Yeats plays Unicorn as before Pot of Broth now-put 'as
written with Lady Gregory.' Rather hard on me not giving my name
with Kathleen ni Houlihan that I wrote all but all of."[8] Lady Gregory's
claim to sole authorship of *Kathleen ni Houlihan* is supported by the
manuscript of the play in the Berg Collection of the New York Public
Library. It is written in Lady Gregory's hand in the kind of 'penny copy
book' that she ordinarily used for both the drafts and final manuscript
versions of her own plays. All the evidence clearly indicates that Lady
Gregory wrote the play in its entirety. . . .

*   *   *

One wonders why, when there was so much evidence of Lady Gregory's involvement in Yeats's work, that they did not at least sign some of

---

5. From an unpublished fragment of a biography
of Lady Gregory, now in the Berg Collection of
the New York Public Library.
6. George Moore, *Hail and Farewell*, *Vale* (London, 1911–1914), p. 145.

7. Yeats, Dedication of volumes one and two of
Plays for an Irish Theatre.
8. Lady Gregory's "Journals," Book 30, p. 296.
These "Journals" are in the Berg Collection of the
New York Public Library.

the plays as co-authors. The answer probably lies in Lady Gregory's enormous productivity. Joseph Holloway, a Dublin architect and diarist who boasted that he attended every play performed in Dublin for some forty years—and wrote about them in a diary of 144 volumes [9]—counted the number of performances given each play at the Abbey between the opening of the Theatre on December 27, 1904, and the departure of the Fays, December 28, 1907. Lady Gregory headed the list with 11 plays and 123 performances. Yeats was next with 8 plays and 123 performances. Excluding Yeats, Lady Gregory had more performances of her plays than the combined total of all other Abbey playwrights in the same amount of time. Any author who writes and has produced eleven plays in three years for a theatre like the Abbey, with its limited audiences, would seem to be monopolizing the stage. Had she been listed—as Yeats suggested—as co-author of two plays by Yeats, it would have been a disaster for the Abbey, which was having a difficult time surviving dissension and desertion by players and authors in the early years.

The emphasis here on Lady Gregory's contributions to Yeats's plays does not mean that Yeats did not help Lady Gregory with some of her own plays. As T. J. Kiernan, former Ambassador to the United States and a friend of Lady Gregory, told the author some years ago, both Lady Gregory and Yeats were constantly helping each other with their writing. Moreover, the chances are very great that Lady Gregory would never have written one line of a play had she not met and been encouraged by Yeats. She was not the least bit interested in the theatre until then. When she and her husband, Sir William Gregory, were dividing their time between London and Ireland, Lady Gregory could not recall having been to the theatre more than twice. Yeats is the spiritual father of Lady Gregory's plays.

ELIZABETH COXHEAD

Lady Gregory: A Literary Portrait †

* * *

If Lady Gregory failed to like Miss Horniman,[1] it was partly for the reason why a good many other people in Ireland failed to like her, that

9. These MS diaries are in the National Library, Dublin.

† From *Lady Gregory: A Literary Portrait* (London: Secker and Warburg, 1966). Copyright © Elizabeth Coxhead 1961, 1966.

1. Ann F. Horniman (1860–1937), English heir to a tea fortune, and supporter of the Irish Literary Theatre, especially in financing construction of its theater on Abbey Street in 1904 [*Editor*].

by Irish standards she was not an ingratiating person. Even by English standards she was outspoken to a degree; and in Ireland, where it is customary to wrap up disagreement or rebuke in soft words, she must have seemed brutally rude almost every time she opened her mouth, or put pen to yellow paper in those acrimonious letters that made Synge say he ever afterwards hated the colour of daffodils.

There was also, more importantly, a cleavage of intention between them, which was widened as time went on. Miss Horniman may or may not have been in love with Yeats, but she was certainly in love with his genius, which she believed to be that of a playwright. In him she saw a second Shakespeare, and her theatre was to be his Globe. She cared nothing for "adding dignity to Ireland", or for any other Irish playwrights or aspirations, which were lumped by her together as "hole-and-corner Irish ideas".

Lady Gregory cared first and foremost for the poetic plays of Yeats; we know this because she says so, in the vital "Playwriting" chapter of *Our Irish Theatre*. but if they were "the apex of the flame, the point of the diamond", they were not with her the only reason for the theatre's existence. There were also Ireland's dignity, and the discovery and encouragement of new authors, and lastly there was her own creative talent and its need for an outlet. Because she invariably speaks of it modestly, because she too often adopts (in my opinion mistakenly) a deprecatory tone, we should not therefore underestimate it as a driving force within her. All talent drives its possessor, and comes in the end to matter more than the genius, be it never so lofty, of a friend.

Miss Horniman's whole attitude to the Abbey, to Lady Gregory, and to the Fays, which their family historian finds so baffling, can be explained, it seems to me, in the light of her increasing disappointment as the poetic plays of Yeats failed to score more than a *succès d'estime*. That Lady Gregory's own plays were meanwhile having a real, popular, side-splitting and tear-jerking success only turned the knife in the wound. But if Lady Gregory had never written a line, she would still have got on to "Miss Horniman's list of truly wicked people", because she stood for Ireland. And that was not what the tea-merchant's granddaughter had ordered when she invested her twenty thousand pounds in an "artistic" theatre of which the major achievement was to be the poetic drama of Yeats.

The double bill of the opening night was Yeats's Cuchulain play *On Baile's Strand*, which contains some of his most beautiful dramatic verse, and *Spreading the News*. One of his curious dramatic theories was that the proper emotion to be induced by tragedy should be "an ever-deepening reverie", which sounds suspiciously like saying that the audience dozed off. If they did, then *Spreading the News* woke them up with a bang.

"We got a tremendous pace into it," says Willie Fay in his autobiography, "the pace of a hard football match." When, later on, it was taken to England, the pace had to be modified. English audiences, less quick-witted than Dublin and with ears not attuned to Irish speech, simply could not take it in.

Flowering as it did so late in her life, the working of her talent always fascinated Lady Gregory, and when she came to print her plays, she included a note on the origins of each, which is of inestimable benefit to her literary biographer. *Spreading the News* was, it seems, intended to be another wistful piece like *Twenty-Five*; the Russian-scandal theme was to be used to rob a girl at a fair of her good name. But Yeats felt that something more amusing was needed to offset the poetic plays which made up most of the theatre's tiny repertory.

Having grown interested in the girl, she found difficulty in substituting another central character with some depth to it, till she hit on the idea of Bartley, the henpecked little man who takes a lugubrious joy in his own misfortunes. Though all he has actually done is to tip over a basket of apples and try to restore a lost hayfork to its owner, these two incidents are magnified by the gossips until he is credited with having committed a murder and eloped with the victim's wife; and he positively basks in the limelight thus drawn upon him as the myth, with a bubbling wealth of comic invention, monstrously grows.

For sheer high spirits perhaps it stands at the top of her list. It is still acted, though at the Abbey more often in Irish than in English. It was translated, pirated, even made (quite unsuitably, one would think) into a comic opera. Nobody could deny its success with the audience, but those whose heads were still in the Celtic twilight spoke of it sneeringly as a pleasing little anecdote, a mere farce. It is true that she was to do better technically, but the thing is the work of a mature dramatic personality, showing us in miniature the kind of playwright she is, and how she differs from her great contemporaries, Yeats and Synge.

They differ widely from each other, but each in his way is a romantic; she is classic. She has gone for her lessons, not to Maeterlinck or to the minor Elizabethans, but to Molière and Congreve. (The plays of Congreve was one of the six books she would have taken in that library legacy at Coole.) She who had been living for the last three years in the cloudy world of the ancient epics shows no trace of their influence when she comes to choose the form in which she will express herself. It is neat, taut, finished; a conundrum has been set and successfully solved. The classic approach was not fashionable in 1904, and neatness was bound to seem anecdotal. What matters, however, is not the form in which you express yourself, but the quality of what you have to express.

And the little play is not a mere farce, firstly because Bartley is a real human being even if the scandal-mongers weaving their web round him are two-dimensional, and secondly because its underlying intention is serious. She is laughing at her characters, as every writer of comedy does, but she is laughing at what is universal in them, not at what is accidental or ephemeral; certainly not at what is "peasant". She is not even merely satirising "the incorrigible Irish genius for mythmaking"; the Irish may bring an extra bravura to the art, but we all practise it. We all relish a scandal, and take care to pass it on in better shape than we receive it. The credulous market folk of *Spreading the News* have their counterparts in the drawing room.

*   *   *

That W. B. Yeats could have written the plays of Lady Gregory, when he felt himself so little of a natural dramatist that he had to call her in to help him write his own, is on the face of it absurd. But no rational objection of that sort hampered the progress of Oliver St John Gogarty's smear-campaign. *How much of her plays did she write? Yeats had spent many months annually in collaboration with her at Coole Park. I almost got him to acknowledge his authorship of "The Rising of the Moon".* And so on. The fact that [Gogarty's] *As I was Going Down Sackville Street* is a highly readable book, original-seeming in its discursive style, too, to those who do not know [George Moore's] *Ave*, gave these insinuations a currency well beyond Dublin.

The only evidence he could have adduced of Yeats's having had a hand in her plays—and as far as I knew he did not adduce it, doubtless preferring to condemn her unread—is the dedication to Yeats of her first collected volume, the *Seven Short Plays*, "because you have taught me my trade."

It is the sort of gesture which should, I suggest, be taken only in the most general sense. In that sense, Yeats had taught all the Abbey dramatists their trade. His enthusiasm and confidence, his sense of the high seriousness of literature and his primary part in getting the theatre founded were the factors which had made it possible for the rest of them to write. He had also evolved an impressive body of dramatic theory, though as I have pointed out, it was a theory which only in effect applied to his own work.

But the implication that he "taught" her in the sense of showing her how to write plays is directly contradicted by the statements of both of them that she worked on the plots and construction of his poetic plays, "for I had learned by this time a good deal about playwriting". If she had learned it from *him*, he would have had no need to summon her aid.

He was interested in her work at the beginning, but his own always came first, both in his estimation and in hers. He had his own writing-room at Coole, at first the library, and after Robert's marriage a specially equipped bedroom, and it was sacred. That his hostess should have intruded on him with demands for help is unthinkable, though he might on occason intrude on her. Her *Journals* prove that in later years he had no idea even of the subject of her plays until they were written; this was probably to a large extent true in the early years also.

He was a judicious critic, but in the nature of things a mainly destructive one. He could tell her what was wrong with a play, but he could not tell her how to set it right. For that, she needed to turn to a natural dramatist. Synge could have helped her had they been closer friends, and had he himself not been working under pressure of anxiety and ill-health; in later years Lennox Robinson supplied a vitalising hint. But for the most part hers was a lonely struggle.

She herself delights to give us, in the notes to each play, the seed from which it germinated in her mind. She is also scrupulous about acknowledging direct help from another writer. Only one such acknowledgment is made to Yeats, in the notes to *The Travelling Man*, and that is really an excess of candour, since we know from *Our Irish Theatre* and from his letters that the original idea had been hers (in any case it is a legend as old as folklore), and that he had taken it from her, worked on it, been dissatisfied and thrown it back. Nor is it among her happiest, being too directly a sermon—perhaps Yeats's didacticism coming through.

But it is *The Rising of the Moon* that calumny is most determined to attribute to Yeats, for the single reason that it is her big success. It is revived not merely oftener than her other plays, but ten times oftener. It is the only work of hers many people know, and it has given its title and the skeleton of its plot to an Irish triple-story film.

The sweeping of the board by a playlet which, though delightful, is slight compared with much else she wrote is as saddening in its way as the success of Yeats's "Lake Isle of Innisfree", but there is nothing mysterious about it. It is an experience which befalls most writers, certainly most writers of fiction, whether in novel or dramatic form. One book or play catches the mass fancy as nothing else before or after it. It is seldom the best, or even the one over which we have worked hardest. It is simply the lucky one; luck sat on our shoulders as we wrote.

The appeal of *The Rising* is easy to understand. To the swiftness of
action she had already achieved in village comedies like *Spreading the
News* (and which the stately Yeats never achieved anywhere) she adds a
"rebelly" flavour which strikes instant echoes in the Irish soul. Night on
the quays, the man on the run, the police-hunt, the sergeant torn by
conflicting loyalties—it is sure-fire stuff. There is about it a tingle of
excitement which, I must concede, she never quite caught again. But
excitement is not everything. The great act of *The White Cockade* has
nearly the same tension, with a subtler development of character, and
in her other one-act masterpieces, *The Workhouse Ward* and *The Gaol
Gate*, irony and poignancy take its place.

It is also perfectly easy to see where *The Rising* comes from. Of some
of her plays, one thinks wonderingly: Now how on earth can she have
known that? But this one is Gregory to a positively autobiographical
extent. The Fenian troubles had been avidly followed in the nursery at
Roxborough. The conflict in the sergeant's mind is the conflict in the
mind of the child, receiving downstairs "the strict Orangism of the draw-
ing-room", and upstairs the imperfectly concealed rebel sentiments of
old Mary Sheridan. All the mature playwright has to do is to transform
the child's age, sex and social class, a simple process to any competent
writer of fiction, and there the sergeant stands. Mary Sheridan's story of
Hamilton Rowan and his escape by boat supplies the rest of the plot.

*   *   *

J. M. Synge

ROBIN SKELTON

[Riders to the Sea] †

* * *

That Synge was aware of the universal nature of the symbolism he was using [in *Riders*], can hardly be doubted. In a review of H. d'Arbois de Jubainville's *The Irish Mythological Cycle and Celtic Mythology* printed in *The Speaker* of 2 April 1904, Synge reveals his longtime familiarity with this material, and refers to the 'Greek kinship of these Irish legends' (II.365)[1], and illustrates his comment by suggesting that Lug is a Celtic Hermes and Balor the Chimaera. He also mentions 'Manannan mac Lir, an Irish sea god' (II. 365). In a review of Lady Gregory's *Cuchulain of Muirthemme* in *The Speaker* of 7 June 1902, Synge again compares Celtic with Homeric story, and here he says: 'The Elizabethan vocabulary has a force and colour that makes it the only form of English that is quite suitable for incidents of the epic kind, and in her intercourse with the peasants of the west Lady Gregory has learned to use this vocabulary in a new way, while she carries with her plaintive Gaelic constructions that make her language, in a true sense, a language of Ireland' (II.368). This passage indicates pretty clearly what Synge was about when he filled *Riders to the Sea* with mythic intimations and reveals also that, even while he was concerned to present accurately the life and dignity of the Aran peasant, he was also interested in creating a more universal picture of man surrounded by natural elements and supernatural forces—or beliefs about those supernatural forces—which he is unable to control.

Seen from this viewpoint, *Riders to the Sea* takes on something of a

† From *The Writings of J. M. Synge* (Indianapolis: Bobbs-Merrill, 1971). Reprinted by permission of Thames and Hudson Ltd.
1. Volume and page references refer to *The Col-*
lected Works of J. M. Synge (New York: Oxford UP, 1962–68). [Page numbers in brackets refer to this edition—*Editor*].

new identity. The very title itself emphasizes the mythic or supernatural
element for there are only two riders in the play, one the doomed Bartley
and the other his spectral brother. We are all, Maurya tells us, doomed
to death, for 'no man can be living for ever'. We are all, sooner or later,
called to destruction. It is one of the messages of Greek tragedy, and the
form of the play has much in common with Greek theatre. The climactic action takes place off-stage and is commented upon by Maurya, who
returns, distraught with her forebodings, as the Greek chorus returns
similarly distraught in so many plays. The old women keening just before
the news of Bartley's death is told, function like a Greek chorus, as also
do the two women who describe Bartley's death. In the Houghton type-
script, which is certainly an earlier version than the established text, the
stage directions give their speeches under the heading WOMEN rather
than ONE OF THE WOMEN which is the heading in all published versions.

The dramatic irony in the play is also similar to that found in Greek
tragedy. Nora reports the priest's words thus: 'she'll be getting her death'
says he 'with crying and lamenting' (III.5) [64]: it is, indeed, Maurya's
lamenting Bartley's going down to the ship that prevents her from giving
her blessing and thus causes his death. A simpler, but still classical, use
of foreboding speech occurs when Maurya says to Bartley:

> It's hard set we'll be surely the day you're drowned with the rest.
> What way will I live and the girls with me, and I an old woman
> looking for the grave?   (III.11) [65]

After a further passage of foreboding, irony returns with a play upon the
vernacular usage of the word 'destroyed'. Nora says:

> And it's destroyed he'll be going till dark night, and he after eating
> nothing since the sun went up.   (III.11) [66]

Cathleen reinforces the effect:

> It's destroyed he'll be, surely.   (III.13) [66]

The pathos and dignity of Maurya's speech on taking Michael's stick to
assist her steps as she goes to the spring to give her blessing to Bartley is
not unlike many of the laments in Aeschylus, Sophocles, and Euripides.

> In the big world the old people do be leaving things after them for
> their sons and children, but in this place it is the young men do be
> leaving things behind them for them that do be old.   (III.13) [67]

The emphasis in this speech upon the way in which the world of Maurya
differs from the 'big world' appears to set the island community apart

from all other communities. Moreover, while in Greek tragedy and story the suffering of the protagonists is the consequence of the sins they or their kin have committed, intentionally or otherwise, in *Riders to the Sea* there appears to be no reason for Maurya's tribulation. The deaths of her sons are not, as are the deaths of Niobe's children, or Medea's, the consequence of acts of blasphemy or evil. In this, *Riders to the Sea* is closer to the world of Sophocles than Euripides; there is an arbitrary quality about the fates of the characters that reminds one of the world of Oedipus. Even here, however, one can find some historical justification for the cruelty of the fates. In *Riders to the Sea*, however, there is no justification. This is not a place in which there is any kind of justice, or mercy. The priest may say that 'the Almighty God won't leave her [Maurya] destitute with no son living' (III.5.) [64], but Maurya tells us, 'It's little the like of him knows of the sea' (III.21) [69]. The sea is, indeed, the 'Almighty God' of the play, an older and more formidable spiritual power than that represented by the priest who, it is emphasized, is 'young.' The priest never enters the action of the play. He is absent physically from the cottage of Maurya just as he is, spiritually, a stranger to her world. His reported words are all comforting, but they do not comfort.

Yet it may be suggested that Christianity plays a part in the play. Does not Maurya sprinkle 'Holy Water' over the clothes of the drowned Michael?

This may be so, but there is some doubt as to the nature of that 'Holy Water', for Maurya refers to 'going down and getting Holy Water in the dark nights after Samhain' (III.25) [71]. It may be that she collects it from a Holy Well, even the Spring Well, mentioned in the play, but it is clear that the only time she does collect it is in the nights after Samhain, for now that Samhain is nearly come round again her supply is almost exhausted; it is the last of the Holy Water she sprinkles over Michael's clothes. Thus the Holy Water is much more the magical water of pre-Christian belief than the water blessed by the priest. Indeed, the priest is not in it at all.

The fusion of pre-Christian and Christian belief is characteristic, of course, of many peasant communities. Synge was not playing fast and loose with the facts. He was, however, portraying a world in which people, insecure and desperate for help against the forces of death and the tyranny of the natural world, seized upon any belief or superstition that might give them comfort and hope. That Maurya finds no comfort or hope for all her observances is the dark message of the play, which ends as a cry, not against God, but against the principle of Mortality. 'No man can be living for ever and we must be satisfied' (III.27) [72].

If this humble, even partly stoic, conclusion of Maurya's is set against the conclusion of Yeats' *Cathleen ni Houlihan*, together with all the other elements in the play that I have mentioned, it becomes clear in just what way *Riders to the Sea* is a counterblast to Yeats. Synge was certainly very much aware that his view of Ireland differed from that of Yeats. Some of his poems seem to be direct retorts to Yeats' early lyrics. On 12 September 1907 he wrote, in a letter to the Irish-American journalist, Frederick J. Gregg: 'I am half inclined to try a play on "Deirdre"— it would be amusing to compare it with Yeats' and [George] Russell's . . .' (IV.xxvii). *Deirdre of the Sorrows* is, certainly, in many ways constructed so as to oppose the vision of Yeats with another. It is therefore not unreasonable to look again at *Riders to the Sea* in these terms.

Cathleen ni Houlihan is, of course, a personification of Ireland, an old woman (the Shan Van Vocht) who has the 'step of a queen'. Maurya, also an old woman, is not an allegorical but a typical figure; she too mourns the past dead though her step is not that of a queen, but weak with age. Cathleen ni Houlihan mourns the loss of her 'four fields'— the four provinces of Ireland. Maurya mourns the loss of her eight menfolk, but without the triumphant tone of Yeats' Old Woman. The ship that brings hope of Irish freedom to Yeats' characters, brings death to the characters of Synge. *Riders to the Sea* is, indeed, a comprehensive drama. It includes, at a more profound level than *Cathleen ni Houlihan*, an awareness of the Irish inheritance of story and belief. Its portrait of the island is that of a place shut off from the 'big world', as Ireland itself is shut off. It is a portrait of a place bewildered by two cultures, the ancient and the new, and by two visions of the nature of the spiritual world.

The island of *Riders to the Sea* is Ireland, but more than Ireland. Its predicaments are those of the Irish peasant, but also those of all men subject to the tyranny of forces they do not understand. Its beliefs are those of the Irish peasant, but they are also those of all people who combine superstition with Christian belief, or who are troubled by thoughts of spiritual realities beyond their ability to understand and control. *Riders to the Sea* is not naturalistic theatre; it is poetic theatre, and it is epic. The figure of man placed against the power of the gods who destroy him is a main theme of epic and of heroic tragedy. Maurya, like Oedipus, bows to the will of the gods, and, like Job, finds at last in humility and endurance a dignity and greatness of spirit, turning down the empty cup of Holy Water in a last symbolic gesture, and asking for mercy upon the souls of all mortal kind.

J. M. SYNGE

Preface to *The Playboy of the Western World* †

In writing *The Playboy of the Western World*, as in my other plays, I have used one or two words only that I have not heard among the country people of Ireland, or spoken in my own nursery before I could read the newspapers. A certain number of the phrases I employ I have heard also from herds and fishermen along the coast from Kerry to Mayo, or from beggar-women and ballad-singers nearer Dublin; and I am glad to acknowledge how much I owe to the folk-imagination of these fine people. Anyone who has lived in real intimacy with the Irish peasantry will know that the wildest sayings and ideas in this play are tame indeed, compared with the fancies one may hear in any little hillside cabin in Geesala, or Carraroe, or Dingle Bay. All art is a collaboration; and there is little doubt that in the happy ages of literature, striking and beautiful phrases were as ready to the story-teller's or the playwright's hand, as the rich cloaks and dresses of his time. It is probable that when the Elizabethan dramatist took his ink-horn and sat down to his work he used many phrases that he had just heard, as he sat at dinner, from his mother or his children. In Ireland, those of us who know the people have the same privilege. When I was writing "The Shadow of the Glen," some years ago, I got more aid than any learning could have given me from a chink in the floor of the old Wicklow house where I was staying, that let me hear what was being said by the servant girls in the kitchen. This matter, I think, is of importance, for in countries where the imagination of the people, and the language they use, is rich and living, it is possible for a writer to be rich and copious in his words, and at the same time to give the reality, which is the root of all poetry, in a comprehensive and natural form. In the modern literature of towns, however, richness is found only in sonnets, or prose poems, or in one or two elaborate books that are far away from the profound and common interests of life. One has, on one side, Mallarmé and Huysmans producing this literature; and on the other, Ibsen and Zola dealing with the reality of life in joyless and pallid words. On the stage one must have reality, and one must have joy; and that is why the intellectual modern drama has failed, and people have grown sick of the false joy of the musical comedy, that has been given them in place of the rich joy found only in what is superb

† From *The Complete Plays of John M. Synge* (New York: Random House, 1935). Vintage Books edition.

and wild in reality. In a good play every speech should be as fully fla-
voured as a nut or apple, and such speeches cannot be written by anyone
who works among people who have shut their lips on poetry. In Ireland,
for a few years more, we have a popular imagination that is fiery and
magnificent, and tender; so that those of us who wish to write start with
a chance that is not given to writers in places where the springtime of
the local life has been forgotten, and the harvest is a memory only, and
the straw has been turned into bricks.

W. B. YEATS

Preface to the First Edition of *The Well of the Saints* †

Six years ago I was staying in a students' hotel in the Latin Quarter [of
Paris], and somebody, whose name I cannot recollect, introduced me to
an Irishman, who, even poorer than myself, had taken a room at the
top of the house. It was J. M. Synge, and I, who thought I knew the
name of every Irishman who was working at literature, had never heard
of him. He was a graduate of Trinity College, Dublin, too, and Trinity
College does not, as a rule, produce artistic minds. He told me that he
had been living in France and Germany, reading French and German
literature, and that he wished to become a writer. He had, however,
nothing to show but one or two poems and impressionistic essays, full
of that kind of morbidity that has its root in too much brooding over
methods of expression, and ways of looking upon life, which come, not
out of life, but out of literature, images reflected from mirror to mirror.
He had wandered among people whose life is as picturesque as the Middle
Ages, playing his fiddle to Italian sailors, and listening to stories in Bavarian
woods, but life had cast no light into his writings. He had learned Irish
years ago, but had begun to forget it, for the only language that interested him was that conventional language of modern poetry which has
begun to make us all weary. I was very weary of it, for I had finished *The
Secret Rose*,[1] and felt how it had separated my imagination from life,
sending my Red Hanrahan, who should have trodden the same roads
with myself, into some undiscoverable country.[2] I said: 'Give up Paris.

---

† Reprinted with permission of Macmillan Publishing Company from *Essays and Introductions*
by W. B. Yeats. Copyright © Mrs. W. B. Yeats
1961.

1. Collection of stories published in 1897 [*Editor.*]
2. Since writing this I have, with Lady Gregory's
help, put *Red Hanrahan* into the common speech.

You will never create anything by reading Racine, and Arthur Symons will always be a better critic of French literature. Go to the Aran Islands. Live there as if you were one of the people themselves; express a life that has never found expression.' I had just come from Aran, and my imagination was full of those grey islands where men must reap with knives because of the stones.

He went to Aran and became a part of its life, living upon salt fish and eggs, talking Irish for the most part, but listening also to the beautiful English which has grown up in Irish-speaking districts, and takes its vocabulary from the time of Malory and of the translators of the Bible, but its idiom and its vivid metaphor from Irish. When Mr. Synge began to write in his language, Lady Gregory had already used it finely in her translations of Dr. Hyde's [3] lyrics and plays, or of old Irish literature, but she had listened with different ears. He made his own selection of word and phrase, choosing what would express his own personality. Above all, he made word and phrase dance to a very strange rhythm, which will always, till his plays have created their own tradition, be difficult to actors who have not learned it from his lips. It is essential, for it perfectly fits the drifting emotion, the dreaminess, the vague yet measureless desire, for which he would create a dramatic form. It blurs definition, clear edges, everything that comes from the will, it turns imagination from all that is of the present, like a gold background in a religious picture, and it strengthens in every emotion whatever comes to it from far off, from brooding memory and dangerous hope. When he brought *The Shadow of the Glen*, his first play, to the Irish National Theatre Society, the players were puzzled by the rhythm, but gradually they became certain that his Woman of the Glen, as melancholy as a curlew, driven to distraction by her own sensitiveness, her own fineness, could not speak with any other tongue, that all his people would change their life if the rhythm changed. Perhaps no Irish countryman had ever that exact rhythm in his voice, but certainly if Mr. Synge had been born a countryman, he would have spoken like that. It makes the people of his imagination a little disembodied; it gives them a kind of innocence even in their anger and their cursing. It is part of its maker's attitude towards the world, for while it makes the clash of wills among his persons indirect and dreamy, it helps him to see the subject-matter of his art with wise, clear-seeing, unreflecting eyes; to preserve the integrity of art in an age of reasons and purposes. Whether he write of old beggars by the roadside, lamenting over the misery and ugliness of life, or of an old Aran

---

3. Dr. Douglas Hyde (1860–1947), writer, translator, founder of the Gaelic league [*Editor*].

woman mourning her drowned sons, or of a young wife married to an old husband, he has no wish to change anything, to reform anything; all these people pass by as before an open window, murmuring strange, exciting words.

* * *

JOSEPH HOLLOWAY

[Journal 1907] †

Saturday, Matinee and Evening, January 12. *The Eloquent Dempsy*[1] wooed back to the Abbey large audiences at both performances, and Henderson beamed on all patrons as they entered the vestibule. He is like a barometer—bad house, he is gloomy and down in the mouth; good house, and a summer day is not more bright and cheerful. . . . The matinee was very well attended, and everyone seemed profoundly impressed with the weird, strange sorrow created by Synge's gem of sadness *Riders to the Sea*. . . . Few things finer than Sara Allgood's portrait of the old mother have been seen on the stage. It was a masterpiece of acting, quite flawless in every detail. To see her return with the bit of bread the girls had sent her with after "Bartley," and totteringly reach the chair by the fire with a look of dread on her face that was thrilling, was to witness as fine a moment of realistic acting as could be desired. . . . *Riders to the Sea* was superbly acted in the evening, and I overheard the author say to D. J. O'Donoghue who sat behind me that he had never seen it better played. When an author thinks the child of his brain realised on the stage, the audience very well may be satisfied.

By the way, a trifle light as air spoiled this almost perfect performance for me, and it was nothing more or less than a label bearing the legend, "National Theatre Co." pasted on the side of the shaft of the stretcher on which the body of "Bartley" was borne into the cottage.

Thursday, January 24. . . . Yeats, before he left for England, told F. J. Fay he did not like his teaching of poetic speaking, and Frank had

† From *Joseph Holloway's Abbey Theatre: A Selection from His Unpublished Journal "Impressions of a Dublin Playgoer,"* edited by Robert Hogan and Michael J. O'Neill. Copyright © 1967 by Southern Illinois University Press.

1. By William Boyle (1853–1922), one of the major popular successes while W. A. Henderson was manager of the Abbey Theatre [*Editor*].

given up doing so in disgust since. There is great dissatisfaction in the camp.

Saturday, January 26. The Abbey was thronged in the evening to witness the first performance of Synge's three-act comedy *The Playboy of the Western World,* which ended in fiasco owing to the coarseness of the dialogue. The audience bore with it for two and a half acts and even laughed with the dramatist at times, but an unusually brutally coarse remark[2] put into the mouth of "Christopher Mahon," the playboy of the title, set the house off into hooting and hissing amid counter applause, and the din was kept up till the curtain closed in.

On coming out, Lady Gregory asked me, "What was the cause of the disturbance?"

And my monosyllabic answer was, "Blackguardism!"

To which she queried, "On which side?"

"The stage!" came from me pat, and then I passed on, and the incident was closed. . . .

"This is not Irish life!" said one of the voices from the pit, and despite the fact that Synge in a note on the programme says, "I have used one or two words only that I have not heard among the country people of Ireland, or spoken in my own nursery before I could read the newspapers," I maintain that his play of *The Playboy* is not a truthful or just picture of the Irish peasants, but simply the outpouring of a morbid, unhealthy mind ever seeking on the dunghill of life for the nastiness that lies concealed there. . . . Synge is the evil genius of the Abbey and Yeats his able lieutenant. Both dabble in the unhealthy. Lady Gregory, though she backs them up when they transgress good taste and cast decency to the winds, keeps clean in her plays, and William Boyle is ever and always wholesome. . . .

W. G. Fay as "Christopher Mahon," the hero, was inimitable in a very disagreeable role. Miss Maire O'Neill as "Margaret Flaherty," the publican's daughter who sets her cap at "Mahon" and gives the cold shoulder to "Shawn Keogh" (F. J. Fay), a sheepish admirer of her (played after the fashion of "Hyacinth Halvey" by Fay) was excellent, and Sara Allgood as "Widow Quin" who had designs on "Mahon" was also good. Two more undesirable specimens of Irish womankind could not be found

---

2. "Widow Quin" wants "Christy" to leave "Pegeen" and go with her—"Come on, I tell you, and I'll find you finer sweethearts at each waning moon." And he answers, "It's Pegeen I'm seeking only, and what'd I care if you brought me a drift of chosen females, standing in their shifts itself, maybe, from this place to the eastern world?" It was made more crudely brutal on the first night by W. G. Fay. "Mayo girls" was substituted for "chosen females" [*Holloway's note*].

in this isle I be thinking. A. Power, repulsively got-up, played "Old Mahon" with some effect. Arthur Sinclair as the drunken bar-keeper, and J. M. Kerrigan as "Jimmy Farrell," a small farmer, interpreted the characters . . . carefully. I only pitied the actors and actresses for having to give utterance to such gross sentiments and only wonder they did not refuse to speak some of the lines.

Sunday, January 27. Met W. G. Fay and Mrs. Fay together with Frank on Pembroke Road while out for a walk, and we chatted about last night's fiasco, and the feeling of the actors during and leading up to the scene. The players had expected the piece's downfall sooner, and W. G. Fay expressed it that "Had I not cut out a lot of the matter, the audience would not have stood an act of it." I praised the acting and said it was a fine audience to play to. It frankly did not like the play and frankly expressed itself on the matter, having patiently listened to it until the fatal phrase came and proved the last straw. Frank excused Synge on the score that he has had no joy in his life, and until he has had some you may expect drab plays from him. . . . The influence of the Elizabethan dramatists was on Synge, and he loved vigorous speech. Frank partly defended him on this score. He told me Lawrence came round after the comedy and was in a terrible state about the piece. Both brothers wondered what would be the result of last night's scene, and I said, "Bad houses next week, but a return when the right stuff would be forthcoming again."

Monday, January 28. . . . Henderson and I went down to the Abbey . . . and on our way spoke of Synge's nasty mind—to store those crude, coarse sayings from childhood and now present them in a play. The influence of Gorki must be upon him. Henderson also told me that the new English manager had arrived, and he was thinking of retiring before being dismissed. The new man was to get £5 a week; he was only getting 30 / -.

By this time we arrived at the Abbey. Two stalwart police at the vestibule suggested trouble, and we found plenty and to spare when we went in. The performance was just concluding amid a terrific uproar (the piece had not been listened to, we were told). The curtains were drawn aside, and W. G. Fay stood forward amid the din. After some minutes, in a lull, he said, "You who have hissed to-night will go away saying you have heard the play, but you haven't."

"We heard it on Saturday!" came from the back of the pit, and the hissing and hooting were renewed.

The scene which followed was indescribable. Those in the pit howled for the author, and he with Lady Gregory and others held animated conversation in the stalls. Denis O'Sullivan made himself very conspicuous railing against the noise producers, and Signor Esposito gesticulated abundantly. Small knots of people argued the situation out anything but calmly, and after about a quarter of an hour's clamour, the audience dispersed hoarse. "Heblon," [3] in a half-tight state, blackguarded the Irish people and upheld the dramatist, and George Roberts said, "The play is the finest ever written if you had only the wit to see it!" I wished him joy of the dungheap of a mind he must possess to arrive at that conclusion, and Lawrence and I departed.

Tuesday, January 29. . . . Arrived at the Abbey when *Riders to the Sea* was half through. D. J. O'Donoghue was going in at the same time. We waited in the side passage near the radiator until it was over. A number of youths were dimly seen in the stalls. The piece was well received. We joined W. J. Lawrence in the back row of the stalls during the interval. I noticed that the youths in the stalls were mostly under the influence of drink (and learned that the management had allowed them in for nothing to back up the play that the crowded pit had come there to howl down). This precious gang of noisy boys hailed from Trinity, and soon after *The Playboy* commenced one of their number (Mr. Moorhead) made himself objectionable and was forcibly removed by Synge and others, after a free fight amongst the instruments of the orchestra.

W. B. Yeats came before the curtain after *Riders to the Sea*, and made a speech "inviting a free discussion on the play on Monday night next in the theatre." Shortly after the commencement of the police-protected play, a remark from the pit set the college boys to their feet, and for a moment they looked like going for those in the pit, but didn't. The uproar was deafening, and it was here Moorhead got put out. One of the theatre's bullies removed by the people who wanted him in struck me as a funny sight. This set the noise in motion, and W. B. Yeats again came on the scene and with raised hand secured silence. He referred to the removal of one drunken man and hoped all that were sober would listen to the play. The noise continued, and shortly after a body of police led on by W. B. marched out of the side door from the scene dock and ranged along the walls of the pit. Hugh Lane now made himself very conspicuous by pointing out some men in the pit and demanding their

3. Joseph O'Connor, police office clerk and feature writer of "Studies in Blue" as Heblon of *The Evening Herald.* From 1933–47 he was a brilliant criminal lawyer and circuit judge of Cork.

arrest as disturbers of the peace. Yeats also was busy just now as a spy aiding the police in picking out persons disapproving of the glorification of murder on the stage. . . . A gent addressed the audience from the stalls, and the students with Hugh Lane in their midst behaved themselves like the drunken cads they were. At the end chaos seemed to have entered the Abbey, and the college youths clambered onto the seats and began the English national anthem, while those in the body of the hall sang something else of home growth. I felt very sad while the scene continued. The college boys had ultimately to be forcibly ejccted by the police, and they marched off in a body singing, police-protected, to the college. One of them was arrested for beating the police and fined £5. Two of those were were ejected from the pit were fined 40 / - each, W. B. Yeats prosecuting.

Despite all, *The Playboy* was not heard!

Wednesday, January 30. I sauntered down about 7:45 to Abbey Street, and saw an immense crowd awaiting the pit-door to be opened, and police everywhere. Met Sinclair in the crowd and had a chat about the turn things had taken. He was hopeful that the success of scandal would be the makings of the theatre, and said Miss Horniman had telegraphed over her delight at the turn things had taken. . . .

A loud-voiced, glorified music-hall patron took up his seat in front of me after *Riders to the Sea* had been perfectly played and enthusiastically received, and commenced shouting in grating, piercing tones, "Shut up!" making more noise than all the house put together. He was a distinctly vulgar type and began to call the play "rotten" during Act III. The house listened to the piece in patches to-night. Every time Synge would appear, he was hissed. Over fifty police were in the theatre, and uproar was frequent; nevertheless, a few were ejected from the pit. W. B. Yeats was eager to get people charged. . . .

The theatre was full to-night to witness a row, and was very disappointed that they did not get value for their money. Several I spoke to thought the play a poor one—the first act having some slight merit, but the others none whatever, and as to the plot it was too absurd for words. All the very nasty bits have vanished. Mr. Short is of opinion that the excitement will do the theatre good. I have my doubts. Outside the theatre in Abbey Street, the place was thronged with people and police, but I did not wait developments. Did I ever think I would see the Abbey protected from an Irish audience by the police!

Thursday, January 31. The police-protected drama by the dramatist of the dungheap . . . got a fair hearing tonight, and was voted by those around me very poor, dull, dramatic stuff indeed. After the first act all interest of any kind ceases, and were it not for the claque imported into the stalls very little applause would be forthcoming. A Free Theatre is a droll cry where police line the walls and block the passages . . . ready to pounce on anyone who dares say "boo" to the filth and libels of the Irish peasant girl on the stage. "Free" indeed! The theatre is forever damned in the eyes of all right-thinking Irishmen. One sack, one sample. Yeats, Synge, and Gregory are all degenerates of the worst type; the former pair indulge in sensuality in their later work, and the latter condones with them. . . .

Over two hundred police guarded the Abbey to-night, with the only result of two arrests for leaving the theatre before the programme was ended. The prestige of the theatre has fled, and Henderson's work of creating an audience frustrated.

Friday, February 1. William Boyle has publicly withdrawn his plays from the Abbey. As an Irish Theatre, the Abbey's knell is rung. This was the biggest blow to the National Theatre Society received since it became a police-protected society.

Saturday, February 2. . . . After dinner I went to the matinee at the Abbey, and found the police in large numbers around the building. The first act had concluded as I went in. Everything was quiet and matinee-like inside, except the number of police lining the walls and blocking up the passages. The audience was not very large and mostly ladies. W. B. Yeats came and had a few words with me about the arrest last night, and I told him what I thought of it and others, and also of the drunken Trinity students of Tuesday night.

He replied, "There were plenty of drunken men in the pit, and I prefer drunken men who applaud on in the right than drunken men who hiss in the wrong." A beautiful sentiment quite worthy of his pal Synge, I thought.

When I pressed him further about the freedom of every man to judge for himself, and yet if a man hissed or left the theatre before the play was over he was likely to be taken, he fled. He would not work in the art-for-art's-sake theory into an answer to that question, and so his flowers of speech did not blossom on the subject. "Humbug," thy name is Yeats.

* * *

W. B. YEATS

The Controversy over *The Playboy of the Western World* †

We have claimed for our writers the freedom to find in their own land every expression of good and evil necessary to their art, for Irish life contains, like all vigorous life, the seeds of all good and evil, and a writer must be free here as elsewhere to watch where weed or flower ripens. No one who knows the work of our theatre as a whole can say we have neglected the flower; but the moment a writer is forbidden to take pleasure in the weed, his art loses energy and abundance. In the great days of English dramatic art the greatest English writer of comedy was free to create *The Alchemist* and *Volpone*,[1] but a demand born of Puritan conviction and shopkeeping timidity and insincerity, for what many second-rate intellects thought to be noble and elevating events and characters, had already at the outset of the eighteenth century ended the English drama as a complete and serious art. Sheridan and Goldsmith, when they restored comedy after an epoch of sentimentalities, had to apologise for their satiric genius by scenes of conventional lovemaking and sentimental domesticity that have set them outside the company of all—whether their genius be great or little—whose work is pure and whole. The quarrel of our theatre to-day is the quarrel of the theatre in many lands; for the old Puritanism, the old dislike of power and reality have not changed, even when they are called by some Gaelic name.

[On the second performance of *The Playboy of the Western World*, about forty men who sat in the middle of the pit succeeded in making the play entirely inaudible. Some of them brought tin trumpets and the noise began immediately on the rise of the curtain. For days articles in the Press called for the withdrawal of the play, but we played for the seven nights we had announced; and before the week's end opinion had turned in our favour. There were, however, nightly disturbances and a good deal of rioting in the surrounding streets. On the last night of the play there were, I believe, five hundred police keeping order in the theatre and in its neighbourhood. Some days later our enemies, though

---

† From *Explorations* by W. B. Yeats (New York: Macmillan / Collier Books, 1973).
1. Plays by Ben Jonson (1572–1637); Richard Brinsley Sheridan (1751–1816) and Oliver Goldsmith (1730–74), named below, English Restoration playwrights of Irish birth [*Editor*].

beaten so far as the play was concerned, crowded into the cheaper seats for a debate on the freedom of the stage. They were very excited, and kept up the discussion until near twelve. The last paragraphs of my opening statement ran as follows.]

From Mr. Yeats's opening Speech in the Debate on February 4, 1907, at the Abbey Theatre.

The struggle of the last week has been long a necessity; various paragraphs in newspapers describing Irish attacks on theatres had made many worthy young men come to think that the silencing of a stage at their own pleasure, even if hundreds desired that it should not be silenced, might win them a little fame, and, perhaps, serve their country. Some of these attacks have been made on plays which are in themselves indefensible, vulgar and old-fashioned farces and comedies. But the attack, being an annihilation of civil rights, was never anything but an increase of Irish disorder. The last I heard of was in Liverpool, and there a stage was rushed, and a priest, who had set a play upon it, withdrew his play and apologised to the audience. We have not such pliant bones, and did not learn in the houses that bred us a so suppliant knee. But behind the excitement of example there is a more fundamental movement of opinion. Some seven or eight years ago the National movement was democratised and passed from the hands of a few leaders into those of large numbers of young men organised in clubs and societies. These young men made the mistake of the newly enfranchised everywhere: they fought for causes worthy in themselves with the unworthy instruments of tyranny and violence. Comic songs of a certain kind were to be driven from the stage; everyone was to wear Irish cloth; everyone was to learn Irish; everyone was to hold certain opinions; and these ends were sought by personal attacks, by virulent caricature and violent derision. It needs eloquence to persuade and knowledge to expound; but the coarser means come ready to every man's hand, as ready as a stone or a stick, and where these coarse means are all, there is nothing but mob, and the commonest idea most prospers and is most sought for.

Gentlemen of the little clubs and societies, do not mistake the meaning of our victory; it means something for us, but more for you. When the curtain of *The Playboy* fell on Saturday night in the midst of what *The Sunday Independent*—no friendly witness—described as 'thunders of applause', I am confident that I saw the rise in this country of a new thought, a new opinion, that we had long needed. It was not all approval of Mr. Synge's play that sent the receipts of the Abbey Theatre this last week to twice the height they had ever touched before. The generation of young men and girls who are now leaving schools or colleges are weary of the tyranny of clubs and leagues. They wish again for individual sincerity, the eternal quest of truth, all that has been given up for so long that all might crouch upon the one roost and quack or cry in the one flock. We are beginning once again to ask what a man is, and to be content to wait a little before we go on to that further question: What is a good Irishman? There are some who have not yet their degrees that will say to friend or neighbour, 'You have voted with the English, and that is bad'; or 'You have sent away your Irish servants, or thrown away your Irish clothes, or blacked your face for your singing. I despise what you have done, I keep you still my friend; but if you are terrorised out of doing any of these things, evil things though I know them to be, I will not have you for my friend any more.' Manhood is all, and the roof of manhood is courage and courtesy.

UNA ELLIS-FERMOR

[John Millington Synge] †

*   *   *

What Synge made of this material is known throughout the English-speaking world. *Riders to the Sea* and *The Playboy of the Western World* are played wherever Irish drama is known, and *Deirdre*, especially the last act, which is the only part he left in finished form, is read wherever tragic poetry is honoured. His development as a dramatist is swift. Scope and humour broaden and deepen successively from play to play; structural subtlety and irony define more and more clearly the grim, the paradoxical and the tragic implications of life. Yet at no time was he uncertain, and if *The Shadow of the Glen* is slighter, as I think it is, than any part of the last two he wrote, it is already clear and complete as a play. His tragedies are untouched by comedy; relief, in them, comes, as with the Greeks, in poetry, and the relief of poetic thought grows more comprehensive as we go from the hard condensation of the early *Riders to the Sea* to the wide and sunny beauty of *Deirdre*. But his comedies are either a frank mixture of the two elements or such laughter as trembles always on the verge of tragedy, and the intimacy of the blending

† From Una Ellis-Fermor, *The Irish Dramatic Movement* (London: Methuen, 1939).

becomes subtler, more bewildering, as we go from the simple contrasts and balances of *The Shadow of the Glen* through *The Well of the Saints* and *The Tinker's Wedding* to *The Playboy of the Western World*. There is at work a watchful mind, slowly observant, grave and capacious. It is never didactic, never abstract, never philosophical, yet full of that intent vigilance which science and tragedy share. It is concrete and dramatic; it works through the human individuals of its creating whose experience is yet universal, and values above all else the inwardness and individuality of that experience.

Because of this steady progression through the six years of Synge's career, it is probably *The Playboy* that shows his dramatic power at its ripest; for *Deirdre*, left unfinished at his death, lacks the final shaping. But the earlier play is a triumphant consummation of the form, perhaps essentially Irish in its material and so in its shape, which subsidiarizes event and takes for its main theme the growth of fantasy in a mind or a group of minds. It is often described by English audiences as 'nothing but talk', and this (which they do not necessarily mean as depreciation) seems true if we compare it with much English comedy, in which character, event and situation interlock and react upon each other; for here character is sometimes no more than the necessary foundation upon which situation can be built and dialogue as much occupied with the service of event and situation as with the revelation of character. If we compare *The Playboy* with a fair, representative comedy by Lyly, Chapman, Ben Johnson, Middleton, Marston, Fletcher, Congreve, Sheridan, Pinero, Jones or Galsworthy, this is clear. For the new Irish comedy of the early twentieth century does something which might else seem only possible to a certain kind of psychological tragedy (such as Ibsen's *John Gabriel Borkman*); it dispenses with all but the minimum of outward event and takes for its theme a mind's exploration and discovery of itself. This, which can carry weight and even passion when the events are tragic, is by no means easy in comedy and except in the comedy of Irish life, where the 'incorrigible genius for myth-making' provides its material, it is liable to relapse into revelation by event. Continuous self-revelation is only possible in comedy where the characters all have a natural tendency to find the processes of their own and other people's minds of absorbing interest, an astounding succession of shocks—'What business would the people here have but to be minding one another's business?' Mrs. Tarpey is right; this is the essential pre-supposition. From this characteristic of the dramatist's originals comes not only that comic, poetic imagery and description which is the main substance of Lady Gregory's shorter plays, but that delighted exploration of his own unfolding personality which Christy Mahon pursues breathlessly through *The Play-boy*. Moreover, the central figure can rely upon the equally delighted co-operation of a society of fantasy-builders as expert and as fruitful as himself, whether in the construction of the tale of catastrophic conflicts between Bartley Fallon and Red Jack Smith or in the creation of a hitherto nonexistent Christopher Mahon. And here Synge, both in *The Well of the Saints* and in *The Playboy*, advances upon Lady Gregory, who was the originator of this kind of comedy; he sees that the genius for myth-making finds its supreme expression in creating the most satisfying myth of all, that of personality. The substance and scope of his comedies at once becomes greater than hers and he can create a full length play out of that very habit which, when used to create only a myth of event, runs to no more than one act.

The form of *The Playboy*, then, its succession of conversations and narrations (slenderly interspersed with episodes) which leads up to the double reversal of the climax, comes directly from its main theme, the growth, like a Japanese paper flower dropped into a bowl of water, of Christopher Mahon's new self.

His evolution from what his father brutally but succinctly describes as a dribbling idiot, not merely into "a likely man', but into a poet-hero, 'the only playboy of the western world', is rapid but sure. So sure that when the reversal comes the new Christy is capable of ousting the original and perpetuating itself. It is the favouring atmosphere of a world of fantasy-builders that starts the process, a world in which whatever is unknown is presumed to be magical and where no talker is without honour, provided he has the luck or sense not to carry on his craft in his own country. Christy creeps into Flaherty's inn and the fostering warmth is enough. The 'polis' never come there; 'it is a safe house, so', and the crime for which he had fled in terror on the roads of Ireland since 'Tuesday was a week', becomes 'maybe something big'. The mystery quickens the blood of his audience, they 'draw nearer with delighted curiosity' and, looking into his own mind for the first time by the illumination of this tribute to his art, he perceives that there is not 'any person, gentle, simple, judge or jury, did the like of me'. From that moment a glorious and brilliant magnification of his deed and his situation sets in, he has 'prison behind him, and hanging before, and hell's gap gaping below'. Once the confession is out his audience contributes royally. They perceive that he is no 'common, week-day kind of a murderer', but a man 'should be a great terror when his temper's roused' and 'a close man' into the bargain. (In fact, a complete Machiavellian, lion and fox together.) As the legend expands at the hands of his audience he accepts the additions, assimilating them so rapidly that they soon become part of his own memory of the event. With becoming modesty he gives the glory to God, but soon realizes that, 'up to the day I killed my father there wasn't a person in Ireland knew the kind I was, and I there drinking, waking, eating, sleeping, a quiet, simple poor fellow with no man giving me heed'. Before the evening is out the widow Quinn has completed the first stage of his development; 'It's great luck and company I've won me in the end of time—two fine women fighting for the likes of me— till I'm thinking this night wasn't I a foolish fellow not to kill my father in the years gone by.'

In the second act the blossoming begins, to pass rapidly on to the fruits of confidence in Christy's victory at the sports at the beginning of the third act: 'Didn't I know rightly I was handsome, though it was the divil's own mirror we had beyond, would twist a squint across an angel's brow.' Christy enters upon a romantic career of bardic self-glorification. Each time he tells his story ('and if it was not altogether the same, anyway it was no less than the first story') he gathers in adroitly whatever had been contributed to the saga by each preceding audience. It is 'a grand story', and 'he tells it lovely'. Honor's comment is true; whichever of his two antithetical selves Christy is at bottom, he is always a fine dramatic raconteur; herein lies his power of convincing himself and giving con-viction, of sinking utterly into the myth that he is acting. In the love scenes with Pegeen he sorts the somewhat conflicting elements in his memory, rationalizing and explaining away the old Christy until finally, after the victory at the sports has given him incontestable proof, he grasps the new self so powerfully that it cannot be shaken even by the father he has dreaded all his life. 'I'm master of all fights from now.' He acknowl-edges the part his admiring audience has played, and whether it has contributed to self-realization, as he thinks, or to the expansion of a superb fantasy, as we half suppose, matters little, 'for you've turned me a likely gaffer in the end of all, the way I'll go romancing through a romping life-time from this hour to the dawning of the judgment day'.

The audience, led by Pegeen, with a reaction common to most romancers when romance presents itself on their doorstep, draw back in horror from the killing which they had glorified so long as it happened in 'a windy corner of high, distant hills'. They have learnt, for the moment, 'that there's a great gap between a gallows story and a dirty deed'. But Pegeen at least is won round at the last, for, after all, what she (and indeed all of them) has loved has been not so much the deed but the man 'that has such poet's talking, and such bravery of heart'. Beside this gift, with its power to bring glory and stir into a world of bog and stone, dirty shebeens and drunken wakes, little else matters. Any other man, beside Christy, is but 'a middling kind of a scarecrow with no savagery or fine words in him at all'. It is Synge's supreme skill in mixing the elements of comedy and tragic irony that leaves us at the end understanding not only how the hero-myth has been created but why. It is not Christy only, but the whole population of the small community he lights upon that has gone 'romancing through a romping life-time', at least for the space of two days. The starved imaginations have made themselves drunk on fantasy as an alternative (or accompaniment) to the 'flows of drink' at Kate Cassidy's wake, and when the curtain falls on the dreary public bar and the dishevelled, half-drunk men, we see what Pegeen and they have lost in the man 'who'd capsize the stars'. The life, aspirations and frustration of a whole country-side is in the play.

* * *

NICHOLAS GRENE

Approaches to *The Playboy* †

* * *

Comic convention throughout [*Playboy*] grows into a different sort of dramatic reality. Take, for example, the use of violence in the play. We can laugh at the story of Christy's deed in the opening scenes, by virtue of the comic immunity which dissociates violence from pain. 'I just riz the loy and let fall the edge of it on the ridge of his skull, and he went down at my feet like an empty sack, and never let a grunt or groan from him at all.' Our moral self-respect is protected by the comic guarantee of painlessness. It is a straightforward comic attitude which Synge encourages us to adopt to the story of the parricide, not 'black' or 'sick' comedy where the laughter has an undercurrent of guilt. It is not even a satire on the specifically Irish sympathy for criminals. In spite of Synge's own professions and the instance of the Lynchehaun case which he said suggested the idea for the play, he does not focus directly on the rural Irish opposition to law. The comic convention established is basically independent of the local setting, and the unusual attitude to violence in Ireland is only of incidental relevance.

We can see this if we compare *The Playboy* with its 'source' in *The*

† From *Synge: A Critical Study of the Plays.* Reprinted by permission of Macmillan, London and Basingstoke.

Aran Islands. Synge tells the story of the parricide whom the people sheltered, and then comments on the islanders' attitude:

> If a man has killed his father, and is already sick and broken with remorse, they see no reason why he should be dragged away and killed by the law.
>
> Such a man, they say, will be quiet all the rest of his life, and if you suggest that punishment is needed as an example, they ask, 'Would any one kill his father if he was able to help it?'

This is a profoundly moral response to a crime of violence: it implies both an appreciation of the dreadfulness of the action, and the deep remorse it must necessarily bring to the criminal. Synge also comments on the fact that the islanders dispatch a man judged guilty of a crime, alone, to present himself at the jail in Galway where he is to serve his sentence. This is not a lawless people, but one whose attitude to law is more sensitive than that of ordinary society.

Nowhere in *The Playboy* is the tone anything like that of the simple unanswerable question, 'Would any one kill his father if he was able to help it?' Instead we have the interrogation of Christy leading up to the splendid interchange:

> *Pegeen*. Is it killed your father?
> *Christy*. With the help of God I did surely, and that the Holy Immaculate Mother may intercede for his soul.

Of course Synge is putting to ironic effect the Irish custom of the promiscuous invocation of the deity. But just as surely he is signalling from the start that this is comedy, that we are not to consider Christy's deed in its full moral implication. The inversion of values indicated by Michael James's 'great respect' for the parricide is part of the comic convention. It is neither a direct nor a satiric portrayal of the Irish peasants, in so far as they may be characterised as condoning violence. Nobody outside a comedy, however anarchic, would say as Pegeen does of a man who has killed his father—'That'd be a lad with the sense of Solomon to have for a pot-boy.' The very absurdity of the logic makes it impossible to take this seriously.

The Playboy starts with a comic hypothesis: a man who thinks himself a parricide finds that he is not regarded with horror but with respect, that he has come by means of his deed to a brave new world of glory. What happens to the man as a result? Synge undoubtedly took his cue for this hypothesis from the abnormal attitude to crime among the Irish country people, but it remains essentially a hypothesis, agreed between author and audience, as remote from ordinary reality as the absurd *mal-entendus* of farce. We can shamelessly enjoy Christy's full-scale account of the murder in Act II:

> Christy . . . Then I turned around with my back to the north, and I hit a blow on the ridge of his skull, laid him stretched out, and he split to the knob of his gullet. (He raises the chicken bone to his Adam's apple.)

At this climactic moment, any tendency we might have to consider the implications of splitting a man's head open is subverted by the gesture with the chicken bone. Long before Old Mahon appears on stage, we have realised that there is something unreal about Christy's deed, or at least attention has been comically arrested, so that we do not fully examine the reality of the murder.

Yet there is more than mock violence in *The Playboy*. Incidental remarks disturb the audience's attitude of comic anaesthesia. 'Where now will you meet the like of Daneen Sullivan knocked the eye from a peeler, or Marcus Quin, God rest him, got six months for maiming ewes', says Pegeen complaining of the degeneracy of the times. Or again from Pegeen:

> You never hanged him, the way Jimmy Farrell hanged his dog from the licence and had it screeching and wriggling three hours at the butt of a string, and himself swearing it was a dead dog, and the peelers swearing it had life?

The same image is picked up when she frightens Christy with hanging in Act II: 'it'd make the green stones cry itself to think of you swaying and swiggling at the butt of a rope.' These lines are comic but it is a sardonic humour, for the description is rather too vivid for comfortable laughter. Where the fantastic absurdity of the playboy / parricide ensures a comic reaction, the hanging of the dog and the savagery of the 'patriots' is closer to truth, less simply funny. Even more upsetting, because quite casual, is Widow Quin's warning to Old Mahon on the dangers of madness: 'them lads caught a maniac one time and pelted the poor creature till he ran out raving and foaming and was drowned in the sea.' We are given a horrifying glimpse of a community where madness is still laughable and cruelty commonplace.

Our comic attitude is unsettled by such passages, but it is only in the final act that violence suddenly becomes immediate and real. With the reappearance of Old Mahon and the exposure of Christy the emotional level of the play rises. Christy's humiliation is initially comic, but as

Pegeen and the crowd turn on him, their cruelty becomes apparent. The climax comes as the taunted victim 'swings round with a sudden rapid movement and picks up a loy'. This loy has been used several times in the earlier scenes, when it needed only one look at it to start Christy off: 'It was with a loy the like of that I killed my father'. The comic prop now becomes a real instrument of violence, and the effect of Christy's movement on the audience is that of complete bewilderment. With the scene of the burning of Christy's leg, we are a long way from the comic security with which we received the news of his deed. Synge leads us across the 'great gap between the gallous story and a dirty deed', from mock murder to real violence.

There is some evidence to suggest that it was this shattering of comic convention which provoked the reaction of the first-night audience. 'The first act went well,' according to Maire Nic Shiublaigh, 'there was laughter at the right places and the correct degree of solemnity was maintained when it was demanded.' The audience evidently accepted the fantastic plot—in this act as much as anywhere Irish men and women are shown hero-worshipping a parricide—and Lady Gregory was able to send a telegram to Yeats after the first act, announcing the play's success. But, Maire Nic Shiublaigh continues, 'during the second act I began to feel a tenseness in the air around me.'[1] Padraic Colum, who was also present, thought that the audience started 'growing hostile to the play from the point where Christy's father enters. That scene was too representational. There stood a man with horribly-bloodied bandage upon his head, making a figure that took the whole thing out of the atmosphere of high comedy'.[2] The line which actually started the row is well known (though it was apparently slightly altered on the night):

> what'd I care if you brought me a drift of chosen females, standing in their shifts itself maybe, from this place to the Eastern world.

It has been generally assumed that the puritanical Dubliners objected instantly to this vision of a nation-wide harem, but it is worth noticing where the line comes in the play. Christy has just returned to the stage, apparently having murdered his father. It may well be that, after a few moments of stunned amazement, the audience reacted against this display of violence, and that it was all but accidental that the delayed response came at the word 'shifts'.

When the Abbey revived the play after Synge's death, they took care to avoid similar reactions:

1. Nic Shiublaigh and Kenny, *The Splendid Years* (Dublin, 1955), p. 83.

2. Padraic Colum, *The Road Round Ireland* (New York, 1926), p. 368.

Originally that excellent actor W. G. Fay was in the part of the Playboy. He made the role a little sardonic, and this . . . took from the extravagance of the comedy. Afterwards the Playboy's father was made a less bloody object, and the part of the Playboy in the hands of another actor was given more charm and gaiety, and there was no trouble with the audience.[3]

(A photograph of Fred O'Donovan as the playboy in 1910 makes clear the sort of conventional juvenile lead the part became.) In later productions *The Playboy* was played fast as a comedy, whereas 'when it was given for the first time it was played seriously, almost sombrely'.[4] These remain the basic alternatives for directing the play. Both extravagant comedy and a more realistic form of drama are there and the central effect of the play depends upon the relation between the two.

---

3. Ibid., pp. 268–9.

4. Nic Shiublaigh and Kenny, *The Splendid Years*, p. 81.

Bernard Shaw

Preface for Politicians †
(To the First Edition in 1906)

John Bull's Other Island was written in 1904 at the request of Mr William Butler Yeats, as a patriotic contribution to the repertory of the Irish Literary Theatre. Like most people who have asked me to write plays, Mr Yeats got rather more than he bargained for. The play was at that time beyond the resources of the new Abbey Theatre, which the Irish enterprise owed to the public spirit of Miss A. E. F. Horniman (an Englishwoman, of course), who, twelve years ago, played an important part in the history of the modern English stage as well as in my own personal destiny by providing the necessary capital for that memorable season at the Avenue Theatre which forced my Arms and The Man and Mr Yeats's Land of Heart's Desire on the recalcitrant London playgoer, and gave a third Irish playwright, Dr John Todhunter, an opportunity which the commercial theatres could not have afforded him.[1]

There was another reason for changing the destination of John Bull's Other Island. It was uncongenial to the whole spirit of the neo-Gaelic movement, which is bent on creating a new Ireland after its own ideal, whereas my play is a very uncompromising presentment of the real old Ireland. The next thing that happened was the production of the play in London at the Court Theatre by Messrs. Vedrenne and Barker, and its immediate and enormous popularity with delighted and flattered English audiences. This constituted it a successful commercial play, and made it unnecessary to resort to the special machinery or tax the special resources of the Irish Literary Theatre for its production.

† Printed by permission of The Society of Authors on behalf of the Estate of George Bernard Shaw. All rights reserved. Space limitations prevent inclusion of the entire text; the full preface is essential to serious study of the play.

1. Todhunter (1839–1916), poet as well as "Ibsenite" playwright, whose "Comedy of Sighs," generally ridiculed, was paired with Yeats's play in 1894 [*Editor*].

How Tom Broadbent Took It

Now I have a good deal more to say about the relations between the Irish
and the English than will be found in my play. Writing the play for an
Irish audience, I thought it would be good for them to be shewn very
clearly that the loudest laugh they could raise at the expense of the
absurdest Englishman was not really a laugh on their side; that he would
succeed where they would fail; that he could inspire strong affection and
loyalty in an Irishman who knew the world and was moved only to
dislike, mistrust, impatience and even exasperation by his own countrymen; that his power of taking himself seriously, and his insensibility to
anything funny in danger and destruction, was the first condition of
economy and concentration of force, sustained purpose, and rational
conduct. But the need for this lesson in Ireland is the measure of its
demoralizing superfluousness in England. English audiences very naturally swallowed it eagerly and smacked their lips over it, laughing all
the more heartily because they felt that they were taking a caricature of
themselves with the most tolerant and large-minded goodhumor. They
were perfectly willing to allow me to represent Tom Broadbent as infat-
uated in politics, hypnotized by his newspaper leader-writers and parliamentary orators into an utter paralysis of his common sense, without
moral delicacy or social tact, provided I made him cheerful, robust,
goodnatured, free from envy, and above all, a successful muddler-through
in business and love. Not only did no English critic allow that the success in business of Messrs English Broadbent and Irish Doyle might
possibly have been due to some extent to Doyle, but one writer actually
dwelt with much feeling on the pathos of Doyle's failure as an engineer
(a circumstance not mentioned nor suggested in my play) in contrast
with Broadbent's solid success. No doubt, when the play is performed in
Ireland, the Dublin critics will regard it as self-evident that without Doyle
Broadbent would have become bankrupt in six months. I should say,
myself, that the combination was probably much more effective than
either of the partners would have been alone. I am persuaded further—
without pretending to know more about it than anyone else—that
Broadbent's special contribution was simply the strength, self-satisfac-
tion, social confidence and cheerful bumptiousness that money, comfort, and good feeling bring to all healthy people; and that Doyle's special
contribution was the freedom from illusion, the power of facing facts,
the nervous industry, the sharpened wits, the sensitive pride of the imaginative man who has fought his way up through social persecution and
poverty. I do not say that the confidence of the Englishman in Broad-

bent is not for the moment justified. The virtues of the English soil are not less real because they consist of coal and iron, not of metaphysical sources of character. The virtues of Broadbent are not less real because they are the virtues of the money that coal and iron have produced. But as the mineral virtues are being discovered and developed in other soils, their derivative virtues are appearing so rapidly in other nations that Broadbent's relative advantage is vanishing. In truth I am afraid (the misgiving is natural to a by-this-time slightly elderly playwright) that Broadbent is out of date. The successful Englishman of today, when he is not a transplanted Scotchman or Irishman, often turns out on investigation to be, if not an American, an Italian, or a Jew, at least to be depending on the brains, the nervous energy, and the freedom from romantic illusions (often called cynicism) of such foreigners for the management of his sources of income. At all events I am persuaded that a modern nation that is satisfied with Broadbent is in a dream. Much as I like him, I object to be governed by him, or entangled in his political destiny. I therefore propose to give him a piece of my mind here, as an Irishman, full of an instinctive pity for those of my fellow-creatures who are only English.

What Is An Irishman?

When I say that I am an Irishman I mean that I was born in Ireland, and that my native language is the English of Swift and not the unspeakable jargon of the mid-XIX century London newspapers. My extraction is the extraction of most Englishmen: that is, I have no trace in me of the commercially imported North Spanish strain which passes for aboriginal Irish: I am a genuine typical Irishman of the Danish, Norman, Cromwellian, and (of course) Scotch invasions. I am violently and arrogantly Protestant by family tradition; but let no English Government therefore count on my allegiance: I am English enough to be inveterate Republican and Home Ruler. It is true that one of my grandfathers was an Orangeman [2]; but then his sister was an abbess; and his uncle, I am proud to say, was hanged as a rebel. When I look round me on the hybrid cosmopolitans, slum poisoned or square pampered, who call themselves Englishmen today, and see them bullied by the Irish Protestant garrison as no Bengalee now lets himself be bullied by an Englishman; when I see the Irishman everywhere standing clearheaded, sane, hardily callous to the boyish sentimentalities, susceptibilities, and cre-

2. Protestant, loyalist sympathizer; hence, like Shaw's other contrasts here, opposed to a Catholic abbess or Republican rebel [*Editor*].

dulities that make the Englishman the dupe of every charlatan and the idolater of every numskull, I perceive that Ireland is the only spot on earth which still produces the ideal Englishman of history. Blackguard, bully, drunkard, liar, foulmouth, flatterer, beggar, backbiter, venal functionary, corrupt judge, envious friend, vindictive opponent, unparalleled political traitor: all these your Irishman may easily be, just as he may be a gentleman (a species extinct in England, and nobody a penny the worse); but he is never quite the hysterical nonsense-crammed, fact-proof, truth-terrified, unballasted sport of all the bogey panics and all the silly enthusiasms that now calls itself "God's Englishman." England cannot do without its Irish and its Scots today, because it cannot do without at least a little sanity.

The Protestant Garrison

The more Protestant an Irishman is—the more English he is, if it flatters you to have it put that way, the more intolerable he finds it to be ruled by English instead of Irish folly. A "loyal" Irishman is an abhorrent phenomenon, because it is an unnatural one. No doubt English rule is vigorously exploited in the interests of the property, power, and promotion of the Irish classes as against the Irish masses. Our delicacy is part of a keen sense of reality which makes us a very practical, and even, on occasion, a very coarse people. The Irish soldier takes the King's shilling and drinks the King's health; and the Irish squire takes the title deeds of the English settlement and rises uncovered to the strains of the English national anthem. But do not mistake this cupboard loyalty for anything deeper. It gains a broad base from the normal attachment of every reasonable man to the established government as long as it is bearable; for we all, after a certain age, prefer peace to revolution and order to chaos, other things being equal. Such considerations produce loyal Irishmen as they produce loyal Poles and Fins, loyal Hindus, loyal Filipinos, and faithful slaves. But there is nothing more in it than that. If there is an entire lack of gall in the feeling of the Irish gentry towards the English, it is because the Englishman is always gaping admiringly at the Irishman as at some clever child prodigy. He overrates him with a generosity born of a traditional conviction of his own superiority in the deeper aspects of human character. As the Irish gentleman, tracing his pedigree to the conquest or one of the invasions, is equally convinced that if this superiority really exists, he is the genuine true blue heir to it, and as he is easily able to hold his own in all the superficial social accomplishments, he finds English society agreeable, and English houses very comfortable,

Irish establishments being generally straitened by an attempt to keep a park and a stable on an income which would not justify an Englishman in venturing upon a wholly detached villa.

Our Temperaments Contrasted

But however pleasant the relations between the Protestant garrison and the English gentry may be, they are always essentially of the nature of an *entente cordiale* between foreigners. Personally I like Englishmen much better than Irishmen (no doubt because they make more of me) just as many Englishmen like Frenchmen better than Englishmen, and never go on board a Peninsular and Oriental steamer when one of the ships of the Messageries Maritimes is available. But I never think of an Englishman as my countryman. I should as soon think of applying that term to a German. And the Englishman has the same feeling. When a Frenchman fails to make the distinction, we both feel a certain disparagement involved in the misapprehension. Macaulay, seeing that the Irish had in Swift an author worth stealing, tried to annex him by contending that he must be classed as an Englishman because he was not an aboriginal Celt. He might as well have refused the name of Briton to Addison because he did not stain himself blue and attach scythes to the poles of his sedan chair.[3] In spite of all such trifling with facts, the actual distinction between the idolatrous Englishman and the fact-facing Irishman, of the same extraction though they be, remains to explode those two hollowest of fictions, the Irish and English "races." There is no Irish race any more than there is an English race or a Yankee race. There *is* an Irish climate, which will stamp an immigrant more deeply and durably in two years, apparently, than the English climate will in two hundred. It is reinforced by an artificial economic climate which does some of the work attributed to the natural geographic one; but the geographic climate is eternal and irresistible, making a mankind and a womankind that Kent, Middlesex, and East Anglia cannot produce and do not want to imitate.

How can I sketch the broad lines of the contrast as they strike me? Roughly I should say that the Englishman is wholly at the mercy of his imagination, having no sense of reality to check it. The Irishman, with a far subtler and more fastidious imagination, has one eye always on things as they are. If you compare [Thomas] Moore's visionary "Minstrel

---

3. Thomas Babington Macaulay (1800–59), MP, writer, colonial administrator of India; Jonathan Swift (1667–1745), Dubliner by birth, career, and burial; Joseph Addison (1672–1719), impeccably English essayist who twice served as aide to the lord lieutenant of Ireland [*Editor*].

Boy" with Mr Rudyard Kipling's quasi-realistic "Soldiers Three," you may yawn over Moore or gush over him, but you will not suspect him of having had any illusions about the contemporary British private; whilst as to Mr Kipling, you will see that he has not, and unless he settles in Ireland for a few years will always remain constitutionally and congenitally incapable of having, the faintest inkling of the reality which he idolizes as Tommy Atkins. Perhaps you have never thought of illustrating the contrast between English and Irish by Moore and Mr Kipling, or even by Parnell and Gladstone. Sir Boyle Roche and Shakespeare may seem more to your point. Let me find you a more dramatic instance. Think of the famous meeting between the Duke of Wellington, that intensely Irish Irishman, and Nelson, that intensely English Englishman.[4] Wellington's contemptuous disgust at Nelson's theatricality as a professed hero, patriot, and rhapsody, a theatricality which in an Irishman would have been an insufferably vulgar affectation, was quite natural and inevitable. Wellington's formula for that kind of thing was a well-known Irish one: "Sir: dont be a damned food." It is the formula of all Irishmen for all Englishmen to this day. It is the formula of Larry Doyle for Tom Broadbent in my play, in spite of Doyle's affection for Tom. Nelson's genius, instead of producing intellectual keenness and scrupulousness, produced mere delirium. He was drunk with glory, exalted by his fervent faith in the sound British patriotism of the Almighty, nerved by the vulgarest anti-foreign prejudice, and apparently unchastened by any reflections on the fact that he had never had to fight a technically capable and properly equipped enemy except on land, where he had never been successful. Compare Wellington, who had to fight Napoleon's armies, Napoleon's marshals, and finally Napoleon himself, without one moment of illusions as to the human material he had to command, without one gush of the "Kiss me, Hardy" emotion which enabled Nelson to idolize his crews and his staff, without forgetting even in his dreams that the normal British officer of that time was an incapable amateur (as he still is) and the normal British soldier a never-dowell (he is now a depressed and respectable young man). No wonder Wellington became an accomplished comedian in the art of anti-climax, scandalizing the unfortunate Croker,[5] responding to the demand

---

4. Again, Irish figures of British careers contrasted with English: Parliamentarians Charles Stewart Parnell (1846–91) and William Ewart Gladstone (1809–98); rhetoricians Sir Boyle Roche (1743–1807), said to have perpetrated the inflated, senseless "Irish Bull," and Shakespeare; military commanders the duke of Wellington (1769–1852) and

Viscount Nelson (1758–1805) [Editor].
5. John Wilson Croker (1780–1857), a comical literary figure who published his own papers, including letters from Wellington; "Kiss me, Hardy," above, are said to have been Nelson's last words [Editor].

for glorious sentiments by the most disenchanting touches of realism, and, generally, pricking the English windbag at its most explosive crises of distention. Nelson, intensely nervous and theatrical, made an enormous fuss about victories so cheap that he would have deserved shooting if he had lost them, and, not content with lavishing splendid fighting on helpless adversaries like the heroic De Brueys or Villeneuve (who had not even the illusion of heroism when he went like a lamb to the slaughter), got himself killed by his passion for exposing himself to death in that sublime defiance of it which was perhaps the supreme tribute of the exquisite coward to the King of Terrors (for, believe me, you cannot be a hero without being a coward: supersense cuts both ways), the result being a tremendous effect on the gallery. Wellington, most capable of captains, was neither a hero nor a patriot: perhaps not even a coward; and had it not been for the Nelsonic anecdotes invented for him—"Up guards, and at em" and so forth—and the fact that the antagonist with whom he finally closed was such a master of theatrical effect that Wellington could not fight him without getting into his limelight, nor overthrow him (most unfortunately for us all) without drawing the eyes of the whole world to the catastrophe, the Iron Duke would have been almost forgotten by this time. Now that contrast is English against Irish all over, and is the more delicious because the real Irishman in it is the Englishman of tradition, whilst the real Englishman is the traditional theatrical foreigner.

The value of the illustration lies in the fact that Nelson and Wellington were both in the highest degree efficient, and both in the highest degree incompatible with one another on any other footing than one of independence. The government of Nelson by Wellington or of Wellington by Nelson is felt at once to be a dishonorable outrage to the governed and a finally impossible task for the governor.

I daresay some Englishman will now try to steal Wellington as Macaulay tried to steal Swift. And he may plead with some truth that though it seems impossible that any other country than England could produce a hero so utterly devoid of common sense, intellectual delicacy, and international chivalry as Nelson, it may be contended that Wellington was rather an eighteenth century aristocratic type, than a specifically Irish type. George IV and Byron, contrasted with Gladstone, seem Irish in respect of a certain humorous blackguardism, and a power of appreciating art and sentiment without being duped by them into mistaking romantic figments for realities. But faithlessness and the need for carrying off the worthlessness and impotence that accompany it, produce in all nations a gay, sceptical, amusing, blaspheming, witty fashion which suits the flexibility of the Irish mind very well; and the contrast between this fashion and the energetic infatuations that have enabled intellectually ridiculous men, without wit or humor, to go on crusades and make successful revolutions, must not be confused with the contrast between the English and Irish idiosyncrasies. The Irishman makes a distinction which the Englishman is too lazy intellectually (the intellectual laziness and slovenliness of the English is almost beyond belief) to make. The Englishman, impressed with the dissoluteness of the faithless wits of the Restoration and the Regency, and with the victories of the willful zealots of the patriotic, religious, and revolutionary wars, jumps to the conclusion that willfulness is the main thing. In this he is right. But he overdoes his jump so far as to conclude also that stupidity and wrong-headedness are better guarantees of efficiency and trustworthiness than intellectual vivacity, which he mistrusts as a common symptom of worthlessness, vice, and instability. Now in this he is most dangerously wrong. Whether the Irishman grasps the truth as firmly as the Englishman may be open to question; but he is certainly comparatively free from the error. That affectionate and admiring love of sentimental stupidity for its own sake, both in men and women, which shines so steadily through the novels of Thackeray, would hardly be possible in the works of an Irish novelist. Even Dickens, though too vital a genius and too severely educated in the school of shabby-genteel poverty to have any doubt of the national danger of fatheadedness in high places, evidently assumes rather too hastily the superiority of Mr Meagles to Sir John Chester and Harold Skimpole.[6] On the other hand, it takes an Irishman years of residence in England to learn to respect and like a blockhead. An Englishman will not respect nor like anyone else. Every English statesman has to maintain his popularity by pretending to be ruder, more ignorant, more sentimental, more superstitious, more stupid than any man who has lived behind the scenes of public life for ten minutes can possibly be. Nobody dares to publish really intimate memoirs of him or really private letters of his until his whole generation has passed away, and his party can no longer be compromised by the discovery that the platitudinizing twaddler and hypocritical opportunist was really a man of some perception as well as of strong constitution, peg-away industry, personal ambition, and party keenness.

* * *

6. Characters from Dickens's novels, respectively, *Little Dorrit*, *Barnaby Rudge*, and *Bleak House* [Editor].

M. J. SIDNELL

Hic and Ille: Shaw and Yeats †

*   *   *

In 1901 with the Irish Literary Theatre well launched and Dublin already stirring, Yeats asked Shaw to come to Ireland and help 'stir things up still further.' Yeats had neglected Shaw's suggestion that *The Devil's Disciple* might be performed in Dublin. 'It was the very play for this country,' wrote Yeats, 'as indeed you said to me—but I did not understand.'

The recognition of Shaw's ability to stir things up in a profitable way is characteristic, but the comment on Shaw's play is not. This new and short-lived enthusiasm for Shaw's work arises apparently from the Irish response to the end of *The Man of Destiny:* [1]

> Some of the young men of the Extreme National Party are reading you just now with great satisfaction. 'The United Irishman' had a long quotation from your 'Napoleon' about English characters a few weeks ago. They would welcome you over with enthusiasm. [2]

That both Yeats and the extreme nationalists would welcome Shaw seems, in the light of subsequent events, to arise from Shaw's adoption of an Irish point of view without, mercifully, talking about Ireland.

*   *   *

Shaw did not come to Dublin and he did not want the Irish Literary Theatre to do *The Man of Destiny* where his attack on the English and his praise of the Irish would lose their critical point, for the play is of course addressed to an English audience. Instead he agreed to write a play especially for Yeats's theatre and an Irish audience. According to Shaw:

> *John Bull's Other Island* was written in 1904 at the request of Mr William Butler Yeats, as a patriotic contribution to the repertory of the Irish Literary Theatre. Like most people who have asked me to write plays, Mr Yeats got rather more than he bargained for. The

† From *Theatre and Nationalism in Twentieth-Century Ireland*, ed. Robert O'Driscoll. Copyright © University of Toronto Press 1971. Reprinted by permission of University of Toronto Press.

1. Shaw's play of 1895 [*Editor*].
2. This essay is based on unpublished correspondence between Shaw and Yeats [*Editor*].

play was at that time beyond the resources of the new Abbey Theatre . . .[3]

The irony of that 'patriotic' with its peculiarly Shavian connotations and
the ambiguity of 'resources' partly give the game away. It was volun-
teered rather than requested according to Yeats, but whatever the
arrangement Shaw's promise was received by Yeats with great enthusiasm, an enthusiasm that lasted until he read the play. Having read it,
Yeats was in a quandary. Here was the opportunity for the Abbey Theatre to launch itself with the work of an internationally known playwright. The play would excite the Dublin audience in ways that no play
of Yeats, Synge, or Lady Gregory could. However, the work would be
difficult to stage and Yeats disliked it.

When he received a copy of the play Yeats read it and gave it to Synge
and to William Fay for their opinions before replying to Shaw. Fay's
response was that it was:

> a wonderful piece of work. But as to our using it I would like a
> longer time to consider it. . . . It is full of fine things but the diffi-
> culty of getting a cast for it would be considerable. I don't know
> how [Shaw] expects to get a show of it in London for with the
> exception of the Englishman and his valet the rest would have to
> be Irish born and bred to get the hang of what he wants.[4]

Synge thought some cuts necessary and Yeats in replying to Shaw made
much of the need for cutting. I quote part of Yeats's long letter:

> I was disappointed by the first act and a half. The stage Irishman
> who wasn't an Irishman was very amusing but then I said to myself
> 'What the devil did Shaw mean by all this Union of Hearts-like
> conversation? What do we care here in this country, which despite
> the Act of Union is still an island, about the English liberal party
> and the Tariff, and the difference between English and Irish char-
> acter, or whatever else it was all about? Being raw people,' I said,
> 'we do care about human nature in action, and that he's not giving
> us.'

The Irish interest in descriptions of national character which had waxed
so strong with *The Man of Destiny* is now on the wane as Shaw's bright
sun rises over Ireland:

---

3. *Complete Plays with Prefaces* (New York, 1963),
II, p. 43 [471]. [Page numbers to this volume are
given in brackets.]

4. From an unpublished letter, W. G. Fay to
W. B. Yeats.

No debauchery that ever coarsened and brutalised an Englishman
can take the worth and usefulness out of him like that dreaming.
An Irishman's imagination never lets him alone, never convinces
him, never satisfies him; but it makes him that he can't face reality
nor deal with it nor handle it nor conquer it: he can only sneer at
them that do. He can't be religious. The inspired Churchman that
teaches him the sanctity of life and the importance of conduct is
sent away empty; while the poor village priest that gives him a miracle or a sentimental story of a saint, has cathedrals built for him
out of the pennies of the poor. He can't be intelligently political:
he dreams of what the Shan Van Vocht said in ninetyeight. If you
want to interest him in Ireland you've got to call the unfortunate
island Kathleen ni Hollihan and pretend she's a little old woman.
It saves thinking. It saves working.[5]

So says Shaw's Doyle, one of the real Irishmen in the play. That reference to 'raw people'—an uncharacteristic phrase to come from Yeats at
this time—seems to be an adjustment of his attitude to the Irish people
which will make possible a better defensive stance from which to respond
to this kind of description of an Irish peasant:

The real tragedy of Haffigan is the tragedy of his wasted youth, his
stunted mind, his drudging over his clods and pigs until he has
become a clod and a pig himself—until the soul within him has
smouldered into nothing but a dull temper that hurts himself and
all around him. I say let him die, and let us have no more of his
like.[6]

Yeats continues his critique, finding more to praise, balancing his respect
for Shaw's sense of comedy and intelligent concern for Ireland against
that logical straightness he hated:

Then my interest began to awake. That young woman who persuaded that Englishman, full of impulsiveness that comes from a
good banking account, that he was drunk on nothing more serious
than poteen, was altogether a delight. The motor car too, the
choosing the member of Parliament, and so on right to the end,
often exciting and mostly to the point. I thought in reading the first
act that you had forgotten Ireland, but I found in the other acts that
is the only subject on which you are entirely serious. In fact you
are so serious that sometimes your seriousness leaps upon the stage,

5. *Complete Plays*, 11, p. 517 [130–31].   6. *Ibid.*, p. 605 [198].

knocks the characters over, and insists on having ιl the conversation to himself. However the inevitable cutting (the play is as you say immensely too long) is certain to send your seriousness back to the front row of the stalls. You have said things in this play which are entirely true about Ireland, things which nobody has ever said before, and these are the very things that are most part of the action. It astonishes me that you should have been so long in London and yet have remembered so much. To some extent this play is unlike anything you have done before. Hitherto you have taken your situation from melodrama, and called up logic to make them ridiculous. Your process here seems to be quite different, you are taking your situations more from life, you are for the first time trying to get the atmosphere of a place, you have for the first time a geographical conscience. (For instance you have not made the landlords the winning side, as you did the Servians in the first version of *Arms and the Man*.)

The criticism is not so much a view of the whole work as a record of Yeats's changing impressions as the play unfolded for him: a tribute to its author's sheepdog skill in herding his audience. And Yeats's response is not unlike in kind, though different in quality, that description of the way in which the boobies who had gone to disrupt *Arms and the Man* fell into Shaw's trap. Yeats steers clear of Shaw's professional Irishman handily enough, but is irritated and confused by the sentimental English celticist and the really Irish internationalist, as he was meant to be. Shaw's Doyle deplores his father's ambition 'to make St George's Channel a frontier and hoist a flag on College Green'. 'Ireland,' insists Yeats, 'is still an island.' Having expended his energy reacting to the early part of the play Yeats is softened for indoctrination by Shaw with new and, he acknowledges, true comments on Ireland.

In his 'Preface for Politicians,' Shaw later put succinctly the attitude to nationalism that permeates *John Bull's Other Island*:

> The great movements of the human spirit which sweep in waves over Europe are stopped on the Irish coast by the English guns of the Pigeon House Fort. Only a quaint little offshoot of English pre-Raphaelitism called the Gaelic movement has got a footing by using Nationalism as a stalking-horse, and popularising itself as an attack on the native language of the Irish people, which is most fortunately also the native language of half the world, including England.[7]

7. *Ibid.*, 471.

Shaw's blow is shrewdly aimed at Yeats. Far from being a poet drawing strength from the native culture, Yeats is implicitly characterised as one bamboozled by a sentimental, affected, and effete primitivism. In sharing a platform with the Gaelic League Yeats saw himself authenticating his Irishness but Shaw, who had little interest in sharing platforms, demolishes the one that Yeats had laboured to construct.

* * *

NORMA JENCKES

The Rejection of Shaw's Irish Play:
John Bull's Other Island †

* * *

Yeats conceived and created the Abbey Theatre as a vehicle for a certain type of dramaturgy. Ten years earlier Shaw had been able to see the value of much that Yeats attempted. He concluded in a letter to Florence Farr written in 1894 at the time of the production of *The Land of Heart's Desire*, that Yeats was a gifted playwright and that his play was exquisite.[1] Yeats was never able to be so generous. Although he can admit the talent and energy of Shaw's *Arms and the Man*, his judgment is never unmixed. He cannot resist noting what is for him the play's "inorganic, logical straightness."[2] Ten years only intensified Yeats's hatred of the logical and unromantic presentation of the world that Shaw represented. When Shaw turned his sights to Ireland, he created *John Bull's Other Island*, with its attack on the mood of dreaminess, Celticism, and escapism. In 1904 too much of the repertory of the Irish Literary Theatre included those plays that treated Celticism and the Irish past as staples. Yeats might later, as described in "The Circus Animals' Desertion," leave behind his gay and heroic images of Ireland, but in 1904 these were still central to his poetic inspiration. Also, he believed that any political improvement in Ireland would only come through a revitalization of the figures of Ireland's heroic past.

Once the Abbey had rejected Shaw's play as diplomatically as possible, and when it was finally produced in London, Yeats expressed his dislike for it in a letter to Lady Gregory he wrote after seeing that perfor-

† From *Eire-Ireland* 10 (Spring 1975). *Eire-Ireland* is the publication of the Irish American Cultural Institute, St. Paul, Minnesota.
1. *Florence Farr, Bernard Shaw, W. B. Yeats:* *Letters*, ed. Clifford Box (London, 1946), p. ix.
2. W. B. Yeats, *Autobiographies* (New York: Doubleday, 1958), p. 283.

mance: "I have seen Shaw's play; it acts very much better than one could
have foreseen, but is immensely long. It begins at 2:30 and ends at 6. I
don't really like it. It is fundamentally ugly and shapeless, but certainly
keeps everybody amused."[3]

William Fay, the director of the amateur acting group that joined
with Yeats in reviving Irish drama, registers an equally amazing shift of
opinion. When he first read it he found it "a wonderful piece of work."
When he saw it in London, his only objections were to the difficulty of
casting it:

> Our company could not do it adequately in their present circum-
> stances. Their experience was far too limited. To my thinking the
> play depends on having a Broadbent who can carry the weight of
> it, for without him it is *Hamlet* without the Prince. Besides, he
> must both look and sound English, and we had nobody who could
> take the part of the Cockney valet, Hodson. In Frank I had a splen-
> did Keegan, but I had no Larry. The rest of the cast I might have
> managed, though my people were really too young for the parts.
> Rather reluctantly I had to advise against attempting the play.[4]

But by 1930 Fay had turned against it violently. In the 1912 revival of
the play under the direction of Granville-Barker, and with the famous
William Poel as Keegan, Fay's wife had "the genteel but not very exciting part of Nora, while I burbled along about 'me sufferings' as old
Haffigan." Remembering this, he pronounces a sweeping condemnation of the play and convicts Shaw of garrulity and of ignorance of his
subject:

> . . . *John Bull's Other Island* ranks among Shaw's failures. It is
> interesting as the first play of his later manner, where action is
> nothing and talk everything, but its talk was out of date before it
> was written down. Mr. Shaw left Ireland in 1876, and it was only
> by hearsay that he knew of the Land League, the Plan of Cam-
> paign, and what Parnell meant to Ireland. By the time he had grasped
> the significance of all these things, Ireland had put them away and
> was busy organizing the Gaelic League which produced Sinn Fein,
> followed by two revolutions and the formation of the Free State.
> There is half a century between the Ireland of *John Bull's Other
> Island* and the Ireland of Sean O'Casey, and yet to O'Casey's name
> one might add with profound reverence, the name of J. M. Synge.[5]

3. *Letters*, ed. Allan Wade (London: Rupert Hart-   ard, 1935), pp. 206–07.
Davis, 1954), p. 442.   5. *The Abbey Theatre*, p. 251.
4. *The Abbey Theatre* (London: Rich and Cow-

More recent critics, who should know better, have likewise belittled the play. Writing in 1971, Michael J. Sidnell conjectures that "the initial rejection of his *John Bull's Other Island* by the Abbey-to-be may even be a matter of rejoicing." He relegates Shaw to the position of a kind of middle-man in Anglo-Irish literary life: "Like Swift, Shaw was to be most useful and dear to Ireland when addressing England or at least seeing Ireland in its relation to England." Sidnell concludes his comments with the note that "Dublin in 1904 according to the best testimony for that year, Joyce's farraginous chronicle, stood more in need of unifying vision than analytical criticism: more in need of creative image than the intellectual structure erected by Shaw as a gallery in which to hand the caricatures of the time."[6] Like Fay, Sidnell performs a feat of literary second-guessing, and he encourages the notion that Shaw could not write a truly Irish play because he was remote from the cultural events of his native land.

This notion, though a persistent one, will not withstand an objective perusal of the events of Shaw's career. Shaw's experience of Irishness and its effect upon his career was quite different from that of Yeats's. At an early age, in 1875, Shaw had felt that he must leave Dublin if he was to make a career as a writer. He perceived that "My business in life could not be transacted in Dublin out of an experience confined to Ireland. I had to go to London just as my father had to go to the Corn Exchange. London was the literary centre for the English language, and for such culture as the realm of the English language (in which I proposed to be king) could afford. There was no Gaelic League in those days, nor any sense that Ireland had in herself the seed of culture."[7] Shaw's concern for Ireland continued throughout his life, but it was the concern of an Irishman residing in England. His English experience greatly affected his view of Ireland. When Shaw turned to analyze the woes of that "most distressful country," he did so with an intimacy that birth can bestow and an objectivity that distance made possible.

Shaw's politics also colored his view of his native land. His Fabian studies, which had taught him that class oppression was common to all nations, made him immune to the "fanatical" Irish nationalism that saw England as the source of all Irish woes and emancipation from England as the solution to all Irish problems. Shaw insisted that there was nothing peculiar or special about the misery of the Irish people. It was the result of British imperialism and feudal land relations, and Ireland shared her miseries with other British colonies. He saw nothing magical or

6. "Hic and Ille: Shaw and Yeats," *Theatre and Nationalism in 20th Century Ireland*, ed. Robert O'Driscoll (Toronto: University of Toronto Press, 1971), pp. 157, 161, 168.

7. "Preface to *Immaturity*," Ayot St. Lawrence Edition of *Collected Works*, I, pp. xxxvii–xxxviii.

charming in the superstition and backwardness of the Irish peasant, but only an ignorance that must be removed. He agreed with the nationalists that Ireland must sever her connection with England to realize her nationhood. But, once accomplished, this first advance must be followed by the removal of all classes and class oppression and the achievement of socialism. Shaw explains his movement from nationalism to internationalism thus: "I was drawn into the Socialist revival of the early eighties, among Englishmen intensely serious and burning with indignation at every real and very fundamental evil that affected all the world; so that the reaction against them bound the finer spirits of all the nations together instead of making them cherish hatred of one another as a national virtue."[8] Shaw's internationalism did not preclude nationalism; it transcended it.

Throughout the 1880's and 1890's Shaw continued to comment on the Irish scene from his Fabian perspective. Repeatedly in articles with such titles as "The Making of the Irish Nation" (1886), "A Balfour Ballad" (1888), "The Tories and Ireland" (1888), "A Crib for Home Rulers" (1888), "The Parnell Forger" (1889), "Shall Parnell Go?" (1890), he used a Marxist analysis to sort out the complexities of the Irish political scene and insisted that "there is no federating nationalities without first realizing them."[9] Shaw remained an Irishman in the thirty years between his departure from Ireland and his re-creation of Ireland in *John Bull's Other Island*, but an Irishman with a difference: a socialist and an internationalist.

Artistically Shaw's interest in Irish subjects finds its highest expression in the play the Abbey Theatre rejected. The fate of Ireland and the Irish, of those who leave Ireland and those who remain, dominates this play, which is a kind of dramatic collision of dreams of Ireland's future. Doyle, Broadbent, and Keegan present their separate hopes and plans for the future of Ireland. Their dreams are juxtaposed against a scathingly realistic picture of Irish rural poverty and exploitation. Shaw had not forgotten Ireland. Perhaps it would be more accurate to say that he remembered things that Yeats had never known. With his reverence for the "Big Houses" and the aristocracy, Yeats could never agree with the insight that illuminated Shaw's work: that class oppression weighed as heavily as national oppression on the Irish poor.

The rejection of Shaw's "uncongenial play," although probably inevitable considering the aims of the new theatre and the biases of its directors, has been seen as a mistake by commentators close to the events.

8. "Preface to *Immaturity*," p. xxxvi.
9. Collected in *The Matter with Ireland*, eds. David Greene and Dan H. Laurence (London: Rupert Hart-Davis, 1962).

Lennox Robinson considered the rejection to be an error in the Abbey management equalled only by the rejection of *The Silver Tassie* by O'Casey.[1] George Moore, who had parted from active involvement in the theatre by 1902, wrote a great deal about Yeats's attempts to keep out the works of playwrights other than those he had discovered. Although Moore does not mention *John Bull's Other Island*, he would say by 1908 that "The Celtic Renaissance does not exist, it is a myth."[2] O'Casey also saw the rejection of Shaw's play as a loss to the Abbey Theatre and a surrender to Yeats's narrowness.[3]

The question of Yeats's personal antipathy to Shaw and the influence of this attitude on his rejection of Shaw's play is a difficult and delicate one. In an oft-quoted passage from his *Autobiographies*, Yeats remembers his nightmare vision of Shaw: "Presently I had a nightmare that I was haunted by sewing machines, that clicked and shone, but the incredible thing was that the machine smiled, smiled perpetually." The image of Shaw which this conjures up is not attractive. But that was not Yeats's whole opinion. He goes on to record his admiration of and debt to Shaw: "Yet I delighted in Shaw, the formidable man. He could hit my enemies and the enemies of all I loved, as I could never hit, as no living author that was dear to me could ever hit."[4] Yeats appreciated Shaw's powers and wanted him as an ally. But when Shaw denounced the twilight dreaming of the neo-Celtic revival, he struck too close to Yeats, and seemed to give aid and support to the enemy.

The differences over his Irish play did not stifle Shaw's relationships with the directors of the Abbey Theatre. Lady Gregory's journals witness her continuing and close relationship with the Shaws. She was a frequent guest at their home and considered Shaw to be her most gentle friend. Shaw's later play, *The Shewing-Up of Blanco Posnet*, was presented at the Abbey in 1909 and occasioned one of the famous battles with censors. In a letter to James Joyce, years later, Yeats notes that Shaw and he are founding an Irish Academy in which they hope to include Joyce. And Shaw's defense of the maligned Roger Casement must have vindicated him in Yeats's eyes.[5]

Bernard Shaw was undeterred by the rejection of his play. Even while awaiting Yeats's decision he was busy planning the London opening with Granville-Barker. Lennox Robinson and O'Casey may have been

1. *Ireland's Abbey Theatre* (London: Sedgwick and Jackson, 1951), p. 152.
2. *Hail and Farewell* (London: Heinemann, 1947).
3. Letter to O'Casey, June 19, 1928; quoted by

Eileen O'Casey in *Sean* (New York: Coward-McCann, 1972), pp. 84–85.
4. *Autobiographies*, p. 134.
5. *Letters*, p. 442.

right in their judgment that the play reflected more on the Abbey management than on Shaw. But, from the vantage point of 70 years, perhaps
it would be more accurate to say that the rejection of the play actually
reflected on neither.

Shaw had a very special feeling for the play which he had written
about his native land. In a letter to Siegfried Trebitsch he ranks it as one
of his "big three."[6] At the time of the play's composition he writes to
Ada Rehan with enthusiasm: "This is the first time I have tried my hand
on Ireland; and of course, being an Irishman, I get a quality into the
play that is quite unlike anything in any other plays. It is not particularly
complimentary to either the Irish or the English; but it is fascinating."[7]
In these lines Shaw refers to the main problem with the play as seen by
those who were trying to establish an Irish National Theatre. This same
problem was in turn to split the Abbey and cause innumerable internal
struggles on the questions of art versus politics. It was the question of
nationalism. Shaw's play was not partisan enough to suit the needs of
the hour. Like some by Yeats, Shaw's play claims to be political but is
not nationalist, and so it was an anomaly in the Ireland of 1904. In a
historical sense, its rejection marks the spirit of the time more than the
theatrical aims of any particular group. Events in Ireland, which were
to culminate in the Easter Rising of 1916, a bloody civil war, and the
declaration of the Irish Free State, demanded that a partisan position at
least pro-Irish, but also anti-British, be reflected in every aspect of Irish
cultural life. The Abbey plays were usually pro-Irish. When they were
not, they occasioned riots. But Shaw's play did not satisfy either half of
this demand, and so it would not do. Nationalism is a simple creed with
simple slogans—"A nation once again" and "Ireland her own"—but
Shaw's politics, as dramatized in *John Bull's Other Ireland*, were more
complex.

DAVID KRAUSE

[*John Bull's Other Island*] †

At the reluctant invitation of Yeats, Shaw tried to provide a play for the
early Abbey Theatre, and the result, *John Bull's Other Island* (1904),
though it had to be rejected because the modest little theater company

6. MS. Berg Collection, New York Public Library.
7. Letters to Ada Rehan, *Collected Letters, 1898–1910*, ed. Dan H. Laurence (London: Max Rein-hardt, 1972), p. 458.

† Reprinted from David Krause: *The Profane Book of Irish Comedy*. Copyright © 1982 by Cornell University. Used by permission of the publisher, Cornell University Press.

could not cast or stage it, deserves a significant place in the tradition of Irish comedy. The only Irish play that Shaw wrote, it has many elements of the irreverent joking and ironic humor that are so typical of barbarous comedy, as well as a number of mock-heroic characters who illustrate the Pelagian or uniquely Irish heresy of comic autonomy, which in Shavian terms could also be described as the liberating spirit of the comic life force. There are no conventional heroes and no villains at all in this antiromantic comedy, unless mother Ireland herself, the intractable Cathleen Ni Houlihan, can once again serve as the villainous old sow who symbolically devours or frustrates all the Irish characters. One might have anticipated that the British Tom Broadbent should have been the villain of the piece, but such an obvious concession to Irish nationalism would have carried with it the melodramatic machinery to undermine Shaw's unique dramatic strategy of characteristically mocking all sides of the conflict in his game of comic cross-purposes. So the nominal enemy Broadbent must share a central position with the disenchanted Irishmen Larry Doyle and Father Keegan, all of them, three in one and one in three, mock heroes who represent aspects of Shaw's ambivalent attitude toward the Irish question at the turn of the century. Perhaps Keegan speaks for all three, and for Shaw, when he says, "My way of joking is to tell the truth. It's the funniest joke in the world." [1]

The unamused Yeats was undoubtedly relieved about the expedient rejection because he considered the play to be too didactic and tainted by naturalistic Ibsenism, and therefore not appropriate for his poetic theater. For his part, Shaw, like Joyce, was an avowed Ibsenite and therefore skeptical about the pre-Raphaelite Yeats's theater, dedicated to the "cultic twalette"—as Joyce laughingly called it—of legendary and romantic Ireland. Shaw had intentionally set out to mock the Ireland of legend and romance in his play, and if he was a disciple of Ibsen in his apparent pursuit of truth, he also projected a broadly comic spirit that was calculated to provoke more ironic laughter than naturalistic dogma. Actually, the enigmatic truth about Ireland is hidden in a variety of Shavian jokes; in the blundering common sense of Broadbent, in the sardonic sermons of Doyle, and in the apocalyptic visions of Keegan. Most profoundly, however, it is in the prophecies of the mad Father Keegan that we find the symbolic and impossible truth; "Saint" Peter, the rock of Rosscullen, and the ostracized fool as defrocked priest who is one of the most poetic and visionary characters Shaw created. The

---

1. Bernard Shaw, *Collected Plays with Their Prefaces* (London: Bodley Head, 1971), 2:930 [Page numbers in brackets refer to this edition—*Editor.*] And I should point out that Joyce apparently agreed with Shaw that profound truths are often hidden in jokes. "Not 'in vino veritas,' " said Joyce, "but 'in risu veritas,'—in laughter, truth" (quoted by W. R. Rodgers in *Irish Literary Portraits* [New York: Taplinger, 1973], p. 132).

best and last joke comes when we realize that Keegan's wild dream of a new secular trinity is finally and hopelessly the thematic heart of the play: an Irish trinity of church and state and people—"It is a godhead in which all life is human and all humanity divine: three in one and one in three. It is, in short, the dream of a madman." [2]

It is one of those rare instances when Shaw allowed the poetry of drama to take precedence over propaganda, and so he concentrates on the comedy of defeat as the isolated Keegan remains magnificently mad and mockingly untriumphant at the end. Keegan has the saintly vision of Shaw's Joan without the vindicating glory of her beatitude. He is the village jester or sublime fool of the play. As a failed priest he is a mock-heroic figure, a failed saint without miracles or martyrdom, without any disciples in Rosscullen except, ironically, for an animated grasshopper and a half-witted Patsy Farrell, though Shaw may have hoped that some loyal Keeganites might one day emerge in modern Ireland. In light of the violent course of twentieth-century Irish history, however, that would have to remain a vain hope, one Shavian joke that is still untrue, similar to his wild forecast in the Preface of the play that the Irish Catholic church would probably liberate itself from Rome when the Irish nation liberated itself from England. [3]

What this means is that the comedy of the play is more convincing than any of Shaw's propaganda; or that his comic-ironic view of Ireland is more dramatic than didactic. Shaw's comic point of view is established at the beginning in the farcical scene between Tom Broadbent and Tim Haffigan, the pompous Anglo-Saxon who sounds like a stage Englishman, and the pseudo-Celt who sounds like a stage Irishman. This alliance of fools is promptly exposed when Larry Doyle, speaking as an ironic chorus voice, as he often does, scolds Broadbent:

2. Shaw, *Collected Plays*, 2:1021 [203]. The saintly Keegan's mad dream of a divine humanity has significant parallels to the heretical dreams of Shaw's St. Joan. They are both holy fools whose private visions are aimed at the salvation of their people. They are both essentially comic characters in a state of grace, wise fools who are so free from sin they cannot be seen as tragic. Joan especially has been mistakenly interpreted as a tragic heroine by most critics. On the contrary, I would go so far as to suggest that she is a comic-rogue heroine, a barbarous peasant girl who must profane all that passes for sacred belief in a corrupted world in order to reveal her divinely inspired and liberating faith in God through the individual conscience. That act of affirmation can only be a comic vision of humanity's potential power and glory. The tragedy of her martyrdom is ours, not hers.
3. In his 1906 Preface to the play, in "Irish Cath-

olic forecast," Shaw disclosed his misunderstanding of the Catholic faith in Ireland when he predicted: "Home rule will herald the day when the Vatican will go the way of Dublin Castle, and the island of saints assume the headship of her own Church (ibid., p. 835). He presented a similarly forlorn hope in the play in the following exchange between Doyle and Father Dempsey (p. 965) [166]:

Doyle. Aye; and I would have Ireland compete with Rome itself for the chair of St Peter and the citadel of the Church; for Rome, in spite of all the blood of the martyrs, is pagan at heart to this day, while in Ireland the people is the Church and the Church the people.
Father Dempsey [startled, but not at all displeased] Whisht, man! youre worse than mad Pether Keegan himself.

But when a thoroughly worthless Irishman comes to England, and finds the whole place full of romantic duffers like you, who will let him loaf and drink and sponge and brag as long as he flatters your sense of moral superiority by playing the fool and degrading himself and his country, he soon learns the antics that take you in. [4]

To learn the antics of the master-slave game is the main purpose of the clown's self-deprecating masquerade. But while romantic duffers like Broadbent encourage stage-Irish parasites like Haffigan to play the fool for fools in England, native Irishmen, according to the sardonic Doyle, suffer from another and more incisive form of folly, which in his most important speech in the play he calls the curse of dreaming, though some farcical ironies will later temper these hard judgments:

Oh, the dreaming! the dreaming! the torturing, heart-scalding, never satisfying dreaming, dreaming, dreaming, dreaming! [*Savagely*] No debauchery that ever coarsened and brutalized an Englishman can take the worth and usefulness out of him like that dreaming. An Irishman's imagination never lets him alone, never convinces him, never satisfies him; but it makes him that he cant face reality nor deal with it nor handle it nor conquer it. . . .

If you want to interest him in Ireland youve got to call the unfortunate island Kathleen ni Houlihan and pretend she's a little old woman. It saves thinking. It saves working. It saves everything except imagination, imagination, imagination; and imagination's such a torture that you cant bear it without whisky. . . .

And all the while there goes on a horrible, senseless, mischievous laughter. When youre young, you exchange vile stories with them; and as youre too futile to be able to help or cheer them, you chaff and sneer and taunt them for not doing the things you darent do yourself. And all the time you laugh! laugh! laugh! eternal derision, eternal envy, eternal folly, eternal fouling and staining and degrading, until, when you come at last to a country where men take a question seriously and give a serious answer to it, you deride them for having no sense of humor, and plume yourself on your own worthlessness as if it made you better than them. [5]

Shaw betrays his own distress in this devastating speech, but he was seldom more brilliantly diagnostic and tragicomic than he is in this dra-

---

4. Shaw, *Collected Plays*, pp. 905–6 [128].
5. Ibid., pp. 909–11 [130–31]. I sometimes think of Larry Doyle as an original for O'Neill's Larry Slade in *The Iceman Cometh*. Both Larrys know too much, see both sides of every argument, and are paralyzed by their excess of fatalistic knowledge. As a result they are both "grandstand Foolosophers."

matic assessment of the Irish malaise of frustrated dreaming and savage laughing. There is no sharper revelation of this barbarous knowledge that haunts the imaginative Irishman and exposes the ironic sense in his seemingly senseless laughter: it provides the only way to go on living in an unlivable world. There are no serious answers; there are only defensive jokes. Fortunately Shaw was a comic genius as well as a puritan preacher, so that he could have it both ways be being seriously didactic and wildly satiric. He could therefore laugh with as well as at his stricken clowns by providing an abundance of vivid jokes that illustrate the liberating Irish folly of psychic release through prevarication and self-deprecation. If there is an element of damnation as well as salvation in that type of dark Irish humor, it might be called making the best of a bad situation. Joyce called the Irish situation a state of "paralysis," O'Casey called it a world of "chassis," and Beckett said there was "nothing to be done" about it. Nothing except survival games of mischievous laughter and gallows humor, as Shaw illustrates in his play. Freud and Eric Bentley have wisely reminded us that one can only grin and bear it, because only the grinning makes it bearable.

*   *   *

Sean O'Casey

JOSEPH HOLLOWAY

[Journal 1923–24] †

* * *

Monday, September 10. . . . I went on to the Abbey and was just in time to see the curtains rise on *Cathleen ni Houlihan* . . . Sara Allgood was impressive in the title role. Sean O'Casey was behind me, and I joined him after Yeats's play and had a chat with him between whiles. He told me he had been raided several times lately. Last week he was awakened out of his sleep with hands pulling the sheet off him, and a light full in his eyes, and three revolvers pointed out. He was hauled out of bed and roughly handled, as they queried his name, etc. He knew of a young fellow, a member of the I.R.A., who was on the run, being taken in the middle of the night by the C.I.D. men and brought out towards Finglas and brutally beaten with the butt end of their revolvers, and then told to run for his life while they fired revolver shots after him, taking bits off his ears, etc., and catching up on him again renewed their beating. Next day O'Casey saw the chap and could hardly recognise him, so battered and bruised was he. Such brutality demoralises a country. Flogging demoralises, but does not correct. . . .

* * *

Monday, March 3. "It is powerful and gripping and all that, but too damned gruesome; it gets you, but it is not pleasant," is the way Dan

† From *Joseph Holloway's Abbey Theatre: A Selection From His Unpublished Journal "Impressions of a Dublin Playgoer,"* ed. Robert Hogan and Michael J. O'Neill. Copyright © 1967 by Southern Illinois University Press.

Maher summed up *Juno and the Paycock*, O'Casey's new play at the Abbey. . . . The last act is intensely tragic and heart-rendingly real to those who passed through the terrible period of 1922. . . . The tremendous tragedy of Act III swept all before it, and made the doings on the stage real and thrilling in their intensity. The acting all round was of the highest quality, not one in the long cast being misplaced or for a moment out of the picture. [Barry] Fitgerald and [F. J.] McCormick as "Captain Jack Boyle" and his bar-room pal "Joxer Daly," an old Forester, make a splendid pair of workers who never work. Sara Allgood as "Juno Boyle," with all the worries of trying to keep everything together was excellent, and in Act III she had great moments of heart-rending sorrow. Arthur Shields as the haunted, maimed boy "Johnny," got the right note of dread into his study from the very first, and Eileen Crowe as "Mary" presented every side of the character cleverly and realistically, and her singing of the duet, "Home to our Mountains," with her mother at the hooley was deliciously droll. Maureen Delaney, as the talkative "Mrs. Maisie Madigan" was most amusing, and Christine Hayden, as the sorrowing mother "Mrs. Tancred" sorrowed for her son most touchingly. . . .

In Act III some in the pit were inclined at first to laugh at the tragedy that had entered into the "Boyle" family, but they soon lost their mirth and were gripped by the awful actuality of the incidents enacted so realistically and unassumingly before them. As I left the theatre, cries of "Author, Author!" were filling the air, and I suppose O'Casey had to bow his acknowledgment. He sat with a friend in the second row of the stalls with his cap on all the while, I noticed. He is a strange, odd fish, but a genius in his way.

*   *   *

Tuesday, March 18. . . . I had a chat with Sean O'Casey in the vestibule. He told me that when he started to write plays he thought he was a second Shaw sent to express his views through his characters, and was conceited enough to think that his opinions were the only ones that mattered. It was Lady Gregory who advised him to cut out all expression of self, and develop his peculiar aptness for character drawing. At first he didn't take kindly to her advice, but afterwards on consideration felt she was right.

He was so poor when he took to writing first that he hadn't the money to supply himself with paper to write his stuff on, and a pal supplied him with paper filched from his employer's store. His first two plays were written in his cramped handwriting, and yet the Abbey directors read his script and expressed sorrow at having to reject both plays, and gave him sound critical advice which he resented at first, but on second thought accepted, and was determined to profit by and did. He was determined to succeed. . . .

He has a small typewriter now. He intends to stick to playwriting; he thinks Robinson has too many irons in the fire to do himself justice. O'Casey reads [Lennox] Robinson's *Observer* article each week, but doesn't think very much of it. He should concentrate more; only those do who reach the very top. This is the age of the specialist.

Friday, March 21. . . . I had a chat with lame Maguire.[1] . . . Speaking of Sean O'Casey, he remembered him as being one of the first to join the Piper's Band and wear the kilt, and an ungainly figure he cut in it. He was more like a country lad than a Dubliner. He always walked with a near-sighted bend of the head. He was always strong and energetic, and when he played hurling he looked a guy in short knickers, and once in a match in the park—so it is said—he killed a sparrow, thinking he was swiping at the ball. He agreed with nobody and believed in nothing. He was strangely distant and silent always. He wrote for *The Irish Worker* and was secretary to the Citizen Army. The book he wrote about the Citizen Army wasn't thought much of by those connected with it.[2] He was a shunter on the Northern Railway in those days. He was always sore-eyed and took an active part in the Gaelic movement. He was very energetic in all he undertook. Now he has struck oil as a playwright, he is determined to work hard to reach the top in that branch of literature. His friend out of Webb's joined us in the latter part of our conversation about O'Casey. It was he told the sparrow incident.

Friday, March 28. A bitterly sharp evening with an icy cutting wind about. I had a long chat with O'Casey in the vestibule of the Abbey. He thinks the Government is proving a set of woeful incompetents—egotistical and intolerant of criticism. They are going from bad to worse. They'll be nobody's friend shortly. He spoke of the hypocrisy over the shooting of the soldier at Cork. "The honour of Ireland is at stake over it, people say who don't know what honour is!"

He witnessed terrible deeds during recent years; a friend of his was riddled with bullets and mutilated in a horrible way by the Green and Tans, a young Tipperary lad. Nothing could be more brutal than the

1. Maguire was the proprietor of a book barrow on the quays.
2. *The Story of the Irish Citizen Army* (1919), by "P. O'Cathasaigh," faulted the organization for stressing nationalism more than labor reform [Editor].

treatment he got. It is hard to think Irish people capable of such savagery. Savages would be decent in comparison to them. After the inquest his remains were brought to his digs, and O'Casey helped to carry in the coffin to his friend's upstairs. Another lad he knew was taken out and tied up by his hands—his feet dangling some distance from the ground, while they poured salts through a tin dish down his throat. The poor fellow was cut down alive, but he is a human wreck ever since—always shaking, though as brave as ever.

* * *

Thursday, August 14. . . . I witnessed a strange incident last night in seeing W. B. Yeats and Mrs. Yeats being crowded out of the Abbey, and having to seek the pictures to allay their disappointment. O'Casey's play, *The Shadow of a Gunman,* had been staged for three nights with the usual result—that crowds had to be turned away each performance. This and his other play, *Juno and the Paycock,* have wonderful drawing power. The same people want to see them over and over again. . . . And the author stood chatting to me in the vestibule the other night as the audience came thronging in, proud of the fact, but in no way swell-headed, his cloth cap cocked over his left eye, as his right looked short-sightedly at the audience's eager rush. Certainly he has written the two most popular plays ever seen at the Abbey, and they both are backgrounded by the terrible times we have just passed through, but his characters are so true to life and humourous that all swallow the bitter pill of fact that underlies both pieces. The acting in both reaches the highest watermark of Abbey acting. It looks as if the Abbey is coming into its own at long last, and it's about time. In December next it will reach its twentieth year of existence. [Padraic] Colum was present in the front row of the stalls last night, and he became so excited during the events in the second act that he kept unconsciously jumping up and down in his seat, and even at times went over to the stage front and placed his elbows on the stage ledge as he gazed intently at what was taking place thereon.

* * *

LADY GREGORY

[Journal 1923–24] †

* * *

12 APRIL 1923   At the Abbey I found an armed guard; there has been one ever since the theatres were threatened if they kept open.[1] And in the green room I found one of them giving finishing touches to the costume of Tony Quinn, who is a Black and Tan in the play, and showing him how to hold his revolver. *The Shadow of a Gunman* was an immense success, beautifully acted, all the political points taken up with delight by a big audience. Sean O'Casey the author only saw it from the side wings the first night but had to appear to make his bow. I brought him into the stalls the other two nights and have had some talk with him. Last night there was an immense audience the largest I think since the first night of [Shaw's] *Blanco Posnet*. Many, to my grief, had to be turned away from the door. Two seats had been kept for Yeats and me, but I put Casey in one of them and sat in the orchestra for the first act, and put Yeats in the orchestra for the second. I had brought Casey round to the door before the play to share my joy in seeing the crowd surging in (Dermod O'Brien caught in the queue) and he introduced me to two officers, one a Colonel. (Yeats has wanted me to go with them to a *ball* given by the army, "good names being wanted"!)

Casey told me he is a labourer, and as we talked of masons said he had "carried the hod". He said "I was among books as a child, but I was sixteen before I learned to read or write. My father loved books, he had a big library, I remember the look of the books high up on shelves". I asked why his father had not taught him and he said "He died when I was three years old, through those same books. There was a little ladder in the room to get to the shelves, and one day when he was standing on it, it broke and he fell and was killed". I said "I often go up the ladder in our library at home" and he begged me to be careful. He is learning what he can about Art, has bought books on Whistler and Raphael, and takes *The Studio*. All this was as we watched the crowd. I forget how I came to mention the Bible, and he asked "Do you like it"? I said "Yes,

---

† From *Lady Gregory's Journals: Volume I*, Coole Edition (New York: Oxford University Press; Bucks: Colin Smythe Ltd, 1978).
1. That is, during the Irish Civil War threatened by Republicans if they opened, thus suggesting a state of normalcy, and by Free Staters if they did not open [*Editor*].

I read it constantly, even for the beauty of the language". He said he admires that beauty, he was brought up as a Protestant but has lost belief in religious forms. Then, in talking of our war here, we came to Plato's *Republic*, his dream-city, whether on earth or in heaven not far away from the city of God. And then we went in to the play. He says he sent us a play four years ago *Frost and Flowers* and it was returned, but marked "Not far from being a good play". He has sent others, and says how grateful he was to me because when we had to refuse the Labour one "The Crimson in the Tri-Colour" I had said "I believe there is something in you" and "your strong point is characterisation". And I had wanted to pull that play together and put it on to give him experience, but Yeats was down on it. Perrin says he has offered him a pass sometimes when he happened to come in, but he refused and said "No one ought to come into the Abbey Theatre without paying for it". He said "All the thought in Ireland for years past has come through the Abbey. You have no idea what an education it has been to the country". That, and the fine audience on this our last week, put me in great spirits.

* * *

8 MARCH 1924   In the evening to the Abbey with W.B.Y. *Juno and the Paycock* a long queue at the door, the theatre crowded, many turned away, so it will be run on next week. A wonderful and terrible play of futility, of irony, humour, tragedy. When I went round to the green-room I saw O'Casey and had a little talk with him. He is very happy. I asked him to come to tea after the next day matinée as I had brought up a barmbrack for the players, but he said "No I can't come, I'll be at work till the afternoon, and I'm working with cement, and that takes such a long time to get off". "But after that?" "Then I have to cook my dinner. I have but one room and I cook for myself since my mother died." He is of course happy at the great success of the play and I said "You must feel now that we were right in not putting on that first one you sent in *The Crimson in the Tricolour*. I was inclined to put it on because some of it was so good and I thought you might learn by seeing it on the stage, though some was very poor, but Mr. Yeats was firm". He said "You were right not to put it on. I can't read it myself now. But I will tell you that was a bitter disappointment for I not only thought at the time it was the best thing I had written, but I thought that no one in the world had ever written anything so fine". Then he said "You had it typed for me, and I don't know how you could have read it as I sent it in with the bad writing and the poor paper. But at that time it was hard for me to afford even the paper it was written on". And he said "I owe a great deal to you

and Mr. Yeats and Mr. Robinson, but to you above all. You gave me encouragement. And it was you who said to me upstairs in the office— I could show you the very spot where you stood—'Mr. O'Casey, your gift is characterisation'. And so I threw over my theories and worked at characters, and this is the result."

Yeats hadn't seen the play before, and thought it very fine, reminding him of Tolstoi. He said when he talked of that imperfect first play "Casey was bad in writing of the vices of the rich which he knows nothing about, but he thoroughly understands the vices of the poor". But that full house, the packed pit and gallery, the fine play, the call of the mother for the putting away of hatred—"give us Thine own eternal love!" made me say to Yeats "This is one of the evenings at the Abbey that makes me glad to have been born".

* * *

GABRIEL FALLON

[Juno and the Paycock] †

* * *

I didn't see much of Sean O'Casey during the rehearsals of *Juno and the Paycock*. The Abbey's work of weekly repertory went on and I was kept fairly busy. In the week preceding the dress rehearsal of *Juno* Lady Gregory came to town. If she attended rehearsals I didn't see her. My part of Bentham was almost wholly rehearsed at the 1 o'clock luncheon break; the old difficulty of getting the professionals and the 'part-timers' together saw to that. I have no doubt that the Old Lady, as we called her, spent some time in the company of her beloved actress, 'Sally' Allgood, but whatever views she may have expressed about the play I had no means of finding out. Not, indeed, that I was particularly interested. The play would go on and that was that.

The dress-rehearsal was planned for Sunday March 2nd at 11.30 a.m. That would give everyone ample time for Mass, or Church, or a long sleep. But there was a difficulty. For some time past an Abbey party had been planned to take place on the night of Saturday March 1st, after the final curtain. Now an Abbey party was a party that *was* a party; at least it was so in those far-off days and nothing was ever allowed to stand in

† From *Sean O'Casey: The Man I Knew* (Boston: Little, Brown, 1965). Copyright © Gabriel Fallon 1965. Reprinted by permission of Routledge & Kegan Paul.

the way of it, neither civil wars nor fights for freedom. Abbey parties had been held under armed guards of various political persuasions and as often as not the guards themselves added much to the revelry. Sometimes directors were present; sometimes not; but whatever the company one thing was certain and that, to use the popular phrase, was that a good time was had by all. But what was to be done on this occasion? Obviously, no one could be expected to dress-rehearse at such an unearthly hour as 11.30 a.m. after a party the night before. Indeed, it was as much as some of us could do to put in a sleepy attendance at the 6 a.m. Mass in the Pro-Cathedral down the street. Sean O'Casey or no Sean O'Casey this dress-rehearsal would have to be postponed, that was all about it. Someone approached the directors, and the directors agreed to postponement. The dress-rehearsal of *Juno and the Paycock* would be held at 5 p.m. on the Sunday.

I arrived at the theatre at 4.30 p.m. and found the author there before me looking rather glum and wondering if a rehearsal would take place since so far as he could find out there was no one else in the theatre. I assured him that everything would be all right even though I privately thought otherwise. Sara Allgood, who had spent the night feasting us with song and story, had left the theatre in or around 3 a.m. a very tired woman. I tried to persuade Sean that dress-rehearsals were always like this but he was only half convinced. Although I did not know it at the time he was suffering much pain with his eyes and was attending the Royal Eye and Ear Hospital where he was a patient of the Senior Surgeon, the sensitive and perceptive Mr. Joe Cummins, who took a particular interest in the dramatist and in the theatre.

Gradually the players filed in and quietly went to their dressing-rooms. Lennox Robinson arrived shortly before 5 o'clock and was followed by Yeats and Lady Gregory. Under the direction of Seaghan Barlow the stage staff were putting finishing touches to the setting. Yeats, Lady Gregory and Robinson took seats in the stalls. The author sat a few seats away from them. The curtain rose about 5.36 p.m. So far as I could see and hear while waiting for my cue in the wings the rehearsal seemed to be proceeding smoothly. As soon as I had finished my part of Bentham at the end of the second act I went down into the stalls and sat two seats behind the author. Here for the first time I had an opportunity of seeing something of the play from an objective point of view. I was stunned by the tragic quality of the third act which the magnificent playing of Sara Allgood made almost unbearable. But it was the blistering irony of the final scene which convinced me that this man sitting two seats in front of me was a dramatist of genius, one destined to be spoken of far beyond the confines of the Abbey Theatre.

The third act had been dominated by Allgood's tragic quality even though Barry Fitzgerald and F. J. McCormick were uproariously funny as Captain Boyle and Joxer. This was always so with Allgood in the part of Juno. She had the quality of pinning down preceding laughter to freezing point. When Juno returns from the doctor with Mary the author's simple directions are: 'Mrs. Boyle enters: it is apparent from the serious look on her face that something has happened. She takes off her hat and coat without a word and puts them by. She then sits down near the fire, and there is a few moments pause.' That is all. Yet Sara Allgood's entrance in this scene will never be forgotten by those who saw it. Not a word was spoken: she did not even sigh: her movements were few and simply confined to the author's directions. She seemed to have shrunken from the Juno we saw in Acts 1 and 2 as if reduced by the catalytic effect of her inner consciousness.

We watched the act move on, the furniture removers come and go, the ominous entry of the I.R.A. men, the dragging of Johnny to summary execution, the stilted scene between Jerry Devine and Mary Boyle, and then as with the ensnaring slow impetus of a ninth great wave Allgood's tragic genius rose to an unforgettable climax and drowned the stage in sorrow. Here surely was the very butt and sea-mark of tragedy! But suddenly the curtain rises again: are Fitzgerald and McCormick fooling, letting off steam after the strain of rehearsal? Nothing of the kind; for we in the stalls are suddenly made to freeze in our seats as a note beyond tragedy, a blistering flannel-mouthed irony sears its maudlin way across the stage and slowly drops an exhausted curtain on a world disintegrating in 'chassis'.

I sat there stunned. So, indeed, so far as I could see, did Robinson, Yeats and Lady Gregory. Then Yeats ventured an opinion. He said that the play, particularly in its final scene, reminded him of a Dostoievsky novel. Lady Gregory turned to him and said: 'You know, Willie, you never read a novel by Dostoievsky.' And she promised to amend this deficiency by sending him a copy of *The Idiot*. I turned to O'Casey and found I could only say to him: 'Magnificent, Sean, magnificent.' Then we all quietly went home.

*   *   *

* * * What shocked me about the author was that he was by no means as certain as I was about the validity of [the final] scene. Indeed, he left me with the impression that he was by no means as knowledgeable about his play as I was for he seemed to be quietly surprised when I drew attention to what I considered to be this excellence or that. I was to learn in time, of course, that an artist is seldom conscious of the effect of what he has created. I recalled O'Casey's insistence that he was writing a play about a young man called Johnny Boyle. Yet Johnny was only one character amongst other and greater characters. We were seeing much more of each other than formerly and on each occasion *Juno* and the craft of the playwright provided the main talking-point. The critics, public and private, with the exception of [W. V.] Lawrence had used as a whip the mixture of tragedy with comedy. There was some talk of Aristotle and I took my first glance into the *Poetics*. While I was not prepared to agree with O'Casey that 'Aristotle was all balls', I conceded that the Greeks were great in their own time and fashion but that there were great playwrights since that time who had thrown Aristotle's *Poetics* (or rather the misconception derived from them by Italian and French theorists) to the winds. Shakespeare had mixed tragedy and comedy and what had been good enough for Shakespeare ought to be good enough for a 'neo-Elizabethan'.

During one of our conversations he told me that when he submitted *Juno and the Paycock* to the Abbey it had an additional scene which the directors cut. He gave me the impression that he was rather aggrieved at this. I asked him what the scene was and he told me it was the shooting of Johnny Boyle which took place in darkness in a roadside setting. I tried to assure him that the directors were perfectly right and that the shooting of Johnny Boyle was in the imagination of the audience infinitely more terrible in those lines where the Second Irregular asks him: 'Have you your beads?' and Johnny replies, 'Me beads! Why do you ass me that, why do you ass me that?' At this point the audience knows only too well what is going to happen, and hardly needs Johnny's agonised 'Mother o' God, pray for me—be with me now in the agonies o' death . . .' to convince them that judicial murder is afoot. After this an actual shooting scene would be truly anti-climax. After some argument on my part he seemed satisfied. Again it was borne in on me that the artist is not always the best judge of his work.

It was obvious that one of the effects of these conversations was to blunt the remarks of the critics. I still maintained that what made this play something greater than great was its final scene and I repeatedly told him so. The fact was that I couldn't get this play and its author out of my mind. The play itself had stirred up all kinds of problems for me. I suppose in a sense it heralded the birth of a drama critic. I was conscious of the play's faults, the poverty of Bentham as a character, the mawkish artificiality of the scenes between Jerry Devine and Mary Boyle. Yet these faults, and I could find no others, were far outweighed by the play's greatness. One of the critics said that O'Casey knew nothing about the art of construction. On this point what struck me about *Juno* was that its characters came and went without let or hindrance. 'Construction' as it was seen in the work of Abbey dramatists had hitherto consisted of situations in which A, B and C are on stage and the dramatist invents some plausible or (as in most cases) implausible reason to get rid of B in order that A and C may discuss something not intended for B's hearing. If this was 'construction' they could keep it so far as I was concerned, for I reasoned that when one could see a man's framework sticking out there was something wrong with the man. There is nothing particularly attractive about a skeleton and no one wants to see the bones of a play.

I believed I saw the reason why Sean O'Casey was not fully conscious of the value of what he had achieved. This work of his was not art for Art's sake, a phrase very much in fashion in the literary Dublin of those days. It was something much more akin to what Paul Claudel had in mind when he wrote to Jacques Riviere in 1912: 'Do you believe for a moment that Shakespeare or Dostoievsky or Reubens or Titian or Wagner did their work for art's sake? No! They did it to free themselves of a great incubus of living matter, *opus non factum*. And certainly not to colour a cold artificial design by borrowings from reality.' *Juno and the Paycock*, I reflected, was an outstanding example of a play which simply had to be written, which, so to speak, erupted from its author, a fact which gave it that 'red-hot contemporaneity' which Lawrence praised. It pulsed with what Henry James had in mind when he demanded 'felt life' from the writer. No doubt Sean O'Casey sat down consciously to write a play about a tragic young man called Johnny Boyle, but underneath other forces were at work and the total result emerged in a blistering indictment of the stupidity of men and (as I thought then on that March evening in 1924 and think so still) in one of the great tragic masterpieces of our time.

This man Sean O'Casey was attracted towards me (I didn't know why) but from that dress-rehearsal of *Juno and the Paycock* I was forcibly attracted towards him. Like him I was a Dubliner who loved my native city. He had lived most of his years in grinding poverty and I had lived mine on the fringe of it. In *Juno and the Paycock* I had found an overwhelming sense of pity which I myself had sometimes felt but was unable to express. I had also, I believed, found a very great dramatist, one who was destined, I said to him, to write very many great plays. I looked back on my theatre-going experience but could recall nothing which equalled this. The highest peak point in the graph of Abbey Theatre dramaturgy was undoubtedly John Millington Synge's *The Playboy of the Western World*. *Juno and the Paycock*, I believed, was as high if not higher.

DAVID KRAUSE

[The Tragi-comic Muse] †

* * *

O'Casey's world is chaotic and tragic but his vision of it is ironically comic. It is in this war-torn world of horrors and potential tragedy that he finds the rowdy humour which paradoxically satirizes and sustains his earthy characters: they are the victims of their follies yet they revel in their voluble absurdities. And it is clear that O'Casey himself enjoys his people no less for their follies, as he intends his audiences to enjoy them. There is a sharp tone of outrage in his Daumier-like portraits of life in the slums of a beleaguered city, and this tone becomes even stronger in his later plays, but he was not dramatizing case histories. His plays do not follow the documentary principles of Naturalism—of Hauptmann's *Weavers* or Galsworthy's *Strife*. Low comedy is not one of the handmaidens of Naturalism. Even when he is in a serious mood O'Casey is likely to be satiric not solemn, poignant not pathetic. And when the tragic events or consequences of war and poverty become most crucial he will open up the action and counterbalance the incipient tragedy with a music-hall turn or a randy ballad or a mock-battle. While everyone awaits a terrifying raid by the Black and Tans in *The Gunman* the well-oiled Dolphie Grigson parades into the house spouting songs and biblical rhetoric in drunken bravado. Just when Mrs Tancred is on her way to bury her ambushed son in *Juno* the Boyles have launched their wild drinking and singing party. While the streets ring with patriotic speeches about heroic bloodshed in *The Plough* the women of the tenements have a free-for-all fight about respectability in a Pub.

* * *

Juno Boyle has the name of a classical heroine, and she has many of the qualities of that Roman goddess, but O'Casey uses the allusion in such a way as to give her the heroic stature of her namesake and the earthy reality of a Dublin housewife of the tenements. When Bentham hears her name he is reminded of the 'ancient gods and heroes', however, the Captain explains how she got her name: 'You see, Juno was born an' christened in June; I met her in June; we were married in June, an' Johnny was born in June, so wan day I says to her, "You should ha'

---

† From *Sean O'Casey: The Man and His Work*, rev. ed. Copyright © David Krause 1960, 1975.

been called Juno', an' the name stuck to her ever since".' Furthermore, O'Casey was aware of the fact that the classical Juno was always associated with peacocks, the patron birds who are often near her or draw her chariot, but he used this aspect of the legend in a completely ironic way by giving his Juno a peacock of a husband who takes his name from the common association of strutting vanity. Thus, the 'Paycock' becomes Juno's parasite not her protector.

The women in O'Cascy's plays are realists from necessity, the men are dreamers by default. The men are frustrated and gulled by dreams which they are unable and unwilling to convert into realities. And as if in mock-defence of those dreams they revel in their romanticizing and bragging and drinking. In *John Bull's Other Island* Shaw may have gone to the root of the Irishman's curse when he made Larry Doyle pour out his embittered confession:

> Oh, the dreaming! dreaming! the torturing, heart-scalding, never satisfying dreaming, dreaming, dreaming, dreaming! No debauchery that ever coarsened and brutalized an Englishman can take the worth and usefulness out of him like that dreaming. An Irishman's imagination never lets him alone, never convinces him, never satisfies him; but it makes him that he cant face reality nor deal with it nor handle it nor conquer it; he can only sneer at them that do, and be 'agreeable to strangers', like a good-for-nothing woman on the streets. It's all dreaming, all imagination. He cant be religious. The inspired Churchman that teaches him the sanctity of life and the importance of conduct is sent away empty; while the poor village priest that gives him a miracle or a sentimental story of a saint, has cathedrals built for him out of the pennies of the poor. He cant be intelligently political; he dreams of what the Shan Van Vocht said in ninetyeight. If you want to interest him in Ireland you've got to call the unfortunate island Kathleen ni Houlihan and pretend she's a little old woman. It saves thinking. It saves working. It saves everything except imagination, imagination, imagination; and imagination's such a torture that you cant bear it without whisky. [1]

O'Casey's Irishmen suffer from the symptoms of this outcry, and as a result there is an undercurrent of tragedy in the plays. But most of O'Casey's Irishmen possess the grotesque symptoms without Larry Doyle's awareness of them, and as a result there is also an abundance of comedy in the plays. Herein lies one of the many differences between tragedy

1. Bernard Shaw, *John Bull's Other Island* (London: Constable, 1931), pp. 84–85.

and comedy: the tragic figure becomes truly tragic when he is able to see his own image; the comic figure becomes absurdly comic when he is unable, or pretends to be unable, to see his own image. When the women in O'Casey's plays finally see themselves and their world clearly they become tragic figures, like Juno Boyle and Bessie Burgess. Of the men, only Davoren as the self-confessed 'poltroon' makes Larry Doyle's discovery, at the very end of the *Gunman* after he has fully indulged his aery dreams, but he is the only non-comic character in the play.

There is, however, one unique figure who dominates all three plays, the mock-heroic character who proudly wears his motley and is satisfied to see as much of himself and the world as he expediently chooses to see. This character is first formulated in Seumas Shields in the *Gunman*, and he is fully developed in Captain Jack Boyle in *Juno* and Fluther Good in the *Plough*—those two falstaffian rogues who epitomize the triumphant anti-hero.

Captain Jack Boyle may lack the girth of [Shakespeare's] Captain Jack Falstaff, but he has the same flamboyant humour and glorious mendacity, the ingenious sense of self-indulgence and self-preservation. Both men are bragging scoundrels whose disrespect for the truth stems not only from an instinctive love of licence but from an empirical conviction that a virtuous life invariably leads to dullness and an heroic life often leads to death. Falstaff can point to a corpse on the battlefield and say, 'there's honour for you', or counterfeit death because 'The better part of valour is discretion, in the which better part I have saved my life'. Boyle, living like Falstaff in a time of Civil War when men's lives are valued cheaply, sets too high a price on his own sweet skin to care about honour or become involved in the fighting. And he has his counterfeit game for saving himself from the deadly virtues of work: he automatically develops a powerful pain in his legs at the mere mention of a job. When Jerry Devine goes looking for him in all the Pubs with news of a job, his discretionary wrath erupts and protects him: 'Is a man not to be allowed to leave his house for a minute without havin' a pack o' spies, pimps an' informers cantherin' at his heels? . . . I don't want the motions of me body to be watched the way an asthronomer ud watch a star. If you're folleyin' Mary aself, you've no pereeogative to be folleyin' me.' *(Suddenly catching his thigh.)* 'U-ugh, I'm afther gettin' a terrible twinge in me right leg!' Furthermore, Boyle has what he considers a good reason to regard a man like Devine with suspicion: 'I never heard him usin' a curse word; I don't believe he was ever dhrunk in his life—sure he's not like a Christian at all!'

Captain Boyle's account of his adventures on the sea has that comic touch of fantastic imagination which characterized Captain Falstaff's version of his exploits on Gadshill. Juno Boyle knows her husband for the 'struttin' paycock' that he is, and she pointedly explains his seafaring record; 'Everybody callin' you "Captain"', an' you only wanst on the wather, in an oul' collier from here to Liverpool, when anybody, to listen or look at you, ud take you for a second Christo For Columbus!' But this fact does not prevent the 'Captain' from telling his 'buttie' Joxer what it was like to be an adventurous sailor on the high seas.

> BOYLE.   Them was days, Joxer, them was days. Nothin' was too hot or too heavy for me then. Sailin' from the Gulf o' Mexico to the Antanartic Ocean. I seen things, I seen things, Joxer, that no mortal man should speak about that knows his Catechism. Often, an' often, when I was fixed to the wheel with a marlin-spike, an' the wins blowin' fierce an' the waves lashin' an' lashin', till you'd think every minute was goin' to be your last, an' it blowed, an' blowed—blew is the right word, Joxer, but blowed is what the sailors use——
>
> JOXER.   Aw, it's a darlin' word, a daarlin' word.
>
> BOYLE.   An' as it blowed an' blowed, I often looked up at the sky an' assed meself the question—what is the stars, what is the stars?
>
> JOXER.   Ah, that's the question, that's the question—what is the stars?

A clever parasite full of comic platitudes, the ingratiating Joxer is a perfect foil for the braggart Captain; he spaniels at the Captain's heels most of the time, but he too sees as much of himself and the world as it is profitable for him to see. Joxer is capable of reversing the game and fooling the Captain when he has something to gain. Together they insulate themselves from the world of terrible realities by living in an illusory world of fantasies and drunken bravado. O'Casey satirizes them unsparingly for the shiftless rascals that they are, yet because he also sees the amusement of a universal frailty in them—they are fools not knaves—he is able to laugh with as well as at their hilarious mischief. And audiences laugh with as well as at them because they too recognize the common frailties of man in the Boyles and Joxers of this world—Boyle the universal braggart-warrior, Joxer the universal parasite-slave, both of them derived from the well-known clowns of Roman and Elizabethan comedy. It is also possible that many men are more than amused by the 'paycock's' game and secretly envy the Captain and his 'buttie' their merry pranks. The average man who realizes he cannot cope with his besetting problems on an heroic scale may well have an unconscious desire to get rid of his problems entirely by emulating the Captain in his irresponsible and therefore irresistible dreaming and singing and drinking. A frustrated non-hero might if he dared forsake his responsible suffering and seek the unihibited pleasures of a clowning anti-hero; however, he probably settles for the vicarious pleasure of sitting in a theatre and watching a Captain Boyle thumb his red nose at responsibility. Much is made of the frustrated clown who yearns to play Hamlet, but the average man is more likely a frustrated Hamlet who if he had the strength of his weakness would cheerfully assume the role of an uninhibited Falstaff or Boyle.

The women in O'Casey's plays may be uninhibited creatures, too, but they always remain close to the realities of life and when there is a call for responsible action they put aside self-gratification and act. Even Juno has her fling. When the Boyles have their wild party Juno joins the celebration on borrowed money and time, and after the mourning Mrs Tancred interrupts them, Juno temporarily agrees with the Captain and remarks that maybe Mrs Tancred deserved to lose her Die-hard son. But when her own son is killed, when her daughter is seduced, Juno assumes her burdens; she repeats Mrs Tancred's prayer and rejects the Captain. When her daughter cries out against a God who would allow such tragic things to happen, Juno replies: 'These things have nothin' to do with the Will o' God. Ah, what can God do agen the stipidity o' men!' And she abandons the Captain. When Prince Hal becomes King he assumes the burdens of state and rejects the dissolute Falstaff.

> I know thee not, old man: fall to thy prayers:
> How ill white hairs become a fool and jester!
> I have long dream'd of such a king of man,
> So surfeit-swell'd, so old, and so profane.
> But being awak'd, I do despise my dream.

In a somewhat similar manner, Juno, being awake, forsakes all dreams and rejects her foolish jester of a husband. Her elegaic prayer brings her to a condition of tragic awareness.

Yet O'Casey does not end the play with Juno. Maintaining the anti-heroic theme and contrapuntal rhythm of the whole work, he concludes on a tragi-comic note by contrasting Juno's heroic condition with the Captain's mock-heroic condition. For it is his play as well as Juno's; together they represent the tragi-comic cycle of O'Casey's world; together they reveal the ironic cross-purposes of life. As Juno and Mary leave to start a new life, the Captain and Joxer stagger drunkenly into the barren room, roaring patriotic slogans as they collapse in a state of semi-coherent bravado. It is a final scene of horrible humour. The Captain remains the 'struttin' paycock' in his glorious deterioration; even in his drunken raving he remains a magnificently grotesque anti-hero. Juno must reject him, yet we can forgive him, for he maintains his falstaffian spirit to the end.

* * *

SEAMUS DEANE

O'Casey and Yeats: Exemplary Dramatists †

* * *

* * * Yeats wrote plays which were meant to counter everything that Shaw, Ibsen and Pinero represented; his attitude to the drama of ideas was very much of a piece with the attitude of Virginia Woolf to Arnold Bennett, of Joyce to Zola. Yeats was participating in the modernist repudiation of the kind of deathly realism which he associated with these names at the same time as he was being influenced by the whole literary reaction away from the pallid languages of Georgian poetry, Pre-Raphaelite nuance, sub-Tennysonian reverberation. In other words, while he developed a new and starker realism of language, he repudiated the forms in which realism, as a literary movement and principle, had made its mark.

In this respect he is more acute in his perception than O'Casey whose realism is very much that of the Edwardian dramatists, more hectically coloured indeed than they are by the fever of the Irish political situation. O'Casey's sensibility is that of someone born before the magic mark of December 1910. His mentors are Shaw and Boucicault. He was one of the finest of the Edwardian moralist-dramatists fallen among German Expressionists. But, essentially, his career is that of a powerful dramatic instinct struggling in the toils of anachronistic or unamenable forms. In this respect, he makes a startling contrast with Yeats and could hardly be viewed now as an exemplar save by those who wish to use him as an exponent of pacifism or as a specimen of the proletarian revolutionary. For obvious reasons, Germany has been the country in which these versions of O'Casey have been most popular, although the pacifist O'Casey has fairly recently and not unexpectedly had a vogue in Dublin.

† From "O'Casey and Yeats: Exemplary Dramatists," in *Celtic Revivals: Essays in Modern Irish Literature, 1880–1980,* copyright © Seamus Deane 1985. Reprinted by permission of Faber and Faber Ltd.

The question which needs answering, however, is this: granted that Yeats was, as a dramatist, part of the modernist avant-garde and that O'Casey was not, is it not nevertheless true that O'Casey dealt more passionately and directly with the Irish situation than Yeats ever did? There seems to be no doubt in most minds that Juno and Bessie Burgess (although not, surely, the dreary Davoren or the dopey Minnie Powell) are more memorable and now, in the glare of contemporary Belfast, more recognizable figures than the Queens and Swineherds, the Emers and Forgaels of Yeats's dramas. In fact are these women not the living consequence of the pre-revolutionary Countess Cathleen and Kathleen Ni Houlihan, those literary poseurs who perhaps helped send out 'certain men (and women) the English shot'?

The drift of such questions implies that the Yeatsian figures, however avant-garde the form of the plays in which they occur, are essentially literary fabrications beside which O'Casey's women stand, branded with the suffering of the actual. At any rate, my answer to such questions has to be no. They are all of them literary creations and it seems to me that the significance of these heroic O'Casey women or of the non-heroic men is in large part the result of a kind of emotional proselytizing on O'Casey's part, the effect of which is reduced by the contradictory form of the plays in which he relays his missionary appeal. Where Yeats's plays command the audience to participate in a vision of the world, O'Casey's demand that it have or share his opinions about it.

Part of the renewed respect for O'Casey comes from audiences which are more impatient than usual with artists who do not supply an immediate set of approved sentiments for meeting a political crisis. O'Casey seems to do that; Yeats does not. But then it was Yeats who wrote 'Lapis Lazuli'.

> I have heard that hysterical women say
> They are sick of the palette and fiddle-bow,
> Of poets that are always gay,
> For everybody knows or else should know
> That if nothing drastic is done
> Aeroplane and Zeppelin will come out,
> Pitch like King Billy bomb-balls in
> Until the town lie beaten flat.

There is no need to rehearse what is already known about O'Casey's politics and the division in his plays between sympathetic women and egoistic men which makes it impossible for us to conceive of any political commitment not hostile to human feeling. He was a strange sort of pacifist, being inclined to repudiate the violence of his Ireland, not on principle but on the ground that this was not a violence which would lead to any improvement in the lot of those who most needed to benefit from real social and political change. His constituency was tenement Dublin, not the select audience for Yeats's Noh drama. But, while these are certainly views which belong to at least some of the volumes of his *Autobiographies*, they are not at all integral to his plays. Is *The Silver Tassie* an anti-war play, or is it a play about an almost sadistic human selfishness? Or is it essentially about the plight of the demobbed and wounded soldier?

The combination of tragedy and comedy in O'Casey's early work is an unhappy one, since their coexistence renders the first sentimental and the other farcical. They divide from one another so completely that we feel he has managed to divorce rather than reconcile the mixed elements. Whether the oppositions be those of politically egoistic men or heroically humane women, of black clerics or the poetic sex of young lovers, O'Casey can finally deal with them only as schismatic statements in which he takes the side of heresy against official rule. He is in fact a Zhdanovite, making his literature conform to a stereotyped party line, using all the resources of a very stagey Irish rhetoric to support those on the side of Life against the dealers in Death. There is a similarity between his career and that of D.H. Lawrence, in that each of them abandoned the native ground upon which their quarrel with the world began for an exile in which the missionary sense became predominant and sought expression in a crusade—the instinctual life of the dark gods against the white mythologies of officialdom. The fact that O'Casey and Lawrence are generally assumed to be on opposite sides of the political divide makes the similarity all the more startling.

Political thought predicated on utopian premises has to assume a highly utilitarian attitude towards literature. The reduction of the human personality to a stereotype, the homiletic approach to language, the puritan suspicion of formal complexity, are all examples of the reaction against modernism in literature which reached such intellectually bankrupt but politically powerful culminations in the writings of Zhdanov, Stalin and the German fascists. From today's vantage point, O'Casey seems closer to the school of socialist realism than to any other. Even his adaptation of German expressionism is merely the adaptation of a technique; it does not signal a change in sensibility. However progressive his opinions may sound, especially when contrasted with those of Yeats, O'Casey as a writer was part of the reactionary movement against the 'decadence' of literary modernism which is part of the political history of the twentieth century. The world in which his writings are admired is a world which has no time for Joyce, Proust, Beckett or Kafka.

When we look to see which authors have most effectively protested against what Lukács calls 'the dismemberment of human consciousness by capitalism',[1] it is surely to writers like these and to Yeats that we turn. O'Casey spoke out against Irish nationalist-populist violence; he also spoke out against Irish clericalism. His range of reference scarcely extends beyond those things. He is a provincial writer whose moment has come again in the present wave of revisionist Irish history, itself a provincial phenomenon. He belongs to the Abbey Yeats tried not to have. The dispute between them over *The Silver Tassie* was, in effect, a dispute over modernist literature and the role which literature should have in relation to the culture out of which it arose initially and to which it must continually return. O'Casey lost the battle but won the war. He deprived the Abbey of his plays even though the Abbey was and is the sort of theatre for which ideally his plays were written. For the theatre in Ireland, by its rejection of Yeatsian forms of drama, by its repudiation of those gestures of body, colour, form and speech which he alone revivified in the early part of this century, has joined with the dull reaction of the thirties, both right and left wing, against all that was important and innovative in the modern arts. Yeats's defence of Synge in 1907 and of O'Casey in 1926 reminds us, however, that there need be no exclusive choice made between these three Abbey dramatists. All that I have argued for here is a recognition of the fact that Yeats is a more profoundly political dramatist than O'Casey, that it is in his plays that we find a search for the new form of feeling which would renovate our national consciousness, and that he, more than O'Casey, stands therefore as a great exemplar for the present moment. O'Casey's virtues as a dramatist are sufficiently recognized but these should not be confused with his usefulness as an example.

1. G. Lukacs, *Studies in European Realism*, trans. E. Bone (London, 1972), p. 234.

Brendan Behan

SEAMUS de BURCA

Brendan Behan: A Memoir †

* * *

The Quare Fellow was originally written in Irish as a one-act play, and
was titled "Casadh an tSugain" or "The Twisting of Another Rope" after
a play by Douglas Hyde, "Casadh an tSugain" or "The Twisting of the
Rope." Brendan submitted the play to Ernest Blythe, Managing Director of the Abbey Theatre, who returned it with the curt comment that
the author might "some day write a play." Mr. Blythe cannot claim at
any time to have encouraged Brendan in his literary career, and Brendan
said to me finally, "The only thing I ever had in common with Ernest
Blythe was that I could tell him to 'fuck off' in Irish."

But it would take more than a rebuff to discourage Brendan, so he sat
down and wrote the same play in English and extended it to three acts.
He submitted this play, *The Twisting of Another Rope*, to Mr. Blythe,
and this time was asked to come along to see Miss Ria Mooney, the
Abbey producer, and discuss the possibility of making the play actable.
Brendan retorted indignantly, "I am a playwright, and Ria Mooney is a
producer, and we don't speak the same language. If there are any revisions in my play, I can do the revisions myself." He took the script
home, sat on it for a month but made no revisions whatever, and returned
the script to Blythe. This time, when Blythe realised Brendan had done
nothing with the play, he very promptly sailed it back.

So began the impossible task for Brendan of trying to find another
venue in Dublin. The tragedy, as I see it, of a rejection by the Abbey is
that there is no alternative. At least, at that time there was no alternative.

† From *Brendan Behan: A Memoir* (Newark, Delaware: Proscenium Press, 1971). First published by
Proscenium Press. Reprinted by permission of publisher and author.

One could wash dishes or become a whore's ponce,[1] but once the Abbey rejected you there was nothing left.

However, Brendan sent the play to Hilton Edwards, through Micheál Mac Liammóir's niece, Sally Travers. I was walking along Pembroke Road one afternoon with my blind friend Tom Pugh, and Brendan hailed me from across the road. "Hey, Jimmy!" You could hear him in heaven. He ran across the street to talk to us; he was calling on Sally to find out the fate of his play.

"How long is it since you sent the play?" I asked him.

"A month."

"They will keep you waiting two years," I told him.

"Not foggin' likely, they won't keep me waiting two years," he said.

I know he left the play another fortnight and then took it back.

Cyril Cusack was offered the play and turned it down. He said himself it was one of the mistakes he regretted.

In 1954, Alan Simpson and Carolyn Swift opened a theatre, The Pike, a converted coach-house in Herbert Lane. It was a tiny theatre seating sixty or seventy people. The Simpsons accepted the play and paid Brendan £30 for an agreed twenty-eight performances, one performance each night, including Sundays. Less than 2000 people crowded into the tiny theatre for the twenty-eight performances, and those of us who saw the play will keep the memory with us for the rest of our lives. The company was run as a kind of commonwealth, each actor receiving as wages about 9 / - weekly; it took the stigma of amateurism out of it, I suppose. The cast was excellent; they were not acting; they were living in the precincts of a prison. I saw the play twice later in the Queen's by the Abbey,[2] but it was the Pike that gave the definitive performance of *The Quare Fellow.*

The scene is Mountjoy in the twenty-four hours preceding the execution of a man for carving up his brother. This man was Bernard Kirwan, and the drama took place while Brendan was in the Joy.[3] The political prisoners were normally isolated from the other prisoners, and exercised in a small yard overlooking the window of the Governor's office. Here the condemned man took his visits, and Kirwan became acquainted with Brendan. They often spoke together, and it is said Kirwan embraced Brendan the day before he was hanged. Be that as it may, Brendan in the play created a wonderfully sympathetic character through the eyes of the prisoners and the warders, although we never actually see the doomed man on the stage.

1. Pimp [*Editor*].
2. The Abbey Theatre was destroyed by fire in 1951; the company performed at The Queen's

Theatre and elsewhere until the new theater opened in 1966 [*Editor*].
3. In Mountjoy Prison [*Editor*].

The play in The Pike had such an overwhelming effect on me I found I could not rise from my seat when it was over. The homosexual character, however, pathetic as he was, offended me. You will recall the criminals are shocked to find themselves with a "Sexual mechanic," and the unfortunate outcast is distressed to find himself harboured with those he thinks beneath him. Act One ends with the homosexual hanging himself. But to me the play was a powerful indictment of society in its inhumanity to man. An atmosphere of doom pervaded the Pike that night, and a feeling of claustrophobia, perhaps helped by the smallness of the theatre. I never recaptured the same feeling in the Queen's Theatre, and this I am sorry to say.

The performance in the Pike did one thing. It meant that the bogey of a possibly ruinous libel action that always haunted theatrical managements in Dublin—particularly since the Louis D'Alton play, *The Money Doesn't Matter*, when [actor] Denis O'Dea took an action against a critic for saying he impersonated Lennox Robinson in that play—had been dispelled. One word from any of the officials in Mountjoy who fancied himself represented on the stage, and the play would have been stopped. But be it said to the credit of the staff of Mountjoy, no complaint was made. Besides they all liked Brendan. But then, of course, there was no mention of Mountjoy on the programme, and we didn't pretend to copy the actual uniforms when we dressed the warders or the prisoners. Sean Kavanagh described the play to me at the time as a fantasy, though he knew very well the background.

For another eighteen months, Alan Simpson hawked *The Quare Fellow* round Dublin, trying to find a bigger theatre. For six months of this time, however, he was enjoying the success of Samuel Beckett's *Waiting for Godot*. The Olympia management, Stanley Illsley and Leo McCabe, wouldn't have it. They didn't admire Brendan. Brendan's brother Sean worked there. As long as my brother Lorcan was there, Sean would always have a job, but he had become a nuisance to the new management by insisting on union rights, and had been thrown out. So there was no love lost between Brendan and Messrs. Illsley and McCabe, although later they allowed a touring version of *The Hostage* to be shown with certain cuts.

I have heard that Brendan sent *The Quare Fellow* to the London Workshop Theatre, Stratford East by post. How long did Joan Littlewood keep the author waiting? I don't know, but when the news broke in London that she had accepted it, theatrical and literary circles were simply flabbergasted. Most considered *The Quare Fellow* had been successfully and decently interred after its airing in the Pike and would never be heard of again. Brendan himself told me he was helped by the anti-hanging campaign then at its height. "I object to a gratuitous insult to my friend the hangman," he said to me in the Gate, referring to a line in my play *Mrs. Howard's Husband,* "He has the face of a hangman."

On his way to London Brendan asked for and got permission to visit Cathal Goulding,[4] who was serving a sentence in an English prison. Cathal was delighted to see his old friend, and told him he had got a copy of my book *The Soldier's Song* for the prison library.

We have all heard of the famous television interview in London. Though Brendan was drunk, the British public took him to their heart. Malcolm Muggeridge has said it was the final corruption of Brendan when he discovered he had not got to write any more—he hadn't even got to talk. Joan Littlewood told Muggeridge the West End ignored the performance until the interview.

When the play opened in the Comedy Theatre, Brendan sang the song "The Old Triangle" live. During the first interval he went across the road to have a pint, and when he got into the bar he saw an old lag from Mountjoy sitting there. They exchanged greetings. The lag said, "You're a nice fucker. You never wrote that song." Brendan rocked with laughter.

On his return home, he again asked for permission to visit Goulding, and this time he was refused. The Governor, a retired British Army major, explained his reason to Goulding. "Do you know I saw that fellow Behan on television, and you won't believe it, he was drunk. Stoned!"

"Drunk or sober, you will never be on television," Goulding told him.

According to Val Iremonger, poet and diplomat, Brendan started to drink spirits at this time, and his constitution simply could not stand up to it. At this time, too, diabetes, the complaint that was to kill him, had manifested itself. He was admitted to the City of Dublin Hospital in Baggot Street. There he wrote the introduction to my book *The Soldier's Song* and went through the galleys. He had one complaint, my reticence about the Civil War. I told him I felt the quality of the book was uneven, but it represented twenty years' work, and he said if he had done it it would have been more uneven. He was in very good humor and said beaming, "If you hadn't invited me to do the foreword I would have had to rustle my way into the book." * * *

4. A leader of the Irish Republican Army [*Editor*].

COLIN MacINNES

The Writings of Brendan Behan †

There are artists whose public performance is so flamboyant—Byron, Alfred Jarry or Erik Satie are examples—that their contemporaries, repelled or dazzled by the man, have failed to measure his artistic quality. This has been the fate of Brendan Behan. The ex-Borstalian, the rebel in trouble with two governments, the interrupter of his own plays in London and New York, the drinker, the singer, the "broth of a boy" persona, have been a gift to columnists and the shame of those who expect of artists that their loftiest aim be the Order of Merit (or its Irish equivalent if there is one—as I hope there isn't). That Behan's writings have some virtue is allowed—but of what kind is it? For in all assessments I have read of writing in English in the past decade, while significance is bestowed on many a dullard whose productions are deemed, by the critical investigator, to conform to the "trend" or "pattern" he discerns, the name of Behan somehow gets forgotten. This surprises me, for of all the writers of my generation, including myself, the only one who I am certain will be read a century from now, is he.

Or rather, this does not surprise me; for the reasons that make the unwary undervalue his achievement are so evident. Chief of these is that he's an Irish writer. Now towards Irish writers (by which, for the moment, I mean writers in English of whatever race and faith who have drawn their essential strength from Ireland) we have a divided attitude. We can admit, as we must, that without them "English" writing of the past and present would lose half its weight. Yet we also seem to believe a benevolent magic makes it so easy for Irishmen to be fine writers, that this gift of nature deprives them of true merit. To be Jonson or Johnson or Daniel Defoe is the consequence of worthy labour. To be Congreve or Swift or Sheridan . . . why, they had only to loosen their delightful Irish tongues, and out it all came pouring like a blackbird's song! Shaw, Wilde, Synge, Joyce, O'Casey—they had only to talk, as in a trance, and the accumulation of generations of sweet grog-shop blarney (sufficiently transmuted by these writers to be artistically acceptable across the Irish Sea) came tumbling out to dazzle us; but we saw through the trick and, while bewitched, refused to bestow the severer kind of praise that

† First published *London Magazine*, August 1962. Reprinted with permission.

Englishmen reserve for work manifestly resulting from qualities of character, labour, scholarship and earnest moral purpose.

I exaggerate, of course; but with to suggest this patronizing attitude to Irish writing, largely unconscious and totally detestable, has as its basis—even in the most enlightened English minds—a political motivation. All our obsessions with India, Africa, Suez, Cyprus and the Caribbean, and the rights and wrongs of what we did and do there, serve somehow to mask from ourselves the fundamental fact of English social and political history, which is our centuries' old war with Ireland. It strikes me as significant, for example, that while dozens of Irish writers (including, of course, Brendan Behan) have found in this theme the chief material of their creations, not one English writer, so far as I know, has tackled it on the scale that it deserves. A *Passage to India* or *Mr Johnson*[1] may not be profound analyses of the Anglo-Indian or Anglo-African disputes, but at least they are gestures, by Englishmen, in the right direction. But what English study have we of those centuries of bloodshed and oppression nearer home?

Having failed in this task of self-assessment—as much in our national thinking as more particularly in our writing—we have fallen back, in both these areas of consciousness, on the negative device of patronage and denigration. The Irish (without whose labour force, even today, our armies, hospitals and transportation system would collapse) remain worthy and slightly comical; and Ireland (whose dreadful division is exclusively an English responsibility, however much we try to hide behind the Orange lodges) a place of rapture and futility. We have forgiven the Irish for all the crimes we have committed on them; and the nastiest form this charitable gesture takes is to refuse to look Ireland in the eyes. Failing to do so saves us from the pain accompanying genuine repentance; but it also inhibits national self-knowledge, for until we have understood what we have done in Ireland, and are doing yet, we shall never understand ourselves.

* * *

In *The Quare Fellow* Behan confronted a theme of daunting difficulty. An exclusively male cast, a principal character who is never seen, a setting of unrelieved gloom. From these unpromising materials (or, of course, being the artist he is, because of them) Behan has made a drama that is funny, humane, and a profound affirmation of the life that everything in the prison is trying to destroy.

The play opens with a song (and closes with a variant of it):

1. By the novelists E. M. Forster and Joyce Cary, respectively *[Editor]*.

A hungry feeling came o'er me stealing
And the mice were squealing in my prison cell,
And that old triangle
Went jingle jangle,
Along the banks of the Royal Canal.

Behan has been criticized for his addiction to incidental songs in his plays—in my view quite mistakenly (though perhaps his own occasional contributions from the stalls were somewhat excessive—but I do wish I'd heard them). It would seem that a people who once loved *The Beggar's Opera* (and to whom its modern transformation by Brecht and Weill is more or less acceptable) are embarrassed by the convention of mixed speech and singing, particularly in a "serious" play. I cannot account for this objection (or rather, don't want to bother to try to) if only because all theatre is in one sense illusion, and everything depends on the conviction with which the artist uses any theatrical device. In *The Quare Fellow* Behan introduces song sparingly, with great tact and dramatic effect. From the outset, the very fact that an invisible prisoner is singing, and that the first character we see, a warder, stops him, establishes at once his central theme which is the conflict of life and joy with cruelty and death, and the triumph of life despite judicial murder:

> The screw was peeping.
> And the lag was weeping . . .
> *Warder:* The screw is listening as well as peeping, and you'll be bloody well weeping if you don't give over your moaning. We might go down there and give you something to moan about. . . .
> B Wings: two, three and one. Stand to your doors. Come on, clean up your cells there.

As we meet the prisoners and warders we are made aware that the forthcoming execution of the "quare fellow" is a shared obsession: the warders, the active party in the matter, being far more disturbed by it than the inmates. Snobberies, resentment and frustrations of the prisoners are conveyed with comic irony, reminding us that a jail population differs from that outside in no essential respect whatever. The first Act ends with an attempted suicide by a reprieved prisoner; and the dramatic effect of this, by bringing us so close to death so early, and by contrasting its "voluntary" nature in this instance with the irrevocable killing that must come, reinforces the gathering sensation of impending horror.

The central "character" of the second Act is the grave the prisoners are digging for tomorrow's victim: a riveting theatrical device, since the

condemned man, though still unseen, becomes even more visible to the
audience's imagination; and a device saved from the merely macabre by
the intensity of feeling with which Behan invests this gruesome emblem,
and by the speed and point of the sardonic dialogue he gives to the
prisoners and warders who surround it. As time passes (by now we too
are counting the hours till the execution) we meet in later Acts, and in
increasing order of seniority, the hierarchy who are going to destroy this
human life (and, by implication, meet the invisible judges, ministers
and the society who have willed the deed). The warders at first seemed
omnipotent, but now we see their Chief, their Governor and the Hangman: an imported Englishman (since the "violent" Irish do not care,
apparently, for this task) and, without doubt, one of the most revolting
personages yet to be created by an English-writing dramatist. The one
character we are drawn to is the young Gaelic-speaking warder Crimmin, who is as yet an innocent. It was a bold and characteristic device
of Behan's to put the only really likeable man in the play among the
oppressors, and he brings this off without a trace of sentiment or artifice.
As the hour approaches, there are detailed physical descriptions by the
prisoners of exactly what will happen to the quare fellow, so clinical as
to be unbearable. Nervous tension rises, and the warders become openly
the victims:

> Warder Regan (almost shouts):   I think the whole show should
> be put on in Croke Park; after all, it's at the public expense and
> they let it go on. They should have something more for their money
> than a bit of paper stuck up on the gate.
> Chief: Goodnight, Regan. If I didn't know you, I'd report what
> you said to the Governor.
> Warder Regan: You will anyway.
> Chief: Goodnight, Regan.

As the clock sounds the hour, the prison is bedlam: warders and prisoners, locked in the same disaster, become indistinguishable, and the
bars melt in the heat. The play ends with a brief and calculated dying
fall . . . a life has been snatched, but life will go on forever.

Considered as a drama that soars from initial apparent *grand guignol*
to authentic lyric tragedy, the play is beyond praise. Viewed as a demonstration that any alternative to judicial murder must be better—and,
as forcefully, that prisons defeat their own supposed ends of humiliation
or redemption—it will carry conviction to anyone capable of being convinced. Yet so fine is it as a play that, just as Greek tragedy haunts us
still despite the moral mainsprings of the drama being quite different

from our own, so I am sure *The Quare Fellow*, in whatever kind of social
order that may replace our own, will never lose its human relevance.

*   *   *

COLBERT KEARNEY

[*The Quare Fellow*] †

*   *   *

In Mountjoy [Prison] Behan had met two men who were condemned to
death by hanging, one for butchering his brother, the other for drowning
his wife. (It is said that Behan saved the latter's life by jeering him so
much that he was declared insane and sent to an asylum.[1]) Bernard
Kirwan, who dissected his brother, was a strange person who embraced
Behan the day before his death and promised that he would pray for him
in heaven. Few people could easily forget such a kiss, least of all Behan
who was aware how horrifyingly close his own offence had brought him
to execution. Later on in Mountjoy, Behan lived through another execution and on this occasion the circumstances were even more disturbing: the victim was a young man who had fired a shot at the police—a
charge on which Behan himself had been found guilty.[2] On the eve of
the execution he must have recalled his agony in Walton Jail in 1940
when the IRA men, Barnes and McCormack, were hanged in Birmingham for their alleged part in causing explosions in Coventry. There again
he had been tormented by the knowledge that he had come to England
to plant bombs, that it could so easily have been his neck in the noose.[3]
Is it any wonder that death figures so prominently in his writings? The
play which was set in *the black cell* was entitled *Casadh Súgáin' Eile*
(The Twisting of Another Rope). 'Casadh an tSúgáin' *(The Twisting of*
the Rope), is a beautiful love-song which tells how the lover was deprived
of his girl: her parents invited him to make a rope in her house and,
when he moved his chair out the doorway, they locked him out. The
theme of the song does not seem to be particularly relevant to Behan's
play but the title was. Douglas Hyde had dramatised the story and this
little one-acter is normally considered the first play of the Irish-language

---

† From *The Writings of Brendan Behan* (New York:
St. Martin's Press, 1977).
1. Ulick O'Connor, *Brendan* (London 1970), 81.
2. Behan, *Confessions of an Irish Rebel*, 56.
3. When his publisher was unsure as to the suit-
ability of the title *Borstal Boy*, Behan suggested *This
Young Neck* as an alternative. See Rae Jeffs, *Brendan Behan: Man and Showman* (London 1966),
41.

theatre; Behan, perhaps unconsciously, hoped that his play would be the first of a revived Irish theatre. One also suspects that the emphasis on the *other* rope indicates his awareness of the rope which was to be used, not on Barnes or McCormack or Kirwan, but on the spectre which haunted Behan—his imagined self who had not escaped.

Casadh Súgáin Eile was rejected by the Abbey but the raw material was too much a part of Behan to be forgotten. Shortly after his release from the Curragh [jail] it came to the surface again. In January 1947 he attended a meeting of IRA men who were planning a concert in commemoration of the deaths of Barnes and McCormack. When it was suggested that the programme should include a one-act play on the subject of the 1798 Insurrection, Behan argued that what was needed was a play about Barnes and McCormack and, when it was pointed out that no such play existed, promised to provide one himself within forty-eight hours, which he did. The play was entitled *Gretna Green* and showed three people outside a prison on the eve of a double execution; it would be clear to anybody at such a concert that the prison was Winson Green and that the two to be executed were Barnes and McCormack. No copy of the play survives but those involved recall that there was little action and that the impact of the play was hindered by the freezing cold weather which left the organisers with a half-empty house.[4]

When Behan promised a play in two days, he clearly had some idea of what it would be like. His confidence must have been based on his work on *Casadh Súgáin Eile* and on his awareness of the part played by Barnes and McCormack in the complex of feelings which had found expression in a play about the hanging of Bernard Kirwan. The fact that he himself had not been in the prison where they died led him (if he had not done so previously) to set the scene outside *the black cell* so that the victims and the execution exist only in the minds and words of the chorus without—a device which was to shape *The Quare Fellow*.

Although Behan was happy that his play had had a production, he was not content to leave it at that. He persisted with the play as set in Mountjoy on the eve of the Kirwan hanging. When working for Radio Éireann in the early fifties, he hoped that it would be broadcast. He showed Francis MacManus a draft of a one-act entitled *The Twisting of Another Rope* but it must have been a fairly rough draft for MacManus remembered it as 'a few pages of a play about a man who was condemned to death for boiling his brother.' Having made no impression on Radio Éireann, Behan turned yet again to the Abbey where de Blaghd

4. Seamus G. O'Kelly, "I Knew the Real Brendan Behan," *The Irish Digest*, June 1964, 69f.

advised him to develop it into a full-length play. When Behan had done this, de Blaghd suggested that Behan might go over the play with an Abbey producer to see if it could be made shorter and more suitable for staging; de Blaghd was also worried that some official in Mountjoy would consider the play actionable. Behan, reacting to what he felt to be a superfluity of advice, undertook to revise the play himself but it was the same script he sent back to the Abbey and it was rejected.[5] The play did the rounds of the theatres in Dublin, unsuccessfully until it fell into the hands of Alan Simpson and Carolyn Swift who had recently converted an old coach-house into a theatre, the Pike.

Behan found the Pike much more congenial that the Abbey: the play was accepted on condition that he made some revisions and he did so willingly, even to the extent of changing the title of which he was so fond into the much more striking *The Quare Fellow*, the name given by the prisoners to the condemned man.[6] The Pike production was excellent and the play very well received, yet none of the larger Dublin theatres was willing to take it over when offered. Though it was an unqualified success, the Pike production actually lost money because of the large cast and the tiny capacity of the converted coach-house. However, *The Quare Fellow* had far to go. In 1956 Joan Littlewood put it on at the Theatre Workshop in London and after a three months run and critical acclaim it moved to the West End.

Whether they like it or not, the people who come to see *The Quare Fellow* take an important part. There is a short interval of darkness between the switching off of the auditorium lights and the rise of the curtain during which is heard a resigned voice singing a melancholy song. When the curtain rises, the audience sees a prison landing. 'On the wall and facing the audience is printed in large block shaded Victorian lettering the word "SILENCE".'(1) [256] [7] This is as much a test of the audience as an instruction to the prisoners. The audience is examining an institution which it has created, sanctioned and maintained itself. The audience is society: it must respect its own security system, must certainly not laugh at it. The audience may seek to escape its role by claiming that it knows nothing of prisons and allows them to be run by experts. Behan's play makes them expert in at least one field of penology, hanging.

5. *Confessions of an Irish Rebel*, 239f.; de Burca, *Brendan Behan* (Newark: Delaware) 24; and Michael O hAodha's introduction to *Moving Out and A Garden Party*, ed. Robert Hogan (California 1967), 4f.

6. The story of the Pike production is told in Alan Simpson, *Beckett and Behan and a Theatre in Dublin* (London 1962).

7. Figures in parentheses refer to pages in the first edition of *The Quare Fellow* (London 1956). [Page numbers in brackets refer to this edition—*Editor*.]

The man that feels it worst, going into that little house with the red door and the silver painted gates at the bottom of D. Wing, is the man that has been in the nick before, when some other merchant was topped; or he's heard screws or old lags in the bag shop or at exercise talking about it. A new chap that's never done anything but murder, and that only once, is usually a respectable man, such as this Silver-top here. He knows nothing about it, except the few lines that he'd see in the papers. 'Condemned man entered the hang-house at seven fifty-nine. At eight three the doctor pronounced life extinct.' (7) [260]

An indication of the power of the play is the manner in which it alters the audience from the respectable 'new chap' to the experienced lag. After *The Quare Fellow* it is impossible to see judicial hanging as an element in an argument on crime and punishment: Behan has infixed in our minds the physicality of the action and the actuality of the hours before it.

Though we never see it, the hang-house has a *red* door and the gates are painted *silver*. The operation which takes place inside is as lively as the paintwork. The dynamics of hanging are complicated, relating the weight of the body to the length of the drop, allowing for variations in the dimension and texture of the neck. (79f.) [305f] It is beyond the scope of pure science and indeed it demands the personal attention and intuitive eye of the craftsman: 'He says he can judge better with the eye. If he gave him too much one way he'd strangle him instead of breaking his neck, and too much the other way he'd pull the head clean off his shoulders.' (65) [296] Every care is taken to ensure the success of the victim in his next life: in the case of a Catholic, the hood is slit and socks taken off immediately to facilitate anointing. (81) [307] A young Protestant clergyman showed himself guilty of weak faith while attending one of his persuasion to the gallows: although he saw the washer being correctly placed under the victim's ear he was unable to watch the hanging body and fainted. (63) [295] Nor is it only during the actual hanging that the welfare of the subject is taken into account. His last hours on earth are filled with luxuries which are the envy of other prisoners—special food and more cigarettes than he can smoke. The warders are strictly instructed to prevent any depression. 'An air of cheerful decorum is indicated, as a readiness to play such games as draughts, ludo, or snakes and ladders; a readiness to enter into conversation on sporting topics will also be appreciated.' (66) [297] Regulations also stipulate that nobody is supposed to know the right time.

Despite the elaborate machinery, some are not impressed, especially those with long experience of prisons.

> In the first place the doctor has his back turned after the trap goes down, and doesn't turn and face it until the screw has caught the rope and stopped it wriggling. Then they go out and lock up the shop and have their breakfast and don't come back for an hour. Then they cut your man down and the doctor slits the back of his neck to see if the bones are broken. Who's to know what happens in the hour your man is swinging there, maybe wriggling to himself in the pit. [260]

It is reported that one man lived for seventeen minutes at the end of the rope. (8) [260] A prisoner who had actually seen a body after hanging would not like to do so again: 'his head was all twisted and his face black, but the two eyes were the worst; like a rabbit's; it was fear that had done it.' (22) [269] The audience may not be inclined to believe the testimony of prisoners, some of it based on rumour, but it is corroborated by one of the warders:

> And you're not going to give me that stuff about just shoving over the lever and bob's your uncle. You forget the times the fellow gets caught and has to be kicked off the edge of the trap hole. You never heard the warders below swinging on his legs the better to break his neck, or jumping on his back when the drop was too short. (76) [303]

This is disturbing and the person of the executioner does not help to exorcise the spectre of such inhuman bungling. He is drunk and, despite his apparent know-how, his total lack of any feeling for his subject is frightening. And who is to say that he has made a mess?

It has been objected that the play 'lacks the unifying focus of a central character'.[8] Surely the central character is, as the title suggests, 'the quare fellow' himself. He is to be hanged and the theme of the play is the effect which his fate has on the people within the prison and, by the extension already mentioned, on the audience. The dialogue is seldom far removed from 'the quare fellow'. He does not appear on the stage but this does not prevent him from dominating it in the minds of others. We do not know his name or anything personal about him: all we know is his crime and his punishment. A great deal of the dramatic tension in the play arises from this. The prison system has devised a procedure

---

8. Raymond J. Porter, *Brendan Behan* (New York 1973), 20.

whereby the condemned man is kept apart. One wonders why. Can it be that they who are about to kill him are acting in his interest? Is it not more likely that they are trying to keep the business as quiet and as secret as possible? That they feel that there is something shameful, something obscene, in the idea of legal execution? And is this why the prisoners and staff refuse to mention the victim by any personal name? The 'quare fellow' is taboo: all attempts to hide him and to dehumanise him are attempts to disguise the fact that he is a human being who is about to be killed in a careful calculated manner. The audience does not see him; all society ever sees is 'the few lines in the papers'.

Yet everybody knows he is there in the little house with the red door and the silver painted gates, that the warders bring him attractive meals and so many cigarettes that his throat is parched, that the hangman will peep in at him and note the strength of his neck, that he will be taken out in the morning and be left dangling at the end of a rope until dead. The dramatist does not allow us to *see* him on the stage despite the fact that he is the principal participant in the action. The audience should not be surprised: society, that is they themselves, ordains that a similar technique be used in real life.

The Quare Fellow is a play within a play, and structurally much more sophisticated than it is often thought. [9] There are two audiences: those in the theatre watch those on the stage who witness the externals of the closet-drama. Those on the stage react in various ways to the ritual in which they play or are forced to play some part. Some of them, prisoners mostly, seem to be callously unconcerned with the fate of the unknown victim; others, most of the people who are part of the system, accept the procedure as sanctioned by religion, morality and social necessity. The theatre-audience cannot resist judging the behaviour of those on stage and invariably they laugh at the black humour of the prisoners and dissociate themselves from the strict principles of the prison regime. At some point during or after the play the theatre-audience must realise that they have been tricked into a position which is critical of the very institution which they support outside the theatre.

* * *

9. See, for example, Ted E. Boyle, *Brendan Behan* (New York 1969).

D. E. S. MAXWELL

[*The Quare Fellow*] †

Brendan Behan was born in Dublin on 9 February 1923, a child of the tenements, and died there after a rambunctiously alcoholic life on 20 March 1964. His father was a house painter, as was Brendan Behan himself, and the family had strong connections both with Republicanism and Dublin Theatre.

Behan once remarked, 'When Samuel Beckett was in Trinity College listening to lectures, I was in the Queen's Theatre, my uncle's music hall. That is why my plays are music hall and his are university lectures.' Behan's judgment is very partial. Beckett's fantastics are at times songsters, and they can juggle with hats, ladders, and knick-knacks as elaborately as Laurel and Hardy. Referring to his own affinity with Joan Littlewood's sense of theatre, Behan said that 'the thing to aim for is to amuse people and any time they get bored, divert them with a song or a dance'. Yet Behan could organise his music hall beyond self-indulgent song and dance. Written originally in Irish (*Casadh Sugáin Eile—The Twisting of Another Rope*), *The Quare Fellow*'s English version was rejected by the Abbey, then by Hilton Edwards—partly because of Behan's own dilatoriness. Alan Simpson was more patient. In its final shape *The Quare Fellow* is in debt to him, though he claims only that 'we rearranged rather then rewrote some of the play'. It entirely avoids the wasteful 'turns' of *The Hostage* (1958), the result largely of Joan Littlewood's Theatre Workshop production at Stratford East.

Before curtain rise on *The Quare Fellow*, a prisoner's sardonic song gives human voice to the stage set's images of confinement: the severe lines of cell doors and the administrative circle, the women's section visible but beyond reach, the notice in Victorian lettering which says, 'SILENCE'. All except the voice is institutional, correctional. The play, like the voice, challenges the restraints: morning stand-to, the line-up for inspection, the filing out to dig the grave for the condemned man. These dreary rituals, to which the inmates pay mocking observance, stand against the antic caperings of the two Young Prisoners, who 'samba out with their brushes humming the Wedding Samba'. Like the choreographed coal-stealing in Wesker's *Chips with Everything* (1962), the parade

† From *A Critical History of Modern Irish Drama, 1891–1980*. Copyright © Cambridge University Press 1984. Reprinted with the permission of Cambridge University Press.

drill in McGrath's *Events While Guarding the Bofors Gun* (1966), *The Quare Fellow*'s chores and disciplines evade the intentions of their supervisors. 'By the left, laugh', as Dunlavin says.

The one song, 'that old triangle', sounds the play's strict chronology, from 'To begin the morning / The warder bawling' through 'On a fine spring evening / The lag lay dreaming' to 'The day was dying / And the wind was sighing.' Apart from this there are a few snatches of song only. Thus discreetly used, the song generalises on the passage of time, which is the main 'action' of the play. The prisoners return obsessively to it—particularly the coming hour of execution, but generally as the focus of their lives: 'Healey is coming up today', 'the small hours of this morning', 'long months here', 'out again this day week', 'three days of No. 1', 'the death watch coming on at twelve o'clock'. Hardly a page lacks such a confining definition by hours, days, years. Time and space impose their restrictions, brought together in the final song:

> In the female prison
> There are seventy women
> I wish it was with them that I did dwell,
> Then that old triangle
> Could jingle jangle
> Along the banks of the Royal Canal.

The crude pun, in the diminuendo after the hanging, revives the sexual antithesis to death.

For the prisoners the Quare Fellow is not a Cause. He is a victim, a sacrifice, the ceremonies of his death detailed in their minds. Only through them has the audience access to the condemned cell and to knowledge of its occupant, whom we never see, and who is deprived of individuality. He is all the Quare Fellows who have met this death.

Much of the conversation about the Quare Fellow is in the past tense. It refers to him only indirectly, through prison lore of the gruesome mechanics of hanging and of the hours before it. Warders and prisoners agree on its messiness. What do we learn about it? The duty warders make futile attempts to conceal the passage of time. The washer is put beneath the condemned man's ear, the hood is donned. The prisoner's weight and build may be wrongly estimated: decapitation or strangulation—'his head was all twisted and his face black, but the two eyes were the worst, like a rabbit's; it was fear that had done it'. The prisoners' view is unsentimental, almost clinical, with a colouring of macabre fascination. Most feel some compassion. But the compassion is for a man seen as his own executioner—'Begod, he's not being topped for nothing—to cut his own brother up and butcher him like a pig.'

These responses are far from the absolutes of reformist opinion. Their power is the greater for an anguish—and an appetite—which does not come from any sense of Virtue Crucified. The personification is not to suggest any symbolic association between the Quare Fellow and Christ. Christ, however, did share his crucifixion with two outcasts more of the Quare Fellow's persuasion. Without urging, Behan's play hints at some such extension.

As the Quare Fellow's superior last meal is taken to him, the other prisoners crowd the yard in an antiphonal chorus:

PRISONER A. Pork Chops
PRISONER B. Pig's feet.
PRISONER A. Salmon.
NEIGHBOUR. Fish and chips.
MICKSER. Jelly and custard.
NEIGHBOUR. Roast lamb.
PRISONER A. Plum pudding.
PRISONER B. Turkey.
NEIGHBOUR. Goose.
PRISONERS A., B., AND NEIGHBOUR. Rashers and eggs.
ALL. Rashers and eggs, rashers and eggs, and eggs and rashers and eggs and rashers it is.

The hangman and his sober attendant deliver a litany which tastelessly but formally solemnises the soul and body of the Quare Fellow:

JENKINSON *(sings).* My brother, sit and think
While yet some time is left to thee
Kneel to thy God who from thee does not shrink
And lay thy sins on Him who died for thee.
HANGMAN. Take a fourteen stone man as a basis and giving him a
drop of eight foot. . . .

Finally the prisoners enter the rite. Their wordless howling at the moment of execution, and Mickser's parody of a race-course commentator determine their presence at a mystery, not a demonstration against capital punishment.

Structurally, as Colbert Kearney has remarked, the play is subtly made. We observe the prisoners, who are observing 'the externals of the closet drama',[1] luring us to experience the condition of the outcast and the pressure of the social defences against him. The play represents the psychological defences which people set up against violent death, and at an

1. Colbert Kearney, *The Writings of Brendan Behan* (New York 1977), p. 71.

even deeper level its fascination. The emotions which welcome barbaric revenge in whatever form—execution, feud, assassination, war—enter the play's ambit, recorded with remarkable neutrality of tone. Even Warder Regan who comes closest to explicit condemnation of the whole process, never fully interrogates its motives. One of his speeches, towards the end, refers to the pandering to a lust for death and spectacle, now hypocritically muted with the hanging removed from public to private view, from mass audience to its secular and ecclesiastical representatives. Almost shouting, Regan says, 'I think the whole show should be put on in Croke Park; after all, it's at the public expense and they let it go on. They should have something more for their money than a bit of paper stuck up on a gate.' but he continues in his office.

The Quare Fellow epitomises—almost *is*—Behan's achievement in the theatre. It is localised by language, and through language escapes to its wider applications. The music-hall styles are there, but refined to subtle purposes. The play has a message, but the message is not the play. It is entertainment, but entertainment is not its substance. *The Quare Fellow*, classically restricted to one day's action, disturbs in its audience's imagination longer scopes of time and experience. It takes us into the presence of individuals who merge into a voice beyond their individualities.

*   *   *

Behan had a short life and wrote only two plays of value. Nevertheless he deserves attention. Around the time of his first play Dubliners were seeing Shaw (*St Joan*, *The Doctor's Dilemma*), a Eugene O'Neill (*Anna Christie*), an Elmer Rice (*Not for Children*); from the home dramatists Lady Longford's *The Hill of Quirke*, and at the Abbey, Tomelty's *Is The Priest at Home?*, Molloy's *The Will and the Way*, and *Twenty Years A-Wooing* by John McCann, a prolific and successful writer of soap operas: revivals, safe new works, potboilers. *The Quare Fellow* is of a superior order. It is basically realistic, yet with chorus, song, mime, a language that transforms the vernacular it draws on, redeems realism from hand-me-down imitation; and is genuinely continuous with a tradition, the urban drama of O'Casey, because it is re-phrasing, not merely aping, a style. Nothing, of course, immediately came of the example. Behan himself was destroyed by financial success and personal excess. Dublin theatre was inattentive to him. Alan Simpson remembers that 'respectable' managements were dubious about Behan.[2] The Abbey did not stage

2. Alan Simpson, *Beckett and Behan and a Theatre in Dublin* (London 1962), pp. 55–6.

The Quare Fellow until 1958, after its acclaim in London; nor *The Hostage*, which Ernest Blythe considered filthy rubbish, until 1970. But even though his native city did not take him up, Behan's work remained a standing intimation of theatrical alternatives to the 'grim, grey similarity', as Tomas MacAnna called it, 'of the plays that went on at the Queen's'.[3]

* * *

3. Tomas MacAnna, "New Abbeys for Old," *The Irish Times*, 4 September 1969.

Samuel Beckett

ALEC REID

[Krapp's Last Tape] †

* * *

Before we turn to the plays, we must say something about the author himself. Throughout his life, quietly but uncompromisingly, Beckett has avoided every form of personal publicity.[1] He is naturally reticent, unassertive, with a deep respect for the privacy of others, and a considerable impatience with the spurious, impersonal world of press parties, public relations and the rest. On one of the rare occasions when he has talked to a journalist, he remarked that writers are never interesting, and for himself at least, it is the work that matters. Only one justification, therefore, is possible for any discussion of Beckett the private individual as distinct from Beckett the writer. Over the past fifteen years a legend has grown up about him which leads to a fundamental misconception of his work. Thousands of people—billions as Estragon would say—will unhesitatingly identify him as the author of *Waiting for Godot*, and, although they know nothing else of him or of his writing, they yet have a clear, insistent image of him as a gloomy, arrogant, desiccated egghead, the dramatist of dustbins, cripples, and cosmic despair, comprehensible, if at all, only to the highest of highbrows. To Beckett personally this would not matter in the least. As he wrote to Alan Schneider, his American director, after the disastrous opening of *Godot* in Miami, "Success and failure on the public level never mattered much to me, in fact I feel much more at home with the latter, having breathed deep of its vivifying air all my writing life up to the last couple of years. . . . For the moment all I can say and all I want to say is that this Miami fiasco does not distress me in the smallest degree, or only in so far as it dis-

† From *All I Can Manage, More Than I Could: An Approach to the Plays of Samuel Beckett* (New York: Grove Press, 1968).

1. Samuel Beckett died in 1989 [*Editor*].

tresses you." A man who can think, feel, and write like this needs no one to fight his battles for him, but unfortunately the widespread image of Beckett as an inhuman intellectual affects the general appreciation of his work. It frightens people away, and to no purpose. While writing this study I have become increasingly convinced that if more were known about Beckett himself, more people would come to his plays and come with that open approach which the work demands. That is why these personal details have been added.

Those who do not know much about Beckett are usually very surprised to hear that he took an active part in the French Resistance for nearly two years, and that for the next two and a half he was in hiding from the Gestapo. The circumstances under which he came to join the Resistance are highly illuminating. At the end of 1931 Beckett, then a lecturer in French at Trinity College, Dublin, suddenly resigned, left Ireland, and spent the next five years moving about Europe, now in Germany, now in Austria, now in England, finally settling in Paris in 1937. When the Germans invaded Poland in 1939, Beckett happened to be in Ireland spending a month's holiday with his mother. He hurried back to his flat in Montparnasse, but at first he declined to involve himself in a war which, as he insisted, was no concern of a neutral Irishman like himself. Once the Germans occupied Paris in 1940, however, this attitude of detachment did not last long. Beckett soon became incensed at the Nazi treatment of the Jews, among whom he had many close friends. The constant public humiliations—every Jew was forced to wear a yellow Star of David stitched onto his clothing—and the almost daily shooting of hostages presented a situation in which, as Beckett has said almost apologetically, "I couldn't stand with my arms folded." Anger led to action. By the end of 1940 he had become actively involved with a Resistance group with agents dotted all over France gathering details of enemy troop movements. The information, some of it seemingly very trivial, found its way to Beckett scribbled on bus tickets, old envelopes, cigarette packets, anything, and his job was to collate it, edit it, type as much as possible onto two sheets of paper, and forward them to another agent to be micro-filmed and eventually transmitted to London. Beckett refuses to attach any importance to this work—"boy-scout stuff" he calls it—but in August, 1942, the group was betrayed, and out of eighty members, less than twenty survived. Beckett and his wife Suzanne were alerted and got away barely half an hour before the Gestapo came for them. For the next four months they were, as Sam puts it, "on the trot", making their way through enemy territory, liable at any moment to be recognised or denounced, executed then and there, or sent to almost certain death in the concentration camps. At last they crossed into Unoccupied France ending up at Roussillon, a village high in the mountains behind Avignon. Here they remained in semi-hiding until the German collapse, Beckett working as a farm labourer during the daytime while in the evenings he wrote *Watt*, a strange, fantastical, comic novel set in the country round Foxrock, County Dublin, where he had been brought up. As he has explained, this helped to take his mind off the war and the German Occupation. For these two and a half years Beckett's life and Suzanne's depended literally on his ability to pass himself off as a French peasant, and to earn enough money by the sweat of his brow to pay for their food. As soon as he could move about freely again, he hurried back to Ireland to see his mother, but he was now so thin and so gaunt that many of his old friends failed to recognize him. These are things which we should remember when we hear Beckett described as a remote intellectual in an ivory tower. More than most people he has lived close to death every minute of the day and has seen those around him butchered suddenly and ruthlessly. He has known fear, suffering, hardship, but also that indestructible determination to stay alive and go on, which we find again and again in his work.

People who have formed their picture of Beckett only through the legend are also greatly surprised to hear of his genius for companionship, a remarkable ability to make those coming in contact with him feel the richer for his mere presence. "Sam," said one colleague who worked with him in difficult circumstances just after the war, "is the sort of person you could wander off with and watch rats swimming in the river, and you'd both feel you'd spent a useful afternoon." The word "both" is significant, for Beckett always imparts this sense of something shared, of someone coming along with you. The same friend goes on to describe him at a tea party in Dublin talking to some students, "giving them everything he could, all they wanted; with it, with them, although there was a whole generation between them."

This gift comes from an instinctive recognition of what the other person needs and a remarkable generosity in providing it. In this context Brendan Behan, whom Beckett liked and admired, had a characteristic story. Once, in Paris, Behan found himself under lock and key due to some temporary financial embarrassment. Beckett hearing of it, sought him out, and then, in Brendan's words, "He paid them what I owed them, and he took me away, and he gave me ten thousand francs, and a double brandy, and a lecture on the evils of drinking." A nicer sense of priorities would be hard to imagine.

* * *

If we are to grasp the [theatrical] process fully we must be at an actual performance; anything less is like trying to appreciate an Impressionist painting from a verbal description or a black and white reproduction. We can get some faint idea of it, however, through a brief extract from *Krapp's Last Tape*. First of all, let us imagine ourselves in a theatre. Then, when we have understood how the passage relates to what has gone before, let us read it aloud, paying faithful attention to the pauses marked in the text.

The stage in front of us is dark except for a pool of strong white light shed by a lamp hanging over a table in the centre. At this table we see Krapp, a shabby old man whom we have already watched fumbling short-sightedly with his keys, and have already heard talking to himself in a cracked but distinctive voice. Now he switches on a tape-recording which he had made on his birthday many years ago. We *hear* Krapp-at-39, "sound as a bell", as the tape claims, and "intellectually at the crest of the wave—or thereabouts;" but at the same time we *see* the old man on the stage, short-sighted, shuffling, coughing, no longer able to remember what the tape was about. In that moment Krapp's words are immaterial; sight and sound combine to make us know in one brief second the flight of thirty years. Time was, time is; to this favour must we all come.

The voice on the tape is describing how Krapp sat by the canal one cold November afternoon, throwing a rubber ball for a small dog as he watched the house where his mother lay dying and waited for the blind in her room to be pulled down for the last time. By playing on our senses Beckett evokes the whole experience for us very vividly; we feel the wind, see the dull, wintry colours, finger the ball, hear the dog yelping. But as we listen, we become aware of something else, of three distinct sound-patterns. Gradually we distinguish an even-paced measure for narrative speech, a slower, long-drawn-out lyrical tempo, and a brisker, harsh, sardonic tone, and we notice the periods of silence marking the change from one rhythm to the next. From the interplay of these rhythms we gradually realize that Krapp-at-39 is torn by two radically opposed elements in his character, and that the conflict still racks the old man sitting at the table in front of us. The sound-patterns do not depend on any "interpretation" imposed by the actor or the director. They are inevitable, deliberately constructed by Beckett through the words he has chosen, the way he has arranged them, and the pauses which he has put down to separate them. We must hear the passage if we are to feel the texture of the whole experience.

*   *   *

A pool of light on a dark stage, a tape-recorder, an old man listening to a story about a dog and a ball * * * —what could be simpler? Yet we have watched a human being tear himself to pieces, and we have suffered with him. There is nothing highbrow or abstruse here, no symbols or learned allusions, nothing calling for specialized knowledge of any kind. All we need is to watch and to listen in the same way as we watch and listen to any other play or film, or to the television. Beckett has often said that his plays are very simple; the difficulties are of our making, not his.

*   *   *

RUBY COHN

[Krapp's Last Tape]†

At first entitled "the Magee Monologue," *Krapp's Last Tape* was written after Beckett heard a radio broadcast of Pat Magee reading from his fiction. Like Beckett's earlier plays, *Krapp's Last Tape* shows awareness of its genre. But there are differences. *Godot* and *Fin de partie [Endgame]* show through word and gesture that they are what they are—stage plays. *All That Fall*, a radio play, presents sounds but not a radio. *Krapp's Last Tape*, a stage play, puts a tape-recorder on stage. The earlier plays play with the techniques of their genre, but *Krapp's Last Tape* plays against its genre by using the techniques of another medium. *Krapp's Last Tape* employs the tape-recorder as a stage metaphor for time past. Unlike Proust's Marcel, Krapp does not have to depend on involuntary memory for lost time. He can find it on spools of tape, methodically numbered, titled, and catalogued.

In *Godot* everything that happens has happened before, but the characters cannot remember. In *Fin de partie* most things that happen have happened before, and the characters remember the past more vividly than they live in the present. In *Krapp's Last Tape* a form of what happens has happened before, but the memory of it has been codified. Krapp calls his tape a "retrospect," and we witness his reaction to retrospects.

After Krapp's initial reading of tape numbers and titles, the dialogue of *Krapp's Last Tape* may be trisected: 1) Krapp listens to a tape made thirty years ago; 2) he records a tape; 3) he listens to part of the first tape.

† From *Back to Beckett* (Princeton: Princeton UP, 1973).

The actions overlap, and from that overlap emerges Beckett's most direct character. By that I mean that Krapp is not estranged from us—not by appearance, setting, or medium. Gogo and Didi wait on a stage no man's land; shroud-sheets and ashbins distance us from the characters of *Fin de partie*; invisible Ma and Da Rooney grow to size through sound. But ordinary Krapp is at once spotlighted at his ordinary table. Through the course of the play, he most habitually makes the gesture of listening. Finally he faces us more naked than if he were naked, because he is so utterly alone. He is as familiar as the California bumper sticker: "Dirty old men need love too."

The play-long familiarity is a subtle achievement, where, for once, everything is on the surface. Neither Bible, Descartes, Dante, nor even Proust helps us to know Krapp. A hymn and *Effie Briest* are the only literary references, and the play tells us all we need know about them to understand this old man in whom desire is stronger than memory, as the spotlight is stronger than the nonsuffering of darkness.

We see before us unkempt Krapp at the age of sixty-nine, addicted to bananas that constipate him, to alcohol that he drinks offstage, to desire for women in fact (Fanny) and fantasy (Effie Briest). Sixty-nine-year-old Krapp listens to a tape made on his thirty-ninth birthday, in which he laments his addiction to bananas and alcohol and lingers over his farewell to love. In that tape Krapp speaks of a tape made ten or twelve years earlier, in which he recalls his constipation and his addiction to alcohol and sex. Each age is scornful of those that precede it: in his twenties Krapp sneered at his youth; at thirty-nine Krapp finds it "hard to believe [he] was ever that young whelp" in his twenties; at sixty-nine he begins to record: "Just been listening to that stupid bastard I took myself for thirty years ago, hard to believe I was ever as bad as that." Each age has its ambition: in his twenties Krapp spoke ironically of "the opus . . . magnum"; when he is thirty-nine, we hear fragments of his vision of darkness, impatiently interrupted by Krapp; sixty-nine-year-old Krapp comments sardonically on what may be the magnum opus resulting from his vision; it has sold seventeen copies. Each age has its love: in his twenties Krapp lived off and on with Bianca; at thirty-nine Krapp recalls the eyes of a nursemaid, but he dwells longer on a nameless woman in a boat; at sixty-nine Krapp has to be content with a "Bony old ghost of a whore" whom he perhaps moulds into a fantasy of Effie Briest in Fontane's novel. Each age brings its loss: in his twenties Krapp's father died; at thirty-nine he meticulously describes his surroundings when his mother dies; by the time he is sixty-nine Krapp has no one to lose.

Unlike other Beckett stage characters, Krapp is rooted in a familiar world whose every detail is realistically plausible. Packets of letters or photograph albums are perhaps more usual than tape collections in an effort to retain the past, but the collector's impulse is common to all. A reel on a machine recreates two scenes that move us by the homespun quality of their truth. In a death scene we do not see Krapp's dying mother, but through Krapp's tape we envision how death is surrounded by trivia. In a love scene we have no physical picture of the beloved woman, but Krapp conveys a feeling of belonging to the universe through union with the beloved.

At one level, Krapp is a living emblem of our age of mass media; at another, he converts a machine into a tool for introspection. In the stage present, Beckett makes slapstick comedy of Krapp's weak eyes, but Krapp himself finds eyes seductive. In his twenties Bianca's eyes were "incomparable." At thirty-nine, eyes "like chrysolite," intrude upon his memory of his mother's death. At sixty-nine he can still remember the eyes of his unnamed love: "The eyes she had!"

White-faced and purple-nosed, Krapp vaguely resembles a clown, and his clothes vaguely relate him to the music-hall tramp—rusty-black trousers that are too short, and rusty-black waistcoat with four large pockets; dirty white shirt and dirty white boots. Near-sighted, hard of hearing, he walks laboriously. His stage business is with keys and bananas, providing opportunity for comic mime. Slipping on a banana-skin is one of the oldest slapstick jokes, but Krapp is its victim only once on this day; the second skin he tosses offstage out of his way. Like the actor of Acte sans paroles I, he learns.

Krapp's opening mime as written is sexually suggestive—inserting keys in locks, handling the phallic bananas in a masturbatory manner. The gestures predict the dialogue of a dirty old man. When Krapp breaks into speech about his tapes, he speaks of them as animate objects—"the little rascal! . . . the little scoundrel!." But when he begins to read the titles of the tapes, he is puzzled. His past is on tape, not in his head. When the slapstick is over, memories begin. After Krapp listens to the tape within the tape, about the girl in a shabby green coat, he looks at his watch, then disappears backstage, from where we hear three corks pop. In a brief burst of quavering song, he returns to his spotlighted table, to listen again.

During the course of his listening, Krapp stops the machine at the word "viduity." Krapp disappears and reappears with an enormous dictionary, to help him with this word he knew thirty years ago, but knows no longer. His third exit is made after he hears the love scene in the boat; glancing first at an envelope, then at his watch, he disappears backstage. We hear the sound of a bottle against a glass, brief siphon, then *"bottle against glass alone."* The graduation from wine to whiskey is indicated, as in radio drama, by sounds—and not as in radio drama, by the visible effect on Krapp, who comes unsteadily into view, to tape the present.

Krapp is a writer, and yet his speech calls less attention to itself than that of Maddy Rooney, housewife. Krapp singles out for emphasis the words "spooool," "viduity," and "vidua-bird." The first and third give him sensuous pleasure, and we see them as symbols for aspects of Krapp, the spools containing his consciousness and the bird reflecting his virility—"Black plumage of male."

Krapp is not so echoic as Hamm or Clov, but his rare repetitions are also meaningful. Eyes form a leitmotif, and the moment of Krapp's mother's death is marked when the *blind* goes down on her window. On Krapp's thirty-ninth birthday there is "Not a soul" in the winehouse; at his mother's death there is "hardly a soul." Krapp describes the tape recorded in his twenties as ending with a yelp to Providence, and after his mother dies, a dog yelps for a black ball. The dog takes the ball from Krapp "gently, gently," and in the boat of the love scene, "all moved, and moved us, gently." Krapp's relation to Bianca was "Hopeless business," and to his love in the boat Krapp says, "It was hopeless and no good going on." A fire lit Krapp's vision of darkness on the Memorable Equinox, and the play ends on an ironic reference to "the fire in me now." Repetitions emphasize contrasts, as the sixty-nine year old relic before us contrasts with the vigorous voice on tape.

On stage the most telling contrast is played by Krapp against his tape. When listening to thirty-nine year old Krapp denigrate Krapp in his twenties, old Krapp twice joins in the taped laugh, once laughs alone, once listens to the taped laugh, and finally joins in a prolonged laugh at the aspirations of the youngest of the three Krapps. Elsewhere, Krapp switches off to brood, or to wind the tape forward. He is most impatient with the chief item of his thirty-ninth year—the Memorable Equinox—so that we hear mere fragments of a vision that emanates from darkness. Only once before he records does Krapp wind the tape back—to replay the love scene in the punt. Its lyricism fresh in our minds, we hear the sad contrast of Krapp's present tape. Subject and style have faded with the years.

Krapp begins as the younger Krapp began, by jeering at a still younger Krapp. In tough abrupt sentences, Krapp salvages a few details of memory, then gives himself orders. More frequently than in the earlier tape, Krapp refers to himself in the third person. Once we are involved with

Krapp, he proclaims his own detachment from himself through his use of the third person. Coming to the meager present, Krapp uses a heat-cold opposition that underlines the poignancy of his situation: "Crawled out once or twice, before the summer was cold. Sat shivering in the park, drowned in dreams and burning to be gone." Krapp completes a hymn that summarizes the play, as Didi's round song summarizes *Godot*, and Hamm's anecdote of the engraver summarized *Fin de partie*: "Now the day is over, / Night is drawing nigh, / Shadows of the evening / Steal across the sky." But through his imagination that is prodded by tapes, Krapp rebels against the shadows—a rebellion that is climaxed by a self-command, four times repeated: "Be again."

This is Krapp's ultimate order, which he cannot obey. No one can "be *again*," though once is never enough. Significantly, the order to be again is coupled with youthful memories that seem to predate Krapp's involvement with women or writing. His memories are immersed in nature—"in the dingle on a Christmas Eve . . . on Croghan on a Sunday morning." Even as an adult, Krapp recalls love in a scene of natural beauty.

Only in his third playback does Krapp react to the lyrical love scene of his thirty-ninth year. Only this third time does Krapp allow the tape to run to its end, in which he boldly claims that he would not want his best years back. The end of the replay is the end of Beckett's play, and it links the three Krapps: thirty-nine-year-old Krapp has mocked a younger Krapp thanking God that his youth was over, and he has commented: "False ring there." Sixty-nine-year-old Krapp has concluded his recording: "No, I wouldn't want [my best years] back." The pattern of Krapp's life, the pattern of his two tapes, belies the claim. Whatever his best years are, he does want earlier years back, and the tapes cannot bring them. Memory is not life, which is rather a series of successive selves, heard on tapes. Finally, even memory ceases, as the stage recorder tapes the stillness.

In 1969 Beckett directed a German translation of *Krapp's Last Tape* in the Werkstatt of Berlin's Schiller Theater. Working through the large tough frame of actor Martin Held, Beckett amplified his stage directions even while he simplified the stage picture. He pared the opening mime of clown suggestions, stressing the worn rather than the farcical quality of Krapp's clothes. He eliminated clown-business with keys and envelopes, but he added rheumatic fingers for fumbling. Krapp's first gesture was new and moving: Krapp hugs himself and shivers slightly—cold, lonely, lovelorn. Because of the poverty of business, the similarity between the sixty-nine- and the thirty-nine-year-old Krapp is more striking. The man whom we have seen eat two bananas tells us that he just ate three. The man whom we have seen step slowly from his spotlight into darkness tells us that he loves to return from the darkness to himself, Krapp. And yet sixty-nine-year-old Krapp looks in astonishment at the tape-recorder when he hears his voice saying: "Me. *(Pause.)* Krapp."

In building Krapp's role, Beckett gave some attention to triplets: At the beginning Krapp walks three times out of his spotlight into darkness and back. At the beginning Beckett has Krapp disappear backstage three times—for ledger, tapes, and tape-recorder. In the later action Beckett changes the three backstage disappearances for offstage drinking, for a dictionary, for offstage drinking and a microphone. Krapp consults his watch three times during the course of the play. After he records, he looks at the machine three times before he wrenches off his last tape. (He does not throw it away.)

During the course of the play Beckett often separated speech from movement. When Krapp moves about, he says nothing. But when taped speech is heard, Krapp listens with immobile intensity. Beckett made almost no changes in the dialogue, but he did add "That voice!" to Krapp's taped comment on his thirty-nine-year-old tape. "A kick in the crutch" was changed to "between thumb and index." The price of Krapp's book was omitted, and several mocking self-laughs were added.

Most of Beckett's changes made stage movement more precise. Krapp slams objects more frequently, and wordless murmurs accompany his discontent. His slouching walk is unbalanced. Before assuming the listening posture, Krapp looks over his right shoulder into the darkness. At the mention of Bianca, the girl in green, the nursemaid, the nameless love (three times), Krapp bends his head to the machine in the same intent way. In the most extended playing of the love scene—the second—Krapp's head sinks down upon the table. When he switches off, he hugs himself and shivers, as at the beginning. In his own recording, each "Be again" rises in intensity, but not in volume. Then Krapp strikes his head as he explodes: "Once wasn't enough for you." But he subsides into his final listening position, the same as at the start. Finally, the lights go out, and it is dark except for the tape-recorder light, the machine turning in silence.

Most of Beckett's memorable characters are old, but Krapp alone conveys the weight of his years. The play was inspired by Pat Magee's distinctive whispering voice with its evocation of unrelieved weariness. Roger Blin, who was to have taken the role in the original French production, bowed out because it made him feel too old. Martin Held, who was physically wrong for the part, seemed to shrink visibly by the end of his forty-five-minute performance. Jean Martin bordered on senility, with red eyes, twitching cheek, and drooling mouth. Old age assaults them all.

ENOCH BRATER

[Krapp's Last Tape] †

* * *

Krapp's Last Tape was written in early 1958 for the Irish actor Patrick Magee (an early draft of the piece is in fact labelled "Magee Mono-logue"). That October Donald McWhinnie's production opened at the Royal Court Theatre on a double-bill with George Devine's *Endgame*. Beckett thought Magee's interpretation of Krapp, which he saw during rehearsals in London, was "terrific." He said this was his "best experi-ence in theater ever." Set in Krapp's den, Beckett's scene for this play begins with a mime accompanied by a wry repertory of amplified sound effects: keys jingle, corks pop, drawers spring, hands rub, feet shuffle, a ledger thumps on a table, a banana peel slithers to the floor. A "wearish old man" heaves a heavy sigh, stumbles, and breathes with difficulty as he moves about this deliberately circumscribed space. But this time we see as well as hear; Beckett's script is now as complicated visually as it had previously been aurally. In this act without words the player's move-ment has been calculated to hold the stage with authority. Krapp looks at his watch, searches in his pockets, takes out an envelope, puts it back, fumbles again, takes out a small bunch of keys, raises it to his eyes, chooses a key, gets up and moves to front of table. He stoops, unlocks first drawer, peers into it, feels about inside of it, takes out a reel of tape, peers at it, puts it back, locks drawer, unlocks second drawer, peers into it, feels about inside it, takes out a large banana, peers at it, locks drawer, puts keys back in his pocket. He turns, advances to edge of stage, halts, strokes banana, peels it, drops skin at his feet, puts end of banana in his mouth and remains motionless, staring vacuously before him. Finally he bites off the end, turns aside and begins pacing to and fro, medita-tively eating the banana. He treads on skin, slips, nearly falls, recovers himself, stoops and peers at skin and finally pushes it, still stooping, with his foot over the edge of the stage into the pit. I am of course repeating

† From *Why Beckett* (London: Thames and Hudson, 1989).

Beckett's precise direction for enactment: his mime calls for the complete arrangement of a visual field in perfect harmony with acoustics that are so palpably—and electronically—rendered. In the opening moments of *Krapp's Last Tape* it's as though Beckett has almost succeeded in *visualizing* a radio play's soundscape. "The basic problem of both production and acting lies in the listening," observed Pierre Chabert, who played Krapp under Beckett's direction in Paris. "How can a play which is based on the act of listening be made to work in the theatre? How can the act of listening be dramatized?" "Listening is here communicated," Chabert elaborated, "by the look. It is literally the eye which is listening."

The sight-sound relations at the beginning of the play serve as a kind of prologue for all that is to follow. This is, after all, a performance text that will place its premium on sound. Krapp-at-69 searches for "box three . . . spool five," a tape of thirty years ago. But the occasion for that "old P.M." (post-mortem) was in a sense a reaction to yet another recording session dated a decade or so before, when Krapp was in his twenties: "Just been listening to an old year, passages at random," we hear along with Krapp. "Hard to believe I was ever that young whelp. The voice! Jesus! And the aspirations! . . . And the resolutions! . . . To drink less, in particular." In this play the irony involves three, not two, ages of man. On tape we hear Krapp chuckling at his younger self; onstage we see Krapp laughing bitterly at his recorded laugh. The protagonists in this action, however, are merely two voices: the one we hear recited live by the actor onstage, the other disembodied, but forever imprinted on magnetic tape which the same actor has prerecorded. When Krapp switches on his machine, the audience discovers him in a private act of listening. The sound of his younger voice evokes moments from a past which he experiences anew each time he listens to the tape. Proustian memory is made manifest, tangible, and real. The dynamics is both simple and pointed: we watch Krapp, and we listen with him. The image we see onstage, however, makes an explicit comment on everything that is heard as well as on everything that no longer needs to be said. On this platform every "retrospect" is literally seen in the bitter perspective framed by this mediating tableau. The play of voices therefore makes of an intangible past a concrete staged presence. When he picks up a reel of tape, Krapp can even hold his history in his hands. And what remains this time is not some "old stancher," but a "girl in a shabby green coat, on a railway-station platform." The darkness of Krapp's world, and of the audience's bleak horizon, is suddenly illuminated by a verbal image whose visual potential is far more riveting than anything we will see in this stubborn proscenium. A voiced-image on the voice-over defies time. It defines it, too: "The face she had! The eyes! Like . . . *hesitates* . . . chrysolite!" Beckett draws Krapp's simile from *Othello;* fragments from a dramatic past can still be reworked into fresh material for a new repertory. Language can always be counted on to resound in a human voice, the proper vehicle for stage dialogue.

In *Krapp's Last Tape* Beckett's lines still carry the inner determinacy of an Irish melody. Though the playwright once said that "the Krapp text has nothing to do with Dublin," it's Old Miss McGlome Krapp remembers singing ("Connaught, I fancy"); and Krapp's mother, like Beckett's, "lay-a-dying" in a house on a canal that *seems* to be Dublin's. Tired and drunk, this old boozer waxes lyrical. It's his birthday, that "awful occasion," after all: "Be again on Croghan on a Sunday morning, in the haze, with the bitch, stop and listen to the bells . . . Be again, be again." And sex with Fanny, the "bony old ghost of a whore" who "came in a couple of times," is still better than "a kick in the crutch." The Protestant hymn Krapp intones, "Now the day is over, / Night is drawing nigh," foreshadows a twilight that will be once again familiarly Celtic. Several critics have read the Irishness of *Krapp's Last Tape* in a distinctly autobiographical way, especially the "memorable night in March, at the end of the jetty, in the howling wind, never to be forgotten" (Krapp-at-39). On a visit to Ireland to see his mother Beckett is reported to have had some sort of insight on the wharf at Dun Laoghaire resembling his character's "vision, at last" about facing the darkness within. It was like "resolving to go naked," Beckett confided to one friend. To John Calder he said, somewhat apologetically, that it was "something like revelation." Krapp's "crest of the wave," however, is only "—or thereabouts," and Beckett is not Krapp. Whatever Beckett may have experienced on a Dublin wharf during a storm was certainly "less Wordsworthy," to quote from his own *Murphy.* Krapp-at-69 can't stand listening to this overblown passage anyway; the pretension, not to mention the romantic rhetoric of ⅃ landscape wallowing in the sublime (complete with lighthouse, foam, and obligatory granite rocks), is simply unbearable. When Krapp is forced to listen to "that stupid bastard" that was himself, he curses before switching off.

Krapp's Last Tape moves not only in time, but through time. Every second in the presentness of performance is quickly turning into Krapp's past. On his playback Krapp retrieves time; an image memorialized on tape resists mutability. That moment on the lake, in a punt, comes back more than once to "be again, be again," reifying and reasserting his existence in a frail attempt at communion:

I thought it was hopeless and no good going on, and she agreed, without opening her eyes. *(Pause.)* I asked her to look at me and after a few moments—*(pause)*—after a few moments she did, but the eyes just slits, because of the glare. I bent over her to get them in the shadow and they opened. *(Pause. Low.)* Let me in. *(Pause.)* We drifted in among the flags and stuck. The way they went down, sighing, before the stem! *(Pause.)* I lay down across her with my face in her breasts and my hand on her. We lay there without moving. But under us all moved, and moved us, gently, up and down, and from side to side.

Krapp is 69; he has long ago taped his "Farewell to love." This year, like so many others, there is not much news to report, just the "sour cud and the iron stool." The recording we see him make tonight, however, will be his very last tape. The voice from the past might be, finally, prophetic: this earth may soon be "uninhabited." Krapp stares motionless before him as "*the tape runs on in silence.*" Who will bother to listen to all those reels when he, too, is gone?

This play, of course, is set in the future. Beckett was worried that his critics might pick up on the fact that, thirty to forty years before 1958 (the date of composition for *Krapp's Last Tape*), there were indeed no tape recorders. He nearly called the work *Ah Well*, the sigh that adds a poetic refrain to so much in his actor's separate but related monologues. In his own production of the piece in Germany, *Das letzte Band*, Beckett decided to place the accent on lyricality by restricting the comic elements specified in his published text. Krapp's purple nose was gone, as was the emphasis on a clown's oversized boots (*"size ten at least"*). But to make sure that the atmosphere might never become maudlin, Beckett kept the slapstick routine of man and cosmic banana, a reassuring touch of humor in this otherwise somber work.

* * *

JOHN P. HARRINGTON

The Irish Beckett †

When *Waiting for Godot* was in its first productions, the matter of its universal and humanist or local and Irish import was an issue. Expec-

---

† From *The Irish Beckett*. (Syracuse: Syracuse UP, 1990). Printed courtesy of Syracuse University Press.

tation of local import was as axiomatic then as the humanistic image of Beckett is now. In Dublin the issue was of some particular interest because of the author's Irish portfolio and the general configuration of Irish drama in the 1950s around privileged regionalism, a.k.a. Peasant Quality. The case was not closed, as it has been since. *Godot* had affinities with modern Irish drama that were apparent to frequenters of the Abbey. But the play came from an author who in their memory had been branded in court a bawd and blasphemer from Paris, and the play left them, like others, with the enigma of Godot. A. J. Leventhal, who years later could be more decisive, presented the case without verdict in *The Dublin Magazine* on the occasion of The Pike Theatre's Dublin premiere of *Godot* in 1956. Familiar with the previous Paris and London productions, Leventhal took up the issue because "the real innovation in the Irish production lies in making the two tramps (Austin Byrne and Dermot Kelly faithfully efficient) speak with the accent of O'Casey's Joxer tempered by Myles na gCopaleen's 'Dubalin' man." Locally, at least, Leventhal wrote with the authority of personal familiarity: years later Denis Johnston, a notable omission from Beckett's memory of Dublin's drama of the late 1920s, would always refer to Leventhal as Beckett's secretary as Beckett had been Joyce's. Perhaps with support or on instructions from the author, Leventhal responded to the "Dubalin" accents somewhat imperiously: "It seemes [sic] evident that the author had in mind a universal rather than a regional application of his vision of mankind in perpetual expectation, desperately endeavouring to fill the hiatus between birth and death" (52). His sole printed rationale for that claim was that the names of the four characters indicate different nationalities. (It is interesting to note that Sigfried Unseld reports a luncheon with T. W. Adorno, who proposed the same theory of names in *Endgame*, and Beckett, who denied any such use of names in that play [93].) Responding to local hearsay, Leventhal observed in his review of the Dublin production of *Godot* that:

> Mr. Beckett's origin has caused the view to be widely accepted that the whole conception of *Waiting for Godot* is Irish, a fact which the original French has been unable to conceal, it is claimed. The Pike Theatre production lends support to this view, and it may well be that *Waiting for Godot* will go down in the local records as a lineal descendant of the works of the high literary kings of the Irish dramatic renascence. It is understood that there is a proposal to translate the play into Irish which would assist in bringing about a general acceptance here of this theory. Indeed later literary histori-

ans might align Mr. Beckett with George Moore, who, in his efforts to help in the revival of the Irish language, suggested that he might compose his work in French which could be translated into English for the convenience of the Gaelic Leaguers who would then, in their turn, have little difficulty in turning the text into Irish. (52–53)

In 1956 Leventhal only offered by way of verdict the speculation that "the point might be made that the effective use of local idiom would also be a proof of the universal applicability of the play since its intrinsic quality would lose nothing by the change" (52). That is wholly ambiguous, of course, if the point was made: if local idiom was a change, then it would prove little about the intrinsic quality of the play. In any case, the assumption of the strictly universal contexts of *Godot*, argued somewhat uneasily by Leventhal in 1956, eventually became as axiomatic in Ireland as elsewhere.

That axiom, though, needs examination. Production lore is replete with incidental evidence of Beckett's working links with Irish drama. A number of works were written for Irish actors; Beckett's favorite actors included a string of Irish ones; and Roger Blin's qualifications for the first Paris production of *Godot*, however universal its intention, seem to have included his previous appearance in a French production of *The Playboy of the Western World* (Bair 404). Irish actors, if they thought Beckett not Irish, thought he was something other than universal. Jack MacGowran was performing O'Casey's *The Shadow of a Gunman* in London when he was recruited for the BBC taping of *All That Fall*. "I didn't know then who Beckett was," MacGowran said. "I'd never heard of him. I thought he was a Frenchman whose work had been translated into English" (Young 52). Beckett, though, knew what to make of an Irish character actor like MacGowran. Beckett adds to these suggestive links his multiple tributes to Irish dramatists, his willing information about his formative encounters with productions of plays at the Abbey and Gate Theatres, and even use of fundamental local images in works like *Not I*: " 'I knew that woman in Ireland,' Beckett said, 'I knew who she was—not 'she' specifically, one single woman, but there were so many of those old crones, stumbling down the lanes, in the ditches, beside the hedgerows. Ireland is full of them. And I heard 'her' saying what I wrote in *Not I*. I actually heard it' " (Bair 622). None of this is to suggest that Samuel Beckett was aspiring to be an Abbey playwright. His relation to Irish theater in the 1950s was, rather, as impatient and as antagonistic as his dudgeon on Irish censorship in the 1930s. That was clear enough when he withdrew mimes from the 1958 Dublin Theatre Festival as part of a dispute provoked by the Archbishop of Dublin's disapproval of O'Casey's *The Drums of Father Ned* and of a stage adaptation of *Ulysses*. O'Casey and others managed to shut down the festival because of perceived censorship. Beckett's mimes were not generally missed, but he extended his own ban to productions of any of his works in Ireland. That lasted until 1960: "it is now time I fell off my high Eire moke" (Murray 108). Relation by antagonism is relation nonetheless. Specialized criticism of Beckett, assuming the universal frame of reference, and never entertaining MacGowran's assumption that the author was really French, often quite clearly contradicts that assumption or at least opens the way for qualification. In his formidable study *The Intent of Undoing in Samuel Beckett's Dramatic Texts*, S. E. Gontarski takes as problem the principle that "Beckett is unable to slough his literary past, the culturally coded forms of literature, as easily as he would like. As much as Beckett might resist the notion, he finds himself already written into the text of Western literature. In much of his creative process, he struggles to undo himself" (xiv). This is instructive and useful. There are niches of cultural forms within Western literature, though, and Gontarski's persuasive theory of Beckett's plays, undoing, also has reference to literary pasts and cultural codes more specific than Western literature.

In "the French period" Beckett's dramatic productions are, in a decade, two plays in French, *En attendent Godot* and *Fin de partie*, which he translated into English; two plays in English, *Krapp's Last Tape* and *Happy Days*, which he translated into French; and a pivotal radio play, *All That Fall*, in English, set in Ireland, and only translated into French by another hand. Beckett's novels, roughly contemporary with the same "period," are consistently about place and more often than not about Ireland. Drama differs from the maieutics of Beckett's narrative fiction in easy effacement of specific locale: it is more conducive, in the phrase of the narrator of *Watt*, to very interesting exercises. But those plays most effaced of geographically identifiable setting also refer to Ireland's features, such as Connemara in *Godot* or Connaught in *Krapp*. Like Beckett's novels, these plays also draw on more personal, autobiographical material, always Irish, like the revelation on the pier in Dun Laoghaire in *Krapp*. But such connections as have been made about Beckett's plays and Irish drama are often glosses of the sort that at this time of heightened awareness of the mechanics of cultural relativity can be taken as patronizing. Katherine Worth in *The Irish Drama of Europe*, for example, adds to the national definitions of Beckett: "an Irishman who lives in

France, writes with equal facility in French and English, regularly translates himself from one to the other and always keeps in his English an
Irish lilt" (241). In 1983 Hugh Kenner wrote that Beckett "is not Irish as
Irishness is defined today by the Free State" and that Beckett is instead
"willing to be the last Anglo-Irishman" (270).

Argument for the "Irishness" of Beckett's plays might take two tacks.
One would be examination of the Irish material in Beckett's plays,
including such as the helpfully flagged vision of the Irish crone in *Not I*
and also less obvious representations of action constructed in and refined
out of local material. Another would be examination of the place of
Beckett's plays in Irish drama, of, in Gontarski's terms, the plays' relations to culturally coded forms of literature distinctly Irish. There is
interesting secondary evidence for this argument. When the Irish-language version of *Godot* promised by Leventhal finally materialized for
two nights in 1971, the *Irish Times* reviewer of *Ag Fanacht Le Godot*
offered the opinion, in Irish, that "Until I saw *Godot* in Irish I didn't
properly understand how exactly Beckett takes hold of the Irish literary
heritage" (Murray 107 n9)—the literary heritage, that is, rather than the
general cultural heritage.

Contemporary with the admission of Beckett's works such as *More
Pricks Than Kicks* into Irish studies was an Irish Theatre Company production of *Godot* in 1982 accompanied by revivals of Yeats's *On Baile's
Strand* and Synge's *The Well of the Saints*. The artistic director of the
company announced its thesis that "these plays show Irish drama as
firmly rooted in the European tradition" (Murray 121). The subject of
Katherine Worth's book was a strain in modern Irish drama derived from
the Continent, usually in circumnavigation of England, as represented
by Wilde, Synge, Yeats, and O'Casey, all leading to Beckett. This is a
select list of Irish playwrights, and it has in mind a selection of their
works, but it is a provocative selection. Synge, Yeats, and O'Casey are
the names most prominent in Beckett's own memories of the Abbey
Theatre in his student days. For a gallery catalogue, *Samuel Beckett: An
Exhibition*, Beckett offered to James Knowlson the information that the
Irish dramas most vivid in his memory were "several" of O'Casey's plays,
Yeats's plays including but not limited to two Sophocles "versions," "most"
productions of Synge in the late 1920s, and two plays by Lennox Robinson (22–23). Shaw appeared in Beckett's comments as a negative aside,
and Beckett's well-known response to a request for a tribute to Shaw,
also recorded in Knowlson's catalogue, brought forth again a preference
for specific works by Yeats, Synge, and O'Casey: "What I would do is
give the whole unupsettable applecart for a sup of the Hawk's Well, or

the Saints', or a whiff of Juno, to go no further" (23). As he was selective in his praise for Yeats's poetry and the state of Irish writing in "Recent Irish Poetry" in 1934, so Beckett was selective on these later dates in reference to Irish drama. Those names—Yeats, Synge, and O'Casey— may at this date seem a fairly comprehensive compendium, but a reading of Joseph Holloway's theater diaries from the late 1920s gives a corrective sense of the great mass of productions that go unmentioned by Beckett. Certainly, those recollections owe something to the moment of the question, which as posed by Knowlson was forty years or so after the fact. But they also point to the degree to which Beckett's plays constitute an extension of one strain in Irish drama, a strain most antithetical to a local dramatic "realism," and a strain generally ignored by the Abbey in the years between first productions of that trinity of Irish playwrights and of Beckett. That gap in time, between the 1920s and the 1950s, helps account for the interesting local effect of Beckett's dramatic work as retroactive influence. Beckett's plays help extricate a strain in the national drama for a time obscured. That retroactive action is evident in the new proposals for ideal programs of Irish plays lately offered by many critics. John Rees Moore would join *The Cat and the Moon* with *Godot* (246); Worth would join *Godot* with *The Well of the Saints* or *At the Hawk's Well* with *Endgame* (260); Robin Skelton would join *The Shadow of the Glen, Juno and the Paycock,* and *Godot* (63). For better or worse, these groupings shift the canon of Irish drama, alter the sense of individual plays, and suggest that the exclusively universal "application," as Leventhal said of *Godot,* may be arbitrary.

Works Cited

Bair, Dierdre. *Samuel Beckett: A Biography.* New York: Harcourt Brace Jovanovich, 1978.
Gontarski, S. E. *The Intent of Undoing in Samuel Beckett's Dramatic Texts.* Bloomington: Indiana UP, 1985.
Kenner, Hugh. *A Colder Eye: The Modern Irish Writers.* New York: Knopf, 1983.
Knowlson, James. *Samuel Beckett: An Exhibition.* London: Turret Books, 1971.
Leventhal, A. J. "Dramatic Commentary." *The Dublin Magazine* ns 31.1 (1956): 52–54.
Moore, John Rees. *Masks of Love and Death: Yeats as Dramatist.* Ithaca: Cornell UP, 1971.
Murray, Christopher. "Beckett Productions in Ireland: A Survey." *Irish University Review* 14.1 (1984): 103–25.
Skelton, Robin. *The Writings of J. M. Synge.* Indianapolis: Bobbs-Merrill, 1971.
Unseld, Siegfried. "To the Utmost: To Samuel Beckett on His Eightieth Birthday." *As No Others Dare Fail: For Samuel Beckett on His Eightieth Birthday By His Friends and Admirers.* New York: Riverrun, 1986. 91–95.
Worth, Katherine. *The Irish Drama of Europe from Yeats to Beckett.* Atlantic Highlands: Humanities Press, 1978.
Young, Jordan R. *The Beckett Actor: Jack MacGowran, Beginning to End.* Beverly Hills: Moonstone Press, 1987.

Brian Friel

FIELD DAY THEATRE COMPANY

[Program Notes for *Translations*] †

Extract from The Hedge Schools of Ireland *by P. J. Dowling*

'The Hedge Schools owed their origin to the suppression of all the ordinary legitimate means of education, first during the Cromwellian regime and then under the Penal Code introduced in the reign of William III and operating from that time till within less than twenty years from the opening of the nineteenth century . . .

'The Hedge Schools were clearly of peasant institution. They were maintained by the people who wanted their children educated; and they were taught by men who came from the people . . .

'The poorest and humblest of the schools gave instruction in reading, writing and arithmetic; Latin, Greek, Mathematics and other subjects were taught in a great number of schools; and in many cases the work was done entirely through the medium of the Irish language. Though the use of the vernacular was rapidly falling into decay during the eighteenth century, it was owing to the greater value of English on the fair and market rather than to any shifting of ground on the part of the schools . . .

'The Hedge Schools were the most vital force in popular education in Ireland during the eighteenth century. They emerged in the nineteenth century more vigorous still, outnumbering all other schools, and so profoundly national as to hasten the introduction of a State system of education in 1831 . . .'

† Courtesy Field Day Theatre Company.

Extract from The Autobiography of William Carleton *(born in County Tyrone, 1794):*–

'The only place for giving instruction was a barn. The barn was a loft over a cowshed and stable . . . It was one of the largest barns in the parish.

'(At the age of fourteen) I had only got as far as Ovid's *Metamorphoses*, Justin, and the first chapter of John in the Greek Testament.'

Extract from the memoirs of the Reverend Mr Alexander Ross, Rector, Dungiven, County Derry. 1814:–

'Even in the wildest districts, it is not unusual to meet with good classical scholars; and there are several young mountaineers of the writer's acquaintance, whose knowledge and taste in the Latin poets, might put to the blush many who have all the advantages of established schools and regular instruction.'

Extract from A History of Ireland *by Edmund Curtis:*–

'In 1831 Chief Secretary Stanley introduced a system of National Education . . . The system became a great success as an educational one but it had fatal effects on the Irish language and the old Gaelic tradition. According to Thomas Davis, at this time the vast majority of the people living west of a line drawn from Derry to Cork spoke nothing but Irish daily and east of it a considerable minority. It seems certain that at least two millions used it as their fireside speech . . . But the institution of universal elementary schools where English was the sole medium of instruction, combined with the influence of O'Connell, many of the priests, and other leaders who looked on Irish as a barrier to progress, soon made rapid inroads on the native speech . . .'

Extract from Ordnance Survey of Ireland *by Thomas Colby, Colonel, Royal Engineers (1835.):*–

'To carry on a minute Survey of all Ireland no collection of ready instructed surveyors would have sufficed. It, therefore, became indispensable to train and organise a completely new department for the purpose. Officers and men from the corps of Royal Engineers formed the basis of this new organisation, and very large numbers of other persons possessing various qualifications, were gradually added to them to expedite the great work . . .

'The mode of spelling the names of places was peculiarly vague and unsettled, but on the maps about to be constructed it was desirable to establish a standard orthography, and for future reference, to identify the several localities with the names by which they had formerly been called . . .'

Extract from the Spring Rice Report (advocating a general survey of Ireland) to the British Government; 21 June 1824:—

'The general tranquillity of Europe, enables the state to devote the abilities and exertions of a most valuable corps of officers to an undertaking, which, though not unimportant in a military point of view, recommends itself more directly as a civil measure. Your committee trust that the survey will be carried on with energy, as well as with skill, and that it will, when completed, be creditable to the nation, and to the scientific acquirements of the present age. In that portion of the Empire to which it more particularly applies, it cannot but be received as a proof of the disposition of the legislature to adopt all measures calculated to advance the interests of Ireland.'

Extracts from the letters of John O'Donovan, a civilian employee with the Ordnance Survey, later Professor of Celtic Studies, Queen's College, Belfast:—

Buncrana
23 August 1835
'On Friday we travelled through the Parish of Clonmany and ascended the Hill of Beinnin. Clonmany is the most Irish Parish I have yet visited; the men only, who go to markets and fairs, speak a little English, the women and children speak Irish only. This arises from their distance from Villages and Towns and from their being completely environed by mountains, which form a gigantic barrier between them and the more civilized and less civil inhabitants of the lower country.'

Dun Fionnchada? Dun Fionnchon?
Dunfanaghy
9 September 1835
'I am sick to death's door of the names on the coast, because the name I get from one is denied by another of equal intelligence and authority to be correct. The only way to settle these names would be to summon a Jury and order them to say and present 'uppon ther Oathes" what these

names are and ought to be. But there are several of them such trifling places that it seems to me that it matters not which of two or three appelations we give them. For example, the name Timlin's Hole is not of thirty years standing and will give way to another name as soon as that dangerous hole shall have swallowed a fisherman of more illustrious name than Tim Lyn.'

Glenties
15 October 1835
'Yesterday being a fair-day at Dunglow we were obliged to leave it in consequence of the bustle and confusion. We directed our course southwards through the Parish of Templecroan, keeping Traigh Eunach (a name which I find exceedingly difficult to Anglicise) to the right . . . On the road we met crowds of the women of the mountains who were loaded with stockings going to the stocking fair of Dunglow and who bore deep graven on their visages the effects of poverty and smoke, of their having been kept alive by the potatoe only . . . I have seen several fields of oats on this coast, some prostrated and rotting, others with the grain completely blown off the stalk—and some so green in October as to preclude the possibility of ripening at all.'

Ballyshanny
1 November 1835
'I have met in this town a fine old man named Edward Quin, from whom I have received a good deal of information. He has been employed by Lieutenant Vickers to give the Irish names of places about Ballyshannon, and has saved me a good deal of trouble—I wish you could induce Mr Vickers to take him to his next district, and keep him employed writing in the Name Books, and taking down the names from the pronounciation of the country people.'

DESMOND RUSHE

Derry *Translations* †

Derry is an ancient and storied city. Its history can be traced back to 546 when the great St. Colmcille, or Columba, founded a monastery at a

---

† Reprinted by permission of the author and *Eire-Ireland* from *Eire-Ireland*, Winter 1980. *Eire-Ireland* is the publication of the Irish American Cultural Institute, St. Paul, Minnesota.

place called Doire Calgaich, or "Calgach's oak-wood," close to the River Foyle. Today, more than fourteen centuries later, its name in English is Derry or Londonderry, largely depending on the political persuasion of the user. The Doire Calgaich monastery thrived. Indeed, it was of such importance in the 12th century that it replaced Kells, County Meath, as the metropolis of the chain of monasteries established by St. Colmcille's followers. In 1566, Derry was the scene of a fierce battle between Seán the Proud O'Neill and the English, and, in 1608, Sir Cahir O'Doherty attacked and destroyed the English garrison. And then, in 1613, King James I magnanimously granted Derry and a vast tract of adjacent estates to the citizens of London. The London companies laid out a new city on the banks of the Foyle and planted the surrounding land with Protestant settlers. Derry had become Londonderry.

In the war between the Royalists and Parliamentarians in the 1640s, Derry sided with the latter. In the struggle between the Jacobites and the Williamites in the 1680s, it staunchly supported William of Orange. A long and celebrated siege by Jacobite forces was broken on July 28, 1689, and is now annually commemorated by Apprentice Boys' marches. Down all the years, Doire, or Derry, or Londonderry, has witnessed divisions—political, cultural, religious, social. It witnesses them today.

What has all this to do with theatre? A great deal. For, on a mellow Autumn evening, Derry's Guildhall was the scene of a quite remarkable theatrical event which, at its thematic core, explored those conflicting elements etched in the city's long and turgid history. The occasion was the première of a new play by Ireland's outstanding playwright, Brian Friel. The venue was the often bombed center of civic administration— a setting, incidentally, used by Friel in his Bloody Sunday play *The Freedom of the City*. A new theatre company called Field Day—founded by Mr. Friel with Belfast-born actor, Stephen Rea—was making its debut, and there was *no* evidence of a sectarian divide in a distinguished audience. There was a generous sprinkling of artists, playwrights, poets, critics, novelists, church dignitaries and politicans from Dublin, Belfast, London and elsewhere, and the atmosphere was charged with emotion, and not a little pride, because a world première was being staged, and the author was an international figure who had once taught school in Derry. There were tears shed during the performance, and the standing ovation at the end was initiated by the Unionist lord mayor.

Translations is set in a Donegal hedge school and the time is August, 1833. It is written in the English language, yet seven of the ten characters speak in their native tongue, which is Irish. The suggestion of a paradox here does not intrude: there is no linguistic confusion on the part of the audience, for Mr. Friel is a very excellent craftsman and there is no difficulty in accepting that the language spoken is, where necessary, Irish. There are two important points in the play's construction. One is that a new system of national education introduced by the English will make the hedge school redundant and wean Irish speakers away from their native tongue. Another is that the first Ordnance Survey map of Ireland is being prepared under the control of the military, and old and untranslatable Irish placenames are being Anglicized. A culture is in a state of transition, in the process of being absorbed, and traditional values are being disturbed creating an identification dilemma. The conflict postulated by Mr. Friel still exists, unresolved. The scene, set in a Donegal townland close to 150 years ago, has a peculiar relevance to community divisions that exist today. The point was not missed by Derry audiences.

The play has historical, social, and cultural connotations, but it is also human, and, in one scene, beautifully and delicately so. A young English army officer on Ordnance Survey duty falls in love with the quiet, dreamy countryside, and also with a young peasant girl. Mr. Friel involves them in a love scene which is remarkable. He can talk only in English, which she does not understand, and she can speak in Irish, and haltingly in Latin, both of which are meaningless to him. But they articulate through the universal language of eyes and heart. It is a jewel of a scene, and significant threads lead to and from it. The girl has expressed a desire to learn English, because she hopes to emigrate to America. The boy later disappears, murdered perhaps by a jealous rival, and his commanding officer promises brutal reprisals if he is not found. Some of Mr. Friel's interweaving elements are there: an ancient tongue in decay, an imposed and resented authority, violence. The brief idyll of innocent love stands out.

To what extent a lack of knowledge of the Ireland of the 1830s may inhibit appreciation of the play is debatable. The hedge school, a unique phenomenon, flourished because education had been proscribed under pain of vicious penalty by the Penal Laws. In the hedge school, elementary subjects such as reading, writing and arithmetic were taught, and then, as a general rule, there was an extraordinary preoccupation with Greek and Roman classicism. The Donegal peasant in Mr. Friel's play is as familiar with the flashing-eyed Athene of Greek mythology as with the Grainne of Irish legend. While the master and his students cannot speak English, they can converse in the languages of Homer and Virgil. They know nothing of Shakespeare, but they can quote Ovid. While this is an authentic reflection of how things were, it may raise questions of dramatic credibility. Indeed, it already has raised an objection which also has much to do with injured ethnic pride. The critic of the London *Sunday Times* referred to the fact that the English officers "were unable to translate, let alone distinguish between, the classical languages and Gaelic," and he later added:

> I would have believed more readily in the historical accuracy of the picture had the English officers been less oafishly unlatined. As it was, I took the piece as a vigorous example of corrective propaganda: immensely enjoyable as theatre if, like much else in Ireland, gleamingly tendentious.

Perhaps Mr. Friel should have taken some license in relation to historical accuracy as a sop to the sensitivities of English critics. As it is, his splendid and incisive work is hardly likely to have the doors of London theatres flung open to it.

SEAMUS HEANEY

[Review of *Translations*] †

Brian Friel's *Translations*, which has just finished its very successful run at the Dublin Theatre Festival, plays elaborate variations on an old theme. Perhaps Joyce stated it most succinctly in the classic passage towards the end of *A Portrait of the Artist* where the English Jesuit confuses Stephen Dedalus by calling a tundish a funnel, and Stephen goes on to meditate on the consequences of the language shift in Ireland from Irish to English: "The language we are speaking is his before it is mine . . . my soul frets in the shadow of his language". For a moment Joyce allows Stephen to indulge the myth of dispossession, though he is careful to allow him another, steelier moment when Stephen tells Davin that his people threw off their own language willingly.

The play is set in Irish-speaking Donegal in the 1830s, at a time when the dispossession or abandonment began to accelerate. A corps of the Royal Engineers is at work on the Ordnance Survey of Ireland, anglicizing and standardizing the place-names—"making sense" of them. Captain Lancey and Lieutenant Yolland are being assisted in their work by Owen, son of the local hedge-schoolmaster, Hugh O'Donnell, while being resented by his other son, Manus. Yolland falls for Manus's fian-

† ". . . English and Irish," *TLS* 24 Oct. 1980, p. 1199. Reprinted by permission of the author and The Times Literary Supplement.

cée (or perhaps one should translate this to his "intended"), tribal lines
get tangled and things fall apart.

Traditional characters (redcoat soldier, shawled girl, hedge-schoolmaster—this last a drily realized portrait by Ray McAnally) and traditional motifs (eviction, potato-blight, poteen) are woven together with a
mixture of irony and elegy. Friel knows that there were certain inade-
quacies within the original culture that unfitted it to survive the impact
of the English presence and domination, but the play is not simply a
historical entertainment. What the schoolmaster says to Lieutenant Yolland in Act 2 is symptomatic of Friel's vigilant concern with the way we
still use language in Ireland (and in England?). "It can happen that a
civilization can be imprisoned in a linguistic contour that no longer
matches the landscape of fact."

In the 1830s the landscape of fact included the new National Schools
where the instruction was free and in English, but Friel's scene is a
hedge-school—a kind of fit-up classical academy—where the first language is Irish, although Latin and Greek are to be heard almost as frequently. We do not hear Irish on the stage, of course—and that "of
course" tells us how successful the National School system was—yet
once the English soldiers arrive we understand that it is the language of
the Donegal characters, because Owen, the son who has arrived back
from Dublin with them, begins to act as go-between and interpreter.
This allows Friel to show, at times comically and at times angrily, that
there are still two kinds of speech within what appears to be a common
language shared by the two islanders. It also allows him to show Owen
assisting in the annihilation of the place he came from as he translates
the place-names into English and literally changes the map.

Owen (played with brio and a proper bewilderment by Stephen Rea)
is a key figure in the dispossession / abandonment uncertainty. His brother
Manus sees him as a betrayer, his father, more cautiously, sees him as
a kind of success, and he cannot quite manage to see himself. Significantly, he cannot settle for a name: he is Owen to the natives but his
soldier friends call him Roland and he does not quite deny them their
mistake. There is a lovely moment at the end when the place-names he
has anglicized are read out by Captain Lancey in their new versions and
Owen must translate them back into Irish for the benefit of his neighbours. It is a list of places that the army is now intent on devastating in
retaliation for the presumed killing of Lieutenant Yolland. The betrayer
is betrayed.

Brian Friel has by now [1980] produced a more significant body of
work than any other playwright in Ireland, and it is time that he was, as

it were, translated. I am sure this piece would come home like a remembrance in, for example, Derek Walcott's theatre in Trinidad. His recent plays—*Aristocrats* and *Faith healer* last year, and now *Translations*— show him in the grip of a major theme. He has come in from different angles but with a constant personal urgency upon the need we have to create enabling myths of ourselves and the danger we run if we too credulously trust to the sufficiency of these myths. In the opening moment of *Translations*, a girl who has been mute is being taught by Manus to say: "My name is Sarah". Nothing can stop her now, Manus assures her, she can say who she is so she is safe. Towards the end of the play, however, when the English captain demands who she is, his command and strangeness scare her: "My name . . . my name is . . ." is all she can manage. It is as if some symbolic figure of Ireland from an eighteenth-century vision poem, the one who once confidently called herself Cathleen Ni Houlihan, has been struck dumb by the shock of modernity. Friel's work, not just here but in his fourteen preceding plays, constitutes a powerful therapy, a set of imaginative exercises that give her the chance to know and say herself properly to herself again.

RICHARD KEARNEY

[*Translations*] †

* * *

In the second act of *[Translations]*, Friel provides us with two dramatic instances of translation. The first is a translation of labour (between Owen and Yolland); the second a translation of love (between Yolland and Máire).

The act opens with Yolland and Owen, bent over a Name Book and large map, embarked upon their task of transposing the Gaelic toponymy of Baile Beag into an English alternative. The translation of names also involves a translation of namers—the roles of colonizer and colonized are reversed, as Yolland and Owen undergo an exchange of identity.

While Owen is patently engrossed by the mapping process, Yolland is lost in a world of dreams, savouring each Gaelic word upon his tongue, reluctant to 'traduce' it into its Anglo-Saxon equivalent. So that when Owen offers the practical suggestion of rendering *Bun na hAbhann* (in

---

† From *Transitions: Narratives in Modern Irish Culture* by Richard Kearney (Dublin: Wolfhound Press, 1988). Reprinted by permission of Wolfhound Press.

Irish, mouth of the river) as *Burnfoot*, Yolland's reaction is one of protective deference towards the original: 'Let's leave it alone. There's no English equivalent for a sound like that'. But it is not just the sound that is at stake. It is the stored heritage of local history which each Gaelic name recollects and *secretes*. The translation of these placenames closes off rather than discloses their mnemonic secrets, distorts their former meaning.

Yolland describes his first encounter with the Gaelic language as a quasi-mystical revelation. The linguistic divide is experienced by him as a threshold demarcating fundamentally heterogeneous modes of consciousness. He speaks of discovering a new continent of feeling, one belonging to 'a totally different order. I had moved into a consciousness that wasn't striving nor agitated, but at its ease and with its own conviction and assurance'.

But the threshold is also a frontier. It cannot be crossed with impunity, as Yolland will discover to his cost. Already he has intimations of the impenetrable barrier of words which no translation, however well-intentioned, can traverse. 'Even if I did speak Irish', concedes Yolland, 'I'd always be an outsider here, wouldn't I? I may learn the password but the language of the tribe will always elude me, won't it? The private core will always be . . . hermetic, won't it?' Owen's reassuring rejoinder—'you can learn to decode us'—has an ominous ring, its scarcely veiled sarcasm reflecting his private complicity with his own native tribe. In short the commercial collusion between Planter and Gael cannot be immunized against the cultural-linguistic conflict which opposes them.

If language unites people by permitting communication, it divides them by cultivating the possibility of separate tribal identities. This paradox is a heritage of the *felix culpa* of our first parents: their fall from the edenesque *Logos* which enabled God and man to speak with one voice. And this original sin of language—the sin of speaking in a multiplicity of conflicting tongues—finds its ultimate nemesis in the subsequent biblical account of the Tower of Babel.

*   *   *

Yolland cannot help recognizing that the whole business of toponymic translation constitutes an 'eviction of sorts': an 'erosion' of the traditional Gaelic pieties in the name of Imperial progress. But Yolland's disapproval is counterbalanced by his naive belief that there might exist an ideal system of translation where the obstacles thrown up by tribal dialects could be transcended. Yolland is hankering after a prelapsarian naming process, similar to that of Adam when he named the animals, capable of achieving an exact correspondence between word and thing. When Owen finally confesses to Yolland that his real name is not *Rolland* but *Owen*—or better still *Oland* by way of a perfect compromise between the nominal differences of Irish (Owen) and English (Yolland)—they celebrate their newfound confraternity of naming:

> *Owen:*   A christening! . . .
> *Yolland:* A thousand baptisms! Welcome to Eden!
> *Owen:*   Eden's right! We name a thing and—bang!—it leaps into existence!
> *Yolland:* Each name a perfect equation with its roots.
> *Owen:*   A perfect congruence with its reality. Take a drink.
> *Yolland:* Poteen—beautiful.
> *Owen:*   Lying Anna's poteen.
> *Yolland:* Anna na mBraeg's poteen. . . . I'll decode it yet'.

Once again, Friel reminds us that the magical equation of word and world is achieved by the power of a lie! The fact that Owen and Yolland consecrate their new transliteral unity (as *Oland*) with Anna's illusionist brew is itself a hint of the disillusioning reality to follow.

Friel juxtaposes this 'translation of labour' sequence between Owen and Yolland with a scene featuring a 'translation of love' between Yolland and Máire. In this second exchange Friel highlights the impossibility of attaining an ideal system of language capable of decoding semantic differences into some common transcultural identity. Yolland and Máire meet at the local dance. Ever since Yolland arrived in the village they have been admiring each other from a distance. Now at last together they try to transcend this distance, stealing away to the fields so that they might communicate their mutual love. But if their love is mutual their dialect is not. Máire begins by speaking Latin which Yolland mistakes for Gaelic. Then she stammers forth the only three English words in her possession—water, fire, earth. But even though Yolland congratulates Máire on her 'perfect English', his lie of encouragement cannot alter the fact that they continually misunderstand each other's words. Finally they do appear to reach some level of communication by lovingly reciting to each other the litany of Gaelic placenames. The irony is of course that this source of semantic agreement is precisely the issue which so tragically divides their respective tribes. Their commonly uttered words still consign them to separate worlds as Friel himself indicates in a textual note: 'Each now speaks almost to himself / herself'. (One recalls Frank's and Grace's equally discrepant invocation of place-names in

[Friel's] *Faith Healer*). As each name is intoned by one lover and anti-phonally echoed by the other, they move closer together and embrace. This climactic touch serves as a sort of leitmotif reiterating the opening exchange between Manus and Sarah. The order is reversed, however, in so far as speech now becomes touch whereas in the former scene touch had become speech.

When Yolland and Máire finally kiss, their moment of loving silence is no more than a provisional reprieve from the decree of language. Sarah enters; and shocked by what she witnesses she rushes off calling out the name of Máire's suitor—'Manus!'. Thus in a cruel twist of dra-matic fortunes, Sarah's initial transition from silence to speech—her initiation into the naming process in the opening love scene between herself and Manus—becomes the condition for the betrayal of love.

According to the local code, Máire has been promised to Manus and this tacit tribal contract cannot be gainsaid or 'decoded' by an outsider—even in an act of love. As Jimmy Jack explains in his final speech, enun-ciating his own fictitious betrothal to the Goddess Athene: 'The word *exogamein* means to marry outside the tribe. And you don't cross those borders casually—both sides get very angry. Now, the problem is this: Is Athene sufficiently mortal or am I sufficiently godlike for the marriage to be acceptable to her people and to my people?'. Whatever about trans-gressing the mythological boundaries between the human and the divine, the real boundaries between one human code and another cannot be ignored with impunity. Yolland is assassinated by the Donnelly twins—renegade pupils from the hedge school; and Captain Lancey promises retribution on the whole community—he orders their livestock to be slaughtered and their abodes levelled.

Friel's irony excels itself at this point: Lancey's threat to destroy the very locality which his own Ordnance Survey was proposing to civilize and advance, renders the whole 'translation' process null and void. Nominal eviction has been replaced by its literal equivalent. This rever-sal of plot also extends to a reversal of character. Summoned before a local gathering, Owen is now compelled to give a literal translation of Lancey's punitive intentions, his compromising role as go-between now made embarrassingly plain. For the dubious benefit of his own tribe, Owen is forced to *retranslate* Lancey's English rendition of the names of the local villages to be destroyed back into their Gaelic originals. Owen's own labour of words has backfired; he is hoist with his own petard.

Máire also becomes a victim of this reverse play of language. Exposed in the abrupt polarization of the two rival tribes, she can no longer feel at home in her own community and yet has no other home to go to now that Yolland is dead. Employing again his dramatic technique of reverse repetition, Friel reinvokes the idiom of mapping to emphasize Máire's dilemma. Tracing out an imaginary map on that very spot on the hedge school floor where Owen's Ordnance Survey map had been spread, she lists off the placenames of Yolland's native Norfolk which he had taught her to recite during their love-duet the previous night—Winfarthing, Barton, Bendish, Saxingham etc. 'Nice sounds', she muses, as Yolland had done before her with reference to Gaelic names, 'just like Jimmy Jack reciting Homer'. But there is a fundamental difference between the recitation of Jimmy Jack and that of Máire and Yolland. Since the Greeks had no historic quarrel with the Gaels their two tongues could peacably conjugate in a way that English and Gaelic cannot. In one particularly striking moment, Máire recalls that Yolland's parting message to her was in fact a mistranslation: 'He tried to speak in Irish, he said—'I'll see you yesterday'—he meant to say, 'I'll see you tomorrow'.' This mistranslation is a poignant signal of the fact that in the colonial conflict between England and Ireland the time was out of joint. In such a context, linguistic discrepancies are the inevitable consequence of historical ones.

These reversals of *plot, persona,* and *time,* are reinforced by a more generalized reversal of *perception.* The disarticulation of language brought about by the various abortive attempts at translation, also expresses itself at the level of the characters' distorted perception of the world about them. The last scene of the play is littered with misidentifications, on a par with the most convoluted comedies of Wilde or Shakespeare. Manus, who flees to Mayo, is mistaken for the assassins (the Donnellys); the fumes from the burning army tents are mistaken for the sweet smell of potato blight; Doalty is mistaken for the arsonist; a bacon-curing schoolmaster from Cork is mistaken for the village schoolmaster, Hugh—the National school replacing the old hedge school; and the anglicized Owen is mistaken for (in the sense of taking over from) his inveterately Gaelic brother, Manus, as faithful son to their father, Hugh.

All these instances of displacement consolidate Friel's message about the mis-taken substitution of Irish by English. But Friel, like Hugh, recognizes that this mistake is an irreversible, if regrettable, inevitability of history. 'We like to think we endure around truths immemorially posited', Hugh explains with rueful wisdom, 'but we remember that words are signals, counters. They are not immortal. And it can happen . . . that a civilization can be imprisoned in a linguistic contour which no longer matches the landscape of . . . fact'. The rich mytho-poetic resources of the Gaelic tongue, Hugh adds, were themselves a response to the painful historical circumstances which conditioned its development: 'Yes, it is a rich language . . . full of mythologies of fantasy and hope and self-deception—a syntax opulent with tomorrows. It is our response to mud cabins and a diet of potatoes; our only method of replying to . . . inevitabilities'. Thus in stoical acknowledgement that what is done cannot be undone, Hugh determines to make a virtue of necessity by creatively refashioning the English language so as to make sense of the new landscape of historical fact. At one point Owen tries to revoke the repercussions of translation, dismissing the whole sorry business as '*my* mistake—nothing to do with us'. But Hugh has had enough of self-deception. Pointing to the Name Book, he counsels his community to reclaim in and through the English language that which has been lost to it. 'We must learn those new names', he soberly challenges, 'we must learn to make them our own, we must make them our new home'.

* * *

ERIC BINNIE

[Friel and Field Day] †

In the ancient and troubled frontier city of Derry, Brian Friel established the Field Day Theatre Company in 1980. He was joined in this bold endeavour by a number of other artists, including the actor Stephen Rea and the poet Seamus Heaney. All of the Board of Directors are Northerners. Their motives, in founding the new company, were to reappraise the political and cultural situation in Northern Ireland as it affects the whole of Ireland. They aim to examine and analyze the established opinions, slogans, myths and war-cries which have gone to the creation of the present troubles in Ireland. Like Brecht's Galileo in his final exchange with Andrea, perhaps like Brecht himself in his final years, on a not dissimilar frontier, Friel and his fellow directors clearly believe that there can, indeed, be a new age, despite all the evidence to the contrary.

The name Field Day has several implications—a day spent away from normal activities, a day spent outdoors, a sports day, a festival, a brawl, and, for example, in such popular usage, as "the critics had a field day," it suggests the chance to assert oneself to the fullest and most triumphant

† "Brecht and Friel," *Modern Drama* 31.3 (1988):365–70. Reprinted by permission of *Modern Drama*, University of Toronto.

or pleasurable extent. In terms of famous paintings, one thinks of Breughel's rustic holidays, the topsy-turvy world of periodic and necessary excess by which means rampant vitality is contained—a safety valve on the darker, less manageable energies of the people. Brian Friel has chosen the title Field Day wisely, having in mind most of the implications just listed. It is a theatre company which flourishes defiantly in the face of a grim, relentless, daily existence; festive, certainly, but also portentous.

Just as Brecht chose to create his ensemble company right on the border between East and West, in order fully to exploit each side's fears and suspicions of the other in ways which were, ultimately, uniquely creative, so Friel founded his company in the strife-torn city of Derry, right on the edge of British Ireland, artificially cut off from its hinterland of Donegal, now in the Republic (Southern Ireland). During his East Berlin years Brecht used the paradoxical invulnerability provided by the East / West dichotomy to create a theatrical system which now rightly bears his name. Brechtian theatre, or dialectical theatre, became a mature form during these frontier years. As yet, Brian Friel's plays are too diverse in form to be compared to Brecht's later works, yet they may be comparable, in terms of their similar origins on border locations, which are, by their very nature, dialectical.

The aims of Field Day Theatre Company are to create a shared context which might make possible communication across Ireland's border; to give all Irishmen an artistic "fifth province" rising above and covering the whole island, an hypothetical province which would neither accept the North / South division, nor ignore the separate traditional strengths of those on either side.[1] Thus Field Day is located in the North (British Ireland) and works in both North and South, yet has strong reservations about both. The intention is to create an awareness, a sense of the whole country, North and South together, and to examine predominant attitudes to the island as a whole. Friel's artistic development since the formation of Field Day has moved steadily towards a closer integration of historical considerations and contemporary themes, achieved, for example, by examining the role of language as a reflection of national character. He expresses this concern for language in the statement, "We [Irish playwrights] are talking to ourselves as we must, and if we are overheard in America or England, so much the better."[2]

Friel sees contemporary Ireland as being in a state of uneasy confu-

1. Quoted in Ulf Dantanus, Brian Friel: The Growth of an Irish Dramatist (Goteborg, 1985), p. 170.

2. " 'Talking to Ourselves.' Brian Friel Talks to Paddy Agnew," Magill, December 1980, pp. 59–61: p. 60.

sion, in which it is the dramatist's overwhelming duty to clarify, eluci-
date, and establish agreed codes, for purposes of communication and
discussion. In explicating Friel's play *Translations*, Seamus Heaney points
to the speechless character, Sarah, as a type of Kathleen ni Houlihan (a
symbolic figure for Ireland itself), whose difficult struggle to pronounce
her own name "constitutes a powerful therapy, a set of imaginative exercises that give her [Ireland] a chance to know and say herself properly to
herself again."[3]

The creation of Field Day has forced Friel into a more prominent
public role, yet he shuns easy political labels or pat solutions. He sees
his role as that of one who creates self-awareness through the critical
examination of Irish beliefs, as these are expressed in the contours of
everyday speech. For this reason his translation of Chekhov's *The Three
Sisters* avoids the many fine English versions and attempts to make the
play accessible to his audience by using identifiably Irish forms of English
speech. Reaching his audience through adaptation to Irish speech should
not be confused with any belated twitterings over a new Celtic Twilight.
In his most recent play, *The Communication Cord*, Friel makes farcical
use of the sentimentalism of artificial traditional. The stage directions
read:

> *Every detail of the kitchen and its furnishings is accurate of its time
> (from 1900 to 1930). But one quickly senses something false about
> the place. It is too pat, too 'authentic.' It is in fact a restored house,
> a reproduction, an artefact of today making obeisance to a home of
> yesterday.*[4]

His satire makes it clear that there is no going back, that uncritical restoration of the Irish past is no solution to the contemporary malaise.
This latest play acts as a humorous corrective to any superficial impression wrongly created by the elegiac mood of the earlier play *Translations*.

To what extent can we call Friel a political writer? He is not committed to any particular party or faction. Yet his later plays, especially, are
dependent upon the dialectical method to the extent that the spectator
may feel that he is watching a particularly fine debate. Undoubtedly
Friel himself would not describe himself as a Brechtian, yet the effect
he and his company are having on audiences in contemporary Ireland
is not far removed from the political excitement achieved by Brecht during his consciously ambivalent Berliner Ensemble years.

3. Seamus Heaney, *Translations* (review), *The Times Literary Supplement*, 24 Oct. 1980, p. 1199. [See p. 559 in this volume—*Editor*.]

4. *The Communication Cord* (London, 1983), p. 11.

Perhaps a sense of the directors' intentions can be gathered from the series of pamphlets published by Field Day as a separate activity from that of play production. The aim of the pamphleteers is to re-examine those aspects of Irish life which have come to be accepted uncritically. Twelve pamphlets have so far[5] been issued by Field Day, and the public response has been exciting. Naturally, many reviews have been polemical, but the over-all result has been to raise the level of critical debate about issues which have for far too long been shrouded in blind, partisan myth. Looking over the titles, or sub-titles, of these pamphlets one is reminded of nothing so much as of the theatre songs or scene captions from such Brecht plays as *The Measures Taken* or *The Mother*.[6] Typical pamphlet headings are "An Open Letter," "Civilians and Barbarians," "Myth and Motherland," "Dynasties of Coercion," and "The Apparatus of Repression." It is characteristic of Field Day, that, when the first half-dozen pamphlets were collected and published in one volume, this included, by invitation, an afterword by Denis Donoghue, whose comments were far from laudatory.[7] This is a telling detail about the publishing aspect of the company. Clearly, as with the plays, the purpose of the pamphlets is to encourage discussion and to question mindless obedience to any one cause. Despite this intention, there has been a tendency to berate Field Day simply for raising such issues. One is reminded that it has taken a critic of the stature of John Willett something like thirty years to shake up popular notions about Brecht's hard-line adherence to one unique system of belief, by repeatedly drawing attention to Brecht's inbred scepticism and detachment. Let us hope that the detachment of the Field Day Company and its directors will be accepted more readily.

The theatrical function of Field Day is organised on lines more akin to the early productions of Planchon in Lyon, or even to the pre-war productions of Brecht, than to those of the Berliner Ensemble. Using tiny budgets, mostly raised from the Arts Councils of both Northern Ireland and the Republic, the company manages to commission one new play each year, to workshop this production extensively and to tour the play to every variety of make-shift venue, before audiences at every level of theatrical experience, holding diverse political or religious persuasions, and living on both sides of the border.

Friel is not the only playwright whose works are produced by Field Day. The directors have encouraged younger writers both in the creating

---

5. By 1986 [*Editor*].

6. For example: "Praise of Illegal Work," "The Blotting Out," "The Song of Supply and Demand," "The Mother Learns to Read," "Praise of Learn-ing," "Praise for the Common Cause."

7. Field Day Theatre Company, *Ireland's Field Day* (London, 1985).

of new works, such as Thomas Kilroy's *Double Cross*, and in the writing of Irish adaptations of foreign classics, such as Derek Mahon's *High Time*—a version of Moliere's *The School for Husbands*.[8] The plays are first presented in the town hall, or Guildhall, of Derry, on an improvised stage which provides little more than Frank Fay's "two planks and a passion."[9] After their initial run they go on tour. The latest production, Kilroy's *Double Cross*, transferred to the Royal Court Theatre, London, for a very successful run. The company has few constant elements: there is no permanent roster of actors or crew, rather members are hired to meet the demands of each play. Nevertheless, Stephen Rea, one of the founders of Field Day, has either directed or acted in all of the plays produced so far, and a number of other actors re-appear fairly frequently. Clearly this does not constitute an ensemble in any sense that Brecht would have used the term, but, given the financial constraints of producing theatre in such seemingly unfavourable conditions, there is still a remarkable element of continuity. Friel and Rea are closely involved in all planning and selection. The plays produced so far demonstrate considerable variety of form, yet there appears to be a consistency of purpose—to challenge accepted notions, to counteract lethargy or despair, to make Irish men and women more aware of their own responsibilities and potentiality, to create open-ended speculation, and to do so with wit and style.

There can be few dramatists writing during the last thirty years who have not felt the impact of Brecht's theatrical innovations. Brian Friel is no exception. One need only think of the use of the double (or alter-ego) in *Philadelphia Here I Come*, the separate but interlocking mono-logues of *Faith Healer*, or the chorus of speaking corpses which ends *The Freedom of the City*, to recall Friel's attention to experimental form.[1] While his more recent plays, *Translations* and *The Communication Cord*, depend upon more conventionally realistic settings, experimentation continues in the plays of younger writers within the group. With considerable success, Thomas Kilroy's *Double Cross* explores the complexity of the Irish / English relationship. One actor plays both the sycophantic Brendan Bracken (Churchill's Minister of Information) and the quisling, William Joyce (Lord Haw-Haw). The juxtaposition of these two Irish characters within the performance of a single actor, manifesting different

8. *Double Cross* (London, 1985); *High Time* (Dublin, 1985).
9. Frank Fay, one of the founders of what came to be known as The Abbey Theatre, frequently used this phrase from Lope de Vega to define the basic

elements of theatre.
1. All of these plays, together with *Translations*, are collected in *Selected Plays of Brian Friel* (London, 1984).

aspects of the love-hate relationship between the Irish and the English, is a dramaturgical conceit worthy of Brecht, and in the tradition of Brecht's doubling of Shen Te and Shui Ta in the *Good Person of Setzuan*.

This fine new play by one of the younger Field Day writers has a unique structure and effectiveness. Thematically, it raises the same questions as Friel's best known play, *Translations*. Both plays present the effects of Irish emotionalism in face of the rationality of the more powerful and ponderous neighbour, England. While Kilroy's play examines this characteristic in terms of personality, Friel's treatment uses historical incident as his starting point. The early nineteenth-century process of standardization which the central British government imposes upon the local inhabitants, in particular the systematic Anglicizing of Irish place-names, becomes a telling metaphor for the relationship of one country to the other. Friel presents the resultant loss of Irish self-confidence in socio-linguistic terms—briefly, language creates history; a people who do not keep faith with the historical names of their location lose their identity; a people without a sense of their own history become vulnerable for take-over. Vagueness about the past leads from a loss of self-confidence either to hopelessness or to violent crisis. Thus, without spelling it out, the relationship between the historic context and present Irish problems is relayed to the contemporary audience. Yet the structure of the play is complex, its subtle effects unfolding with reflection rather than immediately. Friel was concerned that the play should not be received as a simple lament for what is past, that it should make its political point quietly but clearly. His fears were unwarranted. The play became a new national classic almost immediately. Though the play is not Brechtian in structure or style, its theme reminds one of Brecht's warning "one must not build on the good old things, but on the bad new ones."[2] Its historical setting does not detract from its relevance to the contemporary audience. Its immense popularity may owe something to its elegiac charm, but its gentle satire on Irish passivity has not been lost. If we try to evaluate the play in Brechtian terms, it must be through the Brecht of quiet subversion rather than the Brecht of chilling rationality and didacticism.

Each playwright, Brecht and Friel, has mastered the implication of his own frontier location, and has used it in his own way. Brecht's ambitions were greater—his concern was with global, rather than with local issues; though the larger questions can be seen, at least in part, as having arisen out of his specific situation. Each playwright has shown his genius

---

2. Quoted in John Willett, *Brecht in Context: Comparative Approaches* (London, 1984), p. 197.

in the individuality of his plays, but, also, in the important effect he has
had on younger dramatists. Brecht's legacy is all about us; Friel's is best
described by Thomas Kilroy, in the preface to his recently published text
of *Double Cross*:

> This play could not have been written without Field Day. Some
> years ago Field Day asked me to write one of their *Pamphlets* and I
> completely failed to do so. It was round about that time that I decided
> to try and write a play for the company instead, addressing the kind
> of topics which Field Day has restored to serious debate in Ireland.
> For me, Field Day is the most important movement of its kind in
> Ireland since the beginning of this century. It has provided a plat-
> form for the life of the mind, of whatever persuasion, at a time
> when mindlessness threatens to engulf us all.[3]

Chronology

1913 Establishment Ulster Volunteer Force, Irish Citizen Army, Irish Volunteers
Dublin labor lock-out and strike
Third Home Rule Bill rejected twice by House of Lords

1914 James Joyce stories, *Dubliners*
Irish Parliamentarian Party pledges support for England in World War I
Irish Republican Brotherhood contemplates wartime rising

1915 Padraig Pearse's eulogy of O'Donovan Rossa

1916 Easter Rising
Joyce novel, A *Portrait of the Artist as a Young Man*
Boyd's study, *Ireland's Literary Renaissance*

1918 Joyce play, *Exiles*
Overwhelming Sinn Fein support in general election

1919 Dial Eireann ratifies provisional constitution
Anglo-Irish War (through 1921)

1922 Anglo-Irish Treaty approved
Irish Civil War (through 1923)
Joyce novel, *Ulysses*

1923 Yeats awarded Nobel Prize
O'Casey, *Shadow of a Gunman*
Dublin Magazine

1924 O'Casey, *Juno and the Paycock*
Corkery study, *The Hidden Ireland*

1925 Abbey subsidized by Irish Free State government

1926 O'Casey's *Plough and the Stars* theater riots
Fianna Fail republican party founded

1928 Gate Theatre Company founded
O'Casey's *The Silver Tassie* rejected by Abbey
Yeats poems, *The Tower*

1929 Censorship of Publications Act
Denis Johnston, *The Old Lady Says 'No!'* rejected by Abbey, produced by the Gate Theatre Company
Elizabeth Bowen novel, *The Last September*
Shannon River hydroelectric project

1931 Frank O'Connor stories, *Guests of the Nation*

1932 Death of Lady Gregory
Fianna Fail wins general election
Sean O'Faolain stories, *Midsummer Night Madness*

1933 Fine Gael opposition party founded

1934 Beckett stories, *More Pricks Than Kicks*

1935 Prohibition of importation of contraceptives

1936 IRA declared illegal
1937 New constitution of the Irish Free State
1938 Douglas Hyde becomes president
1939 Death of Yeats
Yeats, *The Death of Cuchulain*
Joyce, *Finnegans Wake*
O'Casey autobiography, *I Knock at the Door*
IRA bombing campaign in England
Declaration of Irish neutrality in World War II
1940 *The Bell*, literary journal
1949 Republic of Ireland declared
1950 Industrial Development Authority
1951 Abbey Theatre accidentally burned
Free Presbyterian Church (Unionist)
Beckett novel, *Molloy*, first of trilogy
1952 Bord Failte (Irish Tourist Board)
1953 Pike Theatre opened, Dublin
1954 Beckett, *Waiting for Godot*
Behan, *The Quare Fellow*
1955 Ireland joins United Nations
1956 IRA campaign on border of Northern Ireland
1957 Beckett, *Endgame*
1958 Second Dublin Theatre Festival canceled after censorship disputes
Beckett, *Krapp's Last Tape*
Behan, *The Hostage*
1961 RTE television
1964 Friel, *Philadelphia, Here I Come!*
1966 Opening of newly constructed Abbey Theatre
Bombing of Nelson's Pillar, Dublin
Ulster Volunteer Force (Unionist) campaign
1968 Northern Ireland Civil Rights Association
1969 Troops quell sectarian riots in Northern Ireland
Beckett awarded Nobel Prize
1970 IRA splits into Provisional (unification of Ireland) and Official (Marxist)
1972 "Bloody Sunday" riots in Derry
1973 Republic joins European Economic Community
Friel, *Freedom of the City*
1980 Field Day Theatre Company, Derry, founded
Friel, *Translations*

Selected Bibliography

Books excerpted and articles reprinted in this volume are not here included.

HISTORY

Bartlett, Thomas, ed. *Irish Studies: A General Introduction*. Totowa: Barnes and Noble, 1988.
Beckett, J. C. *The Making of Modern Ireland*. New York: Knopf, 1966.
Bottigheimer, Karl S. *Ireland and the Irish: A Short History*. New York: Columbia UP, 1982.
Brown, Terence. *Ireland: A Social and Cultural History, 1922–1985*. London: Fontana, 1985.
Boyce, D. George. *Nationalism in Ireland*. Baltimore: Johns Hopkins UP, 1982.
Edwards, R. Dudley. *A New History of Ireland*. Dublin: Gill and Macmillan, 1972.
Foster, R. F. *Modern Ireland, 1600–1972*. New York: Penguin, 1988.
Hutchinson, John. *The Dynamics of Cultural Nationalism: The Gaelic Revival and the Creation of the Irish Nation State*. London: Allen and Unwin, 1987.
Kee, Robert. *The Green Flag: A History of Irish Nationalism*. New York: Delacorte, 1972.
Lyons, F. S. L. *Culture and Anarchy in Ireland, 1870–1939*. Oxford: Clarendon, 1979.
——. *Ireland Since the Famine*. Rev. ed. London: Fontana, 1973.
Moody, T. W., and F. X. Martin, eds. *The Course of Irish History*. Cork: Mercier Press, 1967.
O'Brien, Conor Cruise. *States of Ireland*. New York: Pantheon, 1972.

IRISH LITERARY HISTORY

Brown, Malcolm. *The Politics of Irish Literature: From Thomas Davis to W. B. Yeats*. Seattle: U of Washington P, 1972.
Cairns, David, and Shaun Richards. *Writing Ireland: Colonialism, Nationalism, and Culture*. Manchester: Manchester UP, 1988.
Costello, Peter. *The Heart Grown Brutal: The Irish Revolution in Literature from Parnell to the Death of Yeats, 1891–1939*. Totowa: Rowman and Littlefield, 1977.
Deane, Seamus. *A Short History of Irish Literature*. Notre Dame: Notre Dame UP, 1986.
Fallis, Richard. *The Irish Renaissance*. Syracuse: Syracuse UP, 1977.
Finneran, Richard J., ed. *Anglo-Irish Literature: A Review of Research*. Rev. ed. New York: MLA, 1983.
Howarth, Herbert. *The Irish Writers, 1880–1940: Literature and Nationalism*. New York: Hill and Wang, 1959.
Jeffares, A. Norman. *Anglo-Irish Literature*. New York: Schocken, 1982.
Kenner, Hugh. *A Colder Eye: The Modern Irish Writers*. New York: Knopf, 1983.
Mercier, Vivian. *The Irish Comic Tradition*. New York: Oxford UP, 1962.
O'Connor, Frank. *A Short History of Irish Literature: A Backward Look*. New York: Putnam, 1967.
O'Connor, Ulick. *All the Olympians: A Biographical Portrait of the Irish Literary Renaissance*. New York: Holt, 1984.
Skelton, Robin. *Celtic Contraries: Selected Essays*. Syracuse: Syracuse UP, 1989.

IRISH DRAMA

Bell, Sam Hanna. *The Theatre in Ulster.* Dublin: Gill and Macmillan, 1972.
Edwards, Philip. *Threshold of a Nation: A Study in English and Irish Drama.* New York: Cambridge UP, 1979.
Fay, W. G., and Catherine Carswell. *The Fays of the Abbey Theatre.* London: Rich and Cowan, 1935.
Flannery, James W. *Miss Annie F. Horniman and the Abbey Theatre.* Dublin: Dolmen Press, 1970.
Hogan, Robert. *After the Irish Renaissance: A Critical History of the Irish Drama Since "The Plough and the Stars."* Minneapolis: Minnesota UP, 1967.
———, ed. *Modern Irish Drama.* 4 vols. Dublin: Dolmen Press, 1975–79.
Hunt, Hugh. *The Abbey, Ireland's National Theatre.* Dublin: Gill and Macmillan, 1979.
———. *Theatre and Nationalism in Ireland.* Swansea: University College, 1974.
Kavanagh, Peter. *The Story of the Abbey Theatre.* New York: Devin-Adair, 1950.
Malone, Andrew E. *The Irish Drama.* London: Constable, 1929.
O'Driscoll, Robert, ed. *Theatre and Nationalism in Twentieth-Century Ireland.* Toronto: Toronto UP, 1971.
O hAodha, Micheal. *Theatre in Ireland.* London: Blackwell, 1974.
Robinson, Lennox. *Ireland's Abbey Theatre: A History, 1899–1951.* London: Sidgwick and Jackson, 1951.
Worth, Katherine. *The Irish Drama of Europe from Yeats to Beckett.* Atlantic Highlands: Humanities Press, 1978.

W. B. YEATS

Ellmann, Richard. *Yeats: The Man and the Masks.* London: Macmillan, 1949.
Hone, Joseph. *W. B. Yeats: 1865–1939.* New York: Macmillan, 1943.
Moore, James Rees. *Masks of Love and Death: Yeats as Dramatist.* Ithaca: Cornell UP, 1971.
Qamber, Akhtar. *Yeats and the Noh.* New York: Weatherhill, 1974.
O'Driscoll, Robert, and Lorna Reynolds, eds. *Yeats and the Theatre.* Niagara Falls: Maclean-Hunter Press, 1975.
Skelton, Robin, and Ann Saddlemyer, eds. *The World of W. B. Yeats.* Rev. ed. Seattle: U of Washington P, 1967.
Ure, Peter. *Yeats the Dramatist.* New York: Barnes and Noble, 1963.
Vendler, Helen. *Yeats' Vision and the Later Plays.* Cambridge: Harvard UP, 1963.

J. M. SYNGE

Corkery, Daniel. *Synge and Anglo-Irish Literature: A Study.* 1931. New York: Russell and Russell, 1965.
Gerstenberger, Donna. *John Millington Synge.* New York: Twayne, 1964.
Greene, David H., and Edward M. Stephens. *J. M. Synge, 1871–1909.* New York: Macmillan, 1959.
Harmon, Maurice, ed. *J. M. Synge Centenary Papers.* Dublin: Dolmen Press, 1971.
Kiberd, Declan. *Synge and the Irish Language.* London: Macmillan, 1979.
King, Mary C. *The Drama of J. M. Synge.* Syracuse: Syracuse UP, 1985.
Price, Alan. *Synge and Anglo-Irish Drama.* London: Methuen, 1961.
Saddlemyer, Ann. *J. M. Synge and Modern Comedy.* Dublin: Dolmen Press, 1968.
Skelton, Robin. *J. M. Synge and His World.* New York: Viking, 1971.
Stephens, Edward. *My Uncle John: Edward Stephens' Life of J. M. Synge.* Ed. Andrew Carpenter. London: Oxford UP, 1974.
Whitaker, Thomas R., ed. *Twentieth-Century Interpretations of* The Playboy of the Western World. Englewood Cliffs: Prentice-Hall, 1969.

LADY GREGORY

Adams, Hazard. *Lady Gregory*. Lewisburg: Bucknell UP, 1973.
Coxhead, Elizabeth. *J. M. Synge and Lady Gregory*. New York: London House, 1962.
Gregory, Ann. *Me and Nu: Childhood at Coole*. Gerrards Cross: Colin Smythe, 1970.
Kohfeldt, Mary Lou. *Lady Gregory: A Biography*. New York: Atheneum, 1985.
Mikhail, E. H. *Lady Gregory: Interviews and Recollections*. London: Macmillan, 1977.
Saddlemyer, Ann. *In Defense of Lady Gregory, Playwright*. Dublin: Dolmen Press, 1966.
Saddlemyer, Ann, and Colin Smythe, eds. *Lady Gregory: Fifty Years After*. Totowa: Barnes and Noble, 1987.

G. B. SHAW

Eric Bentley. *Bernard Shaw*. Rev. ed. London: Methuen, 1967.
Berst, Charles A. *Bernard Shaw and the Art of Drama*. Urbana: U of Illinois P, 1973.
Ervine, St. John. *Bernard Shaw: His Life, Work and Friends*. New York: William Monroe, 1956.
Ganz, Arthur F. *George Bernard Shaw*. New York: Grove, 1983.
Greene, David H., and Dan Laurence, eds. *Bernard Shaw: The Matter with Ireland*. London: Rupert Hart-Davis, 1962.
Greene, Nicholas. *Bernard Shaw: A Critical View*. New York: St. Martin's, 1984.
Holroyd, Michael. *Bernard Shaw*. 3 vols. New York: Random House, 1988–.
———, ed. *The Genius of Shaw: A Symposium*. New York: Rinehart and Winston, 1979.
Kaufman, R. J., ed. *G. B. Shaw: A Collection of Critical Essays*. Englewood Cliffs: Prentice-Hall, 1965.

SEAN O'CASEY

Ayling, Ronald, ed. *Sean O'Casey*. London: Macmillan, 1969.
Benstock, Bernard. *Sean O'Casey*. Lewisburg: Bucknell UP, 1970.
Hogan, Robert. *The Experiments of Sean O'Casey*. New York: St. Martin's Press, 1960.
Kilroy, Thomas, ed. *Sean O'Casey: A Collection of Critical Essays*. Englewood Cliffs: Prentice-Hall, 1975.
McCann, Sean. *The World of Sean O'Casey*. London: New English Library, 1966.
O'Casey, Eileen. *Sean*. London: Macmillan, 1971.
O'Connor, Gary. *Sean O'Casey: A Life*. New York: Atheneum, 1988.

BRENDAN BEHAN

Behan, Beatrice. *My Life with Brendan*. New York: Twayne, 1969.
Behan, Dominic. *My Brother Brendan*. New York: Simon and Schuster, 1966.
Boyle, Ted E. *Brendan Behan*. New York: Twayne, 1969.
Jeffs, Rae. *Brendan Behan: Man and Showman*. London: Hutchinson, 1966.
McCann, Sean, ed. *The World of Brendan Behan*. New York: Twayne, 1966.
Mikhail, E. H., ed. *The Art of Brendan Behan*. New York: Barnes and Noble, 1979.
O'Connor, Ulick. *Brendan*. London: Hamish Hamilton, 1970.
Simpson, Alan. *Beckett and Behan and a Theatre in Dublin*. London: Routledge and Kegan Paul, 1962.

SAMUEL BECKETT

Bair, Dierdre. *Samuel Beckett: A Biography*. New York: Harcourt Brace Jovanovich, 1978.
Cohn, Ruby. *Just Play: Beckett's Theater*. Princeton: Princeton UP, 1980.
Gontarski, S. E. *The Intent of Undoing in Samuel Beckett's Dramatic Texts*. Bloomington: Indiana UP, 1985.
Fletcher, John, and John Spurling. *Beckett: A Study of His Plays*. New York: Hill and Wang, 1972.

Kenner, Hugh. *A Reader's Guide to Samuel Beckett*. New York: Farrar, Straus, Giroux, 1973.
————. *Samuel Beckett: A Critical Study*. Rev. ed. Berkeley: U California P, 1968.
Knowlson, James, and John Pilling. *Frescoes of the Skull: The Later Prose and Drama of Samuel Beckett*. New York: Grove Press, 1980.
Mercier, Vivian. *Beckett / Beckett*. New York: Oxford UP, 1977.
O'Brien, Eoin. *The Beckett Country: Samuel Beckett's Ireland*. Monkstown, County Dublin: Black Cat Press, 1986.
Simpson, Alan. *Beckett and Behan and a Theatre in Dublin*. London: Routledge and Kegan Paul, 1962.
Webb, Eugene. *The Plays of Samuel Beckett*. Seattle: U of Washington P, 1972.

BRIAN FRIEL

Dantanus, Ulf. *Brian Friel: A Study*. London: Faber and Faber, 1988.
Deane, Seamus. *Celtic Revivals: Essays in Modern Irish Literature, 1880–1980*. Winston-Salem: Wake Forest UP, 1987.
————. "Introduction." *Brian Friel: Selected Plays*. Washington, DC: Catholic UP, 1986.
Hickey, Des, and Gus Smith. *Flight From the Celtic Twilight*. Indianapolis: Bobbs-Merrill, 1973.
Maxwell, D. E. S. *Brian Friel*. Lewisburg: Bucknell UP, 1973.
Pine, Richard. *The Diviner: The Art of Brian Friel*. Mullingar, County Westmeath: Lilliput Press, 1988.